Skill	Use	Procedure	Example
The process of determining a thesis statement, selecting the main ideas and supporting material, and developing an introduction and a conclusion.	To organize and develop material in a way that is best suited to your particular audience.	1. Write a thesis statement that identifies your main ideas.	The three aspects of romantic love are passion, intimacy, and commitment.
		2. Order, outline, and revise the main points.	I. Passion is the first aspect of romantic love to develop. II. Intimacy is the second. III. Commitment is the third.
		3. Select and outline support material for each main point.	Example for "passion": A. Passion is a compelling feeling of love. B. (Focus on function.) C. (Discuss maintenance.)
		4. Prepare section transitions.	From I to II: Although passion is essential to a relationship, passion without intimacy is just sex.
		5. Create introductions and select the best one.	What does it mean to say "I'm in love?" And how can you know whether what you are experiencing is not just a crush?
		6. Create conclusions and select the best one.	Developing romantic love involves passion, intimacy, and commitment.
		7. List sources.	Sample entry: Strenberg, Robert J. and Michael L. Barnes, eds. *The Psychology of Love.* New Haven, CT: Yale University Press, 1988.

Skill Builders

 PULL OUT SECTION

Interpersonal Communication

Politeness (page 110)

Skill	Use	Procedure	Example
Relating to others in ways that meet their need to be appreciated and protected.	To determine the degree of politeness necessary to achieve your objective.	1. Recognize when what you are planning to say is likely to be recognized as a face-threatening act. 2. Consider how well you know each other, whether one person holds power over the other, and the risk of hurting the other person. 3. Construct the wording of a positive politeness (shows appreciation, approval, honor, affection) or a negative politeness (acknowledges imposition or intrusion) statement based on the issues of relationship, power, and risk.	Chris thinks her boss did not consider all that he should have in determining her year's bonus. She might construct the following negative politeness statement: "Mr. Seward, I know you put considerable time into your bonus decisions, but you have been willing to talk about your decisions in the past. I was hoping you'd be willing to take a few minutes to discuss your decision with me."

Paraphrasing (page 129)

Skill	Use	Procedure	Example
A response that conveys your understanding of another person's message.	To increase listening efficiency; to avoid message confusion; to discover the speaker's motivation.	1. Listen carefully to the message. 2. Notice what images and feelings you have experienced from this message. 3. Determine what the message means to you. 4. Create a message that conveys these images or feelings.	Grace says, "At two minutes to five, the boss gave me three letters that had to be in the mail that evening!" Bonita replies, "If I understand, you were really resentful that your boss dumped important work on you right before quitting time when she knows you have to pick up the baby at day care."

Skill Builders

Gather and Evaluate Material for Your Speech (page 326)

Skill	Use	Procedure	Example
The process of collecting, evaluating, and recording information items that may be appropriate for use in a speech.	To search and evaluate sources of information that may contain items related to the speech goal and to document them in a form that allows easy access to items while providing documentation for the origin of an item.	1. Locate potential sources of information including books, periodicals, reference works, Web sites, observations, and interviews.	In her research on West Nile virus, Tamika found three books, six magazine articles, one journal article, sixteen newspaper articles, several statistics from the Center for Disease Control, three Web site pages, and she interviewed a doctor who specialized in infectious disease control.
		2. Scan the information to access its relevance to your speech goal.	After scanning the resources she determined that two of the books and the journal article were too technical for her specific goal.
		3. Evaluate each resource for its authority, objectivity, and currency.	Tamika eliminated five magazine articles because in the article the source of the information was not identified. She eliminated three more because they were dated. She eliminated two of the Web pages that seemed to be hysterical responses to the illness.
		4. Read all the sources and use note cards to record each item of information that might be useful in developing your speech along with the relevant bibliographic information on that source.	After reading her sources, she prepared sixteen note cards.
		5. Develop a phrase that you can use to verbally cite the source of an item in your speech.	On the back of each note card she wrote a phrase that verbally described the source of the item.

Describing Feelings (page 160)

Skill	Use	Procedure	Example
Putting an emotional state into words.	For self-disclosure; to teach people how to treat you.	1. Identify the behavior that has triggered the feeling. 2. Identify the specific emotion you are experiencing as a result of the behavior. Anger? Joy? Be specific. 3. Frame your response as an "I" statement. "I feel _____." 4. Verbalize the specific feeling.	"I just heard I didn't get the job, and I feel cheated and bitter" or "Because of the way you defended me when I was being belittled by Leah, I feel both grateful and humbled."

Assertiveness (page 167)

Skill	Use	Procedure	Example
Standing up for yourself and doing so in interpersonally effective ways that describe your feelings honestly and exercise your personal rights while respecting the rights of others	To show clearly what you think or feel.	1. Identify what you are thinking or feeling. 2. Analyze the cause of these feelings. 3. Identify what your real preferences and rights are. 4. Use describing feelings and describing behavior skills to make "I" statements that politely explain your position.	When Gavin believes he is being unjustly charged, he says, "I have never been charged for a refill on iced tea before—has there been a change in policy?"

Describing Behavior, Consequences, and Feelings (b-c-f) (page 196)

Skill	Use	Procedure	Example
Describing the basis of a conflict in terms of behavior, consequences, and feelings (b-c-f).	To help the other person understand the problem completely.	1. Own the message. 2. Describe the behavior that you see or hear. 3. Describe the consequences that result.	Jason says, "I have a problem that I need your help with. When I tell you what I'm thinking and you don't respond (b), I start to think you don't care about me or what I think (c), and this causes me to get very angry with you (f)."

Group Communication

Brainstorming (page 245)

Skill	Use	Procedure	Example
An uncritical, nonevaluative process of generating associated ideas.	To generate a list of potential solutions to a problem.	1. Verbalize ideas as they come to mind. 2. Refrain from evaluating the merits of ideas. 3. Encourage outrageous and unique ideas. 4. Build on or modify the ideas of others. 5. Use extended effort to generate more ideas. 6. Record the ideas.	Problem: "What should we do to raise money to help a child who needs a liver transplant?" Ideas: sell cookies, sell candy, sell wrapping paper; wrap packages at mall for donations; find corporate sponsors; have a corporate golf outing, a youth golf outing, a tennis tournament, a bowling tournament, a paint-ball tournament; auction donated paintings; do odd jobs for money.

Problem Solving in Groups (page 247)

Skill	Use	Procedure	Example
Using a systematic six-step process to work out difficulties or resolve issues.	A guide for groups to follow in arriving at conclusions to fact or value questions.	1. Define the problem in specific and precise language as a question of fact, value, or policy containing one central idea. The question is: "What textbook should we adopt for the required Human Communication course?"	The question is: "What textbook should we adopt for the required Human Communication course?"
		2. Analyze the problem using the experiences of group members, information obtained from public sources, and through interviews with other knowledgeable people.	Members who have taught the course before recount their experiences with various texts. We read the publishers' information packets, and we talk to the sales reps.
		3. Determine the solution criteria.	The criteria we will use are coverage, writing style, Web support, and cost.
		4. Identify possible solutions through brainstorming.	We identify six books that might work.
		5. Evaluate the solutions by comparing them to the criteria.	We compare the books to one another using our criteria.
		6. Decide using expert opinion, average group opinion, majority, unanimity, or consensus method.	We adopt a consensus method for deciding.

Public Speaking

Crafting a Specific Speech Goal That Meets Audience Needs (page 298)

Skill	Use	Procedure	Example
The process of identifying a speech purpose that draws on speaker's knowledge and interests and is adapted to a specific audience and setting.	To identify a speaking goal where speaker interest and expertise, audience needs and interests, and setting overlap.	1. Identify topics within subject areas in which you have interest and expertise.	Subject: Exercising Topics: Yoga, Kick Boxing, Walking, Weight Training
		2. Analyze your audience's demographic characteristics, interests, and attitudes toward your subject.	Older lower income black women with little experience in exercising. Likely to be unknowledgeable and indifferent.
		3. Understand the occasion and the location for the speech.	Women's Health Fair at local community center. About twenty women will attend.
		4. Select a topic that will meet the interests and needs of your audience and setting.	Topic: Walking (easy to do, has benefits)
		5. Write a specific speech goal that clearly states the exact response you want from your audience.	I want the audience to understand four major benefits of walking three times a week.

Foundations of Communication

Perception Checking (page 45)

Skill	Use	Procedure	Example
Making a verbal statement that reflects your understanding of another person's behavior.	To enable you to test the accuracy of your perceptions.	1. Describe the behaviors of the other that have led to your perception. 2. Add your interpretation of the behavior to your statement.	After taking a phone call, Shimika comes into the room with a completely blank expression and neither speaks to Donnell nor acknowledges that he is in the room. Donnell says, "Shimika, from your blank look, I get the feeling that you're in a state of shock. Has something happened?

Using Specific Language (page 59)

Skill	Use	Procedure	Example
Clarify meaning by narrowing what is understood from a general category to a particular group within that category, by appealing to the senses, or by choosing words that symbolize exact thoughts and feelings, or by using concrete details or examples.	To help the listener picture thoughts analogous to the speaker's.	1. Assess whether the word or phrase to be used is less specific (or concrete or precise) than it can be. 2. Pause to consider alternatives. 3. Select a more specific (or concrete or precise) word, or give an example or add details.	Instead of saying, "Bring the stuff for the audit," say, "Bring the records and receipts from the last year for the audit. "Or, instead of saying, "I was really cold," say, "I nearly froze; my fingers were numb."

COMMUNICATE!

RUDOLPH F. VERDERBER

Distinguished Teaching Professor of Communication
University of Cincinnati

KATHLEEN S. VERDERBER

Northern Kentucky University

ELEVENTH EDITION

THOMSON
＊
WADSWORTH

Australia • Canada • Mexico • Singapore • Spain • United Kingdom • United States

Publisher: Holly J. Allen

Editor: Annie Mitchell

Senior Development Editor: Greer Lleuad

Assistant Editor: Aarti Jayaraman

Editorial Assistant: Trina Enriquez

Senior Technology Project Manager: Jeanette Wiseman

Senior Marketing Manager: Kimberly Russell

Marketing Assistant: Andrew Keay

Advertising Project Manager: Shemika Britt

Project Manager, Editorial Production: Mary Noel

Print/Media Buyer: Judy Inouye

Permissions Editor: Sommy Ko

Production Service: Cecile Joyner, The Cooper Company

Text Designer: Lisa Delgado, Delgado and Company

Photo Researcher: Terri Wright

Copy Editor: Kay Mikel

Cover Designers: Robert Pizzo, Ross Carron

Cover Illustration: Robert Pizzo

Compositor: New England Typographic Service

Printer: R.R. Donnelley, Willard

For more information about our products, contact us at:
Thomson Learning Academic Resource Center
1-800-423-0563
For permission to use material from this text or product, submit a request online at http://www.thomsonrights.com. Any additional questions about permissions can be submitted by email to thomsonrights@thomson.com.

Library of Congress Control Number: 2003116436

Student Edition: ISBN 0-534-63936-4

Instructor's Edition: ISBN 0-534-63937-2

Thomson Wadsworth
10 Davis Drive
Belmont, CA 94002-3098
USA

Asia
Thomson Learning
5 Shenton Way #01-01
UIC Building
Singapore 068808

Australia/New Zealand
Thomson Learning
102 Dodds Street
Southbank, Victoria 3006
Australia

Canada
Nelson
1120 Birchmount Road
Toronto, Ontario M1K 5G4
Canada

Europe/Middle East/Africa
Thomson Learning
High Holborn House
50/51 Bedford Row
London WC1R 4LR
United Kingdom

Latin America
Thomson Learning
Seneca, 53
Colonia Polanco
11560 Mexico D.F.
Mexico

Spain/Portugal
Paraninfo
Calle Magallanes, 25
28015 Madrid, Spain

BRIEF CONTENTS

CONTENTS

I t is with great excitement that we present you with the eleventh edition of *Communicate!*, a text that remains a market leader because of our commitment to helping students master the concepts, theories, and skills that careful research and scholarship demonstrates are essential for effective human communication.

When we begin a revision, we carefully consider feedback from instructors across the country that informs us about the changing needs of their students. We review the latest scholarship to see how concepts and theories of communication have been refined, and we then update the text so that what students learn represents the best and latest thinking. Additionally, we revise our examples and illustrations so they correspond to changes in theory and practice and reflect the changing social and cultural landscapes to which students are exposed. Finally, we continue to ensure that we are at the forefront of integrating computer-mediated resources into the text so that students are encouraged to be interactive learners, adept at utilizing the vast resources available on the World Wide Web.

This new edition of *Communicate!* continues to combine theory, skills practice, and competency evaluation so students (1) understand the major concepts from communication theory and research, (2) recognize how these concepts and theories provide a basis for applying communication skills, (3) develop a range of communication skills, and (4) begin to apply what they learn in class to real-life situations, resulting in increasing communication competence in all settings.

Strengths of the Text

A major challenge with any revision is to be sensitive to the burgeoning research in communication while still providing a manageable, coherent introduction to the field that makes a real difference to the development of students' skills. This edition, like previous editions, overcomes this challenge by clearly describing well-accepted scholarship that is specifically related to understanding and practicing communication competence—we work very hard to accurately translate scholarship into language that is easily understood by introductory students. This revision continues to use what previous users have said is a reliable learning model. This model has six integrated steps:

1. **Theoretical understanding** of communication theories that provide the foundation for specific skills

2. **Examples** that enable students to identify effective skill usage

3. **Steps** involved in the performance of skills

4. **Practice** in using skills

5. **Self-assessment–based learning goals** through which students are encouraged to assess their current skill levels and write specific goals to help them master key skills

6. **Review**

New to This Edition

This new edition incorporates many conceptual and pedagogical changes, including the following significant chapter-by-chapter revisions:

Chapter 5, "Holding Effective Conversations," includes updated discussions of the characteristics of conversations and the guidelines for effective conversations. In addition, the section on electronically-mediated conversations has been substantially revised to reflect the growing scholarship in this area.

Chapter 6, "Listening and Responding," includes a new section on responding supportively to give comfort that reflects the substantial body of research on comforting and the skills associated with supportive communication.

Chapter 9, "Interviewing," has been heavily revised in response to feedback from instructors. This chapter now discusses both informational and employment interviewing from the perspectives of both interviewer and interviewee.

Chapter 16, "Practicing the Presentation of Your Speech," Chapter 17, "Informative Speaking," and Chapter 18, "Persuasive Speaking" all feature new speeches and analyses. Additionally, Chapters 12–16 now include Speech Plan Action Steps that guide students through a step-by-step preparation process that results in significantly better speeches. These Action Step activities are supplemented by examples of each activity prepared by other students, available for students to view at the *Communicate!* Web site.

In addition, the eleventh edition includes the following updated technological features, all highlighted at the end of each chapter in the Communicate! Online section:

- The Communicate! CD-ROM is packaged free with each new book. This dynamic multimedia learning tool brings the text content to life with video clips of communication scenarios and samples speeches. The Communicate! In Action clips are enactments of the conversation scenarios presented in Chapters 5–9 and 11 of the text so students can see and hear how the skills they are studying can be used to create effective conversations in difficult circumstances. New to this edition's CD-ROM are video clips for Chapters 9 and 11, which depict a job interview and a group communication scenario. Also new to this edition are CNN Situation Analysis video clips, which feature CNN news stories that highlight key concepts discussed in the text. The Speech Interactive clips allow students to see the authors of the new sample student speeches included in Chapters 16–18 as they present their speeches. The Communicate! CD-ROM also provides access to the Communicate! Web site, InfoTrac® College Edition, and Speech Builder Express™.

■ The extensive and revamped Communicate! Web site provides students with a multitude of text-specific learning aids, including interactive electronic versions of all text exercises. From the Web site students can download worksheets, data collection sheets, and speech checklists as well as complete activities online, email them to their instructors if requested, and compare their responses to activities with models provided by the authors. The Web site also features study aids such as chapter outlines, flash cards and other resources for mastering glossary terms, and chapter quizzes that help them check their understanding of key concepts.

■ Web Resource Web links and InfoTrac® College Edition activities have been integrated into the text to expand skills practice and learning online. These Web Resources are highlighted in the text with colored text and icons and are easily accessed from the Communicate! Web site. All the links are monitored to ensure that they remain active.

■ Many Speech Plan Action Steps can be completed with Speech Builder Express™, a dynamic online speech organization and outlining tool. This interactive software enables students to complete speech assignments and generate a complete speech outline, including a works cited section.

Revised Features

■ **Spotlight on Scholars** boxes feature the work of nine eminent communication scholars. Based on interviews with the scholars, these short articles "put a face" on scholarship by telling each scholar's "story," including a description of what motivated the scholar to follow the line of research discussed in the text. Each article also includes a brief summary of the findings and methods of research used by the scholar so that students are exposed to how communication research is conducted. This unique and highly praised feature helps students understand the research and theory-building process by providing a glimpse of some of the people who have been especially influential in developing communication theories.

- **Diverse Voices** are excerpts of longer, previously published articles that give voice to the communication experiences of people from a wide range of social and cultural backgrounds. These excerpts highlight the personal thoughts and experiences of the individuals featured on topics related to concepts discussed in the chapter, helping students to understand and appreciate how culture affects communication.

- **Skill Builder** boxes visually reinforce learning of many specific skills described and exemplified in the text. Each box includes the definition of the skill, a brief description of its use, the steps for enacting the skill, and an example that illustrates the skill. A convenient tear-out chart at the beginning of the book provides a summary of all the Skill Builders. The skills in the chart are grouped into categories for easy reference.

- **Observe and Analyze** activities require students to observe a specific event or series of events related to concepts they are learning. They are then asked to analyze what happened, using the theories and concepts from the chapter. With this edition students are able to download worksheets and data collection forms at the Communicate! Web site as well as write, edit, and, if requested, email reports of their findings to their instructors.

- **Test Your Competence** activities allow students to practice the skills they are learning. With this edition, students are able to complete these exercises online and then compare their answers with models provided by the authors.

- **Self-Review** quizzes appear at the end of each part. In accord with the findings of learning motivation research, students are encouraged to set specific goals for skill improvement by writing skills-improvement plans for interpersonal, group, and public settings. With this edition, students are able to complete these quizzes online at the Communicate! Web site and, if requested, email them to their instructors.

- **What Would You Do? A Question of Ethics** boxes are short case studies that appear toward the end of chapters. These cases present ethical challenges and require students to think critically, sorting through a variety of ethical dilemmas faced by communicators. Conceptual material presented in Chapter 1 lays groundwork for the criteria on which students may make their assessments. But in each case the dilemma posed focuses on issues raised in the specific chapter.

Supplementary Materials

In addition to the *Communicate!* CD-ROM and Web site, the eleventh edition is accompanied by a suite of integrated resources for students and instructors.

Student Resources

Speech Builder Express™

A Web-based tool that coaches students through the speech organization and outlining process. By completing interactive sessions based on the in-text Speech Plan Action Steps, students can prepare and save their outlines, including a plan for visual aids and a works cited section, formatted according to the principles presented in the text. Text and video models reinforce their interactive practice.

InfoTrac® College Edition

An easy to use online library is also packaged with each new edition.

A *free* four-month subscription to this extensive easy-to-use database of reliable, full-length articles (not abstracts) from hundreds of top academic journals and popular sources is ideal for helping your students master online research and is especially useful when students are preparing speeches.

Student Workbook

by Leonard E. Assante of Volunteer State Community College. The student workbook offers chapter-by-chapter skill-building exercises, vocabulary lists, quizzes, and copies of the worksheets, data collection sheets, and speech checklists featured in the text. The workbook can be bundled with the text at a discount.

Thomson Learning WebTutor™ Toolbox for WebCT and Blackboard

A Web-based teaching and learning tool that takes a course beyond classroom boundaries to an anywhere, anytime environment. *WebTutor Toolbox for Communicate!* corresponds chapter-by-chapter and topic-by-topic with the book, including flash cards (with audio), practice quizzes, and online tutorials. Instructors can use WebTutor Toolbox to provide virtual office hours, post syllabi, set up threaded discussions, and track student progress on the practice quizzes.

Speech Interactive: Student Speeches for Critique and Analysis

This multimedia CD-ROM can be used in addition to the Speech Interactive program featured on your Communicate! CD-ROM. The original Speech Interactive CD-ROM features six sample speeches for interactive critique and analysis.

Service Learning in Communication Studies: A Handbook

by Rick Isaacson, Bruce Dorries, and Kevin Brown. This handbook can be bundled with the text and is an invaluable resource for students in the basic course that integrates or is planning to integrate a service learning component. The handbook provides guidelines for connecting service learning work with classroom concepts and advice for working effectively with agencies and organizations. The handbook also provides model forms and reports and a directory of online resources.

A Guide to the Basic Course for ESL Students

by Esther Yook, Mary Washington College. Available bundled with the text, this guide assists the non-native speaker. Features FAQs, helpful URLs, and strategies for accent management and overcoming speech apprehension.

Instructor Resources

Instructor's Resource Manual with Test Bank

by Nader Chaaban, Montgomery College, Rockville, Maryland. This indispensable manual features changes from the tenth edition to the eleventh edition, sample syllabi, chapter-by-chapter outlines, summaries, vocabulary lists, suggested lecture and discussion topics, classroom exercises, and assignments, as well as a comprehensive Test Bank with answer key and rejoinders.

ExamView®

is a fully integrated collection of test creation, delivery, and classroom management tools that feature all of the test items found in the Instructor's Resource Manual.

Multimedia Presentation Manager: Microsoft® PowerPoint® Presentation Tool for Human Communication

This presentation tool contains a searchable database of PowerPoint slides tailored to the eleventh edition, including text art and cued video clips, many from CNN. Instructors can import information from previously created lectures into the program.

CNN® Today Videos

Organized by topics covered in a typical course, this multivolume video series is available to qualifying adopters. Videos are divided into short segments—perfect for introducing key concepts.

Student Speeches for Critique and Analysis

This multivolume video series offers both imperfect and award-winning sample student speeches. The speeches presented in this text are available in this series.

Communication Scenarios for Critique and Analysis

This video provides faculty and students with real-life contexts of interpersonal communication in action. A great tool for helping students learn to critique and analyze interpersonal communication skills, this video features scripted, videotaped scenarios including the conversations featured on the Communicate! CD-ROM.

Wadsworth Communication Video Library

Available to qualifying adopters. The Video Library includes a variety of instructional videos as well as the Great Speeches video series.

Media Guide for Interpersonal Communication

by Charles G. Apple, University of Michigan-Flint. This guide provides a faculty with media resource listings focused on general interpersonal communication topics. Each listing provides compelling examples of how interpersonal communication concepts are illustrated in particular films, books, plays, Web sites, or journal articles. Discussion questions are provided.

The Teaching Assistant's Guide to the Basic Course

by Katherine G. Hendrix, University of Memphis. Based on leading communication teacher training programs, the guide covers general teaching and course management topics as well as specific strategies for communication instruction, such as providing effective feedback on performance, managing sensitive class discussions, and conducting mock interviews.

Acknowledgments

The eleventh edition could not have been completed without the help of many people. Most important are the reviewers, whose insights, candor, and suggestions for refining the book were invaluable: Cheryl Beese, Rock Valley College; Richard D. Britton, Suffolk Community College; Dale Davis, University of Texas at San Antonio; Michael Elkins, Texas A&M University; Jim D. Hughey, Oklahoma State University; Shirley Maase, Chesapeake College; Michael O'Brien, Northwestern College; William J. Planner, Fox Valley Technical College; Maurice Watson, Brooklyn College CUNY; and David Wohl, West Virginia State College. Many of these reviewers have been faithful adopters of *Communicate!* We are grateful for their support.

We would also like to express our gratitude to the Thomson Wadsworth Communication Team: Annie Mitchell, Acquisitions Editor; Jeanette Wiseman, Senior Technology Project Manager; Mary Noel, Production Project Manager; Aarti Jayaraman, Assistant Editor; Trina Enriquez, Editorial Assistant; and Andrew Keay, Marketing Assistant. Others at Wadsworth, including Edward Wade, Editorial Production Manager; Shemika Britt, Advertising Project Manager; and Holly Allen, Publisher, have offered their support and expertise. Cecile Joyner of The Cooper Company oversaw the production of this book, and we continue to value her ability to keep our books on schedule. A special word of appreciation to Greer Lleuad, Senior Developmental Editor, a truly remarkable professional, who oversaw all of the work on this revision. Her kindness, wisdom, patience, guidance, expertise, and eye for detail nurtured us through this revision and the preparation of the materials for the Web site. She was always "home" when we needed counsel. We also want to note the contributions of Kim Russell, Senior Marketing Manager, who keeps us up to date on emerging trends in the market and so helps us to better serve students. Finally, we want to thank students who have used the text and who have communicated their ideas about how we can make the book better. We encourage you to follow their example and to use the Communicate! Web site to contact us with questions, ideas, and suggestions. We only hope that you will find this book to be one that not only stimulates your intellect, but also improves your ability to understand and be understood by others.

Rudy and Kathie Verderber

COMMUNICATE!

ELEVENTH EDITION

RPIZZO

Martin Barraud/Getty Images

OBJECTIVES

After you have read this chapter, you should be able to answer these questions:

- What is the definition of communication?
- How does the communication process work?
- Why do we communicate?
- What characterizes each of the communication settings you will study in this course?
- What are seven basic principles of communication?
- Why should a communicator be concerned about diversity?
- What major ethical issues face communicators?
- What is communication competence?
- How can you improve your communication skills?

1

Communication Perspectives

Mimi and Marcus finished interviewing the fifth life insurance agent.

"From what I could understand, most of the basic policies are about the same," said Mimi. "So, for me, it comes down to who we'd feel most comfortable with."

"Yeah, that's pretty much the way I see it. And from that standpoint, I'd pick Carrie's policy," Marcus responded.

"She really seemed nice, didn't she?" said Mimi. "She seemed friendly, approachable, and—unlike Paul—she talked to both of us, not just you."

Marcus replied, "What I noticed was how well her presentation of her policy was tailored to our specific needs, unlike Dempsey who spent most of his time talking about a plan that really didn't relate to our needs."

"Yeah, and Gloria, I think that was her name, was so disorganized . . ."

"Right, and she was so engrossed in the PowerPoint™ presentation that she didn't even notice when you tried to ask a question!"

"I sort of liked Steve, but when we suggested that the rates he was quoting were just out of our budget, he didn't offer much help. Once he got off his 'script,' he seemed lost."

"Well," said Marcus, "not only did Carrie offer a policy I could understand, she talked about it in a way that made me think we could call her about other types of insurance and financial advice."

"OK," Mimi said as she nodded. "So we agree; Carrie gets our insurance business!"

hy was Carrie successful? Was it her insurance policy? Her specialized expertise in the insurance business? Not necessarily. From this conversation it appears that Carrie's success was due to her ability to communicate with Mimi and Marcus. Carrie's success is not unusual. Studies done over the years have concluded that, for almost any job, two of the most important skills sought by employers are oral communication skills and interpersonal abilities (Goleman, 1998, pp. 12–13). Even in fields not usually thought of as requiring strong communication skills, employers look for competence. For instance, an article on the role of communication in the workplace found that in engineering, a highly technical field, 72 percent of the employers surveyed indicated that speaking skills were very important (Darling & Dannels, 2003, p. 12). So this course can significantly increase your ability to get a job and to be successful in your chosen career.

How effective you are in your communication with others is important to your career, but it is also the foundation for all of your personal relationships. Your ability to make and keep friends, to be a good family member, to have satisfying intimate relationships, to participate in or lead groups, and to prepare and present speeches depends on your communication skills. During this course you will learn about the communication process and have an opportunity to practice basic communication skills that will help you improve your relationships.

In this first chapter we explain the basic communication process, provide an overview of the functions communication serves, and explore the settings in which our communications occur. Then we describe the major principles of communication. Finally, we discuss communication competence and a process you can use for improving your communication skills.

The Communication Process

communication
the process of creating or sharing meaning in informal conversation, group interaction, or public speaking.

Communication is the process of creating or sharing meaning in informal conversation, group interaction, or public speaking. To understand how this process works, we begin by describing its essential elements: participants, context, messages, channels, presence or absence of noise, and feedback.

Participants

participants
individuals who take turns assuming the roles of senders and receivers during an interaction.

The **participants** are the individuals who take turns assuming the roles of senders and receivers during an interaction. As senders, participants form and transmit messages using verbal symbols and nonverbal behavior. As receivers, they process the messages and behaviors that have been transmitted to them.

Contexts

Contexts are the physical, social, historical, psychological, and cultural settings in which communication occurs.

Physical context The **physical context** of a communication event includes its location, the environmental conditions (temperature, lighting, noise level), the physical distance between communicators, any seating arrangements, and time of day. Each of these factors can affect the communication. For instance, a manager sitting behind her desk in her office talking with members of her staff creates a different context than talking with those same people while sitting at a round table in the conference room.

Social context The **social context** is the expressed purpose of the event as well as the nature of the relationships between and among the participants. Whether a communication event takes place at a family dinner, a formal wedding, or a business meeting, and whether it occurs among family members, friends, acquaintances, work associates, or strangers, influences what and how messages are formed, shared, and understood. For instance, most of us interact differently when talking with family members across the dinner table than we do when talking with a customer at work.

Historical context The **historical context** includes the background provided by previous communication episodes between the participants that influence understandings in the current encounter. For instance, suppose one morning Chad tells Shelby that he will get the draft of the report that they had left for their boss to read. As Shelby enters the office that afternoon, she sees Chad and says, "Did you get it?" Another person listening to the conversation

contexts
the physical, social, historical, psychological, and cultural settings in which communication occurs.

physical context
the location, environmental conditions (temperature, lighting, noise level), physical distance between communicators, any seating arrangements, and time of day of a communication event.

social context
the expressed purpose of the event as well as the nature of the relationships between and among the participants.

historical context
The background provided by previous communication episodes between the participants that influence understandings in the current encounter.

How might the conversation of these people differ if they were in the library working on a class project?

Karen Kapoor/Getty Images

would have no idea what the "it" is to which Shelby is referring. Yet Chad may well reply, "It's on my desk." Shelby and Chad understood one another because of the content of the earlier exchange.

Psychological context The **psychological context** encompasses the mood and feelings each person brings to the conversation. Suppose Corinne is under a great deal of stress as she tries to finish a paper that is due the next morning. If her boyfriend jokingly suggests that she take a speed-typing course, Corinne, who is normally good natured, may explode with an angry tirade. Why? Because her stress level provides the psychological context within which she hears this message, and it taints what she understands.

Cultural context The **cultural context** is the beliefs, values, attitudes, meanings, social hierarchies, religion, notions of time, and roles of a group of people that help participants form and interpret messages (Samovar & Porter, 2003, p. 8). In the United States the privileged ethnic culture is European American. Although many "white" Americans may not think of themselves as "ethnic," as Sonia Nieto (2000) points out, "we are all ethnic, whether we choose to identify ourselves in this way or not" (p. 27). Because the United States is a nation of immigrants, its citizens are quite culturally diverse. As a result, a wide variety of other cultural contexts also exist and influence communication. Today effective communicators recognize and are sensitive to the cultural context of others.

Messages

Messages are the verbal utterances and nonverbal behaviors that senders use to convey their meanings. To understand how messages are created and received, we need to understand meaning, symbols, encoding and decoding, and form or organization.

Meaning **Meaning** is the combination of ideas and feelings that exist in a sender's mind. You may have ideas about how the study group should prepare for your next exam, or whether taxes should be raised or lowered; you also may experience feelings such as jealousy, anger, and love. The meanings you have within you, however, are not transferred magically into another's mind. To share your meanings, they must be transformed into messages.

Symbols **Symbols** are words, sounds, and actions that are recognized by others as representing specific content meaning. To share meanings, you form messages comprising verbal and nonverbal symbols. As you speak, you choose words to convey your meaning. At the same time facial expressions, eye contact, gestures, and tone of voice—all nonverbal cues—accompany your words and also affect the meaning your listener receives from the symbols you use. As you listen, you use both the verbal symbols and the nonverbal cues to make sense of what is being said.

psychological context
the mood and feelings each person brings to the conversation.

cultural context
the beliefs, values, attitudes, meanings, social hierarchies, religion, notions of time, and roles of a group of people that help participants form and interpret messages.

messages
verbal utterances and nonverbal behaviors that senders use to convey their meanings.

meaning
the combination of ideas and feelings that exist in a sender's mind.

symbols
words, sounds, and actions that are recognized by others as representing specific content meaning.

Encoding and decoding   **Encoding** is the cognitive thinking process of transforming ideas and feelings into symbols and organizing them into a message; **decoding** is the process of transforming messages from another back into one's own ideas and feelings. Ordinarily you do not consciously think about either the encoding or the decoding process. But when you have difficulty communicating, you become more aware of them. For example, if you are giving a speech and see puzzled frowns, you may reencode your message by selecting words that better convey your meaning. Likewise, you may become aware of the decoding process when you must figure out the meaning of an unfamiliar word based on its use in a particular sentence.

encoding
the cognitive thinking process of transforming ideas and feelings into symbols and organizing them into a message.

decoding
the process of transforming messages from another back into one's own ideas and feelings.

Form or organization   When the meaning we wish to share is complex, we may need to organize it in sections or in a certain order. Message form is especially important when one person talks without interruption for a relatively long time, such as in a public speech or when reporting an event to a colleague at work.

Channels

A **channel** is a sensory route used to transmit messages. Face-to-face communication has two basic channels: sound (verbal symbols) and light (nonverbal cues). People can and do communicate using all five sensory channels. A fragrant scent or a firm handshake may contribute as much to meaning as what is seen or heard. In general, messages that use multiple channels are more likely to be understood.

channel
a sensory route used to transmit messages.

Noise

Noise is any external, internal, or semantic stimulus that interferes with sharing meaning.

External noises are sights, sounds, and other stimuli in the environment that draw people's attention away from what is being said or done. For instance, while listening to a lecture, you may be distracted by a passing fire engine.

Internal noises are unrelated thoughts and feelings that draw attention away from what is said or done. When you tune out what is being said and focus instead on a past conversation, you are experiencing internal noise.

Semantic noises are the unintended meanings aroused by certain symbols and behaviors that distract your attention from what your friend has to say. Use of ethnic slurs, profanity, and vulgar speech are common causes of semantic noise.

noise
any external, internal, or semantic stimulus that interferes with sharing meaning.

external noises
sights, sounds, and other stimuli in the environment that draw people's attention away from what is being said or done.

internal noises
unrelated thoughts and feelings that draw attention away from what is said or done.

semantic noises
unintended meanings aroused by certain symbols and behaviors that distract your attention from what another person has to say.

Feedback

Feedback is a receiver's response to a message. Feedback indicates to the sender whether and how that message was heard, seen, and understood. If the verbal or nonverbal response indicates to the sender that the intended

feedback
a receiver's response to a message.

meaning was not heard or understood, the originator may try again to encode a message that the receiver might better understand.

A Model of the Basic Communication Process

Figure 1.1 illustrates the communication process between two people. In the minds of these people are meanings, thoughts, or feelings that they intend to share. The nature of those thoughts or feelings is created, shaped, and affected by their total field of experience, including such special factors as values, culture, environment, experiences, occupation, sex, interests, knowledge, and attitudes. To turn meaning into a message, the sender encodes thoughts or feelings into a message that is sent using one or more channels.

Meanings that have been encoded into symbols are turned back into meaning by the receiver through the decoding process. This decoding process is affected by the receiver's total field of experience—that is, by all

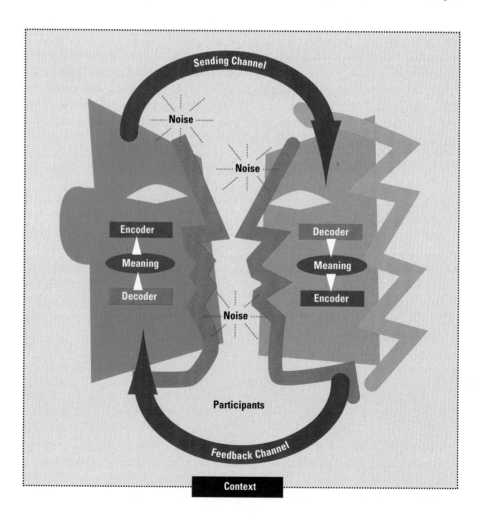

Figure 1.1
A model of communication between two individuals

Test Your Competence ▶

Identifying Elements of the Communication Process

For the following interaction, identify the context, participants, channel, message, noise, and feedback.

Maria and Damien are meandering through the park talking and drinking bottled water. Damien finishes his bottle, replaces the lid, and tosses the bottle into the bushes at the side of the path. Maria, who has been listening, comes to a stop, puts her hands on her hips, stares at Damien, and says angrily, "I can't believe what you just did!" Damien blushes, averts his gaze, and mumbles, "Sorry, I'll get it—I just wasn't thinking." As the tension drains from Maria's face, she gives her head a playful toss, smiles, and says, "Well, just see that it doesn't happen again."

 You can complete this activity online and compare your answer to the authors'. Use your Communicate! CD-ROM to access Skill Learning Activity 1.1 at the Communicate! Web site. When you get to the Communicate! home page, click on "Student Book Companion Site" in the Resource box at right. Select the chapter resources for Chapter 1, then click on "Activities."

the same factors that shape the encoding process. Feedback messages complete the process and provide information on how well the receiver understood the message.

The model depicts the context as the area around the participants. The physical, social, psychological, and cultural context permeates all parts of the process. Similarly the model shows that during conversation external, internal, and semantic noise may be occurring at various points that affect the people's ability to share meanings. As you might imagine, the process becomes much more complex when more than two people are conversing or when someone is speaking to a larger audience.

Communication Functions and Settings

Communication serves many functions and takes place in a variety of settings. When we know its various purposes, we are equipped to better understand the motives of those we talk with. When we recognize how settings affect the process, we can adapt our behavior so that we are more effective.

Communication Functions

Communication serves several important functions for us.

1. **We communicate to meet our social needs.** Just as we need food, water, and shelter, so too do we as social animals need contact with other people. Two people may converse happily for hours, gossiping and chatting about inconsequential matters that neither remembers afterward. When they

part, they may have exchanged little real information and they may never meet again, but their communication has functioned to meet the important need simply to talk with another human being. Similarly, we greet others as we pass by to meet social obligations.

2. **We communicate to enhance and maintain our sense of self.** Through our interactions, we learn who we are, what we are good at, and how people react to how we behave. We explore this important function of communication in detail in Chapter 2, "Perception of Self and Others."

3. **We communicate to develop relationships.** Not only do we get to know others through our communication with them but, more important, we develop relationships with them—relationships that grow and deepen or stagnate and wither away. We discuss how relationships begin and develop in Chapter 8, "Communicating in Relationships."

4. **We communicate to exchange information.** Some information we get through observation, some through reading, some through television, and a great deal through direct communication with others. Whether we are trying to decide how warmly to dress or whom to vote for in the next presidential election, all of us have countless exchanges that involve sending and receiving information. We discuss communication as information exchange in Chapter 5, "Holding Effective Conversations"; Chapter 10, "Participating in Group Communication"; and Chapter 17, "Informative Speaking."

5. **We communicate to influence others.** It is doubtful whether a day goes by in which you don't engage in behavior such as trying to convince your friends to go to a particular restaurant or to support a political candidate, to persuade your spouse to quit smoking, or (an old favorite) to convince an instructor to change your course grade. We discuss the role of influencing others in Chapter 11, "Member Roles in Leadership in Groups," and in Chapter 18, "Persuasive Speaking."

Communication Settings

While the basic communication process describes how meanings are shared, various communication skills can be learned so that you are effective across a variety of settings. In this book you will be introduced to skills to help you achieve communication competence in interpersonal, problem-solving group, public speaking, and electronically mediated settings.

Interpersonal communication settings Most of our communication takes place in **interpersonal communication settings** that are characterized by informal conversations between two or more people. Talking to a friend on campus, chatting on the phone with your mother, arguing the merits of a movie with friends, talking online, and comforting someone who has suffered a loss are all examples of interpersonal communication.

interpersonal communication settings *informal conversations between two or more people.*

Our study of interpersonal communication includes holding effective conversations; listening and responding empathically; sharing personal information; self-disclosure and feedback; developing, maintaining, or improving relationships; talking with people online; and interviewing.

Problem-solving group settings

Problem-solving group settings are characterized by participants who come together for the specific purpose of solving a problem or arriving at a decision. Much of this kind of communication takes place in formal or informal meetings.

Our study of problem-solving group settings includes a discussion of the characteristics of effective groups, the stages of group development, problem solving and decision making, and the roles participants play, including leadership.

problem-solving group settings
participants come together for the specific purpose of solving a problem or arriving at a decision.

Public speaking settings

Public speaking settings are characterized by one participant, the speaker, who delivers a prepared message to a group or audience who has assembled to hear the speaker.

Our discussion of public speaking settings focuses on the speech preparation and delivery process, including determining goals, gathering and evaluating material, organizing and developing material, adapting material to a specific audience, and presenting the speech, as well as variations in procedure for information exchange and persuasion.

public speaking settings
one participant, the speaker, delivers a prepared message to a group or audience who has assembled to hear the speaker.

Electronically mediated communication settings

Today interpersonal communication, group discussion, and public speaking can all take place in **electronically mediated communication settings** that are characterized by participants who do not share a physical context but communicate through the use of technology.

electronically mediated communication settings
participants who do not share a physical context but communicate through the use of technology.

Steve Dunwell/Getty Images

Interpersonally, we may keep in touch with distant family and friends through **email,** electronic correspondence conducted between two or more users on a network. Likewise, an increasing number of us are communicating with people we don't know but with whom we share a common interest through newsgroups and online chat. A **newsgroup** is "an electronic gathering place for people with similar interests" (Miller, 1999, p. 187). Think of a newsgroup as a collecting place for

email
electronic correspondence conducted between two or more users on a network.

newsgroup
an electronic gathering place for people with similar interests.

Email has taken the place of letter writing in most settings.

Internet chat
an interactive message exchange between two or more people in a chat room where the message and typed responses appearing instantly on participants' computer screens.

messages on a common topic. **Internet chat** is an interactive message exchange between two or more people in a chat room where the messages and typed responses appear instantly on participants' computer screens.

Finally, if the written communication revolution is taking place online, the oral communication revolution is taking place on cellular and digital telephones. In the past, telephone use was restricted to where a phone was wired. Now people can make and receive telephone calls from wherever they happen to be—in a car, on a bus, in a classroom, or on the street.

Communication Principles

Principles are general truths. Understanding the principles of communication is important as you begin your study. In this section we discuss seven principles: communication has purpose, communication is continuous, communication messages vary in conscious thought, communication is relational, communication is guided by culture, communication has ethical implications, and communication is learned.

Communication Has Purpose

When people communicate with one another, they have a purpose for doing so. The purpose of a given transaction may be serious or trivial. One way to evaluate the success of the communication is to ask whether it achieved its purpose. When Beth calls Leah to ask whether she'd like to join her for lunch to discuss a project they are working on, her purpose may be to resolve a misunderstanding they've had. Depending on the speaker's purpose, even an apparently successful transaction may fail to achieve its goal. And, of course, different purposes call for different communication strategies.

Speakers may not always be aware of their purpose. For instance, when Jamal passes Tony on the street and says lightly, "Tony, what's happening?" Jamal probably doesn't consciously think, "Tony's an acquaintance and I want him to understand that I see him and consider him worth recognizing." In this case the social obligation to recognize Tony is met spontaneously with the first acceptable expression that comes to Jamal's mind. Regardless of whether Jamal consciously thinks about the purpose, it still motivates his behavior. In this case Jamal will have achieved his goal if Tony responds with an equally casual greeting.

Communication Is Continuous

Because communication is nonverbal as well as verbal, we are always sending behavioral messages from which others draw inferences or meaning. Even silence or absence are communication behaviors if another person infers meaning from them. Why? Because your nonverbal behavior represents reactions to your environment and to the people around you. If you are cold, you shiver; if you are hot or nervous, you perspire; if you are bored, happy, or confused, your face or body language probably will show it. As skilled communicators, we need to be aware of the explicit and implicit messages we are constantly sending to others.

Communication Messages Vary in Conscious Thought

As we discussed earlier in this chapter, sharing meaning with another person involves presenting verbal and nonverbal messages. Our messages (1) may occur spontaneously, (2) may be based on a "script" we have learned or rehearsed, or (3) may be carefully constructed based on our understanding of the unique situation in which we find ourselves.

Many of our messages are **spontaneous expressions,** spoken without much conscious thought. For example, when you burn your finger, you may blurt out "Ouch." When something goes right, you may break into a broad smile.

At other times, our messages are **scripted,** phrasings that we have learned from our past encounters and judge to be appropriate to the present situation. Many of these scripts are learned in childhood. For example, when you want the sugar bowl but cannot reach it, you may say, "Please pass the sugar," followed by "Thank you" when someone complies. This conversational sequence comes from your "table manners script," which may have been drilled into you at home. Scripts enable us to use messages that are appropriate to the situation and are likely to increase the effectiveness of our communication. One goal of this text is to acquaint you with general scripts (or skills) that can be adapted for use in your communication encounters across a variety of relationships, situations, and cultures.

Finally, our messages may be carefully constructed to meet the unique requirements of a particular situation. **Constructed messages** are those that we put together with careful thought when we recognize that our known scripts are inadequate for the situation.

Communication Is Relational

Saying that communication is relational means that in any communication setting, in addition to sharing content meaning, our messages also reflect two important aspects of our relationships: immediacy and control (dominance/submissiveness).

Immediacy is the degree of liking or attractiveness in a relationship. For instance, when José passes by Hal on campus he may say, "Hal, good to see you" (a verbal expression of friendliness); the nonverbal behavior that accompanies the words may show Hal whether José is genuinely happy to see him or is only expressing recognition. For instance, if José smiles, has a sincere sound to his voice, looks Hal in the eye, and perhaps pats him on the back or shakes hands firmly, then Hal will recognize these signs of friendliness. If, however, José speaks quickly with no vocal inflection and with a deadpan facial expression, Hal will perceive the comment as solely meeting some social expectation.

spontaneous expressions
spoken without much conscious thought.

scripted messages
phrasings learned from past encounters that we judge to be appropriate to the present situation.

constructed messages
messages put together with careful thought when we recognize that our known scripts are inadequate for the situation.

immediacy
the degree of liking or attractiveness in a relationship.

Michael Keller/The Stock Market

What messages about affect and control do wedding couples send as they feed each other cake? Power in relationships is influenced by both verbal and nonverbal messages.

control
the degree to which one participant is perceived to be more dominant or powerful.

Control is the degree to which one participant is perceived to be more dominant or powerful. Thus, when Tom says to Sue, "I know you're concerned about the budget, but I'll see to it that we have money to cover everything," his words and the sound of his voice may be saying that he is "in charge" of finances—that he is in control. How Sue responds to Tom determines whether on this issue she submits to his perception of control. If Sue says, "Thanks, I know you have a better handle on finances than I do," then she accepts that on this issue she is willing to submit to Tom at this time. A few days later, if Tom says to Sue, "I think we need to cut back on credit card expenses for a couple of months," and Sue responds, "No way! I need a new suit for work, the car needs new tires, and you promised we could replace the couch," then the nature of the relationship will require further discussion.

Communication Is Guided by Culture

cultural diversity
variations between and among people that affect every aspect of communication.

How messages are formed and how they are interpreted depends on the cultural background of the participants. **Cultural diversity,** variations between and among people, affects every aspect of communication. In our conversations, even though we both speak English, our cultural differences will influence the meanings we share.

Because the people who live in the United States come from a variety of cultures, opportunities for misunderstanding abound. Cultural diversity in the United States continues to grow. According to the U.S. Census Bureau, between 1990 and 2002 the foreign-born percentage of the U.S. population grew from 8 percent to 11.5 percent—about 8.6 million people. Moreover, in 2000 five metropolitan areas (Los Angeles, New York, San Francisco, Miami, and Chicago) together were home to *half* of the U.S. foreign-born population. To read more about the U.S. foreign-born population, use your Communicate! CD-ROM to access Web Resource 1.1: Profile of Foreign Born Population at the Communicate! Web site. Select the chapter resources for

Chapter 1, then click on "Web Resources." We are increasingly likely to encounter people who are culturally different from us, and if we are not sensitive to cultural considerations, we may hurt our relationships.

When we think of cultural diversity, ethnicity and race quickly come to mind. But cultural diversity in communication is also a result of gender, age, sexual orientation, class, education, and religious differences among people. Just as people of different ethnicity may have different rules that guide message construction and interpretation, so too do people who differ in age or sex or who profess different religions. Slang terms are often generation specific. And conversation and touching behavior between people of the opposite sex may be dictated by religious norms.

According to Samovar and Porter (2003), "three cultural elements have the potential to affect situations in which people from different backgrounds come together: (1) perception, (2) verbal processes, and (3) nonverbal processes" (p. 11). Because cultural concerns permeate all of communication, in each chapter of this book we will point out when the concepts and skills you are learning are viewed differently by other cultural groups. In addition, the Diverse Voices feature found in many chapters presents excerpts from articles whose authors explain how they or their culture views a concept presented in the text. In this chapter Harlan Cleveland describes how the diverse peoples in the United States have learned to live together.

DIVERSE VOICES

Lessons from American Experience

by Harland Cleveland

Harland Cleveland, former president of the University of Hawaii, is president of the World Academy of Art and Science. In this selection Cleveland explains how Hawaii, the most diverse of our fifty states, achieves ethnic and racial peace. He argues that the Hawaiian experience is no different from the experience of immigrants to the mainland; the ability to tolerate diversity is not unique in the world.

We Americans have learned, in our short but intensive 200-plus years of history as a nation, a first lesson about diversity: that it cannot be governed by drowning it in "integration."

I came face-to-face with this truth when, just a quarter of a century ago, I became president of the University of Hawaii. Everyone who lives in Hawaii, or even visits there, is impressed by its residents' comparative tolerance toward each other. On closer inspection, paradise seems based on paradox: Everybody's a minority. The tolerance is not despite the diversity but because of it.

It is not through the disappearance of ethnic distinctions that the people of Hawaii achieved a level of racial peace that has few parallels around our discriminatory globe. Quite the contrary. The glory is that Hawaii's main ethnic groups managed to establish the right to be separate. The group separateness in turn helped establish the rights of individuals in each group to equality with individuals of different racial aspect, different ethnic origin, and different cultural heritage.

Hawaii's experience is not so foreign to the transatlantic migrations of the various more-or-less white Caucasians. On arrival in New York (passing that inscription on the Statue of Liberty, "Send these, the homeless, tempest-tost, to me"), the European immigrants did not melt into the open arms of the white Anglo-Saxon Protestants who preceded them. The reverse was true. The new arrivals stayed close to their own kind, shared religion and language and humor and discriminatory treatment with their soul brothers and sisters, and gravitated at first into occupations that did not too seriously threaten the earlier arrivals.

The waves of new Americans learned to tolerate each other—first as groups, only thereafter as individuals. Rubbing up against each other in an urbanizing America, they discovered not just the old Christian lesson that all men are brothers, but the hard, new, multicultural lesson that all brothers are different. Equality is not the product of similarity; it is the cheerful acknowledgement of difference.

What's so special about our experience is the assumption that people of many kinds and colors can together govern themselves without deciding in advance which kinds of people (male or female, black, brown, yellow, red, white, or any mix of these) may hold any particular public office in the pantheon of political power.

For the 21st century, this "cheerful acknowledgement of difference" is the alternative to a global spread of ethnic cleansing and religious rivalry. The challenge is great, for ethnic cleansing and religious rivalry are traditions as contemporary as Bosnia and Rwanda in the 1990s and as ancient as the Assyrians.

In too many countries there is still a basic if often unspoken assumption that one kind of people is anointed to be in general charge. Try to imagine a Turkish chancellor of Germany, an Algerian president of France, a Pakistani prime minister of Britain, a Christian president of Egypt, an Arab prime minister of Israel, a Jewish president of Syria, a Tibetan ruler of Beijing, anyone but a Japanese in power in Tokyo. Yet in the United States during the twentieth century, we have already elected an Irish Catholic as president, chosen several Jewish Supreme Court justices, and racially integrated the armed forces right up to the chairman of the Joint Chiefs of Staff. . . .

I wouldn't dream of arguing that we Americans have found the Holy Grail of cultural diversity when in fact we're still searching for it. We have to think hard about our growing pluralism. It's useful, I believe, to dissect in the open our thinking about it, to see whether the lessons we are trying to learn might stimulate some useful thinking elsewhere. We do not yet quite know how to create "wholeness incorporating diversity," but we owe it to the world, as well as to ourselves, to keep trying.

Excerpted from Harland Cleveland, "The Limits to Cultural Diversity." In Larry A. Samovar and Richard E. Porter (Eds.), Intercultural Communication: A Reader *(10th ed., pp. 433–436). Belmont, CA: Wadsworth, 2003. Reprinted by permission of the World Future Society.*

Communication Has Ethical Implications

ethics
a set of moral principles that may be held by a society, a group, or an individual.

In any encounter we choose whether or not we will communicate ethically. **Ethics** is a set of moral principles that may be held by a society, a group, or an individual. Although what is considered ethical is a matter of personal judgment, various groups still expect members to uphold certain standards. These standards influence the personal decisions we make. When we choose to violate the standards that are expected, we are viewed to be unethical. Here are five ethical standards that influence our communication and guide our behavior.

1. **Truthfulness and honesty** mean refraining from lying, cheating, stealing, or deception. "An honest person is widely regarded as a moral person, and honesty is a central concept to ethics as the foundation for a moral life" (Terkel & Duval, 1999, p. 122). Although most people accept truthfulness and honesty as a standard, they still confess to lying on occasion. We are most likely to lie when we are caught in a **moral dilemma,** a choice involving an unsatisfactory alternative such as not telling a person that our sister committed a minor infraction if we know that the person asking is looking for any excuse to cause our sister considerable harm.

    To understand more about how and why people lie, read the article "Lying and Deception," available through InfoTrac College Edition. Use your Communicate! CD-ROM to access **Web Resource 1.2: "Lying and Deception"** at the Communicate! Web site. Select the chapter resources for Chapter 1, then click on "Web Resources."

truthfulness and honesty
refraining from lying, cheating, stealing, or deception.

moral dilemma
a choice involving an unsatisfactory alternative.

2. **Integrity** means maintaining a consistency of belief and action (keeping promises). Terkel and Duval (1999) say, "A person who has integrity is someone who has strong moral principles and will successfully resist the temptation to compromise those principles" (p. 135). Integrity then is the opposite of hypocrisy. A person who had promised to take a friend to the doctor would live up to this promise even if he or she had an opportunity to go out with a friend.

integrity
maintaining a consistency of belief and action (keeping promises).

3. **Fairness** means achieving the right balance of interests without regard to one's own feelings and without showing favor to any side in a conflict. Fairness implies impartiality or lack of bias. To be fair to someone is to listen with an open mind, to gather all the relevant facts, consider only circumstances relevant to the decision at hand, and not let prejudice or irrelevancies affect how you treat others. For example, if two of her children are fighting, a mom is exercising fairness if she listens openly as the children explain "their side" before she decides what to do.

fairness
achieving the right balance of interests without regard to one's own feelings and without showing favor to any side in a conflict.

4. **Respect** means showing regard or consideration for others and their ideas, even if we don't agree with them. Respect is not based on someone's affluence, job status, or ethnic background. We demonstrate respect by listening to and really trying to understand others' points of view, even when they are vastly different from our own.

respect
showing regard or consideration for others and their ideas, even if we don't agree with them.

5. **Responsibility** means being accountable for one's actions and what one says. Responsible communicators recognize the power of words. Messages can hurt and messages can soothe. Information is accurate or it may be faulty. Responsible communicators hold themselves accountable for how their messages affect others.

responsibility
being accountable for one's actions and what one says.

To learn more about ethics, check out the Web site for the Markkula Center for Applied Ethics at Santa Clara University. Use your Communicate! CD-ROM to access **Web Resource 1.3: Ethics Connection** at the Communicate! Web site. Select the chapter resources for Chapter 1, then click on "Web Resources."

In our daily lives we often face ethical dilemmas and must sort out what is more or less right or wrong. In making these decisions we usually reveal our ethical standards. At the end of each chapter of this book, the feature What Would You Do? A Question of Ethics will ask you to think about and resolve an ethical dilemma that relates to that chapter's content. Your instructor may use these as a vehicle for class discussions, or you may be asked to prepare a written report.

Communication Is Learned

Just as you learned to walk, so too you learned to communicate. But talking is a complex undertaking. You may not yet have learned all of the skills you will need to develop healthy relationships. Because communication is learned, you can improve your ability. Throughout this text we identify interpersonal, group, and public speaking skills that can help you become a more competent communicator.

Just as children learn how to behave from their parents, so too do they learn to communicate. What specific communication behaviors can you identify that you learned at home?

© George Simian/CORBIS

Increasing Our Communication Competence

communication competence
the impression that communicative behavior is both appropriate and effective in a given situation.

Communication competence is the impression that communicative behavior is both appropriate and effective in a given situation (Spitzberg, 2000, p. 375). Communication is *effective* when it achieves its goals; it is *appropriate* when it conforms to what is expected in a situation. We create the perception that we are competent communicators through the verbal messages we send and the nonverbal behaviors that accompany them.

Because communication is at the heart of how we relate to one another, one of your goals in this course will be to learn those things that will increase the likelihood that others will view you as competent. In the

Spotlight on Scholars we feature Brian Spitzberg on Interpersonal Communication Competence. Spitzberg believes perceptions of competence depend in part on personal motivation, knowledge, and skills (2000, p. 377).

Motivation is important because we will only be able to improve our communication if we are *motivated*—that is, if we want to. People are likely to be more motivated if they are confident and if they see potential rewards.

Knowledge is important because we must know what is involved in increasing competence. The more knowledge people have about how to behave in a given situation, the more likely they are to be able to develop competence.

Spotlight on Scholars ▶ Brian Spitzberg

Professor of Communication, ◆ ◆
San Diego State University, ◆ ◆
on Interpersonal
Communication Competence

A lthough Brian Spitzberg has made many contributions to our understanding of interpersonal communication, he is best known for his work in interpersonal communication competence. This interest in competence began at the University of Southern California. For an interpersonal communication seminar assignment, he read the available research on interpersonal competence and found that the conclusions went in different directions. Spitzberg believed the time was ripe for someone to synthesize these perspectives into a comprehensive theory of competence. His final paper for the seminar was his first effort toward constructing a competence theory.

Today, the model of interpersonal communication competence Spitzberg formulated guides most of our thinking and research in this area. He views competence neither as a trait nor as a set of behaviors. Rather, Spitzberg says that interpersonal communication competence is a perception people have about themselves or another person. If competence is a percep-

tion, then it follows that your perception of your interpersonal communication competence or that of your relationship partner would affect how you feel about that relationship. So people are more likely to be satisfied in a relationship when they perceive themselves and the other person as competent. According to Spitzberg, we make these competence judgments based on how each of us acts when we talk together. But what determines how we act in a particular conversation?

As Spitzberg was trying to organize his thinking about competence, he was taking another course in which he became acquainted with theories of dramatic acting. These theories held that an actor's performance depended on the actor's motivation, knowledge of the script, and acting skills. Spitzberg found that these same variables could be applied to communication competence, and he incorporated them into his theory. How we behave in a conversation depends first on how personally motivated we are to have the conversation; second, on how personally knowledgeable we are about what behavior is appropriate in situations like this; and third, on how personally skilled we are at actually using the appropriate behaviors during the conversation. In addition, Spitzberg's theory suggests that context variables, such as those previously discussed in this chapter, also affect how we choose to act in a conversation and the perceptions of competence that they create.

Spitzberg formed most of these ideas while he was still in graduate school, but he and others have spent more than twenty years refining the theory, conducting programs of research based on his theory, and measuring the effectiveness of the theory. The research has fleshed out parts of the theory and provided some evidence of the theory's accuracy. Over the years Spitzberg has developed about a dozen specific instruments to measure parts of the theory. One of these measures, the Conversational Skills Rating Scale, has been adopted as the standard measure of interpersonal communication skills by the National Communication Association (a leading national organization of communication scholars, teachers, and practitioners). His most recent work involves translating the model and measures of competence into the computer-mediated context. To what extent are the skills we use in face-to-face communication similar to those we use in computer-based interaction? Several research projects are currently investigating this question.

Whether the situation is a first date or a job interview, a conflict with a roommate or an intimate discussion of your feelings, Spitzberg believes it is important that others perceive you to be competent. For a list of a few of Spitzberg's publications on competence, see the References section at the end of this book.

For more information about Brian Spitzberg, log on to http://www-rohan.sdsu.edu/dept/schlcomm/Spitzbergbbio.html.

skills
goal-oriented actions or action sequences that we can master and repeat in appropriate situations.

Skill is important because we must know how to act in ways that are consistent with our communication knowledge. **Skills** are goal-oriented actions or action sequences that we can master and repeat in appropriate situations. The more skills you have, the more likely you are to be able to structure your messages effectively and appropriately.

The combination of our motivation, knowledge, and skills lead us to perform confidently in our encounters with others. The rest of this book is aimed at helping you increase the likelihood that you will be perceived as competent. In the pages that follow, you will learn about theories of interpersonal, group, and public speaking that can increase your knowledge and your motivation. You will also learn how to perform specific skills, and you will be provided with opportunities to practice them. Through this practice, you can increase the likelihood that you will be able to perform these skills when needed.

Writing Goal Statements

To get the most from this course, we suggest that you write personal goals to improve specific skills in your own interpersonal, group, and public communication repertoire. Why written goal statements? A familiar saying goes, "The road to hell is paved with good intentions." Regardless of how serious you are about changing some aspect of your communication, bringing about changes in behavior takes time and effort. Writing specific goals makes it more likely that your good intentions to improve won't get lost in the busyness of your life.

Before you can write a goal statement, you must first analyze your current communication skills repertoire. After you read each chapter and practice the skills described, select one or two skills to work on. Then write down your goal statement in four parts.

1. **State the problem.** Start by stating a communication problem that you have. For example: "Problem: Even though my boss consistently gives all the interesting tasks to coworkers, I haven't spoken up because I'm not very good at describing my feelings."

2. **State the specific goal.** A goal is specific if it is measurable and you know when you have achieved it. For example, to deal with the problem stated above, you might write, "Goal: To describe my feelings about task assignments to my boss."

3. **Outline a specific procedure for reaching the goal.** To develop a plan for reaching your goal, first consult the chapter that covers the skill you wish to hone (for instance, Describing Feelings in Chapter 7). Then translate the general steps recommended in the chapter to your specific situation. This step is critical because successful behavioral change requires that you state your objective in terms of specific behaviors you can adopt or modify. For example: "Procedure: I will practice the steps of describing feelings. (1) I will identify the specific feeling I am experiencing. (2) I will encode the emotion I am feeling accurately. (3) I will include what has triggered the feeling. (4) I will own the feeling as mine. (5) I will then put that procedure into operation when I am talking with my boss."

4. **Devise a method of determining when the goal has been reached.** A good goal is measurable, and the fourth part of your goal-setting effort is to determine your minimum requirements for knowing when you have achieved a given goal. For example: "Test of Achieving Goal: This goal will be considered achieved when I have described my feelings to my boss on the next occasion when his behavior excludes me."

Once you have completed all four parts of this goal-setting process, you may want to have another person witness your commitment and serve as a consultant, coach, and support person. This gives you someone to talk to about your progress. A good choice would be someone from this class because he or she is in an excellent position to understand and help. (Also, perhaps you can reciprocate with your support for his or her goal statements in return.)

At the end of each section you will be challenged to develop a goal statement related to the material presented. Figure 1.2 provides another example of a communication improvement plan, this one relating to a public speaking problem.

Problem: When I speak in class or in the student senate, I often find myself burying my head in my notes or looking at the ceiling or walls.

Goal: To look at people more directly when I'm giving a speech.

Procedure: I will take the time to practice oral presentations aloud in my room. (1) I will stand up just as I do in class. (2) I will pretend various objects in the room are people, and I will consciously attempt to look at those objects as I am talking. (3) In giving a speech, I will try to be aware of when I am looking at my audience and when I am not.

Test of Achieving Goal: This goal will be considered achieved when I am maintaining eye contact with my audience most of the time.

Figure 1.2
Communication improvement plan

What Would You Do?   ▶ A QUESTION OF ETHICS

olly has just been accepted at Stanford University and calls her friend Terri to tell her the good news.

MOLLY: Hi Terri! Guess what? I just got accepted to Stanford Law School!

TERRI [*Surprised and disappointed*]: Oh, cool.

MOLLY: Thanks—you sound so enthusiastic!

TERRI: Oh, I am. Listen, I have to go—I'm late for class.

MOLLY: Oh, OK. See you.

The women hang up, and Terri immediately calls her friend Monica.

TERRI: Monica, it's Terri.

MONICA: Hey, Terri. What's up?

TERRI: I just got some terrible news—Molly got into Stanford!

MONICA: So, what's wrong with that? I think it's great. Aren't you happy for her?

TERRI: No, not at all. I didn't get in, and I have better grades and a higher LSAT score.

MONICA: Maybe Molly had a better application.

TERRI: Or maybe it was what was on her application.

MONICA: What do you mean?

TERRI: You know what I mean. Molly's black.

MONICA: Yes, and . . . ?

TERRI: Don't you see? It's called affirmative action.

MONICA: Terri, give it a rest!

TERRI: Oh, please. You know it, and I know it. She only got in because of her race and because she's poor. Her GPA is really low and so is her LSAT.

MONICA: Did you ever stop to think that maybe she wrote an outstanding essay? Or that they thought the time she spent volunteering in that free legal clinic in her neighborhood was good background?

TERRI: Yes, but we've both read some of her papers, and we know she can't write. Listen, Monica, if you're black, Asian, Native American, Latino, or any other minority and poor, you've got it made. You can be as stupid as Forrest Gump and get into any law school you want. It's just not fair at all.

MONICA [*Angrily*]: No, you know what isn't fair? I'm sitting here listening to my so-called friend insult my intelligence and my ethnic background. How dare you tell me that the only reason I'll ever get into a good medical school is because I'm Latino. Listen, honey, I'll get into medical school just the same way that Molly got into law school, because of my brains, my accomplishments, and my ethical standards. And based on this conversation, it's clear that Molly and I are way ahead of you.

Describe how well each of these women followed the ethical standards for communication discussed in this chapter.

Adapted from "Racism," a case study posted on the Web site of the Ethics Connection, Markkula Center for Applied Ethics, Santa Clara University. http://www.scu.edu/ethics/practicing/focusareas/education/racism.html. Used with permission.

Summary

We have defined communication as the process of creating or sharing meaning, whether the context is informal conversation, group interaction, or public speaking.

The elements of the communication process are context, participants, messages, channels, noise, and feedback.

Communication plays a role in all aspects of our lives. First, communication serves many important functions. People communicate to meet needs, to enhance and maintain a sense of self, to develop relationships, to fulfill social obligations, to exchange information, and to influence others. Second, communication occurs in interpersonal, group, and public speaking settings, and increasingly in electronically mediated settings.

Our communication is guided by at least seven principles. First, communication is purposeful. Second, interpersonal communication is continuous. Third, interpersonal communication messages vary in degree of conscious encoding. Messages may be spontaneous, scripted, or constructed. Fourth, interpersonal communication is relational, defining the power and affection between people. Fifth, communication is guided by culture. Sixth, communication has ethical implications. Ethical standards that influence our communication include truthfulness, integrity, fairness, respect, and responsibility. And seventh, interpersonal communication is learned.

A primary issue in this course is competence—we all strive to become better communicators. Competence is the perception by others that our communication behavior is appropriate as well as effective. It involves increasing our knowledge of communication and our understanding of the situations we face, identifying and attaining goals, and being able to use the various behavioral skills necessary to achieve our goals. Skills can be learned, developed, and improved, and you can enhance your learning this term by writing goal statements to systematically improve your own skill repertoire.

Communicate! Online

N ow that you have read Chapter 1, use your Communicate! CD-ROM for quick access to the electronic resources that accompany this text. Your CD-ROM gives you access to InfoTrac College Edition and the Communicate! Web site. When you get to the Communicate! home page, click on "Student Book Companion Site" in the Resource box at right to access the online study aids for this chapter, including a digital glossary, review quizzes, chapter activities, and chapter Web Resources.

Key Terms

At the Communicate! Web site, select chapter resources for Chapter 1. Print a copy of the glossary for this chapter and test yourself with the electronic flash cards or complete the crossword puzzle to help you master these key terms:

communication (4)	external noises (7)	scripted messages (13)
participants (4)	internal noises (7)	constructed messages (13)
contexts (5)	semantic noises (7)	immediacy (13)
physical context (5)	feedback (7)	control (14)
social context (5)	interpersonal communication	cultural diversity (14)
historical context (5)	settings (10)	ethics (16)
psychological context (6)	problem-solving group settings	truthfulness and honesty (17)
cultural context (6)	(11)	moral dilemma (17)
messages (6)	public speaking settings (11)	integrity (17)
meaning (6)	electronically mediated com-	fairness (17)
symbols (6)	munication settings (11)	respect (17)
encoding (7)	email (11)	responsibility (17)
decoding (7)	newsgroup (11)	communication competence
channel (7)	Internet chat (12)	(18)
noise (7)	spontaneous expression (13)	skills (20)

Review Quiz

Test your knowledge of the concepts in this chapter by taking the online quiz at the Communicate! Web site. Select the chapter resources for Chapter 1, then click on "Review Quiz." When you have completed the quiz, submit it for scoring.

Skill Learning Activities

Complete the Observe & Analyze and Test Your Competence activities for Chapter 1 online at the Communicate! Web site. Select the chapter resources for Chapter 1, then click on "Activities." You can submit your Observe & Analyze answers to your instructor, and you can compare your Test Your Competence answers to those provided by the authors.

1.1: Test Your Competence: Identifying Elements of the Communication Process (9)
1.2: Observe & Analyze: Communication Functions (10)

Web Resources

Access the Web Resources for this chapter online at the Communicate! Web site. Select the chapter resources for Chapter 1, then click on "Web Resources."

1.1: Profile of Foreign-Born Population (14)
1.2: Lying and Deception (17)
1.3: Ethics Connection (17)

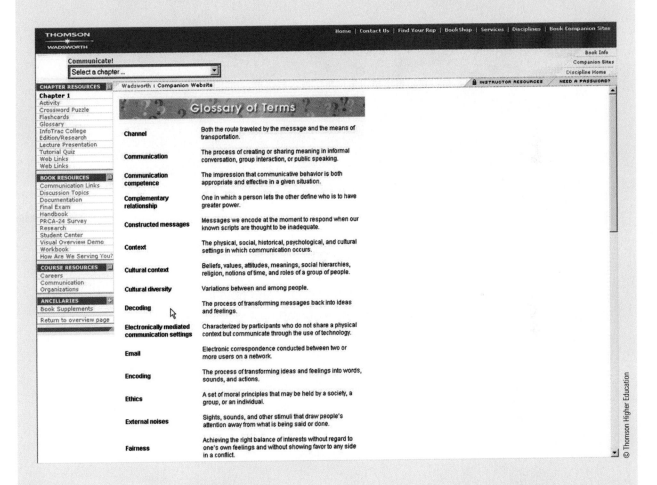

After you have read this chapter, you should be able to answer these questions:

- What is perception?
- How does your mind select, organize, and interpret information?
- What is the self-concept, and how is it formed?
- What is self-esteem, and how is it developed?
- How do self-concept and self-esteem affect our communication with others?
- What affects how accurately we perceive others?
- What are some methods for improving the accuracy of your social perception?

2

Perception of Self and Others

A s Dwayne and Miguel leave their Spanish Literature class on the first day of the semester, Dwayne comments: "Man, I can't believe it! This course is going to be impossible—I don't know if I can do it."

"Really?" replies Miguel. "I thought the course sounded really interesting. The professor was interesting to listen to, and I really liked the idea that we could choose our own term paper topic."

"But Miguel, did you see what we're reading. We've got five books to read—with a test over each book, and then we're supposed to write a term paper!"

"But Dwayne, they're fiction. I mean we start with *Don Quixote* and then read four other books written over a two-hundred-year period—we'll really get an interesting look at Spanish history and culture. And since the professor is so knowledgeable—I mean he was born and educated in Spain—he'll really be able to give us an insider's look."

"Right—as if I need an insider's look. I'm taking four other courses that look pretty heavy. Sure, I wouldn't have signed up for the course if I didn't like Spanish, but five books and a term paper!"

"I think we'll see real contrasts among the writers from different time periods, and writing the paper is going to be fun."

"Fun? Shooting baskets, playing video games, going out on dates—that's fun. Writing a term paper? That's work."

Have you had this kind of disagreement with a friend after a first day of class? How do we come to have different takes on the same event? As we analyze this conversation we can see that Dwayne focuses on the time requirements and workload in the class whereas Miguel focuses on what he can learn. They attended the same class but carried away different perceptions. Because much of the meaning we share with others is based on our perceptions, the study of interpersonal communication begins with understanding the general perceptual process and the social perceptions that affect how we view others.

In this chapter we discuss the perception process, perceptions of self (self-concept and self-esteem), and perceptions of others.

The Perception Process

perception
the process of selectively attending to information and assigning meaning to it.

Perception is the process of selectively attending to information and assigning meaning to it. Your brain selects the information it receives from your sense organs, organizes the information selected, and interprets and evaluates it.

Attention and Selection

Although we are subject to a constant barrage of sensory stimuli, we focus attention on relatively little of it. How we choose depends in part on our needs, interests, and expectations.

Needs   We are likely to pay attention to information that meets our biological and psychological needs. When you go to class, how well in tune you are to what is being discussed is likely to depend on whether you believe the information is important to you—that is, does it meet a personal need?

Interests   We are likely to pay attention to information that pertains to our interests. For instance, you may not even recognize that music is playing in the background until you find yourself suddenly listening to some "old favorite." Similarly, when you are really attracted to a person, you are more likely to pay attention to what that person is saying.

Expectations   Finally, we are likely to see what we expect to see and to miss information that violates our expectations. Take a quick look at the phrases in the triangles in Figure 2.1. If you have never seen these triangles, you probably read "Paris in the springtime," "Once in a lifetime," and "Bird in the hand." But if you reexamine the words, you will see that what you perceived was not exactly what is written. Do you now see the repeated words? It is easy to miss the repeated word because we don't *expect* to see the word repeated.

Figure 2.1
A sensory test of expectation

Organization of Stimuli

Even though our attention and selection process limits the stimuli our brain must process, the absolute number of discrete stimuli we attend to at any one moment is still substantial. Our brains follow certain organizing principles to arrange these stimuli so that they make sense. Two common principles we use are simplicity and pattern.

Simplicity If the stimuli we attend to are very complex, the brain simplifies the stimuli into some commonly recognized form. Based on a quick perusal of what someone is wearing, how she is standing, and the expression on her face, we may perceive her as "a successful businesswoman," "a doctor," or "a soccer mom." Similarly, we simplify the verbal messages we receive. So, for example, Tony might walk out of an hour-long performance review meeting with his boss in which the boss described four of Tony's strengths and three areas for improvement and say to Jerry, his coworker, "Well, I better shape up or I'm going to get fired!"

Pattern A second principle the brain uses when organizing information is to find patterns. A **pattern** is a set of characteristics used to differentiate some things from others. A pattern makes it easy to interpret stimuli. For example, when you see a crowd of people, instead of perceiving each individual, you may focus on a characteristic of sex and "see" men and women, or you may focus on age and "see" children, teens, adults, and seniors. When someone asks you what you noticed about people, you are being asked to discuss pattern.

pattern
a set of characteristics used to differentiate some things from others.

In our interactions with others we try to find patterns that will enable us to interpret and respond to their behavior. For example, each time Jason and Bill encounter Sara, she hurries over to them and begins an animated conversation. Yet when Jason is alone and runs into Sara, she barely says "Hi." After a while Jason may detect a pattern to Sara's behavior. She is warm and friendly when Bill is around and not so friendly when Bill is absent. Based on this pattern, Jason may interpret Sara's friendly behavior as "flirting with Bill."

Interpretation of Stimuli

As the brain selects and organizes the information it receives from the senses, it also **interprets** the information by assigning meaning to it. Look at these three sets of numbers. What do you make of them?

interpret
assigning meaning to information.

A. 631 7348

B. 285 37 5632

C. 4632 7364 2596 2174

In each of these sets, your mind looked for clues to give meaning to the numbers. Because you use similar patterns of numbers every day, you probably interpret A as a telephone number. How about B? A likely interpretation is a Social Security number. And C? People who use credit cards may interpret this set as a credit card number.

Our interpretation of others' behavior in conversation affects how we interact with them. If Jason believes that Sara is only interested in Bill, he may not participate in conversations that she initiates.

In the remainder of this chapter we will apply this basic information about perception to the study of perceptions of self and others in our communication.

Perceptions of Self: Self-Concept and Self-Esteem

self-concept
your self-identity.

self-esteem
your overall evaluation of your competence and personal worthiness.

Self-concept and self-esteem are the two self-perceptions that have the greatest impact on how we communicate. **Self-concept** is your self-identity (Baron & Byrne, 2000, p. 160). It is the idea or mental image that you have about your skills, your abilities, your knowledge, your competencies, and your personality. **Self-esteem** is your overall evaluation of your competence and personal worthiness (based on Mruk, 1999, p. 26). In this section we describe how you come to understand who you are and how you determine whether what you are is good. Then we examine what determines how well these self-perceptions match others' perceptions of you and the role self-perceptions play when you communicate with others.

Forming and Maintaining a Self-Concept

How do we learn what our skills, abilities, knowledge, competencies, and personality are? Our self-concept comes from the unique interpretations about ourselves that we have made based on our experience and from others' reactions and responses to us.

Self-perception We form impressions about ourselves based on our own perceptions. Through our experiences, we develop our own sense of our skills, our abilities, our knowledge, our competencies, and our personality. For example, if you perceive that it is easy for you to strike up conversations with strangers and that you enjoy chatting with them, you may conclude that you are outgoing or friendly.

We place a great deal of emphasis on the first experience we have with a particular phenomenon. For instance, someone who is rejected in his first try at dating may perceive himself to be unattractive to the opposite sex. If additional experiences produce results similar to the first experience, this first perception will be strengthened. Even if the first experience is not immediately repeated, it is likely to take more than one contradictory experience to change the original negative perception.

When we have positive experiences, we are likely to believe we possess the personal characteristics that we associate with that experience, and these characteristics become part of our picture of who we are. So if Sonya quickly debugs a computer program that Jackie has struggled with, she is more likely to incorporate "competent problem solver" into her self-concept. Her positive experience confirms that she has that skill, so it is reinforced as part of her self-concept.

Reactions and responses of others In addition to our self-perceptions, our self-concept is formed and maintained by how others react and respond to us (Rayner, 2001, p. 43). We use other people's comments as a check on our own self-descriptions. They serve to validate, reinforce, or alter our perception of who and what we are. For example, if during a brainstorming session at work, one of your coworkers tells you "You're really a creative thinker," you may decide that this comment fits your image of who you are. And, as Rayner suggests, such comments are especially powerful in affecting your self-perception if you respect the person making the comment. And the power of such comments is increased when the praise is immediate rather than delayed (Hattie, 1992, p. 251).

Some people have very rich self-concepts; they can describe numerous skills, abilities, knowledge, competencies, and personality characteristics that they possess. Others have weak self-concepts; they cannot describe the skills, abilities, knowledge, competencies, or the personality characteristics that they have. The richer our self-concept, the better we know and understand who we are and the better able we will be to cope with the challenges we will face as we interact with others.

Our self-concept begins to form early in life, and information we receive from our families shapes our self-concept (Demo, 1987). One of the major responsibilities that family members have is to talk and act in ways that will help develop accurate and strong self-concepts in other family members. For example, the mom who says, "Roberto, your room looks very neat. You are very organized," or the brother who comments, "Kisha, lending Tomika five dollars really helped her out. You are very generous," is helping Roberto or Kisha to recognize important parts of their personalities.

Our family members shape our self-concept. Can you recall a time when someone in your family praised you for something you had done? Is that something you still consider yourself to be good at?

© David Young-Wolff/PhotoEdit

Observe&Analyze

Who Am I?

First ask, *How do I see myself?* List the skills, abilities, knowledge, competencies, and personality characteristics that describe how you see yourself. To generate this list, try completing the sentences: "I am skilled at . . . ," "I have the ability to . . . ," "I know things about . . . ," "I am competent at doing . . . ," and "One part of my personality is that I am. . . ." List as many characteristics in each category as you can think of. What you have developed is an inventory of your self-concept.

Unfortunately, in many families the members damage each other's self-image and especially the developing self-concepts of children. Blaming, name-calling, and repeatedly pointing out another's shortcomings are particularly damaging. When dad shouts, "Terry, you are so stupid! If you had only stopped to think, this wouldn't have happened," he is damaging Terry's belief in his own intelligence. When big sister teases, "Hey Dumbo, how many times do I have to tell you, you're too clumsy to be a ballet dancer," she is undermining her younger sister's perception of her gracefulness.

Developing and Maintaining Self-Esteem

You'll recall that our self-esteem is our overall evaluation of our competence and personal worthiness—it is our positive or negative evaluation of our self-concept. Our evaluation of our personal worthiness is rooted in our values and develops over time as a result of our experiences. As Mruk (1999) points out, self-esteem is not just how well or poorly we do things (self-concept) but the importance or value we place on what we do well or poorly (p. 27). For instance, as part of Chad's self-concept, he believes he is physically strong. But if he doesn't believe that physical strength or other characteristics he possesses are worthwhile or valuable to have, then he will not have high self-esteem. Mruk explains that it takes both the perception of having a characteristic and a personal belief that the characteristic is of positive value to produce high self-esteem.

When we successfully use our skills, abilities, or knowledge in worthwhile endeavors, we raise our self-esteem. When we are unsuccessful in using our skills and abilities, or when we use them in unworthy endeavors, we lower our self-esteem.

Accuracy of Self-Concept and Self-Esteem

The accuracy of our self-concept and self-esteem depends on the accuracy of our own perceptions and how we process others' perceptions of us. All of us experience success and failure, and all of us hear praise and criticism. If we are overly attentive to successful experiences and positive responses, our self-concept may become overdeveloped and our self-esteem inflated. If, however, we perceive and dwell on failures and give little value to our successes, or if we only remember the criticism we receive, our self-image may be underformed and our self-esteem low. In neither case does our self-concept or self-esteem accurately reflect who we are.

Incongruence, the gap between our inaccurate self-perceptions and reality, is a problem because our perceptions of self are more likely than our true abilities to affect our behavior (Weiten, 1998, p. 491). For example, Sean may actually possess all the skills, abilities, knowledge, competencies, and personality characteristics for effective leadership, but if he doesn't perceive that he has these characteristics, he won't step forward when leadership is needed. Unfortunately, individuals tend to reinforce their self-perceptions by adjusting their behavior to conform with their perceived self-conceptions. That is, people with high self-esteem tend to behave in ways that lead to more affirmation, whereas people with low self-esteem tend to act in ways that confirm the low esteem in which they hold themselves. The inaccuracy of a distorted picture of oneself is magnified through self-fulfilling prophecies and by filtering messages.

Self-fulfilling prophecies
Self-fulfilling prophecies are events that happen as the result of being foretold, expected, or talked about. They may be self-created or other-imposed.

Self-created prophecies are those predictions you make about yourself. We often "talk ourselves into" success or failure. For example, Stefan sees himself as quite social and able to get to know people easily. So, in talking to himself, he says, "I'm going to have fun at the party tonight." As a result of his positive self-esteem and prophecy, he looks forward to encountering strangers and, just as he predicted, makes several new acquaintances and enjoys himself. In contrast, Aaron sees himself as unskilled in establishing new relationships; he says, "I doubt I'll know hardly anyone—I'm going to have a miserable time." Because he fears encountering strangers, he feels awkward about introducing himself and, just as he predicted, spends much of his time standing around alone thinking about when he can leave.

Self-esteem has an important effect on the prophecies people make. For instance, people with positive self-esteem view success positively and confidently prophesy that they can repeat successes; people with low self-esteem attribute their successes to luck and so prophesy that they will not repeat them (Hattie, 1992, p. 253).

The prophecies others make about you also affect your performance and self-image. For example, when teachers act as if their students are bright, students "buy into" this expectation and learn. Likewise, when teachers act as if students are not bright, students may live "down" to these imposed prophecies and fail to achieve. So how we talk to ourselves and how we treat others affects self-concepts and self-esteem.

Filtering messages
A second way that our self-perceptions can become distorted is through the way we filter what others say to us. We are prone to pay attention to messages that reinforce our current self-image

Second ask, *How do others see me?* List the skills, abilities, and so on that describe how you think others see you by completing the sentences: "Other people believe I am skilled at . . . ," "Other people believe I have the ability to . . . ," "Other people believe I know things about . . . ," "Other people believe I am competent at doing . . . ," and "One part of my personality is that other people believe I am. . . ."

Compare your two lists. How are they similar? Where are they different? Do you understand why they differ? After you have thought about each, write a paragraph titled "Who I am, and how I know this."

 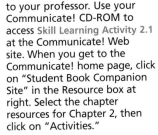 You can use your Student Workbook to complete this activity, or you can complete it online and, if requested, email it to your professor. Use your Communicate! CD-ROM to access Skill Learning Activity 2.1 at the Communicate! Web site. When you get to the Communicate! home page, click on "Student Book Companion Site" in the Resource box at right. Select the chapter resources for Chapter 2, then click on "Activities."

incongruence
the gap between our inaccurate self-perceptions and reality.

self-fulfilling prophecies
events that happen as the result of being foretold, expected, or talked about.

whereas messages that contradict this image may not "register" or may be downplayed. For example, suppose you prepare an agenda for your study group. Someone comments that you're a good organizer. If you spent your childhood hearing how disorganized you were, you may not really hear this comment, or you may downplay it. If, however, you think you are good at organizing, you will pay attention to the compliment and may even reinforce it by responding, "Thanks, I've worked hard to learn how to do this, but it was worth it. It comes in handy."

Changing self-concepts and self-esteem Self-concept and self-esteem are enduring characteristics, but they can be changed. In his analysis of numerous research studies, Christopher Mruk (1999, p. 112) found that self-esteem is increased through hard work and practice, practice, practice—there is simply no escaping this basic existential fact. So why is this important to communication? Because our self-esteem affects with whom we choose to form relationships. Researchers have found that "people with high self-esteem are more committed to partners who perceive them very favorably, while people with low self-esteem are more committed to partners who perceive them less favorably" (Leary, 2002, p. 130).

Many books have been written to help people raise their self-esteem, and there are rich sources of information available on the World Wide Web. To check out one such source, Coping.org's Model of Self-Esteem program, use your Communicate! CD-ROM to access **Web Resource 2.1: Self-Esteem Model** at the Communicate! Web site. Select the chapter resources for Chapter 2, then click on "Web Resources."

In this book we consider many specific communication behaviors that are designed to increase your communication competence. As you begin to practice and to perfect these skills, you may begin to receive positive responses to your behavior. If you continue to work on these skills, the positive responses you receive will help improve your self-concept and increase your self-esteem.

Self-Concept, Self-Esteem, and Communication

Just as our self-concept and self-esteem affect how accurately we perceive ourselves, so too do they influence our communication by moderating competing internal messages in our self-talk and influencing our personal communication style.

self-talk
the internal conversations we have with ourselves.

Self-perceptions moderate self-talk **Self-talk** is the internal conversations we have with ourselves. People who have high self-esteem are likely to engage in positive self-talk, such as "I know I can do it" or "I did really well on that test." Listen to the self-talk Corey had upon returning from a job interview.

> **I think I made a pretty good impression on the personnel director—I mean, she talked with me for a long time. Well, she talked with me, but**

maybe she was just trying to be nice. After all, it was her job. No, she didn't have to spend that much time with me. And she really lit up when I talked about the internship I had at Federated. So, she said she was interested in my internship. But talking about that is not exactly telling me that it would make a difference in her view of me as a prospective employee.

Notice that several of the messages in this internal conversation are competing. What determines which voice Corey listens to is likely to depend on his self-perceptions. If Corey has high self-esteem, he will probably conclude that the interviewer was sincere, and he'll feel good about the interview. If, on the other hand, he has low self-esteem and his self-concept doesn't include competence in the skills and abilities relevant to the job, he is more likely to "listen" to the negative voices in his head and conclude that he doesn't have a chance for the job.

Self-perception influences how we talk about ourselves with others If we feel good about ourselves, we are likely to communicate positively. For instance, people with a strong self-concept and higher self-esteem usually take credit for their successes. Likewise, people with healthy self-perceptions are inclined to defend their views even in the face of opposing arguments. If we feel bad about ourselves, we are likely to communicate negatively by downplaying our accomplishments.

Why do some people put themselves down regardless of what they have done? People who have low self-esteem are likely to be unsure of the value of their contributions and expect others to view them negatively. As a result, people with a poor self-concept or low self-esteem may find it less painful to put themselves down than to hear the criticism of others. Thus, to preempt the likelihood that others will comment on their unworthiness, they do it first.

Presenting Ourselves

We present ourselves to others through the roles we enact. A **role** is a pattern of learned behaviors that people use to meet the perceived demands of a particular context. For instance, during a single day you may enact the roles of "student," "brother/sister," and "employee."

Roles that we enact may result from our own needs, relationships that we form, cultural expectations, the expectations of groups we choose to be part of, and our own conscious decisions. For instance, the oldest child in a large family may be cast in the role of surrogate parent or role model for younger siblings. Or, if peers cast you as the "nerd," you may play along with your role, laughing and telling corny stories even though you really feel hurt or imposed on. Everyone enacts numerous roles each day, and we draw on different skills and attributes as we enact these roles. With each new situation we may test a role we know how to enact, or we may decide to try to enact a new role.

role
a pattern of learned behaviors that people use to meet the perceived demands of a particular context.

How do you suppose this dentist's behavior changes when she goes on a vacation with her brothers and sisters?

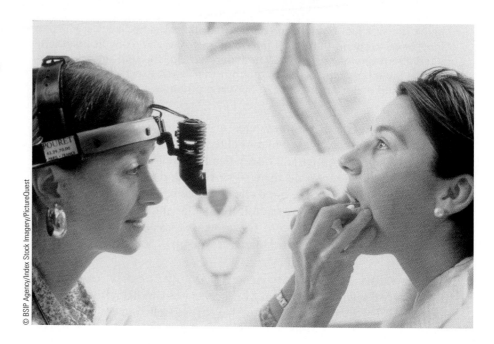

© BSIP Agency/Index Stock Imagery/PictureQuest

Monitor Your Enacted Roles

For three days, record your roles in various situations such as "lunch with a best friend" or "meeting professor about term paper." Describe the roles you chose to enact in each setting such as "student," "confidant," "jokester," or customer."

At the conclusion of this three-day observation period, analyze what you observed. To what extent does your role behavior change across situations? What factors seem to trigger you to enact a particular role? Are there certain roles that you take on more than others? Are there roles

Cultural and Gender Differences

Your cultural background influences your perception and affects your views of self. Many Americans share what is called the "Western view of self." This says that the individual is an autonomous entity with distinct abilities, traits, motives, and values, and that these attributes cause behavior. Moreover, people with this Western view see the individual as the most basic social unit. So, the notion of self-concept and self-esteem are built on the notions of independence from others and discovering and expressing individual uniqueness (Samovar & Porter, 2001, pp. 61–65).

People who share an "Eastern view of self" believe the family, not the individual, is the smallest social unit. In these cultures the skills, abilities, knowledge, and personality characteristics that are valued are profoundly different. Children raised in Western cultures will come to value those personal characteristics that are associated with independence and will develop high self-esteem from them. In Eastern cultures, however, the child is acculturated toward greater interdependency (Samovar & Porter, 2001, p. 120). These children will develop higher self-esteem when they perceive themselves to be cooperative, helpful, and self-effacing.

Similarly, men and women are socialized to view themselves differently and to value who they are based on whether their behavior corresponds to the behavior expected of their sex in their culture. In cultures where women are expected to be nurturing caregivers who attend to home and family life, women who perceive that they have the skills, abilities, knowledge, competencies, and personality characteristics needed for these jobs will have enriched self-concepts and high self-esteem. But women who do not have these attributes are likely to be less confident of who they are and are likely to have lower self-esteem.

The Internet offers a variety of sources on the topics of self-concept and self-esteem. Many of them offer suggestions that people have found useful. You can use a search engine like Google to find and view such sites. To read a particularly provocative article about self-esteem, Dr. Richard O'Connor's "Self-Esteem: In a Culture Where Winning Is Everything and Losing Is Shameful," use your Communicate! CD-ROM to access Web Resource 2.2: Real Self-Esteem? at the Communicate! Web site. Select the chapter resources for Chapter 2, then click on "Web Resources." What points does O'Connor make? How does his conclusion coincide with what you have observed?

Perception of Others

As we encounter others, we are faced with a number of questions: Do we have anything in common? Will others accept and value us? Will we be able to get along? Because this uncertainty makes us uneasy, we try to alleviate it. Charles Berger describes the process we use to overcome our discomfort as **uncertainty reduction,** the process of monitoring the social environment in order to learn more about self and others (Littlejohn, 2002, p. 243). As people interact, they gain information and form impressions of others. These perceptions will be reinforced, intensified, or changed as relationships develop. Just as with our self-perceptions, our social perceptions of others are not always accurate. The factors likely to influence your perceptions of others include their physical characteristics and social behaviors, your use of stereotyping, and your emotional state.

Observing Physical Characteristics and Social Behaviors

Social perceptions, especially the important first impressions, are often made on the basis of physical characteristics and social behaviors. We use our first impressions to help us make sense of others. We use physical characteristics in this order: race, gender, age, appearance, facial expressions, eye contact, movement, personal space, and touch. On the basis of people's physical attractiveness (facial characteristics, height, weight, grooming, dress, sound of voice), we are likely to categorize people as friendly, courageous, intelligent, cool, or their opposites (Aronson, 1999, p. 380). In one study, professional women dressed in jackets were assessed as more

you need to modify? Are there roles you are reluctant to enact that would help you be a more effective communicator? How satisfied are you with the roles you took? With which are you most and least pleased?

Write a paragraph explaining what you have learned. You can use your Student Workbook to complete this activity, or you can complete it online, print out a data collection sheet, write your analysis, and, if requested, email your work to your instructor. Use your Communicate! CD-ROM to access Skill Learning Activity 2.2 at the Communicate! Web site. When you get to the Communicate! home page, click on "Student Book Companion Site" in the Resource box at right. Select the chapter resources for Chapter 2, then click on "Activities."

uncertainty reduction
the process of monitoring the social environment to learn more about self and others.

powerful than professional women dressed in other clothing (Temple & Loewen, 1993, p. 345). Show a friend a picture of your child, uncle, or grandmother, and your friend may well form impressions of your relative's personality on the basis of that photo alone!

Early impressions are also made on the basis of a person's social behaviors. At times our impressions may be formed by observing only a single behavior. For instance, after a company party Caleb asked Sara what she thought of Gavin, the customer service rep. Sara, who had noticed Gavin interrupt Yolanda once, replied, "Gavin? Oh, he thinks he's really important."

implicit personality theories
assumptions people have developed about which physical characteristics and personality traits or behaviors are associated with another.

Some judgments of other people are based on **implicit personality theories,** which are assumptions people have developed about which physical characteristics and personality traits or behaviors are associated with another (Michener & DeLamater, 1999, p. 106).

Because your own implicit personality theory says that certain traits go together, you are likely to generalize and perceive that a person has a whole set of characteristics when you have actually observed only one characteristic, trait, or behavior. When you do this, your perception is exhibiting what is known as the **halo effect.** For instance, Heather sees Martina personally greeting and welcoming every person who arrives at the meeting. Heather's implicit personality theory views this behavior as a sign of the characteristic of warmth. She further associates warmth with goodness, and goodness with honesty. As a result, she perceives that Martina is good and honest as well as warm.

halo effect
to generalize and perceive that a person has a whole set of characteristics when you have actually observed only one characteristic, trait, or behavior.

In reality, Martina may be a con artist who uses her warmth to lure people into a false sense of trust. This example demonstrates a "positive halo" (Heather assigned Martina positive characteristics), but we also use implicit personality theory to inaccurately impute bad characteristics. In fact, Hollman (1972) found that negative information more strongly influences our impressions of others than does positive information. So we are more likely to negatively halo others than to positively halo them.

Halo effects seem to occur most frequently under one or more of three conditions: (1) when the perceiver is judging traits with which he or she has limited experience, (2) when the traits have strong moral overtones, and (3) when the perception is of a person that the perceiver knows well.

Given limited amounts of information, then, we fill in details. This tendency to fill in details leads to a second factor that explains social perception, stereotyping.

Using Stereotypes

stereotypes
attributions that cover up individual differences and ascribe certain characteristics to an entire group of people.

Perhaps the most commonly known factor that influences our perception of others is stereotyping. **Stereotypes** are "attributions that cover up individual differences and ascribe certain characteristics to an entire group of people" (Hall, 2002, p. 198). So, when we find out that someone is Hispanic or Muslim, a skateboarder, a chess player, an elementary school teacher, or a nurse—in short, any "identifiable group"—we use this information to attribute to the person a host of characteristics. These perceived group characteristics, taken as a whole, may be positive or negative, and they may be accurate or inaccurate (Jussim, McCauley, & Lee, 1995, p. 6).

We are likely to develop generalized perceptions about any group we come in contact with. Subsequently, any number of perceptual cues—skin color, style of dress, a religious medal, gray hair, sex, and so on—can lead us to stereotype our generalizations onto a specific individual. According to Hall (2002, p. 201), we don't form most of the stereotypes we use from our personal experience. Instead we learn them from family, friends, coworkers, and the mass media. So we adopt stereotypes before we have any personal "proof." And because stereotypes guide what we perceive, they can lead us to attend to information that confirms them and to overlook information that contradicts them.

Stereotyping contributes to perceptual inaccuracies because it ignores individual differences. For instance, if part of Dave's stereotype of personal injury lawyers is that they are unethical, then he will use this stereotype when he meets Denise, a highly principled woman, who happens to be a successful personal injury lawyer. You may be able to think of instances when you have been the victim of a stereotype based on your gender, age, ethnic heritage, social class, physical characteristics, or other group identity. If so, you know how hurtful the use of stereotypes can be.

When we use stereotypes as the basis of our social interaction, we risk miscommunicating and hurting feelings. A friend of ours who was raised in a middle-class, African American home tells the following story about his first day at college. He was at the registration center, where he had just completed selecting his classes. As he was about to walk over to the cashier's line to write a check for his tuition, the dean of the college greeted him warmly, welcomed him to campus, and directed him to the financial aid line. He was stung. It seems that part of the dean's stereotype was that black students go to college on financial aid.

As this example suggests, stereotyping can lead to prejudice and discrimination. According to Hall (2002), **prejudice** is "a rigid attitude that is based on group membership and predisposes an individual to feel, think, or act in a negative way toward another person or group" (p. 208). Notice the distinction between a stereotype and a prejudice. Whereas a stereotype is a set of beliefs or expectations, a prejudice is a positive or negative attitude; both relate to group membership. Stereotypes and prejudice are cognitive—that is, things we think.

Discrimination, on the other hand, is a negative action toward a social group or its members on account of group membership (Jones, 2002, p. 8). Whereas prejudice and stereotype deal with attitudes, discrimination

prejudice
a rigid attitude that is based on group membership and predisposes an individual to feel, think, or act in a negative way toward another person or group.

discrimination
a negative action toward a social group or its members on account of group membership.

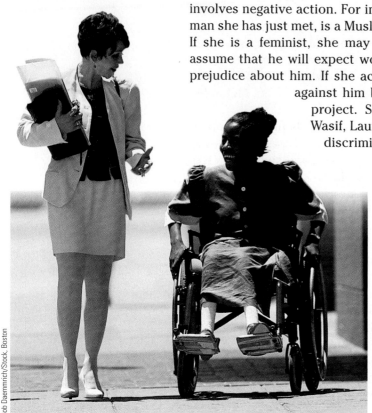

Bob Daemmrich/Stock, Boston

involves negative action. For instance, when Laura discovers that Wasif, a man she has just met, is a Muslim, she may stereotype him as a chauvinist. If she is a feminist, she may use this stereotype to prejudge him and assume that he will expect women to be subservient. Thus she holds a prejudice about him. If she acts on her prejudice, she may discriminate against him by refusing to partner with him on a class project. So, without really having gotten to know Wasif, Laura uses her stereotype to prejudge him and discriminate. In this case, Wasif may never get the chance to be known for who he really is, and Laura may have lost an opportunity to get to work with the best student in class.

The Diverse Voices selection in this chapter turns the situation around. What if you are the subject of prejudice or discrimination because you are, in the words of Arturo Madrid, "the other"?

Stereotypes, prejudice, and discrimination, like self-concept and self-esteem, can be difficult to change. People are likely to maintain their stereotypes and prejudices and continue to discriminate against others even in the face of evidence that disproves their stereotypes.

What is the relationship between these women? How did stereotyping influence your perception?

"-isms"
racism, ethnocentrism, sexism, ageism, ableism, and other "-isms" occur when a powerful group believes its members are superior to those of another group and that this superiority gives the powerful group the right to dominate or discriminate against the "inferior" group.

To read about balancing actions you can take to counteract stereotypes, use your Communicate! CD-ROM to access Web Resource 2.3: Peace Center at the Communicate! Web site. Select the chapter resources for Chapter 2, then click on "Web Resources."

Racism, ethnocentrism, sexism, ageism, able-ism, and other **"-isms"** occur when a powerful group believes its members are superior to those of another group and that this superiority gives the powerful group the right to dominate or discriminate against the "inferior" group. Because "-isms" can be deeply ingrained and subtle, it is easy to overlook behaviors we engage in that are racist, sexist, or ableist.

All people can be prejudiced and can discriminate. Nevertheless, "prejudices of groups with power are farther reaching in their consequences than others" (Sampson, 1999, p. 131).

To read more about stereotyping, read the article "You May Be Stereotyping Your Co-Workers, and That Hurts All of Us," available through InfoTrac College Edition. Use your Communicate! CD-ROM to access Web Resource 2.4: Stereotyping at Work at the Communicate! Web site. Select the chapter resources for Chapter 2, then click on "Web Resources."

DIVERSE VOICES

Social Perception

by Arturo Madrid

Arturo Madrid is the Murchison Distinguished Professor of Humanities at Trinity University. He served as founding President of Tomas Rivera Center, a national institute for policy studies on Hispanic issues. In this selection Madrid describes the conflicting experiences of those who see themselves as different from what has stereotypically been described as "American." Experiencing oneself and being perceived as "other" and "invisible" are powerful determinants of one's self-concept and form a very special filter through which one communicates with others.

My name is Arturo Madrid. I am a citizen of the United States, as are my parents and as were my grandparents, and my great-grandparents. My ancestors' presence in what is now the United States antedates Plymouth Rock, even without taking into account any American Indian heritage I might have.

I do not, however, fit those mental sets that define America and Americans. My physical appearance, my speech patterns, my name, my profession (a professor of Spanish) create a text that confuses the reader.

I am very clearly the *other,* if only your everyday, garden-variety, domestic *other.* I've always known that I was the *other,* even before I knew the vocabulary or understood the significance of otherness.

Despite the operating myth of the day, school did not erase my *otherness.* The true test was not our speech, but rather our names and our appearance, for we would always have an accent, however perfect our pronunciation, however excellent our enunciation, however divine our diction. That accent would be heard in our pigmentation, our physiognomy, our names. We were, in short, the *other.*

Being the *other* involves a contradictory phenomenon. On the one hand, being the *other* frequently means being invisible. On the other hand, being the *other* sometimes involves sticking out like a sore thumb. What is she/he doing here?

If one is the *other,* one will inevitably be seen stereotypically; will be defined and limited by mental sets that may not bear much relation to existing realities.

There is sometimes a darker side to otherness as well. The *other* disturbs, disquiets, discomforts. It provokes distrust and suspicion. The *other* frightens, scares.

For some of us being the *other* is only annoying; for others it is debilitating; for still others it is damning. For the majority otherness is permanently sealed by physical appearance. For the rest otherness is betrayed by ways of being, speaking, or of doing.

The first half of my life I spent downplaying the significance and consequences of otherness. The second half has seen me wrestling to understand its complex and deeply ingrained realities; striving to fathom why otherness denies us a voice or visibility or validity in American society and its institutions; struggling to make otherness familiar, reasonable, even normal to my fellow Americans.

One of the principal strengths of our society is its ability to address on a continuing and substantive basis the real economic, political, and social problems that have faced and continue to face us. What makes the United States so attractive to immigrants are the protections and opportunities it offers; what keeps our society together is tolerance for cultural, religious, social, political, and even linguistic difference; what makes us a unique, dynamic, and extraordinary nation are the power and creativity of our diversity.

The true history of the United States is the one of struggle against intolerance, against oppression, against xenophobia, against those forces that have prohibited persons from participating in the larger life of the society on the basis of their race, their gender, their religion, their national origin, their linguistic and cultural background. These phenomena are not only consigned to the past. They remain with us and frequently take on virulent dimensions.

If you believe, as I do, that the well-being of a society is directly related to the degree and extent to which all of its citizens participate in its institutions, then you will have to agree that we have a challenge before us. In view of the extraordinary changes that are taking place in our society, we need to take up the struggle again, unpleasant as it is. As educated and educator members of this society, we have a special responsibility for assuring that all American institutions, not just our elementary and secondary schools, our juvenile halls, or jails, reflect the diversity of our society. Not to do so is to risk greater alienation on the part of a growing segment of our society; is to risk increased social tension in an already conflictive world; and, ultimately, is to risk the survival of a range of institutions that, for all their defects and deficiencies, provide us the opportunity and the freedom to improve our individual and collective lot.

Let me urge you, as you return to your professional responsibilities and to your personal spaces, to reflect on these two words—*quality* and *diversity*—and on the mental sets and behaviors that flow out of them. And let me urge you further to struggle against the notion that quality is finite in quantity, limited in its manifestations, or is restricted by considerations of class, gender, race, or national origin; or that quality manifests itself only in leaders and not in followers, in managers and not in workers; or that it has to be associated with verbal agility or elegance of personal style; or that it cannot be seeded, or nurtured, or developed.

Excerpted from Arturo Madrid, "Diversity and Its Discontents." In L. A. Samovar & R. E. Porter (Eds.), Intercultural Communication: A Reader (7th ed., pp. 127–131). Belmont, CA: Wadsworth, 1994. Reprinted by permission of Black Issues in Higher Education.

Emotional States

A final factor that affects how accurately we perceive others is our emotional state at the time of the interaction. Based on his research, Joseph Forgas (1991) has concluded that "there is a broad and pervasive tendency for people to perceive and interpret others in terms of their (own) feelings at the time" (p. 288). If, for example, you received the internship you had applied for, your good mood—brought on by your good fortune—is likely to spill over so that you perceive other things and other people more positively than you might under different circumstances. If, however, you receive a low grade on a paper you thought was well written, your perceptions of people around you are likely to be colored by your disappointment or anger due to this grade.

Our emotions also cause us to engage in selective perceptions, ignoring inconsistent information. For instance, if Donna is physically attracted to Nick, she is likely to focus on the positive aspects of Nick's personality and may overlook or ignore the negative ones that are apparent to others.

Our emotional state also affects our attributions (Forgas, 2000, p. 397). **Attributions** are reasons we give for others' behavior. In making judgments about people, we attempt to construct reasons to explain why people behave as they do. According to attribution theory, what we determine—

attributions
reasons we give for others' behavior.

rightly or wrongly—to be the causes of others' behavior has a direct impact on our perceptions of them. For instance, suppose a coworker with whom you had made a noon lunch date has not arrived by 12:20. If you like and respect your coworker, you may attribute his lateness to something out of his control: an important phone call at the last minute, the need to finish a job before lunch, or some accident that may have occurred. If you are not particularly fond of your coworker, you are more likely to attribute his lateness to something in his control: forgetfulness, inconsiderateness, or malicious intent. In either case, your attribution will affect your perception of him and probably how you treat him.

Like prejudices, the attributions we make can be so strong that we ignore contrary evidence. If you are not particularly close to your coworker, when he does arrive and explains that he had an emergency long-distance phone call, you may believe he is lying or discount the urgency of the call.

Understanding that our physical characteristics and social behaviors, stereotyping, and emotional states affect our perceptions of others is a first step in improving our perceptual accuracy. Now we want to describe three guidelines and a communication skill you can use to improve the accuracy of your social perceptions of others.

Improving Social Perception

Because inaccuracies in perception are common and because they influence how we communicate, improving perceptual accuracy is an important first step in becoming a competent communicator. The following guidelines can aid you in constructing a more realistic impression of others as well as in assessing the validity of your own perceptions.

1. **Question the accuracy of your perceptions.** Questioning accuracy begins by saying, "I know what I think I saw, heard, tasted, smelled, or felt, but I could be wrong. What other information should I be aware of?" By accepting the possibility that you have overlooked something, you will become interested in increasing your accuracy. In situations where the accuracy of perception is important, take a few seconds to double-check. It will be worth the effort.

2. **Seek more information to verify perceptions.** If your perception is based on only one or two pieces of information, try to collect further information so that your perceptions are better grounded. Note that your perception is tentative—that is, subject to change.

    The best way to get additional information about people is to talk with them. Unfortunately, we tend to avoid people who are different from us, so we don't know much about them. As a result, we base our perceptions (and then our behavior) on stereotypes. It's OK to be unsure about how to treat someone from another group. But rather than letting your uncertainty cause you to make mistakes, talk with the person and ask for the information you need to become more comfortable.

3. **Realize that your perceptions of a person will change over time.** People often base their behavior on perceptions that are old or based on incomplete information. Just as you have changed, so too have other people. When you encounter someone you haven't seen for a while, as you become reacquainted, let their current behavior rather than their past actions or reputation inform your perceptions. Just because a former classmate was "wild" in high school does not mean that the person has not changed and become a mature responsible adult.

Perception Checking

perception check
a message that reflects your understanding of another person's behavior.

One way to assess the accuracy of a perception is to verbalize it and see whether others agree with what you see. A **perception check** is a message that reflects your understanding of another person's behavior. To use the skill of perception checking, follow these steps: (1) watch the behavior of the other person, (2) ask yourself "What does that behavior mean to me?" and (3) form a message that describes the behavior you have observed and your interpretation of the behavior. Notice the perception check in each of these two examples:

> **Tad, the company messenger, delivers a memo to Erin. As Erin reads the note, her eyes brighten and she breaks into a smile. Tad says, "Hey, Erin, you look really pleased. Am I right?"**

> **Cesar, speaking in short, precise sentences with a sharp tone of voice, gives Bill his day's assignment. Bill says, "From the sound of your voice, Cesar, I get the impression that you're upset with me. Are you?"**

Perception checking allows you to verify your perception or have it corrected before you act on it. For instance, when Bill says, "I get the impression that you're upset with me. Are you?" Cesar may say (1) "No, whatever gave you that impression?" in which case Bill can further describe the cues he received; (2) "Yes, I am," in which case Bill can get Cesar to talk about what has caused the feelings; or (3) "No, it's not you; it's just that three of my team members didn't show up for this shift." If Cesar is not upset with him, Bill can reconsider what caused him to misinterpret Cesar's feelings. If Cesar is upset with him, Bill has created an opportunity for the two to clear the air. Although your initial perceptions may be correct, when you do not verbally perception check, you risk acting on faulty assumptions.

CNN Situation Analysis

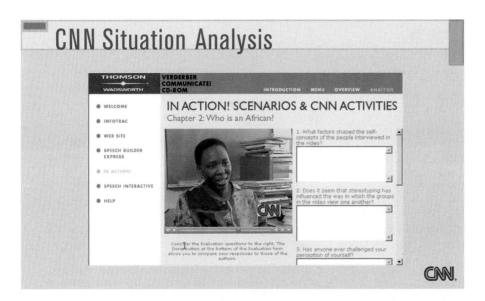

Use your Communicate! CD-ROM to access the CNN video clip "Who Is an African?" Click on the In Action icon in the menu at left, then click on the Conversation Menu in the menu bar at the top of the screen. Select "Who Is an African?" to watch the video (it takes a minute for the video to load). As you watch the video, think about the factors that influence self-concept. What factors shaped the self-concepts of the people interviewed in the video? Does it seem that stereotyping has influenced the way in which the groups in the video view one another? Has anyone ever challenged your perception of yourself? You can respond to these analysis questions by clicking on Analysis in the menu bar at the top of the screen. When you've answered all the questions, click "Done" to compare your answers to those provided by the authors.

Skill Builders — Perception Checking

Skill	Use	Procedure	Example
Making a verbal statement that reflects your understanding of another person's behavior.	To enable you to test the accuracy of your perceptions.	1. Describe the behaviors of the other that have led to your perception. 2. Add your interpretation of the behavior to your statement.	After taking a phone call, Shimika comes into the room with a completely blank expression and neither speaks to Donnell nor acknowledges that he is in the room. Donnell says, "Shimika, from your blank look, I get the feeling that you're in a state of shock. Has something happened?

Test Your Competence

Perception Checking

For each of the following situations, write a well-phrased perception check.

When Franco comes home from the doctor's office you notice that he looks pale and is slump shouldered. Glancing at you with a forlorn look, he shrugs his shoulders.
You say:

As you return the basketball you borrowed from Liam, you smile and say, "Thanks, here's your ball." You notice Liam stiffen, grab the ball, and, turning abruptly, walk away.
You say:

Natalie, who has been waiting to hear about a scholarship, dances into the room with a huge grin on her face.
You say:

You see your adviser in the hall and ask her if she can meet with you on Wednesday afternoon to discuss your schedule of classes for next term. You notice that she pauses, frowns, sighs, turns slowly, and says, "I guess so."
You say:

Compare your written responses to the guidelines for effective perception checking discussed earlier. Edit your responses where necessary to improve them. Now say them aloud. Do they sound "natural"? If not, revise them until they do.

 You can complete this activity online and compare your answers to the authors'. Use your Communicate! CD-ROM to access **Skill Learning Activity 2.4** at the Communicate! Web site. When you get to the Communicate! home page, click on "Student Book Companion Site" in the Resource box at right. Select the chapter resources for Chapter 2, then click on "Activities."

What Would You Do?

A QUESTION OF ETHICS

UniConCo, a multinational construction company, successfully bid to build a new minor league stadium in a Midwestern city that had very little diversity. Miguel Hernandez was assigned to be the Assistant Project Manager, and he moved his family of seven to town. He quickly joined the local Chamber of Commerce, affiliated with the local Rotary group, and was feeling the first signs of acceptance. One day Mr. Hernandez was working at his desk when he accidentally overheard a group of local Anglo construction workers who were on the project talking about their Mexican American coworkers. Miguel was discouraged to hear the negative stereotypes that were being used. The degree of hatred expressed was clearly beyond what he was used to, and he was further upset when he recognized several of the voices as belonging to men he had fought to hire.

A bit shaken, Mr. Hernandez returned to his office. He had a problem. He recognized his workers' prejudices, but he wasn't sure how to change them. Moreover, he wanted to establish good work relationships with his Anglo workers for the sake of the company, but he also wanted to create a good working atmosphere for the other Latino workers who would soon be moving to town to work on the project. What could Mr. Hernandez do?

Devise a plan for Mr. Hernandez. How could he use his social perceptions to address the problem in a way that is within ethical interpersonal communication guidelines?

Summary

Perception is the process of selectively attending to information and assigning meaning to it. Our perceptions are a result of our selection, organization, and interpretation of sensory information. Inaccurate perceptions cause us to see the world not as it is but as we would like it to be.

Self-concept is our self-identity, the idea or mental image that we have about our skills, abilities, knowledge, competencies, and personality. Self-esteem is our overall evaluation of our competence and personal worthiness. Self-concepts come from interpretations of self based on our own experience and on the reactions and responses of others. The inaccuracy of a distorted picture of oneself becomes magnified through self-fulfilling prophecies and filtering messages. Our self-concept and self-esteem moderate competing internal messages in our self-talk, influence our perception of others, and influence our personal communication style.

Perception also plays an important role in forming impressions of others. We form these impressions based on others' physical characteristics and social behaviors, our stereotyping, and our emotional states. Because research shows that the accuracy of people's perceptions and judgments varies considerably, your communication will be most successful if you do not rely entirely on your impressions to determine how another person feels or what that person is really like. You will improve (or at least better understand) your perceptions of others if you take into account physical characteristics and social behaviors, stereotyping, and emotional states.

You can learn to improve perception if you actively question the accuracy of your perceptions, seek more information to verify perceptions, talk with the people about whom you are forming perceptions, realize that perceptions of people need to change over time, and check perceptions verbally before you react.

Communicate! Online

N ow that you have read Chapter 2, use your Communicate! CD-ROM for quick access to the electronic resources that accompany this text. Your CD-ROM gives you access to the CNN Situation Analysis video activity featured on page 45, InfoTrac College Edition, and the Communicate! Web site. When you get to the Communicate! home page, click on "Student Book Companion Site" in the Resource box at the right to access the online study aids for this chapter, including a digital glossary, review quizzes, chapter activities, and chapter Web Resources.

Key Terms

At the Communicate! Web site, select chapter resources for Chapter 2. Print a copy of the glossary for this chapter and test yourself with the electronic flash cards or complete the crossword puzzle to help you master these key terms:

perception (28)
pattern (29)
interpret (29)
self-concept (30)
self-esteem (30)
incongruence (33)
self-fulfilling prophecies (33)

self-talk (34)
role (35)
uncertainty reduction
    theory (37)
implicit personality
    theories (38)
halo effect (38)

stereotypes (38)
prejudice (39)
discrimination (39)
"-isms" (40)
attributions (42)
perception check (44)

Review Quiz

Test your knowledge of the concepts in this chapter by taking the online quiz at the Communicate! Web site. Select the chapter resources for Chapter 2, then click on "Review Quiz." When you have completed the quiz, submit it for scoring.

Skill Learning Activities

Complete the Observe & Analyze and Test Your Competence activities for Chapter 2 online at the Communicate! Web site. Select the chapter resources for Chapter 2, then click on "Activities." You can submit your Observe & Analyze answers to your instructor, and you can compare your Test Your Competence answers to those provided by the authors.

2.1: Observe & Analyze: Who Am I? (32)
2.2: Observe & Analyze: Monitor Your Enacted Roles (36)
2.3: Observe & Analyze: Stereotyping (42)
2.4: Test Your Competence: Perception Checking (46)

Web Resources

Access the Web Resources for this chapter online at the Communicate! Web site. Select the chapter resources for Chapter 2, then click on "Web Resources."

2.1: Self-Esteem Model (34)
2.2: Real Self-Esteem? (37)
2.3: Peace Center (40)
2.4: Stereotyping at Work (40)

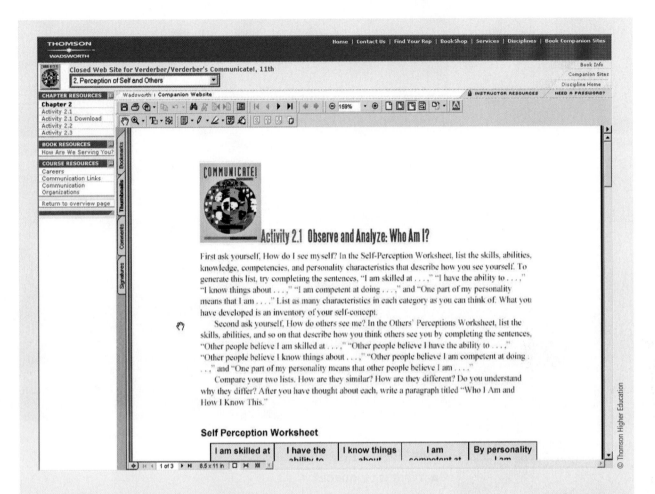

Closed Web Site for Verderber/Verderber's Communicate!, 11th

2. Perception of Self and Others

Book Info
Companion Sites
Discipline Home

CHAPTER RESOURCES

Chapter 2
Activity 2.1
Activity 2.1 Download
Activity 2.2
Activity 2.3

BOOK RESOURCES
How Are We Serving You?

COURSE RESOURCES
Careers
Communication Links
Communication Organizations

Return to overview page

Wadsworth | Companion Website

INSTRUCTOR RESOURCES   NEED A PASSWORD?

Activity 2.1 Observe and Analyze: Who Am I?

First ask yourself, How do I see myself? In the Self-Perception Worksheet, list the skills, abilities, knowledge, competencies, and personality characteristics that describe how you see yourself. To generate this list, try completing the sentences, "I am skilled at . . . ," "I have the ability to . . . ," "I know things about . . . ," "I am competent at doing . . . ," and "One part of my personality means that I am . . . ." List as many characteristics in each category as you can think of. What you have developed is an inventory of your self-concept.

Second ask yourself, How do others see me? In the Others' Perceptions Worksheet, list the skills, abilities, and so on that describe how you think others see you by completing the sentences, "Other people believe I am skilled at . . . ," "Other people believe I have the ability to . . . ," "Other people believe I know things about . . . ," "Other people believe I am competent at doing . . . ," and "One part of my personality means that other people believe I am . . . ."

Compare your two lists. How are they similar? How are they different? Do you understand why they differ? After you have thought about each, write a paragraph titled "Who I Am and How I Know This."

Self Perception Worksheet

I am skilled at	I have the ability to	I know things about	I am competent at	By personality I am

1 of 3   8.5 x 11 in

© Thomson Higher Education

Swahili = English

mtoto = a child

mwanadamu = a man

mwanamke = a woman

toto mchanga = baby

...anaa = family

OBJECTIVES

After you have read this chapter, you should be able to answer these questions:

- What is language?
- What is a speech community?
- What is the relationship between language and meaning?
- How does language change?
- What is the difference between denotative and connotative meaning?
- How do cultural differences affect language use?
- How do gendered language differences affect social perceptions?
- How can you increase the clarity of your messages?
- How can you improve your language usage so that it is more specific?
- How can you use the skills of dating and indexing generalizations to increase the accuracy of your messages?
- How can you phrase messages so that they are perceived as appropriate for the situation?

3

Verbal Communication

Jeff leaned over the ladder, tapped the wall lightly, and called to Sonya, "Would you bring me the um whatdoyacallit over there?"

"Sure," Sonya replied. "Is that the thing you find the doohickies with?" she asked as she handed him a small plastic object.

"Right—like, those little fellows are hard to find without one. And, um, would you also get me the string thingamabob—I'll need it in a few minutes."

"Got ya. Be back," Sonya said.

When Sonya returned, Jeff said, "I was just wondering about something Morrison said at work today."

"What, Jeff?"

"Well, we were working on the Whatshisface account when out of the blue, he says to me, 'Jeff, I have a hard time following what you're trying to say sometimes.' You could have, you know, knocked me over with a feather."

"Wow, what in the world was he talking about? I never have any trouble understanding you."

"Thanks. Well, you know, I guess it's just his problem. I don't think it's worth losing any sleep over. Hey," Jeff continued, "we need a couple more of these gizmos."

"No problemo," Sonya answered. "I'm on it!"

Does Jeff have a problem? Sonya doesn't think so—she understands him perfectly. Did you understand? Jeff is hanging a picture on the living room wall. He needs a stud finder to locate the metal nails that indicate where the two-by-fours are so that he'll have a strong base when he pounds the nails. He also needs a simple "plumb line" to help him make sure that he's hanging the picture straight.

Sonya has known Jeff long enough that she can anticipate what he's talking about. But that's not the case at work. Jeff's verbal problems may seem a little more dramatic than most, but they're not all that different. For, as Thomas Holtgraves (2002), a leading scholar in language use reminds us, "Language is one of those things that we often take for granted" (p. 8). Yet we could all improve the accuracy of our messages.

In this chapter we discuss the nature and use of language, speaking more clearly, and speaking more appropriately.

The Nature and Use of Language

language
a body of symbols (most commonly words) and the systems for their use in messages that are common to the people of the same speech community.

speech community
a group of people who speak the same language (also called a language community).

words
symbols used by a speech community to represent objects, ideas, and feelings.

Language is both a body of symbols (most commonly words) and the systems for their use in messages that are common to the people of the same speech community.

A **speech community,** also called a language community, is a group of people who speak the same language. There are between 3,000 and 4,000 speech communities in the world, with the number of native speakers in a community ranging from a hundred million or more to communities with only a few remaining native speakers. Around 60 percent of the world's speech communities have fewer than 10,000 speakers. The five largest speech communities in order are Mandarin Chinese, English, Spanish, Arabic, and Hindi (Encyclopedia.com, 2002).

Words are symbols used by a speech community to represent objects, ideas, and feelings. While the exact word used to represent the object or idea is arbitrary, for a word to be a symbol it must be recognized by members of the speech community as standing for a particular object, idea, or feeling. So different speech communities use different word symbols for the same phenomenon. For example, the season for planting is called "spring" in English-speaking communities but "pretemps" in French-speaking communities.

Speech communities vary in the words that they use, and they also vary in how words are put together to form messages. The structure a message takes depends on the rules of grammar and syntax that have evolved in a particular speech community. For example, in English a sentence must have at least a subject (a noun or pronoun) and a predicate (a verb). To make a statement in English, the subject is placed before the predicate.

Uses of Language

Although language communities vary in the words that they use and in their grammar and syntax systems, all languages serve the same purposes.

1. **We use language to designate, label, define, and limit.** So, when we identify a house as a "Tudor," we are differentiating it from another that may be identified as an "A-frame."

2. **We use language to evaluate.** Through language we convey positive or negative attitudes toward our subject. For instance, if you see Hal taking more time than others to make a decision, you could describe Hal positively as "thoughtful" or negatively as "dawdling."

3. **We use language to discuss things outside our immediate experience.** Language enables us to speak hypothetically, to talk about past and future events, and to communicate about people and things that are not present. Thus, we can use language to discuss where we hope to be in five years, to analyze a conversation two acquaintances had last week, or to learn about the history that shapes the world we live in.

4. **We can use language to talk about language.** We can use language to discuss how someone phrased a statement and whether better phrasing would have resulted in a clearer meaning or a more positive response. For instance, if your friend said she would see you "this afternoon," but she didn't arrive until 5 o'clock, when you ask her where she's been, the two of you are likely to discuss the meaning of "this afternoon."

Language and Meaning

On the surface, the relationship between language and meaning seems perfectly clear: We select the correct words, structure them using the rules of syntax and grammar agreed upon by our speech community, and people will interpret our meanings correctly. In fact, the relationship between language and meaning is not nearly so simple for several reasons.

One reason is that word meanings change over time. Because we are not born knowing a language, each generation within a speech community learns the language anew. We learn much of our language early in life from our families; much more we learn in school. But we do not all learn to use the same words in the same way.

A second reason is that language is a creative act. When we speak, we use language to create new sentences that represent our meaning. Although on occasion we repeat other people's sentence constructions to represent what we are thinking or feeling, some of our talk is unique.

A third reason is that people interpret words differently. Words have two kinds of meaning: denotative and connotative. Thus, when Melissa tells Trisha that her dog died, what Trisha understands Melissa to mean depends on both the denotative and connotative meaning of the word.

denotation
the direct, explicit meaning a speech community formally gives a word; it is the meaning found in a dictionary.

Denotation is the direct, explicit meaning a speech community formally gives a word—it is the meaning found in a dictionary. So denotatively, when Melissa said her dog died, she meant that her domesticated canine no longer demonstrates physical life. In some situations the denotative meaning of a word may not be clear. Why? First, different dictionaries may define words in slightly different ways. For instance, whereas the *Encarta World English Dictionary* defines "bawdy" as "ribald in a frank, humorous often crude way," the *Cambridge American English Dictionary* defines "bawdy" as "containing humorous remarks about sex." Similar? Yes, but not the same. Second, for many words there are multiple definitions. For instance, the *Random House Dictionary of the English Language* lists 23 definitions for the word "great."

syntactic context
the position of a word in a sentence and the other words around it.

In addition, meaning may vary depending on the **syntactic context** (the position of a word in a sentence and the other words around it) in which the word is used. For instance, in the same sentence a person might say, "I love to vacation in the mountains where it's really cool in mornings and when you hike you're likely to see some really cool animals." Most listeners would understand that "mornings are really cool" refers to temperature and "see some really cool animals" refers to animals that are uncommon or special.

connotation
the feelings or evaluations we associate with a word.

Connotation, the feelings or evaluations we associate with a word, may be even more important to our understanding of meaning than denotation. C. K. Ogden and I. A. Richards (1923) were among the first scholars to consider the misunderstandings resulting from the failure of communicators to realize that their subjective reactions to words are based on their life experiences. For instance, when Melissa tells Trisha that her dog died, Trisha's understanding of the message depends on the extent to which her feelings about pets and death—her connotations of the words—correspond to the feelings that Melissa has about pets and death. Melissa, who sees dogs as truly indispensable friends, may be trying to communicate a true sense of grief, but Trisha, who has never had a pet and doesn't particularly care for dogs, may miss the sense of Melissa's statement.

Word denotation and connotation are important because senders and receivers may differ in the meanings they assign. But from an effectiveness standpoint, the only message that counts is the message that is understood, regardless of whether it is the message you intended.

Meaning Varies across Subgroups in the Speech Community

Within a larger speech community, subgroups with somewhat diverse language use and culture emerge. These subgroups develop variations on the core language that enable them to share meanings unique to their subcultural experience. People from different subcultures approach the world from different perspectives, so they are likely to experience some difficulty sharing meaning when they talk with each other.

In addition to subgroups based on race, religion, and national origin, there are also subgroup cultures associated with generation, social class, and political interests. The need for awareness and sensitivity in applying our communication skills does not depend on someone's being an immigrant or from a different ethnic background. Rather, the need for being aware of potential language differences is important in every type of communication. Developing our language skills so that the messages we send are clear and sensitive will increase our communication effectiveness in every situation.

Cultural Differences in Verbal Communication

Cultures vary in how much meaning is embedded in the language itself and how much meaning is interpreted from the context in which the communication occurs.

In **low-context cultures,** such as in northern Europe or the United States, meaning (1) is embedded mainly in the messages transmitted and (2) is presented directly. In low-context cultures, people say what they mean and get right to the point (Gudykunst & Matsumoto, 1996, pp. 29–30). So, in a low-context culture, "Yes" means "Affirmative, I agree with what you have said."

low-context cultures
meaning is embedded mainly in the messages transmitted and is presented directly.

In **high-context cultures,** such as Asian or Middle Eastern countries, meaning is interpreted based on the physical, social, and relational context. People from high-context cultures expect others to use context cues to interpret meaning. As a result, they present meanings indirectly. In a high-context culture, "Yes" may mean "Affirmative, I agree with what you have said," or it may mean "In this setting it would embarrass you if I said 'No,' so I will say 'Yes,' to be polite, but I really don't agree and you should know this, so in the future don't expect me to act as if I have just agreed with what you said." People from high-context cultures expect others to understand unarticulated feelings and subtle nonverbal gestures that people from low-context cultures don't even process. As a result, misunderstandings often occur.

high-context cultures
meaning is interpreted based on the physical, social, and relational context.

The United States has a low-context national culture, as described previously. But the United States is a country of immigrants, and we know that there are a multitude of cultures represented in this country—even though most Americans speak English. So we have ample opportunity to misunderstand each other.

Gender Differences in Verbal Communication

Over the last two decades, stirred by such book titles as *Men Are from Mars, Women Are from Venus,* people have come to believe gender differences in verbal messages are genetic. Yet research strongly states that differences in gender behaviors are learned rather than biological and that the differences are not nearly as large as portrayed (Wood & Dindia, 1998, pp. 34–36).

There is no evidence to suggest that the differences that have been identified between women's message construction patterns and those of men cause "problems" for either group (Canary & Hause, 1993, p. 141). Nevertheless, a number of specific differences between women's and men's speech patterns have been found, and understanding what has led to them has intrigued scholars. Mulac (1998) notes two differences in language usage between men and women that seem to have the greatest support (pp. 133–134):

1. **Women tend to use both more intensifiers and more hedges than men.** Intensifiers are words that modify other words and serve to strengthen the idea represented by the original word. So, according to studies of the actual speech practices of men and women, women are more likely to use words such as *awfully, quite,* and *so* (as in "It was quite lovely" or "This is so important"). Hedges are modifying words that soften or weaken the meaning of the idea represented by the original word. According to the research, women are likely to make greater use of such words as *somewhat, perhaps,* or *may be* (as in "It was somewhat interesting that . . ." or "It may be significant that . . .").

2. **Women ask questions more frequently than men.** Women are much more likely to include questions like "Do you think so?" and "Are you sure?" In general, women tend to use questions to gain more information, get elaboration, and determine how others feel about the information.

But are these differences really important? Mulac (1998) goes on to report that "our research has shown that language used by U.S. women and men is remarkably similar. In fact, it is so indistinguishable that native speakers of American English cannot correctly identify which language examples were produced by women and which were produced by men" (p. 130). If this is so, then why even mention differences? Even though the differences are relatively small, they have judgmental consequences: "Observers perceive the female and male speakers differently based on their language use" (p. 147). Female speakers are rated higher on *sociointellectual status* and *aesthetic quality.* Thus people perceive women as having high social status, being literate, and being pleasant as a result of perceived language differences. Men rated higher on *dynamism.* That is, people perceive men to be stronger and more aggressive as a result of their language differences. These judgments tend to be the same whether observers are male or female, middle-aged or young (p. 148).

Julia Wood (2003) explains these differences in language usage as resulting from differences in the basic psychological orientation each sex acquires in growing up. Women learn to use communication as a way of establishing and maintaining relationships with others (p. 119). Men learn to use talk as a way to "exert control, preserve independence, and enhance status" (p. 122).

Speaking More Clearly

Regardless of whether we are conversing, communicating in groups, or giving speeches, we speak more clearly by reducing ambiguity and confusion. Compare these two descriptions of a close call in an automobile: "Some nut almost got me with his car a while ago" versus "A gray-haired man in a banged-up Honda Civic crashed the light at Calhoun and Clifton and came within inches of hitting me last week while I was waiting to turn left at the cross street." The differences are in clarity. We are able to express our ideas more clearly when we have a good vocabulary, use specific language, date information, and index generalizations.

Using Specific Language

Specific language clarifies meaning by narrowing what is understood from a general category to a particular item or group within that category. Often, as we try to express our thoughts, the first words that come to mind are general, abstract, and imprecise. The ambiguity of these words makes the listener choose from many possible images rather than picturing the single, focused image we have in mind. The more listeners are called on to provide their own images, the more likely they are to see meanings different from what we intend.

> **specific language**
> *language that clarifies meaning by narrowing what is understood from a general category to a particular item or group within that category.*

Specific words are more concrete and precise than are general words. Saying "It's a Honda Civic" is more specific than saying "It's a car." **Concrete words** appeal to the senses. In effect we can see, hear, smell, taste, or touch concrete words. Thus we can picture that "banged up" Civic. Abstract ideas, such as justice, equality, or fairness, can be made concrete through examples or metaphors. **Precise words** narrow a larger category. For instance, if Nevah says that Ruben is a "blue-collar worker," you might picture any number of occupations that fall within this broad category. If, instead, she is more precise and says he's a "construction worker," the

> **concrete words**
> *words that appeal to the senses and help us see, hear, smell, taste, or touch.*
>
> **precise words**
> *words that narrow a larger category.*

Frank and Ernest

Frank & Ernest reprinted by permission of NEA, Inc.

number of possible images you can picture is reduced. Now you select your image from the subcategory of construction worker, and your meaning is likely to be closer to the one she intended. If she is even more precise, she may say, "Ruben is a bulldozer operator." Now you are even clearer in visualizing Ruben's occupation.

In the preceding example, the continuum of specificity goes from blue-collar worker to construction worker to construction vehicle operator to bulldozer operator. Figure 3.1 provides another illustration of increasing precision.

Choosing specific language is easier when we have a large working vocabulary. As a speaker, the larger your vocabulary, the more choices you have from which to select the word you want. As a listener, the larger your vocabulary, the more likely you are to understand the words used by others.

One way to increase your vocabulary is to study one of the many vocabulary building books on the shelves of most any bookstore, such as *Merriam Webster's Vocabulary Builder* (Cornog, 1998). You might also study magazine features such as "Word Power" in the *Reader's Digest.* By completing this monthly quiz and learning the words with which you are not familiar, you could increase your vocabulary by as many as twenty words per month.

A second way to increase your vocabulary is to make note of words that you read or that people use in their conversations with you and look them up. For instance, suppose you read or hear, "I was inundated with phone calls today!" If you wrote inundated down and looked it up in a dictionary later, you would find that "inundated" means *overwhelmed* or *flooded.* If you then say to yourself, "She was inundated—overwhelmed or flooded—with phone calls today," you are likely to remember that meaning and apply it the next time you hear the word. If you follow this practice, you will soon notice the increase in your vocabulary.

Gambling

Games of Skill

Card Games

Poker

Seven Card Stud

Figure 3.1
Levels of precision

A third way to increase your vocabulary is to use a thesaurus (a list of words and their synonyms) to identify synonyms that are more concrete and precise than the word you may have chosen. An easy way to consult a thesaurus is to access Merriam-Webster's online Collegiate Thesaurus. For instance, when you type "difficult" into the search box, you'll find such synonyms as "hard," "laborious," "arduous," and "strenuous." Use your Communicate! CD-ROM to access **Web Resource 3.1: Merriam-Webster Online** at the Communicate! Web site. Select the chapter resources for Chapter 3, then click on "Web Resources."

Providing Details and Examples

Sometimes the word we use may not have a concrete or precise synonym. In these situations clarity can be achieved by adding detail or examples. For instance, Linda says, "Rashad is very loyal." The meaning of "loyal" (faithful to an idea, person, company, and so on) is abstract, so to avoid ambiguity and confusion, Linda might add, "He defended Gerry when Sara was gossiping about her." By following up her use of the abstract concept of loyalty with a concrete example, Linda makes it easier for her listeners to "ground" their idea of this personal quality in a concrete or "real" experience.

Likewise by providing details, we clarify our messages. Saying, "He lives in a really big house," can be clarified by adding details: "He lives in a fourteen-room Tudor mansion on a six-acre estate."

Skill Builders ▶ Using Specific Language

Skill	Use	Procedure	Example
Clarify meaning by narrowing what is understood from a general category to a particular group within that category, by appealing to the senses, or by choosing words that symbolize exact thoughts and feelings, or by using concrete details or examples.	To help the listener picture thoughts analogous to the speaker's.	1. Assess whether the word or phrase to be used is less specific (or concrete or precise) than it can be. 2. Pause to consider alternatives. 3. Select a more specific (or concrete or precise) word, or give an example or add details.	Instead of saying, "Bring the stuff for the audit," say, "Bring the records and receipts from the last year for the audit." Or, instead of saying, "I was really cold," say, "I nearly froze; my fingers were numb."

Test Your Competence ▶

Clarifying General Statements

Rewrite each of these statements to make it more specific by making general and abstract words more concrete and precise. Add details and examples.

1. My neighbor has a lot of animals that she keeps in her yard.
2. When I was a little girl, we lived in a big house in the Midwest.
3. My husband works for a large newspaper.
4. She got up late and had to rush to get to school. But she was late anyway.
5. Where'd you find that thing?
6. I really liked going to that concert. The music was great.
7. I really respect her.
8. My boyfriend has long hair and a tattoo.
9. She was wearing a colorful scarf and bright shirt that was a little short.
10. We need to have more freedom to choose our courses.

 You can complete this activity online and compare your answers to the authors'. Use your Communicate! CD-ROM to access Skill Learning Activity 3.1 at the Communicate! Web site. When you get to the Communicate! home page, click on "Student Book Companion Site" in the Resource box at the right. Select the chapter resources for Chapter 3, then click on "Activities."

Dating Information

dating information
specifying the time or time period that a fact was true or known to be true.

Dating information is specifying the time or time period that a fact was true or known to be true. Because nearly everything changes with time, not dating our statements can lead someone to conclude that what we are saying is current, when it is not. For instance, Parker says, "I'm going to be transferred to Henderson City." Laura replies, "Good luck—they've had some real trouble with their schools." On the basis of Laura's statement, Parker may worry about the effect his move will have on his children. What he doesn't know is that Laura's information about this problem in Henderson City is over five years old! Henderson City still may have problems, but again, the situation may have changed. Had Laura replied, "Five years ago, I know they had some real trouble with their schools. I'm not sure what the situation is now, but you may want to check," Parker would look at the information differently.

Here are two additional examples:

Undated: Professor Powell is really enthusiastic when she lectures.

Dated: Professor Powell is really enthusiastic when she lectures—at least she was *last quarter* in communication theory.

Undated: You think Mary's depressed? I'm surprised. She seemed her regular, high-spirited self when I talked with her.

Dated: You think Mary's depressed? I'm surprised. She seemed her regular, high-spirited self when I talked with her *last month*.

Have you ever been inconvenienced by information that was out of date? As you form messages, the skill of dating can help you be more accurate with the information you share.

To date information, before you make a statement, (1) consider or find out when the information was true and (2) verbally acknowledge the date or time period when the information was true. When we date our statements, we increase the effectiveness of our messages and enhance our own credibility.

Indexing Generalizations

Generalizing—drawing a conclusion from particulars—enables people to use what they have learned from one experience and apply it to another. For instance, when Glenda learns that tomatoes and squash grow better if the ground is fertilized, she generalizes that fertilizing will help all of her vegetables grow better. Glenda has used what she learned from one experience and applied it to another.

generalizing
drawing a conclusion from particulars.

Indexing is the practice of acknowledging the presence of individual differences when voicing generalizations. For instance, we know that *in general* men are stronger than women. Therefore, *in general* a specific man is likely to be stronger than a specific woman. But we must recognize that although Fred may be stronger than Barbara, we can't say that for sure. So, instead of saying "Fred can out bench press Barbara—after all, he's a guy," we would be wiser to index our statement by saying, "Fred can probably out bench press Barbara because men are generally stronger than women. But, it's certainly possible that he can't."

indexing
the practice of acknowledging the presence of individual differences when voicing generalizations.

Let's consider another example:

Generalization: Your Chevrolet should go 50,000 miles before you need a brake job; Jerry's did.

Indexed Statement: Your Chevrolet may well go 50,000 miles before you need a brake job; Jerry's did, *but of course, all Chevrolets aren't the same.*

To index, consider whether what you are about to say applies a generalization to a specific person, place, or thing. If so, qualify it appropriately so that your assertion does not go beyond the evidence that supports it.

Test Your Competence ▸

Dating and Indexing Messages

Rewrite each of these messages so that they are dated, indexed, or both.

1. Oh, Jamie's an accounting major, so I'm sure she keeps her checkbook balanced.
2. Forget taking statistics; it's an impossible course.
3. Never try talking to Jim in the morning; he's always grouchy.
4. Don't bother to buy that book for class. You'll never use it.

5. I can't believe you bought a dog. I mean, all they do is shed.

 You can complete this activity online and compare your answers to the authors'. Use your Communicate! CD-ROM to access Skill Learning Activity 3.2 at the Communicate! Web site. When you get to the Communicate! home page, click on "Student Book Companion Site" in the Resource box at right. Select the chapter resources for Chapter 3, then click on "Activities."

Speaking Appropriately

During the last few years, we have had frequent discussions and disagreements in the United States about "political correctness." Colleges and universities have been on the forefront of this debate. Although several issues germane to the debate on political correctness go beyond the scope of this chapter, at the heart of this controversy is the question of what language behaviors are appropriate—and what language behaviors are inappropriate.

speaking appropriately means choosing language and symbols that are adapted to the needs, interests, knowledge, and attitudes of the listeners and avoiding language that alienates them. Through appropriate language, we communicate our respect and acceptance of those who are different from us. In this section, we discuss specific strategies that will help you craft appropriate verbal messages.

speaking appropriately *choosing language and symbols that are adapted to the needs, interests, knowledge, and attitudes of the listeners and avoiding language that alienates them.*

Adapt Formality to the Situation

Language should be appropriately formal for the situation. In interpersonal settings, we are likely to use more informal language when we are talking with a spouse and more formal language when we are talking with a stranger. In group settings, we are likely to use more informal language when we are talking with a group of our peers and more formal language when we are talking with a group of managers. In a public speaking setting, we are likely to use more formal language than in either interpersonal or group settings.

One type of formality in language that we usually observe is the manner by which we address others. In formal settings, we address others by their titles followed by their surnames unless they invite us to do something else. So in business settings or at formal parties, it is appropriate to call people "Mr. X," "Ms. B," "Rabbi Z," "Dr. S," or "Professor P." In addition, we generally view it as appropriate to refer to those older than we are, those of higher status, or those whom we respect by title and surname unless otherwise directed.

Limit Use of Jargon and Slang

Appropriate language makes limited use of **jargon** (technical terminology) and **slang** (informal, nonstandard vocabulary). We form language communities as a result of the work we do, our ethnic group, our hobbies, and the subcultures with which we identify. Slang and jargon are so pervasive that there are special dictionaries devoted to the specialized vocabulary of different communities. You can even find slang dictionaries online. To access one maintained by California State University at Pomona, use your Communicate! CD-ROM to access Web Resource 3.2: Slang Dictionary at the Communicate! Web site. Select the chapter resources for Chapter 3, then click on "Web Resources."

jargon
technical terminology.

slang
informal, nonstandard vocabulary.

We can forget that people who are not in our same line of work or who do not have the same hobbies or are not from our group may not understand slang language that seems to be such a part of our daily communication. For instance, when Jenny, who is sophisticated in the use of cyber language, starts talking with her computer-illiterate friend Sarah about "Social MUDs based on fictional universes," Sarah is likely to be totally lost. If, however, Jenny recognizes Sarah's lack of sophistication in cyber language, she can work to make her language appropriate by discussing the concepts in words that her friend understands. In short, when talking with people outside your language community, you are appropriate when you limit your use of jargon or slang or when you explain in-group terms to your listener.

Shoe by Jeff MacNelly; reprinted by permission of Tribune Media Services.

Observe&Analyze

Crude Language Audit

For the next three days, keep a log of each time you use crude or vulgar language or hate speech. Record where you were, who you were with, what you said, and why you chose to use the language you did. At the end of the three days, review your log and analyze your data. Based on your analysis, write a paragraph that describes your crude language behavior. How pervasive is your use of
(continued on p. 65)

Avoid Profanities and Vulgarities

Appropriate language avoids profanity and vulgar expressions. Fifty years ago a child was punished for using "hell" or "damn," and adults used profanity and vulgarity only in rare situations as an expression of strong emotions. Today "casual swearing"—profanity injected into regular conversation—is epidemic in some language communities, including college campuses (DuFrene & Lehman, 2002, p. 48). In some settings even the crudest and most offensive terms are so commonly used that speakers and (as a result) listeners alike have become desensitized, and the words have lost their ability to shock and offend.

Despite the growing, mindless use of crude speech, many people are still shocked and offended by swearing. And people who casually use profanity and vulgarities to pepper their speech are often perceived as abrasive and lacking character, maturity, intelligence, manners, and emotional control (O'Connor, 2000). The problem of swearing has become so acute that some employers have instituted anti-swearing policies for fear of sexual harassment and discrimination lawsuits. To read an InfoTrac College Edition article about anti-swearing policies at work, use your Communicate! CD-ROM to access Web Resource 3.3: Anti-Swearing Policies at the Communicate! Web site. Select the chapter resources for Chapter 3, then click on "Web Resources." Do a PowerTrac search on the title "Watch Your Language!"

Unfortunately, profanity and vulgarity are habits that are easily acquired and hard to extinguish. If you have acquired a "potty mouth," you're going to have to work very hard to clean up your act as verbal habits are hard to break. For tips on how to "tame your tongue," use your Communicate! CD-ROM to access Web Resource 3.4: Cuss Control Academy at the Communicate! Web site. Select the chapter resources for Chapter 3, then click on "Web Resources."

Use Inclusive Language

Language is appropriate when you avoid usages that others perceive as derogatory and exclusionary. Language that our receivers perceive as sexist, racist, or otherwise biased is inappropriate. Two common types of exclusionary language are generic and nonparallel language.

generic language
using words that may apply only to one sex, race, or other group as though they represent everyone.

Generic language **Generic language** uses words that may apply only to one sex, race, or other group as though they represent everyone. This language is a problem since in essence it excludes a portion of the population. Let's consider some examples.

Traditionally, English speakers used the masculine pronoun *he* to stand for all humans regardless of gender. For example, "When a person shops, *he* should have a clear idea of what *he* wants to buy." Now, when you read that sentence, what did you picture? Did you picture a woman shopping? Probably not. Despite traditional usage, it is hard to picture people of both sexes when we hear the masculine pronoun *he*.

So inclusive language avoids using male pronouns when no specific gender reference is intended. You can avoid this in one of two ways. First, you can use plurals. For instance, saying "When people shop, they should have a clear idea of what they want to buy." Alternatively, you can use both male and female pronouns: "When a person shops, he or she should have a clear idea of what he or she wants to buy." Stewart, Cooper, Stewart, and Friedley (1998, p. 63) cite research to show that using "he and she," and to a lesser extent "they," gives rise to listeners' including women in their mental images, thus increasing gender balance in their perceptions. These changes are small, but they are more accurate and demonstrate inclusiveness.

A second problem of noninclusive language results from the traditional use of *man*. Consider the term *man-made*. What this really means is that a product was produced by human beings, but its underlying connotation is that a male human being made the item. Some people try to argue that just because a word has "man" within it does not really affect people's understanding of meaning. But just as with the use of masculine pronouns, research has demonstrated that people usually visualize men (not women) when they read or hear these words. Moreover, when job titles end in "man," their occupants are assumed to have stereotypically masculine personality traits (Gmelch, 1998, p. 51).

For most noninclusive expressions, we have suitable inclusive alternatives—for instance, *police officer* versus *policeman*, *synthetic* versus *man-made*, and *humankind* versus *mankind*. Not only is inclusive language more appropriate, it is also more accurate.

Nonparallel language Nonparallel language is language in which terms are changed because of the sex, race, or other characteristic of the individual. Because it treats groups of people differently, nonparallel language is also belittling. Two common forms of nonparallelism are marking and unnecessary association.

Marking is the addition of sex, race, age, or other designations to a description. For instance, a doctor is a person with a medical degree who is licensed to practice medicine. Notice the difference between the following two sentences:

Jones is a good doctor.

Jones is a good black doctor.

In the second sentence, use of the marker "black" is offensive; it has nothing to do with doctoring. Marking is inappropriate because you trivialize the person's role by introducing an irrelevant characteristic. The speaker may be intending to praise Jones, but listeners may interpret the sentence as saying that Jones is a good doctor "for a black person" (or woman, or old person, and so on) but not that Jones is as good as a white doctor (or a male or young person, and so forth).

A second form of nonparallelism is emphasizing one person's relationship to another when that relationship is irrelevant. Introducing a speaker

crude speech? Are there particular settings in which or certain people with whom you are more likely to swear? Are there settings in which or people with whom you are less likely to swear? What words are your "favorites"? Why do you use crude speech? Then evaluate how satisfied you are with the frequency with which you use vulgar language and with your reasons for using crude speech. Do you think that you are more crude and vulgar in your speech practices today, or has your use of crude language improved? To what do you attribute any change?

 You can use your Student Workbook to complete this activity, or you can complete it online, download a log sheet to use during your data collection, and, if requested, email your work to your professor. Use your Communicate! CD-ROM to access Skill Learning Activity 3.3 at the Communicate! Web site. When you get to the Communicate! home page, click on "Student Book Companion Site" in the Resource box at the right. Select the chapter resources for Chapter 3, then click on "Activities."

nonparallel language
terms are changed because of the sex, race, or other characteristic of the individual.

marking
the addition of sex, race, age, or other designations to a description.

as "Gladys Thompson, whose husband is CEO of Acme Inc., is the chairperson for this year's United Way campaign," for example, is inappropriate. Using her husband's status implies that Gladys Thompson is chairperson because of her husband's accomplishments, not her own.

Shun Hate Speech

You've heard the old child's saying, "Sticks and stones will break my bones, but words will never hurt me." As children we all knew that this statement was a lie. Still it gave us psychological comfort in the face of cruel name-calling. Unfortunately, name-calling can take on even uglier forms in adult speech. Think of the damage caused by the use of words like "nigger," "cracker," "kike," or "fag."

hate speech
the use of words and phrases to demean another person or group and to express the speaker's hatred and prejudice toward that person or group.

Hate speech is the use of words and phrases to demean another person or group and to express the speaker's hatred and prejudice toward that person or group. Under the Constitution of the United States, people usually are afforded free speech protection. From a communication perspective, however, hate speech is always unethical and should be shunned.

By monitoring yourself, you can become more inclusive in your language choices. How can you speak more appropriately? (1) Use language geared to the formality of the relationship and setting; (2) limit use of jargon and slang; (3) avoid crude language; (4) use inclusive language, and (5) shun hate speech.

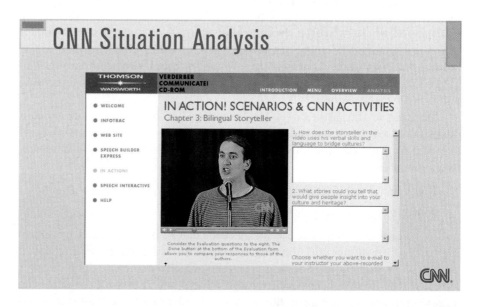

Use your Communicate! CD-ROM to access the CNN video clip "Bilingual Storyteller." Click on the In Action icon in the menu at left, then click on the Conversation Menu in the menu bar at the top of the screen. Select "Bilingual Storyteller" to watch the video (it takes a minute for the video to load). How does the storyteller in the video use his verbal skills and language to bridge cultures? What stories could you tell that would give people insight into your culture and heritage? You can respond to these analysis questions by clicking on Analysis in the menu bar at the top of the screen. When you've answered all the questions, click "Done" to compare your answers to those provided by the authors.

What Would You Do?   A QUESTION OF ETHICS

ne day Heather, Terry, Paul, and Martha stopped at the Student Union Grill before their next class. After they had talked about their class for a few minutes, the conversation shifted to students who were taking the class.

"By the way," Paul said, "do any of you know Porky?"

"Who?" the group responded in unison.

"The really fat guy who was sitting a couple of seats from me. We've been in a couple of classes together—he's a pretty nice guy."

"What's his name?" Heather asked.

"Carl—but he'll always be Porky to me."

"Do you call him that to his face?" Terry asked.

"Aw, I'd never say anything like that to him—Man, I wouldn't want to hurt his feelings."

"Well," Martha chimed in, "I'd sure hate to think that you'd call me 'skinny' or 'the bitch,' when I wasn't around."

"Come on—what's with you guys," Paul retorted. "You trying to tell me that you never talk about another person that way when they aren't around?"

"Well," said Terry, "maybe a couple of times—but I've never talked like that about someone I really like."

"Someone you like?" queried Heather. "Why does that make a difference? Do you mean it's OK to trash talk someone so long as you don't like the person?"

1. Sort out the ethical issues in this case. How ethical is it to call a person you supposedly like by an unflattering name that you would never use if that person were in your presence?

2. From an ethical standpoint, is whether you like a person or not what determines when such name-calling is OK?

Summary

Language is a body of symbols and the systems for their use in messages that are common to the people of the same language community. Through language we designate, label, and define; we evaluate; we discuss things outside our immediate experience; and we talk about language.

The relationship between language and meaning is complex because word meanings change over time, language is a creative act, people interpret words differently based on both denotative and connotative word meanings, and meaning can vary across subgroups within a language community. Denotative meanings are those found in a dictionary. One word may have several meanings assigned, and the description of meanings will vary across dictionaries. Connotative meaning is the emotional and value significance that a word has for a listener in a particular situation. In high-context cultures much of the meaning of a message resides in the context in which it is said, and the words used need to be interpreted in light of the setting. In low-context cultures the message can be interpreted with little regard to the setting. There is also evidence that men and women use language differently.

Effective communicators form messages that are clear and appropriate. We can speak more clearly by using specific language, providing details and examples, dating information, and indexing generalizations. We can speak more appropriately by adapting to the formality of the situation, limiting our use of jargon and slang, avoiding profanity and vulgarity, using inclusive language, and shunning hate speech.

Communicate! Online

N ow that you have read Chapter 3, use your Communicate! CD-ROM for quick access to the electronic resources that accompany this text. Your CD-ROM gives you access to the CNN Situation Analysis video activity featured on page 66, InfoTrac College Edition, and the Communicate! Web site. When you get to the Communicate! home page, click on "Student Book Companion Site" in the Resource box at the right to access the online study aids for this chapter, including a digital glossary, review quizzes, chapter activities, and chapter Web Resources.

Key Terms

At the Communicate! Web site, select the chapter resources for Chapter 3. Print a copy of the glossary for this chapter and test yourself with the electronic flash cards or complete the crossword puzzle to help you master these key terms:

language (52)	high-context cultures (55)	speaking appropriately (62)
speech community (52)	specific language (57)	jargon (63)
words (52)	concrete words (57)	slang (63)
denotation (54)	precise words (57)	generic language (64)
syntactic context (54)	dating information (60)	nonparallel language (65)
connotation (54)	generalizing (61)	marking (65)
low-context cultures (55)	indexing (61)	hate speech (66)

Review Quiz

Test your knowledge of the concepts in this chapter by taking the online quiz at the Communicate! Web site. Select the chapter resources for Chapter 3, then click on "Review Quiz." When you have completed the quiz, submit it for scoring.

Skill Learning Activities

Complete the Observe & Analyze and Test Your Competence activities for Chapter 3 online at the Communicate! Web site. Select the chapter resources for Chapter 3, then click on "Activities." You can submit your Observe & Analyze answers to your instructor, and you can compare your Test Your Competence answers to those provided by the authors.

3.1: Test Your Competence: Clarifying General Statements (60)
3.2: Test Your Competence: Dating and Indexing Messages (62)
3.3: Observe & Analyze: Crude Language Audit (64)

Web Resources

Access the Web Resources for this chapter online at the Communicate! Web site. Select the chapter resources for Chapter 3, then click on "Web Resources."

3.1: Merriam-Webster Online (59)
3.2: Slang Dictionary (63)
3.3: Anti-Swearing Policies (64)
3.4: Cuss Control Academy (64)

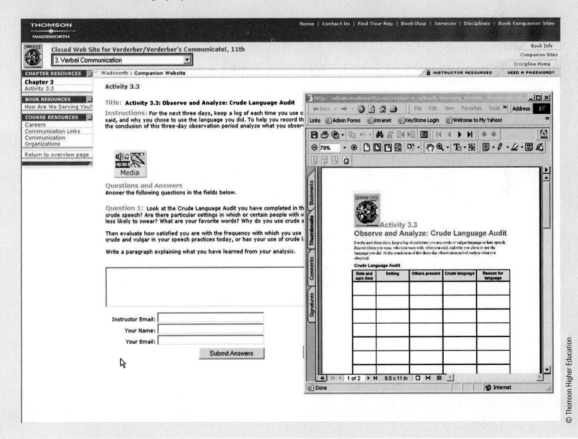

© Thomson Higher Education

Adam Crowley/Getty Images

OBJECTIVES

After you have read this chapter, you should be able to answer these questions:

- What are the differences between verbal and nonverbal communication?

- What types of body motions have communication functions?

- What is paralanguage?

- What are the elements of paralanguage, and how does each affect message meaning?

- How do body type, clothing, poise, touching behavior, and use of time affect self-presentation?

- How is communication affected by the use of physical space?

- How do temperature, lighting, and color affect communication?

- What are some cultural variations that affect our interpretation of nonverbal communication behaviors?

4

Communicating through Nonverbal Behavior

"**Y**ou don't want me to buy that leather jacket we looked at this morning, do you?" Clay asked.

"What do you mean, 'I don't want you to'?" Maya replied.

"You've got that look on your face."

"What look?"

"You know the look—the one you always get on your face when you don't want me to do something I want to do. But forget it, I'm going to get that jacket."

"I still don't know what look you're talking about, Clay."

"Sure you do—you know how I can tell you do? Because now you're embarrassed that I know, and so you're raising your voice."

"I'm not raising my voice, Clay."

"Oh yes you are."

"Clay, you're making me angry."

"You're just saying that because I'm on to you."

"'On to me?' Clay, I don't care whether you get that jacket or not."

"You're right. I can tell—you don't have to spell it out."

"Clay, give it a rest. It's up to you. If you want to get the jacket, get it."

"Well, I don't think I'll buy it—but don't think you talked me out of it."

We've all heard—and said—"actions speak louder than words." Actions are very important to our communication. Researchers estimate that in face-to-face communication "upward of 60 percent of meaning in any social situation is communicated nonverbally" (Burgoon & Bacue, 2003, p. 179). What this means is that the meaning we assign to any communication is based on both the content of the verbal message and our interpretation of the nonverbal behavior that accompanies and surrounds the verbal message. And, as Clay found out, interpreting these nonverbal actions is not always the easiest thing to do.

In this chapter we discuss the nature of nonverbal behavior, body motions, paralanguage, self-presentation, and management of the communication environment.

The Nature of Nonverbal Communication Behavior

nonverbal communication behaviors
bodily actions and vocal qualities that typically accompany a verbal message.

In the broadest sense the term *nonverbal communication* is commonly used to describe all human communication events that transcend spoken or written words (Knapp & Hall, 2002, p. 5). Specifically, **nonverbal communication behaviors** are those bodily actions and vocal qualities that typically accompany a verbal message. The behaviors are usually interpreted as intentional and have agreed-upon interpretations in a particular speech community (Burgoon & Hoobler, 2002, p. 244).

When we say that nonverbals are interpreted as intentional, we mean that people act as if they are intended even if they are performed unconsciously or unintentionally (p. 231). So, when Anita says "I've had it" as she slams a book down on the table, we interpret the loudness of her voice and the act of slamming the book down as intentionally emphasizing the meaning of her words.

Likewise, when we refer to agreed-upon interpretations in a culture or speech community, we recognize that although people from around the world use many of the same nonverbal cues they may interpret them differently. For instance, a smile may acknowledge a pleasant reaction to what has been said or done, or it may simply be a face-saving behavior to mask discomfort in an awkward situation.

In addition to bodily actions and vocal qualities that accompany verbal messages, nonverbal commu-

nication also includes the messages sent by our choices of clothing, use of physical space, furniture, lighting, temperature, and color.

Since much of what is considered appropriate nonverbal behavior depends on culture, we begin by discussing each type of behavior from a U.S. cultural perspective. Then we describe some of the most important ways nonverbal communication behavior is interpreted differently in other cultures and communities.

Body Motions

Body motions, or **kinesics,** include the use of eye contact, facial expression, gesture, and posture to communicate.

body motions or kinesics
the use of eye contact, facial expression, gesture, and posture to communicate.

Eye Contact

Eye contact, also referred to as **gaze,** is how and how much we look at people with whom we are communicating. Eye contact serves many functions in our communication. Its *presence* shows that we are paying attention. *How* we look at a person can reveal a range of emotions from affection to anger or fear. For instance, we describe people in love as looking "doe eyed," and we comment on "looks that could kill." The intensity of eye contact may also be used to exercise dominance, such as when someone "stares another person down" (Knapp & Hall, 2002, pp. 430–431).

eye contact or gaze
how and how much we look at people with whom we are communicating.

Moreover, through our eye contact we monitor the effect of our communication. By maintaining eye contact, you can tell when or whether people are paying attention to you, when people agree with what you are saying, and whether what you are saying is eliciting feelings.

Although people differ in their use of eye contact, studies show that U.S. speakers maintain eye contact about 38 to 41 percent of the time and listeners 62 to 75 percent of the time (p. 350).

We generally maintain better eye contact when we are discussing topics with which we are comfortable, when we are genuinely interested in a person's comments or reactions, or when we are trying to influence the other person. We will talk more about eye contact in Chapter 16, "Practicing the Presentation of Your Speech."

Facial Expression

Facial expression is the arrangement of facial muscles to communicate emotional states or reactions to messages. The three sets of muscles that are manipulated to form facial expressions are (1) the brow and forehead; (2) the eyes, eyelids, and root of the nose; and (3) the cheeks, mouth, remainder of the nose, and chin. Our facial expressions are especially

facial expression
the arrangement of facial muscles to communicate emotional states or reactions to messages.

important in conveying the six basic emotions of happiness, sadness, surprise, fear, anger, and disgust.

Gesture

gestures
the movements of hands, arms, and fingers that alone or in concert with a verbal message convey meaning.

Gestures are the movements of hands, arms, and fingers that alone or in concert with a verbal message convey meaning. Thus, when a person says, "about this high" or "nearly this round," we expect to see a gesture accompanying the verbal description. Likewise, when a person says, "Put that down" or "Listen to me," a pointing finger, pounding fist, or some other gesture often reinforces the point. People do vary, however, in the amount of gesturing that accompanies their speech. Some people "talk with their hands" far more than others.

Our facial expressions are especially important in conveying emotion. What is the message on this face?

© Mark L. Stephenson/CORBIS

Posture

posture
the position and arrangement of the body.

Posture is the position and arrangement of the body. Changes in posture can also communicate. For instance, suddenly sitting upright and leaning forward show increased attention, whereas standing up may signal "I'm done now," and turning one's back to the other conveys a redirection of attention away from the other person.

How Body Motions Are Used

Body motions in general and gestures in particular may be used in the following five ways (Ekman & Friesen, 1969, pp. 49–98).

1. **Body motions take the place of a word or phrase.** We can make a long list of the nonverbal symbols we use frequently to take the place of words or phrases. For instance, in the United States a fisted hand with the thumb pointing up means "everything is go"; first and second fingers held up in a V-shape means "peace" or "victory"; shaking your head from side to side means "no" and up and down means "yes"; shrugging the shoulders means "maybe," "I don't care," or "I don't know."

sign language
systems of body motions used to communicate, which include sign languages of the deaf and alternate sign languages used by Trappist monks in Europe and some women of Australia.

In some cases, emblems are used as a complete language. **Sign language** refers to systems of body motions used to communicate, which include sign languages of the deaf and alternate sign languages used by Trappist monks in Europe and some women of Australia (Leathers, 1997, p. 70).

2. **Body motions illustrate what a speaker is saying.** We use gestures to illustrate in at least five ways:

   ■ To *emphasize* an idea: A man may pound the table in front of him as he says, "Don't bug me."

   ■ To show the *path* or *direction* of thought: A professor may move her hands on an imaginary continuum when she says, "The papers ranged from very good to very bad."

   ■ To show *position:* A waiter may point when he says, "Take that table."

   ■ To *describe:* People may use their hands to indicate size as they say, "The ball is about three inches in diameter."

   ■ To *mimic:* People may nod their heads as they say, "Did you see the way he nodded?"

3. **Body motions display the nonverbal expression of feelings.** These body motions will take place automatically and are likely to be quite noticeable. For instance, if you stub your toe on a chair as you drag yourself out of bed in the morning, you are likely to grab your foot and grim-ace in pain. Occasionally we are led to misinterpret these displays when people purposely mask, deintensify, or overreact. For example, a student may smile to hide the fact that he received a failing grade; a friend may simply shrug her shoulders when asked about breaking off her engagement; or a youngster may howl "in pain" when her older sister bumps her by accident.

4. **Body motions control or regulate the flow of a conversation.** We use shifts in eye contact, slight head movements, shifts in posture, raised eyebrows, and nodding head to tell a person when to continue, to repeat, to elaborate, to hurry up, or to finish. Effective communicators learn to adjust what they are saying and how they are saying it on the basis of such cues.

5. **Body motions relieve tension.** As they speak, people will sometimes fidget or change posture as a means to relax.

Cultural Variations

Several cultural differences in body motions are well documented.

Eye contact In the United States and in other western European cultures, people expect those with whom they are communicating to "look them in the eye." But Samovar and Porter (2001) point out that direct eye contact is not universally appropriate (p. 178). In fact in some cultures direct eye contact is considered rude. For example, in Japan people direct their gaze to a position around the Adam's apple and avoid direct eye contact. Chinese, Indonesians, and rural Mexicans lower their eyes as a sign of deference—to them too much direct eye contact is a sign of bad manners. Arabs, in contrast, look intently into the eyes of the person with whom they are talking—to them direct eye contact demonstrates keen interest. There are also differences in use of eye contact in the subcultures of the United States. For instance, African

Observe&Analyze

▼ Body Motions

Find a public setting (for example, a restaurant) where you can observe two people having a conversation. They should be close enough to you so that you can observe their eye contact, facial expression, and gesture, but not close enough that you can hear what they are saying.

Carefully observe the interaction with the goal of answering the following questions: What is their relationship? What seemed to be the nature of the conversation (social chitchat, plan making, problem solving, argument, intimate discussion)? How did each person feel about the conversation? Did feelings change over the course of the conversation? Was one person more dominant? Take note of the specific nonverbal behaviors that led you to each conclusion, and write a paragraph describing this experience and what you have learned.

You can use your Student Workbook to complete this activity, or you can complete it online. Download an observation sheet to use during your data collection, and, if requested, email your analysis to your instructor. Use your Communicate! CD-ROM to access Skill Learning Activity 4.1.

Americans use more continuous eye contact than whites when they are speaking but less when they are listening (p. 159).

Facial expression, gestures, and movements Studies show that there are many similarities in nonverbal communication across cultures, especially in facial expressions. For instance, several facial expressions seem to be universal, including a slight raising of the eyebrow to communicate recognition, wriggling one's nose, and a disgusted facial look to show social repulsion (Martin & Nakayama 2000, pp. 183–184). In fact, at least six facial expressions (happiness, sadness, fear, anger, disgust, and surprise) carry the same basic meaning throughout the world (Samovar & Porter, 2001, p. 177).

Cultures also differ in the meaning assigned to various gestures. For instance, forming a circle with the thumb and forefinger is the OK sign in the United States, but it means zero or worthless in France, is a symbol for money in Japan, and is a vulgar gesture in Germany and Brazil (Axtell, 1999, pp. 44, 143, 212). Check out some common Brazilian gestures by using your Communicate! CD-ROM to access Web Resource 4.1: Maria Brazil at the Communicate! Web site.

The use of nonverbal displays of emotion also vary. For instance, in some Eastern cultures people have been socialized to deintensify emotional behavior cues, whereas members of other cultures have been socialized to amplify their displays of emotions.

Gender Variations

Men and women differ in their use of nonverbal communication behavior (Canary & Hause, 1993, p. 141), and they also differ in how they interpret the nonverbal communication behaviors of others. Major difficulties in male–female relationships are often created by inaccurately encoding and decoding nonverbal messages. A number of studies have shown that women are better than men at decoding nonverbal vocal and facial cues (Knapp & Hall, 2002, p. 83).

Eye contact In the United States women tend to have more frequent eye contact during conversations than men do (Cegala & Sillars, 1989). Moreover, women tend to hold eye contact more than men regardless of the sex of the person they are interacting with (Wood, 2003, p. 141).

Facial expression and gesture In general, women tend to smile more than men, but their smiles are harder to interpret. Men's smiles generally mean positive feelings, whereas women's smiles tend to be responses to affiliation and friendliness (Hall, 1998, p. 169).

Gender differences in the use of gestures are so profound that people have been found to attribute masculinity or femininity on the basis of gesture style alone (Pearson, West, & Turner, 1995, p. 126). For instance, women are more likely than men to keep their arms close to the body, are less likely to lean forward with the body, more often play with their hair or clothing, and tap their hands more often.

Paralanguage

Paralanguage, or **vocalics,** is the nonverbal "sound" of what we hear—how something is said. Four vocal characteristics comprise paralanguage, and they influence the meaning we convey in our messages.

paralanguage or vocalics
the nonverbal "sound" of what we hear; how something is said.

Vocal Characteristics

By controlling the pitch, volume, rate, and quality of our voice, we can complement, supplement, or contradict the meaning conveyed by the language of our message.

Pitch is the highness or lowness of tone of voice. People tend to raise and lower pitch to accompany changes in volume. They may also raise the pitch when they are nervous or frightened and lower the pitch when they are trying to be forceful.

pitch
the highness or lowness of tone of voice.

Volume is loudness or softness of tone. Some people have booming voices that carry long distances; others are normally soft spoken. Regardless of their normal volume level, people vary their volume depending on the situation and the topic of discussion. People are louder when excited and softer when sad or thoughtful.

volume
the loudness or softness of tone.

Rate is the speed at which a person speaks. People tend to talk more rapidly when they are happy, frightened, nervous, or excited and more slowly when they are problem solving out loud or are trying to emphasize a point.

rate
the speed at which a person speaks.

Quality is the timbre or character of voice. Each human voice has a distinct timbre: some voices are raspy, some smoky, some have bell-like qualities, and others are throaty. However, we can vary our voice quality to communicate a particular state of mind. We may use a nasal quality when we whine, a soft breathy quality to be seductive, and a strident, harsh quality when we are angry.

quality
the timbre or character of voice.

Some of us have developed vocal characteristics that lead others to consistently misinterpret what we say. For instance, a person may use a tone of voice that causes others to believe he is being sarcastic when he is not. If you are concerned about your vocal characteristics, consult with your professor. Your professor can evaluate your voice and, if needed, direct you to additional help.

Vocal Interferences

Most of us are occasionally guilty of using **vocal interferences**—extraneous sounds or words that interrupt fluent speech. These interferences can become a problem, however, when they are perceived by others as excessive and when they begin to call attention to themselves and so prevent listeners from concentrating on meaning. The most common interferences that creep into our speech include "uh," "er," "well," "OK," and those nearly universal interrupters of Americans' conversation, "you know" and "like."

vocal interferences
extraneous sounds or words that interrupt fluent speech.

Vocal interferences may initially be used as "place markers" designed to fill in momentary gaps in speech that would otherwise be silence. In this way they indicate that we are not done speaking and it is still our "turn." So we may use an "um" when we need to pause momentarily to search for the right word or idea. For some speakers the customary filler sounds are "uh" or "er"; for others they are "well" or "um." Although the chance of being interrupted may be real (some people will seek to interrupt at any pause), the intrusion of an excessive number of fillers can lead to the impression that you are unsure of yourself or confused in what you are attempting to say.

Equally prevalent, and perhaps even more disruptive than "uh" and "um," is the overuse of "you know" and "like." The "you know" habit may begin as a genuine way to find out whether what is being said is already known by others. For some, "you know" may be a source of identification—a way to establish common ground with the person being spoken to. Similarly, the use of "like" may start from making comparisons such as "Tom is hot; he looks like Denzel Washington." Soon the comparisons become shortcuts, as in "He's like really hot!" Finally, the use of "like" becomes pure filler: "Like, he's really cool, like I can't really explain it, but I'll tell you he's like wow!" For most people flooding sentences with "you know" and "like" has become a bad habit that results in disjointed messages and sloppy encoding. Instead of working to clarify their thoughts by choosing precise words, they use "like" and "you know" to abdicate their responsibility to encode their ideas. Soon they are using so many fillers that their messages become unintelligible, shifting most of the responsibility for discerning meaning to the receiver.

Curiously, no matter how irritating the use of "you know" or "like" may be to listeners, they are unlikely to verbalize their irritation. Even though listeners may not acknowledge irritation and these interferences may be "accepted" between peers in everyday speech, their habitual use is a handicap in many settings. For example, excessive use of vocal interferences during job interviews, at work, or in class can affect the impression you make. For the most part, speech habits persist from one setting to another. If you use fillers excessively in your everyday speech, you are unlikely to be able to control them easily in more formal settings.

Self-Presentation

People learn a great deal about us and judge us based on how we choose to present ourselves through our body type, clothing and personal grooming, poise and self-confidence, use of touching, and treatment of time.

Body Type

One of the first things others notice about you is your body type. People fall into one of three basic body types: endomorph, mesomorph, or ectomorph. The endomorph shape is soft, round, and fat; the mesomorph is muscular, angular, and hard; the ectomorph is lanky, fragile, and thin. Studies have found that others often perceive endomorphs as sluggish, sociable, dependent, and relaxed; mesomorphs as dominant, confident, energetic, competitive, assertive, hot-tempered, enthusiastic, and optimistic; and ectomorphs as tense, self-conscious, meticulous, precise, sensitive, awkward, and withdrawn (Knapp & Hall, 2002, p. 195).

In the United States the media's idealization of the ectomorph body type for women has contributed to the rise in eating disorders, and the idealization of the mesomorph shape for men has led to the dangerous use of steroids. But preferences for body type varies by culture as Christy Haubegger explains in the Diverse Voices feature, "I'm Not Fat, I'm Latina."

Clothing and Personal Grooming

Your clothing and personal grooming communicate a message about you. Successful professionals understand the message power of dress and grooming. For instance, a person charged with drug peddling would be foolish to show up in the courtroom wearing a starter jacket, heavy gold chains, oversized pants, and a backward-facing baseball cap. Likewise a sales representative may wear khakis and a golf shirt in the office but will don a formal blue suit to make a major presentation to a potential client group. Many businesses have reintroduced dress codes because in the words of Korn-Ferry International, "We found that casual dress fostered a casual attitude" (Geyer, 1999, p. A12).

What three adjectives would you use to describe the personality of each of these people? What about their clothing and personal appearance led you to draw these conclusions?

Today, more than ever, people use clothing choices, body art, and other personal grooming to communicate. From "retro" fashions to hip-hop styles, from blue hair and nail colors to dreadlocks and Mohawks, from tattooing to body piercing, people are choosing to use their physical appearance to differentiate themselves from some groups and to identify closely with others.

Competent communicators recognize that their physical appearance sends a message and adapt their style to the setting. While each of us has the right to express our individuality and

© Matthew McKee/Eye Ubiquitous/CORBIS

DIVERSE VOICES

I'm Not Fat, I'm Latina

by Christy Haubegger

"Beauty is in the eye of the beholder." But when you are a "large" person, whether your size enhances or detracts from your own or others' perceptions of your beauty may depend on your cultural group.

 recently read a newspaper article that reported that nearly 40 percent of Hispanic and African-American women are overweight. At least I'm in good company. Because according to even the most generous height and weight charts at the doctor's office, I'm a good twenty-five pounds overweight. And I'm still looking for the panty-hose chart that has me on it (according to Hanes™ I don't exist). But I'm happy to report that in the Latino community, my community, I fit right in.

Latinas in this country live in two worlds. People who don't know us may think we're fat. At home, we're called *bien cuidadas* (well cared for).

I love to go dancing at Cesar's Latin Palace here in the Mission District of San Francisco. At this hot all-night salsa club, it's the curvier bodies like mine that turn heads. I'm the one on the dance floor all night while some of my thinner friends spend more time waiting along the walls. Come to think of it, I wouldn't trade my body for any of theirs.

But I didn't always feel this way. I remember being in high school and noticing that none of the magazines showed models in bathing suits with bodies like mine. Handsome movie heroes were never hoping to find a chubby damsel in distress. The fact that I had plenty of attention from Latino boys wasn't enough. Real self-esteem cannot come from male attention alone.

My turning point came a few years later. When I was in college, I made a trip to Mexico, and I brought back much more than sterling-silver bargains and colorful blankets.

I remember hiking through the awesome ruins of Maya and the Aztecs, civilizations that created pyramids as large as the ones in Egypt. I loved walking through the temple doorways whose clearance was only two inches above my head, and I realized that I must be a direct descendant of those ancient priestesses for who those doorways had originally been built.

For the first time in my life, I was in a place where people like me were the beautiful ones. And I began to accept, and even like, the body that I have.

I know that medical experts say that Latinas are twice as likely as the rest of the population to be overweight. And yes, I know about the health problems that often accompany severe weight problems. But most of us are not in the danger zone; we're just *bien cuidadas.* Even the researchers who found that nearly 40 percent of us are overweight noted that there is a greater "cultural acceptance" of being overweight within Hispanic communities. But the article also commented on the cultural-acceptance factor as if it were something unfortunate, because it keeps Hispanic women from becoming healthier. I'm not so convinced that we're the ones with the problem.

If the medical experts were to try to get to the root of this so-called problem, they would probably find that it's part genetics, part enchiladas. Whether we're Cuban-American, Mexican-American, Puerto Rican or Dominican, food is a central part of Hispanic culture. While our food varies from fried plaintains to tamales, what doesn't change is its role in our lives. You feed people you care for, and so if you're well cared for, *bien cuidada,* you have been fed well.

I remember when I used to be envious of a Latina friend of mine who had always been on the skinny side. When I confided this to her a while ago, she laughed. It turns out that when she was growing up, she had always wanted to look more like me. She had trouble getting dates with Latinos in high school, the same boys I dated. When she was little, the other kids in the neighborhood had even given her a cruel nickname: *la seca,* "the dry one." I'm glad I never had any of those problems.

Our community has always been accepting of us well-cared-for women. So why don't we feel beautiful? You only have to flip through a magazine or watch a movie to realize that beautiful for most of this country still means tall, blond, and underfed. But now we know it's the magazines that are wrong. I, for one, am going to do what I can to make sure that *mis hijas,* my daughters, won't feel the way I did.

Reprinted from Christy Haubegger, "I'm Not Fat, I'm Latina." In M. Adams, W. J. Blumenfeld, R. Castañeda, H. W. Hackman, M. L. Peters, & X. Zúñiga (Eds.), Readings for Diversity and Social Justice: An Anthology on Racism, Anti-Semitism, Sexism, Heterosexism, Ableism, and Classism (pp. 242–243). New York: Routledge, 2000.

to communicate our political feelings in our dress and personal grooming, we must realize that when we stretch norms and conventions, we create barriers.

Poise

Poise is a manner of bearing that indicates a person's level of self-confidence. As much as 20 percent of the population experiences a high degree of nervousness when encountering strangers, speaking in a group, or making a speech (Richmond & McCroskey, 2000, p. 35). Some people may be comfortable interacting with strangers one on one but still get tense when in a group or when speaking in public. For most people, nervousness decreases as they gain confidence in their ability to interact in a particular setting. As you master the skills discussed in this text, you are likely to learn to cope with the nervousness you might face in various interpersonal communication situations.

poise
a manner of bearing that indicates a person's level of self-confidence.

Touch

Through **touch,** or **haptics** (the use of hands, arms, and other body parts to pat, hug, slap, kiss, pinch, stroke, hold, embrace, and tickle), we communicate a variety of meanings. In Western culture, we shake hands to be sociable and polite, we pat a person on the back for encouragement, we hug a person to show love, and we clasp raised hands to demonstrate solidarity. Our touching can be gentle or firm, perfunctory or passionate, brief or lingering. And how we touch can communicate our power, our empathy, or our understanding. To learn more about touch, read the article "Just the Right Touch," available through InfoTrac College Edition. Use your Communicate! CD-ROM to access Web Resource 4.2: Just the Right Touch at the Communicate! Web site.

touch or haptics
the use of hands, arms, and other body parts to pat, hug, slap, kiss, pinch, stroke, hold,embrace, and tickle.

People differ in their touching behavior and in their reactions to unsolicited touch from others. Some people like to touch and be touched; other people do not. Women tend to touch others less than men do, but women value touching more than men do. Although women view touch as an expressive behavior that demonstrates warmth and affiliation, they are unlikely to touch men because "Women are taught that for them to initiate the touch could mislead the man into thinking the woman is promiscuous" (Richmond & McCroskey, 2000, p. 251).

Although U.S. culture is relatively noncontact oriented, the kinds and amounts of touching behavior within our society vary widely. Touching behavior that seems innocuous to one person may be perceived to be overly intimate or threatening to another. Touch that is perceived to be OK in private may embarrass a person when done in public or with a large group of people. What you communicate by touching may be perceived positively or negatively. Thus, if you want to be perceived as sensitive and caring, it is a good idea to ask the other person before touching.

Time

Our self-presentation also includes how we manage time. Our use of "informal time," as Edward T. Hall (1959, p. 135) calls it, includes duration, activity, and punctuality.

duration
the amount of time we regard as appropriate for certain events or activities.

Duration is the amount of time we regard as appropriate for certain events or activities. For instance, we may expect a sermon to last twenty to thirty minutes, a typical class to run fifty minutes, and a week night dinner with the family to be thirty minutes. When the length of an event differs significantly from our expectations, we begin to attribute meaning to its duration. For example, if we are told that a job interview will take one hour and it is over in twenty minutes, we may conclude that we didn't get the job. Similarly, if the interview stretches to two hours, we may believe that we are in strong contention for the job. Because our use of time creates its own meanings, we need to learn to attend carefully to polite conventions about the "appropriate duration" of events and activities.

activity
what people perceive should be done in a given period.

Activity refers to what people perceive should be done in a given period. Many of us work during the day, sleep at night, eat a light meal around midday, and so on. When someone engages in behavior at a time that we deem unusual, we are likely to see it as inappropriate. For instance, Susan, who prides herself on being available to her employees at work, may be annoyed when Sung Lei calls her at home during the dinner hour to discuss a presentation that is to be delivered at the end of the month. While Sung Lei may believe that by calling her manager at home she is presenting herself as hard working and dedicated in her work, Susan may view Sung Lei as rude and insensitive.

punctuality
the extent to which one adheres strictly to the appointed or regular time.

Punctuality is the extent to which one adheres strictly to the appointed or regular time. It may be the dimension of time that most closely relates to self-presentation. If you make an appointment to meet your manager in her office at 10 A.M., her opinion of you may differ depending on whether you arrive at 9:50, 10:00, 10:10, or 10:30. Similarly, your opinion of her will differ depending on whether she is there or not. In the United States, strict punctuality is the dominant cultural imperative. When a date is made or an appointment set, others will expect you to arrive on time. If you are late, your arrival may be misinterpreted as meaningful.

Cultural Variations in Self-Presentation

Just as the meanings of body motions and paralanguage are culturally determined, so too are self-presentation behaviors and the meanings assigned to them in various cultures.

Touch According to Gudykunst and Kim (2003, p. 256), differences in touching behavior are highly correlated with culture. In some cultures lots of contact and touching is normal behavior, whereas in other cultures individual space is respected and frequent touching is not encouraged. Latin American, Mediterranean, and Arab countries are high-contact cultures, northern European cultures are medium to low in contact, and Asian cultures are for the most part low-contact cultures. The United States, which is a country of immigrants, is generally perceived to be medium-contact, though there are wide differences between individual Americans because of their family heritage.

Time A particularly important area of cultural differences concerns perceptions of time. Some cultures view time monochronically; that is, they see time as compartmental, irreversible, and one-dimensional. In these cultures time is a scarce resource to be "spent," "saved," and "budgeted," not "wasted" or "misspent." The dominant culture of the United States is monochronically oriented, and calendars, schedules, and appointments govern human interaction—one event at a time (Gudykunst & Kim, 2003, p. 179). Thus, in this culture when someone is even a few minutes late, an apology or explanation may be expected.

People from Latin America, Asia, or the Middle East view time more polychronically, seeing time as continuous and allowing people to engage in several activities at the same time. To those with a polychronic view of time, the concept of "being late" has no meaning. One arrives when one has completed what came before. While the dominant culture in the United States is monochronic to the extreme, we again experience wide variations because of our immigrant heritage. In some of our subcultures, a polychronic view of time still influences behavior. Those from Latin American or African American backgrounds are likely to use time in a polychronic way.

Managing Your Communication Environment

In addition to the way we use body motions, paralanguage, and self-presentation cues, we communicate nonverbally through how we manage the physical environment in which our interactions occur. The principal elements of the environment over which we can exercise control are the space we occupy, the temperature of the surroundings, the lighting levels, and the colors used in the interior decorations.

Space

As a study, space includes permanent structures, the movable objects within these structures, and the informal space that separates the participants.

Managing permanent structures The buildings in which we live and work and the parts of those buildings that cannot be moved fall into the category of permanent structures. Although we may not have much control over the creation of such elements, we do exercise control in our selection of them. For instance, when you rent an apartment or buy a condominium or a home, you consider whether or not it is in tune with your lifestyle. People who select a fourth-floor loft may view themselves differently from those who select one-room efficiencies. Doctors, lawyers, and other professionals usually search with care to find homes that fit the image they want to communicate.

In addition, specific features affect our communication within that environment. For instance, people who live in apartment buildings are likely to become better acquainted with neighbors who live across the hall and next door than with those who live on other floors. Similarly, people who share common space such as laundry facilities or garages are more likely to become acquainted than those who do not.

Managing movable objects within space Whether the space is a dormitory room, a dining room, a seminar room, or a classroom, we have the opportunity to arrange and rearrange movable objects to achieve the effect we want. For example, a manager's office arranged so that the manager sits behind the desk and the employee chair is on the other side of that desk says, "Let's talk business—I'm the boss and you're the employee." In contrast, if the employee chair is at the side of the desk (creating an absence of a formal barrier), the arrangement says, "Don't be nervous—let's just chat." Interior designers are skilled at helping people choose colors, fabrics, and furnishings that enhance space and encourage interaction. To understand more about the design considerations in planning a welcoming dining room, use your Communicate! CD-ROM to access Web Resource 4.3: Welcoming Dining Rooms.

Managing informal space Managing informal space includes the space around us at the moment. In the dominant U.S. culture, four distinct distances represent what most people consider appropriate or comfortable in various situations (Hall, 1969):

- *Intimate distance,* up to eighteen inches, is appropriate for private conversations between close friends.
- *Personal distance,* from eighteen inches to four feet, is the space in which casual conversation occurs.
- *Social distance,* from four to twelve feet, is where impersonal business such as job interviews is conducted.
- *Public distance* is anything more than twelve feet.

Of greatest concern to us is the intimate distance, that which we regard as appropriate for intimate conversation with close friends, parents, and younger children. If you have become uncomfortable because a person you were talking with was standing too close to you, you are already aware of how attitudes toward intimate space influence people's conversation. People usually become uncomfortable when "outsiders" violate this intimate distance.

Intrusions into our intimate space are acceptable only in certain settings and then only when all involved follow the unwritten rules. For instance, people will tolerate being packed into a crowded elevator or subway and even touching others they do not know provided the others follow such "rules" as standing rigidly, looking at the floor or the indicator above the door, and not making eye contact with others. Only occasionally will people who are forced to invade each other's intimate space acknowledge the other as a person. Then they are likely to exchange sheepish smiles or otherwise acknowledge the mutual invasion of intimate distance. The Spotlight on Scholars features Judee Burgoon, who has focused a great deal of her research on the effects of such intrusions into our intimate space. Her findings develop and test what she calls "expectancy violation theory."

Interpersonal problems occur when one person's use of space violates the behavioral expectations of another. For instance, Abdul may come from a family that conducts informal conversations with others at a range closer than the eighteen-inch limit many European

People have differing concepts of informal space. Although you might find it rude for nonintimates to get this close to you in conversation, these men would find it rude if you backed away.

Spotlight on Scholars ▶ Judee K. Burgoon

With seven books and more than 150 articles and book chapters to her credit, Judee K. Burgoon is a leading scholar who has helped shape how we now think about nonverbal communication. Her fascination with nonverbal behavior dates back to a graduate school seminar assignment at the University of West Virginia; she was asked to find out what was known about *proxemics*, the study of space. From that assignment, she says, "I just got hooked. Nonverbal is more elusive and difficult to study, and I've always enjoyed a challenge!"

At the time, scholars believed the road to interpersonal success lay in conforming one's behaviors to social norms about the distances that are appropriate for certain types of interactions and the types of touch that are appropriate for individuals in different kinds of relationships. Thus people would be successful in their interactions as long as they behaved in accord with these norms.

Encouraged by one of her professors to "look for the counterintuitive," Burgoon's research uncovered situations where violations of these norms resulted in positive rather than negative consequences. For example, in settings where two people were not well acquainted and one of them began "flirting" by moving closer to the other, thus "violating" that person's space, the other person did not always react by moving away from the violator as expected. In fact, at times the person seemed to welcome the violation and at times may even have moved closer. Similarly, she noticed that touching behavior that violated social norms was sometimes rejected and at other times accepted.

To explain what she saw happening, Burgoon developed and began to test what she named "expectancy violation theory," which is based on the premise that we have strong expectations about how people ought to behave when they interact with us. Whether they meet our expectations affects not only how we interact with them but also such outcomes as how competent, credible, and influential we perceive them to be and what we think of our relationship. She found that how we interpret a violation depends on how we feel about that person. If we like the person, we are likely to read the nonverbal violation as positive ("Gee, she put her arm around me—that means she's really interested in me"). If we don't like the person, we are likely to read the same nonverbal violation as negative ("He better take his arm off of me, this is a clear case of harassment"). And, because we have become sensitized to the situation, the violations will be subject to strong evaluations ("Wow, I really like the feel of her arm around my waist" versus "He's making me feel really uncomfortable"). As Burgoon continued to study violations, she discovered that when a person we really like violates our expectation we are likely to view the interaction as even more positive than we would have if the person had conformed to our expectations. Over the years, Burgoon and her students' numerous research studies have provided strong support for expectancy violation theory.

Burgoon's scholarship has developed like a river. Her first work was a narrow stream with a focus on proxemics, which grew with expectancy violation theory to include all of nonverbal behavior, and it continues to branch. Presently, in one stream of work she is studying what determines how people adapt their behavior when they experience any type of communication violation. Why and when do people reciprocate the violation (for example, if someone shouts, you shout back) or compensate for it (for example, if someone comes too close to you, you step back)? In a second stream, Burgoon is focusing on a specific type of expectancy violation: deception. Here she is trying to sort out the role nonverbal behavior plays in deceitful interactions. Finally, she has begun a stream of work whose purpose is to identify the essential properties of interpersonal communication that are different from the properties of media communication.

Whatever branch her research takes, Judee Burgoon brings the same readiness to challenge the current thinking that has been the hallmark of her work. For complete citations of four of her recent publications in these areas, see the References section at the end of this book.

In addition to teaching a number of courses, Burgoon serves as Director of Graduate Studies, where her role of helping students learn how to conduct research and formulate theory gives her great satisfaction. "Mentoring others is among the major gratifications of doing research. The fun is to teach others what I was taught: always challenge the current assumptions."

To learn more about Judee Burgoon's work, log on to her home page at www.u.arizona.edu/~judee.

Americans place on intimate space. When he talks to a colleague at work and moves in closer than eighteen inches, the coworker may back away from him during the conversation. Unfortunately, there are times when one person intentionally violates the space expectations of another. When the violation is between members of the opposite sex, it may be considered sexual harassment. Glen may, through violations of informal space, posture, movements, or gestures, "come on" to Donnice. If Donnice does not welcome the attention, she may feel threatened. In this case, Glen's nonverbal behavior may be construed as sexual harassment. To avoid perceptions of harassment, people need to be especially sensitive to others' definitions of intimate space.

Whereas our intimate or personal space moves when we move, we seek to claim other space as well, whether or not we are currently occupying it. That is, we are likely to look at certain space as our **territory**—space over which we may claim ownership. If Marcia decides to eat lunch at the company commissary, the space at the table she selects becomes her territory. Suppose that during lunch Marcia leaves her territory to get butter for her roll. The chair she left, the food on the table, and the space around that food are "hers," and she will expect others to stay away. If, when she returns, Marcia finds that someone at the table has moved a glass or a dish into the area that she regards as her territory, she is likely to feel resentful.

territory
space over which we may claim ownership.

Many people stake out their territory with markers. For example, Ramon arrives early for the first day of class, finds an empty desk, and puts his backpack next to it on the floor and his coat on the seat. He then makes a quick trip to the restroom. If someone comes along while Ramon is gone, moves his backpack and coat, and sits down at the desk, that person is violating what Ramon has marked as his territory.

As a student of nonverbal communication, however, you understand that other people may not look at either the space around you or your territory in quite the same way as you do. That the majority of U.S. residents have learned the same basic rules governing the management of space does not mean that everyone shares the same respect for the rules or treats the consequences of breaking the rules in the same way.

Violating Intimate Space Norms

Enter a crowded elevator. Get on it and face the back. Make direct eye contact with the person you are standing in front of. When you disembark, record the person's reactions. On the return trip, introduce yourself to the person who is standing next to you and engage in an animated conversation. Record the reaction of the person and others around you. Get on an empty elevator and stand in the exact center. Do not move when others board. Record their reactions. Be prepared to share what you have observed with your classmates.

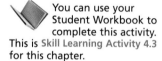 You can use your Student Workbook to complete this activity. This is Skill Learning Activity 4.3 for this chapter.

Temperature, Lighting, and Color

Three other elements of the environment that can be controlled and that affect communication are temperature, lighting, and color.

Temperature can stimulate or inhibit effective communication. Temperature can alter people's moods and change their level of attentiveness. Can you recall the difficulty you have had listening to a teacher in a hot stuffy classroom? Have you found that you become "edgy" when you are cold?

Lighting levels also add meaning to communication messages. In lecture halls and reading rooms, bright light is expected—it encourages good listening and comfortable reading. By contrast, in a chic restaurant, a jazz club music listening room, or a coffee bar, you expect the lighting to be soft and rather dim, which makes for a cozy atmosphere and invites intimate conversation (Knapp & Hall, 2002, p. 126). We often change the lighting level in a room to change the mood and indicate the type of interaction that is expected. Bright lights encourage activity and boisterous conversations, whereas softer lighting levels calm and soothe, encouraging quiet and more serious conversations.

Color may stimulate both emotional and physical reactions. For instance, red excites, blue comforts and soothes, and yellow cheers and elevates mood. Professional interior designers who understand how people react to colors may choose blues when they are trying to create a peaceful, serene atmosphere for a living room, whereas they will decorate in reds and yellows in a playroom.

In addition, specific colors also convey information about people and events. For instance, youth gangs often use colors to signal membership. In some communities gang members wear bandannas or other articles of clothing in a specific color.

Cultural Variations in Environment Management

As you would expect, the environments in which people feel comfortable depend on their cultural background. In the United States, where we have ample land, many people live in single-family homes or in large apartments. In other countries, where land is scarce, people live in closer quarters and can feel "lonely" or isolated in larger spaces. In Japan and Europe, most people live in spaces that by our U.S. standards feel cramped. Similarly, people from different cultures have different ideas about what constitutes appropriate distances for various interactions. Recall that in the dominant culture of the United States, the boundary of personal or intimate space is about eighteen inches. In Middle Eastern cultures, however, men move much closer to other men when they are talking (Samovar & Porter, 2001, p. 186). Thus, when an Arab man talks with an American man, one of the two is likely to be uncomfortable. Either the American will feel uncomfortable and invaded or the Arab will feel isolated and too distant for serious conversation.

We also differ in the temperature ranges that we find comfortable. People who originate from warmer climates can tolerate heat more than people who originate in cooler climates. Even the meanings that we assign to colors vary by national culture and religion. In India white, not black, is the color of mourning, and Hindu brides wear red.

What Would You Do? ▸ A QUESTION OF ETHICS

fter the intramural mixed-doubles matches on Tuesday evening, most of the players adjourned to the campus grill for a drink and a chat. Marquez and Lisa sat down with Barry and Elana, whom they had lost to that night largely because of Elana's improved play. Although Marquez and Lisa were only tennis friends, Barry and Elana had been going out together for much of the season.

After some general conversation about the tournament, Marquez said, "Elana, your serve today was the best I've seen it this year."

"Yeah, I was really impressed. And as you saw, I had trouble handling it," Lisa added.

"And you're getting to the net a lot better too," Marquez added.

"Thanks, guys," Elana said in a tone of gratitude, "I've really been working on it."

"Well, aren't we getting the compliments today," sneered Barry in a sarcastic tone. Then after a pause, he said, "Oh, Elana, would you get my sweater—I left it on that chair by the other table."

"Come on, Barry, you're closer than I am," Elana replied.

Barry got a cold look on his face, moved slightly closer to Elana, and said emphatically, "Get my sweater for me, Elana—now."

Elana quickly backed away from Barry as she said, "OK, Barry—it's cool," and she then quickly got the sweater for him.

"Gee, isn't she sweet," Barry said to Marquez and Lisa as he grabbed the sweater from Elana.

Lisa and Marquez both looked down at the floor. Then Lisa glanced at Marquez and said, "Well, I'm out of here—I've got a lot to do this evening."

"Let me walk you to your car," Marquez said as he stood up.

"See you next week," they both said in unison as they hurried out the door leaving Barry and Elana alone at the table.

1. Analyze Barry's nonverbal behavior. What was he attempting to achieve?

2. How do you interpret Lisa's and Marquez's nonverbal reactions to Barry?

3. Was Barry's behavior ethically acceptable? Explain.

Summary

Nonverbal communication refers to how people communicate through the use of body motions, paralanguage, self-presentation cues, and the physical environment.

Perhaps the most familiar methods of nonverbal communication are what and how a person communicates through body motions and paralanguage. Eye contact, facial expression, gesture, and posture are four major types of body motions. Body motions take the place of words, illustrate what a speaker is saying, display feelings, control or regulate conversations, and relieve tension. Whereas a person's vocal characteristics (volume, rate, pitch, and quality) help us interpret the meaning of the verbal message, a person's vocal interferences ("ah," "um," "you know," and "like") often impede our ability to understand and become annoying.

Although verbal and nonverbal communication work together best when they are complementary, nonverbal cues may replace or even contradict verbal symbols. Generally, nonverbal communication is more to be trusted when verbal and nonverbal cues are in conflict.

Through self-presentation cues, such as clothing, touching behavior, and use of time, people communicate about themselves and their relationship to others. The physical environment is often overlooked even though we set the tone for conversations and nonverbally communicate through it. The choices people make in their permanent spaces, the way they arrange the objects in those spaces, and the way they control or react to temperature, lighting, and color contribute to the quality and meaning of the communication episodes that occur.

Your understanding of nonverbal communication can contribute to clearer encoding and decoding. Armed with this knowledge, you are equipped to be more effective in all settings. Increasing the accuracy with which we use and understand nonverbal communication behavior is even more critical when we are interacting with people who are different from us.

Communicate! Online

N ow that you have read Chapter 4, use your Communicate! CD-ROM for quick access to the electronic resources that accompany this text. Your CD-ROM gives you access to InfoTrac College Edition and the Communicate! Web site. When you get to the Communicate! home page, click on "Student Book Companion Site" in the Resource box at right to access the online study aids for this chapter, including a digital glossary, review quizzes, chapter activities, and chapter Web Resources.

Key Terms

At the Communicate! Web site, select the chapter resources for Chapter 4. Print a copy of the glossary for this chapter and test yourself with the electronic flash cards or complete the crossword puzzle to help you master these key terms:

nonverbal communication
   behaviors (72)
body motions or kinesics (73)
eye contact or gaze (73)
facial expression (73)
gestures (74)
posture (74)

sign language (74)
paralanguage or vocalics (77)
pitch (77)
volume (77)
rate (77)
quality (77)
vocal interferences (77)

poise (81)
touch or haptics (81)
duration (82)
activity (82)
punctuality (82)
territory (87)

Review Quiz

Test your knowledge of the concepts in this chapter by taking the online quiz at the Communicate! Web site. Select the chapter resources for Chapter 4, then click on "Review Quiz." When you have completed the quiz, submit it for scoring.

Skill Learning Activities

Complete Observe & Analyze Activities 4.1 and 4.2 online at the Communicate! Web site. Select the chapter resources for Chapter 4, then click on "Activities." You can submit your Observe & Analyze answers to your instructor.

4.1: Observe & Analyze: Body Motions (76)
4.2: Observe & Analyze: Self-Presentation Audit (83)
4.3: Observe & Analyze: Violating Intimate Space Norms (88)

Web Resources

Access the Web Resources for this chapter online at the Communicate! Web site. Select the chapter resources for Chapter 4, then click on "Web Resources."

4.1: Maria Brazil (76)
4.2: Just the Right Touch (81)
4.3: Welcoming Dining Rooms (84)

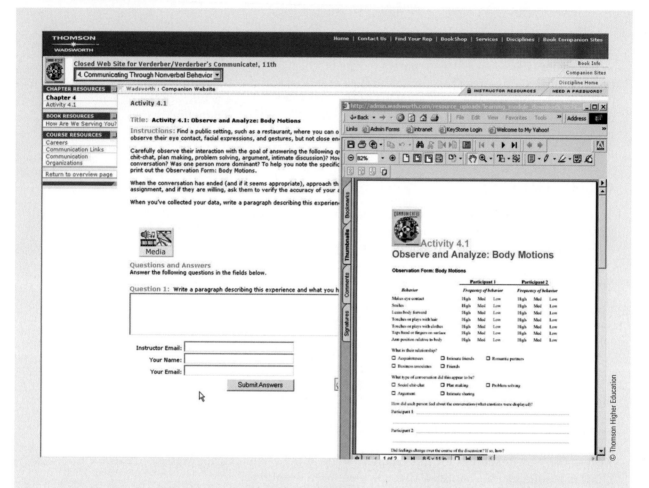

Establishing a Communication Foundation from Chapters 2 through 4

What kind of a communicator are you? This review looks at ten specifics that are basic to effective communicators. On the line provided for each statement, indicate the response that best captures your behavior: 1, almost always; 2, often; 3, sometimes; 4, rarely; 5, never.

_____ When I speak, I tend to present a positive image of myself. (Ch. 2)

_____ In my behavior toward others, I look for more information to confirm or negate my first impressions. (Ch. 2)

_____ Before I act on perceptions drawn from people's nonverbal cues, I seek verbal verification of their accuracy. (Ch. 2)

_____ My conversation is helped by a large vocabulary. (Ch. 3)

_____ I speak clearly, using words that people readily understand. (Ch. 3)

_____ When I am speaking with people of different cultures or of the opposite sex, I am careful to monitor my word choices. (Ch. 3)

_____ I tend to look at people when I talk with them. (Ch. 4)

_____ Most of my sentences are free from such expressions as "uh," "well," "like," and "you know." (Ch. 4)

_____ I consider the effect of my dress on others. (Ch. 4)

_____ I try to control my environment in ways that help my communication. (Ch. 4)

Based on your responses, select the communication behavior you would most like to change. Write a communication improvement goal statement similar to the sample improvement plan in Chapter 1 (page 22). If you would like verification of your self-analysis before you write a goal, have a friend or fellow worker complete this same analysis for you.

You can complete this Self-Review online and, if requested, email it to your instructor. Use your Communicate! CD-ROM to access **Part I Self-Review.** Select the chapter resources for Chapter 4, then click on "Part I Self-Review."

OBJECTIVES

After you have read this chapter, you should be able to answer these questions:

- What is a conversation?
- How does a casual social conversation differ from a pragmatic problem-consideration conversation?
- What are conversational rules, and what are their distinguishing features?
- What is the cooperative principle?
- How do the maxims of the cooperative principle apply to conversation?
- What skills are associated with effective conversations?
- What guidelines regulate turn-taking behavior?
- What is conversational coherence, and how can it be achieved?
- Why is politeness important in conversation?
- What additional skills are important for electronically mediated conversations?

5

Holding Effective Conversations

Gwen agreed to drive Doris to work. As Doris got into the car, Gwen said, "I think it's really going to be a hot one today."

"Looks like it," Doris replied.

As they drove down Main Street, Gwen said, "Look, Capri's seems to be closed. I thought it was one of the best restaurants on this side of town. Have you eaten there?"

"No," Doris replied.

After several minutes of quiet, Gwen said, "I'm rather concerned about the way Glen has been acting lately. I always thought he was a good manager."

Doris nodded.

"Do you think he might be having some problems?" Gwen asked.

"Don't know," Doris said as she looked at her fingernails.

"Well," Gwen added, "let's hope he gets back to his old self soon."

"Um," Doris responded seriously.

After more minutes of silence Gwen said, "Have you watched the new *Survivor*?"

"No," said Doris.

"I think it's getting worse," Gwen said. "I know I'm not going to watch it anymore."

The women rode in silence until Gwen announced, "Well, here we are." Doris turned to Gwen and said sincerely, "Thanks for the ride. I really enjoyed talking with you!"

"Uh, yeah, right," Gwen stuttered.

onversations are the medium of interpersonal communication and the building blocks of good interpersonal relationships. When conversations go well, they are informative, stimulating, and often just good fun. Yet, like the one between Gwen and Doris, some conversations can be difficult to sustain and are frustrating. By understanding how a conversation works and by taking advantage of its dynamics, we all can become more skillful in the everyday talks we have with others.

In this chapter, we define conversation and discuss the types and structure, consider the rules that conversations follow, look at the cooperative principle that helps to explain how conversation works, and consider the guidelines for effective conversation. Finally, we offer a competence test of conversation and supply a sample conversation and analysis for your consideration.

Characteristics of Conversation

conversation
the ordinary kind of communicating people do in a variety of settings.

Conversation, or "everyday talk" as labeled by Karen Tracy (2002, p. 5), is the ordinary kind of communicating people do in a variety of settings. Although conversations are spontaneous communication, most have some structure. When people find a conversation satisfying, they tend to seek out the others for additional conversations. If, for instance, Dan meets Carl at a party and both find the talk they had about politics stimulating, they are likely to look forward to additional conversations on this topic.

How conversations are structured depends on the type of conversation taking place. Let's look at two common types of conversations: the casual social conversation and the pragmatic problem-consideration conversation.

Casual Social Conversation

casual social conversations
interactions whose purpose is to meet participants' interpersonal needs and to enhance or maintain a relationship through spontaneous interactions about nonspecific topics.

Casual social conversations are interactions whose purpose is to meet participants' interpersonal needs and to enhance or maintain a relationship through spontaneous interactions about nonspecific topics. For instance, when Connie, Jeff, Wanda, and Trevor get together for dinner together, their conversation will encompass a variety of topics. All four will participate in discussing some of the topics while two sets of two may converse on others. During dinner they may spend most of the time talking about the upcoming presidential election, or they may scatter their talk over multiple topics including their reviews of a new movie, gossip about a wedding they attended, last week's football game, the current election news, the recent terror alert, or the latest gossip circulating among their friends.

As you can see, gossip is a staple of casual social conversation. Although at times it can be malicious and unethical, gossip is often seen as a harmless form of small talk. In fact, Eggins and Slade (1997, p. 279) point out that gossip is a powerful socializing force. It reflects a sociocultural world and at the same time helps to shape that world.

Casual social conversations are loosely structured. A topic introduced by one person will be accepted or rejected by other participants. Others accept a topic by providing additional information or opinions, agreeing, disagreeing, and so forth. That topic continues to be discussed until another topic is introduced and captures the attention of the participants. A topic is rejected when others do not respond to what has been said and instead begin to discuss a different topic. The topic change process occurs throughout the conversation. When more than two people are part of the conversational group, side conversations may develop on different topics.

Figure 5.1 provides the dialogue and a commentary of a conversation between Donna and Juanita who are attending a play together.

Conversation	Commentary
As she looks around the theater, Donna says, "They really did an Art Deco thing with this place didn't they?"	Donna introduces a possible topic.
"Yeah . . . Hey," Juanita says as she surveys the audience, "it looks as if this is going to be a sellout."	Juanita acknowledges Donna's statement, chooses not to discuss it, and introduces a different topic.
"Certainly does—I see people in the last row of the balcony."	Donna accepts the topic and extends discussion by adding a detail.
"I thought this would be a popular show. It was a hit when it toured Louisville . . . and I hear the attendance has been good all week."	Juanita continues the topic by providing additional information.
"Yeah," Donna adds, "Lots of people I've talked with were trying to get tickets."	Donna and Juanita continue the topic for two more turns.
"Well, it's good for the downtown."	
"I agree," Donna says as she glances at the notes on the cast. After a few seconds she exclaims, "I didn't know Gloria VanDell was from Cincinnati!"	Donna acknowledges Juanita's reply and then introduces a different topic.

Figure 5.1
A casual conversation

Pragmatic Problem-Consideration Conversation

Pragmatic problem-consideration conversations are interactions that require the participants to deliberate and reach a joint conclusion. Sometimes, the problem topic is known before the conversation begins. For instance, if Glen is concerned about the fairness of workloads, he may ask Susan, his coworker, to meet with him to generate some ideas about what can be done to better balance the jobs assigned to each person on the team. At other times, the need to consider a particular topic or problem may arise spontaneously during the discussion. For instance, while office mates are talking over lunch, one of them might say, "Garret has really been stressed out lately." This might stimulate the group to consider what they might do to help alleviate Garret's stress.

Pragmatic problem-consideration conversation has as many as five distinguishable parts.

1. **Greetings and small talk.** Pragmatic problem-consideration conversations may begin with a greeting followed by brief conversation on social topics to develop rapport.

2. **Topic introduction and acceptance of need for discussion.** In the second stage, the problem or issue is introduced by someone, and the participants accept it as the focus of the conversation. How this topic is presented or framed affects how the discussion will proceed.

3. **Information exchange and processing.** In a series of speaking turns, participants share information and opinions, generate alternative solutions, and argue the advantages and disadvantages of different options.

4. **Summarizing decisions and clarifying next steps.** As the partners appear to converge on one solution, someone is likely to summarize what appears to be agreed on. The others will either accept the summary or will amend it to clarify the areas of agreement as well as any remaining disagreements. Sometimes conversational partners skip this step, which is risky because each person will act on what he or she perceives has been decided.

5. **Formal close.** Once the participants have reached a decision, they change topics. Conversationalists have discussed the issue and clarified the next steps that will be taken, and they end discussion of the problem. An ending statement provides a transition that enables participants to move to a social conversation topic, begin a new problem consideration, or simply disengage from one another. The formal closing often includes showing appreciation for the conversation, such as "I'm glad we took some time to share ideas. I think we'll be far more effective if the two of us are on the same page." Or the closing might leave the door open for later conversation, such as "If you have any second thoughts, give me a call."

Because problem-consideration conversations are spontaneous, they don't follow a linear problem-solving format. The conversationalists may begin by generating some alternatives, then, while discussing advantages and disadvantages, they may share information that might lead to the suggestion of additional alternatives, and so on. In the midst of this discussion, they may digress, changing the topic to something unrelated to the problem at hand before circling back to identifying and evaluating alternatives. They may agree to a plan, then continue to debate it, and eventually reconsider their decision. Problem-solving conversations will include these five types of talk, but the discussion is likely to jump back and forth between types talk. The dialogue and analysis in Figure 5.2 is an example of a simple pragmatic problem-consideration conversation between April and Yolanda.

Conversation	Analysis

"Hi, Yolanda. How are you doing?"
    "Oh, I can't complain too much."
    "Yeah, I feel much the same. Listen, I'm glad I ran into you—I need your help on something."
    "Can we do this quickly, April? I've really got to get working on the speech I'm doing for class."
	1. Greeting is short.

"Oh, this will just take a minute, Yolanda. If I remember right, you said that you'd been to the Dells for dinner with Scot. I'd love to take Rob there to celebrate his birthday, but I wanted to know whether we'd really feel comfortable there."	**2.** Topic introduction.
"Sure. It's pretty elegant, but the prices aren't bad, and the atmosphere is really romantic." "So you think we can really do dinner on sixty or seventy dollars?"	**3.** Information exchange and processing.
"Oh, yeah. We had a salad, dinner, and dessert, and our bill was under seventy dollars even with the tip."	**4.** Summarizing.
"Thanks, Yolanda. I wanted to ask you 'cause I know you like to eat out when you can."	**3.** More information exchange and processing.
"No problem, April. Gotta run. Talk with you later—and let me know how Rob liked it."	**5.** Formal closing.

Figure 5.2
A pragmatic problem-consideration conversation

© Rhoda Sidney/PhotoEdit

Problem-consideration conversations are more ordered than casual social conversations. What part of a problem-consideration conversation does it appear these people are in?

Rules of Conversation

conversational rules
unwritten prescriptions that indicate what behavior is obligated, preferred, or prohibited in certain contexts.

Conversations may appear to have little form or structure, but they usually follow certain rules. **Conversational rules** are "unwritten prescriptions that indicate what behavior is obligated, preferred, or prohibited in certain contexts" (Schimanoff, 1980, p. 57).

Let's take a closer look at this definition using the common conversational rule: "If one person is talking, then another person should not interrupt." First, a rule *prescribes:* it tells what (or what not) to do. So one should not begin talking when someone else is already speaking. Second, a rule is *contextual.* This means that conversational rules can change depending on the situation or culture. So the rule about interrupting is true in an ordinary situation but in an emergency, it's OK to interrupt. Because rules are contextual, they can differ by culture. For example, in some cultures the rule is to look the speaker in the eye; in other cultures, it is a sign of respect to avert your eyes. Finally, rules specify *what should be done,* but each conversational partner is still free to follow or violate the rule. But people who violate conversational rules risk alienating others and being perceived as rude. Figure 5.3 provides some examples of common conversational rules.

If your mouth is full of food, then you must not talk.
If you are spoken to, you must reply.
If another does not hear a question you ask, then you must repeat it.
If more than two people are conversing, then each should have equal time.
If your conversational partners are significantly older than you, then you should refrain from using profanities and obscenities.
If you can't say something nice, then don't say anything at all.
If you are going to say something that you don't want overheard, then lower the volume of your voice.

Figure 5.3
Some common conversational rules

Effective Conversations Follow the Cooperative Principle

H. Paul Grice (1975, pp. 44–46) described the **cooperative principle,** which states that conversations will be satisfying when the contributions made by conversationalists are in line with the purpose of the conversation. Based on this principle, Grice identified four conversational **maxims,** or rules of conduct, that cooperative conversational partners follow.

cooperative principle
states that conversations will be satisfying when the contributions made by conversationalists are in line with the purpose of the conversation.

maxims
rules of conduct that cooperative conversational partners follow.

1. The **quality maxim** calls for us to provide information that is truthful. When we purposely lie, distort, or misrepresent, we are not acting cooperatively in the conversation. Being truthful means not only avoiding deliberate lies or distortions but also taking care to avoid misrepresentation. Thus, if a classmate asks you what the prerequisites for Bio 205 are, you should share them if you know them, but you should not guess and offer your opinion as though it were fact. If you don't know or if you have only a vague recollection, you follow the quality maxim by honestly saying, "I'm not sure."

quality maxim
provide information that is truthful.

2. The **quantity maxim** calls for us to tailor the amount of information we provide so that it is sufficient and necessary to satisfy others' information needs and keep the conversation going. But we are not supposed to become so lengthy and detailed that we dominate the conversation and undermine the informal give-and-take that is characteristic of good conversations. So, when Saul asks Randy how he liked his visit to St. Louis, Randy's answer, "fine," is uncooperatively brief as it makes it difficult for Saul to continue the conversation. On the opposite extreme, should Randy launch into a twenty-minute monologue that details everything he did including recounting what he ate each day, he would also be violating the maxim.

quantity maxim
tailor the amount of information we provide so that it is sufficient and necessary to satisfy others' information needs and keep the conversation going.

3. The **relevancy maxim** calls for us to provide information that is related to the topic currently being discussed. Comments that are only tangential to the subject, or that seek an abrupt subject change when other conversational partners are still actively engaged with the topic, are uncooperative. For example, Hal, Corey, and Li-Sung are in the midst of a lively discussion about the upcoming 5K walk/run for the local homeless shelter when Corey asks whether either Hal or Li-Sung has taken Speech 101. Because Corey's change of subject disrupts an ongoing discussion, he is violating the relevancy maxim.

relevancy maxim
provide information that is related to the topic currently being discussed.

4. The **manner maxim** calls for us to be specific and organized when communicating our thoughts. We cooperate with our conversational partners when we choose specific language so our partners can easily understand our meaning. When D'wan asks Remal how to download a computer file, Remal will comply with the manner maxim by explaining the process one step at a time using language that D'wan can understand. Obviously observing the manner maxim doesn't mean that you have a specific outline for every comment you make. Conversations, after all,

manner maxim
be specific and organized when communicating thoughts.

are informal. But following the manner maxim does mean that you organize what you are saying thoughtfully so that others don't have to work too hard to understand you.

In addition to these four maxims, Bach and Harnish (1979, p. 64) have proposed two additional maxims that cooperative partners follow.

morality maxim
be moral and ethical when we speak.

5. The **morality maxim** calls for us to be moral and ethical when we speak. For example, in the United States violations of the morality maxim would include repeating information that had been disclosed confidentially, purposefully deceiving someone as to the truthfulness or accuracy of another's statements, or persuading someone else to do something that the speaker knows is wrong or against the other's personal interests.

politeness maxim
demonstrate respect for other participants by behaving courteously.

6. The **politeness maxim** calls for us to demonstrate respect for other participants by behaving courteously. In our conversations we should attempt to observe the social norms of politeness in the dominant culture and not purposefully embarrass ourselves or others during the interaction. In the Diverse Voices feature, Gwendolyn Gong describes how politeness is enacted in her cultural community. In the next section we will discuss means of practicing politeness.

DIVERSE VOICES

When Mississippi Chinese Talk

by Gwendolyn Gong, Ph.D.

Dr. Gong, an associate professor at Texas A&M, explains how Mississippi Chinese use conversational accommodation and topic shifting to politely reduce conversational discomfort for their conversational partners and themselves. This excerpt focuses on the use of accommodation or deference.

Though my family heritage traces back to an ancestral village in Canton, China, I am a Chinese American, born and reared in the Mississippi Delta. Given that my siblings—in truth, my entire immediate family—served as classic, prolific producers of Southern speech, I found it peculiar that, when I went to graduate school in Indiana, my Hoosier peers and professors saw me as some sort of enigma—an oddity. They would joke, "The picture's fine but adjust the sound." This same type of remark followed me to Texas, where indeed another version of English is spoken. "Adjust the sound." What did that mean? Hadn't these folks

ever encountered a Mississippian before? The truth was that they had. But I was different. I was a Mississippi Chinese. Since the 1800s this lush farming area has served as a homeland for approximately 1,200 Cantonese Chinese from Southern China who have gradually assimilated into being Southerners of another ilk: Mississippi Chinese (MC). In my experience, one of the most interesting ways by which I have observed how Southern Genteelism and Confucianism reveal themselves is in the talk of the MC.

A major feature that typifies MC speech is deference, the courteous submission or acquiescence to the opinions, wishes, or judgment of another speaker, which may manifest itself in two forms: accommodation (that is, making the non-MC speaker feel comfortable and welcome) and topic shifting (changing the subject of a conversation). Ironically, accommodation that may provide comfort for the non-MC listener may, on occasion, result in discomfort for the MC speaker; conversely, topic shifting oftentimes provides relief and control for the MC speaker but frustration for the non-MC listener. For non-MC speakers and listeners, understanding how deference operates among the MC helps to provide a more effective informed exchange between these two groups.

A number of years ago at the institution where I was teaching, I developed a friendship with a colleague. This woman was a master teacher who spoke with authority and often openly revealed to me her earnest but prejudicial concerns about me as a person. Occasionally, we would see each other in passing and chat:

"Hi, Gong. I went to a Thai restaurant on Sunday. I asked for some soy sauce, and the waiter looked at me like I was crazy. What was wrong with asking for some soy sauce? The food was so bad—like bad Chinese food—that I covered it with everything. Why was that guy so mad at me?"

"Asking for soy sauce isn't a crime. I don't know why your waiter was upset," I replied sheepishly. I was not certain why she was broaching me on the topic of Thai food; I'm not expert on it, though I do enjoy that particular cuisine.

"We ought to have lunch. What's your schedule?" my colleague inquired.

"I've already eaten. Plus I've got so much work to finish in my office today. Sorry that I can't join you while you eat." I was uncomfortable, yet truthful.

"What'd ya eat? Betcha had egg rolls, eh? Gong, you're always eating egg rolls—at least you used to.

Remember when you first came here years ago? I couldn't believe it—a Chinese, teaching English—with a Southern accent, too. I used to share an office with a fellow named Joe, who'd eat tacos and avocados all the time, and then I'd see you across the hall, eating egg rolls. Right, Gong? Don't ya remember?"

"Well, no I really don't remember, but I suppose it's true," I replied, trying to go along with my colleague. "I do recall Joe and I ate take-out food sometimes. It was a quick way to have lunch," I added, my voice trailing off, diminishing with every syllable. I wished I were anywhere else but here, "talking" with this person. It was embarrassing enough that she made these kinds of remarks to me at all, much less within earshot of other faculty and students. Where could I hide? I thought to myself: "Hang in there; it'll be over soon."

This is only one conversation among many that this professor and I have shared. Out of my deep belief that she did care about me and out of my respect for her professional accomplishments, I always accommodated this individual's topic selection and conversational moves. I self-consciously defended her, rationalizing that she was just "tone-deaf" and didn't understand her audience very well. She admitted that she had never known an American-born Asian like me before. As a result, I reasoned to myself that I should give her a break, help her avoid "losing face," and prevent her from feeling awkward. Yet I always experienced regret that I voluntarily subjected myself to being bullied, demeaned, and belittled by someone espousing true friendship.

Excerpted from Dr. Gwendolyn Gong, "When Mississippi Chinese Talk." In A. Gonzalez, M. Houston, & V. Chen (Eds.), Our Voices: Essays in Culture, Ethnicity, and Communication *(pp. 110–116). Los Angeles: Roxbury, 1994. Reprinted by permission.*

Guidelines for Effective Conversationalists

Regardless of how well we think we converse, almost all of us can learn to be more effective conversationalists. In this section, we discuss several guidelines for improving your conversational skills.

Observe&Analyze

Following the Cooperative Principle

For the next three days keep a log of two or three conversations you have had. After you complete each conversation, take a few moments to record your observations and perceptions. At the end of the three days, analyze your log. Then write a paragraph in which you answer these questions: How well did I adhere to the maxims of the cooperative principle? Did the extent to which I and my conversational partners adhered to these maxims affect my satisfaction with the conversation? Is there a particular maxim that is more difficult for me to follow?

 You can use your Student Workbook to complete this activity, or you can complete it online, download a log to use, and, if requested, email it to your instructor. Use your Communicate! CD-ROM to access Skill Learning Activity 5.1.

Prepare to Contribute Interesting Information

Curious people make interesting conversationalists. The more you know about a range of subjects, the greater the chances are that you will be able to participate effectively in social conversations. Here are some ways to increase what you are able to contribute:

1. Keep up to date on current events and issues.

    ■ Read a newspaper every day.
    ■ Read one weekly news or special-interest magazine.
    ■ Follow the news online or through television or radio.
    ■ Watch television documentaries and news specials as well as entertainment and sports programs.

2. Increase your cultural IQ.

    ■ Attend live theater and a variety of concerts in addition to going to movies.
    ■ Attend cultural festivals sponsored by different ethnic groups.
    ■ Study the music, art, or history of another nationality.
    ■ Visit museums and historical sites.
    ■ Read a variety of novels including the classics.

3. Develop special expertise.

    ■ Learn a craft.
    ■ Start a collection.
    ■ Become proficient at a game or sport.

Following these suggestions will provide you with a fountain of quality information you can share in social conversations.

To be an effective conversationalist, you need to build your information base. When was the last time you attended a concert, visited a museum exhibit, or participated in a similar cultural event?

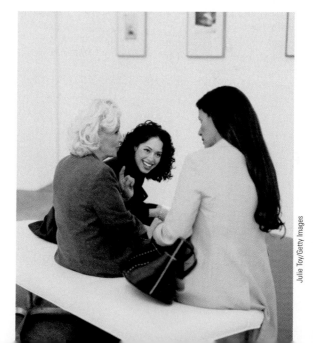

Julie Toy/Getty Images

Ask Questions That Motivate Others to Respond

What happens in the first few minutes of a conversation can have a profound effect on how well a social conversation develops. Although asking questions comes easy to some, many people seem at a loss for what to do to get a conversation going. There are countless ways to start a conversation; here are four question lines commonly used to get a conversation started. Notice that none of these is a "yes" or "no" question. Each question is designed to motivate the respondent to share specific information that will contribute to continuing the conversation.

1. *Questions about the other's family:* How is Susan getting along this year at college? How is your dad feeling? Do you have children? How long have you been married?

2. *Questions about a person's work:* What do you do for a living? What projects have you been working on lately? What are you majoring in?

3. *Questions about sporting or cultural events:* How was the fishing trip you went on last week? Did you see how Tiger Woods got out of that impossible situation at last week's tournament? Have you seen the new *Star Wars* movie?

4. *Questions about current events:* What do you think about the airlines using racial profiling? Can you believe the amount of money CEOs make? Did you see that there was another carload of kids killed on I-75 last Saturday?

These four types of questions are commonly used to open conversations with acquaintances, but there are obviously many others as well.

Provide Free Information

Effective conversationalists make it easy for others to continue the conversation by making comments that provide new information to which the partner can respond. **Free information** is extra information offered during a message that can be used by the responder to continue the conversation.

Many people have difficulty sustaining conversations because in replying to questions they give one-word or very brief responses. Suppose Paul asks Jack, "Do you like tennis?" and Jack answers "Yes," and then just looks at Paul. Paul has nowhere to go. To keep the conversation going (or to get it started), Paul has to think of a new line to pursue. If Jack continues supplying only short responses, Paul will eventually become tired and bored and may terminate the conversation.

Suppose, however, that Jack answers "Yes" and goes on to say, "I've only been playing for about a year, but I really enjoy it." Now Paul has a direction to follow. He might turn the conversation to his own experience: "I haven't been playing long myself, but I'm starting to get more confidence, especially with my forehand." Or he might use the information to ask another question: "Have you taken any lessons or clinics?"

free information
extra information offered during a message that can be used by the responder to continue the conversation.

As a respondent, it's important to give free information. As the initiator, it's important to listen for the free information provided and use it. The better the quality of the free information, the more likely it is that the conversation will continue and prove rewarding to both participants.

Practice Appropriate Turn-Taking

Researchers point out that in ordinary conversation people often speak at the same time and that turns are not always easy to identify. However, participants in interactions do treat the concept of "turn" as "relevant, real, and consequential in an individual's speaking time/space" (Ford, Fox, & Thompson, 2002, p. 8). We balance speaking and listening in a conversation by practicing these turn-taking techniques:

1. **Take the appropriate number of turns.** In any conversation, the ideal is for all to have approximately the same number of turns. If you discover that you are speaking more than your fair share, try to restrain yourself by mentally checking whether everyone else has had a chance to talk once before you talk a second time. Similarly, if you find yourself being inactive in a conversation, try to increase your participation level. Remember, if you have information to contribute, you are cheating yourself and the group when you do not share it.

2. **Speak an appropriate length of time on each turn.** People are likely to tune out or become annoyed with those conversational partners who make speeches, filibuster, or perform monologues rather than engaging in the ordinary give-and-take of conversation. Similarly, it is difficult to carry on a conversation with someone who gives one- or two-word replies to questions designed to elicit meaningful information. Turns do, of course, vary in length depending on what is being said. If your average statements are much longer or shorter than those of your conversational partners, however, you need to adjust.

3. **Recognize and heed turn-exchanging cues.** Patterns of vocal tone, such as decreasing loudness or lowering pitch, and use of gestures that indicate the end of statements are the most obvious turn-taking cues. When you are trying to get into a conversation, look for them.

    By the same token, be careful of giving inadvertent turn-exchanging cues. For instance, if you tend to lower your voice when you are not really done speaking or take long pauses for emphasis when you expect to continue, you may be interrupted because others are likely to act on these cues.

4. **Use conversation-directing behavior and comply with the conversation-directing behavior of others.** In general, a person who relinquishes his or her turn may define who speaks next. For instance, when Paul concludes his turn by saying, "Susan, did you understand what he meant?" Susan has the right to the floor. Skillful turn-takers use conversation-

directing behavior to balance turns between those who freely speak and those who may be more reluctant to speak. Similarly, effective turn-takers remain silent and listen politely when the conversation is directed to someone else.

Of course, if the person who has just finished speaking does not verbally or nonverbally direct the conversation to a preferred next speaker, then the turn is up for grabs and goes to the first person to speak.

5. **Interrupt rarely.** Although interruptions are generally considered inappropriate, interrupting for "clarification" and "agreement" (confirming) are interpersonally acceptable (Kennedy & Camden, 1983, p. 55). For instance, interruptions that are likely to be accepted include relevant questions or paraphrases intended to clarify, such as "What do you mean by 'presumptuous'?" or "I get the sense that you think presumptuous behavior is especially bad," and reinforcing statements such as "Good point, Max" or "I see what you mean, Suzie." Interruptions that are likely to be viewed as disruptive or incomplete include those that change the subject or that seem to minimize the contribution of the interrupted person.

Maintain Conversational Coherence

Conversational coherence is the extent to which the comments made by one person relate to those made by others previously in the conversation. Littlejohn (2002) points out that conversational coherence is "how communicators create clear meaning [in conversation]" (p. 83). The more directly messages relate to those that precede them, the more coherent or meaningful is the conversation.

Although many topics of conversation just "come up," we can still work at maintaining conversational coherence while a particular topic is being discussed. In social conversations, where the primary goal is to enjoy each other's company, topics may change and will cover a wide variety of issues. Nevertheless, to maintain coherence, what we say should be related to what was said before. If what we want to say is only tangentially related or is unrelated, then we should defer the turn to someone else who may have more relevant comments. If there are only two of us conversing, then we should respond to the speaker's message before introducing a change in topic.

Practice Politeness

Politeness, relating to others in ways that meet their need to be appreciated and protected, is universal to all cultures (Brown & Levinson, 1987). Although levels of politeness and ways of being polite vary, all people have **positive face needs** (the desire to be appreciated and approved, liked, and honored) and **negative face needs** (the desire to be free from imposition or intrusion).

politeness
relating to others in ways that meet their need to be appreciated and protected.

positive face needs
the desire to be appreciated and approved, liked, and honored.

negative face needs
the desire to be free from imposition or intrusion.

To meet people's positive face needs, we make statements that show concern, compliment, or use respectful forms of address. For example, it is polite to greet your instructor as "Professor Reynolds" (to use a respectful form of address) or to say "Thanks for the tip on how to work that problem, it really helped" (to compliment).

To meet people's negative face needs, we make statements that recognize that we are imposing or intruding on the time of another. For instance, to recognize that you are imposing, you might say to your professor, "I can see you're busy, but I wonder whether you could take a minute to . . ." or "I know you don't have time to talk with me now, but I wanted to see whether there was a time that we could meet later today or tomorrow."

Although politeness is always important, it is especially so whenever we must say something to a person that might cause the person to "lose face." The goal of politeness theory is not to avoid face threatening—it is normal. Rather, the goal is to lessen or eliminate potential conversational or relationship problems that could result from these statements.

Suppose your professor returned a set of papers and you believe the grade you received was not reflective of the quality of the paper. You could, of course, say, "I don't think you graded my paper fairly, and I want you to reconsider the grade you gave me," a statement that is face threatening without consideration for politeness. So, what might you say to your professor that would be more appropriate? You have three choices:

1. **You can make a statement that includes some form of positive politeness.** "I would appreciate it if you could look at my paper again. I've marked the places I'd like you to consider. My roommate said that you were fair and usually willing to reconsider if there seemed to be a good reason." Although the request still contains a direct imposition on the professor, "I would appreciate it" is much softer than "I want you to." Moreover, the effort to include a positive politeness statement that shows the professor has been kind enough to do favors when there might be a good reason is helpful as well.

2. **You can make a statement that includes negative politeness.** "I'm sure you're very busy and don't have time to reread and remark every paper, but I'm hoping you'll be willing to look at my paper again. To minimize the time it might take, I've marked the places I'd like you to consider. I've also written comments to show why I phrased those sections as I did." Although the request is still a direct imposition, it makes the statement that you recognize that you are imposing. It also suggests that you wouldn't do it if there weren't at least, potentially, good reasons. Moreover, you've taken time not only to limit how much the professor

needs to look at but also to show why you thought the sections were in keeping with the assignment.

3. **You can make a statement that is indirect or off the record.** "Please don't take this the wrong way, but I was surprised by a few of your comments." By saying this in a casual way, you hope your professor might be curious enough to ask what caused you to be surprised. With this opening you can move to one of the more direct face-saving approaches.

So the question is, how do we choose whether to be polite and, if so, which of the three strategies do we use? Brown and Levinson (1987) believe this decision is affected by a combination of three factors.

1. **How well people know each other and their relative status.** The less familiar we are with someone and the higher the person's social status, the more effort we will put into being polite.

2. **The power that the hearer has over the speaker.** Most of us will work harder to be polite to those who are powerful than to those who are powerless.

3. **The risk of hurting the other person.** Most of us will work harder to be polite to people we believe to be more vulnerable than to those whom we perceive as less likely to be hurt by our impoliteness.

Test Your Competence ▶

Practicing Politeness

Rephrase each of these face-threatening statements using some form of positive or negative politeness. To get you started, the authors' model answer is provided for the first statement.

1. "Tommy, turn down your stereo. You're playing that music too loud."

   Positive Politeness: "Tommy, I'd really appreciate it if you could turn the stereo down. I have trouble listening to music when it's this loud."

   Negative Politeness: "Tommy, I know it's your room and you have every right to play your music as loud as you want, but could you turn it down a bit. I've got a splitting headache."

2. "Lisa, you need to finish your part of the paper so I can get it typed before the weekend."

3. "I disagree with what you just said."

4. "Can you stop on your way home and pick up some milk and bread?"

5. "I don't want to see that movie."

6. "I think we should stop seeing each other."

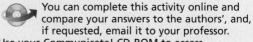 You can complete this activity online and compare your answers to the authors', and, if requested, email it to your professor. Use your Communicate! CD-ROM to access Skill Learning Activity 5.3.

Skill Builders

Politeness

Skill	Use	Procedure	Example
Relating to others in ways that meet their need to be appreciated and protected.	To determine the degree of politeness necessary to achieve your objective.	1. Recognize when what you are planning to say is likely to be recognized as a face-threatening act. 2. Consider how well you know each other, whether one person holds power over the other, and the risk of hurting the other person. 3. Construct the wording of a positive politeness (shows appreciation, approval, honor, affection) or a negative politeness (acknowledges imposition or intrusion) statement based on the issues of relationship, power, and risk.	Chris thinks her boss did not consider all that he should have in determining her year's bonus. She might construct the following negative politeness statement: "Mr. Seward, I know you put considerable time into your bonus decisions, but you have been willing to talk about your decisions in the past. I was hoping you'd be willing to take a few minutes to discuss your decision with me."

To show how you might use these three factors in determining how polite you are, let's consider two examples. First, suppose you want to impose on your roommate to take a look at your paper before you turn it in to your professor. Your roommate is your friend, and you get along quite well, so the imposition is relatively minor and only mildly threatening. Moreover, your roommate has no special power over you. In light of these considerations, you might not put much effort into trying to be polite. You might make this request without much regard to your roommate's negative face needs and say, "Danny, take a look at this paper. I need to hand it in tomorrow."

Second, suppose that you want to ask your professor to preread the same paper before you submit it for a grade. Because your professor is not your friend (you are socially more distant) and because your professor has considerable power over you (he controls your grade), you will probably want to approach your professor more politely than you did your friend. As a result, you are likely to make a statement that includes a form of positive politeness or one that includes a form of negative politeness.

As you come to better understand face needs, you will become better able to accurately diagnose situations in which you should take particular care to engage in polite behavior. In addition, each of us can make the world a bit more humane by working at being polite regardless of situational imperatives. Certainly one important aspect of politeness is courtesy. To understand more about communication courtesy, read the article "What's the Message of Your Manners?" available through InfoTrac College Edition. Use your Communicate! CD-ROM to access Web Resource 5.1: Message of Your Manners.

Electronically Mediated Conversations

In our fast-paced world, we spend some of our conversational time interacting with others with the help of communication technology. The use of cell phones, electronic messaging systems, email, newsgroups, and chat lines have all enhanced our ability to "converse" with others who are not physically close to us. Yet electronically mediated conversations present their own challenges.

Cell Phones and Electronic Messaging

In a matter of a few years, cell phones and electronic messaging systems use has become commonplace. Today children as well as adults have their own personal phones and pagers that enable them to talk with others regardless of where they are. In fact, it has become commonplace for people to interrupt a face-to-face conversation to take a cell phone call or check a page. And at times conversational partners will take turns talking to the person at the other end of a cell phone. Cell phone and messaging technology have brought many advantages, but we are still learning how to use these mediated communication devices effectively in ways that do not harm our relationships with those who are present. Check out the "ten commandments" of cell phone etiquette by using your Communicate! CD-ROM to access Web Resource 5.2: Cell Phone Etiquette.

Email

Email, the most widespread application of Internet technology, is electronic correspondence that is part letter writing and part conversation. Surprisingly, for the 75 percent of teens who are online, email accounts for most of their one-on-one contact (Globus, 2002, p. 13). According to a study by Waldeck, Kearney, and Plax (2001), students find that email is a great way to clarify. Students are most likely to use email rather than face-to-face meetings or telephone calls to ask teachers for information. And email is making it easy for distant family members to stay in daily contact.

Although you probably have used email for a long time, you can improve the quality of your email conversations by following these guidelines:

Cell phones allow people who are not present to be part of a conversation. How do you feel when someone you are talking with takes a social cell phone call?

1. **Take advantage of delayed feedback.** One advantage of email over face-to-face conversation is the delay between receiving a message and responding to it. We can capitalize on this if we edit what we write. Never send an email before you have reread what you have written and analyzed it in terms of both what you've said and how you've said it. Don't just correct typos.

2. **Include the wording that you are responding to in your email.** Even though email exchanges may occur quickly, the originator may not remember exactly what he or she wrote to you. When you respond to specific points people made in their messages, summarize or paraphrase what they said before you respond.

3. **Take into account the absence of nonverbal cues to meaning.** Nonverbal communication may provide as much as 66 percent of the social meaning of a message, so you must determine what you can do in writing that will "fill in the gaps" of meaning. Most specialists advise that you choose your words carefully and add more adjectives when appropriate. For instance, instead of writing, "What you said really bugged me," you might write, "What you said had some merit, but the way you said it really hurt my feelings." Now the reader will have a much better idea of your feelings about the response.

   Icons that are used in email to express emotions are called "emoticons." For a listing of the various ways you can express nonverbal emotions online, use your Communicate! CD-ROM to access Web Resource 5.3: Emoticons.

4. **Use common abbreviations sparingly, if at all.** Commonly used abbreviations may make your message shorter, but they don't necessarily make it more meaningful. Although some frequent email users can easily decode

these cryptic notations, many who receive these shorthand citations are at a loss to make sense of them. For instance, abbreviations such as BTW (by the way), FWIW (for what it's worth), IMHO (in my humble opinion) may be common in chat rooms but uninterpretable by other users. Avoid using all capital letters for emphasis. On the Internet, messages that are in capitals are the equivalent of shouting in face-to-face conversations.

5. **Keep in mind that email messages are not secure.** Because email is so easy to use, at times we may write email messages that include very confidential material—information that we'd ordinarily guard carefully. Keep in mind that a message you write is copied and stored (at least temporarily) on many computers between yours and the recipient's, and with the click of a mouse our email can be sent to people we never intended to see it. "In some ways, email messages are like postcards. Anyone 'carrying' the message can read it, even if most would never do so" (Crumlish, 1997, p. 132). If you have something to say that is confidential, could be used against you in some way, or could be totally misinterpreted, it is better to convey that message in a written letter or a private phone call. For additional guidelines on the effective use of email, use your Communicate! CD-ROM to access Web Resource 5.4: Email Etiquette.

Conversing via Newsgroups and Internet Chat

Two other forms of Internet messages are newsgroups and chat or instant messaging. A **newsgroup** is an electronic "bulletin board" for people with similar interests, and **Internet chat** and **instant messaging** are online interactive message exchanges. In newsgroups you post articles and people post responses. In a chat room typed responses appear instantly on all participants' computer screens. Internet messages are exchanged between two people in real time. Thus chat rooms and instant messaging approximate face-to-face conversation because feedback is relatively instantaneous.

Several of the recommendations for email conversations are equally important in newsgroups and chat rooms. Still, both newsgroups and chat rooms are significantly different from email. For instance, once you have subscribed to a newsgroup, you can spend your time "listening," posting articles, and responding to articles.

Listening without participating is called **lurking,** which gives you a kind of pseudo-interaction with others. For instance, suppose you join a sports newsgroup that is formed to discuss golfing. You will find that various people will have posted and responded to newsgroup articles or "threads" on issues related to golf. These may range from threads that discuss a particular pro golfer (such as Tiger Woods, Phil Michelson, Julie Inkster, or Sri Pak) to those that focus on improving your game (driving, putting, chipping), and so forth. You can "lurk" by reading the threads, but you need not respond yourself. In this way, you get to learn a little about the personalities of posters and repliers.

You may post a response or start a new thread. A posted article may generate little if any response. But it may touch a nerve and receive many replies, some of which may take the form of **flaming,** a hostile or negative

newsgroup
an electronic "bulletin board" for people with similar interests.

Internet chat
online interactive message exchanges.

instant messaging
online interactive message exchanges.

lurking
listening without participating online.

flaming
a hostile or negative response to what has been written online.

response to what has been written. Some of these result in "flame wars" where rude and hostile messages are alternatingly posted. Some people enjoy anonymous verbal combat, but flame wars can undermine the purpose of a newsgroup or chat room.

In newsgroups (as well as in some chat rooms) you are expected to observe newsgroup **netiquette** (Internet etiquette). "Not observing etiquette in a Newsgroup will result in almost instant criticism and reprimand, usually by more than one participant" (Banks, 1997, p. 106). Many newsgroups post **FAQs** (frequently asked questions) that list the rules followed by a list of participants in that particular newsgroup.

netiquette
Internet etiquette.

FAQs
frequently asked questions on a Web site.

In chat rooms everything that is typed by any participant appears on the screen. And just like any gathering, several conversations are likely to be occurring at once. So it is sometimes difficult to follow what is being said to whom. With instant messaging you are able to exchange messages with another person—usually someone you know. But as with other forms of Web-based interaction, instant messaging restricts the information we receive because the nonverbal parts of the message are missed. To learn more about the pros and cons of instant messaging, read "Instant Messaging, Pressuring Teens, Spreading Good and Bad Information" available through InfoTrac College Edition. Use your Communicate! CD-ROM to access Web Resource 5.5: Instant Messaging.

In addition, in chat rooms the real identity of people is usually masked by using nicknames rather than real names. You can be whomever you want—so can everyone else. As a result, you really have no idea whether a person you are talking with is male or female, young or old, rich or poor.

Email from family and friends makes being far from home less lonely.

AP/Wide World Photos

Cultural Variations in Effective Conversation

Throughout this chapter we have considered the guidelines for conversational behavior that assumes a Western low-context cultural perspective. Just as what is considered appropriate verbal and nonverbal behavior varies between low-context and high-context cultures, so do the guidelines for effective conversation. Gudykunst and Masumoto (1996, pp. 30–32) explain four differences in conversational patterns between people of low-context and high-context cultures.

First, low-context culture conversations (like those in Germany) are likely to include greater use of such categorical words as *certainly, absolutely,* and *positively,* whereas high-context culture conversations (like those in Japan) are likely to include greater use of qualifiers such as *maybe, perhaps,* and *probably.*

Second, low-context cultures strictly adhere to the relevancy maxim by valuing relevant comments that are perceived by listeners to be directly to the point. In high-context cultures, however, individuals' responses are likely to be more indirect, ambiguous, and apparently less relevant, because listeners rely more on nonverbal cues to help them understand the speaker's intentions and meaning.

Third, in low-context cultures, the quality maxim is operationalized in truth telling. People are expected to verbally communicate their actual feelings about things regardless of how this affects others. Conversationalists in high-context cultures operationalize the quality maxim differently. They define quality as maintaining harmony and saving face so messages may mask a conversationalist's true feelings.

Finally, in low-context cultures, periods of silence are considered uncomfortable because little information is being shared when no one is speaking. In high-context cultures, silence in conversation is often meaningful. When three or four people sit together and no one talks, the silence may indicate truthfulness, disapproval, embarrassment, or disagreement, depending on the situation.

Conversation and Analysis

Use your Communicate! CD-ROM to access the video clip of Susan and Sarah's conversation. Click on the In Action icon in the menu at left, then click on Conversation Menu in the menu bar at the top of the screen. Select "Susan and Sarah Overview" to watch the video (it takes a minute for the video to load). As you watch the conversation, notice to what extent each of the women follow the six conversational maxims. How does each exemplify the guidelines for effective conversationalists? You can answer this and other analysis questions by clicking on Analysis in the menu bar at the top of the screen. When you've answered all the questions, click "Done" to compare your answers to those provided by the authors.

A transcript of the conversation is printed here. You can also find a copy of this transcript online, which enables you to take notes as you watch the video. Use your Communicate! CD-ROM to access Skill Learning Activity 5.5. When you have finished viewing the video and taking notes, compare your notes to the detailed conversational analysis provided by the authors below.

Susan and Sarah are close friends who share the same religious background and the occasional frustrations that their family beliefs cause.

Jason Harris/© Thomson Higher Education

Conversation

SUSAN: So how are you and Bill getting along these days?

SARAH: Oh, not too well, Suze. I think we've got to end the relationship. There are so many issues between us that I just don't have the same feelings.

SUSAN: Yeah, you know, I could tell. Is there one specific thing that's a problem?

SARAH: And it's ironic because early on I didn't think it would be a problem, but it is. You know, he's not Jewish, and since we've started talking about marriage I've realized that it is a problem. While Bill's a great guy, our backgrounds and beliefs just don't mesh. I never realized how important my Jewishness was to me until I was faced with converting. And Bill feels similarly about it.

SUSAN: I think I'm kind of lucky, well, in the long run. Remember in high school my parents wouldn't let me go out with anybody who wasn't Jewish? At the time I resented that and we both thought they

Analysis

Susan initiates the conversation with a meaningful question.

Sarah answers the question and gives "free information" about her lack of feelings and the presence of multiple problems.

Susan poses a question that suggests the potential for problem consideration.

Sarah accepts Susan's willingness to discuss a problem by sharing specific information that becomes the topical focus of the rest of the conversation—information that meets the Grice conversational maxims.

Susan shifts the topic a bit by speaking about her experiences. This seems to violate the relevancy maxim, but in so doing, she lays the groundwork for later exchanges.

Conversation

were reactionary, but now I'm kind of glad. At the time my parents said, "you never know what's going to come out of a high school relationship." Well, they never got that far, but it did force me to think about things.

SARAH: Yes, I remember that. You hated it. It's amazing to realize your parents can actually be right about something.

SUSAN: Right, it was the pits at the time, but at least it spared me the pain you and Bill are going through. It must be awful to be in love with someone that you realize you don't want as a life partner.

SARAH: Exactly, but I'm glad that my parents didn't restrict my dating to Jewish guys. I've learned a lot by dating a variety of people and I know that I've made this decision independently. Bill's a great guy, but for me to be me, I need to partner with a Jewish man—and Bill knows he can't be that. Making this choice has been hard, but it's helped me to grow. I guess I understand myself better.

SUSAN: So where have you guys left it? Are you going to still see each other? Be friends?

SARAH: We hope so. But right now, it's too fresh. It hurts to see him, so we're trying to give each other some space. I think it will really be tough when I hear he's seeing someone else. But I'll get by.

SUSAN: Well, you know I'm here for you. And when you're ready, there are some real hotties at Hillel. I'll be glad to introduce you.

Analysis

Sarah shows that she recalls what was said. She then adds additional free information to keep the conversation flowing.

Susan confirms her parents' wisdom that spared her pain. She then makes a statement that stimulates further discussion from Sarah.

Sarah agrees, but then shows the value of being free to date a variety of people.

Here Sarah confirms that it was her decision to partner with a man of her religion. But she also confirms that the decision was a hard one.

Susan pursues the topic by asking questions to probe the consequences of Sarah's decision.

These questions lead Sarah to disclose the difficulties she's experienced as a result of her decision.

Here Sarah opens the door for Susan's support.

Susan picks up on Sarah's need by stating she stands by her and is even willing to help.

Conversation

SARAH: Thanks Suze. So how's your new job?

SUSAN: Oh, it's great. I really like my boss, and I've gotten a new assignment that fits right in with my major. Plus my boss has been flexible in assigning my hours. I just wish it wasn't so far away.

SARAH: I thought it was downtown.

SUSAN: It is, it takes me over an hour because I have to change buses three times.

SARAH: Wow—are you at least able to study while you ride?

SUSAN: Not really. I get carsick.

SARAH: Oh, I forgot. Bummer.

SUSAN: Yeah, but I'll survive. Listen, I hate to leave but I've got a class in ten minutes, and if we're late, the professor glares when we walk in. I don't need that.

SARAH: What a jerk.

SUSAN: Yeah, well, I've got to run.

SARAH: Same time tomorrow?

SUSAN: Sure.

Analysis

Sarah's thanks serves as a close to the topic. She then asks a question suggesting a change of topics.

Although Susan could probe further, she accepts the change of topic by giving information to support her generalization of "It's great."

Here Sarah could comment on the free information Susan provided. Instead she focuses on location.

Sarah continues the side issue by asking another question.

Susan shows why she can't study.

Sarah tries to save face.

Susan sees no value in continuing this discussion so she cites a reason for ending the discussion.

The girls agree to meet again the next day. As you can see, discussion of this second issue is far less productive than discussion of the first issue.

What Would You Do?   A QUESTION OF ETHICS

 arah, John, Louisa, Naima, and Richard all met at a party that the university sponsored during First Year Orientation. During a break, they began sharing where they were from, where they were work-ing, what classes they were taking, and their potential majors. John was having fun talking with Louisa—he thought she was cute, and he wanted to impress her. When she mentioned that she had been involved in theater during high school and was considering majoring in drama, he began to share his own theater experiences. Everyone was politely listening, and interested at first, but he kept talking and talking. Finally, Naima interrupted John and changed the subject, for which the rest of the group was quite grateful.

Throughout their twenty-minute conversation, whenever someone would bring up a new subject, John would immediately take center stage and expound on some wild story that remotely applied. Not only was he long-winded, but his stories seemed to be fabricated. He was the hero in every one—either through his intellect or his strength. Besides all this, as he talked he included completely inappropriate side comments that were turnoffs to all of the listeners. One by one, each person found a reason to excuse him- or herself.

Soon John was standing alone. Several minutes later, John heard the other four around the corner talking. Before he could round the corner and come into their sight, he heard one of them say, "Do you guys want to go down to the coffee house so we can talk in peace? That John was really too much—but I think we can avoid seeing him if we zip out the side door. That way the rest of us can have a chance to talk."

1. Have you ever talked with someone like John? Where did John go wrong in his conversational skills? What should he have done differently?

2. What are the ethical implications of Louisa and the rest of the group sneaking out the side door without saying anything to John? Defend your position.

Summary

Conversations are informal interchanges of thoughts and feelings that usually occur in face-to-face settings. There are two types of conversations, social conversations and problem-consideration conversations, each of which has a general structure.

Conversations are guided by rules, prescriptions that indicate what behavior is obligated, preferred, or prohibited. Effective conversations are governed by the cooperative principle, which suggests that conversations "work" when participants join together to accomplish conversational goals and make the conversation pleasant for each participant. The cooperative principle is characterized by six maxims: quality, quantity, relevancy, manner, morality, and politeness.

Effective conversationalists prepare to contribute information, ask questions that motivate others to respond, provide free information, practice appropriate turn-taking behavior, maintain conversational coherence, and practice politeness through engaging in positive and negative face-saving strategies.

People are making increased use of electronically mediated conversations including cell phones, instant messaging, email, newsgroups, and chat rooms.

Communicate! Online

N ow that you have read Chapter 5, use your Communicate! CD-ROM for quick access to the electronic resources that accompany this text. Your CD-ROM gives you access to the video of the conversation between Susan and Sarah on pages 116–118, InfoTrac College Edition, and the Communicate! Web site. When you get to the Communicate! home page, click on "Student Book Companion Site" in the Resource box at the right to access the online study aids for this chapter, including a digital glossary, review quizzes, chapter activities, and chapter Web Resources.

Key Terms

At the Communicate! Web site, select the chapter resources for Chapter 5. Print a copy of the glossary for this chapter and test yourself with the electronic flash cards or complete the crossword puzzle to help you master these key terms:

conversation (96)
casual social conversations (96)
pragmatic problem-consideration conversations (98)
conversational rules (100)
cooperative principle (101)
maxims (101)

quality maxim (101)
quantity maxim (101)
relevancy maxim (101)
manner maxim (101)
morality maxim (102)
politeness maxim (102)
free information (105)
politeness (107)
positive face needs (107)

negative face needs (108)
newsgroup (113)
Internet chat (113)
instant messaging (113)
lurking (113)
flaming (113)
netiquette (114)
FAQs (114)

Review Quiz

Test your knowledge of the concepts in this chapter by taking the online quiz at the Communicate! Web site. Select the chapter resources for Chapter 5, then click on "Review Quiz." When you have completed the quiz, submit it for scoring.

Skill Learning Activities

Complete the Observe & Analyze, Test Your Competence, and Conversation and Analysis activities for Chapter 5 online at the Communicate! Web site. Select the chapter resources for Chapter 5, then click on "Activities." You can submit your Observe & Analyze answers to your instructor, compare your Test Your Competence answers with those provided by the authors, and do both for the Conversation and Analysis activity.

5.1: Observe & Analyze: Following the Cooperative Principle (104)
5.2: Observe & Analyze: Developing Topics for Conversation (105)
5.3: Test Your Competence: Practicing Politeness (109)

Web Resources

Access the Web Resources for this chapter online at the Communicate! Web site. Select the chapter resources for Chapter 5, then click on "Web Resources."

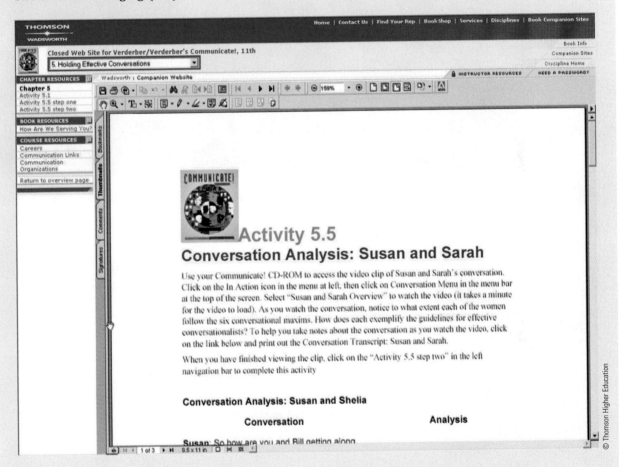

Mark Richard/PhotoEdit

OBJECTIVES

After you have read this chapter, you should be able to answer these questions:

- What five processes are used during listening?
- How can you focus your attention?
- How can you increase your understanding?
- What is empathy?
- How can questioning increase understanding?
- What is paraphrasing?
- What are three tactics that can help you remember what you hear?
- How can you evaluate what you've heard?
- What characterizes support messages?
- What specific verbal messages provide comfort?

6

Listening and Responding

"**G**arson, do you have an extra key to the document cabinet? I misplaced mine, and I have to get into it right away."

"No, I don't have a key, but it doesn't matter because . . ."

"I can't believe it. When I left home this morning, I was sure I had it."

"Bart, it's OK . . ."

"I pulled out my keys—but I just had my car key and main door key."

"Bart, I've been trying to tell you, just try the . . ."

"It's just like me. I think I've got everything, but just before I check the last time Sue will say something to me and I get sidetracked. Then I just take off."

"Bart, calm down. The door's . . ."

"Calm down?! If I can't get those documents to the meeting, there's going to be hell to pay. We've got six people coming from all over the city just to look at the documents. What am I supposed to say to them?"

"Bart, you don't have to say anything. I've been trying to . . ."

"Oh sure—I just go in there and say, 'By the way, the documents are locked up in the cabinet and I left my key at home.' Come on, Garson—who's got the other key?"

"Bart, listen!!! I've been trying to tell you—Miller was in the cabinet and, knowing you'd be along in a minute, he left the door open."

"Well, why didn't you tell me?"

A re you a good listener when you are under pressure like Bart? Or do you occasionally find that your mind wanders when others are talking to you? Listening is a key communication skill, yet less than 2 percent of us have had any formal listening training (Listening Factoid, 2003). Most of us can improve our listening skills.

In her recent book, Judi Brownell (2002) points out that a little more than ten years ago members of the International Listening Association gained consensus on this definition: "**Listening** is the process of receiving, constructing meaning from, and responding to spoken and/or nonverbal messages" (p. 48). Incorporated within this definition are the processes of attending, understanding, evaluating, remembering, and responding. You can begin your study of listening by completing an inventory of your listening skills. Use your Communicate! CD-ROM to access Web Resource 6.1: Listening Inventory. The feedback from this inventory may help you pinpoint specific processes you need to improve.

listening
the process of receiving, constructing meaning from, and responding to spoken and/or nonverbal messages.

Attending

attending
the perceptual process of selecting and focusing on specific stimuli from the countless stimuli reaching the senses.

Attending is the perceptual process of selecting and focusing on specific stimuli from the countless stimuli reaching the senses. Recall from Chapter 2 that we attend to information that interests us and meets physical and psychological needs. But to be a good listener, we have to train ourselves to attend to what people are saying regardless of our interest or needs. Let's consider three techniques for consciously focusing attention.

1. **Get physically and mentally ready to listen.** Physically, good listeners adopt a listening posture. For instance, when good listeners have been told that the next bit of information will be on the test, they are likely to sit upright in their chairs, lean slightly forward, cease any extraneous physical movement, and look directly at the professor. Likewise, mentally they will focus their attention by blocking out miscellaneous thoughts that pass through their minds. Although what you are thinking about may be more pleasant to attend to than what someone is saying to you, you must compel yourself to focus on what is being said.

2. **Make the shift from speaker to listener a complete one.** In conversation we are called on to switch back and forth from speaker to listener so frequently that we may find it difficult at times to make these shifts completely. Instead of listening, it is easy to rehearse what you are going to say as soon as you have a chance. Especially when you are in a heated conversation, you will consciously need to pull yourself away from preparing speeches instead of listening.

3. **Hear a person out before you react.** Far too often we stop listening before the person has finished speaking because we think we know what the person is going to say. Yet often we are wrong. In addition, we often

stop listening to people because their mannerisms and words "turn us off." For instance, we may be turned off by a speaker's accent, use of profanity, or advocacy for ideas we find repugnant.

Understanding

Understanding is decoding a message accurately to reflect the meaning intended by the speaker. Sometimes we do not understand because the message is encoded in words that are not in our vocabulary, but most of our misunderstanding stems from passive listening. *Active listening* requires us to use empathy, questioning, and paraphrasing so that we understand both the message content and the speaker's intent.

understanding
decoding a message accurately to reflect the meaning intended by the speaker.

Empathy

Empathy is intellectually identifying with or vicariously experiencing the feelings or attitudes of another. Or, as Jon Hayes (2002) says, letting people "know that they have been understood from within their own frame of reference and that they can see the world as they see it while remaining separate from it" (p. 183). To empathize, we generally try to put aside our own feelings or attitudes about another. Three approaches people use when empathizing are empathic responsiveness, perspective taking, and sympathetic responsiveness (Weaver & Kirtley, 1995, p. 131).

empathy
intellectually identifying with or vicariously experiencing the feelings or attitudes of another.

Empathic responsiveness occurs when you experience an emotional response parallel to, and as a result of observing, another person's actual or anticipated display of emotion (Omdahl, 1995, p. 4; Stiff et al., 1988, p. 199). For instance, when Monique tells Heather that Brad broke off their engagement, Heather will have used empathic responsiveness if she senses the sadness that Monique feels and experiences a similar sense of loss.

empathic responsiveness
experiencing an emotional response parallel to, and as a result observing, another person's actual or anticipated display of emotion.

"Cheer up, Nicole! What does Princeton know? Say, you got any plans for that last bit of cobbler?"

perspective taking
imagining yourself in the place of another; the most common form of empathizing.

sympathetic responsiveness
feeling concern, compassion, or sorrow for another because of the other's situation or plight.

respect
paying serious attention to others' ideas and feelings.

Perspective taking, imagining yourself in the place of another, is the most common form of empathizing. Although perspective taking is difficult for many of us (Holtgraves, 2002, p. 122), with conscious effort we can learn to imagine ourselves in the place of another. For example, if Heather personalizes the message by picturing herself being told that her engagement is off, anticipates and experiences her own emotions were this to occur, and then assumes that Monique must be feeling the same way, Heather is exemplifying perspective taking.

Sympathetic responsiveness is feeling concern, compassion, or sorrow for another because of the other's situation or plight. Having *sympathy* differs from the other two approaches. Rather than attempting to experience the feelings of the other, when you sympathize, you translate your intellectual understanding of what the speaker has experienced into your own feelings of concern, compassion, and sorrow for that person. For instance, imagine that Heather understands that Monique is sad and disappointed. Instead of trying to "feel Monique's pain" or experience how she herself would feel in a similar situation, Heather feels concern and compassion for her friend. This is showing sympathy. Because of this difference in perspective, many scholars differentiate sympathy from empathy.

Although people vary in their ability to empathize, most of us need to learn ways to practice it more effectively. To begin with, we need to **respect** the people who are speaking by paying more serious attention to their ideas and feelings. Respecting others focuses our time and energy on the other, not on the self.

How well you empathize also depends on how observant you are of others' behavior and how clearly you "read" the nonverbal messages they are sending. To improve your observational skills, try this. When another person begins a conversation with you, develop the habit of silently posing two questions to yourself: (1) What emotions do I believe the person is experiencing right now? and (2) What are the cues the person is giving that I am using to draw this conclusion? Consciously asking these questions helps you focus your attention on the nonverbal aspects of messages; this is where most of the information on the person's emotional state is conveyed.

To further increase the accuracy of reading emotions, we can use the skill of perception checking (introduced in Chapter 2). This is especially helpful when the other person's culture is different from our own. Let's consider an example. Suppose Jerry says that he really feels embarrassed when people comment on how old he is to be wearing braces. His friend Mary might empathize by concentrating on the feelings he shows with both his verbal and nonverbal messages, and then she may show that she understands by saying, "I can understand your embarrassment—I might even be depressed if that kept happening to me." To explore additional suggestions for developing empathy, use your Communicate! CD-ROM to access Web Resource 6.2: Listening and Empathy Responding.

Questioning

Active listeners ask questions to get the information they need to understand. A **question** is a statement designed to get further information or to clarify information already received. Although you may have asked questions for as long as you can remember, you may notice that at times your questions either don't get the information you want or irritate, fluster, or cause defensiveness. We can increase the chances that our questions will get us the information we want and reduce negative reactions if we observe these guidelines.

1. **Recognize the kind of information you need to increase your understanding.** Suppose Maria says to you, "I am totally frustrated. Would you stop at the store on the way home and buy me some more paper?" At this point, you may be a bit confused and need more information to understand. Yet if you simply respond "What do you mean?" Maria, who is already uptight may become defensive. To solicit the information you need, you might recognize one of the three types of information needs you have, and form a question to meet that need. You probably will not know precisely what it is you do not understand. To increase your understanding, you might ask Maria one of these three types of questions:

   ■ *Get details:* "What kind of paper would you like me to get, and how much will you need?"

   ■ *Clarify word meanings:* "Could you tell me what you mean by 'frustrated'?"

   ■ *Clarify feelings:* "What's frustrating you?"

2. **Phrase questions as complete sentences.** Under pressure our tendency is to use one- or two-word questions that may be perceived as curt or abrupt. For instance, when Miles says "Molly just told me that I always behave in ways that are totally insensitive to her needs," instead of asking "How?" you might ask, "Did she give you specific behaviors or describe specific incidents when this happened?" Curt, abrupt questions often seem to challenge the speaker instead of focusing on the kind of information the respondent needs to understand the statement. By phrasing more complete questions, the questioner shows the respondent that he or she has been heard.

3. **Monitor your nonverbal cues so that they convey genuine interest and concern.** Ask questions with a tone of voice that is sincere—not a tone that could be interpreted as bored, sarcastic, cutting, superior, dogmatic, or evaluative. We need to constantly remind ourselves that the way we speak may be even more important than the words we use.

4. **Put the "burden of ignorance" on your own shoulders.** To minimize defensive reactions, especially when people are under stress, phrase your questions to put the burden of ignorance on your own shoulders. Preface your question with a short statement that suggests that any

Observe&Analyze

Empathizing Effectively

Write a paragraph describing a time when you effectively empathized with another person. What was the person's emotional state? How did you recognize it? What were the nonverbal cues? Verbal cues? What type of relationship do you have with this person? How similar are the two of you? What type of empathizing did you use? Why?

 You can complete this activity online and, if requested, email it to your instructor. Use your Communicate! CD-ROM to access Skill Learning Activity 6.1.

problem of misunderstanding may be the result of *your* listening skills. For instance, when Drew says "I've really had it with Malone screwing up all the time," you might say, "Drew, I'm sorry, I'm missing some details that would help me understand your feelings better—what kinds of things has Malone been doing?"

Here are two more examples that contrast inappropriate with more appropriate questioning responses.

TAMARA: They turned down my proposal again!

ART [*Inappropriate*]: Well, did you explain it the way you should have? [*This question is a veiled attack on Tamara in question form.*]

  [*Appropriate*] Did they tell you why? [*This question is a sincere request for additional information.*]

RENEE: With all those executives at the party last night, I really felt strange.

JAVIER [*Inappropriate*]: Why? [*With this abrupt question, Javier is making no effort to be sensitive to Renee's feelings or to understand them.*]

  [*Appropriate*] Gee, what is it about your bosses' presence that makes you feel strange? [*Here the question is phrased to elicit information that will help Javier understand, and it may help Renee understand as well.*]

Paraphrasing

paraphrasing
putting into words the ideas or feelings you have perceived from the message.

In addition to being skilled questioners, active listeners are also adept at **paraphrasing,** putting into words the ideas or feelings you have perceived from the message. For example, during a meeting with his professor to discuss his performance on the first exam, Charley says, "Well, it looks like I really blew this first test—I had a lot of things on my mind, but I'm really going to study next time." If Professor Jensen responds by saying, "If I understand you, you're saying that for this next test you are going to outline the chapters and review your notes after each class," she would be paraphrasing.

content paraphrase
one that focuses on the denotative meaning of the message.

Paraphrases may focus on content, on feelings underlying the content, or on both. In the previous example, the professor's paraphrase is a **content paraphrase,** one that focuses on the denotative meaning of the message. If Professor Jensen had said, "So you were pretty upset with your grade," her response would have been a **feelings paraphrase**—that is, a response that captures the emotions attached to the content of the message.

feelings paraphrase
a response that captures the emotions attached to the content of the message.

By paraphrasing, you give the speaker a chance to verify your understanding. If Professor Jensen's paraphrase coincides with what Charley meant, Charley might say, "Right." But if her image is at odds with what he meant, he can clarify it by saying, "Well, I'm going to read and highlight chapters carefully, but I wasn't going to outline them." The longer and more complex the message, the more important it is to paraphrase. When the speaker appears to be emotional or when English is not the speaker's native language, paraphrasing is also important.

Skill Builders — Paraphrasing

Skill	Use	Procedure	Example
A response that conveys your understanding of another person's message.	To increase listening efficiency; to avoid message confusion; to discover the speaker's motivation.	1. Listen carefully to the message. 2. Notice what images and feelings you have experienced from this message. 3. Determine what the message means to you. 4. Create a message that conveys these images or feelings.	Grace says, "At two minutes to five, the boss gave me three letters that had to be in the mail that evening!" Bonita replies, "If I understand, you were really resentful that your boss dumped important work on you right before quitting time when she knows you have to pick up the baby at day care."

To paraphrase effectively, (1) listen carefully to the message, (2) notice what images and feelings you have experienced from the message, (3) determine what the message means to you, and (4) create a message that conveys these images or feelings.

Test Your Competence

Questions and Paraphrases

Provide an appropriate question and paraphrase for each of these statements. To get you started, look at this authors' model:

Example: "It's Dionne's birthday, and I've planned a *big* evening. Sometimes I think Dionne believes I take her for granted—well, after tonight she'll know I think she's something special!"

Question: "What specific things do you have planned?"

Paraphrase: "If I'm understanding you, you're really proud that you've planned a night that's going to be a lot more elaborate than what Dionne expects on her birthday."

1. Luis: "It was just another mind-numbing class. I keep thinking one of these days Professor Romero will get excited about something. He is a real bore!"

2. Angie: "Everyone seems to be raving about the new reality show on Channel 5 last night, but I didn't see it. You know, I don't watch the 'boob tube.'"

3. Kaelin: "I don't know if it's me or Mom, but lately she and I just aren't getting along."

4. Aileen: "I've got a report due at work and a paper due in management class. On top of that, it's my sister's birthday, and so far I haven't even had time to get her anything. Tomorrow's going to be a disaster."

 You can complete this activity online and compare your answers to the authors'. Use your Communicate! CD-ROM to access Skill Learning Activity 6.2.

Remembering: Retaining Information

remembering
being able to retain information and recall it when needed.

Remembering is being able to retain information and recall it when needed. Too often people forget almost immediately what they have heard. For instance, you can probably think of many times when you were unable to recall the name of a person to whom you were introduced just moments earlier. Three techniques that can help you improve your ability to remember information are repeating, constructing mnemonics, and taking notes.

Repeat Information

Repetition—saying something two, three, or even four times—helps listeners store information in long-term memory by providing necessary reinforcement (Estes, 1989, p. 7). If information is not reinforced, it will be held in short-term memory for as little as twenty seconds and then forgotten. So, when you are introduced to a stranger named Jack McNeil, if you mentally say "Jack McNeil, Jack McNeil, Jack McNeil, Jack McNeil," you increase the chances that you will remember his name. Likewise, when you receive the directions "Go two blocks east, turn left, turn right at the next light, and it's in the next block," you can immediately repeat to yourself "two blocks east, turn left, turn right at light, next block—that's two blocks east, turn left, turn right at light, next block."

Construct Mnemonics

mnemonic device
any artificial technique used as a memory aid.

Constructing mnemonics helps listeners put information in forms that are more easily recalled. A **mnemonic device** is any artificial technique used as a memory aid. One of the most common ways of forming a mnemonic is to use the first letters of a list of items you are trying to remember to form a word. For example, an easy mnemonic for remembering the five Great Lakes is HOMES (*H*uron, *O*ntario, *M*ichigan, *E*rie, *S*uperior).

Test Your Competence ▶

Creating Mnemonics

Mnemonics are useful memory aids. Construct a mnemonic for the five phases of the listening process: attending, understanding, remembering, evaluating, and responding. Record your mnemonic.

Tomorrow, while you are getting dressed, see whether you can recall the mnemonic you created.

Then see whether you can recall the phases of the listening process from the cues in your mnemonic. How well did you do? Write a brief paragraph describing your experience.

 You can complete this activity online. Use your Communicate! CD-ROM to access Skill Learning Activity 6.3.

When you want to remember items in a sequence, you can form a sentence with the words themselves or assign words using the first letters of the words in sequence to form an easy-to-remember statement. For example, when you studied music the first time, you may have learned the notes on the lines of the treble clef (E, G, B, D, F) with the saying *"every good boy does fine."* (And for the notes on the treble clef spaces, F, A, C, E, you may have remembered the word *face.*) You can read more about mnemonic techniques at MindTools.com. Use your Communicate! CD-ROM to access **Web Resource 6.3: Mnemonics.**

Take Notes

Although note taking would be inappropriate in the most casual interpersonal encounters, it represents a powerful tool for increasing your recall of information when you are involved in conversations where important information you need to remember is being shared. Not only does note taking provide a written record that you can go back to, but it also gives you an active role in the listening process (Wolvin & Coakley, 1996, p. 239).

Useful notes may consist of a brief list of main points or key ideas plus a few of the most significant details. Or they may be a short summary of the entire concept (a type of paraphrase) after the message is completed. For lengthy and rather detailed information, however, good notes likely will consist of a brief outline of what the speaker has said, including the overall idea, the main points of the message, and key developmental material. Good notes are not necessarily very long. In fact, many classroom lectures can be reduced to a short outline of notes. Figure 6.1 is an example of this and is based on the material in this chapter.

Dana White/PictureQuest

Effective managers understand the value of making notes about problems that employees point out. How can you use note taking at work to improve your performance?

Attend—focus
- Get ready (physically & mentally)
- Make complete shift (don't rehearse)
- Hear person out (don't check out or interrupt)

Understand—use active listening
- Empathize
- Ask questions (clarify words & feelings & get details)
- Paraphrase (content & feelings)

Remember
- Repeat info.
- Construct mnemonics (ex., Great Lakes, HOMES)
- Take notes

Evaluate
- Separate facts from inferences

Respond supportively
- Supportive messages characteristics: aim to help, accept other, demonstrate concern, availability to listen, ally, acknowledge & validate feelings, encourage elaboration
- Supporting positive feelings
- Giving comfort: clarify intentions, politeness, other-centered messages, reframe, advice

Figure 6.1
Notes based on a lecture on listening

Test Your Competence

Listening to Remember

Take the listening test provided at the Communicate! Web site to evaluate how well you remember what you hear, with and without notes. The information presented assumes that you are on your first day of a new job working in a college department office. You will hear directions given to you by a fellow work-study student who has been working in that office for some time, and then you'll take a test. This first time you hear the directions, you should not take notes. The second time you listen to the directions, take notes. Then use these notes to help you answer the questions on a second test. Compare how well you score on the tests.

 Complete this activity online and compare your answers to the authors'. Use your Communicate! CD-ROM to access Skill Learning Activity 6.4.

Critical Analysis

The fourth listening process is to critically analyze what has been said. **Critical analysis** is the process of evaluating what you have heard in order to determine its truthfulness. Critical listening is especially important when you are asked to believe, act on, or support what is being said. For instance, if a person is trying to convince you to vote for a particular candidate, or support efforts to legalize gay marriage, or buy an expensive gadget, you will want to listen critically so that you can evaluate the information and arguments presented. If you don't critically analyze what you hear, you risk going along with ideas or plans that may violate your values, are counterproductive to your interests, or mislead others (including the speaker) who value your judgment.

One important skill of critical analysis is to separate statements of fact from statements based on inference. **Factual statements** are those whose accuracy can be verified or proven. **Inferences** are statements made by the speaker that are based on facts or observations. If we comment, "You are reading this sentence" we have stated a fact. If we say, "You are understanding and enjoying what you are reading," we have made an inference.

Separating factual statements from inferences begins by recognizing whether what has been said is an established fact, or whether it is an opinion that may be related to a fact. If the statement is a fact, we need to determine if the fact that was stated is true because people sometimes make things up and pass them off as facts. If the statement is an inference, then we need to further evaluate it to see if the inference is valid. An inference may be false, even when it is based on observable facts. For instance, you are reading this sentence, you may even be nodding your head and smiling, but these facts do not alone provide proof of either your understanding or your enjoyment.

When we have determined that a statement is an inference, we need to test to see whether it is a valid inference. To do this we can ask ourselves (or the speaker) three questions: (1) What are the facts that support this inference? (2) Is this information really central to the inference? (3) Are there other facts or information that would contradict this inference? For example, when we hear "Better watch it, Katie's in one foul mood today. Did you catch the look on her face? That's one unhappy girl," we should stop and think, is Katie really in a bad mood? The "fact" that supports this is her facial expression. Is this fact accurate? Is Katie really looking unhappy or angry? Is the look on her face enough to conclude that she's in a bad mood? Or does Katie normally look unhappy? Is the look on her face really key to determining her mood? Or are there other cues that those of us who know her would expect to see? Is there anything else about Katie's behavior today that could lead us to believe that she's not in a bad mood?

critical analysis
the process of evaluating what you have heard in order to determine its truthfulness.

factual statements
statements whose accuracy can be verified or proven.

inferences
statements made by the speaker that are based on facts or observations.

Test Your Competence

Evaluating Inferences

For each of the following statements, identify the fact(s) and the inference(s). Then, write three specific questions that "test" the validity of the inference.

Example: The campus walk-in health clinic is understaffed. I stopped by the other day and had to wait two hours to be seen.

Fact: I had to wait two hours to be seen at the walk-in clinic.
Inference: The clinic is understaffed.
Questions: 1. Is one person's experience alone enough to support the inference?
2. Are there times when there is not a backup?
3. Are there other things besides staffing levels that could account for the wait?

1. Christy got 96 percent on the first test. She must have crammed all weekend.
2. Kali's pregnant. Just look at how tight her jeans are; she can barely keep them buttoned.
3. You can't get a good job unless you know someone. Mike searched everywhere for six months before he finally talked to his next door neighbor, who hired him for his construction company.
4. If you want to go to dental school when you graduate, forget it. In the past three years, none of the students from this program who applied got in.
5. Kids today are growing up too fast. I mean, they carry cell phones and everything.

 You can complete this activity online and compare your answers to the authors'. Use your Communicate! CD-ROM to access Skill Learning Activity 6.5.

You are listening critically when you (1) separate facts from inferences, (2) analyze the "facts" to determine if they are true, and (3) test to see whether inferences are valid.

Responding Supportively to Give Comfort

comfort
to help people feel better about themselves and their behavior.

Many times as we are listening we recognize that the speaker is emotionally distressed and in need of comfort. We can respond supportively by confirming the speaker's feelings and providing emotional comfort. To **comfort** means to help people feel better about themselves and their behavior. Comforting occurs when one feels respected, understood, and confirmed.

Over the years much of the groundbreaking scholarship on comforting has been done by Brant Burleson and his colleagues. Brant Burleson is featured in this chapter's Spotlight on Scholars.

Spotlight on Scholars ▷ Brant Burleson

Professor of Communication at Purdue University, on Comforting

The seeds for Brant Burleson's interest in comforting behavior were sown during his undergraduate days at the University of Colorado at Boulder where he was taught that all communication was persuasion. This proposition did not square with Burleson's own experiences. As a child of the fifties who came of age during the emotion-filled sixties, Burleson had witnessed lots of hurt and conflict, but he had also seen people engaging in altruism and acts of comforting. These comforting acts, he reasoned, were not aimed at changing anyone's opinion or behavior. They were simply done to help the other person. When Burleson entered graduate school at the University of Illinois, he began to formally study how individuals comfort others. He wanted to establish scientifically whether comforting messages were important and whether they made a difference. Since graduate school, Burleson's work has done much to accomplish this goal.

In his research, Burleson has carefully defined comforting strategies as messages that have the goal of relieving or lessening the emotional distress of others. He has limited his work to looking at how we comfort others who are experiencing mild or moderate sadness or disappointment that happens as a result of everyday events. He has chosen not to study comforting in situations where there is extreme depression or grief because of extraordinary events. He has also chosen to limit his work to the verbal strategies that we use when we comfort. Burleson's care in defining the "domain" of his work is important. By carefully stating the type of emotional distress he is concerned with, and by clearly identifying the limits of his work, Burleson enables those who read his work to understand the types of situations to which his findings apply.

Early on, Burleson worked with James L. Applegate, who had developed a way of judging the sophistication of particular comforting messages. Sophisticated messages were seen as those that acknowledged, elaborated, and legitimized the feelings of another person. Sophisticated comforting strategies are also more listener-centered (aimed at discovering how the distressed person feels), less evaluative, more feeling-centered, more likely to accept the point of view of the other person, and more likely to offer explanations for the feelings being expressed by the other person.

More recently Burleson and others who study comforting have turned their attention to understanding the results of comforting. Previous research has judged comforting messages only on the extent to which they reduce the immediate distress a person is feeling. Burleson believes the effects of comforting extend beyond this simple instrumental effect. He theorizes that effective comforting should also help the other person be able to cope better in the future. Skilled comforting should also benefit the comforter. When we effectively comfort others, Burleson believes we increase our own self-esteem. We also become better liked by the person we comfort and by those who see us effectively comfort others. Finally, Burleson believes those who are effective at comforting others are likely to have better long-term relationships. A growing list of research studies, some conducted by Burleson and his colleagues, provide support for his theory. For complete citations of many of his and his colleagues publications, see the reference list at the end of this book.

To better understand just why comforting messages help people feel better when other messages don't do anything—or even make people feel worse—Burleson has recently studied theories and research on emotion and factors that lead to emotional distress. This study of emotion dynamics has led to a new understanding of comforting as a conversational process that, at its best, helps distressed others make sense of what has happened to them, work through their feelings, and reappraise the upsetting situation. This view of the comforting process emphasizes the role of empathic listening and the importance of getting upset people to talk about their feelings and experiences in detail. People seem to make sense of their distressing experiences by expressing their thoughts and feelings in narratives or stories. Burleson and his graduate students are currently conducting several studies on sense-making narratives and how these narratives contribute to the reduction of emotional distress.

For more information on Burleson's research, go to http://www.sla.purdue.edu/academic/comm/Staff/Faculty.html#Burleson.

Characteristics of Effective and Ineffective Emotional Support Messages

supportive messages
comforting statements whose goal is to reassure, bolster, encourage, soothe, console, or cheer up.

Supportive messages are comforting statements whose goal is to reassure, bolster, encourage, soothe, console, or cheer up. Supportive messages are helpful and provide comfort because they create a conversational environment that encourages the person needing support to talk about and make sense of the situation that is causing distress. In recent studies, Burleson found that effective supportive messages had these characteristics (Burleson, 2003, pp. 565–568):

1. They clearly state that the speaker's aim is to help the other.
   Example: "I'd like to help you, what can I do?"

2. They express acceptance or affection for the other; they do not condemn or criticize.
   Example: "I understand that you just can't seem to accept this."

3. They demonstrate care, concern, and interest in the other's situation; they do not focus on a lengthy recount or a similar situation.
   Example: "What are you planning to do now?" Or "Gosh, tell me more; what happened then?"

4. They indicate that the speaker is available to listen and support the other without intruding.
   Example: "I know we've not been that close, but sometimes it helps to have someone to listen, and I'd like to do that for you."

5. They state that the speaker is an ally.
   Example: "I'm with you on this." Or "Well, I'm on your side, this isn't right."

6. They acknowledge the other's feelings and situation as well as express sincere sympathy; they do not condemn or criticize the other's behavior or feelings.
   Example: "I'm so sorry to see you feeling so badly; I can see that you're devastated by what has happened."

7. They assure the other that what he or she is feeling is legitimate; they do not tell the other how to feel or that the other should ignore his or her feelings.
Example: "With what has happened to you, you have a right to be angry."

8. They encourage the other to elaborate on his or her story.
Example: "Uh huh," "yeah," or "I see. How did you feel about that?" or "Well, what happened before that, can you elaborate?"

Supporting does not mean making false statements or only telling someone what he or she wants to hear. Effective supporting responses are in touch with the facts but focus on how those facts can provide emotional support for the speaker.

Supporting Positive Feelings

We all like to treasure our good feelings. When we share them, we don't want them dashed by a listener's inappropriate or insensitive responses. Supporting someone's positive feelings is generally easy, but it still requires some care. Consider this example:

KENDRA [*hangs up the telephone, does a little dance step, and turns to Selena*]: That was my boss. He said he'd put my name in for promotion. I didn't believe he would really choose me!

Kendra's statement requires an appropriate verbal response. To provide one, Selena can voice her empathic response:

SELENA: Kendra, way to go, girl! That's terrific! You really seem excited. What else did he say?

Selena's response legitimizes Kendra's feelings. Her response also shows that she is happy because Kendra seems happy. And finally, she encourages Kendra to elaborate.

Supporting responses like Selena's are much appreciated. You can probably remember an event that made you feel happy, proud, pleased, soothed,

Brian Bailey/Getty Images

Recall an occasion when you were feeling especially happy and chose to share your feelings with someone. How did the person react? Was it what you hoped for? How did that person's reaction affect your feelings?

or amused, and you should share those feelings. Wasn't it great when others recognized your feelings and affirmed your right to have them? Wasn't it a bummer when they didn't?

Giving Comfort

Providing emotional support for someone who has had something good happen is much easier than responding to someone who is in the midst of a difficult situation or who is experiencing emotional turmoil. Comforting is helping people feel better about themselves, their behavior, or the situation they are in by creating a safe conversational space where they can express their feelings and work out a plan for the future. Comforting rarely happens in single statements. Instead, it usually occurs over several turns in a conversation or over several conversations that span weeks, months, and occasionally years. Supportive messages that comfort have the eight characteristics previously discussed, but they also draw from these five specific comforting message skills

clarify supportive intentions
openly stating that your goal in the conversation is to help your partner.

1. **Clarifying supportive intentions.** When people are experiencing turmoil, they may have trouble understanding the motives of those who want to help. You can **clarify your supportive intentions** by openly stating that your goal in the conversation is to help your partner. Notice how David does this in this conversation:

   DAVID [*noticing Paul sitting in his cubicle with his head in his lap and his hands over his head*]: Paul, is everything OK?

   PAUL [*sitting up with a miserable but defiant look on his face*]: Like you should care. Yeah, everything is fine.

   DAVID: Paul, I do care. You've been working for me for five years; you're one of our best technicians. So if something is going on, I'd like to help, even if all I can do is listen. Now, what's up?

buffering
cushioning the effect of messages by utilizing both positive and negative politeness skills.

2. **Buffering face threats with politeness. Buffering** cushions the effect of messages by utilizing both positive and negative politeness skills (see Practicing Politeness in Chapter 5). The very act of providing comfort can threaten the positive and negative face needs of your partner. On one hand, your partner can feel that you will respect, like, or value him less because of his situation. On the other hand, the very act of comforting suggests that the other person cannot independently handle the situation. So comforting messages are phrased very politely in ways that address the other person's face needs. Notice how David says to Paul, "You're one of our best technicians," which reaffirms his admiration for Paul's work. David also attends to Paul's need for independence by stating that maybe all he "can do is listen," which implies that Paul will be able to do the rest.

3. **Encouraging understanding through other-centered messages.** To reduce emotional distress, people need to "make sense" out of what has happened (Burleson & Goldsmith, 1998). People feel better if they can reevaluate specific parts of the situation or change their opinion about what happened. An important way for people to do this is by repeatedly telling and elaborating on the story (what happened to them). We can help people do this by using **other-centered messages,** those that encourage our partners to talk about and elaborate on what happened and how they feel about it. Many of us find this difficult to do because we have been taught it is rude to pry or we are uncomfortable hearing someone's problems, so our gut reaction is to change the subject.

other-centered messages
statements that encourage our partners to talk about and elaborate on what happened and how they feel about it.

Other-centered messages may ask questions that allow the other to elaborate, they may simply be vocalized encouragement (um, uh huh, wow, I see), they encourage the person to explore their feelings, and they demonstrate understanding and empathy.

4. **Reframing the situation.** When people are vulnerable and are in the midst of strong emotions, they are likely to perceive events in a limited way. At times their limited vision prevents them from viewing the situation in ways that would enable them to reevaluate the situation or their feelings. In these cases it may be helpful for you to **reframe** the situation by offering ideas, observations, information, and alternative explanations that might help your partner understand the situation in a different light. For example, when Travis returns from a date and in a disgusted voice says to his roommate Pete, "Well,

reframing
offering ideas, observations, information, and alternative explanations that might help your partner understand the situation in a different light.

that was certainly a disaster. We had a great time at dinner, saw a funny movie, and I thought we were having a great time, but when we got to her place, she gave me a quick kiss on the cheek, said 'Thanks a lot,' and disappeared inside her door. It's clear she's not interested in me." Pete might comfort Travis by giving him some information he's overlooked and provide

We can support others by framing what has happened to them so that they might see it in a different light. When have you used framing?

Michael Newman/PhotoEdit

a different "window" from which to view the evening. "I can see why you'd think that, it sounds like she was pretty abrupt. But maybe instead of rejecting you, she was protecting herself. You know a lot of guys these days expect to sleep with a woman on the first date. Maybe she's just had bad experiences before."

giving advice
presenting relevant suggestions and proposals that a person can use to satisfactorily resolve a situation.

5. **Giving advice.** At times we can comfort people by **giving advice,** presenting relevant suggestions and proposals that a person can use to satisfactorily resolve a situation. Unfortunately, we often rush to give advice before we really understand the problem. Advice should not be given until our supportive intentions have been understood, we have attended to our partner's face needs, and we have sustained an other-centered interaction for some time. Only when your partner has had time to understand and make his or her own sense out of what has happened should you offer advice to help with unresolved issues. Before giving advice, always ask permission and acknowledge that your advice is only one suggestion of many that might work. Present the potential risks or costs associated with your advice, and let your partner know that it's OK if he or she chooses to ignore what you have said.

Gender and Cultural Considerations in Comforting

It is popularly thought that men and women differ in the value they place on emotional support, with women expecting, needing, and providing more. However, Burleson (2003, p. 572) reports that a growing body of research finds that both men and women of various ages place a high value on emotional support from their partners in a variety of relationships (siblings, same-sex friendships, opposite-sex friendships, and romantic relationships). Studies also find that men and women have similar ideas about what messages do a better or worse job of reducing emotional distress. Both men and women find that messages encouraging them to explore and elaborate on their feelings provide the most comfort. Research has also found that men are less likely to use other-centered messages when comforting.

Researchers have also examined cultural differences in comforting. Burleson (p. 574) reports that members of all social groups find solace strategies, especially other-centered messages, the most sensitive and comforting way to provide emotional support. Burleson has identified these cultural differences:

1. European Americans, more than other American ethnic groups, believe that openly discussing feelings will help a person feel better.

2. Americans are more sensitive to other-centered messages than are Chinese.

3. Both Chinese and Americans view avoidance strategies as less appropriate than approach strategies, but Chinese saw avoidance as more appropriate than Americans did.

4. Both married Chinese and Americans viewed the emotional support provided by their spouse to be the most important type of social support they received.

5. African Americans place lower value on partner emotional support skills than do European or Asian Americans. This was especially true for African American women.

Overall, it appears that we are more alike than different when it comes to our desire to be supported by our partners and the types of messages we find to be emotionally comforting.

Figure 6.2 summarizes how good listeners and poor listeners deal with the five aspects of listening: attending, understanding, remembering, evaluating, and responding empathically.

	Good Listeners	Bad Listeners
ATTENDING	Attend to important information	May not hear what a person is saying
	Ready themselves physically and mentally	Fidget in their chairs, look out the window, and let their minds wander
	Listen objectively regardless of emotional involvement	Visibly react to emotional language
	Listen differently depending on situations	Listen the same way regardless of the type of material
UNDERSTANDING	Assign appropriate meaning to what is said	Hear what is said but are either unable to understand or assign different meaning to the words
	Seek out apparent purpose, main points, and supporting information	Ignore the way information is organized
	Ask mental questions to anticipate information	Fail to anticipate coming information
	Silently paraphrase to solidify understanding	Seldom or never mentally review information
	Seek out subtle meanings based on nonverbal cues	Ignore nonverbal cues

Figure 6.2
A summary of the five aspects of listening

	Good Listeners	Bad Listeners
REMEMBERING	Retain information	Interpret message accurately but forget it
	Repeat key information	Assume they will remember
	Mentally create mnemonics for lists of words and ideas	Seldom single out any information as especially important
	Take notes	Rely on memory alone
EVALUATING	Listen critically	Hear and understand but are unable to weigh and consider it
	Separate facts from inferences	Don't differentiate between facts and inferences
	Evaluate inferences	Accept information at face value
RESPONDING EMPATHICALLY	Provide supportive comforting statements	Pass off joy or hurt; change the subject
	Give alternative interpretations	Pass off hurt; change the subject

Figure 6.2 continued

Conversation and Analysis

Use your Communicate! CD-ROM to access the video clip of Damien and Chris's conversation. Click on the "In Action" icon in the menu at left, then click on "Conversation Menu" in the menu bar at the top of the screen. Select "Damien and Chris Overview" to watch the video (it takes a minute for the video to load). As you watch the interaction, analyze how well Damien uses the skills of active listening and how well his responses demonstrate effective support and comforting. You can respond to this and other analysis questions by clicking on "Analysis" in the menu bar at the top of the screen. When you've answered all the questions, click "Done" to compare your answers to those provided by the authors.

Jason Harris/© Thomson Higher Education

Here is a transcript of the conversation. You can also find a copy of this transcript online, which allows you to take notes as you watch the video. Use your Communicate! CD-ROM to access **Skill Learning Activity 6.6** at the Communicate! Web site. When you have finished viewing the video and taking notes, click on "Authors' Model Analysis" to compare your notes to the detailed conversational analysis provided by the authors.

Damien and Chris work in a small shop selling shirts and gifts. Usually they get along well, but lately Chris has seemed standoffish. Damien decides to talk with Chris to see if anything is wrong. Damien approaches Chris in the break room.

Conversation

DAMIEN: Chris, you've been kind of quiet lately, man. What's been going on?

CHRIS: Nothing.

DAMIEN: Come on, man, what's going on?

CHRIS: Just life. [*shrugs*] I'm just kind of down right now.

DAMIEN: Well, what am I here for? I thought we were friends.

CHRIS [*he thinks about it and decides to talk about it*]: Well, Carl's been on my case the last few weeks.

DAMIEN: Why? Did you do something?

CHRIS: Oh, he says that I'm sloppy when I restock and that I'm not always "polite" to our customers. You know, just 'cuz I don't smile all the time. I mean, what does he want—little Mary Sunshine?

DAMIEN: So you're angry with the boss.

CHRIS: Yeah, I guess . . . no, no, not so angry, I'm just frustrated. I come in to work every day, and I try to do my job, and I don't complain. You know, I'm sick and tired of getting stuck back there in the stock room reorganizing everything. It's not like they're paying us big bucks here. And Carl shouldn't expect us to be charming with everybody who walks through that door. I mean, half of the people who walk through that door are, well, they're totally rude and act like jerks.

DAMIEN: Yeah, I feel like you on that. Some of those people shouldn't be allowed out in public. What is Carl saying about how you're dealing with the customers?

CHRIS: Oh, he just says that I've changed and that I'm not being "nice." I mean, he used to call me his top guy.

DAMIEN: I mean, you know how Carl is. He's a fanatic about customer service. You know how, when we first started, he drilled us about being polite and smiling and being courteous at all times. So maybe when he says "you're not being nice," he just means that you're not doing it the way you used to. I mean, I've noticed a change. I mean, you're just not yourself lately. Is anything going on outside of work?

CHRIS: You could say that. Sarah and I just bought a house, so money's been a bit tight. Now, she wants to quit her job and start a family, and I'm not sure we can afford it. On top of it all, my kid sister shows up a few weeks ago on our doorstep, pregnant, and so she's living with us, so yeah, it is a bit overwhelming. And I'm a bit worried that Carl's going to fire me.

Jason Harris/© Thomson Higher Education

DAMIEN: Wow, that is a lot of stuff! I can understand why you're down, but did Carl really threaten to fire you?

CHRIS: No, no, but I'm not perfect, and he could use my "attitude" as an excuse to fire me.

DAMIEN: Well, did you think about telling him what's been going on? And maybe, you know, he'll understand and cut you some slack.

CHRIS: Or he could see that I really have changed and he'd can me.

DAMIEN: OK, well, just tell me this. Do you like working here?

CHRIS: Yeah, of course I do.

DAMIEN: OK, well, then, you've just got to tough it out. I mean, you've just got to use the game face on these people. You used to be the best at doing that. So you're just gonna have to get back to being a salesman, and leave everything else behind.

CHRIS: I guess I never realized how much my problems were affecting my work. I thought Carl was just out to get me, but now you're noticing something too, then maybe I have changed. Thanks, thanks for talking this out.

What Would You Do?   ▸ A QUESTION OF ETHICS

Janeen always disliked talking on the telephone—she thought it was an impersonal form of communication. Thus college was a wonderful respite. When friends would call her, instead of staying on the phone she could quickly run over to their dorm or meet them at a coffeehouse.

One day during reading period before exams, Janeen received a phone call from Barbara, an out-of-town friend. Before she was able to dismiss the call with her stock excuses, she found herself bombarded with information about old high school friends and their whereabouts. Not wanting to disappoint Barbara, who seemed eager to talk, Janeen tucked her phone under her chin and began straightening her room, answering Barbara with the occasional "uh-huh," "hmm," or "wow, that's cool!" As the "conversation" progressed, Janeen began reading through her mail and then her notes from class. After a few minutes, she realized there was silence on the other end of the line. Suddenly very ashamed, she said, "I'm sorry, what did you say? The phone . . . uh there was just a lot of static."

Barbara replied with obvious hurt in her voice, "I'm sorry I bothered you, you must be terribly busy."

Embarrassed, Janeen muttered, "I'm just really stressed, you know, with exams coming up and everything. I guess I wasn't listening very well; you didn't seem to be saying anything really important. I'm sorry. What were you saying?"

"Nothing 'important'," Barbara answered. "I was just trying to figure out a way to tell you. I know that you were friends with my brother Billy, and you see, we just found out yesterday that he's terminal with a rare form of leukemia. But you're right, it obviously isn't really important." With that, she hung up.

1. How ethical was Janeen's means of dealing with her dilemma of not wanting to talk on the phone but not wanting to hurt Barbara's feelings?

2. Identify ways in which both Janeen and Barbara could have used better and perhaps more ethical interpersonal communication skills. Rewrite the scenario incorporating these changes.

Summary

Listening is the complex process that encompasses attending, understanding, remembering, evaluating, and responding with support and comfort.

Attending is the process of selecting and focusing on specific stimuli from the countless ones that we receive. We can be more effective in attending if we (1) get ready both physically and mentally, (2) make the shift from speaker to listener complete (don't rehearse), and (3) hear a person out before responding.

Understanding is the process of decoding a message so that the meaning accurately reflects that intended by the speaker. Empathizing, which is identifying with or vicariously experiencing the feelings of another, can increase understanding. We can also increase understanding by asking questions to clarify and get details and by paraphrasing the speaker's content and feelings.

Remembering is the process of retaining information so it can be recall when it is needed. By repeating information, using mnemonics, and taking notes, we can increase the likelihood that we will remember what we hear.

Critical analysis is the process of evaluating what has been said to determine its truthfulness. Critical analysis is especially important when a speaker is asking you to believe, act on, or support what is being said. One important skill of critical analysis is to separate statements of fact from inferences. Statements of fact should be analyzed to see if they are true. Inferences should be tested to see if they are valid. Three questions can help us to test inferences: (1) What facts support this inference? (2) Is the information really central to the inference? (3) Are there other facts that would contradict the inference?

Responding with support and comfort helps people feel better about themselves and their behavior. Effective support messages are those that aim to help, accept others, demonstrate concern, show one's willingness to listen and be an ally, acknowledge and validate the speaker's feelings, and encourage elaboration. We need to support people who are experiencing positive feelings as well as comfort those in difficult situations. When we give comfort, we should use messages that clarify our intentions, practice politeness, are other-centered, reframe the situation, and offer advice on issues the speaker cannot seem to resolve.

Communicate! Online

N ow that you have read Chapter 6, use your Communicate! CD-ROM for quick access to the electronic resources that accompany this text. Your CD-ROM gives you access to the video of the conversation between Damien and Chris on pages 143–144, InfoTrac College Edition, and the Communicate! Web site. When you get to the Communicate! home page, click on "Student Book Companion Site" in the Resource box at right to access the online study aids for this chapter, including a digital glossary, review quizzes, the chapter activities, and the chapter Web Resources.

Key Terms

At the Communicate! Web site, select the chapter resources for Chapter 6. Print a copy of the glossary for this chapter and test yourself with the electronic flash cards or complete the crossword puzzle to help you master these key terms:

listening (124)
attending (124)
understanding (125)
empathy (125)
empathic responsiveness (125)
perspective taking (126)
sympathetic responsiveness (126)
respect (126)

question (127)
paraphrasing (128)
content paraphrase (128)
feelings paraphrase (128)
remembering (130)
mnemonic device (130)
critical analysis (133)
factual statements (133)
inferences (133)

comfort (134)
supportive messages (136)
clarify supportive intentions (138)
buffering (138)
other-centered messages (139)
reframing (139)
giving advice (140)

Review Quiz

Test your knowledge of the concepts in this chapter by taking the online quiz at the Communicate! Web site. Select the chapter resources for Chapter 6, then click on " Review Quiz." When you have completed the quiz, submit it for scoring.

Skill Learning Activities

Complete the Observe & Analyze, Test Your Competence, and Conversation and Analysis activities for Chapter 6 online at the Communicate! Web site. Select the chapter resources for Chapter 6, then click on "Activities." You can submit your Observe & Analyze answers to your instructor, compare your Test Your Competence answers to those provided by the authors, and do both for the Conversation and Analysis activity.

6.1: Observe & Analyze: Empathizing Effectively (127)
6.2: Test Your Competence: Questions and Paraphrases (129)
6.3: Test Your Competence: Creating Mnemonics (130)
6.4: Test Your Competence: Listening to Remember (132)

Web Resources

Access the Web Resources for this chapter online at the Communicate! Web site. Select the chapter resources for Chapter 6, then click on "Web Resources."

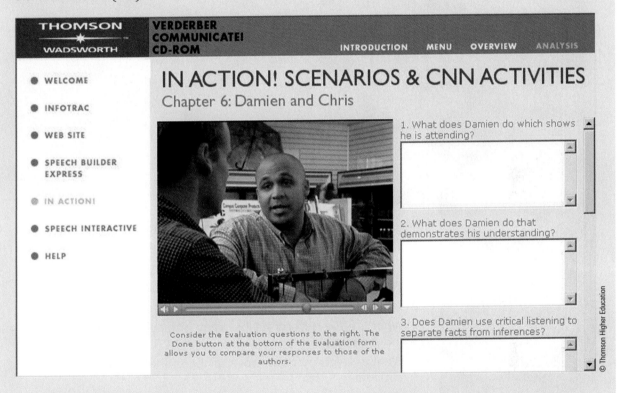

OBJECTIVES

After you have read this chapter, you should be able to answer these questions:

- What is self-disclosure?
- What are the guidelines for effective disclosure?
- When and how does one describe feelings?
- What are the differences between displaying feelings and describing feelings?
- What can you do to improve giving praise and constructive criticism?
- What is assertiveness?
- How does assertiveness differ from passive or aggressive behavior?
- How can you assert yourself appropriately?

7

Sharing Personal Information: Self-Disclosure and Feedback

"Chuck, when that interviewer at the grocery store asked you whether you'd rather have stuffing than potatoes, you said 'Yes'! We've been married more than twenty years, and I'm just now learning that you like stuffing more than potatoes."

"Well, I'm sorry, Susan," Chuck said sheepishly.

"Chuck," Susan asks, "are there other things that you like or don't like that you haven't told me about during these more than twenty years I've been your wife?"

"Well, probably."

"Chuck, why aren't you telling me about these things?"

"Well, I don't know, Susan. I guess I didn't think they were all that important."

"Not important? Chuck, almost every night that I cook we have potatoes. And frankly, I hate potatoes. I wouldn't care if I never saw a potato again. Now I find out you like stuffing better!"

"Sue, why didn't you ever tell me that you don't like potatoes?"

"Well I, uh-uh . . ."

oor Chuck—poor Susan—all those years! But is their experience all that unusual? Do we take the time to tell others what we are really thinking and feeling? For a lot of people, the answer is a resounding *no*.

Self-disclosure and feedback are a means to deepen relationships and are important interpersonal communication processes. In this chapter we take a closer look at these concepts and elaborate on the skills associated with each. We discuss self-disclosure, disclosing feelings, giving personal feedback, and assertiveness.

Self-Disclosure

self-disclosure
sharing biographical data, personal experiences, ideas, and feelings.

We develop and grow our relationships through self-disclosure. It is at the heart of making friends. **Self-disclosure** is sharing biographical data, personal experiences, ideas, and feelings. Statements such as "I was 5' 6" in seventh grade" provide biographical information—facts about you as an individual. "I don't think prisons ever really rehabilitate criminals" discloses a personal idea. "I get scared whenever I have to make a speech" discloses feelings. Biographical disclosures may be the easiest to make, and some biographical information is public. Most of us find it more difficult to talk about our personal ideas and feelings (Rosenfeld, 2000, p. 6).

Guidelines for Appropriate Self-Disclosure

We know that self-disclosure is important, yet Affifi and Guerrero (2000) point out that "individuals often choose to avoid disclosure rather than risk the perceived personal or relational consequences" (p. 179). So disclosure is important—but risky. The following guidelines can help us minimize risk by suggesting appropriate levels of self-disclosure for different interpersonal encounters.

1. **Early in a relationship, self-disclose the kind of information you want others to disclose to you.** When people are getting to know others, they begin by sharing information that they perceive to be low risk. This is information usually shared freely among people with that type of relationship in that culture and might include information about hobbies, sports, school, and views of current events. One way to determine what information is appropriate to disclose is to ask yourself whether you would feel comfortable having the person disclose that kind of information to you.

2. **Self-disclose intimate information only when you feel confident that it is an acceptable risk because your partner is trustworthy and willing to listen.** There is always some risk that disclosure will distress or alarm

your partner and damage your relationship, but the better you know your partner, the more likely it is that a difficult disclosure will be well received. Incidentally, this guideline explains why people sometimes engage in inappropriate intimate self-disclosure with bartenders or with people they meet in travel. They perceive the disclosures as safe (representing reasonable risk) because the person either does not know them or is in no position to use the information against them.

3. **Continue self-disclosure only if it is reciprocated.** Research suggests that people expect a kind of equity in self-disclosure (Derlega, Metts, Petronio, & Margulis 1993, p. 33). When it is apparent that self-disclosure is not being returned, you should consider limiting the amount of disclosure you make. Someone's choice not to reciprocate indicates that the person does not yet feel comfortable with this level of self-disclosure. If the response you receive to your self-disclosure implies that it was inappropriate, try to find out why. In this way you may avoid this problem in the future.

4. **Gradually self-disclose more personal information.** Because receiving self-disclosure can be as threatening as giving it, most people become uncomfortable when the level of disclosure exceeds their expectations. As a relationship develops, the depth of disclosure should gradually increase. So we disclose biographical and demographic information early in a relationship and more closely held personal information in a more developed relationship (Dindia, Fitzpatrick, & Kenny, 1997, p. 408).

5. **Reserve intimate self-disclosure for well-established personal relationships.** Disclosures about intimate matters are appropriate in close, well-established relationships. When people disclose very personal information to acquaintances or business associates, they are not only taking a risk of being exposed but the disclosure may also threaten their partner. Making intimate disclosures before a bond of trust is established risks alienating the other person. Moreover, people are often embarrassed by and hostile toward others who try to saddle them with intimate information in an effort to establish a personal relationship where none exists.

Some people who are extremely shy become inarticulate when they try to self-disclose. For some good advice for those who are extremely reluctant to disclose, read "The Art of Self-Exposure," available through InfoTrac College Edition. Use your Communicate! CD-ROM to access Web Resource 7.1: Self-Disclosure and Shyness.

In the Diverse Voices feature, "Black and White," Linda Howard describes what she has experienced as a person who is multiethnic and biracial. As you read this excerpt from an interview with Ms. Howard, first try to empathize with her frustration at being stereotyped and, second, consider her courage in disclosing information about herself and her feelings.

Black and White

by Linda Howard

Today we tend to label people as black, white, Asian, Hispanic, and so forth. But what if you are half one and half another? Linda Howard is a recent high school graduate who has been awarded a four-year scholarship to a prominent university in New England. Listen to a transcript of an interview with her.

y parents are Black and White American. I come from a long heritage. I am of French, English, Irish, Dutch, Scottish, Canadian, and African descent.

I don't really use race. I always say, "My father's Black, my mother's White, I'm mixed." But I'm American; I'm human. That's my race; I'm part of the human race.

It's hard when you go out in the streets and you've got a bunch of White friends and you're the darkest person there. No matter how light you are to the rest of your family, you're the darkest person there and they say you're Black. Then you go out with a bunch of Black people and you're the lightest there and they say, "Yeah, my best friend's White." But I'm not. I'm both.

I don't always fit in—unless I'm in a mixed group. That's how it's different. Because if I'm in a group of people who are all one race, then they seem to look at me as being the *other* race . . . whereas if I'm in a group full of [racially mixed] people, my race doesn't seem to matter to everybody else. . . . Then I don't feel like I'm standing out. But if I'm in a group of totally one race, then I sort of stand out, and that's something that's hard to get used to.

It's hard. I look at history and I feel really bad for what some of my ancestors did to some of my other ancestors. Unless you're mixed, you don't know what it's like to be mixed.

I've had people tell me, "Well, you're Black." I'm not Black; I'm Black and White. I'm Black and White American. "Well, you're Black!" No, I'm not! I'm both. It's insulting, when they try and . . . bring it right back to the old standards, that if you have anybody in your family who's Black, you're Black. . . . I mean, I'm not ashamed of being Black, but I'm not ashamed of being White either; and if I'm both, I want to be part of both. And I think teachers need to be sensitive to that.

See, the thing is, I mix it at home so much that it's not really a problem for me to mix it outside.

I don't think [interracial identity] is that big of a problem. It's not killing anybody, at least as far as I know, it's not. It's not destroying families and lives and stuff. It's a minor thing. If you learn how to deal with it at a young age, as I did, it really doesn't bother you the rest of your life, like drugs. . . .

I think we're all racist in a sense. We all have some type of person that we don't like, whether it's from a different race, or from a different background, or they have different habits.

But to me a *serious racist* is a person who believes that people of different ethnic backgrounds don't belong or should be in *their* space and shouldn't invade *our* space: "Don't come and invade *my* space, you Chinese person. You belong over in China or you belong over in Chinatown."

Racists come out and tell you that they don't like who you are. Prejudiced people [on the other hand] will say it in like those little hints, you know, like, "Oh, yes, some of my best friends are Black." Or they say little ethnic remarks that they know will insult you but they won't come out and tell you. "You're Black. I don't want anything to do with you." Racists, to me, would come out and do that.

Both racists and prejudiced people make judgments, and most of the time they're wrong judgments, but the racist will carry his one step further. . . . A racist is a person that will carry out their prejudices.

I had a fight with a woman at work. She's White, and at the time I was the only Black person in my department. Or I was the only person who was at *all* Black in my department. And she just kept on laying on the racist jokes. At one point, I said, "You know, Nellie, you're a racist pig!" And she got offended by that. And I was just joking, just like she'd been joking for two days straight—all the racist jokes that she could think of.

I've got a foot on both sides of the fence, and there's only so much I can take. I'm straddling the fence, and it's hard to laugh and joke with you when you're talking about the foot that's on the other side.

She couldn't understand it. We didn't talk for weeks. And then one day, I had to work with her. We didn't say anything for the first like two hours of work. And then I just said, "Smile, Nellie, you're driving me nuts!" and she smiled and laughed. And we've been good friends ever since. She just knows you don't say ethnic things around me; you don't joke around with me like that because I won't stand for it

from you anymore. We can be friends; we can talk about anything else—except race.

Excerpted from "Case Study: Linda Howard, 'Unless you're mixed, you don't know what it's like to be mixed,'" in Sonia Nieto, Affirming Diversity: The Sociopolitical Context of Multicultural Education *(3rd ed., pp. 50–60).* Published by Allyn and Bacon, Boston, MA. Copyright © 2000 by Pearson Education. Adapted by permission of the publisher.

Cultural and Gender Differences

As we might expect, self-disclosure norms vary from culture to culture. Formal cultures engage in less self-disclosure, and informal cultures engage in more self-disclosure. The United States is considered an informal culture (Samovar & Porter, 2001, p. 82). As a result, Americans tend to disclose more about themselves to acquaintances than do those in formal cultures. The level of formality in a culture can also be seen in how people dress and the forms of address they use. Germany, for instance, a country that is like the United States in many ways, has a much higher degree of formality. Germans

Across cultures, when relationships become more intimate, self-disclosure increases.

are likely to dress well even if just visiting friends or going to school. They also use formal titles in their interactions with others, and they have fewer close friends. A German proverb states, "A friend to everyone is a friend to no one." Japan is another country that has a much higher degree of formality. As a result, people from these cultures also engage in less self-disclosure, especially with nonintimates.

Particularly in the beginning stages of a crosscultural friendship, cultural differences can easily lead to misperceptions and discomfort. For instance, an American student may perceive an exchange student from China as reserved and not interested in establishing a "genuine" friendship because the exchange student doesn't volunteer personal information. At the same time, the Chinese exchange student may be feeling embarrassed by the American's personal disclosures. When we are aware of cultural differences, we can vary our level of disclosure so that it is appropriate for our partner.

Regardless of these cultural differences, however, Gudykunst and Kim (2003) have discovered

© Jack Hollingsworth/CORBIS

that, across cultures, as relationships become more intimate, self-disclosure increases. In addition, they found that the more partners disclosed to each other, the more they were attracted to each other, and the more uncertainty about each other was reduced (p. 329).

Women tend to disclose more than men, are disclosed to more than men, and are more aware than men of cues that affect their self-disclosure (Dindia, 2000b, p. 24; Reis, 1998, p. 213). Deborah Tannen (2003) argues that one way to capture the differences between men's and women's verbal styles is by paying attention to "report-talk" and "rapport-talk" (p. 92). Tannen's point is that men in our society are more likely to view conversation as **report-talk**—a way to share information, display knowledge, negotiate, and preserve independence. In contrast, women are more likely to use **rapport-talk**—a way to share experiences and establish bonds with others.

report-talk
a way to share information, display knowledge, negotiate, and preserve independence.

rapport-talk
a way to share experiences and establish bonds with others.

Disclosing Feelings

At the heart of intimate self-disclosure is sharing our personal emotions, which is a risky business. Why? When we share our feelings, we are generally giving the other person potent knowledge about us that he or she might use to harm us. So all of us have to decide whether and how we disclose our feelings. Obviously, one option we have is to withhold our emotions. If we do decide to disclose our feelings, we can either display them or describe them.

Withholding Feelings

withholding feelings
denying feelings by keeping them inside and not giving any verbal or nonverbal cues to their existence.

Withholding feelings is denying them by keeping them inside and not giving any verbal or nonverbal cues to their existence. Psychologists believe habitually withholding feelings can lead to physical problems such as ulcers and heart disease as well as to psychological problems such as stress and depression. Moreover, people who withhold feelings can be perceived as cold, undemonstrative, and difficult to talk with.

In some situations withholding feelings is appropriate. For example, when a situation is inconsequential, you may well choose to withhold your feelings. Likewise, even though a stranger's crude behavior at a party may bother you, you may choose to withhold your irritation to avoid embarrassing your date. Or at work you may withhold your frustration with a difficult customer. And, of course, those who enjoy gambling would argue that withholding feelings is best exemplified by the skilled poker player who displays a "poker face," a neutral look that is impossible to decipher, so as not to give away the quality of his hand.

Displaying Feelings

Displaying feelings is the act of showing feelings through facial expressions, body responses, and verbal outbursts. Cheering over a great play at a sporting event, howling when you bang your head against the car door-jamb, and patting a coworker on the back for doing something well are all displays of feelings.

Feelings displays harm relationships when negative feelings such as anger, disgust, or hatred are displayed in ways that frighten or threaten others. For instance, when Anita tells Jerome "That first paragraph isn't very well written," and Jerome becomes resentful and shouts "Who the hell asked you for your opinion?" this display would probably shock, embarrass, and scare Anita, momentarily damaging their relationship. Although a display of negative feelings may make you feel better temporarily, the frustration or anger that is being vented is likely to make the other person defensive, which will damage the conversational climate.

Displays of feelings often serve as an escape valve for very strong emotions, so in some sense they are a healthier approach to feelings than withholding since we "get them out of our system." Unfortunately, while we may feel better, these displays usually stress our relational partners. Rather than withholding or displaying our emotions, we can use the self-disclosure skill of describing feelings to help us share our feelings with others in an appropriate manner.

Describing Feelings

Describing feelings is the skill of naming the emotions you are feeling without judging them. Describing feelings increases the likelihood of having a positive interaction and decreases the chances of creating defensiveness. Moreover, when we describe our feelings, we teach others how to treat us because we explain how what has happened affects us. This knowledge gives our relational partners information that they can use to help us deal with our emotions. For example, if you tell Paul that you enjoy it when he visits you, your description of how you feel should encourage him to visit you again. Likewise, when you tell Gloria that you are annoyed that she borrows your jacket without asking, she is more likely to ask the next time. Describing your feelings allows you to exercise a measure of control over others' behavior simply by making them aware of the effects their actions have on you.

There are at least six reasons people don't describe feelings regularly.

1. **Many people mistakenly believe that by saying "I feel" they are describing their emotions when they are actually evaluating others.** Consider the following the sentence "I feel like you're better than me." But rather than describing a feeling, the speaker is making an assertion. So the use of "I feel" doesn't automatically lead to a description of an emotional state. Stop and think. When a person says something that

displaying feelings
the act of showing feelings through facial expressions, body responses, and verbal outbursts.

describing feelings
the skill of naming the emotions you are feeling without judging them.

leads you to believe this person thinks he or she is superior, how might you *feel?* Perhaps you feel hurt, rejected, angry, or inferior. If so, then you should describe your feelings by saying "I feel hurt (or rejected, or angry, or inferior)."

Let's consider one more example. Suppose your fiancée has just told you that you should postpone your wedding. If you say, "I feel you don't love me anymore," you haven't described a feeling. But if you say "I feel angry (or dismal, or stunned) by your wanting to postpone the wedding," you are describing how you feel.

2. **Many people have a limited active vocabulary of words that signify a range of emotional states.** They can sense that they are feeling something; however, they may not be able to distinguish between or name the feeling as hatred, annoyance, betrayal, envy, outrage, or shock. Each of these words describes a different feeling, yet people with limited emotional vocabularies may call each of these "anger." Figure 7.1 presents several synonyms for a number of common emotions. To become more effective in describing your feelings, learn and use a wider "vocabulary of emotions."

3. **For many people, describing their feelings is an unacceptable risk because it makes them vulnerable.** If you describe your feelings, it is true that you risk having a partner use this knowledge as a weapon. Perhaps you have had experiences where trust was betrayed. So it is safer to act angry than to be honest and describe the hurt you feel; it is safer to appear indifferent than to share your happiness and risk being made fun of. Yet, if you don't take reasonable risks in your relationships, you are

Describing feelings is difficult for many people because it makes them vulnerable. Can you recall a situation in which you masked your feelings because you didn't trust others? Was your fear justified?

Jason Harris/© Thomson Higher Education

Words Related to *Angry*

annoyed	enraged	incensed	infuriated
irate	livid	mad	outraged

Words Related to *Loving*

affectionate	amorous	aroused	caring
fervent	heavenly	passionate	tender

Words Related to *Embarrassed*

flustered	humiliated	mortified	overwhelmed
rattled	shamefaced	sheepish	uncomfortable

Words Related to *Surprised*

astonished	astounded	baffled	jolted
mystified	shocked	startled	stunned

Words Related to *Fearful*

afraid	anxious	apprehensive	frightened
nervous	scared	terrified	worried

Words Related to *Disgusted*

aghast	appalled	dismayed	horror-struck
nauseated	repulsed	revolted	sickened

Words Related to *Hurt*

abused	damaged	forsaken	hassled
mistreated	offended	pained	wounded

Words Related to *Happy*

cheerful	contented	delighted	ecstatic
elated	glad	joyous	pleased

Words Related to *Lonely*

abandoned	alone	deserted	desolate
forlorn	isolated	lonesome	lost

Words Related to *Sad*

blue	depressed	downcast	gloomy
low	miserable	morose	sorrowful

Words Related to *Energetic*

animated	bouncy	brisk	lively
peppy	spirited	sprightly	vigorous

Figure 7.1
The vocabulary of emotions

likely to miss the joy and peace from healthy, satisfying relationships. If your friend Pete playfully calls you by a nickname, you can tell Pete that you resent (feel resentful) being called that. Then Pete has the option of continuing to call you by that name or, to show that he cares about you, to stop using it. If you don't describe your feelings to Pete, however, he will probably continue calling you by that name simply because he doesn't realize that you don't like it. By saying nothing, you reinforce his behavior; by describing your feelings, you teach Pete how to treat you.

Test Your Competence

Building Your Vocabulary of Emotions

For each of these statements, select three words from Figure 7.1 that might fit the statement but would represent different emotional reactions. As you select the words, try to visualize the feeling that each of the words arouses.

1. I feel _____ when you call me late at night.
2. I was _____ that she told everyone about that.
3. He was _____ when he discovered what she had done.
4. Witnessing that accident really made me feel _____.

5. When my father died, I felt _____.
6. I'm _____ about graduating.
7. I'm _____ about losing my job.
8. I was _____ when the doctor told me I needed surgery.
9. I suppose I should understand that it was a mistake, but I feel _____.
10. When you look at me like that, I feel _____.

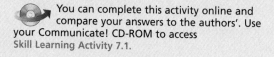 You can complete this activity online and compare your answers to the authors'. Use your Communicate! CD-ROM to access **Skill Learning Activity 7.1.**

 Although the level of risk varies with each situation, in healthy relationships you will more often improve rather than hurt relationships by describing your feelings. To further explore how to increase your ability to be vulnerable, use your Communicate! CD-ROM to access Web Resource 7.2 Becoming Vulnerable. Which of the reasons for avoiding vulnerability ring true to you?

4. **Many people fear that if they describe their real feelings others will judge them or make them feel guilty about having such feelings.** People believe it is tactful to withhold their feelings because "the truth sometimes hurts." You may have learned to avoid the truth by not saying anything or by telling "little" lies. When you were young, perhaps your mother said, "Don't forget to give Aunt Marta a great big kiss." At that time, you may have blurted out, "Ugh—it makes me feel yucky to kiss Aunt Marta. She's got a mustache." If your mother then responded, "That's terrible—your Aunt Marta loves you. Now you give her a kiss and never let me hear you talk like that again!" you probably felt guilty for having this "wrong" feeling. Yet the thought of kissing your Aunt Marta did make you feel "yucky." But you learned to ignore your feelings in order to be tactful.

5. **Many people believe describing feelings causes harm to others or to a relationship.** If it really annoys Fyodor when his girlfriend, Lana, smokes, Fyodor may choose not to confront Lana because he doesn't want to hurt her. If Fyodor says nothing, but is still irritated by Lana's smoking, his irritation may increase and he may begin to avoid spending

time with her. Lana will be bewildered by Fyodor's distant behavior, but she won't understand why. By not describing his feelings, Fyodor may damage their relationship and hurt Lana. If Fyodor describes his feelings to Lana in a nonjudgmental way, she may try to quit smoking. They might get into a discussion in which Lana discloses her struggle with tobacco addiction. Together they might work out a plan that is mutually acceptable. In short, describing feelings does not have to be offensive to your partner. Instead, it can be a catalyst for effectively discussing and resolving issues in the relationship.

6. **Some cultural or ethnic groups favor masking or withholding feelings.** In some cultures, harmony among group members is believed to be more important than individuals' personal feelings. People from these cultures may have been taught that expressing their feelings is selfish and divisive. Men and women also differ in how they handle feelings. To learn more about how they differ, read the article "Gender Differences in Motives for Regulating Emotions," available through InfoTrac College Edition. Use your Communicate! CD-ROM to access Web Resource 7.3: Gender Differences in Emotions.

To describe your feelings: (1) Identify the behavior that has triggered the feeling. The feeling results from some specific behavior—what someone has said or done to or about you. (2) Identify the specific emotion you are experiencing as a result of the behavior. The vocabulary of emotions provided in Figure 7.1 can help you develop your ability to select specific words to describe your feelings. (3) Frame your response as an "I" statement: "I feel *happy, sad, irritated, vibrant.*" "I" statements help neutralize the impact of an emotional description because they do not blame the other or evaluate the other's behavior. Instead, a first person message accurately conveys what you are expressing and why. (4) Verbalize the specific feeling.

Here are two examples of describing feelings. Notice that the first one begins with the trigger, and the second one begins with the feeling—either order is acceptable: (1) "Thank you for your compliment [trigger]; I [the person having the feeling] feel gratified [the specific feeling] that you noticed the effort I made." (2) "I [the person having the feeling] feel very resentful [the specific feeling] when you criticize my cooking on days I've worked as many hours as you have [trigger]."

To begin with, you may find it easier to describe positive feelings: "As a result of your taking me to the movie, I really feel cheered up" or "When you offered to help me with the housework, I really felt relieved." As you become comfortable describing positive feelings, you can move to describing negative feelings caused by environmental factors: "It's cold and cloudy; I feel gloomy" or "When there's a thunderstorm, I get jumpy." Finally, you can risk describing the difficult emotions you feel resulting from what people have said or done: "When you forced me to kiss Aunt Marta, I felt repulsed by her mustache and betrayed by you" or "When you use a sarcastic tone while you are saying that what I did pleased you, I really feel confused."

Skill Builders Describing Feelings

Skill	Use	Procedure	Example
Putting an emotional state into words.	For self-disclosure; to teach people how to treat you.	1. Identify the behavior that has triggered the feeling. 2. Identify the specific emotion you are experiencing as a result of the behavior. Anger? Joy? Be specific. 3. Frame your response as an "I" statement. "I feel _____." 4. Verbalize the specific feeling.	"I just heard I didn't get the job, and I feel cheated and bitter" or "Because of the way you defended me when I was being belittled by Leah, I feel both grateful and humbled."

Giving Personal Feedback

Sometimes in our interactions and relationships it is appropriate to comment on another's message or behavior. When personal feedback is conveyed with sensitivity, it can help the other person to develop a more accurate self-concept and to adapt his or her message and behavior appropriately. First we consider what it means to describe behavior.

Test Your Competence

Identifying Descriptions of Feelings

For each of these statements, determine if the message is a description of feelings. If it is, place a "D" next to it. If you determine that the message is not a description of feelings, supply a message that provides a description of feelings.

1. That was a great movie!
2. I was really cheered by the flowers.
3. I feel that you are not respecting my rights.
4. Yuck!
5. Damn—I screwed that up again. I feel like an idiot.

6. I feel certain I got the job because I was the most qualified person.
7. Congratulations, I feel happy for you.
8. When Pam's around, I feel like a third wheel.
9. I'm ecstatic about winning the award.
10. I'm sick and tired of you.

 You can complete this activity online and compare your answers to the authors'. Use your Communicate! CD-ROM to access **Skill Learning Activity 7.2.**

Then we show how describing behavior enhances praise and constructive criticism.

Describing Behavior

Both effective praising and critiquing are based on being descriptive rather than evaluative. Just as we must learn to describe our feelings as part of effective self-disclosure, so we must learn to describe the specific behavior of others if we are to give effective feedback. Unfortunately, people are quick to share generalized conclusions and evaluations. "You're so mean," "She's a tease," "You're a real friend," and countless statements like these are attempts to provide feedback but are stated as evaluative and vague.

Describing behavior is accurately recounting the specific behaviors of another without commenting on their appropriateness through evaluative language. When we describe behavior, we become accountable for our observations and conclusions. To describe behavior, we move backward through the perceptual process by identifying the specific behaviors that have led to our generalized perception. What led you to conclude someone was "mean"? Was it something the person said? Did? If so, what? What did the person do or say that led you to conclude that he or she is a "real friend"? Once you have identified the specific behaviors, actions, or messages that led to your conclusion, you can share that information as feedback. For example, "Georgio, you called me a liar in front of the team, and you know I have no way to prove that I told the truth." "Shana, you came to my graduation even though it was on your twenty-first birthday. You stayed and comforted me when Tyrone left, and you even volunteered to stay with my son so I could job hunt. You're a real friend."

describing behavior
accurately recounting the specific behaviors of another without commenting on their appropriateness through evaluative language.

Praise

Praise is describing the specific positive behaviors or accomplishments of another and the effect that behavior has on others. Too often we fail to acknowledge the positive and helpful things people say and do. Yet our view of who we are—our identity as well as our behavior—is shaped by how others respond to us. Praise can be used to reinforce positive behavior and to help another develop a positive self-concept.

Praise is not the same as flattery. When we flatter someone, we use insincere compliments to ingratiate ourselves to that person. When we praise, our compliments are sincere. We express only admiration that we genuinely feel.

For praise to be effective, we need to focus the praise on the specific behavior and accomplishments and word the message to be in keeping with the significance or value of the accomplishment or behavior. If your sister, who tends to be forgetful, remembers your birthday, that is a

praise
describing the specific positive behaviors or accomplishments of another and the effect that behavior has on others.

behavior that you will want to praise so that it is reinforced. But saying "You're so wonderful, you're on top of everything" reinforces nothing because it is an overly general statement that does not identify a particular behavior or accomplishment. Gushing "Oh, you remembered to return the pliers! I'm so grateful. That was just unbelievably thoughtful of you" is overkill that will be perceived as insincere. Simply saying something like "Thanks for the birthday card; I really appreciate it" would be appropriate. The response acknowledges the accomplishment by describing the specific behavior and the positive feeling of gratitude that the behavior has caused. While effective praise can enhance self-esteem too much, unnecessary praise can actually lower self-esteem. Check out an interesting article about praise and self-esteem in children, "Do You Praise Your Child Too Much?," available through InfoTrac College Edition. Use your Communicate! CD-ROM to access Web Resource 7.4: Too Much Praise?

Here are two more examples of appropriate praise:

Behavior: Sonya takes responsibility for selecting and buying a group wedding present for a friend. The gift is a big hit.

Praise: "Sonya, the present you chose for Stevie was really thoughtful. Not only did it fit our price range, but Stevie really liked it."

Accomplishment: Cole has just received a letter inviting him to a reception at which he is to receive a scholarship award given for academic accomplishments and community service work.

Praise: "Congratulations, Cole. I'm proud of you. It's really great to see that the effort you put into studying as well as the time and energy you have devoted to the Second Harvest Food Program and Big Brothers is being recognized and valued."

Praise doesn't "cost" much, and it is usually valued and appreciated. Not only does praise provide feedback and build esteem, it can also deepen our relationship with that person because it increases the openness of the relationship. To increase your effectiveness using praise, follow these steps: (1) Identify the specific behavior or accomplishment that you want to reinforce. (2) Describe the specific behavior or accomplishment. (3) Describe any positive feelings or outcomes that you or others experienced as a result of the behavior or accomplishment. (4) Phrase the response so that the level of praise appropriately reflects the significance of the behavior or accomplishment.

Giving Constructive Criticism

constructive criticism
describing specific behaviors of another that hurt the person or that person's relationships with others.

Research on reinforcement theory has found that people learn faster and better through positive rewards such as praise. Nevertheless, there are still times when personal feedback needs to address negative behaviors or actions. **Constructive criticism** is describing specific behaviors of another that hurt the person or that person's relationships with others. Although the word *criticize* can mean judgment, constructive criticism does not condemn or judge but is based on empathy and a sincere desire to help someone understand the impact of his or her behavior. Use the following guidelines when giving constructive criticism.

1. **Ask the person's permission before giving criticism.** Before you give constructive criticism, you should make sure the person wants to hear what you have to say. A person who has agreed to hear constructive criticism is likely to be more receptive to it than is someone who is not accorded respect by being asked.

2. **Describe the behavior by accurately recounting precisely what was said or done without labeling the behavior good or bad, right or wrong.** By describing behavior, you lay an informative base for the feedback and increase the chances that the person will listen receptively. Feedback that is preceded with detailed description is less likely to be met defensively. Your description shows that you are criticizing the behavior rather than attacking the person, and it points the way to a solution. For example, if DeShawn asks, "What did you think of the visuals I used when I delivered my report?" replying "They weren't very effective" would be general and evaluative. Replying "Well, the type on the first two was small, and I had trouble reading them" is descriptive. Notice this constructive criticism does not attack DeShawn's competence. Instead, it points out a problem and in so doing enables DeShawn to see how to improve.

3. **Attend to positive face needs.** Remember, by its nature even constructive criticism threatens the needs all of us have to be liked and admired. So prefacing constructive criticism with statements that bolster our continuing respect or admiration is important. One way to do this is to offer praise before criticism. In our example, you could begin your feedback to DeShawn by saying, "First, the charts and graphs were useful, and the color really helped us to see the problems. Second, the type size on the first two overheads was small, and I had trouble reading them." Here the praise is relevant and significant. If you cannot preface feedback with significant praise, don't try. Prefacing feedback with empty praise will not help the person accept your feedback.

4. **When appropriate, suggest what a person might do in response to the feedback.** Because the focus of constructive criticism is helping, it is appropriate to provide the person with your suggestions that might lead to positive change. In responding to DeShawn's request for feedback, you might also add, "When I make overheads, I generally try to use 18-point type or larger. You might want to give that a try." By including a positive suggestion, you not only help the person by providing honest information, you also show that your intentions are positive.

Observe&Analyze

Praising and Criticizing

Think of someone you need to praise and someone to whom you would like to give constructive criticism. Prepare feedback for each person. Use the following steps:

1. Begin by writing a sentence that identifies your general impression of each person.

2. For each person, recall and write down the specific behaviors, actions, and messages that led to your impression.

3. Identify all the consequences that have resulted from the way this person has acted or spoken.

4. If you have any advice that seems appropriate to give to this person, record it.

5. Write a short feedback message for each person that follows the guidelines for effective praise or criticism.

In the next day or two have a feedback conversation with at least one of these people and use your preparation to help you deliver the feedback. Then write a paragraph describing what happened and how well the feedback was received. Analyze why you believe the feedback was received as it was.

 You can complete this activity online, download a preparation workshop, and, if requested, email it to your instructor. Use your Communicate! CD-ROM to access Skill Learning Activity 7.3.

Assertiveness

assertiveness
standing up for ourselves in interpersonally effective ways.

In addition to helping others understand how we feel, self-disclosure also enables us to state our preferences, needs, and feelings—to be **assertive,** standing up for ourselves in interpersonally effective ways. We can understand the specific qualities of assertive communication best if we contrast it with other ways of interacting when we believe our rights or needs are in danger of being violated or ignored.

Contrasting Methods of Dealing with Needs and Rights

When we believe others are insensitive to our needs and rights, we can respond passively, aggressively, or assertively.

passive behavior
not expressing personal preferences or defending our rights because we fear the cost and are insecure in the relationships, have very low self-esteem, or value the other person above our self.

Passive behavior People behave **passively** when they do not express their personal preferences or defend their rights because they fear the cost and are insecure in the relationships, have very low self-esteem, or value the other person above themselves. People who behave passively submit to other people's demands, even when doing so is inconvenient, against their best interests, or violates their rights. For example, Aaron and Katie have a standing date to go inline skating at 8 A.M. Saturday mornings, but Aaron's Friday work schedule has changed and he doesn't get home until 3 A.M. on Saturday morning. So the 8 A.M. skating date is really inconvenient. If he is passive, he won't say anything to Katie but will drag himself out of bed and go skating even though he'd much rather stay in bed. When people consistently use passive behavior, they can end up short-circuiting their relationships.

aggressive behavior
belligerently or violently confronting another with your preferences, feelings, needs, or rights with little regard for the situation or for the feelings or rights of others.

Aggressive behavior People behave **aggressively** when they belligerently or violently confront another with their preferences, feelings, needs, or rights with little regard for the situation or for the feelings or rights of others. People behave aggressively when they perceive themselves to be powerful, do not value the other person, lack emotional control, or feel defensive. People who behave aggressively risk damaging their relationships. Research shows that people who receive aggressive messages are likely to feel hurt by them regardless of their relationship (Martin, Anderson, & Horvath, 1996, p. 24).

Suppose that without letting her know of his schedule change Aaron has continued to meet Katie to go inline skating. If Katie suggests they meet next week at 7:30, Aaron may explode and aggressively reply, "You've got to be kidding; no way am I going to do that! Forget it." Katie, who has no context for understanding this aggressive outburst, may be momentarily startled and become distant.

Assertive behavior As we mentioned earlier, assertiveness means expressing personal preferences and defending personal rights while respecting the preferences and rights of others. Assertiveness is an important disclosure skill. It helps us to achieve our personal goals while maintaining our relationships, and our assertive messages teach others how to treat us. When we assert our needs and preferences effectively, we provide our partners with the honest and truthful information they need to understand and meet our needs. When Aaron's schedule changed, he would have behaved assertively if he had called Katie, explained his situation, and negotiated a more convenient time for inline skating.

Paulette Dale (1999), a consultant on assertive behavior, contrasts these three behaviors as follows: Whereas a submissive or passive response conveys the message "*I'm* not important, *you're* important," and an aggressive response conveys the message "*I'm* important, *you're* nothing," an assertive response conveys the message "*I'm* important, *you're* important, we're *both* important" (pp. 5–6).

Situations in Which Assertiveness Is Appropriate

There are at least three types of situations where you may need to be assertive.

Refusing a request "Just say 'No'" seems like simple advice. Yet many of us find ourselves overburdened, resentful, or in trouble because we passively say "Yes" to something we really do not want to do. Whether the request is as innocent as babysitting for a

Bruce Ayers/Getty Images

Assertive behavior does not intimidate the other person. How would you feel if you were the woman in this photo? From her nonverbal cues, do you think she will be effective at asserting herself?

Passive and Aggressive Behavior

Describe two incidents in the past where you behaved passively or aggressively. Now analyze each situation. What type of situation was it? Did someone make a request? Did you need to express a preference or right? Was someone imposing on you? What type of relationship did you have with the person (stranger, acquaintance, friendship, business, intimate, romantic)? How did you feel about how you behaved? If you had used assertive messages, what might you have said?

You can complete this activity online and, if requested, email it to your instructor. Use your Communicate! CD-ROM to access Skill Learning Activity 7.4.

friend or as risky as unprotected sex, knowing how to politely refuse is important. For example, Nick's mom calls and asks him to come home this weekend for his brother's birthday, but Nick needs the weekend to catch up on his studies and finish a paper that is due on Monday. If he is assertive, Nick might say, "Gee, Mom, I understand how much you like having everyone together for birthdays, but I can't make it this weekend. I need to catch up on my reading for class and I have a paper due Monday, so I'll be in the library most of the weekend. I'm sorry. I know you're disappointed, but I'm not coming." To learn more about refusing requests, use your Communicate! CD-ROM to access Web Resource 7.5: How to Say No.

Expressing a preference or right There are times when we need to share our personal preferences or stand up for our rights. In our everyday dealings with others, we need to be assertive in telling people what we want. Cerise and Ramon have agreed to go out to dinner on Sunday night. If Ramon suggests they eat at the newest Chinese Restaurant and Cerise dislikes Chinese food, she might assert herself by saying, "Well, I'd prefer going somewhere else. I really don't enjoy Chinese food. How about Carrabbas? We both like Italian!"

Correcting an imposition We all encounter situations where other people knowingly or unknowingly infringe on us. They may behave in ways that are offensive or inappropriate. They may violate our rights, our space, or our personhood. In these instances assertive behavior will enable us to correct the situation so that it becomes one that we find to be acceptable. For example, Karla has brought her six-year-old son to the latest Harry Potter movie. Unfortunately the family in the seats immediately behind them are breaking the mood by loudly talking about what is happening on screen. Karla can attempt to assert herself and correct this imposition by saying something like, "Excuse me. You probably don't realize it, but your conversation distracts from the movie my son and I have been looking forward to. So please stop talking."

In each of these situations—refusing a request, expressing preferences, and correcting impositions—assertive messages balance our rights and needs with the rights and needs of others. For a review of the characteristics of assertive behavior, see Figure 7.2.

Here are some useful guidelines for practicing assertive behavior: (1) identify what you are thinking or feeling; (2) analyze the cause of these feelings; (3) identify what your real preferences and rights are; and (4) use describing feelings and describing behavior skills to make "I" statements that explain your position politely. If you are having trouble taking the first step to being more assertive, begin with situations in which you are likely to have a high potential for success (Alberti & Emmons, 1995). In addition, try to incorporate the characteristics of assertive behavior outlined in Figure 7.2.

Own your feelings	Assertive individuals acknowledge that the thoughts and feelings expressed are theirs.
Avoid confrontational language	Assertive individuals do not use threats, evaluations, or dogmatic language.
Use specific statements directed to the behaviors at hand	Instead of focusing on extraneous issues, assertive individuals use descriptive statements that focus on the issue that is most relevant.
Maintain eye contact and firm body position	Assertive individuals look people in the eye rather than shifting gaze, looking at the floor, swaying back and forth, hunching over, or using other signs that may be perceived as indecisive or lacking conviction.
Maintain a firm but pleasant tone of voice	Assertive individuals speak firmly but at a normal pitch, volume, and rate.
Avoid hemming and hawing	Assertive individuals avoid vocalized pauses and other signs of indecisiveness.

Figure 7.2
Characteristics of assertive behavior

Assertiveness in Cross-Cultural Relationships

Assertiveness, which is based on valuing individual rights, is practiced in Western cultures. As Samovar and Porter (2001) point out, "communication problems arise when cultures that value assertiveness come in contact with cultures that value accord and harmony" (p. 85). For instance, "to maintain harmony and avoid interpersonal clashes, Japanese business has evolved an elaborate process called *nemawashii,* 'binding the roots of a plant before pulling it

Skill Builders ▶ Assertiveness

Skill	Use	Procedure	Example
Standing up for yourself and doing so in interpersonally effective ways that describe your feelings honestly and exercise your personal rights while respecting the rights of others	To show clearly what you think or feel.	1. Identify what you are thinking or feeling. 2. Analyze the cause of these feelings. 3. Identify what your real preferences and rights are. 4. Use describing feelings and describing behavior skills to make "I" statements that politely explain your position.	When Gavin believes he is being unjustly charged, he says, "I have never been charged for a refill on iced tea before—has there been a change in policy?"

out.' In this process, any subject that might cause disorder at a meeting is discussed in advance. Anticipating and obviating interpersonal antagonism allow the Japanese to avoid impudent and discourteous behavior" (p. 85).

In fact, some collectivist societies use "a style of communication in which respecting the relationship through communication is more important than the information exchanged" (Jandt, 2001, p. 37). Jandt goes on to explain that these societies use group harmony, avoidance of loss of face to others and oneself, and a modest presentation of oneself as means of respecting the relationship. "One does not say what one actually thinks when it might hurt others in the group" (p. 37).

Conversely, in Latin and Hispanic societies men, especially, are frequently taught to exercise a form of self-expression that goes far beyond the guidelines presented here for assertive behavior. In these societies, the concept of "machismo" guides male behavior. Thus, the standard of assertiveness considered appropriate in the dominant American culture can seem inappropriate to people whose cultural frame of reference leads them to perceive it as either aggressive or weak.

Test Your Competence

Assertive Messages

For each of the following situations, write an assertive response.

1. You come back to your dorm, apartment, or house to finish a paper that is due tomorrow, only to find that someone else is using your computer.

Assertive response:

2. You work part time at a clothing store. Just as your shift is ending, your manager says to you, "I'd like you to work overtime, if you would. Martin's supposed to replace you, but he just called and can't get here for at least an hour." You have dinner guests arriving in two hours.

Assertive response:

3. During a phone call with your elderly grandmother, she announces, "Your Great Aunt Margie called, and I told her you'd be happy to take us grocery shopping and out to lunch on Saturday." You were planning to spend Saturday working on your portfolio to take to an interview next week.

Assertive response:

4. You and your friend made a date to go dancing, an activity you really enjoy. When you meet, your friend says, "If it's all the same to you, I thought we'd go to a movie instead."

Assertive response:

5. You're riding in a car with a group of friends on the way to a party when the driver begins to clown around by swerving the car back and forth, speeding up to tailgate the car in front, and honking his horn. You believe this driving is dangerous, and you're becoming scared.

Assertive response:

 You can complete this activity online and compare your responses to the authors'. Use your Communicate! CD-ROM to access Skill Learning Activity 7.5.

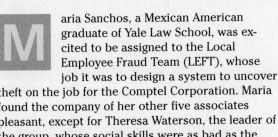

What Would You Do?   A QUESTION OF ETHICS

Maria Sanchos, a Mexican American graduate of Yale Law School, was excited to be assigned to the Local Employee Fraud Team (LEFT), whose job it was to design a system to uncover theft on the job for the Comptel Corporation. Maria found the company of her other five associates pleasant, except for Theresa Waterson, the leader of the group, whose social skills were as bad as the stereotypical queen bee. Maria wondered why she, of all people, had been appointed to head the project. Maria found herself increasingly angered by Theresa's views on issues of affirmative action and abortion. Several times she wanted to confront Theresa on these issues, but Maria felt that the harmonious relationship of the group was at stake, and she didn't want to risk losing the group's cohesiveness.

Although Maria was able to control herself in most settings, she began to be critical of Theresa's views during group meetings, forcefully pointing out what she considered to be illogical thinking and openly upbraiding Theresa for her mistakes. When one of the men on the task force confronted her privately, she considered trusting him with her problem, yet she unconsciously feared that self-disclosure would make her seem weak, particularly to a white male. Several days later, when the two other women in the group confronted her about her behavior toward Theresa, Maria broke down and told them her problem.

1. What are the ethical issues in this case?
2. Did Maria behave ethically in this situation?
3. If you were one of the women advising Maria, what would you recommend that she do?

Conversation and Analysis

Use your Communicate! CD-ROM to access the video clip of Trevor and Meg's conversation. Click on the "In Action" icon in the menu at left, then click on "Conversation Menu" in the menu bar at the top of the screen. Select "Trevor and Meg Overview" to watch the video (it takes a minute for the video to load). As you watch Trevor and Meg discuss the future of their relationship, focus on how effectively they are communicating. How do Trevor and Meg disclose their feelings? Note how effective each is at owning feelings and opinions. How well do Trevor and Meg use praise and constructive criticism? Notice how each demonstrates the characteristics of assertive behavior. What really is Meg's fear? You can respond to these analysis questions by clicking on "Analysis" in the menu bar at the top of the screen. When you've answered all the questions, click "Done" to compare your answers to those provided by the authors.

Jason Harris/© Thomson Higher Education

Here is a transcript of the conversation. You can also find a copy of this transcript online, which enables you to take notes as you watch the video. Use your Communicate! CD-ROM to access **Skill Learning Activity 7.6.** When you have finished viewing the video and taking notes, click on

"Authors' Model Analysis" to compare your notes to the detailed conversational analysis provided by the authors.

Trevor and Meg have been going together for the last several months of their senior year at college. Now that graduation is approaching, they are trying to figure out what to do about their relationship. They sit and talk.

Conversation

TREVOR: Meg, I think it's time we talk about making plans for the future. After all, we'll be graduating next month.

MEG: Trevor, you know how uncomfortable I feel about making any long-range plans at this time. We still need to know a lot more about each other before we even think about getting engaged.

TREVOR: Why? We've both said we love each other, haven't we? [*Meg nods*] So why, why's this too soon? What else do we need to know?

MEG: For starters, I'll be going to law school this fall, and this year is going to be difficult. And, you haven't gotten a job yet.

TREVOR: Come on, Meg. You're going to law school in the city, so I'll have a degree in business, so I can probably get a job most anywhere.

MEG: But Trevor, that's just my point. I know I'll be starting law school; I've always wanted to be a lawyer. And you don't really have any idea what you want to do. And that bothers me. I can't be worrying about you and your career when I'm going to need to focus on my classes.

TREVOR: But I told you, I can get a job anywhere.

MEG: Yes, Trevor, but you need more than a job. You need to figure out what kind of job really turns you on. Or else you risk waking up one day and regretting your life. And, I don't want to be there when that happens. I watched my dad go through a midlife crisis, and he ended up walking out on us.

TREVOR: I'm not your dad, Meg. I won't leave you. And don't worry about me, I'll find a job.

MEG: Really? You knew I was going to law school in the city for over a month, but you still haven't even begun a job search. Trevor, right now is the time when people are hiring, and you haven't even done your résumé. The longer you wait, the more difficult your search is going to be.

TREVOR: Come on Meg, you've already said I'm irresistible. What company wouldn't want me?

MEG: I'm serious, Trevor. Look, I've got a scholarship to law school, but it's only going to pay half of my expenses. I'll be taking a loan to get enough money to pay the rest and to have money to live on. I won't have the money or the time to be very supportive of you if you haven't found work. I need the security of knowing that you've got a job and that you are saving money.

TREVOR: Well, they say that "two can live as cheaply as one." I was thinking that once you got settled, I'd move in and that will save us a lot of money.

MEG: Whoa, Trevor. You know how I feel about that. I do love you, and I hope that we have a future together. But living together this year is not an option. I think we need at least a year of living on our own to get ourselves settled and make sure that we really are compatible. After all, we come from totally different backgrounds. I practically raised myself, and I've paid my own bills since I was eighteen, while you've been lucky enough to have parents who footed your bills. There have been several times when we've talked about important issues and the differences between us have been obvious, and they worry me.

TREVOR: You mean when I was joking around about our different taste in cars?

MEG: No, Trevor, not cars, that's minor. But we also have greatly different feelings about money and family. You've told me that once you get married you want to start a family immediately. As I see it, I've got a three-year commitment to law school, then seven to ten years of hard work in order to make partner at a good firm. So I'm not sure when I want to start a family. But I know it won't be at least for six years.

TREVOR: So, what are you saying, Meg? Is it over? "Thanks for the good time, Trevor, but you're not in my plans?"

MEG: Please don't be sarcastic. I'm not trying to hurt you. It makes me happy to think that we'll spend the rest of our lives together. But I'm worried about several things, so I'm just not ready to commit to that now. Let's just take a year, get settled, and see what happens. I'll love it if you do get a job near where I'm in school. That way we can have time to sort through some of the issues between us.

TREVOR: You mean if you can fit me into your schedule? Meg, if we love each other now, aren't we still going to love each other next year? If we wait until we have everything settled, we might never get married; there'll always be something. After all, we are two different people. We're never going to agree on everything!

MEG: Are you saying that as unsettled as our lives are right now we can shoulder the additional stress of planning for a marriage?

TREVOR: No, what I'm saying is that we live together this year, see how it goes, then if it isn't working, we don't have to get married.

Summary

Self-disclosure reveals information about ourselves that is unknown to others. Guidelines can help us decide when self-disclosure is appropriate.

Disclosing feelings can be difficult. We can deal with our feelings by withholding them, displaying them, or skillfully describing them.

Instead of owning our own feelings and ideas, we often avoid disclosure by making generalized statements.

Personal feedback builds relationships by describing, not evaluating, behavior and its effects. Positive feedback is accomplished through praise. Negative feedback can be delivered effectively through constructive criticism.

Assertiveness is the skill of standing up for ourselves in interpersonally effective ways. Passive people are often unhappy as a result of not stating their needs; aggressive people get their ideas and feelings heard but may create other problems through their aggressiveness. Three types of assertion are refusing a request, expressing a preference or right, and correcting an imposition.

Communicate! Online

Now that you have read Chapter 7, use your Communicate! CD-ROM for quick access to the electronic resources that accompany this text. Your CD-ROM gives you access to the video of the conversation between Trevor and Meg on pages 170–171, InfoTrac College Edition, and the Communicate! Web site. When you get to the Communicate! home page, click on "Student Book Companion Site" in the Resource box at right to access the online study aids for this chapter, including a digital glossary, review quizzes, chapter activities, and chapter Web Resources.

Key Terms

At the Communicate! Web site, select the chapter resources for Chapter 7. Print a copy of the glossary for this chapter and test yourself with the electronic flash cards or complete the crossword puzzle to help you master these key terms:

self-disclosure (150)	displaying feelings (155)	constructive criticism (163)
report-talk (154)	describing feelings (155)	assertiveness (164)
rapport-talk (154)	describing behavior (161)	passive behavior (164)
withholding feelings (154)	praise (161)	aggressive behavior (164)

Review Quiz

Test your knowledge of the concepts in this chapter by taking the online quiz at the Communicate! Web site. Select the chapter resources for Chapter 7, then click on "Review Quiz." When you have completed the quiz, submit it for scoring.

Skill Learning Activities

Complete the Observe & Analyze, Test Your Competence, and Conversation and Analysis activities for Chapter 7 online at the Communicate! Web site. Select the chapter resources for Chapter 7, then click on "Activities." You can submit your Observe & Analyze answers to your instructor, compare your Test Your Competence answers to those provided by the authors, and do both for the Conversation and Analysis activity.

7.1: Test Your Competence: Building Your Vocabulary of Emotions (158)
7.2: Test Your Competence: Identifying Descriptions of Feelings (160)
7.3: Observe & Analyze: Praising and Criticizing (163)
7.4: Observe & Analyze: Passive and Aggressive Behavior (166)
7.5: Test Your Competence: Assertive Messages (168)
7.6: Conversation and Analysis: Trevor and Meg (169)

Web Resources

Access the Web Resources for this chapter online at the Communicate! Web site. Select the chapter resources for Chapter 7, then click on "Web Resources."

7.1: Self-Disclosure and Shyness (151)
7.2: Becoming Vulnerable (158)
7.3: Gender Differences in Emotions (159)
7.4: Too Much Praise? (162)
7.5: How to Say No (166)

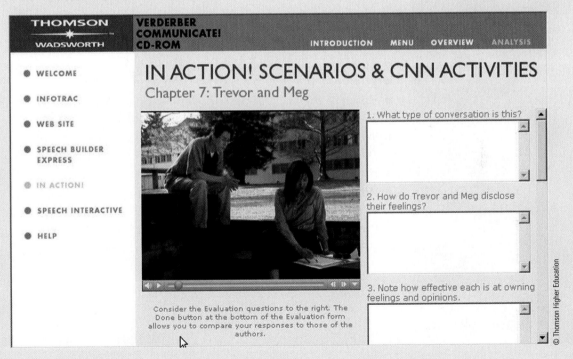

Mark Scott/Getty Images

After you have read this chapter, you should be able to answer these questions:

- What are the major types of relationships?
- What are effective ways of starting a relationship?
- How are the skills of descriptiveness, openness, tentativeness, and equality used in maintaining relationships?
- What are interpersonally effective methods of ending a relationship?
- How are electronically mediated relationships built?
- What are the five conflict styles, and when is each style appropriate?
- What skills are used to initiate conflict effectively?
- What skills are used in responding to a conflict initiated by another?

8

Communicating in Relationships

t was Monday, between classes, and Jennifer had an hour before her next class. She decided to walk over to the bookstore. On the way she looked up and spotted Maria, a woman in her accounting class. "Hey, how you doing?"

"OK," Maria replied. "What did you think of that test we had yesterday?"

"Not sure I want to think about it now," Jennifer replied with a little laugh.

"I know what you mean," Maria said. "I hope we get them back soon. See you in class tomorrow."

"Right," Jennifer replied as Maria made her way across the street.

A minute later, Jennifer was startled as she heard, "Hey beautiful, what are you doing here?"

"Greg," Jennifer said with a big smile on her face. "You startled me. I thought you were off someplace today!"

"Well," Greg replied, "as it turned out, my plans to work with Ken went up in smoke. Have you got time to stop at the cafeteria?"

"You know I've always got time to spend with you."

"Like to decide what we're going to do this weekend?"

"Sounds good to me!"

relationships
sets of expectations two people have for their behavior based on the pattern of interaction between them.

good relationships
ones in which the interactions are satisfying to and healthy for those involved.

I nterpersonal skills help you start, build, and maintain healthy **relationships,** sets of expectations two people have for their behavior based on the pattern of interaction between them (Littlejohn, 2002, p. 234). Relationships run the gamut from acquaintances (like Maria and Jennifer) to intimate friends (like Greg and Jennifer). Regardless of the level of a relationship with a person, we seek **good relationships,** ones in which the interactions are satisfying to and healthy for those involved.

In this chapter, we describe three types of relationships, examine disclosure and feedback ratios, explain the stages that typical relationships flow through, and look at online relationships. Then we examine conflict and explain how to use the conflict process to strengthen relationships.

Types of Relationships

We behave differently depending on whether our relationships are personal or impersonal. Moving on a continuum from impersonal to personal (Dindia & Timmerman, 2003, p. 687), we can classify our relationships as acquaintances, friendships, and close friends or intimates.

Acquaintances

acquaintances
people we know by name and talk with when the opportunity arises but with whom our interactions are largely impersonal.

Acquaintances are people we know by name and talk with when the opportunity arises but with whom our interactions are largely impersonal. We become acquainted with those who live near us, are in our classes, work with us, are part of our religious community, or perform services for us. For example, Jim, an accountant, has been an acquaintance who has been preparing Sung Lee's taxes for three years, but they never meet outside of his office, and they only exchange polite small talk or discuss Sung Lee's taxes.

Friends

friends
people with whom we have negotiated more personal relationships that are voluntary.

Over time, some of our acquaintances become **friends,** people with whom we have negotiated more personal relationships that are voluntary (Patterson, Bettini, & Nussbaum, 1993, p. 145). As friendships develop, people move toward interactions that are less role-bound. That is, Jim and Sung Lee may decide to get together for lunch. If they find that they enjoy each other's company, they may eventually become friends.

What we look for in our friends We tend to choose people as friends who have qualities we find attractive. Sometimes they have similar interests, attitudes, values, and personalities (Vangelisti, 2002, pp.

644–646), but relationships may also develop when there are dissimilarities in personality. The saying "opposites attract" is as accurate as "birds of a feather flock together." Stated theoretically, relationships depend on mutual need fulfillment, so people can be attracted to those who are different from them but who fulfill their needs. Thus, opposites attract when the differences between the people are complementary (Winstead, Derlega, & Rose, 1997, p. 26).

What we expect from our friends
Although people may be drawn to each other for many reasons, research shows that endearing friendships are marked by a high degree of positiveness, assurance, openness, networking, and task sharing (Dindia, 2000a, p. 291; Guerrero & Andersen, 2000, p. 178).

How does race affect friendships? Do you have many friends of different races?

- *Positiveness:* Friends spend time with each other because they reap positive benefits in doing so. They enjoy each other's company, they enjoy talking with each other, and they enjoy sharing experiences.
- *Assurance:* Friends **trust** each other. They risk putting their well-being in the hands of another because they trust the other not to intentionally harm their interests.
- *Openness:* Friends share personal information and feelings with each other.
- *Networking:* Friends show a high level of commitment not only to each other but to each other's friends and family. They are likely to sacrifice their time and energy to engage in activities with family and friends of friends.
- *Task sharing:* Friends help each other with work.

trust
to risk putting your well-being in the hands of another.

Close Friends or Intimates

Close friends or **intimates** are those with whom we share our deepest feelings. People may have countless acquaintances and many friends, but they are likely to have only a few close or intimate friends.

Close friend or intimate relationships differ from others in the degree of commitment, trust, disclosure, and enjoyment partners experience. For instance, although friends engage in some self-disclosure, they are not likely to share the secrets of their lives; intimate friends often gain knowledge of the innermost being of their partner. One type of intimate relationship is a romantic relationship. To read an interesting article about the stages of romantic relationships, use your Communicate! CD-ROM to access Web Resource 8.1: Stages in Healthy Romantic Relationships.

close friends or intimates
those with whom we share our deepest feelings.

Disclosure and Feedback Ratios in Relationships

As people interact in a relationships, they choose to disclose or avoid disclosing personal information. They also give or refrain from giving feedback. It is disclosure and feedback message exchanges that move us from acquaintance relationships to friendships and from friendships to intimate relationships. A healthy relationship is marked by a balance of self-disclosure and feedback between partners.

The Johari window (see Figure 8.1), named after its two originators, Jo Luft and Harry Ingham, is a tool for analyzing the extent of disclosure and feedback you engage in in your relationships (Luft, 1970). The window represents all of the information about you. You and your partner each know some, but not all, of this information. The window has four "panes" or quadrants (the verbal and physical responses to people and their messages), which define the extent of self-disclosure in the relationship.

	Known to self	Not known to self
Known to others	Open	Blind
Not known to others	Secret	Unknown

Figure 8.1
The Johari window

The first quadrant is called the "open" pane because it contains the information about you that both you and your partner know. It includes information you have disclosed and observations about you that your partner has shared with you. If you were preparing a Johari window that represented your side of your relationship with another person, you would include in the open pane all the items of information about yourself that you have shared with that other person as well as observations about you that your partner has made.

The second quadrant is called the "secret" pane. It contains information that you know about yourself but that your partner does not know about you. This information may run the gamut from where you keep your clean underwear to past incidents you are ashamed of. If and when you choose to disclose this secret information to your partner, the information moves from the secret into the open pane of the window. So through disclosure the secret pane becomes smaller and the open pane is enlarged. Disclosure allows others to know more of the "real" you. When the secret pane is large, you are protected, but you are presenting a facade to others.

The third quadrant is called the "blind" pane. It contains information that the other person knows about you but about which you are unaware. Most people have blind spots—aspects of their behavior or effects of their behavior about which they are unaware. For example, Charley may not know that he snores when he sleeps or that he frowns and taps his foot when he is concentrating. Yet his study partner may have observed the behavior and made the connection. Information moves from the blind area of the window to the open area through feedback. Thus, like disclosure, feedback enlarges the open pane of the Johari window, but in this case it is the blind pane that becomes smaller.

The fourth quadrant is called the "unknown" pane. It contains information about you that you do not know and neither does your partner. We know that there is information that is "unknown" because we periodically "discover" it. For instance, do you like to hang glide? Well, if you've never tried it, you don't know—and neither does anyone else. But if someone talks you into trying it, you'll find out. Then this information will move into the secret or open pane of your window.

As you disclose and receive feedback in a relationship, the sizes of the various windowpanes change (Figure 8.2). As a relationship grows, the open pane of both partners' windows becomes larger, and the secret and hidden parts become smaller.

In Figure 8.2a we see an example of a relationship in which little disclosure or feedback is occurring. This person has not shared much information with the other and has received little feedback from this partner as well. We would expect to see this pattern in new relationships or in ones between acquaintances.

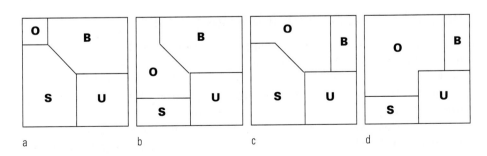

a   b   c   d

Figure 8.2
Sample Johari windows:
(a) low disclosure, low feedback;
(b) high disclosure, low feedback;
(c) low disclosure, high feedback;
(d) high disclosure, high feedback.

Figure 8.2b shows a relationship in which the person is disclosing to a partner but the partner is providing little feedback. As you can see, the secret pane is smaller, but the hidden pane is unchanged. A window like this indicates that the individual is able to disclose information but that the partner is unable or unwilling to give feedback (or perhaps the individual refuses to accept the feedback being given). Part of the way that we learn about who we are comes from the feedback we receive from others, and relationships in which one partner does not provide feedback can become very unsatisfying to the other individual.

Figure 8.2c shows a relationship in which the person is good at providing feedback but does not disclose. Most of us disclose only when we trust our partners, so this pattern may be an indication that the individual does not have confidence in the relational partner.

Figure 8.2d shows a relationship in which the individual has disclosed information and received feedback, and the open pane of the window has enlarged as a result of both processes. Windows that look like this indicate that there is sufficient trust and interest in the relationship that both partners are willing to risk by disclosing and giving feedback.

Obviously, to get a complete "picture" of the relationship, each partner's Johari window would need to be examined. As stated at the beginning of this discussion, the window is a useful tool for helping partners examine and discuss the levels of intimacy and trust in their relationship.

Communication in the Stages of Relationships

Even though no two relationships develop in exactly the same manner, most relationships move through identifiable stages following a "life cycle" that includes beginning and developing, stabilizing, and deterioration (Duck, 1987; Taylor & Altman, 1987). Whether a relationship moves to the next stage depends on how partners interact.

Beginning and Developing Relationships

Fundamental to starting or building a relationship is the need to reduce uncertainty by getting information about our partner (Berger & Brada, 1982; Littlejohn, 2002, p. 243). We get information about others **passively** by observing their behavior, **actively** by asking others for information, and **interactively** by conversing with them directly.

The three communication activities we engage in to start and build relationships are striking up conversation, keeping conversation going, and moving toward intimacy through self-disclosure and feedback.

passive strategy
observing the behavior of others.

active strategy
asking others for information.

interactive strategy
conversing with others directly.

Striking up a conversation No relationship can begin until you talk with the other person. One of the most stressful times for most of us is when we begin a conversation with a complete stranger. For those who find talking to strangers difficult, the conversational openers listed here can help you overcome your anxiety.

1. **Introduce yourself.** "Hi, my name is Gordon. What's yours?"

2. **Refer to the physical context.** "This is awful weather for a game, isn't it?" or "Kim and John have done a great job of remodeling. Did you see the house before they began?"

3. **Share your thoughts or opinions.** "I really like parties, don't you?" "I live on this floor too—do these steps bother you as much as they do me?" or "Doesn't it seem stuffy in here?"

4. **Ask a question about the other person.** "Marge seems to be an excellent hostess—have you known her long?" or "I don't believe I've had the pleasure of seeing you before—do you work in marketing?"

A cheerful response to your opener suggests that the person is interested in continuing. Refusal to answer or a curt reply may mean that the person is not really interested in talking with you at this time. To learn other techniques you can use to begin conversations in large gatherings, read the article "How to Master Networking," available through InfoTrac College Edition. Use your Communicate! CD-ROM to access Web Resource 8.3: Networking.

Keeping the conversation flowing Once two people have begun an interaction, they are likely to engage in "small talk," which is a necessity in early stages of relationships (Dindia & Timmerman, 2003, pp. 692, 696–697). Small talk is conversation that meets social needs with relatively low amounts of risk and is characterized by idea exchange and gossip.

Idea-exchange messages contain facts, opinions, and beliefs. For example, Dan and Walt may talk about the scores from last night's ball games. Or Bonita and Ken may share their opinions about the War on Terror. Although the discussions of the War on Terror are more serious than a conversation about sports, both represent idea exchanges. This type of communication is important in the early stages of a relationship because through it you learn what the other person values and how he or she thinks. Based on this, you can reassess your attraction level and decide whether to invest in growing the relationship.

idea-exchange messages
messages that contain facts, opinions, and beliefs.

Gossip, evaluative talk about people you both know and about "facts" whose accuracy is unknown, is one of the most common forms of interpersonal communication. Gossip appears to be an easy way to talk with people without appearing to share much information about yourself. Statements such as "Do you know Bill? I hear he lost his job" and "Would you believe that Madison Simon and Tim Johnson are going together? I mean, they are so different!" are examples of gossip.

gossip
evaluative talk about people you both know and about "facts" whose accuracy is unknown.

Observe&Analyze

Distinguishing between Types of Relationships

1. List five people you have known for some time who you consider to be acquaintances. Why do you consider these people to be acquaintances rather than friends? What do you talk about with each of these people? What subjects do you avoid? Do any of these relationships have the potential to become friendships? If so, what would you have to do to make that transition?

2. List five people you have known for some time who you consider to be friends. Why do you consider each of these people to be a friend? How does your relationship with each differ from your relationships with your acquaintances? What do you talk about with each of these people? What subjects do you avoid? Do any of these relationships have the potential to become best friendships or intimate relationships? If so, what would you have to do to make the transition?

3. List one to three people you have known for some time who you consider to be your best friends or your inti-

(continued on p. 183)

stabilization
a positive communication climate that encourages mutually satisfying conversations free from defensiveness.

defensiveness
a negative feeling or behavior resulting from a perceived threat from the other.

There are two positions on how gossip affects relationships (Turner et al., 2003, pp. 130–131). One holds that gossip is "social glue," a healthy and harmless form of talk that can bring people closer. The other theory views gossip as "relational ruin," and holds that gossip, which by its nature is untrustworthy, damages relationships because it leads one conversational partner to view the other as less credible, trustworthy, and likeable.

In their recent study, Turner and her colleagues found that regardless of whether the gossip information was positive ("Karen was accepted to Harvard Law School, she's so bright") or negative ("Karen didn't get into Harvard Law School, I can't believe she even applied, she's not that bright"), the gossiper's partner viewed the gossiper as less likeable, trustworthy, and expert. This finding was the same for relationships where the partners were already friends as well as in situations where the individuals had just met.

Gossip occurs during all phases of relationships, and it is frequently used in newer relationships because it is mistakenly considered to be "safe." You may think you can gossip for a long time with another person without really saying anything about yourself, but this research suggests that your gossip is sending messages to your partner about who you are and how well you can be trusted or believed.

Moving conversations to more intimate levels In addition to engaging in small talk, people who seek deeper relationships will also begin to disclose personal information and share feelings about important matters. Through personal disclosure, we come to know and to understand each other.

Expressions of affection are particularly important in developing relationships (Floyd & Morman, 1998, p. 157). Affection is expressed through nonverbal behaviors such as holding hands, staring into each other's eyes, hugging, and kissing. Verbal messages like "You are really special to me," "I like you," or "I really enjoy our time together" directly communicate affection.

Creating a Positive Climate in Stable Relationships

When two people are satisfied with the level of the relationship, whether as acquaintances, as friends, or as close friends/intimates, they begin to **stabilize** it. Stability is maintained if both partners help create a positive communication climate that encourages mutually satisfying conversations free from defensiveness. **Defensiveness** is a negative feeling or behavior resulting from a perceived threat from the other. Unfortunately, as time goes by, people sometimes fall into communication habits that create a defensive climate that can hurt the stability of the relationship. A positive climate is created by sending messages that are descriptive rather than evaluative, open rather than closed, tentative rather than dogmatic, and equal rather than superior.

Speaking descriptively

Speaking descriptively simply means stating what you feel in objective language devoid of evaluation or judgment. In earlier chapters, we explained the skills of describing feelings and behavior, and making "I" statements. When we use these skills, we are descriptive. Compare the climate each of these statements creates:

Evaluative: What a stupid idea—that will never work.

Descriptive: I don't see how that idea will work.

Speaking openly

Speaking openly means honestly sharing thoughts and feelings. Stable relationships exist in a climate where both people are candid. We fear being candid if we think our comments will be perceived as intrusive or will be misinterpreted or rejected. Compare the climate created by these messages:

Open: Marty, if you're not busy on Saturday, would you like to go shopping with me?

Closed: Marty, what are you doing on Saturday?

Speaking tentatively

Speaking tentatively suggests the possibility of inaccuracy and legitimate alternative views. Stable relationships exist in climates where partners verbally acknowledge other ways of thinking. When we are dogmatic in expressing our opinions or present information as "truth," we risk alienating our partner who may have alternative opinions or possess different information. Compare the climate created by these messages:

Tentative: You might want to talk with Jeb about that course. I think he took it last semester, and if I remember correctly, he got an A.

Dogmatic: You've got to talk to Jeb. He knows all about that course. He took it last semester and got an A.

Speaking to others as equals

Speaking as equals means phrasing messages that are plain, down to earth, and convey respect for the other. When messages are condescending and patronizing, they undermine relational stability, creating anger, resentment, and defensiveness in others. Compare the climate created by each of these statements:

Equal: Bethany, I got behind on finishing this letter, but it really should be in the mail by 3:00. Do you think you can bail me out and get it typed by 3:00?

Superior: Bethany, get on this letter right away. I want it on my desk in 20 minutes.

In addition to choosing language carefully, we must also be conscious of the effects of our tone of voice and facial expressions. As we learned earlier, our nonverbal communication can totally negate the meaning of the words we use.

mates. Why do you consider each of these people to be best friends or intimates? What do you talk about with each of these people? What subjects do you avoid? How does each of these relationships differ from those you have with your friends?

Write an essay in which you describe what you have learned about your relationships.

 You can complete this activity online and, if requested, email your essay to your instructor. Use your Communicate! CD-ROM to access Skill Learning Activity 8.2.

speaking descriptively
stating what you feel in objective language devoid of evaluation or judgment.

speaking openly
honestly sharing thoughts and feelings.

speaking tentatively
suggesting the possibility of inaccuracy and legitimate alternative views.

speaking as equals
phrasing messages that are plain, down to earth, and convey respect for the other.

Test Your Competence ▶

Creating Stabilizing Statements

Rephrase each of these messages so that the new message fosters a supportive rather than a defensive communication climate.

1. Don't do it that way. That will never work.
2. Quit bugging me. I'll do it when I'm good and ready.
3. As long as you live in my house, you'll do as I say.
4. I'll pay the bills, after all, I'm an accounting major and you're just an art major.
5. Have you decided where we're going for dinner yet?
6. You should cancel your plans. It's going to rain tomorrow.
7. I can't believe you got a tattoo. It's such a juvenile act of rebellion. You'll be sorry.
8. So, are you dating anyone?
9. Everyone drinks in college.
10. So, when do you think you'll finish that book I lent you?

 You can complete this activity online and compare your answers to the authors'. Use your Communicate! CD-ROM to access Skill Learning Activity 8.3.

How relationships end depends on the interpersonal competence of both people. Do you know people who have amicable divorces? How do they differ from people who have hostile divorces?

Relationship Disintegration

Although poor communication skills may contribute to disintegrating relationships, other factors are likely to be more important (Vangelisti, 2002, p. 663). Over time, a relationship may become less satisfying to one or both partners. When this happens, the partner or partners may change the relationship so that it is less intimate or terminate the relationship altogether.

As partners reduce the level of disclosure and feedback, intimate relationships may devolve to friendships or acquaintances, or may terminate.

Unfortunately, when people decide to end a relationship, they sometimes use strategies that are more hurtful than necessary. Strategies that manipulate the other into ending the relationship or withdrawal and avoidance strategies that leave the partner wondering where you disappeared to (or why you're acting distant) are unethical. Effective communicators use positive tone and directly disclose their feelings and the reasons for changing the level of intimacy in the relationship.

Michael Newman/PhotoEdit

Electronically Mediated Relationships

Thanks to technological innovation, today people are introduced to others they have never seen through electronic newsgroups, chat rooms, and Internet dating services. Moreover, some of these encounters are likely to develop into personal relationships (Barnes, 2003, pp. 138–139).

For example, Andrea and Matt "meet" each other as they communicate in a newsgroup dedicated to the subject of "environmental concerns." They already believe they have at least one thing in common—an interest in environmental issues. As the postings continue, they notice that they are the only ones who hold a specific view on this issue. Moreover, they begin to see that they hold other ideas in common as well. At this point, they decide to "meet" in a private chat room where they "talk" with each other. Now they are able to begin to explore whether they have other common interests. Before long, they have exchanged email addresses and have corresponded directly. If their interest in each other continues to grow, they may arrange to chat on the telephone. If this proves to be satisfactory, they may arrange to meet in person. At some point during this process, they have begun to have a personal relationship that may become a friendship or an intimate relationship.

Of course, many people in electronically mediated (EM) relationships are perfectly content as acquaintances and enjoy the opportunity to talk with each other. EM relationships are attractive to some busy people largely because they do not have time to "do the bar scene." Other people who begin relationships in face-to-face settings use EM communication to sustain these relationships when work or school requires them to live at a distance. Email, which was developed as a tool for conducting business, is now widely used by families, friends, and lovers.

Can EM relationships endure? As Susan Barnes (2003) states, "Transforming an Internet relationship into an actual one can be difficult" (p. 139). EM communicators seem to lack many of the things emphasized in traditional discussion of relationship development: physical proximity, information about physical appearance, cues about group membership, and information about the broader social context. However, people in EM settings can overcome these shortcomings by emailing, by exchanging photographs either electronically or by mail, by talking on the telephone, and, ultimately, by arranging meetings.

What are some of the benefits and drawbacks to relationships that exist at a distance? Some critics of EM relationships argue that face-to-face interaction has more social presence than the Internet; the possibility of immediate feedback with face-to-face interaction conveys greater personal closeness (Flaherty, Pearce, & Rubin, 1998, p. 264). In addition, in most EM forms, some of the nonverbal message is lost. Despite these drawbacks, more and more people are turning to EM communication to develop and maintain relationships.

EM relationships are attractive to those who have for one reason or another had difficulty making strong interpersonal relationships in person. Because EM communication is planned, people are able to show verbal skillfulness and humor in their writing, and they do not have to deal with physical attraction. In fact, some individuals report their EM relationships are even better than face-to-face relationships. From her research, Susan Barnes (2003) reports that "Two advantages of Internet dating are the ability of relationships to build over time and elimination of disruptive nonverbal information" (p. 139).

But there are important differences between in-person and EM communication that can create difficulties for relational development. J. D. Bigelow (1999, pp. 636–637), of Boise State University, focuses on three such problems:

1. **EM communication is less rich than face-to-face, primarily because text messages are primarily verbal.** As a result of not being able to see or hear the way people present their messages, we may misinterpret the message. Only with videoconferencing is the full range of nonverbal messages available.

2. **EM communication, conducted via keyboard entries, is slower paced than face-to-face conversation.** Although this slower rate may provide a person more time for thought, this slower transmission reduces the spontaneity that is an important characteristic of face-to-face interaction.

3. **EM communicators are invisible.** EM communicators often reserve their privacy by using online identities and perhaps by representing themselves differently.

 To read a thorough comparison of the differences between relationships in person and electronically mediated relationships, use your Communicate! CD-ROM to access Web Resource 8.4: In-Person versus Cyberspace Relationships.

Online chat rooms are becoming more animated. People can choose or create avatars that move around and interact with other avatars in a cyber world. How do avatars change electronically mediated relationships?

Bruce Ayers/Getty Images

From Internet to In-Person Relationships

In face-to-face relationships, trust is built over time. We meet a person and then begin interacting. As a result of the behavior we encounter, we then make decisions about trust. For instance, we loan a book and consider when and if it is returned; we make a date and consider whether and how often the person is on time; we tell the person something that is personal and consider whether that person keeps the information to him- or herself or communicates it to others. Through such experiences, we determine whether or not we can trust the person and thus whether or not we want to move toward a more intimate relationship (Goldberg, 1999, p. 113).

In EM relationships, making a trust evaluation is more difficult. Some of the media through which relationships are developed are very opaque. That is, we lose most of the spontaneity and most of the information normally available through nonverbal channels. As a result, our capacity to judge the accuracy of the trustworthiness of the behavior of another is limited.

The Dark Side of Electronically Mediated Relationships

Despite its appeal, using EM communication to form relationships has led to several unethical practices.

Abuse of anonymity One unethical practice for Internet-based relationships is the common practice of assuming a fictitious online persona. A serious question for Internet relationships is, "What kind of relationship can be forged when users are not honest about who they are?" This practice removes both accountability and responsibility. Research shows that women have the most to lose from fictitious identity usage (Kramer & Kramarae 1997, p. 236).

Dishonesty A second unethical practice is the ease with which one can deceive. People lie about their sex, physical attributes, and also create fictitious careers, homes, and so forth. Because we do not "know" our EM partner in person, we are severely limited in our abilities to independently confirm what we are told. Those in EM relationships need to proceed with caution. It is wise to be skeptical of what people tell you about themselves—especially at the beginning of such a relationship. As Jenny Preece (2000) points out, "Online romances of any sort may fail when real-life meetings result in dashed fantasies. For example, online no one is overweight, but in reality a person's extra 25 pounds can make a difference. And dishonesty works only as long as the relationship remains online only" (p. 156).

In the early stages of the relationship, it is also wise to limit the personal information you divulge. Remember, in any communication situation, self-disclosure should occur only if it is reciprocated. Even then, begin slowly and with information that is less personal before moving to more sensitive issues.

technological addictions *nonchemical (behavioral) addictions that involve human–machine interaction.*

interpersonal conflict *when the needs or ideas of one person are at odds or in opposition to the needs or ideas of another.*

Abuse of anonymity and dishonesty are of special concern for EM relationships formed by children; thus it is especially important for parents to monitor children's EM relationships. Interestingly enough, some parents decline to monitor their kids' online chatting, likening it to violating their privacy by eavesdropping on their phone calls. But as Okrent (1999) cautions, "There's a difference: when your child's on the phone, she knows for certain who's on the other end of the line" (p. 41). Parents need to learn how to monitor their children's Internet usage and to use software capable of blocking access to objectionable sites.

Addiction A third potential problem for children and adults alike is **technological addictions,** defined as nonchemical (behavioral) addictions that involve human–machine interaction (Griffiths, 1998, p. 62). The seductiveness of communicating electronically can result in the disruption of ongoing interpersonal relationships. When people spend more and more time on the Internet talking with "unknown" people, they have less time to spend with friends and loved ones. To read a fascinating article on deviant behavior in cyberspace, use your Communicate! CD-ROM to access Web Resource 8.5: The Bad Boys of Cyber Space.

Conflict in Relationships

When two people have an honest relationship, it is inevitable that there will be times when one person's attempt to satisfy his or her own needs will conflict with the other person's desires. When this happens, the partners experience conflict. **Interpersonal conflict** exists when the needs or ideas of one person are at odds or in opposition to the needs or ideas of another. In these conflict situations, participants have choices about how they act and how they communicate with each other.

Many people view conflict as a sign of a bad relationship, but the reality is that conflicts occur in all relationships. Although cultures differ in how they view conflict (for example, Asian cultures see it as dysfunctional), whether conflict hurts or strengthens a relationship depends on how we deal with it. In this section, we discuss five styles people use to manage conflict. Then we describe specific communication strategies that can be used to initiate and respond to conflict episodes in a collaborative style.

Styles of Managing Conflict

When faced with a conflict, people can withdraw, accommodate, force, compromise, or collaborate (Cahn, 1990; Cupach & Canary, 1997; Masters & Albright, 2002). Figure 8.3 outlines the results that flow from each of these styles for managing conflict.

Withdrawal When people **withdraw,** they physically or psychologically remove themselves from the conflict. People may physically withdraw by leaving the site. For instance, when Justina says, "Eduardo, I thought we agreed that you'd pay my folks back the $60 you owe them this week," Eduardo may withdraw physically by walking downstairs. Eduardo would be withdrawing psychologically if he ignores Justina and continues to read the paper. Withdrawal is an uncooperative and unassertive response to conflict because the withdrawer refuses to talk about the issue.

Considered from an individual satisfaction standpoint, withdrawal creates a lose-lose situation because neither party to the conflict really accomplishes what he or she wants. Although Eduardo temporarily escapes from the conflict, he knows it will come up again.

Considered from a relational satisfaction standpoint, withdrawal creates a lose-lose situation. Neither person accomplishes his or her goal. When used repeatedly, withdrawal leads to relationship decline because it doesn't eliminate the problem. Withdrawal may postpone consideration of a problem, but it usually increases tension. Neither party eliminates or attempts to manage the nature of the conflict. Moreover, withdrawal results in what Cloven and Roloff (1991) call "mulling behavior" (p. 136). By **mulling,** they mean thinking about or stewing over an actual or perceived problem until the conflict is perceived as being more severe and results in blaming behavior.

Withdrawal may be used effectively as a temporary effort to create time to cool down and think. For instance, Eduardo might say, "Hold it a minute; let me think about this while I get a cup of coffee, and then we'll talk about

withdraw
to physically or psychologically remove yourself from the conflict.

mulling
thinking about or stewing over an actual or perceived problem until the conflict is perceived as being more severe and results in blaming behavior.

In a long-term relationship, what is likely to happen if both partners use withdrawing as their dominant conflict style?

Jason Harris/© Thomson Higher Education

Approach	Characteristics	Goal	Outlook
Withdrawal	Uncooperative, unassertive	To keep from dealing with conflict	I don't want to talk about it.
Accommodating	Cooperative, unassertive	To keep from upsetting the other person	Getting my way isn't as important as keeping the peace.
Forcing	Uncooperative, assertive	To get my way	I'll get my way regardless of what I have to do.
Compromising	Partially cooperative, partially assertive	To get partial satisfaction	I'll get partial satisfaction by letting the other person get partial satisfaction as well.
Collaborating	Cooperative, assertive	To solve the problem together	Let's talk this out and find the best solution possible for both of us.

this some more." A few minutes later, having calmed down, Eduardo may return, ready to approach and deal with the conflict.

When neither the relationship nor the issue is really important, withdrawing is also a good strategy. For example, at a party at which Josh and Mario have just met, the subject turns to sky diving. Josh may politely excuse himself to go talk with other people when he realizes that he strongly disagrees with the position Mario is advocating. In this case, Josh judges that it simply is not that important to resolve the disagreement for neither the issue nor his relationship with Mario is that important.

accommodating
resolving conflict by satisfying others' needs or accepting others' ideas while neglecting our own.

Accommodating Accommodating is resolving conflict by satisfying others' needs or accepting others' ideas while neglecting our own. So this approach is cooperative but unassertive. For instance, Juan has looked forward to vacationing alone with Mariana, his wife of six months. But when she says, "I think it would be fun to have mom and dad come with us, don't you?" Juan gives in and replies, "Sure, whatever you want."

Considered from an individual satisfaction standpoint, accommodation is a you win–I lose situation. The person who accommodates loses and allows the other person to win.

Individual Satisfaction	Relational Satisfaction	Relational Effects	When Appropriate
Lose/lose: neither party gets satisfaction	Negative: no resolution	Drives wedge into relationship: results in mulling and blaming	Either as temporary disengagement or when issue is unimportant
Lose/win: the other party gets satisfaction	Negative: neither party feels good about the process	Hurts relationship because one person takes advantage	To build social credits or when the issue is unimportant
Win/lose: one party, the forcer, gets satisfaction	Negative: physical and psychological pain for the loser	Hurts relationship because one person feels intimidated	In emergencies; when it is critical to one's or others' welfare; if someone is taking advantage of you
Lose/lose or win/win: neither party is fully satisfied	Neutral to positive: at least partial satisfaction for both	May help or hurt because satisfaction is compromised	When issue is important, when time is short, or when other attempts don't work
Win/win: both parties feel satisfied with the process	Positive: relationship strengthened because of mutual benefits	Helps the relationship because both sides are heard	Anytime

Figure 8.3
Styles of conflict management

From a relational satisfaction standpoint, habitual accommodation has two problems. First, conflicts resolved through accommodation may lead to poor decision making because important facts, arguments, and positions are not voiced. Second, habitual accommodation results in the accommodator consistently receiving less, which may eventually result in feelings of resentment.

Habitually accommodating is a problem, but when the issue really isn't that important but the relationship is, it is appropriate and effective to accommodate. For instance, whether to have chicken or fish for dinner may be unimportant to you, but if your in-laws prefer fish, you may accommodate them.

Accommodating is a preferred style of dealing with conflict in some cultures. In Japanese culture, for instance, it is thought to be more humble and face-saving to accommodate than to risk losing respect through conflict (Lulofs & Cahn, 2000, p. 114).

Forcing Forcing is resolving conflict by attempting to satisfy your own needs or advance your own ideas with no concern for the needs or ideas of others and no concern for the harm done to the relationship. Forcing can

forcing
resolving conflict by attempting to satisfy your own needs or advance your own ideas with no concern for the needs or ideas of others and no concern for the harm done to the relationship.

compromising
resolving conflict by both people altering their position so that the needs of both are partially met.

collaborating
using problem solving to address the needs and issues of each party and arrive at a solution that is mutually satisfying.

be done through physical threats, verbal attacks, coercion, or manipulation. If the other person accommodates, the conflict dies; if not, it escalates.

Forcing is uncooperative but assertive. Considered from an individual satisfaction standpoint, forcing is I win–you lose. Forcers demand their way with little regard to the cost borne by others.

From a relational satisfaction standpoint, forcing usually hurts a relationship. Because of this, forcing is only appropriate when the issue is very important and the relationship is not. It is also a preferred style in emergencies when quick and decisive action must be taken to ensure safety or to minimize harm.

Compromising   Compromising is resolving conflict by both people altering their position so that the needs of both are partially met. Under this approach both people have to give up part of what they really want or believe, or have to trade one thing they want in order to get something else. Compromising is partially cooperative and partially assertive.

From a personal satisfaction standpoint, compromising creates a lose-lose situation, because both people in a sense "lose" even as they "win."

From a relational satisfaction standpoint, compromise may be seen as neutral to positive, because both parties gain some satisfaction.

Although compromising is a popular style, there are significant problems associated with it. One problem of special concern in compromising is that the quality of a decision is affected if one of the parties "trades away" a better solution to effect the compromise. Compromise is appropriate when the relationship is very important, the issues have no simple solution, and both people have strong interests in some parts of the issue.

Collaborating   Collaborating is using problem solving to address the needs and issues of each party and arrive at a solution that is mutually satisfying. During collaboration people treat their disagreement as a problem to be resolved, and they discuss the issues and their feelings about the issues and identify the characteristics that are important for them to find in a solution.

Collaborating is both cooperative and assertive. Thus from an individual satisfaction standpoint, collaboration is win-win because the conflict is resolved to the satisfaction of all.

From a relational satisfaction standpoint, collaboration is positive because both sides feel that they have been heard. They get to share ideas and weigh and consider information. In effect, collaboration proves to be the most appropriate and the most effective means of managing conflict.

In the Spotlight on Scholars feature, you can see how the research of Daniel Canary has validated the importance of both appropriateness and effectiveness in conflict management.

Spotlight on Scholars ▷ Daniel J. Canary

Professor of Communication, ◆ ◆ ◆
Hugh Downs School of Human ◆ ◆ ◆
Communication, Arizona State
University, on Conflict Management

Dan Canary, citing the personal benefit in studying conflict, stated, "I learned how to control my own behavior and become more effective in my personal relationships." Canary's initial curiosity about effective conflict management behaviors was piqued when he was in graduate school at the University of Southern California. At the time, he was a classmate of Brian Spitzberg, who formulated the theory that relational competence is a product of behaviors that are both appropriate and effective, and Bill Cupach, who was studying conflict in relationships. Although Canary saw the connection between their work, it was several years later—after he experienced successful and unsuccessful resolutions of significant conflict episodes in his personal life—that he began in earnest to study how the way people behave during conflict episodes affects their relationships.

Scholars can become well-known by developing a new theory that more clearly describes what really happens when we interact, by carrying out a series of research studies that test and elaborate on the theories developed by others, or by organizing, integrating, and synthesizing the theories and research work that has been done in an area so that people who are not specialists in the particular area can better understand what is known. Dan Canary's reputation has been made in both of the latter types of scholarship.

Canary's research studies are helping to identify the behaviors that lead to perceiving a person as a competent conflict manager. Although people will view some of the communication behaviors to manage conflict as appropriate and some behaviors as effective, Canary argues that both are necessary to be perceived as competent. Drawing on Spitzberg's competence theory, Canary's research studies are designed to identify conflict behaviors that accomplish both of the goals of appropriateness and effectiveness. The results of his studies consistently show that integrative conflict strategies—problem-solving, collaborating, and compromising approaches

that display a desire to work with the other person—are perceived to be both appropriate and effective (that is, competent). Furthermore, his studies have shown that when one partner in a relationship is thought to be a competent conflict manager, the other one trusts him or her more, is more satisfied with the relationship, and perceives the relationship to be more intimate.

His research studies identify specific conflict management behaviors that are viewed as appropriate or effective. Canary has found that when a person acknowledges the arguments of others (for example, "Uh huh, I can see how you would think that") and when a person agrees with the arguments that others make to support their points (for example, "Gee that's a good point that I hadn't really thought about") the person is viewed as having appropriately handled the conflict. To be viewed as effective, however, requires a different set of behaviors.

According to Canary's findings, conflict handling behaviors that are viewed to be effective include stating complete arguments, elaborating and justifying one's point of view, and clearly developing one's ideas. In a conflict situation, Canary noticed that what was viewed as appropriate alone had the potential to be ineffective because appropriate behaviors seemed to involve some sort of agreement with the other person.

Canary reasoned that there must be ways to be both appropriate and effective in conflict situations. This led him to consider methods of sequencing, or ordering, messages in a conflict episode. His preliminary results have revealed that competent communicators (those perceived to be both appropriate and effective) will begin by acknowledging the other's viewpoint or agreeing with part of the other's argument, *before* explaining, justifying, and arguing for their own viewpoint. In using this sequence, Canary believes competent communicators help "frame" the interaction as one of cooperative problem solving rather than as one of competing interests wherein only one party can "win."

Many of Canary's major contributions to the study of conflict in personal relationships are included in two books: *Relationship Conflict* (coauthored with William Cupach and Susan Messman) is a synthesis of the diverse conflict literature that was written for graduate students and other scholars; *Competence in Interpersonal Conflict* (coauthored with Cupach) focuses on how readers can increase their competence at managing interpersonal conflict in a variety of settings. For complete citations of these and other Canary publications, see the references list at the end of this book.

Canary teaches courses in interpersonal communication, conflict management, and research methods. His research involves a quickly applied conflict rating system that people can use to observe conflict in an efficient yet valid way.

Resolving Conflicts through Collaboration

During a conflict episode, one person initiates the conflict, and the other person responds to it. Whether you initiate or respond to conflict, you can practice collaboration through specific communication skills and verbal strategies. In this section, we describe how to initiate conflict and how to respond to conflicts initiated by others.

Skills for Initiating Conflict

Many people avoid conflict because they do not know how to initiate a conflict conversation effectively. The following guidelines for initiating conflict (as well as those for responding to conflict in the next section) are based on work from several fields of study (Adler, 1977; Gordon, 1971; Whetten & Cameron, 2002).

1. **Recognize and state ownership of the apparent problem.** Collaboration seeks to resolve a problem, so the first step is to identify and own the problem. It's your problem—at this time the other person may not be aware that you are at odds. If you are trying to study for a test in your most difficult course and the person next door is playing the stereo so loud that you can't concentrate, it is important to acknowledge that you are the one who is distracted. So, when you approach your neighbor, you might say something like "Hi, I'm having a problem that I need your help with. I'm trying to study for a midterm in a really tough class. . . ." rather than "Your stereo's too loud. Turn it down. I need to study."

2. **Describe the conflict issue in terms of behavior, consequences, and feelings.** The behavior, consequences, and feelings (b-c-f) sequence is a

specific order for communicating your concerns: "When a specific behavior(s) happen(s), the specific consequences result, and I feel (a certain way)" (Gordon, 1971). When you include these three parts, the other person has more information from which to understand the situation. The b-c-f sequence uses skills we discussed earlier: owning ideas and feelings, describing behavior, and describing feelings.

So, in the example of the loud stereo, you might follow up on the opening by saying: "When I hear your stereo [b], I get distracted and can't concentrate on studying [c], and then I get frustrated and annoyed [f]."

Let's review: *The loudness of the stereo* is the behavior (b) you observe that has consequences. *I get distracted and can't concentrate on studying* are the consequences (c) that result from this behavior. *I get frustrated and annoyed* are the feelings (f) you experience.

3. **Avoid evaluating the other person's motives.** Evaluative language leads to defensiveness. Be careful not to accuse or distort what others have done. In most cases they are not intentionally trying to thwart you; they are simply trying to meet their own needs. Your neighbor doesn't know you're studying. He or she is just trying to enjoy the music. So, don't escalate conflict with evaluative statements.

4. **Phrase your preferred solution in a way that focuses on common ground.** Once you have been understood and you understand the other's position, make your suggestion for resolution. This suggestion is more likely to be accepted if you can tie it to a shared value, common interest, or shared constraint. In our example you might say, "I think we both have had times when even little things get in the way of our being able to study. So even though I realize I'm asking you for a special favor, I hope you can help me out by turning down your stereo while I'm grinding through this material." In short, the better you are at initiating conflict appropriately the more likely you will get a beneficial outcome.

©1995 Baby Blues Partnership. Distributed by King Features Syndicate. Reprinted with special permission of King Features Syndicate, Inc.

Skill Builders

Describing Behavior, Consequences, and Feelings (b-c-f)

Skill	Use	Procedure	Example
Describing the basis of a conflict in terms of behavior, consequences, and feelings (b-c-f).	To help the other person understand the problem completely.	1. Own the message. 2. Describe the behavior that you see or hear. 3. Describe the consequences that result.	Jason says, "I have a problem that I need your help with. When I tell you what I'm thinking and you don't respond (b), I start to think you don't care about me or what I think (c), and this causes me to get very angry with you (f)."

5. **Mentally rehearse what you will say before you confront the other person, so that your request will be brief and precise.** Initiating a collaborative conflict conversation requires us to be in control of our emotions. Yet, by nature and despite our good intentions of keeping on track, our emotions can get the better of us, and in the heat of the moment we may say things we shouldn't or go on and on and annoy the other person.

Before you go charging over to your neighbor's room, think to yourself, "What am I going to say?" Take a minute to practice. Say to yourself, "I need to own the problem and then follow the b-c-f sequence." Then mentally rehearse a few statements until you think you can do it when your neighbor comes to the door.

Test Your Competence

Using the B-C-F Sequence

Rephrase each of these conflict messages into a statement that uses the b-c-f sequence of describing behavior, consequences, and feelings.

1. I'm sick and tired of picking up after you. I'm not your maid. I can't go on living in a mess. So either clean up or get out!

2. I'm not going to sit here and let you trash my best friend. Who do you think you are anyway?

3. It figures you would say something like that; you're just a racist.

4. I can't believe you asked someone over for dinner at the last minute without asking me. That's so inconsiderate!

5. You ran up the charge card bill this month. Do you think we're made of money? If you don't stop spending, we're going to go bankrupt!

 You can complete this activity online and compare your answers to the authors'. Use your Communicate! CD-ROM to access Skill Learning Activity 8.6.

Responding to Conflict Effectively

It is more difficult to create a collaborative climate when responding to conflict initiated by another, because it is easy to become defensive if the person does not initiate the conflict effectively. Most initiators are not skilled. To introduce a collaborative environment, use the following guidelines.

1. **Disengage.** If the initiator is aggressively forcing, put your emotional "shields up." When the Enterprise is about to be attacked or has just been fired upon, *Star Trek* buffs know that the captain shouts "Shields up!" With its shields in place the ship is somewhat protected from the enemy's fire, and the captain and crew are able to continue to function normally while they consider their strategy.

   We also need to learn to mentally put our shields up when someone becomes overly aggressive in initiating a conflict. Consciously creating a mental barrier gives you time to disengage emotionally so you can listen and retain your problem-solving ability. Remember, the other person has a problem—not you—but you may be able to help him or her.

2. **Respond empathically with genuine interest and concern.** When someone initiates a conflict inappropriately, that person is still watching you closely to see how you react. Even if you disagree with the complaint, you can demonstrate empathy for the person's feelings. Sometimes you can do this by allowing others to vent their emotions while you listen. Only when someone has calmed down can you begin to problem solve. In our example, you might well start by saying, "I can see you're angry. Tell me about it."

3. **Paraphrase your understanding of the problem and ask questions to clarify issues.** Because most people are unaware of the b-c-f sequence, you may want to form a paraphrase that captures your understanding of b-c-f issues or ask questions to elicit this information. For instance, let's suppose the person says, "What in the world are you thinking?" If information is missing, as with this initiating statement, then you can ask questions that reflect the b-c-f framework: "Is it the volume of the music or the type of music that is distracting?" "So, you were studying all right before I turned on my music?" "Are you angry with me or frustrated by your inability to concentrate—or is something else going on?" Sometimes people initiate a conflict episode on minor issues when what really needs to be considered has not been mentioned.

4. **Seek common ground by finding some aspect of the complaint to agree with.** This does not mean giving in to the other person. Nor does it mean that you should feign agreement on a point that you do not agree with. However, using your skills of supportiveness, you can look for points with which you can agree (Adler, 1977).

   So, in our example "Your loud music is making it hard for me to study this difficult material for the exam" you have several options. You could agree in part: "I agree it's hard to study difficult material." You could agree in principle: "I agree it's best to study in a quiet place." You could agree

Observe&Analyze

Correcting Conflict Failures

Describe a recent conflict you experienced in which the conflict was not successfully resolved (your needs or those of your partner's were unmet, or the relationship was damaged). From memory, write a script of the conversation. Analyze what happened using the concepts you have just studied. What type of conflict was this? What conflict styles were used? What guidelines for collaboration were violated? Imagine that you could redo the conversation using the guidelines for collaboration. Write a script that reflects what might have happened had you been collaborative. Would this outcome have been more satisfying?

 You can complete this activity online and, if requested, email it to your instructor. Use your Communicate! CD-ROM to access Skill Learning Activity 8.7.

with the initiator's perception: "I can see that you are finding it difficult to study with music in the background." Or you could agree with the person's feelings: "It's obvious that you're frustrated and annoyed."

You do not need to agree with the initiator's conclusions or evaluations. You need not concede. But by agreeing to some aspect of the complaint, you create common ground from which a problem-solving discussion can proceed.

5. **Ask the initiator to suggest alternative solutions.** As soon as you are sure that you both have agreed on what the problem is, ask the initiator for alternative ways to resolve the conflict. The initiator has probably spent time thinking about what needs to be done, and your request for alternatives signals a willingness to listen and cooperate. You may find that one of the suggestions seems reasonable to you. If none are, you may be able to craft an alternative that builds on one of the ideas presented. In any case, asking for suggestions communicates your trust in the other person and strengthens the problem-solving climate.

Learning from Conflict Management Failures

Ideally, you want to resolve conflicts as they occur. Nevertheless, there will be times when no matter how hard both persons try, they will not be able to resolve the conflict.

Especially when the relationship is important to you, take the time to analyze your inability to resolve the conflict. Ask yourself these questions: "Where did things go wrong?" "Did one or more of us become evaluative?" "Did I use a style that was inappropriate to the situation?" "Did we fail to implement the problem-solving method adequately?" "Were the vested interests in the outcome too great?" "Am I failing to use such basic communication skills as paraphrasing, describing feelings, and perception checking?" "Did I fall back on what Turk and Monahan (1999, p. 232) label 'repetitive non-optimal behaviors'—verbal abuse, dishonest replies, or sarcasm—automatically when I became angry?"

By taking time to analyze your behavior, you put yourself in a better position to act more successfully in the next conflict episode you experience. Conflict is inevitable; you can count on having opportunities to use this knowledge again.

What Would You Do?   A QUESTION OF ETHICS

Sally and Ed had been seeing each other for more than three years when Ed moved 150 miles away to attend college. When he left, they promised to continue to see each other and agreed that should either of them want to start seeing someone else they would tell the other person before doing so.

During the first five months that Ed was away, Sally became friendly with Jamie, a coworker at the child care center on the campus of the local junior college. Jamie had a great sense of humor, and during working hours he and Sally would often tease each other to the point that other coworkers accused them of flirting. On several occasions they had dinner together before their night class, usually on Jamie's request, and on a couple of the weekends that Ed hadn't come home, they had seen a movie together. As time went on, it became apparent to Sally that Jamie's interest in her was going beyond the point of just being friends. Because she didn't want to risk losing his companionship, Sally had never mentioned Ed.

On Friday of that week, just as Sally and Jamie were about to leave the childcare center and head for a movie, the door swung open and in walked Ed. Sally hadn't been expecting him, but she took one look at him, broke into a big smile, and ran over and gave him a warm embrace. Too absorbed with her own excitement, Sally didn't even notice Jamie's shock and disappointment. She quickly introduced Ed to Jamie and then casually said to Jamie, "See you Monday!" and left with Ed.

That weekend, Ed confessed that he wanted to end their relationship. He had gone out with a woman who lived down the hall from him in his dorm a couple of times and saw the relationship blossoming. Sally was outraged. She accused Ed of acting dishonestly by violating their agreement about seeing other people and told him that he had used her until he was secure at college. Their conversation continued to go downhill, and eventually Ed left.

On Monday, when Sally saw Jamie at work, he was very aloof and curt. She asked him if he wanted to get a bite to eat before class and was genuinely surprised when he answered with an abrupt "No." As she ate alone, she pondered her behavior and wondered if and how she could ever rectify her relationship with Jamie.

1. Sort out the ethical issues in this case. Under which ethical guidelines would Sally's, Ed's, and Jamie's actions be considered ethical or unethical?

2. Using guidelines from this chapter, role-play different key moments in this scenario, changing them to improve the communication ethics and outcome of the situation.

Conversation and Analysis

Use your Communicate! CD-ROM to access the video clip of Jan and Ken's conversation. Click on the "In Action" icon in the menu at left, then click on "Conversation Menu" in the menu bar at the top of the screen. Select "Jan and Ken Overview" to watch the video (it takes a minute for the video to load). As you watch Jan and Ken talk, focus on how the nature of their relationship influences their interaction. What does each person do to help maintain the relationship? How does each person handle this conflict? How well does each person listen to the other? Are Jan and Ken appropriately assertive? Notice how well each provides feedback and describes feelings. You can respond to these analysis questions by clicking on "Analysis" in the menu bar at the top of the screen. When you've answered all the questions, click "Done" to compare your answers to those provided by the authors.

A transcript of the conversation is printed here. You can also find a copy of this transcript online, which allows you to take notes as you watch the video. Use your Communicate! CD-ROM to access

Jason Harris/© Thomson Higher Education

Skill Learning Activity 8.8 at the Communicate! Web site. When you have finished viewing the video and taking notes, click on "Authors' Model Analysis" to compare your notes to the detailed conversational analysis provided by the authors.

Jan and Ken are in their early to middle twenties. They meet at Jan's apartment. Jan and Ken have been good friends for most of their lives. But because of what she said last week, Ken believes Jan has betrayed their friendship.

Conversation

KEN: Jan, we need to talk. Why'd you tell Shannon about what happened between Katie and me? Now Shannon doesn't want to talk to me.

JAN [*Silent for a moment as she realizes he knows*]: Ken, I'm sorry, I didn't mean to tell her. It just kind of slipped out when we were talking.

KEN: Sorry? Sorry is not enough. I told you that in private, and you promised that you'd keep it just between you and me.

JAN: Ken, I told her that long before the two of you started dating. You know, Shannon and I, we've been friends for a long time. We were just talking about guys and cheating and stuff. It wasn't about you specifically.

KEN: It wasn't about me? It was totally about me. You had no right to tell anyone that, under any circumstances. Now Shannon doesn't trust me. She thinks I'm a lowlife that sleeps around.

JAN: Well, I'm sorry, but the two of you weren't even dating yet.

KEN: Oh, that's irrelevant. You know, it would be irrelevant even if Shannon and I weren't dating. But, you know, the point is I thought I could trust you and tell you anything and that it would go no further.

JAN: Yeah, like the time I told you I was thinking about dropping out of school for a semester and you just happened to tell my dad?

KEN: Ah, that's not the same thing.

JAN: You know what, it's *exactly* the same. I trusted you and you squealed. My dad lit into me big-time. He should have never known I was thinking about that. I trusted you, and you betrayed me.

KEN: Well look, I was just trying to look out for you. I knew you were making a big mistake, and I was just trying to stop you. And besides, you know I was right! [*Gets discouraged*] Don't change the subject here. Are you saying that your telling Shannon is some sort of payback for me telling your dad?

JAN: No, I'm just trying to point out that you've got no right to throw stones!

KEN: You know what? Then maybe neither of us can trust the other. Maybe we just shouldn't tell each other anything that we don't want broadcast to the world, huh?

Jason Harris/© Thomson Higher Education

JAN: Don't be such a jerk. I'm sorry, OK?

KEN: Well, that's not good enough. You ruined any chance I had with her.

JAN: Are you saying that something I said about what you did a long time ago is ruining your chances?

KEN: Yeah, it might.

JAN: Ken, if she truly valued your friendship, something that you did a long time ago shouldn't matter.

KEN: Well, maybe you're right.

JAN: Look, I said I'm sorry, and I meant it. I'm also sorry about, you know, throwing in what you told my dad. I know that wasn't fair, but you know, you really hurt my feelings when you blew up at me like that.

KEN: Listen, listen, I shouldn't have, I shouldn't have told your dad. I should have probably encouraged you to talk to him. We still friends?

Summary

Interpersonal communication helps develop and maintain relationships. A good relationship is any mutually satisfying interaction with another person.

We have three types of relationships. Acquaintances are people we know by name and talk with, but with whom our interactions are limited in quality and quantity. Friendships are marked by degrees of warmth and affection, trust, self-disclosure, commitment, and expectation that the relationships will endure. Close or intimate friends are those with whom we share our deepest feelings, spend a lot of time, or mark the relationship in some special way.

A healthy relationship is marked by a balance of self-disclosure and feedback. The Johari window is a tool for analyzing this balance.

The life cycle of a relationship includes starting or building, stabilizing, and ending. In the starting or building stage, people strike up a conversation, keep the conversation going, and move to more intimate levels. People nurture relationships through the skills of describing, openness, tentativeness, and equality. Many relationships end. We may terminate them in interpersonally sound ways or in ways that destroy our chances to continue the relationship on any meaningful level.

Many people develop relationships on the Internet through chat rooms and email. Electronically mediated relationships may be subject to anonymity and dishonesty. Addiction to the Internet can disrupt relationships.

A primary factor leading to termination of a relationship is failure to manage conflict successfully. We cope with conflicts in a variety of ways:

withdrawing, accommodating, forcing, compromising, and collaborating. When we are concerned about the long-term relationship, collaboration is often most appropriate.

When you have a problem with a person, initiate the conflict using basic communication skills. Own the problem; describe the basis of the conflict in terms of behavior, consequences, and feelings; plan what you will say ahead of time; avoid evaluating the other person's motives; phrase your request so that it focuses on common ground, and mentally rehearse what you will say.

When responding to another person's problem, put your shields up, respond empathically with genuine interest and concern, paraphrase your understanding of the problem, seek common ground, and ask the person to suggest alternatives.

Finally, learn from conflict management failures.

Communicate! Online

Now that you have read Chapter 8, use your Communicate! CD-ROM for quick access to the electronic resources that accompany this text. Your CD-ROM gives you access to the video of the conversation between Jan and Ken on pages 200–201, InfoTrac College Edition, and the Communicate! Web site. When you get to the Communicate! home page, click on "Student Book Companion Site" in the Resource box at the right to access the online study aids for this chapter, including a digital glossary, review quizzes, chapter activities, and chapter Web Resources.

Key Terms

At the Communicate! Web site, select the chapter resources for Chapter 8. Print a copy of the glossary for this chapter and test yourself with the electronic flash cards or complete the crossword puzzle to help you master these key terms:

relationships (176)
good relationships (176)
acquaintances (176)
friends (176)
trust (177)
close friends or intimates (177)
passive strategy (180)
active strategy (180)
interactive strategy (180)

idea-exchange messages (181)
gossip (181)
stabilization (182)
defensiveness (182)
speaking descriptively (183)
speaking openly (183)
speaking tentatively (183)
speaking as equals (183)
technological addictions (188)

interpersonal conflict (188)
withdraw (189)
mulling (189)
accommodating (190)
forcing (191)
compromising (192)
collaborating (192)

Review Quiz

Test your knowledge of the concepts in this chapter by taking the online quiz at the Communicate! Web site. Select the chapter resources for Chapter 8, then click on "Review Quiz." When you have completed the quiz, submit it for scoring.

Skill Learning Activities

Complete the Observe & Analyze, Test Your Competence, and Conversation and Analysis activities for Chapter 8 online at the Communicate! Web site. Select the chapter resources for Chapter 8, then click on "Activities." You can submit your Observe & Analyze answers to your instructor, compare your Test Your Competence answers to those provided by the authors, and do both for the Conversation and Analysis activity.

8.1: Observe & Analyze: Johari Window (180)
8.2: Observe & Analyze: Distinguishing between Types of Relationships (182)
8.3: Test Your Competence: Creating Stabilizing Statements (184)
8.4: Observe & Analyze: Advice on Cyber Relating (188)
8.5: Observe & Analyze: Your Conflict Profile (192)
8.6: Test Your Competence: Using the B-C-F Sequence (196)
8.7: Observe & Analyze: Correcting Conflict Failures (198)
8.8: Conversation and Analysis: Jan and Ken (199)

Web Resources

Access the Web Resources for this chapter online at the Communicate! Web site. Select the chapter resources for Chapter 8, then click on "Web Resources."

8.1: Stages in Healthy Romantic Relationships (178)
8.2: Johari Window Self-Test (180)
8.3: Networking (181)
8.4: In-Person versus Cyberspace Relationships (186)
8.5: The Bad Boys of Cyber Space (188)
8.6: Your Conflict Profile (192)

Jeff Cadge/Getty Images

After you have read this chapter, you should be able to answer these questions:

- What is an interview?
- What types of questions are used in an interview?
- What are the characteristics of open and closed, primary and secondary, and neutral and leading questions?
- How do you prepare for and conduct an information interview?
- How do you conduct a job interview?
- How should you prepare a résumé and cover letter so that you are likely to be chosen for a job interview?
- How should you prepare to be interviewed?
- Can you identify typical questions used by job interviewers?
- What can you do to follow up an interview?

9

Interviewing

"Ramsey, I've got a project for you."

"What is it?"

"Parker at City Hall called to tell me that the police are planning on expanding the experimental program in the Garden Projects, and he wants us to be the corporate sponsor."

"What's the Garden Project?"

"It's a community garden tended by residents and police officers. It's been successful in two housing projects in different parts of the city."

"Sounds interesting."

"Well, I want you to find out all you can about it. I want to know how well the experimental project has worked, what kind of outcome statistics are available, how the residents feel about the effectiveness of the program, and anything else you can think of."

"So you want me to do some research, maybe find some articles that explain . . ."

"Well, you might do that, but most of all I want you face to face with both officers and residents. Interview them and get the real story."

"Uh, well, uh . . . OK—I'll give it a shot."

nterviewing is a powerful method for collecting firsthand information that may be unavailable elsewhere, and it is an important interpersonal skill to master. Yet, as Ramsey's less than enthusiastic response suggests, many of us have little experience gaining information this way. An **interview** is a structured conversation where most of the time is spent with one person asking questions and the other person answering them. Unlike most interpersonal communication, interview participants usually prepare for the interview conversation.

We begin this chapter by describing interview planning, especially how good interview questions are constructed. Then we explain how to prepare for and conduct an interview where the goal is to gather information. Finally we discuss employment interviews from the perspective of both the interviewer and the interviewee.

interview
a structured conversation where most of the time is spent with one person asking questions and the other person answering them.

Questions Used in Interviewing

The success of any interview depends on preparing a list of good questions. Questions may ask about (1) behaviors (what a person has done or is doing), (2) demographics (such as age, education), (3) opinion or values, (4) knowledge (facts), (5) experiences, and (6) feelings. But regardless of content, an interview question list is likely to have a mix of open-ended and closed questions, which may be phrased neutrally or may be leading. Some questions will be primary and others secondary or follow-up questions.

Open versus Closed Questions

open questions
broad-based probes that call on the interviewee to provide perspective, ideas, information, feelings, or opinions as he or she answers the question.

Open questions are broad-based probes that call on the interviewee to provide perspective, ideas, information, feelings, or opinions as he or she answers the question. For example, in a job interview you might be asked "What one accomplishment has best prepared you for this job?" In a customer service interview a representative might ask "What seems to be the problem?" or "Can you tell me the steps you took when you first set this product up?" Interviewers ask open questions to encourage the person to talk, allowing the interviewer an opportunity to listen and to observe. Open questions take time to answer and give respondents more control, which means that interviewers can lose sight of their original purpose if they are not careful (Tengler & Jablin, 1983).

closed questions
narrowly focused questions that require the respondent to give very brief (one- or two-word) answers.

By contrast, **closed questions** are narrowly focused and require the respondent to give very brief (one- or two-word) answers. Closed questions range from those that can be answered "yes" or "no," such as "Have you had a course in marketing?" to those that require only a short answer, such as "Where did you buy the product?" By asking closed questions, interviewers can control the interview and obtain specific information quickly. The answers to closed questions cannot reveal the nuances behind responses, nor are they likely to capture the complexity of the story. Effective interview conversations contain a combination of open and closed questions such as those used in employment interviews.

Neutral versus Leading Questions

Open and closed questions may be either neutral or leading. **Neutral questions** do not direct a person's answer. "What can you tell me about your work with Habitat for Humanity?" or "What symptoms did you experience?" are both neutral questions. The neutral question gives the respondent free rein to answer the question without any knowledge of what the interviewer thinks or believes.

By contrast, **leading questions** guide respondents toward providing certain types of information and imply that the interviewer prefers one answer over another. "What do you like about working for Habitat for Humanity?" steers the respondent to describe only the positive aspects of the work. "Was this as painful as a migraine?" directs the answer by providing the standard for comparison. In most types of interviews, neutral questions are preferred.

neutral questions
questions that do not direct a person's answer.

leading questions
questions that guide respondents toward providing certain types of information and imply that the interviewer prefers one answer over another.

Primary versus Secondary Questions

Primary questions are the lead-in questions that introduce one of the major topics of the interview conversation. When planning interview questions, careful thought should be given so that the primary questions cover all of the major topic areas you hope to learn about during the conversation. **Secondary** or follow-up questions are designed to probe the answers given to primary questions. When a specific answer is expected, secondary questions may be preplanned, but usually they are spontaneously constructed in response to an answer to a primary question. Some follow-up questions encourage the person to continue ("And then?" "Is there more?"); some probe into what the person has said ("What does 'frequently' mean?" "What were you thinking at the time?"); and some probe the feelings of the person ("How did it feel to get the prize?" "Did it last longer than fifteen minutes?"). The major purpose of follow-up questions is to encourage the person to expand on an answer that seems incomplete or vague. Sometimes the person may not really understand how much detail you are looking for, and occasionally the person may be purposely trying to be evasive.

primary questions
lead-in questions that introduce one of the major topics of the interview conversation.

secondary or follow-up questions
questions designed to probe the answers given to primary questions.

Interviewing for Information

Interviewing can be a valuable method for obtaining information on nearly any topic. Students interview experts to obtain information for papers; lawyers and policemen interview witnesses to establish facts;

Test Your Competence

Open and Closed Questions

Indicate which of the following questions are open (O) and which are closed (C). If the question is open, write a closed question seeking similar information; if the question is closed, write an open question. Make sure your questions are neutral rather than leading.

___ 1. What leads you to believe that Sheldon will be appointed?

___ 2. How many steps are there in getting a book into print?

___ 3. Will you try out for the Shakespearean play this year?

___ 4. When are you getting married?

___ 5. Have you participated in the Garden Project?

 You can complete this activity online and compare your answers to the authors'. Use your Communicate! CD-ROM to access **Skill Learning Activity 9.1.**

health care providers interview patients to obtain medical histories before making diagnoses; reporters interview sources for their stories; social workers and sales representatives interview clients; and managers interview current and perspective employees. Interviews are more likely to achieve the desired result if they are carefully planned. Planning includes clearly defining the purpose of the interview, selecting the person (people) to interview, planning the interview protocol, and conducting the interview.

Defining the Purpose of the Interview

Informative interviews require a clear, identified purpose that can be summarized in one sentence. Without such a statement of purpose the interviewer's questions more than likely will have no direction, and the information derived from the interview may not fit together well. The purpose may be to obtain expert information, investigate a complaint, get the story of someone's experience, or evaluate someone.

Suppose you wanted to learn about the commercial food service business. Possible specific purposes would be:

1. To find out what criteria were used for selecting a commercial food service provider for this college.

2. To learn the most efficient means for setting up a cafeteria line.

3. To understand how dietitians create cost-effective menus that provide good nutrition.

Each of these topics covers an entirely different aspect of food service and will direct who you interview and the types of questions you prepare to ask.

Selecting the Best Person to Interview

In some situations it is obvious who is to be interviewed; at other times, locating the right person to interview can be a challenge, especially when you need expert answers. You may have to do research before you can identify the right people. Suppose your purpose is to learn how dietitians create cost-effective menus that provide good nutrition. You might begin by asking one of the food service workers at the campus dining hall for the name of the food service manager. Or you could find the manager by calling the student center. In any case, the manager could give you the name

Focus groups are marketing interviews with a group of consumers. What adjustments do you think an interviewer must make in a group versus a one-on-one interview?

and phone number (or email address) of the dietitian. Once you have identified the person or people to be interviewed, you need to contact them to make an appointment. Be sure to clearly state the purpose of the interview, how the interview information will be used, and how long you expect the interview to take. When setting a time and date, be flexible by suggesting several dates and time ranges.

You don't want to bother your interviewee with information you can get elsewhere. So to prepare appropriate questions, you will need to do some research on the topic. If, for instance, you are going to interview a dietitian, you will want to find out what a dietitian is and does. If your purpose is to understand how nutritious cost-effective menus are planned in an institutional setting, you can acquaint yourself with the current FDA nutritional standards and search for articles on cost factors in commercial food service operations. Not only will interviewees be more likely to enjoy talking with you if you're well informed, but familiarity will also enable you to ask better questions.

Developing the Interview Protocol

The heart of the interview plan is the **interview protocol,** an ordered list of questions that have been selected to meet the specific purpose of the interview. Preparation of the interview protocol begins by listing the topic areas to be covered in the interview. Once topics are listed, they need to be prioritized for importance. Figure 9.1 presents a list of topics for the interview with the dietitian.

interview protocol
an ordered list of questions that have been selected to meet the specific purpose of the interview.

Figure 9.1
Topics for an interview with
the dietician

- Demographic information
- Determining portion costs
- Understanding student food preferences
- Deciding on menus

For each topic a list of questions should be generated. Questions should be revised until they are a mixture of open and closed questions that are phrased neutrally. Figure 9.2 shows some questions that could be asked about the topic "Determining Portion Costs."

Once a complete question list has been generated, you will need to estimate how long it will take to ask and answer all of the questions. A rule-of-thumb is to allow four minutes for each open-ended question and one minute for each close-ended question. If your realistic guess exceeds the time you have allotted for the interview, cull your questions by eliminating some from each topic list and by severely trimming those from less important topics.

The final step in creating the interview protocol is to develop a sequence for the questions. Your initial questions should be short and designed to get the interviewee involved in the conversation. In general these opening questions should ask for facts. It is better to leave more complex or controversial questions until later after you have established rapport. Answering fact questions can be boring for the interviewee, so you might consider spreading these throughout the interview. It is usually easier for people to talk about things in the present than it is for them to remember things in the past or to hypothesize about the future, so begin by asking about current practices or events, then work backward or forward. Be sure to place topics of great importance early in the interview so that you have plenty of time for follow-up questions.

When you have finalized your interview protocol, reproduce it leaving enough space between your questions for you to take complete notes of the answers.

Figure 9.2
Questions to determine
portion costs

- Do you know the cost of each portion of all items?
- How are portion costs determined?
- Do you have a budget for each meal plan serving?
- Suppose you'd planned a menu and it turned out to be more expensive than you anticipated, what would happen?
- How important is portion control?
- What are some of the less expensive foods you use that are both nutritious and tasty?

Conducting the Interview

By applying the interpersonal skills we have discussed in this book, you'll find that you can turn your careful planning into an excellent interview.

First, of course, you will want to be courteous during the interview. Start by thanking the person for taking the time to talk to you. Remember, although the interviewee may enjoy talking about the subject, may be flattered, and may wish to share knowledge, that person has nothing to gain from the interview. Encourage the person to speak freely. Most of all, respect what the person says regardless of what you may think of the answers.

Second, listen carefully. At key places in the interview you should paraphrase what the person has said to assure yourself that you really understand him or her.

Third, keep the interview moving. You do not want to rush the person, but you do want to get your questions answered during the allotted time.

Fourth, make sure that your nonverbal reactions—your facial expressions and your gestures—are in keeping with the tone you want to communicate. Maintain good eye contact with the person. Nod to show understanding, and smile occasionally to maintain the friendliness of the interview. How you look and act is likely to determine whether the person will warm up to you and give you an informative interview.

Finally, if you are going to publish the substance of the interview, be sure to get written permission for exact quotes, as a courtesy, offer to let the person see a copy of the article (or at least tell the person exactly when it will be published). Under some circumstances you may want to show the person a draft of your report of the interview before it goes into print if only to double-check the accuracy of direct quotations. If so, provide a draft well before the deadline to give him or her the opportunity to read it and to give you time to deal with any suggestions. At times you may wish to conduct an electronic interview using email. To read some useful tips for these types of interviews, use your Communicate! CD-ROM to access Web Resource 9.1: Email Interviews.

Conducting Employment Interviews

Almost all organizations use interviewing as part of their hiring process. Employment interviews help organizations assess which applicants have the knowledge, experience, and skills to do a job and which applicants will "fit" into the organization's culture. Interviews allow organizations to evaluate personal characteristics (such as ambition, energy, and enthusiasm) and interpersonal skills (such as conversing and listening) that cannot be judged from a résumé.

Historically, most employment interviewing was done by human resource professionals or managers, but today organizations are using coworkers as interviewers. You may have already helped to conduct employment interviews, or you may be asked to do so in the near future.

Preparing for the Interview

As with information interviews, preparation begins by doing research. In the case of employment interviewing, this means becoming familiar with the knowledge, skills, and aptitudes that someone must have to be successful in the job. It also means studying the résumés, references, and, if available, the test scores for each person you will interview.

In most employment interviewing situations you will be seeing several candidates. You will want to make sure that all applicants are asked the same (or very similar) questions and that the questions selected allow applicants to disclose information you will need to know to make an informed hiring decision. To accomplish this, you will want to use a highly to moderately structured interview. This means that you will prepare a general interview protocol to use with all interviewees. Your protocol should have questions designed to probe the interviewees' knowledge, skills, and experiences that are relevant to the job. For potential queries, use your Communicate! CD-ROM to access Web Resource 9.2: 109 Typical Job Interview Questions.

It is important that you avoid questions that violate fair employment practice legislation. The Equal Opportunity Commission has detailed guidelines that spell out what questions are unlawful. To read a generalized discussion of the types of questions that should not be asked in interviews, use your Communicate! CD-ROM to access Web Resource 9.3: Discrimination Laws and Interviewing.

Conducting the Interview

A well-planned employment interview is carefully orchestrated. It has an introduction designed to establish rapport and help the interviewee relax. As the interviewer, you should warmly greet the applicant by name, shake hands, and introduce yourself. If you will be taking notes or recording the interview, you should explain that to the candidate. During the early part of the interview, you will want to "feel out" the applicant. If the applicant is extremely nervous, you may want to ask a couple of "warm-up" questions designed to put the applicant at ease. If the applicant seems comfortable, you may move directly into the body of the interview using the interview protocol.

In the body, or main part of the interview, candidates are carefully questioned to determine whether their knowledge, skills, experiences, personal characteristics, and interpersonal style fits with the demands of the job and with the organizational culture. During this period it is important for you, the interviewer, to keep the interview moving. You will want to give applicants sufficient time to answer your questions, but you don't want to waste time by allowing applicants to over answer questions. One way to help applicants understand the scope of the interview is to preview each of the topic areas to be covered and the time you expect to spend in this conversation.

As you ask the questions, strive to sound spontaneous and to speak in a voice that is easily heard. Be sensitive to the nonverbal messages you are sending. Be careful that you are not "leading" applicants through nonverbal cues. Use follow-up questions to probe answers that are vague. Remember, your goal is to understand the applicant.

Jason Harris;/©Thomson Higher Education

Early in the interview the interviewer should establish rapport. In addition to a welcoming greeting, what other methods have interviewers used to put you at ease?

As the interview comes to an end, tell the applicant what will happen next. Explain how and approximately when the hiring decision will be made, and how the applicant will be notified. Unless you are the person with hiring authority, remain neutral about the candidate. You don't want to mislead the candidate with false hope or discouragement.

Interviewing to Get a Job

Because most organizations use interviews as part of their selection process, you have probably already been an interviewee and know how stressful interviews can be. In this section, we describe strategies and tactics you can use to make your next job search less stressful.

Getting the Interview

Because interviewing is time consuming, most organizations do not interview all the people who apply for a job. Rather, they use a variety of screening devices to eliminate people who don't meet their qualifications. Chief among these are evaluating the qualifications presented on the résumé and in the cover letter. The goal of your résumé and cover letter "is to communicate your qualifications in writing and sell yourself to prospective employers" (Kaplan, 2002, p. 6).

It all begins with research To write an effective cover letter and résumé that highlights your qualifications for a particular job, you need to know something about the job requirements and about the company. The career center advisers at your college or university can assist you with your research. Or use your Communicate! CD-ROM to access Web Resource 9.4: Research Before You Write, which links you to additional sources of information on various companies.

cover letter
a short, well-written letter expressing your interest in a particular job.

Write an effective cover letter A **cover letter** is a short, well-written letter expressing your interest in a particular job. It should include how you learned of the opening, why you are interested in the company, and highlight your skills and experiences that demonstrate how you fit the requirements of the position. In addition, it should directly ask for an opportunity to interview for the position. To learn more about how to write effective cover letters, read "Quick Take Cover," available through InfoTrac College Edition. Use your Communicate! CD-ROM to access Web Resource 9.5: Quick Take Cover. You can also access Web Resource 9.6: Cover Letter Don'ts to find a list of several cover letter faux pas that you will want to avoid.

résumé
a written summary of your skills and accomplishments.

Prepare a professional résumé The **résumé** is a summary of your skills and accomplishments and is your "silent sales representative" (Stewart & Cash, 2000, p. 274). Although there is no universal format for résumé writing, there is some agreement on what should be included. The following information should be included:

1. **Contact information:** Information including your name, addresses (current and permanent), telephone numbers, and email address.

2. **Career Objective:** A one-sentence objective focusing on your job search goals. To read more about formulating career objective statements, use your Communicate! CD-ROM to access Web Resource 9.7: What Is Your Objective?

3. **Employment History:** List of your paid and unpaid experiences beginning with the most recent. List the name and address of the organization, your employment dates, your title, key duties, and noteworthy accomplishments.

4. **Education:** List the names and addresses of the schools you have attended (including specialized military schools), the degrees or certificates earned (or expected), and the dates of attendance and graduation. Also list academic honors received with degrees or certificates.

5. **Relevant professional affiliations:** List the names of the organizations, dates of membership, and any offices held.

6. **Military background:** List branch and dates of service, last rank held, significant commendations, and discharge status.

7. **Special Skills:** List language fluencies, computer expertise, and so forth.

8. **Community Service:** List significant involvement in community service organizations, clubs, and other volunteer efforts.

9. **References:** List or have available the names, addresses, email addresses, and phone numbers of at least three people who will speak well of your ability, your work product, and your character.

Format your résumé so that it is easy to read and highlights your accomplishments. Make sure the résumé is short. If you haven't had much experience, one page is ideal. But regardless of your experience, limit your résumé to three pages at most. Carefully proofread your résumé so that it is error free, then reproduce it on high-quality paper stock. To read about—and avoid—the top twenty résumé pet peeves identified by 2,500 recruiters, use your Communicate! CD-ROM to access Web Resource 9.8: Résumé Pet Peeves.

Figure 9.3 and Figure 9.4 display a sample cover letter and a sample résumé for a recent college graduate.

Electronic cover letters and résumés

Electronic cover letters and résumés are sent online. Electronic résumés have become quite popular with employers and job seekers. For example, from 1995 to 1999 the number of résumés that were received electronically by Microsoft increased from 5 percent to 50 percent (Criscito, 2000, p. 2). Employers like electronic résumés because they can sift through large numbers looking only for particular qualifications or characteristics. Candidates like electronic résumés because they can send essentially the same materials online, saving time and money.

Although electronic cover letters and résumés contain the same content, they may differ in several ways (Schmidt & Conaway, 1999, pp. 98–99). Many of the differences take into account the fact that they will be scanned electronically. Thus, it is wise to avoid such things as boldface, italics, and bullet points because they will "only confuse computerized word searches or interfere with the scanning process" (p. 98). The most important thing to remember for a scannable or email résumé is to keep the format simple.

electronic cover letters and résumés
these contain the same information as traditional cover letters and résumés but are sent online.

Test Your Competence

Résumé and Cover Letter

Read the help wanted ads in your local newspaper until you locate a job you would enjoy. Write a résumé and cover letter applying for this position. To link you to an online résumé service to draft and print your résumé, use your Communicate!

CD-ROM to access Web Resource 9.9: Résumé Builder.

You can complete this activity online and, if requested, submit it to your instructor. Use your Communicate! CD-ROM to access Skill Learning Activity 9.4.

2326 Tower Place
Cincinnati, OH 45220
April 8, 2004

Mr. Kyle Jones
Acme Marketing Research Associates
P.O. Box 482
Cincinnati, OH 45201

Dear Mr. Jones:

I am applying for the position of first-year associate at
Acme Marketing Research Associates, which I learned about
through the Office of Career Counseling at the University of
Cincinnati. I am a senior mathematics major at the University
of Cincinnati who is interested in pursuing a career in marketing research. I am highly motivated, eager to learn, and I
enjoy working with all types of people. I am excited by the
prospect of working for a firm like Acme Marketing Research
Associates where I can apply my leadership and problem-
solving skills in a professional setting.

As a mathematics major, I have developed the analytical proficiency that is necessary for working through complex problems.
My courses in statistics have especially prepared me for data
analysis, and my more theoretical courses have taught me how
to construct an effective argument. My leadership training and
opportunities have given me the ability to work effectively in
groups and have taught me the benefits of both individual and
group problem solving. My work on the Strategic Planning
Committee has given me an introduction to market analysis
by teaching me skills associated with strategic planning.
Finally, from my theatrical experience, I have gained the
poise to make presentations in front of small and large groups
alike. I believe these experiences and others have shaped who
I am and have helped me to develop many of the skills necessary to be successful. I am interested in learning more and
continuing to grow.

I look forward to having the opportunity to interview with
you in the future. I have enclosed my résumé with my school
address and phone number. Thank you for your consideration.
I hope to hear from you soon.

Sincerely,

Elisa C. Vardin

Figure 9.3
Sample cover letter

Elisa C. Vardin

2326 Tower Avenue
Cincinnati, Ohio 45220
Phone: (513) 861-2497
Email: ElisVardin@UC.edu

PROFESSIONAL OBJECTIVE

To use my intellectual abilities, quantitative capabilities, communication skills, and proven leadership to further the mission of a high-integrity marketing research organization.

EDUCATIONAL BACKGROUND

UNIVERSITY OF CINCINNATI, Cincinnati, OH, B.A. in Mathematics June 2004. GPA 3.36. Dean's List.

NATIONAL THEATER INSTITUTE at the Eugene O'Neill Theater Center, Waterford, CT. Fall 2002.
      Acting, Voice, Movement, Directing, and Playwriting.

WORK AND OTHER BUSINESS RELATED EXPERIENCE

REYNOLDS & DEWITT, Cincinnati, OH. Summer 2003. Intern at Brokerage/
      Investment Management Firm. Provided administrative support. Created new databases,
      performance comparisons, and fact sheets in Excel and Word files.

MUMMERS THEATRE GUILD, University of Cincinnati, Spring 2000–Spring 2003. Treasurer. Responsible
      for all financial/accounting functions for this undergraduate theater community.

SUMMERBRIDGE CINCINNATI, Cincinnati Country Day School, Cincinnati, OH. Summer 2002. Teacher in
      program for "at-risk" junior high students. Taught 7th grade mathematics, 6th and 7th grade
      speech communication, sign language; Academic advisor; Club leader. Organized five-hour
      diversity workshop and three-hour tension-reduction workshop for staff.

STRATEGIC PLANNING COMMITTEE, Summit Country Day School, Cincinnati, OH. Fall 1998–1999. One
      of two student members. Worked with the Board of Directors developing the first Strategic Plan
      for a 1,000-student independent school (Pre-K through 12).

AYF INTERNATIONAL LEADERSHIP CONFERENCE, Miniwanca Conference Center, Shelby, MI. Summer
      1999–2001. Participant in international student conference sponsored by American Youth
      Foundation.

PERSONAL
Musical Theater: lifetime involvement, including leads and choreography for several shows. A cappella
singing group, 2000–2003; Director 2002–2004. Swing Club 2002–2004, President and Teacher of
student dance club. Junior High Youth Group Leader, 2001. Math Tutor, 2002. Aerobics Instructor,
2002–2003. University of Cincinnati Choral Society, 2001–2004. American Sign Language Instructor,
Winter 2002, 2003.

TECHNICAL SKILLS AND TRAINING: SAS, SPSS, EXCEL, ACCESS, WORD. Univariate and
Multivariate Statistics (2 courses), Regression Analysis (2 courses).

REFERENCES: Available on request.

Figure 9.4
Sample résumé

There are three kinds of electronic résumés: the paper résumé that becomes an electronic version when it is scanned into a computer; an ASCII text emailable version (a generic computer file that you create especially to send through cyberspace); and a multimedia résumé that is given a home page at a fixed location on the Internet for anyone to visit (Criscito, 2000, p. 2).

A scanned résumé can be attached to an email and sent directly to a company's recruiters over the Internet. If you already have a paper résumé, scanning allows you to send the résumé without retyping it. A résumé that has been prepared, saved, and sent as a generic ASCII text file has the advantage of being able to be read by anyone regardless of the word processing software he or she is using (Criscito, 2000, p. 3). Such a document can be sent as a file to company recruiters or posted to the home page of a company, a job bank, or a newsgroup. Finally, when you post your résumé on a home page, you have dramatically increased the likelihood that someone who is seeking employees with your qualifications will see your résumé and inquire about your interest in their company. For more information on electronic résumés, use your Communicate! CD-ROM to access Web Resource 9.10: Monster.com's Résumé Dos & Don'ts. There you can read four articles that provide detailed information about electronic résumés: "Emailing Text Résumés," "A Scannable Résumé," "ACSII Questions," and "Applying Online FAQs."

Preparing to Be Interviewed

While the résumé and cover letter make you an attractive candidate for an employer, it is your behavior at the interview that will solidify your chances of receiving an offer. The following guidelines will help you prepare for the interview.

1. **Do your homework.** If you haven't yet done extensive research on the position and the company, do so before you go to the interview. Be sure you know the company's products and services, its areas of operation, ownership, and financial health. Nothing puts off interviewers more than applicants who arrive at an interview knowing little about the company.

2. **Based on your research, prepare a list of questions about the organization and the job.** The employment interview should be a two-way street where you size up the company as they are sizing you up. So you will probably have a number of specific questions to ask the interviewer. For example, "Can you describe a typical workday for the person in this position?" or "What is the biggest challenge in this job?" Make a list of your questions and take it with you to the interview.

3. **Rehearse the interview.** Several days before the interview spend time outlining the job requirements and how your knowledge, skills, and experiences meet those requirements. Practice answering questions

commonly asked in interviews, such as those listed in Figure 9.5 or those presented in Web Resource 9.2: 109 Typical Job Interview Questions. To sharpen your interviewing skills, answer sample questions, and receive help to improve your answers, use your Communicate! CD-ROM to access Web Resource 9.11: Virtual Interview.

4. **Dress appropriately.** You want to make a good first impression, so it is important to be well groomed and neatly dressed. Although "casual" or "business casual" is common in many workplaces, some organizations still expect employees to be more formally dressed. If you don't know the dress code for the organization, call the Human Resources Department and ask. Even when the dress code is casual, men should wear collared shirts (not golf or T-shirts), dress slacks, and a tie. In a business casual setting, a sport coat should be worn or carried. Men should be recently shaved with facial hair well groomed. Women should be conservatively attired in skirt and blouse or dress slacks or dress. Bare midriffs and low-cut necklines are not appropriate. If possible, body art should be covered and jewelry should be removed from piercings. Both men and women should wear leather shoes that are clean and polished.

5. **Plan to arrive on time.** The interview is the organization's first exposure to your work behavior, so you don't want to be late. Find out how long it will take you to travel by making a dry run several days before. Plan to arrive ten or fifteen minutes before your appointment.

6. **Bring supplies.** Gather and bring extra copies of your résumé, cover letter, and references as well as the list of questions you plan to ask. You will also want to have a writing tablet and pen so that you can make notes.

Behavior During the Interview

Interviewing can be stressful. Use these guidelines to help you put your best foot forward.

1. **Use active listening.** When we are anxious, we sometimes have trouble listening well. Work on attending, understanding, and remembering what is asked. Remember that the interviewer will be aware of your nonverbal behavior, so be sure to make and keep eye contact as you listen.

- In what ways does your transcript reflect your ability?
- Can you give an example of how you work under pressure?
- What are your major strengths? Weaknesses?
- Can you give an example of when you were a leader and what happened?
- What have you done that shows your creativity?
- What kind of position are you looking for?

Figure 9.5
Frequently asked interview questions

2. **Think before answering.** If you have prepared for the interview, you want to make sure that as you answer the questions posed you also tell your story. So take a moment to consider how your answer will portray your skills and experiences. "Tell me about yourself," is not an invitation to give the interviewer your life history. Rather, you can focus your answer on presenting your experiences and qualifications that are related to the job.

3. **Be enthusiastic.** If you come across as bored or disinterested, the interviewer is likely to conclude that you would be an unmotivated employee.

4. **Ask questions.** As the interview is winding down, be sure to ask the questions you prepared that have not already been answered. You may also want to ask how well the interviewer believes your qualifications match the position, and what your strengths are.

5. **Avoid discussing salary and benefits.** The time to discuss salary is when you are offered the job. If the interviewer tries to pin you down, simply say something like, "I'm really more interested in talking about how my experiences map onto you needs and would like to defer talking about salary until we know we have a match." Similarly, discussions of benefits are best held until an offer is made.

Active listening and enthusiasm are key to being an effective interviewee. What behaviors demonstrate enthusiasm in an interview?

Michael Newman/PhotoEdit

Conversation and Analysis

Use your Communicate! CD-ROM to access the video clip of Elliott Miller's job interview at Community Savings and Loan. Click on the "In Action" icon in the menu at left, then click on "Conversation Menu" in the menu bar at the top of the screen. Select "Elliot Miller Interview" to watch the video (it takes a minute for the video to load). As you watch the video, notice how well both Karen Bourne and Elliott Miller follow the guidelines for effective interviews. You can record your observations and respond to other analysis questions by clicking on "Analysis" in the menu bar at the top of the screen. When you've answered all the questions, click "Done" to compare your answers to those provided by the authors.

A transcript of the conversation is printed here. You can also find a copy of this transcript online, which allows you to take notes as you watch the video. Use your Communicate! CD-ROM to access Skill Learning Activity 9.5 at the Communicate! Web site. When you have finished viewing the video and taking notes, click on "Authors' Model Analysis" to compare your notes to the detailed conversational analysis provided by the authors.

Elliott Miller is a second-semester senior who has double-majored in business and communication. Today he is interviewing with Community Savings and Loan, which is recruiting managerial trainees. Elliott has dressed carefully. He has on his good charcoal suit, a light blue shirt, a conservative necktie, and wingtips. At 10 A.M. sharp he knocks on the office door of Karen Bourne, the person with whom he has an interview. She is in her mid-thirties and dressed in a conservative navy blue suit. She opens the door and offers her hand to Elliott.

Conversation

BOURNE: Mr. Miller, I see you're right on time. That's a good start. [*They shake hands.*]

MILLER: Thank you for inviting me to interview today.

BOURNE: Sit down. [*He sits in the chair in front of her desk; she sits behind the desk.*] So you're about to finish college are you? I remember that time in my own life—exciting and scary!

MILLER: It's definitely both for me. I'm particularly excited about the job here at Community Savings and Loan.

BOURNE [*Smiles*]: Then there's a mutual interest. We had a lot of applications, but we're interviewing only eight of them. What I'd like to do is get a sense of your interests and tell you about our managerial trainee program

Jason Harris/© Thomson Higher Education

here, so that we can see if the fit between us is as good as it looks on paper. Sound good to you?

MILLER: Great.

BOURNE: Let me start by telling you about a rather common problem we've had with our past managerial trainees. Many of them run into a problem—something they have trouble learning or doing right. That's normal enough—we expect that. But a lot of trainees seem to get derailed when that happens. Instead of finding another way to approach the problem, they get discouraged and give up. So I'm very interested in hearing what you've done when you've encountered problems or road blocks in your life.

MILLER: Well, I can remember one time when I hit a real road block. I was taking an advanced chemistry course, and I just couldn't seem to understand the material. I failed the first exam, even though I'd studied hard.

BOURNE: Good example of a problem. What did you do?

MILLER: I started going to all the tutorial sessions that grad assistants offer. That helped a little, but I still wasn't getting the material the way I should. So I organized a study team and offered to pay for pizzas so that students who were on top of the class would have a reason to come.

BOURNE [*Nodding with admiration*]: That shows a lot of initiative and creativity. Did the study team work?

MILLER [*Smiling*]: It sure did. I wound up getting a B in the course, and so did several other members of the study team who had been in the same boat I was in early in the semester.

BOURNE: So you don't mind asking for help if you need it?

MILLER: I'd rather do that than flounder, but I'm usually pretty able to operate independently.

BOURNE: So you prefer working on your own to working with others?

MILLER: That depends on the situation or project. If I have all that I need to do something on my own, I'm comfortable working solo. But there are other cases in which I don't have everything I need to do something well—maybe I don't have experience in some aspect of the job or I don't have a particular skill or I don't understand some perspectives on the issues. In cases like that, I think teams are more effective than individuals.

BOURNE: Good. Banking management requires the ability to be self-initiating and also the ability to work with others. Let me ask another question. As I was looking over your transcript and résumé, I noticed that you changed your major several times. Does that indicate you have difficulty making a commitment and sticking with it?

MILLER: I guess you could think that, but it really shows that I was willing to explore a lot of alternatives before making a firm commitment.

BOURNE: But don't you think that you wasted a lot of time and courses getting to that commitment?

MILLER: I don't think so. I learned something in all of the courses I took. For instance, when I was a philosophy major, I learned about logical thinking and careful reasoning. That's going to be useful to me in management. When I was majoring in English, I learned how to write well and how to read others' writing critically. That's going to serve me well in management too.

BOURNE: So what led you to your final decision to double major in business and communication? That's kind of an unusual combination.

MILLER: It seems a very natural one to me. I wanted to learn about business because I want to be a manager in an organization. I need to know how organizations work, and I need to understand different management philosophies and styles. At the same time, managers work with people, and that means I have to have strong communication skills.

Interview Follow-Up

When the interview is complete, there are several important steps to follow:

1. **Write a thank-you note.** It is appropriate to write a short note thanking the interviewer for the experience and re-expressing your interest in the job. For tips on writing thank-you notes, use your Communicate! CD-ROM to access Web Resource 9.12: Notable Notes.

2. **Self-assess your performance.** Take time to critique your performance. How well did you do? What can you do better next time?

3. **Contact the interviewer for feedback.** If you don't get the job, you might call the interviewer and ask for feedback. Be sure to be polite and to indicate that you are only calling to get some help on your interviewing skills. Actively listen to the feedback, using questions and paraphrases to clarify what is being said. Be sure to thank the interviewer for helping you.

Test Your Competence

Mock Interview

Pair with one of your classmates and conduct mock interviews. You and your classmate should exchange the material you prepared in Skill Learning Activity 9.4. You will prepare and participate in two interviews, one in which you will use your partner's ad, résumé, and cover letter to prepare and interview your partner for a job, and the other in which your partner will use the material you supply to interview you for a job. Your instructor will provide you with additional information regarding this assignment. This is Skill Learning Activity 9.6 for this chapter.

What Would You Do?   A QUESTION OF ETHICS

After three years of working at Everyday Products as a clerk, Mark had decided to look for another job. As he thought about preparing a résumé, he was struck by how little experience he had for the kind of job he wanted.

When he talked with Ken about this, Ken said, "Exactly what have you been doing at Everyday?"

"Well, for the most part I've been helping others look for information—I've also done some editing of reports."

"Hmm," Ken thought for a while. "Why not retitle your job as Editorial Assistant—it's more descriptive."

"But my official title is Clerk."

"Sure, but it doesn't really describe what you do. This way you show major editorial experience. Don't worry, everybody makes these kinds of changes—you're not really lying."

"Yeah, I see what you mean. Good idea!"

1. Is it interpersonally ethical for Mark to follow Ken's advice? Why or why not?

2. How should we deal with statements like "Everybody does it"?

Summary

Interviewing can be a productive way to obtain information from an expert for a paper, an article, or a speech.

The key skill of interviewing is using questions effectively. Open questions allow for flexible responses; closed questions require very brief answers. Primary questions stimulate response; follow-up questions ask for additional information. Neutral questions allow the respondent free choice; leading questions require the person to answer in a particular way.

When you are interviewing for information, you will want to define the purpose, select the best person to interview, develop a protocol, and conduct the interview according to the protocol.

Job interviews are a specific type of communication setting with particular demands for both interviewer and interviewee.

When you are interviewing prospective applicants for a job, structure your interview carefully to elicit maximal information about the candidate. Before the interview starts, become familiar with the data contained in the interviewee's application form, résumé, letters of recommendation, and test scores, if available. Be careful how you present yourself, do not waste time, avoid loaded questions, do not ask questions that violate fair employment practice legislation, and give the applicant an opportunity to ask questions. At the end of the interview explain to the applicant what will happen next in the process.

To get an interview, begin by taking the time to learn about the company and prepare an appropriate cover letter and résumé that are designed to motivate an employer to interview you. Electronic letters and résumés have become popular and need special preparation. For the interview itself you should dress appropriately, be prompt, be alert and look directly at the interviewer, give yourself time to think before answering difficult questions, ask intelligent questions about the company and the job, and show enthusiasm for the position.

Communicate! Online

N ow that you have read Chapter 9, use your Communicate! CD-ROM for quick access to the electronic resources that accompany this text. Your CD-ROM gives you access to the video of Elliott Miller's interview on pages 221–223, InfoTrac College Edition, and the Communicate! Web site. When you get to the Communicate! home page, click on "Student Book Companion Site" in the Resource box at right to access the online study aids for this chapter, including a digital glossary, review quizzes, the chapter activities, and the chapter Web Resources.

Key Terms

At the Communicate! Web site, select the chapter resources for Chapter 8. Print a copy of the glossary for this chapter and test yourself with the electronic flash cards or complete the crossword puzzle to help you master these key terms:

interview (206)
open questions (206)
closed questions (206)
neutral questions (207)
leading questions (207)

primary questions (207)
secondary or follow-up questions (207)
interview protocol (209)
cover letter (214)

résumé (214)
electronic cover letters and résumés (215)

Review Quiz

Test your knowledge of the concepts in this chapter by taking the online quiz at the Communicate! Web site. Select the chapter resources for Chapter 9, then click on "Review Quiz." When you have completed the quiz, submit it for scoring.

Skill Learning Activities

Complete the Observe & Analyze, Test Your Competence, and Conversation and Analysis activities for Chapter 9 online at the Communicate! Web site. Select the chapter resources for Chapter 9, then click on "Activities." You can submit your Observe & Analyze answers to your instructor, compare your Test Your Competence answers to those provided by the authors, and do both for the Conversation and Analysis activity.

9.1: Test Your Competence: Open and Closed Questions (208)
9.2: Observe and Analyze: Information Interviews (211)

Web Resources

Access the Web Resources for this chapter online at the Communicate! Web site. Select the chapter resources for Chapter 9, then click on "Web Resources."

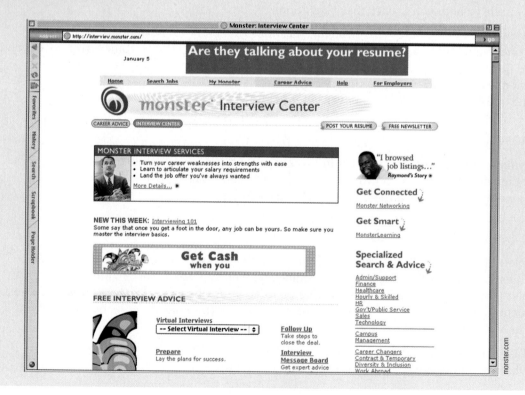

Interpersonal Communication from Chapters 5 through 9

What kind of an interpersonal communicator are you? This analysis looks at specific behaviors that are characteristic of effective interpersonal communicators. On the line provided for each statement, indicate the response that best captures your behavior: 1, almost always; 2, often; 3, occasionally; 4, rarely; 5, never.

_____ In conversation, I am able to make relevant contributions without interrupting others. (Ch. 5)

_____ When I talk, I try to provide information that satisfies others' needs and keeps the conversation going. (Ch. 5)

_____ When I'm not sure whether I understand, I seek clarification. (Ch. 6)

_____ When a person describes an unfortunate experience, I am able to provide appropriate comfort. (Ch. 6)

_____ I listen attentively, regardless of my interest in the person or the ideas. (Ch. 6)

_____ I describe objectively to others my negative feelings about their behavior toward me without withholding or blowing up. (Ch. 7)

_____ I am quick to praise people for doing things well. (Ch. 7)

_____ I criticize people for their mistakes only when they ask for criticism. (Ch. 7)

_____ I am able to maintain a positive communication climate by speaking in ways that others perceive as descriptive, nondogmatic, and nonmanipulative. (Ch. 8)

_____ When I find myself in conflict with another person, I am able to discuss the issue openly without withdrawing or appearing competitive or aggressive. (Ch. 8)

_____ I have an up-to-date résumé ready for immediate use. (Ch. 9)

_____ I present myself well when I am being interviewed. (Ch. 9)

Based on your responses, select the interpersonal communication behavior that you would most like to change. Write a communication improvement plan similar to the sample goal statement in Chapter 1 (page 22). If you would like verification of your self-review before you write a contract, have a friend or a coworker complete this same analysis for you.

You can complete this Self-Review online and, if requested, email it to your instructor. Use your Communicate! CD-ROM to access **Part II Self-Review** at the Communicate! Web site. Select the chapter resources for Chapter 9, then click on "Part II Self-Review."

OBJECTIVES

After you have read this chapter, you should be able to answer these questions:

- What characterizes effective groups?
- How can group discussion lead to improving group goal statements?
- What is the optimum size for a group?
- What factors affect cohesiveness in groups?
- How can a group improve its cohesiveness?
- How do groups form, maintain, and change their norms?
- How does the physical setting affect group interaction?
- What are the stages of group development?
- What are the steps of the problem-solving method?
- What constraints result in groups being ineffective at problem solving, and how can they be managed?

10

Participating in Group Communication

embers of the Alpha Production Team at Meyer Foods were gathered to review their hiring policies. At the beginning of the meeting, Kareem, the team facilitator, began, "You know why I called you together. Each production team has been asked to review its hiring practices. So, let's get started." After a few seconds of silence, Kareem said, "Drew, what have you been thinking?"

"Well, I don't know," Drew replied, "I haven't really given it much thought." (There were nods of agreement all around the table.)

"Well," Jeremy said, "I'm not sure I even remember what our current policies are."

"But when I sent you the email notice of the meeting, I attached a preliminary analysis of our practices and some questions I hoped each of us would think about before this meeting," Kareem replied.

"Oh, is that what that was?" Byron said. "I read the part about the meeting, but I guess I didn't get back to look at the attachment."

Kareem said, "I think the CEO is looking for some specific recommendations from us."

"Anything you think would be appropriate would be OK with me," Dawn added.

"Well, how about if we each try to come up with some ideas for next time," Kareem suggested. "Meeting adjourned."

As the group dispersed, Kareem overheard Drew whisper to Dawn, "These meetings sure are a waste of time, aren't they?"

erhaps you have been part of a work group at school, at work, or at your church. If so, the opening dialogue probably sounds familiar. When group meetings are ineffective, it is easy to point the finger at the leader, but often, as is the case with this group, the responsibility for the "waste of time" or other ineffectiveness lies not with one person but with the complex nature of communication in a group setting. Because most of us spend some of our time interacting in groups, we need to learn how group process works and how to participate in ways that maximize group effectiveness.

In this chapter, we examine the characteristics of effective work groups, the stages of group development, problem solving in groups, and the constraints on effective decision making.

Characteristics of Effective Work Groups

work group
a collection of three or more people who must interact and influence one another to solve problems and to accomplish a common purpose.

A **work group** is a collection of three or more people who must interact and influence one another to solve problems and to accomplish a common purpose. Effective work groups have clearly defined goals, an optimum number of diverse members, cohesiveness, norms, and a good working environment. Let's consider each of these.

Clearly Defined Goals

group goal
a future state of affairs desired by enough members of the group to motivate the group to work toward its achievement.

An effective work group has clearly defined group goals. A **group goal** is a future state of affairs desired by enough members of the group to motivate the group to work toward its achievement (Johnson & Johnson, 2003, p. 73). Goals become clearer to members, and members become more committed to goals, when they are discussed. To read about various methods that can be used to arrive at group goals, use your Communicate! CD-Rom to access Web Resource 10.1: Setting Group Goals. Through goal discussions, members are able to make sure goal statements are specific, consistent, challenging, and acceptable.

specific goal
a precisely stated, measurable, and behavioral goal.

First, goal statements must be specific. A **specific goal** is precisely stated, measurable, and behavioral. For example, the crew at a local fast food restaurant that began with the goal of "increasing profitability of the store" made the goal more specific and meaningful by revising the goal statement to read: "During the next quarter, the second shift night crew will increase the profitability of the store by reducing food costs on their shift by 1 percent through reducing the amount of food thrown away due to precooking."

consistent goals
complementary goals; achieving one goal not prevent the achievement of another.

Second, goal statements must be consistent. **Consistent goals** are complementary; that is, achieving one goal does not prevent the achievement

DILBERT reprinted by permission of United Features Syndicate, Inc.

of another. To meet the consistency test, the team will have to believe that reducing the amount of precooking will not interfere with maintaining their current level of service. If they do not believe that these two goals can be accomplished simultaneously, they will need to reformulate the goals so that they are compatible.

Third, goal statements must be challenging. **Challenging goals** require hard work and team effort; they motivate group members to do things beyond what they might normally accomplish. The crew determined that a goal of 1 percent was a significant challenge.

Fourth, goal statements must be acceptable. **Acceptable goals** are seen as meaningful by team members and are goals to which members feel personally committed. People support things that they help to create. So group members who participate in setting their own goals are likely to exert high effort to see that the goals are achieved. Likewise, a group member who does not believe a goal is reasonable or just is likely to be unmotivated or to resist working toward accomplishing the goal. Because the members of the crew helped to formulate the profitability goal, they are more likely to work to achieve it.

challenging goals
goals that require hard work and team effort; they motivate group members to do things beyond what they might normally accomplish.

acceptable goals
goals to which members feel personally committed.

Optimum Number of Diverse Members

Effective groups are composed of enough diverse members to ensure good interaction but not so many members that discussion is stifled. In general, as the size of a group grows, so does the complexity it must manage. Bostrom (1970) noted that the addition of one member to a group has a geometric effect on the number of relationships. When only Jeff and Sue are in a group, there is only one relationship to manage. But when a third person, Bryan, joins them, the group now has four relationships to manage (Jeff-Sue, Bryan-Jeff, Bryan-Sue, Bryan-Sue-Jeff). As groups grow in size and complexity, the opportunities for each member to participate drop, leading to member dissatisfaction (Gentry, 1980). When many people cannot or will not contribute, the resulting decision is seldom a product of the group's collective thought (Beebe et al., 1994, p. 125).

So what is the "right" size for a group? It depends. In general, research shows that the best size for a group is the smallest number of people capable of effectively achieving the goal (Sundstrom et al., 1990). For many

homogeneous group
group in which members have a great deal in common.

heterogeneous group
group in which various demographics, levels of knowledge, attitudes, and interests are represented.

cohesiveness
the degree of attraction members have to one another and to the group's goal.

As groups become more diverse, achieving cohesiveness becomes more difficult. How can a group develop cohesiveness so that it can benefit from diversity?

situations, this might mean as few as three to five people. As the size of the group increases, the time spent discussing and deciding increases as well. This argues for very small groups because they will be able to make decisions more quickly. However, as the goals, problems, and issues become complex, it is unlikely that very small groups will have the diversity of information, knowledge, and skills needed to make high-quality decisions. For many situations, then, a group of five to seven or more might be desirable.

More important than having a certain number of people in a group is having the right combination of people in the group. Notice the heading of this section was "optimum number of *diverse* members." To meet this test, it is usually better to have a heterogeneous group rather than a homogeneous group. **A homogeneous group** is one in which members have a great deal in common. By contrast, a **heterogeneous group** is one in which various demographics, levels of knowledge, attitudes, and interests are represented. For example, a group composed of seven women accounting students would be considered a homogeneous group; a group composed of male and female students from three different colleges would be considered a heterogeneous group.

Effective groups are likely to be composed of people who bring different but relevant knowledge and skills into the group discussion (Valacich et al., 1994). In homogeneous groups, members are likely to know the same things, come at the problem from the same perspective, and, consequently, be likely to overlook some important information or take shortcuts in the problem-solving process. In contrast, groups composed of heterogeneous members are more likely to have diverse information, perspectives, and values, and, conse-quently, discuss issues more thoroughly before reaching a decision.

Cohesiveness

Nita Winter Photography

Effective work group are also cohesive. **Cohesiveness** is the degree of attraction members have to one another and to the group's goal. In a highly cohesive group, members genuinely like and respect each other, work cooperatively to reach the group's goals, and generally perform better than noncohesive groups (Evans & Dion, 1991). In contrast, a group that is not cohesive may have members who are indifferent toward or dislike each other, have little interest in what the group is trying to accomplish, and may even work in ways that prevent the group from being successful.

Research (Balgopal, Ephross, & Vassil, 1986; Widmer & Williams, 1991) has shown that several factors lead to developing cohesiveness in groups:

attractiveness of the group's purpose, voluntary membership, feeling of freedom to share opinions, and celebration of accomplishments.

1. **Attractiveness of the group's purpose.** Social or fraternal groups, for example, build cohesiveness out of devotion to service or brotherhood. In a decision-making group, attractiveness is likely to be related to how important the task is to members. If Daniel is part of a group of students who must develop a computer program using the language they are learning in class, the cohesiveness of the group will depend in part on how interested the group is in developing such a program.

2. **Voluntary membership.** When we are forming groups, we should give people some control over joining. So important is this for fostering cohesiveness that each recruit in the all-voluntary military of the United States is allowed to choose his or her specialty. Likewise, Daniel's group is likely to develop cohesiveness more easily if they are able to volunteer to work on the task of developing a computer program.

   If group members are appointed, or if group members are having a little difficulty really getting comfortable with working together, a group may benefit from **team building activities** designed to help the group work better together (Clark, 1994). Often this means having the group meet someplace outside of its normal setting where members can engage in activities designed to help them recognize each other's strengths, share in group successes, and develop rituals. As group members learn to be more comfortable with each other socially, they are likely to become more comfortable in the group setting as well.

   team building activities *activities designed to help the group work better together.*

3. **Feeling of freedom to share opinions.** Feeling comfortable in disagreeing with the ideas and positions of others is an important aspect of group cohesion. If Daniel's computer science group is comfortable sharing contrasting ideas without fear of being chastised, they are likely to develop more cohesiveness. Moreover, group members should feel free to converse about their goals very soon after the group is formed. During this discussion, individual members should be encouraged to express their ideas about the goals of the group and to hear the ideas of others. Through this discussion process, the group can clarify goals and build group commitment.

4. **Celebration of accomplishments.** Groups should be encouraged to set subgoals that can be achieved early. Groups that feel good about the work they are accomplishing develop a sense of unity. Once early subgoals are accomplished, the group can celebrate these achievements. Celebrations of early achievements cause members to more closely identify with the group and to see it as a "winner" (Renz & Greg, 2000, p. 54).

Keep in mind that the more heterogeneous the group, the more difficult it is to build cohesiveness. We know that heterogeneous groups generally arrive at better decisions, so we need to structure group conversations that

Cohesiveness in Homogeneous versus Heterogeneous Groups

Identify two groups (for example, a sports team, study group, fraternal or community group, or work team) to which you belong, one should have members you consider to be homogeneous, and the other members you consider to be heterogeneous.

Analyze the demographic differences in each group. When you have completed this analysis, write a paragraph that discusses cohesiveness in each group. How cohesive is each group? Are both groups equally cohesive? Was it easier or more difficult to establish cohesiveness in a particular group? What real or potential pitfalls result from the level of cohesiveness in each group?

You can use your Student Workbook to complete this activity, or you can complete it online, download a demographic analysis worksheet to help you complete it, and, if requested, email it to your instructor. Use your Communicate! CD-ROM to access Skill Learning Activity 10.1.

norms
expectations for the way group members will behave while in the group.

ground rules
prescribed behaviors designed to help the group meet its goals and conduct its conversations.

can develop cohesiveness in all types of groups. This is why team-building activities, development of freedom to express controversial ideas, and celebration of achievements are so important with heterogeneous groups.

In addition, members should be taught to communicate in ways that foster supportive patterns of cooperative interaction. Groups become cohesive when individual members feel valued and respected. By using the skills of active listening, empathizing, describing, and collaborative conflict management, you can help heterogeneous groups become cohesive.

Moreover, groups should set aside specific times during which the group stops working on its task and instead focuses on team relationships, enabling members to discuss and resolve personal differences before these hurt team cohesiveness and team performance.

Norms

Norms are expectations for the way group members will behave while in the group. Effective groups develop norms that support goal achievement (Shimanoff, 1992) and cohesiveness (Shaw, 1981). Norms begin to be developed early in the life of the group. Norms grow, change, and solidify as people get to know one another better. Group members usually comply with norms and are sanctioned by the group when they do not.

Norms can be developed through formal discussions or informal group processes (Johnson & Johnson, 2003, p. 27). Some groups choose to formulate explicit **ground rules,** prescribed behaviors designed to help the group meet its goals and conduct its conversations. These may include sticking to the agenda, refraining from interrupting others, actively listening to others, requiring full participation, focusing argument on issues rather than personalities, and sharing decision making. To read a list of group norms that contribute to group effectiveness, use your Communicate! CD-ROM to access Web Resource 10.2: Setting Group Norms.

In most groups, however, norms evolve informally. When we become part of a new group, we try to act in ways that were considered appropriate in other groups in which we have participated. If the other members of our new group behave in ways that are consistent with our interpretation of the rules for behavior, an informal norm is established. For example, suppose Daniel and two other group members show up late for a meeting. If the group has already begun discussion and the latecomers are greeted with cold looks, showing that other members of this group do not abide by being late, then this group will develop an on-time norm. A group may never discuss informal norms that develop, but all veteran group members understand what they are and behave in line with the expectations of these informally established norms.

When group members violate a group norm, they are usually sanctioned. The severity of the sanction depends on the importance of the norm that was violated, the extent of the violation, and the status of the person who violated the norm. Violating a norm that is central to a group's performance or cohesiveness will generally receive a harsher sanction than will violating a norm that is less central. Minor violations of norms, or violation of a norm by a newcomer, or violations of norms that are frequently violated will generally receive more lenient sanctions. Group members who have achieved higher status in the group (for example, those with unique skills and abilities needed by the group) receive more lenient sanctions or escape sanctioning.

Some norms turn out to be counterproductive. For example, at the beginning of the first meeting of a work group suppose a few folks start cutting up, tell jokes and stories, and generally ignore attempts by others to begin more serious discussion. If the group seems to encourage or does not effectively sanction this behavior, then this dallying behavior will become a group norm. As a result, the group may become so involved in these behaviors that work toward the group's goals is delayed, set aside, or perhaps even forgotten. If counterproductive behavior such as this continues for several meetings and becomes a norm, it will be very difficult to change.

What can a group member do to try to change a norm? Renz and Greg (2000) suggest that you can help your group change a counterproductive norm by (1) observing the norm and its outcome, (2) describing the results of the norm to the group, and (3) soliciting opinions of other members of the group (p. 52). For instance, you might observe whether every meeting begins late, note how long dallying tends to continue, determine whether discussion is productive, and judge whether extra meetings are necessary. Then you could start the next meeting by reporting the results of your observations and asking for reaction from group members.

While norms are important mechanisms for guiding group behavior, social norms also influence our behavior in other less structured group settings. Social norm theory has been used to guide recent successful alcohol, tobacco, and violence interventions on college campuses. To read more about such interventions, use your Communicate! CD-ROM to access Web Resource 10.3: Social Norm Interventions.

The Working Environment

A good **working environment** includes a physical setting that is conveniently located for most members, has a comfortable temperature, has enough space to accommodate the members, is comfortably furnished, and contains the resources the group needs to perform its tasks.

working environment
a physical setting that is conveniently located, has a comfortable temperature, has enough space, is comfortably furnished, and contains the resources the group needs to perform its tasks.

When a group meets on an ongoing basis, it will want to choose a location that is convenient for its members. By choosing a location that is easily accessible, the group makes it easier for all members to attend. When locations are chosen that are inconvenient for members, a norm of lateness or absence may develop.

The temperature of the room in which a group meets affects the way in which the group interacts. People in rooms they perceive to be too warm are not only uncomfortable but may feel crowded, which results in negative behaviors. Similarly, when the temperature of a room or meeting place is too cold, group members tend to become distracted.

The space in which a group meets should be appropriate for the size and composition of the group and the nature of what they are trying to accomplish during their time together. When the space is too big for the group, members will feel overwhelmed and distant from each other. In some cases, they may have trouble hearing one another. When the space is too small, the group will experience feelings of crowding. We have all found ourselves in situations in which room size contributed to negative experiences. Men and women seem to differ on their space preferences. Women generally find smaller rooms more comfortable than do men, who prefer larger spaces (Freedman, Klevansky, & Ehrich, 1971).

The physical setting can affect both group interaction and decision making (Figure 10.1). Seating can be too formal. When seating approximates a board of directors style, as illustrated in Figure 10.1a, where people sit indicates their status. In this style, a dominant-submissive pattern emerges that can inhibit group interaction. People who sit at the head of the table are likely to be looked to for leadership and are seen as having more influ-

Figure 10.1
Which group members do you think will be able to arrive at a decision easily? Why or why not?

ence than those members who sit on the side. People who sit across the table from one another interact with one another more frequently but also find themselves disagreeing with one another more often than they disagree with others at the table.

Seating that is excessively informal can also inhibit interaction. For instance, in Figure 10.1b, the three people sitting on the couch form their own little group; the two people seated next to each other form another group; and two members have placed themselves out of the main flow. In arrangements such as these, people are more likely to communicate with the people adjacent to them than with others. In such settings, it is more difficult to make eye contact with every group member. Johnson and Johnson (2003) maintain that "easy eye contact among members enhances the frequency of interaction, friendliness, cooperation, and liking for the group and its work" (p. 171).

The circle, generally considered the ideal arrangement for group discussions and problem solving, is depicted in Figure 10.1c. Circle configurations increase participant motivation to speak because sight lines are better for everyone and everyone appears to have equal status. When the location of the group meeting does not have a round table, the group may be better off without a table or with an arrangement of tables that makes a square, which approximates the circle arrangement, as shown in Figure 10.1d.

Stages of Group Development

Although some groups are brought together on a one-time-only basis to make a quick decision, most work groups convene regularly to consider a variety of issues. Once assembled, these typical work groups tend to move through stages of development. Although numerous models have been proposed to describe the stages of group development, Tuckman's (1965) model has been widely accepted because it identifies the central issues facing a group at each stage in its development. He named these stages forming, storming, norming, performing, and adjourning. Research by Wheelen and Hochberger (1996) has confirmed that groups can be observed moving through each of these stages. In this section, we describe each of the stages of group development and discuss the nature of communication during each phase.

Forming

Forming is the initial stage of group development during which people come to feel valued and accepted so that they identify with the group. At the beginning of any group, individual members will experience feelings of

forming
the initial stage of group development during which people come to feel valued and accepted so that they identify with the group.

discomfort caused by the uncertainty they are facing in this new social situation. To explore the specific anxieties raised in a new group situation, use your Communicate! CD-ROM to access **Web Resource 10.4: Forming Fears and Uncertainty.**

Politeness and tentativeness on the part of members may characterize group interactions as members try to become acquainted with others, understand how the group will work, and find their place in the group. During forming, any real disagreements between people remain unacknowledged as members strive to be seen as flexible. During this stage, if the group has formally appointed group leaders, group members depend on them for clues as to how they should behave. Members work to fit in and to be seen as likable.

Anderson (1988) suggests that during forming we should express positive attitudes and feelings while refraining from abrasive or disagreeable comments, we should make appropriately benign self-disclosures and wait to see if they are reciprocated, and we should try to be friendly, open, and interested in others. This means using active listening and empathizing skills to become better acquainted with other members of the group, and smiling, nodding, and maintaining good eye contact to make conversations a bit more relaxed.

Storming

storming
the stage of group development during which the group clarifies its goals and determines the roles each member will have in the group power structure.

Storming is the stage of group development during which the group clarifies its goals and determines the roles each member will have in the group power structure. The stress and strain that arise when groups begin to make decisions are a natural result of the conflicting ideas, opinions, and personalities that begin to emerge during decision making. In the forming stage, members are concerned about fitting in, whereas in the storming stage, members are concerned about expressing their ideas and opinions and finding their place. One or more members may begin to question or challenge the formal leader's position on issues. In groups that do not have formally appointed leaders, two or more members may vie for informal leadership of the group. During this phase, the overpoliteness exhibited during forming may be replaced by snide comments, sarcastic remarks, or pointedly aggressive exchanges between some members. While storming, members may take sides, forming cliques and coalitions.

Storming, if controlled, is an important stage in a group's development. During periods of storming, the group is confronted with alternative ideas, opinions, and ways of viewing issues. Although storming will occur in all groups, some will manage it better than others. When storming in a group is severe, it can threaten the group's survival. When a group does not storm, it may experience **groupthink,** a deterioration of mental efficiency, reality testing, and moral judgment that results from in-group pressure (Janis, 1982, p. 9). To avoid groupthink, we should encourage constructive disagreement, self-monitor what we say to avoid name-calling and using

groupthink
a deterioration of mental efficiency, reality testing, and moral judgment that results from in-group pressure.

inflammatory language, and use the active listening skills discussed earlier with emphasis on paraphrasing and honest questioning (Anderson, 1988). To read a comprehensive article on groupthink, use your Communicate! CD-ROM to access **Web Resource 10.5: Groupthink.**

Norming

Norming is the stage of group development during which the group solidifies its rules for behavior, especially those that relate to how conflict will be managed. As the group successfully completes a storming phase, it moves into a phase where members begin to apply more pressure on each other to conform. During this phase, the norms or standards of the group become clear. Members for the most part comply with norms, although those who have achieved higher status or power may continue to occasionally deviate from them. Members who do not comply with norms are sanctioned.

During norming, competent communicators pay attention to the norms that are developing. Then, they adapt their communication styles to the norms of the group. When communicators who are monitoring norm development determine that a norm is too rigid, too elastic, or in other ways counterproductive, they initiate a group discussion about their observations. As you would expect, these conversations are best received when the person initiating them uses the skills of describing behavior using specific and concrete language.

norming
the stage of group development during which the group solidifies its rules for behavior, especially those that relate to how conflict will be managed.

Performing

Performing is the stage of group development when the skills, knowledge, and abilities of all members are combined to overcome obstacles and meet goals successfully. Through each of the stages, groups are working to accomplish their goals. Once members have formed social bonds, settled power issues, and developed their norms, however, they "get in the groove," becoming more effective at creative problem solving and task performance. During this stage, conversations are focused on problem solving and sharing task-related information, with little energy directed to relationship building. Members who spend the group's time in chitchat not only detract from the effectiveness of the group but risk being perceived as unprepared or lazy. Performing is the most important stage of group development. This is the stage in which members freely share information, solicit ideas from others, and work to solve problems.

performing
the stage of group development when the skills, knowledge, and abilities of all members are combined to overcome obstacles and meet goals successfully.

Adjourning

Adjourning is the stage of group development in which members assign meaning to what they have done and determine how to end or maintain interpersonal relations they have developed. Some groups are brought together for a finite time period, whereas for other groups work is continuous.

adjourning
the stage of group development in which members assign meaning to what they have done and determine how to end or maintain interpersonal relations they have developed.

Stages of Group Development

Think of a group to which you have belonged for less than one quarter, semester, or term (if you have an assigned group in this course, use that group). Now, write a paragraph that begins by identifying the stage of development the group is currently in and then describe how this group transitioned through each of the previous stages of group development. What event(s) do you recall as turning points, marking the group's movement from one stage to another. Has the group become "stuck" in a stage, or has it developed smoothly? What factors contributed to that? What can you do to help this group succeed in the stage that it is in and transition to the next stage?

 You can complete this activity online and, if requested, email it to your instructor. Use your Communicate! CD-ROM to access Skill Learning Activity 10.2.

Regardless of whether a group is short term or ongoing, all groups experience endings. A short-term project team will face adjourning when it has completed its work within the time period specified for its existence. Ongoing groups also experience endings. When the team has reached a particular goal, finished a specific project, or lost members to reassignments or resignations, it will confront the same developmental challenges faced by short-term groups in this phase.

Keyton's (1993) study of the adjourning phase of group development points to two challenges that groups face during this phase. First, groups need to construct meaning from their shared experience by evaluating and reflecting on the experience. They may discuss what led to their successes or failures, recall events and share memories of stressful times, and celebrate accomplishments. Second, members will need to find ways to sever or maintain interpersonal relationships that have developed during the group's life together. During this phase, people in the group may explore ways to maintain contact with those they have particularly enjoyed working with. They may continue the relationship on a purely social level or plan to undertake additional work together.

Keyton thinks it is especially important for groups to have a termination ritual, which can range from an informal debriefing session to formalized celebrations with group members and their friends, family, and colleagues. Whatever form the ritual takes, Keyton believes such a ritual "affects how they [members] will interpret what they have experienced and what expectations they will take with them to similar situations" (p. 98).

The phases of group development explain the work that groups must do to aid the socioemotional development of the group. How the group develops through these phases is important to how effectively it works. But achieving group goals is also the result of how well the group uses the problem-solving process. We now turn our attention to understanding the problem-solving process and the communication skills that provide the focus for the performing stage of group development.

Problem Solving in Groups

Research shows that groups follow many different approaches to problem solving. Some groups move linearly through a series of steps to reach consensus, and some move in a spiral pattern in which they refine, accept, reject, modify, and combine ideas as they go along. Whether groups move in something approximating an orderly pattern or go in fits and starts, those groups that arrive at high-quality decisions are likely to accomplish certain tasks during their deliberations. These tasks include identifying a specific problem, analyzing the problem, arriving at criteria that an effective solution must meet, identifying possible alternative solutions to the problem, comparing the alternatives to the criteria, and determining the best solution or combination of solutions.

Defining the Problem

Much wheel-spinning takes place during the early stages of group discussion as a result of members' not understanding their specific goal. It is the duty of the person, agency, or parent group that forms a particular work group to give the group a charge, such as "work out a new way of selecting people for merit pay increases." However, rarely will the charge be stated in such a way that the group does not need to do some clarification of its own. Even when the charge seems clear, effective groups will want to make sure they are focusing on the real problem and not just symptoms of the problem. Let's look again at the charge "work out a new way of selecting people for merit pay increases." What is wrong with this as a problem definition? "Work out a new way of selecting" is too general to be meaningful. A clearer question would be "What are the most important criteria for selecting people for merit pay increases?"

Even when a group is given a well-defined charge, it will need to gather information before it can accurately define the specific problem. Accurately defining the problem requires the group to understand the background, history, and status of the problem. This means collecting and understanding a variety of information. Some groups, however, rush through defining the problem and end up working to solve symptoms, not root causes. To read an article suggesting that later stages of problem solving move more quickly if the group has thoroughly studied, discussed, and agreed on the problem, use your Communicate! CD-ROM to access Web Resource 10.6: What's Your Problem?

It helps if the group formally states the problem in writing. This written statement can help the group avoid being sidetracked by tangential or unrelated issues. Unless the group can agree on a formal definition of the problem, there is little likelihood of the group's being able to work together toward a solution.

Effective problem definitions have these four characteristics.

1. **They are stated as questions.** Problem-solving groups begin from the assumption that solutions are not yet known, so problems should be stated as questions to be answered. For example, the merit pay committee might define the problem it will solve as follows: What are the most important criteria for determining merit pay increases? Phrasing the group's problem as a question furthers the spirit of inquiry.

2. **They contain only one central idea.** If the charge includes two questions—"Should the college abolish its foreign language and social studies requirements?"—the group should break it down into two separate questions: Should the college abolish its foreign language requirement? Should the college abolish its social studies requirement?

3. **They use specific and precise language to describe the problem.** For instance, the problem definition "What should the department do about courses that aren't getting the job done?" may be well intentioned, and participants may have at least some idea about their goal, but such vague wording as "getting the job done" can lead to problems later. Notice how this revision makes the intent much clearer: "What should the department do about courses that receive low scores on student evaluations?"

4. **They can be identified as a question of fact, value, or policy.** How we organize our problem-solving discussion will depend on the kind of question we are addressing: a question of fact, value, or policy.

questions of fact
questions concerned with discovering what is true or to what extent something is true.

Questions of fact are concerned with discovering what is true or to what extent something is true. Implied in such questions is the possibility of determining truth through the process of examining facts by way of directly observed, spoken, or recorded evidence. For instance, "Did Smith steal equipment from the warehouse?" "Did Mary's report follow the written guidelines for the assignment?" and "Do the data from our experiment support our hypothesis?" are all questions of fact. The group will discuss the validity of the evidence it has to determine what is true.

questions of value
questions that concern subjective judgments of what is right, moral, good, or just.

Questions of value concern subjective judgments of what is right, moral, good, or just. Questions of value can be recognized because they often contain evaluative words such as *good, reliable, effective,* or *worthy.* For instance, the program development team for a TV sitcom aimed at young teens may discuss, "Is the level of violence in the scripts we have developed appropriate for programs designed to appeal to children?" or "Is the proposed series of ads too sexually provocative?" Although we can establish criteria for "too sexually provocative" and "effectively" and measure material against those criteria, the criteria we choose and the evidence we accept depend on our judgment. A different group of people using different values might come to a different decision.

questions of policy
questions that concern what courses of action should be taken or what rules should be adopted to solve a problem.

Questions of policy concern what courses of action should be taken or what rules should be adopted to solve a problem. "Should the university support international workers rights?" and "Where should the new landfill be built?" are both questions of policy. The inclusion of the word *should* in questions of policy makes them the easiest to recognize and the easiest to phrase of all problem statements.

Analyzing the Problem

Analysis of a problem entails finding out as much as possible about the problem and determining the criteria that must be met to find an acceptable solution. Three types of information can be helpful in analyzing problems. Most groups begin by sharing the information individual members have acquired through their experience. This is a good starting place, but groups that limit their information gathering to the existing knowledge of members often make decisions based on incomplete or faulty information.

Test Your Competence

Stating Problems

Indicate whether each of the following is a question of fact (F), a question of value (V), or a question of policy (P).

_____ 1. What should we do to increase the quality of finished parts?

_____ 2. Do police stop African American drivers more frequently than other drivers?

_____ 3. Should television news organizations use exit polls to call elections?

_____ 4. Is John guilty of involuntary manslaughter?

_____ 5. Is seniority the best method of handling employee layoffs?

_____ 6. What is the best vacation plan for our family?

 You can complete this activity online and compare your answers to the authors'. Use your Communicate! CD-ROM to access Skill Learning Activity 10.3.

A second source of information that should be examined includes published materials available through libraries, electronic databases, and the Internet. From these sources, a group can access information about the problem that has been collected, analyzed, and interpreted by others. Just because information is published, however, does not mean that it is accurate or valid. Accuracy and validity are especially an issue when the information comes from an Internet source, and the group will also have to evaluate the relevance and usefulness of the information.

A third source of information about a problem can be gleaned from other people. At times, the group may want to interview experts for their ideas about a problem or conduct a survey to gather information from a particular target group.

Once group members have gathered information, it must be shared with other members. It is important for group members to share new information to fulfill the ethical responsibility that comes with group discussion. A study by Dennis (1996) shows that groups tend to spend more time discussing information common to group members if those with information don't work to get the information heard. The tendency to discuss common information while ignoring unique information leads to less effective decisions. To overcome this, groups need to ask each member to discuss the information he or she has uncovered that seems to contradict his or her personal beliefs about the issue. When addressing a complex issue, separate information sharing from decision making by holding separate meetings spaced far enough apart to enable members to think through their information.

Determining Solution Criteria

Once a group understands the nature of the problem, it is in a position to determine what tests a solution must pass in order to solve the problem. The criteria become the decisive factors in determining whether a particular solution will solve the problem. The criteria that are selected should be ones that the information gathered has suggested are critical to successfully solving the problem.

The criteria that the group decides on will be used to screen alternative solutions. Solutions that do not meet the test of all criteria are eliminated from further consideration. For example, a local citizens' committee is charged with selecting a site for a new county jail. The group arrives at the following phrasing for the problem: "Where should the new jail be located?" After the group agrees on this wording, they can then ask the question, "What are the criteria for a good site for a new jail?"

In that discussion, suppose members contribute information related to the county's budget, the need for inmates to maintain family contact, concerns about proximity to schools and parks, and space needs. After considering this kind of information, the group might then select the following criteria for selecting a site:

- Maximum cost of $500,000 for purchasing the land.
- A location no more than three blocks from public transportation.
- A location that is one mile or more from any school, day care center, playground, or youth center.
- A lot size of at least ten acres.

When groups discuss and decide on criteria before they think about specific solutions, Kathryn Young and her colleagues (2000) suggest that groups increase the likelihood that they will be able to avoid becoming polarized and will be more likely to come to a decision that all members can accept.

Identifying Possible Solutions

For most policy questions, many solutions are possible. The trick is to tap the creative thinking of group members so that many ideas are generated. At this stage of discussion, the goal is not to worry about whether a particular solution fits all the criteria but to come up with a large list of ideas.

brainstorming
an uncritical, nonevaluative process of generating associated ideas.

One way to identify potential solutions is to brainstorm for ideas. **Brainstorming** is an uncritical, nonevaluative process of generating associated ideas. It involves verbalizing your ideas as they come to mind without stopping to evaluate their merits. Members are encouraged, however, to build on the ideas presented by others. For a more detailed discussion of the brainstorming process, use your Communicate! CD-ROM to access Web Resource 10.7: Rules for Brainstorming. In a ten- or fifteen-minute brainstorming session, a group may come up with twenty or more possible solutions depending on the nature of the problem. For instance, the group working on the jail site question might mention ten or more in just a few minutes of brainstorming, such as sites that individual members have thought of or that they have heard others mention.

Evaluating Solutions

Once the group has a list of possible solutions, it needs to compare each solution alternative to the criteria that it developed. During this phase, the group must determine whether each criterion is equally important or whether certain criteria should be given more weight in evaluating alternative solutions. Whether a group weighs certain criteria more heavily or not, it should use a process that ensures that each alternative solution is thoroughly assessed against all of the criteria.

Research by Randy Hirokawa (1987) confirmed that high-quality decisions are made by groups that are "careful, thoughtful, and systematic" in evaluating their options (p. 10). In another study, Hirokawa (1988) noted that it is common for groups to begin by eliminating solutions that clearly do not meet important criteria and then to compare the positive features of solutions that remain.

When brainstorming, how difficult is it for you to refrain from judging ideas?

Skill Builders ▶ Brainstorming

Skill	Use	Procedure	Example
An uncritical, nonevaluative process of generating associated ideas.	To generate a list of potential solutions to a problem.	1. Verbalize ideas as they come to mind. 2. Refrain from evaluating the merits of ideas. 3. Encourage outrageous and unique ideas. 4. Build on or modify the ideas of others. 5. Use extended effort to generate more ideas. 6. Record the ideas.	Problem: "What should we do to raise money to help a child who needs a liver transplant?" Ideas: sell cookies, sell candy, sell wrapping paper; wrap packages at mall for donations; find corporate sponsors; have a corporate golf outing, a youth golf outing, a tennis tournament, a bowling tournament, a paintball tournament; auction donated paintings; do odd jobs for money.

Deciding

decision making
the process of choosing among alternatives.

A group brought together for problem solving may or may not be responsible for making the actual decision, but it is responsible for presenting its recommendation. **Decision making** is the process of choosing among alternatives. The following five methods differ in the extent to which they require that all members agree with the decision and the amount of time it takes to reach a decision.

1. **The expert opinion method.** Once the group has eliminated those alternatives that do not meet the criteria, the group asks the member who has the most expertise to select the final choice. This method is quick, and it is useful when one member is much more knowledgeable about the issues or has a greater stake in implementation of the decision.

2. **The average group opinion method.** When using this approach, each member of the group ranks the alternatives that meet all the criteria. These rankings are then averaged, and the alternative receiving the highest average ranking becomes the choice. This method is useful for routine decisions or when a decision needs to be made quickly. It can also be used as an intermediate straw poll to enable the group to eliminate low-scoring alternatives before moving to a different process for making the final decision.

3. **The majority rule method.** When using this method, the group votes on each alternative, and the one that receives the majority of votes (50 percent + 1) is selected. Although this method is considered democratic, it can create problems for implementation. If the majority voting for an alternative is slight, then there may be nearly as many members who do not support the choice as there are those that do. If these minority members object strongly to the choice, they may sabotage implementation of the solution either through active or passive means.

4. **The unanimous decision method.** In this method, the group must continue deliberation until every member of the group believes the same solution is the best. As you would expect, it is very difficult to arrive at truly unanimous decisions, and to do so takes a lot of time. When a group reaches unanimity, however, it can expect that each member of the group will be fully committed to selling the decision to others and to helping implement the decision.

5. **The consensus method.** This method is an alternative to the unanimous decision method. In consensus, the group continues deliberation until all members of the group find an acceptable variation, one they can support and are committed to helping to implement. Members of a consensus group may believe that there is a better solution than the one that has been chosen, but they feel they can support and help implement the one they have agreed to. Although easier to achieve than

reaching unanimity, arriving at consensus is still difficult. Although the majority rule method is widely used, selecting the consensus method is a wise investment if the group needs everyone's support to implement the decision successfully. To read a complete comparison of the advantages and disadvantages of various decision-making methods, use your Communicate! CD-ROM to access Web Resource 10.8: Decision-Making Methods.

In the United States the majority rule method is the one under which many groups function. In Japan the dominant decision-making method is the consensus method. This method is described in the Diverse Voices selection.

Skill Builders — Problem Solving in Groups

Skill	Use	Procedure	Example
Using a systematic six-step process to work out difficulties or resolve issues.	A guide for groups to follow in arriving at conclusions to fact or value questions.	1. Define the problem in specific and precise language as a question of fact, value, or policy containing one central idea. The question is: "What textbook should we adopt for the required Human Communication course?"	The question is: "What textbook should we adopt for the required Human Communication course?"
		2. Analyze the problem using the experiences of group members, information obtained from public sources, and through interviews with other knowledgeable people.	Members who have taught the course before recount their experiences with various texts. We read the publishers' information packets, and we talk to the sales reps.
		3. Determine the solution criteria.	The criteria we will use are coverage, writing style, Web support, and cost.

Skill	Use	Procedure	Example
		4. Identify possible solutions through brainstorming.	We identify six books that might work.
		5. Evaluate the solutions by comparing them to the criteria.	We compare the books to one another using our criteria.
		6. Decide using expert opinion, average group opinion, majority, unanimity, or consensus method.	We adopt a consensus method for deciding.

Test Your Competence

The Problem-Solving Process

Describe how you would use the six steps in the problem-solving process to arrive at a solution to the following situation.

Your manager at work has decided that you and your coworkers should decide whether it is time to upgrade your company-supplied mobile phone

hardware and service. If you decided to upgrade, you are supposed to do the research and choose the equipment and service provider.

 You can complete this activity online and compare your answers to the authors'. Use your Communicate! CD-ROM to access **Skill Learning Activity 10.4.**

DIVERSE VOICES

The Group: A Japanese Context

by Delores Cathcart and Robert Cathcart

One of Japan's most prominent national characteristics is the individual's sense of the group. Loyalty to the group and a willingness to submit to its demands are key virtues in Japanese society.

 his dependency and the interdependency of all members of a group is reinforced by the concept of *on*. A Japanese is expected to feel an indebtedness to those others in the group who provide security, care, and support. This indebtedness creates obligation and when combined with dependency is called *on*. *On* functions as a means of linking all persons in the group in an unending chain because obligation is never satisfied, but continues throughout life. *On* is fostered by a system known as the *oyabun-kobun* relationship. Traditionally the *oyabun* is a father, boss, or patron who protects and provides for a son, employee, or student in return for his or her service and loyalty. This is not a one-way dependency. Each boss or group leader recognizes his own dependency on those below. Without their undivided loyalty he or she could not function. *Oyabun* are also acutely aware of this double dimension because of having had to serve a long period of *kobun* on the way up the hierarchy to the position at the top. All had *oyabun* who protected and assisted them, much like a father, and now each must do the same for their *kobun*. *Oyabun* have one or more *kobun* whom they look after much as if they were children. The more loyal and devoted the "children" the more successful the "father."

This relationship is useful in modern life where large companies assume the role of superfamily and become involved in every aspect of their workers' lives. Bosses are *oyabun* and employees are *kobun*. . . .

This uniquely Japanese way of viewing relationships creates a distinctive style of decision making known as *consensus decision*. The Japanese devotion to consensus building seems difficult for most Westerners to grasp but loses some of its mystery when looked at as a solution to representing every member of the group. In a system that operates on *oyabun-kobun* relationships nothing is decided without concern for how the outcome will affect all. Ideas and plans are circulated up and down the company hierarchy until everyone has had a chance to react. This reactive process is not to exert pressure but to make certain that all matters affecting the particular groups and the company are taken into consideration. Much time is spent assessing the mood of every-one involved and only after all the ramifications of how the decision will affect each group can there be a quiet assent. A group within the company may approve a decision that is not directly in its interest (or even causes it difficulties) because its members know they are not ignored, their feelings have been expressed and they can be assured that what is good for the company will ultimately be good for them. For this reason consensus decisions cannot be hurried along without chancing a slight or oversight that will cause future problems.

The process of consensus building in order to make decisions is a time-consuming one, not only because everyone must be considered, but also because the Japanese avoid verbalizing objections or doubts in order to preserve group harmony. The advice, often found in American group literature, that group communication should be characterized by open and candid statements expressing individual personal feelings, wishes, and dislikes, is the antithesis of the Japanese consensus process. No opposing speeches are made to argue alternate ideas; no conferences are held to debate issues. Instead, the process of assessing the feelings and mood of each work group proceeds slowly until there exists a climate of agreement. This process is possible because of the tight relationships that allow bosses and workers to know each other intimately and to know the group so well that needs and desires are easy to assess.

Excerpted from Delores Cathcart and Robert Cathcart, "The Group: A Japanese Context." In Intercultural Communication: A Reader, *8th ed., Larry A Samovar and Richard E. Porter, eds. (Belmont, CA: Wadsworth, 1997), pp. 329–339. Reprinted by permission of the author.*

Constraints on Effective Decision Making

Following a structured problem-solving process should help groups be more effective, but groups may still face cognitive, affiliative, and social constraints that can interfere with constructive decision making (Gouran & Hirokawa, 1996; Janis, 1989).

cognitive constraints
the pressure a group feels as a result of a difficult task, a shortage of information, or limited time.

Cognitive constraints occur when a group feels under pressure as a result of a difficult task, a shortage of information, or limited time. Signs of cognitive constraints are comments like "How do they expect us to get this done in a week?" or "We've got a ton of material to sift through." Overcoming these constraints requires a group to assure itself that the task is important enough to give the necessary time and compensate for the difficulty. For instance, overhauling the method of producing a product will take more time than most would like to spend, but if the overhaul is a necessity to keep a company afloat, the time is well spent.

affiliative constraints
pressure a group feels when some or all members are more concerned about maintaining harmonious relationships with others than they are about making high-quality decisions.

Affiliative constraints occur when some or all members of the group are more concerned about maintaining harmonious relationships with others than they are about making high-quality decisions. Signs of affiliative constraints are reluctance of some members to talk, backing down for no apparent reason, and reluctance to show any disagreement. Working through these constraints is often a matter of practicing the interpersonal skills we covered in the early part of this book. Dealing with this might also require assigning someone to serve as a **devil's advocate,** taking the opposite side of the argument just to test the apparent consensus. Once a group sees that constructive argument is healthy when it is good-natured, the group is more likely to be honest with its opinions.

devil's advocate
taking the opposite side of the argument just to test the apparent consensus.

egocentric constraints
pressure from members of the group who have high needs for control or are driven by other personal needs.

Egocentric constraints occur when members of the group have high needs for control or are driven by other personal needs. These people see issues in terms of a "win-lose." They feel that by getting the group to accept their position they "win." If the group chooses another alternative, they have suffered a personal loss. What drives egocentric individuals is not necessarily a strong preference for one alternative but the need to be "right." Statements like "Well, I know that most of you are new to the commission and have lots of ideas, but I have served in this capacity for the past five years, and so I know what won't work" are sure signs of egocentrism. Egocentric constraints are difficult to overcome, but egocentric individuals are not incapable of rational thinking. Inviting them to verbalize the information upon which they are basing their conclusions can sometimes help them to modify their position and move into problem solving.

What Would You Do? ▶ A QUESTION OF ETHICS ◆ ◆ ◆ ◆ ◆ ◆ ◆

he Community Service and Outreach committee of Students in Communication was meeting to determine what cause should benefit from the annual fund-raising Talent Contest that SIC held each year.

"So," said Mark, "does anyone have any ideas about whose cause we should sponsor?"

"Well," replied Glenna, "I think we should give it to a group that's doing literacy work."

"Sounds good to me," replied Mark.

"My aunt works at the Boardman Center as the literacy coordinator, so why don't we just adopt them?" asked Glenna.

"Gee, I don't know much about the group," said Reed.

"Come on, you know, they help people learn how to read," replied Glenna sarcastically.

"Well, I was kind of hoping we'd take a look at sponsoring the local Teen Runaway Center," offered Angelo.

"Listen, if your aunt works at the Boardman Center," commented Laticia, "let's go with it."

"Right," said Pablo, "that's good enough for me."

"Yeah," replied Heather, "let's do it and get out of here."

"I hear what you're saying, Heather," Mark responded, "I've got plenty of other stuff to do."

"No disrespect meant to Glenna, but wasn't the Boardman Center in the news because of question-

able use of funds?" countered Angelo. "Do we really know enough about them?"

"OK," said Mark, "enough discussion. I've got to get to class. All in favor of the literacy program at the Boardman Center indicate by saying 'aye.' I think we've got a majority. Sorry, Angelo, you can't win them all."

"I wish all meetings went this smoothly," Heather said to Glenna as they left the room. "I mean, that was really a good meeting."

1. What did the group really know about the Boardman Center? Is it good group discussion practice to rely on a passing comment of one member?

2. Regardless of whether the meeting went smoothly, is there any ethical problem with this process? Explain.

Summary

Effective groups meet several criteria: They develop clearly defined goals, have an optimum number of diverse members, work to develop cohesiveness, establish norms, and establish a good working environment.

Once groups have assembled, they tend to move through five stages of development: forming, getting people to feel valued and accepted so that they identify with the group; storming, clarifying goals while determining the role each member will have in the group power structure; norming, solidifying rules for behavior; performing, overcoming obstacles and meeting goals successfully; and adjourning, assigning meaning to what they have done and determining how to end or maintain interpersonal relations they have developed.

Once the group has reached the performing stage, they begin to move through a series of steps of problem solving, including defining the problem as a question of fact, value, or policy; analyzing the problem; determining solution criteria; identifying possible solutions; evaluating solutions; and deciding.

Throughout the problem-solving process, members need to deal with the cognitive, affiliative, and egocentric constraints that groups encounter.

Communicate! Online

N ow that you have read Chapter 10, use your Communicate! CD-ROM for quick access to the electronic resources that accompany this text. Your CD-ROM gives you access to InfoTrac College Edition and the Communicate! Web site. When you get to the Communicate! home page, click on "Student Book Companion Site" in the Resource box at right to access the online study aids for this chapter, including a digital glossary, review quizzes, the chapter activities, and the chapter Web Resources.

Key Terms

At the Communicate! Web site, select the chapter resources for Chapter 10. Print a copy of the glossary for this chapter and test yourself with the electronic flash cards or complete the crossword puzzle to help you master these key terms:

work group (230)
group goal (230)
specific goal (230)
consistent goals (230)
challenging goals (231)
acceptable goals (231)
homogeneous group (232)
heterogeneous group (232)
cohesiveness (232)
team building activities (233)

norms (234)
ground rules (234)
working environment (235)
forming (237)
storming (238)
groupthink (238)
norming (239)
performing (239)
adjourning (239)
questions of fact (242)

questions of value (242)
questions of policy (242)
brainstorming (244)
decision making (246)
cognitive constraints (250)
affiliative constraints (250)
devil's advocate (250)
egocentric constraints (250)

Review Quiz

Test your knowledge of the concepts in this chapter by taking the online quiz at the Communicate! Web site. Select the chapter resources for Chapter 10, then click on "Review Quiz." When you have completed the quiz, submit it for scoring.

Skill Learning Activities

Complete the Observe & Analyze and Test Your Competence activities for Chapter 10 online at the Communicate! Web site. Select the chapter resources for Chapter 10, then click on "Activities." You can submit your Observe & Analyze answers to your instructor and compare your Test Your Competence answers to those provided by the authors.

10.1: Observe & Analyze: Cohesiveness in Homogeneous versus Heterogeneous Groups (234)
10.2: Observe & Analyze: Stages of Group Development (240)
10.3: Test Your Competence: Stating Problems (243)
10.4: Test Your Competence: The Problem-Solving Process (248)

Web Resources

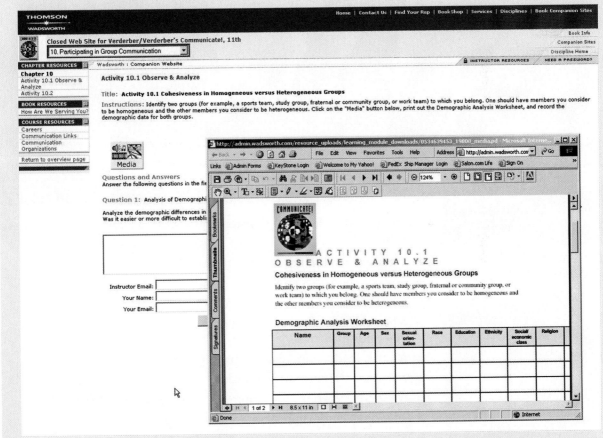

OBJECTIVES

After you have read this chapter, you should be able to answer these questions:

- What are roles, and why are they important in groups?
- How do members choose their roles?
- What types of roles do members of groups enact?
- What behaviors are expected of all members to make group meetings effective?
- What is leadership, and why is it important to a group?
- What are the tasks of leadership?
- What characterizes the communication behavior of leaders?
- How does leadership develop in a group?
- What behaviors can help an individual become a leader?
- What should the leader of a meeting do to make the meeting successful?

11

Members' Roles and Leadership in Groups

"Well, since we're all here, let's get started. The agenda calls for us to begin by reviewing the three bids we received for landscaping services. Dontonio, will you be the recorder again?"

"Sure, Ray, no problem."

"OK. Sarella, we know we can depend on you to have studied the bids. So why don't you start us out by summarizing what you found?"

"Well, only three of the six companies submitted detailed bids in line with our request. After reviewing each, I concluded that they all will provide the same basic services and on similar schedules. Two of the bids came in at about the same amount, but the other one is much higher. The two lower bids were from Wildflowers and from J&M."

"Well, I've never heard of Wildflowers, but my brother-in-law used J&M for a while and dropped them because they ran over his flower beds with their big riding mowers. I don't think we want that here."

"Hey, Jose, be careful, my boyfriend works for J&M, and I don't think his crews are that irresponsible."

"Judith, I don't think Jose meant his comment as a personal attack on your boyfriend. I think he was just trying to share something he had heard."

"Yeah, you're right, Shawn, thanks. Sorry, Jose. It's a good thing we have Shawn to keep us from popping off at each other."

O ur beginning conversation is typical of interactions in groups. If you listened closely, you could hear that the members of this group were not only discussing the topic but were acting in the ways expected of them by others in the group. Our goal in this chapter is to explain how members of groups take on specific roles that help or detract from the effectiveness of the group. We describe the types of roles members assume, and the responsibilities that group members have during meetings. Then we discuss group leadership, including understanding its functions, identifying several leadership roles, describing how members gain and maintain leadership, and the responsibilities of meeting leaders. Finally, we discuss ways to evaluate group effectiveness.

Members' Roles

role
a specific pattern of behavior that one group member performs based on the expectations of other members.

A **role** is a specific pattern of behavior that one group member performs based on the expectations of other members. The roles that group members play depend on their personalities and what is required or needed by the group. Four common types of roles are task-related, maintenance, procedural, and self-centered roles.

Task-Related Roles

task-related roles
specific patterns of behavior that directly help the group accomplish its goals.

Task-related roles require specific patterns of behavior that directly help the group accomplish its goals. Members who play task roles are likely to be information or opinion givers, information or opinion seekers, or analyzers.

information or opinion givers
people who provide content for the discussion.

Information or opinion givers provide content for the discussion. People who perform these roles are expected to have developed expertise or to be well informed on the content of the task and to share what they know with the group. The more material you have studied, the more valuable your contributions will be. "Well, the articles I read seem to agree that . . ." and "Based on the years I've been in the community and given what the recent citizens' poll revealed, I think we should . . ." are statements typical of information and opinion givers.

information or opinion seekers
people who probe others for their ideas and opinions on issues before the group.

Information or opinion seekers are expected to probe others for their ideas and opinions on issues before the group. Typical comments by those performing these roles include, "Before going further, what information do we have about how raising fees is likely to affect membership?" or "How do other members of the group feel about this idea?"

analyzers
people who probe the content and the reasoning of members during discussion.

Analyzers are expected to probe the content and the reasoning of members during discussion. In so doing, their role is to question what is being said and to help members understand the hidden assumptions in their statements. Analyzers make statements such as "Enrique, you're generalizing from only one instance. Can you give us some others?"

Maintenance Roles

Maintenance roles require specific patterns of behavior that help the group develop and maintain good member relationships, group cohesiveness, and effective levels of conflict. Members who play maintenance roles are likely to be supporters, tension relievers, harmonizers, or interpreters.

Supporters are expected to encourage others in the group. When another member contributes to the group, supporters show appreciation through their nonverbal or verbal behavior. Nonverbally, supporters may smile, nod, or vigorously shake their heads. Verbally, they demonstrate support through statements like "Good point, Ming," "I really like that idea, Nikki," or "It's obvious you've really done your homework, Janelle."

Tension relievers are expected to recognize when group members are stressed or tiring and to intervene in some way that relieves the stress or reenergizes the group. People who are effective in this role are able to tell jokes, kid around, and tell light-hearted stories so that the group is refreshed when it returns to the task. In some situations, a single well-placed one-liner will get a laugh, break the tension or the monotony, and jolt the group out of its lethargy. Although the tension reliever momentarily distracts the group from its task, this helps the group remain cohesive.

Harmonizers are expected to intervene in the group's discussions when conflict is threatening to harm group cohesiveness or the relationships between specific group members. Tension relievers distract group members, whereas harmonizers mediate and reconcile differences between group members. Harmonizers are likely to make statements such as "Tom, Jack, hold it a second. I know you're on opposite sides of this, but let's see where you might have some agreement," "Cool it, everybody, we're really coming up with some good stuff; let's not lose our momentum by getting into name-calling."

Interpreters are expected to be familiar with the differences in the social, cultural, and gender orientations of members of the group and to use this knowledge to help group members understand each other. Interpreters are especially important in groups whose members are culturally diverse (Jensen & Chilberg, 1991). For example, an interpreter might say, "Paul, Lin Chou is Chinese, so when she says that she will think about your plan she probably means that she does not support your ideas, but she doesn't want to embarrass you in front of the others." Or an interpreter might say, "Jim, most of us are Latino, and in our culture it is considered impolite to begin business before we socialize and catch up with one another."

Procedural Roles

Procedural roles require specific patterns of behavior that help the group manage its problem-solving process. Members who play procedural roles are likely to be expediters, recorders, or gatekeepers.

maintenance roles
patterns of behavior that help the group develop and maintain good member relationships, group cohesiveness, and effective levels of conflict.

supporters
people who encourage others in the group.

tension relievers
people who recognize when group members are stressed or tiring and intervene in some way that relieves the stress or reenergizes the group.

harmonizers
people who intervene in the group's discussions when conflict is threatening to harm group cohesiveness or the relationships between specific group members.

interpreters
people familiar with the differences in the social, cultural, and gender orientations of members of the group and who use this knowledge to help group members understand each other.

procedural roles
specific patterns of behavior that help the group manage its problem-solving process.

expediters
people who keep track of what the group is trying to accomplish and help move the group through the agenda.

recorders
people who take careful notes of what the group has decided and the evidence upon which the decisions are based.

minutes
A public record of the group's activities.

gatekeepers
people who manage the flow of conversation so that all members have an equal opportunity to participate.

self-centered roles
patterns of behavior that focus attention on individuals' needs and goals at the expense of the group.

Expediters are expected to keep track of what the group is trying to accomplish and to help move the group through the agenda. When the group has strayed, expediters will make statements like "I'm enjoying this, but I can't quite see what it has to do with resolving the issue," or "Let's see, aren't we still trying to find out whether these are the only criteria that we should be considering?"

Recorders are expected to take careful notes of what the group has decided and the evidence upon which the decisions are based. Recorders usually distribute edited copies of their notes to group members prior to the next meeting. Sometimes these notes are published as **minutes,** which become a public record of the group's activities.

Gatekeepers are expected to manage the flow of conversation so that all members have an equal opportunity to participate. If one or two members begin to dominate the conversation, the gatekeeper is expected to acknowledge this and to invite other members of the group to participate. Gatekeepers also notice nonverbal signals that indicate that a member wishes to speak. The gatekeeper is the one who sees that Juanita is on the edge of her chair, eager to comment, and says, "Let me interrupt you, Doug. We haven't heard from Juanita, and she seems to have something she wants to say."

Self-Centered Roles

Self-centered roles reflect specific patterns of behavior that focus attention on individuals' needs and goals at the expense of the group. Task-related, maintenance, and procedural roles must be played for groups to be effective, but self-centered roles detract from group effectiveness. Members who play self-centered roles are likely to be aggressors, jokers, withdrawers, or monopolizers.

Some members provide information to the group, others help maintain harmonious relations among group members, and still others help the group to stay on track. When you are part of a problem-solving group, which roles do you usually assume?

Aggressors seek to enhance their own status by criticizing almost everything or blaming others when things get rough and by deflating the ego or status of others. Aggressors should be confronted and helped to assume a more positive role. They should be asked whether they are aware of what they are doing and of the effect their behavior is having on the group.

Jokers attempt to draw attention to themselves by clowning, mimicking, or generally making a joke of everything. Unlike tension relievers, the joker is not focused on helping the group to relieve stress or tension. Rather, a joker disrupts work when the group is trying to focus on the task. Jokers should also be confronted and encouraged to use their abilities when the group needs a break but to refrain from disrupting the group when it is being productive.

Withdrawers can be expected to meet their own goals at the expense of group goals by not participating in the discussion or the work of the group. Sometimes withdrawers do so by physically missing meetings. At other times, withdrawers are physically present but remain silent in discussion or refuse to take responsibility for doing work. When a person has assumed this role, the group needs to find out why the person is choosing not to participate. When possible, the goals of the withdrawer need to be aligned with the goals of the group. For example, members of a group noticed Marianne came late to meetings and didn't seem to be prepared. The group finally confronted her and learned that she was late arriving because of her job. She also indicated that she did not contribute because she usually missed so much of the discussion. This group was able to change meeting dates, and Marianne became a fully participating member.

Monopolizers can be expected to talk all the time, giving the impression that they are well read, knowledgeable, and of value to the group. They should be encouraged when their comments are helpful and reined in when they are talking too much or when their comments are not helpful.

aggressors
people who seek to enhance their own status by criticizing almost everything or blaming others when things get rough and by deflating the ego or status of others.

jokers
people who attempt to draw attention to themselves by clowning, mimicking, or generally making a joke of everything.

withdrawers
people who meet their own goals at the expense of group goals by not participating in the discussion or the work of the group.

monopolizers
people who talk all the time, giving the impression that they are well read, knowledgeable, and of value to the group.

Normal Distribution of Roles

What proportion of time in a "normal" group should be devoted to the various roles described in this section? According to Robert Bales (1971), a leading researcher in group interaction processes, 40 to 60 percent of discussion time is spent giving and asking for information and opinion; 8 to 15 percent of discussion time is spent on disagreement, tension, or unfriendliness; and 16 to 26 percent of discussion time is characterized by agreement or friendliness (positive maintenance functions). We can apply two norms as guidelines for effective group functioning: (1) approximately half of all discussion time should be devoted to information sharing, and (2) group agreement time should far outweigh group disagreement time.

To complete a survey that will help you find out what combination of roles you are most likely to play in a team or group, use your Communicate! CD-ROM to access Web Resource 11.1: Identifying Your Team Player Style. How are you likely to contribute to group or team effectiveness?

Test Your Competence

Identifying Roles

Match the typical comment to the role it is most characteristic of.

Typical Comment

____ 1. "Did any one discover if we have to recommend only one company?"

____ 2. "I don't have time to help with that."

____ 3. "I think Rick has an excellent idea."

____ 4. "Stupid idea, Katie. Why don't you stop and think before you open your mouth."

____ 5. "Kwitabe doesn't necessarily agree with you, but he would consider it rude to openly disagree with someone who is older."

____ 6. "Josiah, in your plan, weren't you assuming that we'd only need two days for rehearsal?"

____ 7. "Lisa, I understand your point. What do you think about it, Paul?"

____ 8. "OK, so we've all agreed that we should begin keeping time logs. Now shouldn't we be thinking about what information needs to be in them?"

____ 9. "Wow, it's getting tense in here. If we don't chill out soon, we're likely to spontaneously combust. And, hello, that'll be a problem, cuz, we're the only engine company in this area of town. Right?"

____10. "Barb, I don't think that your position is really that different from Saul's. Let me see if I can explain how they relate."

____11. "I've visited that home before, and found that both the mom and dad are trying very hard to help their son."

Roles

a. aggressor

b. analyzer

c. expediter

d. gatekeeper

e. harmonizer

f. information or opinion giver

g. information or opinion seeker

h. interpreter

i. supporter

j. tension reliever

k. withdrawer

 You can complete this activity online and compare your answers to the authors'. Use your Communicate! CD-ROM to access **Skill Learning Activity 11.1.**

Member Responsibilities in Group Meetings

Although members specialize in particular roles during group discussions and problem solving, members of effective groups also assume common responsibilities for making their meetings successful. Here are some guidelines prepared by a class of university students to help group members prepare for, participate in, and follow up on a meeting in order to increase its effectiveness ("Guidelines," 1998).

Preparing

As the chapter opening vignette illustrated, too often people think of group meetings as a "happening" that requires attendance but no particular preparation. Countless times we have observed people arriving at a meeting unprepared even though they are carrying packets of material that they received in advance of the meeting. The reality is that meetings should not be treated as impromptu events but as carefully planned interactions that pool information from well-prepared individuals. Here are some important steps to take prior to attending a meeting.

1. **Study the agenda.** Consider the purpose of the meeting and determine what you need to do to be prepared. The agenda is an outline for your preparation.

2. **Study the minutes.** If this is one in a series of meetings, study the minutes and your own notes from the previous meetings. Since each meeting is not a separate event, what happened at one meeting should provide the basis for preparation for the next meeting.

3. **Prepare for your contributions.** Read the material distributed prior to the meeting and do your own research to become better informed about items on the agenda. If no material is provided, identify the issues yourself and learn what you need to know to be a productive member of the group. Bring any materials you have uncovered that will help the group accomplish the agenda. If appropriate, discuss the agenda with others who will not be attending the meeting and solicit their ideas concerning issues to be discussed in the meeting.

4. **Prepare to play a major role.** Consider which roles you are assigned or which you are interested in playing. What do you need to do to play those roles to the best of your ability?

5. **List questions.** Make a list of questions related to agenda items that you would like to have answered during the meeting.

Participating

Go into the meeting with the expectation that you will be a full participant. If there are five people in the group, all five should be participating.

1. **Listen attentively.** Concentrate on what others are saying so that you can use your material to complement, supplement, or counter what has been presented.

2. **Stay focused.** In a group setting, it is easy to get the discussion going in nonproductive directions. Keep your comments focused on the specific agenda item under discussion. If others have gotten off the subject, do what you can to get people back on track.

3. **Ask questions.** "Honest" questions whose answers you do not already know help to stimulate discussion and build ideas. Review the guidelines for questions presented in Chapters 6 and 9.

4. **Take notes.** Even if someone else is responsible for providing the official minutes, you will need notes that help you follow the line of development. Also, these notes will help you remember what has been said and any responsibilities you have agreed to take on. For useful tips on how to take minutes in meetings, use your Communicate! CD-ROM to access Web Resource 11.2: Taking Notes.

5. **Play devil's advocate.** When you think an idea has not been fully discussed or tested, be willing to voice disagreement or encourage further discussion.

6. **Monitor your contributions.** Especially when people are well prepared, they have a tendency to dominate discussion. Make sure that you are neither dominating the discussion nor abdicating your responsibility to share insights and opinions. If you are a person who finds it difficult to participate in meetings, use your Communicate! CD-ROM to access Web Resource 11.3: Assert Yourself in Meetings, which discusses useful steps for speaking out in meetings.

Some people wait until the last minute to prepare for meetings. Do you find it annoying to attend meetings where people come unprepared to participate?

Following Up

When meetings end, too often people leave and forget about what took place until the next meeting. But what happens in one meeting provides a basis for what happens in the next; be prepared to move forward at the next meeting.

1. **Review and summarize your notes.** Try to do this shortly after you have left the meeting while ideas are still fresh in your mind. Make notes of what needs to be discussed next time. For a detailed discussion of how to process your meeting notes, use your Communicate! CD-ROM to access Web Resource 11.4: Dealing with Your Notes.

2. **Evaluate your effectiveness.** How effective were you in helping the group move toward achieving its goals? Where were you strong? Where were you weak? What should you do next time that you did not do in this meeting?

3. **Review decisions.** Make note of what your role was in making decisions. Did you do all that you could have done?

4. **Communicate progress.** Inform others who need to know about information conveyed and decisions that were made in the meeting.

5. **Follow up.** Make sure you complete all assignments you received in the meeting.

6. **Review minutes.** Compare the official minutes of the meeting to your own notes, and report any significant discrepancies that you find.

Leadership

Although performance of all task, maintenance, and procedural roles aid groups in accomplishing their goals, good leadership is also necessary to accomplish group goals. Scholars have offered numerous definitions of leadership, but common to most definitions is the notion that **leadership** is a process of influencing members to accomplish group goals (Shaw, 1981, p. 317). In this section we will discuss the functions of leadership, types of leaders, and ways of becoming informal leaders.

leadership
is a process of influencing members to accomplish group goals

The Function of Leadership

Napier and Gershenfeld (1999, p. 243) suggest that functional leadership is acting in a way that helps the group achieve its goals. These functions include influencing the group's procedures and task accomplishment and maintaining satisfactory relationships between members. From this perspective, then, all members share leadership because member roles are specifically designed to serve these functions as well. However, in most groups, members do not assume some of the roles that are necessary for effective group functioning. Current thinking is that the leader's role is to step in and assume a combination of roles needed in the group at a particular time that are not being assumed by other group members (Rothwell, 1998, p. 168).

In short, those filling the leadership role must be versatile and able to adapt their behavior to the situation. Leaders are adept at listening to the group and becoming attuned to what the group needs at a particular time. Based on what they have heard, leaders adapt their behavior to the situation and influence the group to behave in ways that will lead to goal accomplishment.

Types of Leaders

formal leader
an assigned, appointed, or elected leader who is given legitimate power to influence others.

informal leaders
members of the group whose authority to influence stems from the power they gain through their interactions in the group.

A group will often have more than one leader. Many groups have a designated **formal leader,** an assigned, appointed, or elected leader who is given legitimate power to influence others. During its work life, a group may have only one formal leader, but several people may play leadership roles. **Informal leaders** are members of the group whose authority to influence stems from the power they gain through their interactions in the group. Informal leaders do not have legitimate power; rather, their influence comes from their expertise or from how much other group members like and respect them.

How Members Gain and Maintain Informal Leadership

According to research by Ernest Bormann (1990), leaders emerge through a two-step elimination process. During the first step of the process, members form crude impressions about one another based on early interactions. During this phase, members who do not demonstrate the commitment or skillfulness necessary to fulfill leadership roles are eliminated. Group members less likely to emerge as leaders include those who do not participate (either due to shyness or indifference); those who are overly strong and bossy in their opinions and positions; those who are perceived to be uninformed, less intelligent, or unskilled; and those with irritating interpersonal styles.

During the second phase, those who are still acceptable to the group may vie for power. Sometimes one contender will become an informal leader because the group faces a crisis that this member recognizes and is better able to help the group remedy than others are. At other times, a contender may become an informal leader because one or more members of the group have come to trust this person and openly support influence attempts made by that contender. To explore seven principles that are useful for maintaining leadership during difficult challenges, read "Leadership Principles for Tough Times," available through InfoTrac College Edition. Use your Communicate! CD-ROM to access Web Resource 11.5: Leadership Principles.

In some groups, most members will eventually recognize one contender as the informal leader. In other groups, two or more contenders may comfortably share informal leadership by specializing and engaging in complementary behavior. For example, one leader might be particularly attuned to group relationships and may use influence to keep conflict at healthy levels. The other leader may be skilled at keeping the group on track and moving through the agenda during meetings. In general, however, the members of the group will be more susceptible to the informal leadership of those contenders who provide appropriate combinations of procedural, task, and relationship maintaining influences.

Students are often interested in how they can exert leadership in a group. Because leadership is demonstrated through communication behaviors, following these recommendations can help you gain influence.

1. **Actively participate in discussions.** When members do not participate, others may view them as disinterested or uninformed. Indicate your interest and commitment to the group by participating in the group's discussions.

2. **Come to group meetings prepared.** Uninformed members rarely achieve leadership, whereas those who demonstrate expertise gain the power to influence us.

3. **Actively listen to the ideas and opinions of others.** Because leadership requires analyzing what a group needs, the leader must understand the ideas and needs of members. When you actively listen, you also demonstrate your willingness to consider a point of view different from your own. We are more likely to accept influence attempts when we believe the person really understands us.

4. **Avoid stating overly strong opinions.** When other members of the group perceive that someone is inflexible, they are less likely to accept that person as a leader.

5. **Actively manage meaning.** During problem solving, members can become unclear about what is happening. As a result, they experience uncertainty. If you have a mental map or framework that can help the group clarify and understand issues it is facing, you can use it to influence the group. Gail T. Fairhurst has explored how leaders manage meaning in groups; she calls this process **framing.** You can read about her work in the Spotlight on Scholars feature.

framing
how leaders manage meaning in groups.

Spotlight on Scholars ▶ Gail T. Fairhurst

Professor of Communication, University of Cincinnati, on Leadership in Work Organizations ◆ ◆ ◆ ◆

ccording to Gail T. Fairhurst, who has been studying organizational communication throughout her career, leadership is not a trait possessed by only some people, nor is it a simple set of behaviors that can be learned and then used in any situation. Rather, Fairhurst's research has convinced her that leadership is the process of creating social reality by managing the meanings that are assigned to certain behaviors, activities, programs, and events. Further, she believes leadership is best understood as a relational process.

Fairhurst's current work is focused on how organizational leaders frame issues for their members. Framing is the process of managing meaning by selecting and highlighting some aspects of a subject while excluding others. When we communicate our frames to others, we manage meaning because we are asserting that our interpretation of the subject should be taken as "real" over other possible interpretations. How leaders choose to verbally frame events at work is one way that leaders influence workers' and others' perceptions.

Framing is especially important when the organization experiences change, such as downsizing. To reduce uncertainty during times of change, members of the organization seek to understand what the change means to them personally and to the way they work in the organization. Leaders are expected to help members understand what is happening and what it means. By framing the change, leaders select and highlight some features of the change while downplaying others, providing a lens through which organizational members can understand what the change means.

In *The Art of Framing* (with Robert A. Sarr, 1996), Fairhurst says that leaders use five language forms or devices to frame information: metaphors, jargon or catch phrases, contrast, spin, and stories. Metaphors show how the change is similar to something that is already familiar. For instance,

leaders may frame downsizing with weight and prizefighting metaphors, suggesting that the organization is "flabby and needs to get down to a better fighting weight so it can compete effectively." Jargon or catch phrases are similar to metaphors because they help us understand the change in language with which we are already familiar. Leaders may use jargon and catch phrases with words such as "lean and mean." Contrast frames help us understand what the change is by first seeing what it is not. Leaders may use contrast frames by suggesting that the downsizing "is not an attempt to undermine the union, it is simply an attempt to remain competitive." Spin frames cast the change in either a positive or negative light. Leaders may use a positive spin frame by pointing out that the company will not use forced layoffs but will instead use early retirements and natural attrition to reduce the size of the workforce. Story frames make the change seem more real by serving as an example, such as recounting the success of another well-known company that used the same strategy.

Fairhurst has also studied how the meaning of a change is continually reframed as members of the organization work out the specifics of how to implement the change. She analyzed the transcripts of tape-recorded conversations between managers and their subordinates during times when a company was undergoing a significant change in the way it worked. Her analysis has revealed that employees' reactions to change are often framed as "predicaments" or "problems," showing that they are confused or unclear about the change. Sometimes employees feel that what they are being asked to do is in conflict with the goals of the change. In response, the leader might counter the employee predicament by using one of several reframes, for example, "personalization." Using personalization, a leader might point out the specific behaviors the member needs to adopt to be in line with the change. Fairhurst suggests that such reframing techniques help members understand what to do next to bring about the change.

Fairhurst's experience in analyzing the real conversations of managers and subordinates indicates that many of those in organizational leadership roles are not very good at framing and, as a result, may need to be trained to develop mental models that they can draw on to be more effective during their day-to-day interactions with workers. For complete citations of many of Fairhurst's publications, see the references list at the end of this book.

Fairhurst served a five-year term as Head of the Department of Communication Arts at the University of Cincinnati. Since then, she has resumed her role as an active member of the faculty. In addition to teaching courses in organizational communication at both the graduate and undergraduate levels, Fairhurst works with the Center for Environmental Communication Studies, a research and consulting organization she helped found.

Gender Differences in Emerging Leaders

A question that has generated considerable research is whether the gender of a leader has any effect on a group's acceptance of leadership. Some research suggests that gender does affect group acceptance, but not because women lack the necessary skills. A persistent research finding is that messages are evaluated differently depending on the source of the message (Aries, 1998, p. 65). Thus, the same behavior may be perceived differently depending on whether it is performed by a woman or a man. For example, a group member says, "I think we are belaboring the point and should move on." If the speaker is a woman, the comment may well be perceived as bossy, dominating, and critical. If a man makes the same comment, he is more likely to be perceived as being insightful and task-oriented. One problem women face is that their efforts to show leadership may be differently interpreted.

Moreover, gender-role stereotypes can lead to devaluing cooperative and supportive behaviors that many women use quite skillfully. Yet, as Sally Helgesen (1990) points out, many female leaders are successful because they respond to people and their problems with flexibility and because they are able to break down barriers between people at all levels of the organization.

Fortunately, changes in perception are occurring as the notion of "effective" leadership changes. Patricia Andrews (1992, p. 90) supports this conclusion, noting that it is more important to consider the unique character of a group and the skills of the person serving as leader than the gender of the leader. She goes on to show that a complex interplay of factors (including how much power the leader has) influences effectiveness more than gender does. As W. E. Jurma and B. C. Wright (1990, p. 110) have pointed out, research studies have shown that men and women are equally capable of leading task-oriented groups.

Moreover, by the mid-1990s, studies were showing that task-relevant communication was the only significant predictor of who would emerge as leaders, regardless of gender. Katherine Hawkins's (1995) study noted no significant gender differences in the production of task-relevant communication. Such communication, it seems, is the key to emergent leadership in task-oriented group interaction—for either gender.

Leading Group Meetings

Most of us will have occasion to be responsible for convening, facilitating, and following up some group meeting. Whether you are leading the meeting of a project group for class, a task force at work, or substitute for your manager as the leader of the monthly department meeting, knowing how to effectively plan, facilitate, and follow up on meetings is a useful skill. Here are guidelines effective leaders follow.

Before the Meeting

1. **Prepare the agenda.** An agenda is an organized outline of the items that need to be covered during a meeting. Items for the agenda come from reviewing the minutes of the last meeting to determine what the group agreed to take as next steps and from new issues that have arisen since the last meeting. Effective leaders make sure the agenda is appropriate for the length of the meeting. Figure 11.1 shows an agenda for a group that is meeting to decide which one of three courses to offer over the Internet next semester. For other ideas about agenda preparation, use your Communicate! CD-ROM to access Web Resource 11.6: Scripting the Agenda.

2. **Decide who should attend the meeting.** In most cases, all members of a group will attend meetings. Occasionally, one or more members of the group may not need to attend a particular meeting but may only need to be informed of the outcomes of the meeting.

3. **Arrange an appropriate location and meeting time.** Be sure that the location has all the equipment and supplies the group will need to work effectively. This may include arranging for audiovisual equipment, computers, and other specialized equipment. Choose a setting where the tables and chairs can be arranged in a manner that suits the group's purpose. Because groups become less effective in long meetings, a meeting should last no longer than ninety minutes. If a meeting must be planned for a longer period of time, schedule hourly breaks to avoid fatigue.

March 1, 2004

To: Campus computer discussion group
From: Janelle Smith
Re: Agenda for discussion group meeting

Date: March 8, 2004
Place: Student Union, Conference Room A
Time: 3:00 p.m. to 4:30 p.m. (Please be prompt.)

Meeting Objectives

1. We will familiarize ourselves with each of three courses that have been proposed for Internet-based delivery next semester.

2. We will evaluate each course against the criteria we developed last month.

3. We will use a consensus decision process to determine which of the three courses to offer.

Agenda for Group Discussion

Review of Philosophy 141
   Report by Justin on Philosophy 141 proposal
   Committee questions
   Comparison of PHIL 141 to criteria

Review of Art History 336
   Report by Marique on Art History 336 proposal
   Committee questions
   Comparison of ARTH 336 to criteria

Review of Communication 235
   Report by Kathryn on Communication 235
   Committee questions
   Comparison of COMM 235 to criteria

Consensus building discussion and decision
   Which proposals fit the criteria?
   Are there non-criteria-related factors to consider?
   Which proposal is more acceptable to all members?

Discussion of next steps and task assignments.

Set date of next meeting.

Figure 11.1
Agenda for Internet course committee

4. **Distribute the agenda.** The agenda should be in the hands of attendees several days before the meeting. Unless group members get an agenda ahead of time, they will not be able to prepare for the meeting.

5. **Speak with each participant prior to the meeting.** It is important to understand members' positions and personal goals. Time spent pre-working issues helps the leader anticipate conflicts that are likely to emerge and plan how to manage them so that the group makes effective decisions and maintains cohesiveness.

During the Meeting

1. **Review and modify the agenda.** Begin the meeting by reviewing the agenda and modifying it based on members' suggestions. Because things can change between when an agenda is distributed and when the meeting is held, reviewing the agenda ensures that the group is working on

items that are still important and relevant. Reviewing the agenda also gives members a chance to control what is to be discussed.

2. **Monitor roles members assume and consciously play that are unfilled by others.** The role of the leader during a discussion is to provide the task or procedural direction and relationship management that the group lacks. Leaders need to maintain awareness of what specific roles are needed by the group at a specific time. When other group members are assuming the necessary roles, the leader need do nothing. But when there is need for a particular role and members are not assuming that role, the leader should perform the necessary behaviors. For example, if the leader notices that some people are talking more than their fair share and that no one else is trying to draw out quieter members, the leader should assume the gatekeeper role and ask reluctant members to comment on the discussion.

3. **Monitor the time so that the group stays on schedule.** It is easy for a group to get bogged down in a discussion. Although another group member may serve as expediter, it is the leader's responsibility to make sure that the group stays on schedule.

4. **Monitor conflicts and intervene as needed.** A healthy level of conflict should be encouraged in the group so that issues are fully examined. But if the conflict level becomes dysfunctional, the leader may need to mediate so that relationships are not unduly strained.

Effective leaders hold informal converstions after the meeting to repair damaged relationships. Is this easy for you to do?

5. **Periodically check to see if the group is ready to make a decision.** The leader of the group should listen for agreement and move the group into its formal decision process when the leader senses that discussion is no longer adding insight.

© Frozen Images/The Image Works

6. **Implement the group's decision rules.** The leader is responsible for overseeing that the decision-making rule the group has agreed to is used. If the group is deciding by consensus, the leader must make sure that all members feel that the chosen alternative is one that they can support. If the group is deciding by majority rule, the leader calls for the vote and tallies the results.

7. **Before ending the meeting, summarize decisions and assignments.** To bring closure to the meeting and to make sure that each member leaving the meeting is clear about what has been accomplished, the leader should summarize what has hap-

pened in the meeting. The leader also should reiterate task assignments made during the meeting and review what is left to accomplish or decide.

8. **Ask the group to decide if and when another meeting is needed.** Ongoing groups should be careful not to meet just for the sake of meeting. Leaders should clarify with members when, and if, future meetings are necessary. The overall purposes of future meetings will dictate the agenda that will need to be prepared.

Meeting Follow-Up

1. **Review the meeting outcomes and process.** A good leader learns how to be more effective by reflecting on and analyzing how well the previous meeting went. Leaders need to think about whether the meeting accomplished its goals and whether group cohesion was improved or damaged in the process.

2. **Prepare and distribute a summary of meeting outcomes.** Although some groups have a member who serves as the recorder and who distributes minutes, many groups rely on their leaders to do this. A written record of what was agreed to, accomplished, and next steps serve to remind group members of the work they have to do. If the group has a recorder, the leader should check to make sure that minutes are distributed in a timely manner.

3. **Repair damaged relationships through informal conversations.** If the debate during the meeting has been heated, it is likely that some people have damaged their relationships with others or left the meeting angry or hurt. Leaders can help repair relationships by seeking out these participants and talking with them. Through empathetic listening, leaders can soothe hurt feelings and spark a recommitment to the group.

4. **Follow up with members to see how they are progressing on items assigned to them.** When participants have been assigned specific task responsibilities, the leader should check with them to see if they have encountered any problems in completing those tasks.

Conversation and Analysis

Use your Communicate! CD-ROM to access the video clip of the Student Government Financial Committee meeting. Click on the "In Action" icon in the menu at left, then click on "Conversation Menu" in the menu bar at the top of the screen. Select Group Communication to watch the video (it takes a minute for the video to load). As you watch the conversation, observe the group's dynamics. Is their goal clear? Do they have sufficient diversity in their membership? What stage of group development do they appear to be in? Are they using the problem-solving method? What roles are being played by each member? Do they appear to be prepared for the meeting? You can answer these and other analysis questions by clicking on "Analysis" in the menu bar at the top of the screen. When you've answered all the questions, click "Done" to compare your answers to those provided by the authors.

Here is a transcript of the conversation. You can also find a copy of this transcript online, which allows you to take notes as you watch the video. Use your Communicate! CD-ROM to access Skill Learning Activity 11.4. When you have finished viewing the video and taking notes, click on "Authors' Model Analysis" to compare your notes to the detailed conversational analysis provided by the authors.

As members of the Student Government Financial Committee, Davinia, Joyce, Thomas, and Pat make decisions on how much funding, if any, to give to various student groups that request support from the funds collected from student fees. They are meeting for the first time in a campus cafeteria.

Conversation

THOMAS: Well, we've got twenty-three applications for funding and a total of $19,000 that we can distribute.

DAVINIA: Maybe we should start by listing how much each of the twenty-three groups wants.

JOYCE: It might be better to start by determining the criteria that we will use to decide if groups get any funding from student fees.

DAVINIA: Yeah, right. We should set up our criteria before we look at applications.

THOMAS: Sounds good to me. Pat, what do you think?

PAT: I'm on board. Let's set up criteria first and then review the applications against those.

JOYCE: OK, we might start by looking at the criteria used last year by the Financial Committee. Does anyone have a copy of those?

THOMAS: I do. [*He passes out copies to the other three people.*] They had three criteria: service to a significant number of students, compliance with the college's nondiscrimination policies, and educational benefit.

DAVINIA: What counts as "educational benefit"? Did last year's committee specify that?

JOYCE: Good question. Thomas, you were on the committee last year. Do you remember what they counted as educational benefit?

THOMAS: The main thing I remember is that it was distinguished from artistic benefit—like a concert or art exhibit or something like that.

PAT: But can't art be educational?

DAVINIA: Yeah, I think so. Thomas, Joyce, do you?

THOMAS: I guess, but it's like art's primary purpose isn't to educate.

JOYCE: I agree. It's kind of hard to put into words, but I think educational benefit has more to do with information and the mind, and art has more to do with the soul. Does that sound too hokey? [*Laughter*]

PAT: OK, so we want to say that we don't distribute funds to any hokey groups, right? [*More laughter*]

DAVINIA: It's not like we're against art or anything. It's just the funding we can distribute is for educational benefit, right? [*Everyone nods.*]

JOYCE: OK, let's move onto another criterion. What is the significant number of students?

THOMAS: Last year we said that the proposals for using money had to be of potential interest to at least 20 percent of students to get funding. How does that sound to you?

PAT: Sounds OK as long as we remember that something can be of potential interest to students who aren't members of specific groups. Like, for instance, I might want to attend a program on Native American customs even though I'm not a Native American. See what I mean?

DAVINIA: Good point—we don't want to define student interest as student identity or anything like that. [*Nods of agreement*]

THOMAS: OK, so are we agreed that 20 percent is about right with the understanding that the 20 percent can include students who aren't in a group applying for funding? [*Nods*] OK, then do we need to discuss the criterion of compliance with the college's policies on nondiscrimination?

© Thomson Higher Education

Evaluating Group Effectiveness

There is an old saying that goes, "A camel is a horse built by a committee." Although this saying is humorous, for some groups it is also true. If we are to avoid ending up with camels when we want horses, we need to understand how to assess a group's effectiveness and how to improve group processes based on those evaluations. Groups can be evaluated on the quality of the decision, the quality of role taking, and the quality of leadership.

The Decision

That a group meets to discuss an issue does not necessarily mean that it will arrive at a decision. As foolish as it may seem, some groups thrash away for hours only to adjourn without having reached a conclusion. Of course, some groups discuss such serious problems that a decision cannot be made without several meetings. In such cases, it is important that the group adjourn with a clear understanding of what the next step will be. When a group "finishes" its work without arriving at some decision, however, the result is likely to be frustration and disillusionment. The Group Effectiveness Rating Sheet in Figure 11.2 provides one method for evaluating the quality of a group's decision based on three major aspects of groups: group characteristics, member relationships, and problem-solving ability. You can download and print a copy of the Group Effectiveness Rating Sheet by accessing Skill Learning Activity 11.5.

Individual Participation and Role Behavior

Although a group will struggle without leadership, it may not be able to function at all without members who are willing and able to meet the task, maintenance, and procedural functions for the group. The Participation and Role Behavior Rating Sheet in Figure 11.3 provides one method for evaluating the behavior and role taking of each participant. You can download and print

---

Rate the group as a whole on each of the following questions using this scale: 1 = always, 2 = often, 3 = sometimes, 4 = rarely, 5 = never.

Group Characteristics

_____ 1. Did the group have a clearly defined goal to which most members were committed?

_____ 2. Did the group's size fit the tasks required to meet its goals?

_____ 3. Was group member diversity sufficient to ensure that important viewpoints were expressed?

_____ 4. Did group cohesiveness aid in task accomplishment?

_____ 5. Did group norms help accomplish goals and maintain relationships?

_____ 6. Was the physical setting conducive to accomplishing the work?

Member Relationships

_____ 1. Did members feel valued and respected by others?

_____ 2. Were members comfortable interacting with others?

_____ 3. Did members balance speaking time so that all members participated?

_____ 4. Were conflicts seen as positive experiences?

_____ 5. Did members like and enjoy each other?

Group Problem Solving

_____ 1. Did the group take time to define its problem?

_____ 2. Was high-quality information presented to help the group understand the problem?

_____ 3. Did the group develop criteria before suggesting solutions?

_____ 4. Were the criteria discussed sufficiently and based on all of the information available?

_____ 5. Did the group use effective brainstorming techniques to develop a comprehensive list of creative solution alternatives?

_____ 6. Did the group fairly and thoroughly compare each alternative to all solution criteria?

_____ 7. Did the group follow its decision rules in choosing among alternatives that met the criteria?

_____ 8. Did the group arrive at a decision that members agreed to support?

Figure 11.2
Group Effectiveness Rating Sheet

a copy of the Participation and Role Behavior Rating Sheet by accessing **Skill Learning Activity 11.5.**

Leadership

Some group discussions are leaderless, although no discussion should be without leadership. If there is an appointed leader—and most groups have one—evaluation can focus on that individual. If the group is truly leaderless, the evaluation should consider attempts at leadership by various members or focus on the apparent leader who emerges from the group. The Leader Behavior Rating Sheet in Figure 11.4 provides one method for evaluating the behavior and role taking of the meeting leader. You can download and print a copy of the Leader Behavior Rating Sheet by accessing **Skill Learning Activity 11.5.**

Name of Participant: _____
For each characteristic listed below, rate the participant on a scale of 1 to 5:
1 = excellent, 2 = good, 3 = average, 4 = fair, 5 = poor.

Meeting Behavior

_____ 1. Prepared and knowledgeable

_____ 2. Contributed ideas and opinions

_____ 3. Actively listened to the ideas of others

_____ 4. Politely voiced disagreement

_____ 5. Completed between-meeting assigned tasks

Performance of Task-Oriented Roles

_____ 1. Acted as information or opinion giver

_____ 2. Acted as information seeker

_____ 3. Acted as analyzer

Performance of Procedural Roles

_____ 1. Acted as expediter

_____ 2. Acted as recorder

_____ 3. Acted as gatekeeper

Performance of Maintenance Roles

_____ 1. Acted as supporter

_____ 2. Acted as tension reliever

_____ 3. Acted as harmonizer

_____ 4. Acted as interpreter

Avoidance of Self-Centered Roles

_____ 1. Avoided acting as aggressor

_____ 2. Avoided acting as joker

_____ 3. Avoided acting as withdrawer

_____ 4. Avoided acting as monopolizer

Qualitative Analysis

Based on the quantitative analysis above, write a two- to five-paragraph analysis of the person's participation. Be sure to give specific examples of the person's behavior to back up your conclusions.

Figure 11.3
Participation and Role Behavior Rating Sheet

Was there a formal group leader? Yes No

If yes, name this person: _____

Who were the informal leaders of the group?

a. _____

b. _____

c. _____

Which of these leaders was most influential in helping the group meet its goals?

_____

Rate this leader on each of the following questions using a scale of 1 to 5:
1 = always, 2 = often, 3 = sometimes, 4 = rarely, 5 = never.

_____ 1. Demonstrated commitment to the group and its goals.

_____ 2. Actively listened to ideas and opinions of others.

_____ 3. Adapted his or her behavior to the immediate needs of the group.

_____ 4. Avoided stating overly strong opinions.

_____ 5. Managed meaning for the group by framing issues and ideas.

_____ 6. Was prepared for all meetings.

_____ 7. Kept the group on task and on schedule.

_____ 8. Made sure that conflicts were handled effectively.

_____ 9. Implemented the group's decision rules effectively.

_____ 10. Worked to repair damaged relationships.

_____ 11. Followed up after meetings to see how members were progressing on
             assignments.

Figure 11.4
Leader Behavior Rating
Sheet

Test Your Competence

Consulting on Meeting Effectiveness

If you are part of an ongoing task group in this class, use this group to complete this activity. If you are not in an ongoing task group in this class, follow your instructor's directions for identifying an appropriate group to use for this activity. You are to act as a consultant to your group by evaluating the last meeting (or the next meeting) of your group using the group effectiveness, participation and role behavior, and leader behavior rating sheets. Based on your ratings, write a short consultant's report in which you identify the group's strengths and weaknesses. Then develop five to seven specific action recommendations for improving the next meeting of the group.

 You can complete this activity online, download copies of the rating sheets, and compare your answers to the authors'. Use your Communicate! CD-ROM to access Skill Learning Activity 11.5.

What Would You Do? A QUESTION OF ETHICS

 ou know, Sue, we're going to be in deep trouble if the group doesn't support Mc-Gowan's resolution about dues reform."

"Well, we'll just have to see to it that all the arguments in favor of that resolution are heard, but in the end it's the group's decision."

"That's very democratic of you, Sue, but you know that if it doesn't pass, you're likely to be out on your tail."

"That may be, Heather, but I don't see what I can do about it."

"You don't want to see. First, right now the group respects you. If you would just apply a little pressure on a couple of the members, you'd get what you want."

"What do you mean?"

"Look, this is a good cause. You've got something on just about every member of the group. Take a couple of members aside and let them know

that this is payoff time. I think you'll see that some key folks will see it your way."

Heather may well have a point about how Sue can control the outcome. Should Sue follow Heather's advice? Why or why not?

Summary

When individuals interact in groups, they assume roles. A role is a specific pattern of behavior that a member of the group performs based on the expectations of other members.

There are four types of roles: task-oriented roles, maintenance roles, procedural roles, and self-centered roles. Members select the roles they will play based on how roles fit with their personality, what is required of them by virtue of a position they hold, and what roles the group needs to have assumed that are not being played by other members. One role that is of particular importance to effective group functioning is the leadership role.

Leadership is the process of influencing members to accomplish goals. As such, leadership is a general role that includes providing whatever is needed by the group that is missing in other members' behavior. Groups may have a single leader, but more commonly leadership is shared among group members. Groups may have both formal and informal leaders. Formal leaders have formal authority given to them either by some entity outside of the group or by the group members themselves. Informal leaders emerge during a two-stage process. Individuals who want to become recognized as informal leaders in a group should come to group meetings prepared, actively participate in discussions, actively listen to others, avoid appearing bossy or stating overly strong opinions, and manage the meaning for other participants by framing.

Using the forms provided, you can evaluate groups on the quality of the decision, the quality of notetaking, and the quality of leadership.

Communicate! Online

ow that you have read Chapter 11, use your Communicate! CD-ROM for quick access to the electronic resources that accompany this text. Your CD-ROM gives you access to the video of the Student Government Financial Committee meeting on pages 272–273, InfoTrac College Edition, and the Communicate! Web site. When you get to the Communicate! home page, click on "Student Book Companion Site" in the Resource box at right to access the online study aids for this chapter, including a digital glossary, review quizzes, the chapter activities, and the chapter Web Resources.

Key Terms

At the Communicate! Web site, select the chapter resources for Chapter 11. Print a copy of the glossary for this chapter and test yourself with the electronic flash cards or complete the crossword puzzle to help you master these key terms:

role (256)
task-related roles (256)
information or opinion givers (256)
information or opinion seekers (256)
analyzers (256)
maintenance roles (257)
supporters (257)

tension relievers (257)
harmonizers (257)
interpreters (257)
procedural roles (257)
expediters (258)
recorders (258)
minutes (258)
gatekeepers (258)
self-centered roles (258)

aggressors (259)
jokers (259)
withdrawers (259)
monopolizers (259)
leadership (263)
formal leader (264)
informal leaders (264)
framing (265)

Review Quiz

Test your knowledge of the concepts in this chapter by taking the online quiz at the Communicate! Web site. Select the chapter resources for Chapter 11, then click on "Review Quiz." When you have completed the quiz, submit it for scoring.

Skill Learning Activities

Complete the Observe & Analyze, Test Your Competence, and Conversation and Analysis activities for Chapter 11 online at the Communicate! Web site. Select the chapter resources for Chapter 11, then click on "Activities." You can submit your Observe & Analyze answers to your instructor, compare your Test Your Competence answers to those provided by the authors, and do both for the Conversation and Analysis activity.

11.1: Test Your Competence: Identifying Roles (260)
11.2: Observe & Analyze: Member Meeting Responsibilities (263)
11.3: Observe & Analyze: Emerging Informal Leadership in CBS's *Survivor* Series (265)
11.4: Conversation and Analysis: Group Communication (272)
11.5: Test Your Competence: Consulting on Meeting Effectiveness (276)

Web Resources

Access the Web Resources for this chapter online at the Communicate! Web site. Select the chapter resources for Chapter 11, then click on "Web Resources."

11.1: Identifying Your Team Player Style (260)
11.2: Taking Notes (262)
11.3: Assert Yourself in Meetings (262)
11.4: Dealing with Your Notes (263)

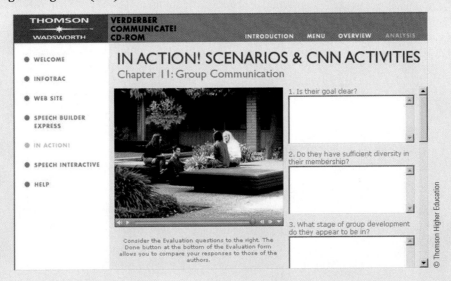

Group Communication | Self-Review

Group Communication from Chapters 10 and 11

How effective are you at working in problem-solving groups? The following statements can help you evaluate your effectiveness in group settings. Use this scale to assess the frequency with which you perform each behavior: 1 = always; 2 = often; 3 = sometimes; 4 = rarely; 5 = never.

_____ I enjoy working with others to accomplish goals. (Ch. 10)

_____ I actively listen and keep an open mind during problem-solving discussions. (Ch. 10)

_____ I adapt my behavior to the norms of the group. (Ch. 10)

_____ I am comfortable with conflict. (Ch. 10)

_____ I avoid performing self-centered roles in the group. (Ch. 11)

_____ I am equally adept at performing task-oriented, procedural, and maintenance roles in the group. (Ch. 11)

_____ I come to group meetings prepared. (Ch. 11)

_____ During group meetings, my active participation makes positive contributions to goal accomplishment and maintaining good relationships. (Ch. 11)

_____ After meetings, I complete tasks I have been assigned and review meeting notes and minutes. (Ch. 11)

To verify this self-analysis, have a friend or fellow group member complete this review for you. Based on what you have learned, select the group communication behavior you would most like to improve. Write a communication improvement plan similar to the sample goal statement in Chapter 1 (page 22).

 You can complete this Self-Review online and, if requested, email it to your instructor. Use your Communicate! CD-ROM to access **Part III Self-Review** at the Communicate! Web site. Select the chapter resources for Chapter 11, then click on "Part III Self-Review."

© Will Hart/PhotoEdit/PictureQuest

After you have read this chapter, you should be able to answer these questions:

- How do you brainstorm for topics?
- How do you compile audience data?
- How do you predict level of audience interest in, knowledge of, and attitude toward a topic?
- What are physical and psychological conditions affecting the speech?
- How do you test your speech goal?

12

Determining Your Speaking Goal

ulia, I have to get up in class tomorrow and give a speech. Help! What in the world do I have to say that anyone wants to hear?"

"Well, let's see, you've had a baseball card collection since you were five, and it's now worth a lot of money. You could talk about that."

"No. That would be boring."

"Or you could talk about the mix-up at the cemetery when Grandpa Jack died, that's a funny story."

"I'd be embarrassed to talk about that."

"Or, you could give a speech on losing weight, after all, you've lost sixty pounds."

"What? And show everyone the picture of me when I was fat? Are you kidding?"

"Or you could give a speech on how your wife never has any good ideas."

"JUULLIAAA!"

"I give up."

This chapter begins our study of public speaking, the third setting in which human communication takes place. Developing your skills at speech making is important for your success in your career and your effectiveness in advocating your ideas in a variety of public forums. It is difficult to think of a career that will not require you to give presentations, and many promotions are based on the impression you make when you present. Skillful speakers are empowered to influence the world around them. From speaking at a local zoning meeting to stop the proposed landfill near your home to advocating for a charitable cause, speech-making skills will allow you to effectively get your personal, social, and political views heard.

Usually we think of a speech as a formal address that is prepared beforehand and presented to an audience that has gathered to hear the speech. But as the Random House dictionary explains, a speech is a "general word, with no implication of kind or length, or whether planned or not" (p. 1833). So we all engage in speech making much more than we realize. You may recall times when you wanted or needed to say something important to another person, so you stopped and thought about precisely what and how you would actually say it. Perhaps you've asked someone to marry you, or you've initiated a breakup, or you've had to fire someone. In all likelihood you spent a fair amount of time thinking about exactly how you would word your "speech." Maybe you witnessed an incident of sexual harassment at work and decided to talk with the union rep about it; you probably took the time to think of exactly what you were going to say. The point is that a "speech" may be a lengthy thoroughly prepared presentation with all kinds of multimedia audiovisual aids given to an audience of five hundred, or it may be a short, well-thought-out statement in which you pour out your heart.

Effective speakers are not born; they are made with lots of hard work. Demosthenes, the great Athenian orator who we think of as the prototype for brilliant speaking, was highly criticized when he entered public life. But with great determination and practice, he became one of the greatest orators in Western culture. Most of us have heard how he even filled his mouth with rocks so he could develop his pronunciation and articulation abilities.

Just as in Demosthenes' day, effective speaking today is the product of a careful preparation process. In the next five chapters we are going to introduce you to the "Speech Plan," a five-step process for preparing to speak. These are the action steps you will study:

1. Selecting a specific speech goal that is appropriate for your audience and occasion (Chapter 12)

2. Gathering and evaluating information to use in the speech (Chapter 13)

3. Organizing and developing information in a way that is best suited to your particular audience (Chapter 14)

4. Developing a strategy for verbally and visually adapting material to your specific audience (Chapter 15)

5. Practicing the speech (Chapter 16)

Following this plan will demystify presentations and enable you to enjoy sharing your ideas with others. In the final two chapters we apply these speech basics to the most common forms of public speaking: informative and persuasive presentations.

Although we will be describing how the speech plan action steps apply to situations in which you face a larger audience, these skills are relevant to other settings too, such as when you need to present the findings of your investigation to your coworkers in a problem-solving session, when you want to persuade your neighbor to join the community cleanup effort, or even when you want to ask your partner to start a family.

In this chapter we describe and explain the first action step of the speech plan: **Selecting a specific speech goal that is adapted to your audience and occasion.** As is true of each of the five action steps, this first one is broken into several substeps: identifying topics, analyzing your audience, understanding the speech setting, choosing a topic, and, finally, developing a specific speech goal. Although we discuss each task separately, in practice they overlap and can be completed in a different order.

Identifying Topics

In real-life settings, people are invited to give speeches because of their expertise on a particular subject, but selecting the best topic is often left in the hands of the speaker. What is the difference between a subject and a topic? A **subject** is a broad area of knowledge, such as NASCAR racing, cognitive psychology, baseball cards, or the Middle East. A **topic** is some specific aspect of a subject. For example, an authority on NASCAR racing might be able to speak on a variety of topics including how the NASCAR point system works or the meaning of NASCAR flags.

subject
a broad area of knowledge.

topic
some specific aspect of a subject.

So in what subject areas do you have expertise? The goal of this section is to help you list subject areas in which you have an interest or knowledge and then to develop a list of specific topics from those subject areas, topics that you may use for the speeches you will be assigned to make in class.

Listing Subjects

When you are asked (or required) to speak, use the same criteria for identifying subjects as those used by professional speakers. Start by listing subject areas (1) that are important to you and (2) that you know something about. Then select suitable topics within those areas.

© Thomson Higher Education

Subjects that meet these criteria probably include such things as your major, prospective profession, or current job; your hobbies or leisure activities; and special interests and concerns (social, economic, educational, or political). So, if health care is your actual or prospective vocation, rock climbing is your favorite activity, and illiteracy, substance abuse, and environmental pollution are your interests and concerns, then these are subject areas you should know something about and from which you could identify topics.

At this point you might be thinking, "Why not just talk about a topic an audience wants to hear about?" Avoid this temptation. The fact is audiences listen to speakers *because of* perceived expertise or insight on a particular subject. Additionally, when speakers really care about their topic, their enthusiasm can encourage others to become interested and involved in topics that they normally would consider dull. We have a son-in-law who is a passionate and very knowledgeable "birder." When he talks about birds, people listen because of the quality of his information as well as the excitement he conveys. We've seen people who have virtually no interest in "birding" getting entranced by listening intently to what he has to say. So choose topics in those subject areas you are truly excited about and in which you have spent months or years developing expertise and insight.

When you brainstorm, you will come up with many topics from one subject. Try it!

brainstorming
an uncritical, nonevaluative process of generating associated ideas.

Brainstorming for Potential Topics

Recall that a topic is a specific aspect of a subject, so each subject has an unlimited number of topics to choose from. To generate a list of specific topics from the subject areas you have identified, use a form of **brainstorming,** an uncritical, nonevaluative process of generating associated ideas. Under the subject of tennis, for example, a person who plays tennis as a hobby might be able to list twenty, thirty, or more potential topics such as player rating systems, equipment improvements, types of serves, net play, and types of courts, to name just a few. For additional details on how to use brainstorming for developing topics, read "Brainstorming by Yourself," available through InfoTrac College Edition. Use your Communicate! CD-ROM to access Web Resource 12.1: Brainstorming. Action Step 1.a presents a three-part process that will help you to brainstorm lists of topics for three subject areas in which you have some expertise and interest that you can use for your speeches in this class. From these lists you should be able to develop speeches for this course and for other occasions. Figure 12.1 is an example of one student's response to this step.

Major/Vocation	Hobby/Activity	Concern/Issue
Geology	*Lacrosse*	*Environment*
faults	*history	*habitat destruction
folds	*rules	rain forests
*Hopper crystals	equipment	extinctions
earthquakes	helmet	jaguars
fluvial systems	pads	air pollution
gems	Crosse	water pollution
*diamond tests	*skills	fertilizers
Morrison formation	ball	*oil wells
geophysics	field	industrialization
*fossils	players	overpopulation
volcanoes	midfield	Washington salmon
archeology	goalie	*littering
soil	strategy	lakes
oil	break-away	rivers
drilling	attack	ozone layer

Figure 12.1
One student's response to brainstorming subject areas for topics

Analyzing the Audience

Because speeches are given for a particular audience, before you can finally decide on your topic you need to understand who will be in your prospective audience. **Audience analysis** is the study of the intended

audience analysis
the study of the intended audience for your speech.

Action Step 1.a

Brainstorming for Topics

1. Divide a sheet of paper into three columns. Label column 1 with your major or vocation, such as "Art History"; label column 2 with a hobby or an activity, such as "Chess"; and label column 3 with a concern or an issue, such as "Water Pollution."

2. Working on one subject column at a time, quickly brainstorm a list of at least fifteen related topics for each column.

3. Place a check mark next to the three topics in each list that you would most enjoy speaking about.

4. Keep these lists for future use in choosing a topic for an assigned speech.

 You can go online to print out a worksheet that will help you complete this activity. Use your Communicate! CD-ROM to access Skill Learning Activity 12.1.

audience for your speech. During your audience analysis, you will want to find out the demographic profile of your audience (their ages, sex, educational level, and so on). You will also want to understand their current knowledge and attitudes toward your topic. This information will help you choose from your topic lists one that is appropriate for a specific audience. The results of your audience analysis will also give you insights for effective **audience adaptation,** the active process of developing a strategy for tailoring your information to the specific speech audience. To read an interesting article on the importance of careful audience analysis, use your Communicate! CD-ROM to access Web Resource 12.2: Defining Your Audience.

audience adaptation
the active process of developing a strategy for tailoring your information to the specific speech audience.

Kinds of Audience Data Needed

The first step is to gather audience demographic data and subject-specific information to determine in what ways audience members are alike and different. From demographic information you will be able to make educated inferences about how familiar the audience is with your subject area and their attitudes toward it. You will want demographic information about the age, education, gender, income, occupation, race, ethnicity, religion, geographic uniqueness, and language of your audience. You will also want to know about the audience members' level of knowledge and attitude toward your subject. Figure 12.2 presents a list of questions to answer when acquiring demographic information about an audience.

What challenges would this audience pose for a speaker running for city council?

Jeff Greenberg/PhotoEdit

Age: What is the age range of your audience, and what is the average age?

Education: What percentages of your audience have high school, college, or postgraduate education?

Gender: What percentage of your audience is male? Female?

Socioeconomic background: What percentage of your audience comes from high-, middle-, or low-income families?

Occupation: Is the majority of your audience from a single occupational group or industry, or do audience members come from diverse occupational groups?

Race: Are most members of your audience of the same race or a mixture of races?

Ethnicity: What ethnic groups are represented in the audience? Are most audience members from the same cultural background?

Religion: What religious traditions are followed by audience members?

Geographic uniqueness: Are audience members from the same state, city, or neighborhood?

Language: What languages do a significant number of members of the audience speak as a first language? What language (if any) is common to all audience members?

Knowledge of subject: What can you expect the audience already knows about your subject? How different is the knowledge level of audience members?

Attitude toward subject: What can you expect your audience's feelings to be about your subject?

Figure 12.2
Demographic audience analysis questions

Ways of Gathering Audience Data

Now that we have considered the kinds of audience data you need, let's consider three ways you can gather demographic information.

1. **You can gather data through observation.** If you are familiar with members of your audience (as you are with members of your classroom audience), you can get much of the significant data about them from personal observation. For instance, from being in class for even a couple of sessions, you will have a good idea of class members' approximate age, the ratio of men to women, and their racial makeup. As you listen to them talk, you will learn more about their interest in, knowledge of, and attitudes about many issues.

2. **You can gather data by questioning the person who invited you to speak.** When you are invited to speak, interview your contact person about the characteristics of the audience. Your contact person should be in a

position to make educated guesses about most demographic information and should also know about the audiences' knowledge level and attitudes.

3. **You can make informed guesses about audience demographics.** If you can't get information in any other way, you will have to make intelligent guesses based on such indirect information as the general makeup of the people who live in a specific community or the kinds of people who are likely to attend the event or occasion. Many organizations poll public opinion on various topics.

Using Audience Analysis to Forecast Audience Reactions

The next step in audience analysis is to use the data you have collected to predict the audience's potential interest in, knowledge of, and attitudes toward your potential subject. These predictions form a basis for your topic selection. We will return to this analysis in Chapter 15 in the discussion of adapting verbally and visually to your audience.

Audience knowledge What type of background does the average audience member have in your subject area? What can you count on them already knowing? What is likely to be new information to most of them? It is important that you choose a topic geared to the background knowledge you can expect audience members to have. For instance, if the subject is folk music, you can expect a baby boomer-aged, better educated audience to have a working knowledge of the tradition and artists. However, you can expect that audience to be less knowledgeable about the subject of rap music.

Audience interest How excited is the audience likely to be about your subject? For instance, suppose you would like to speak on the subject of new cancer drugs; if your audience is comprised of physicians, you can expect that they will be interested in your subject. But if your audience is your classmates in this course, then you can predict that you will have to build audience interest as you speak.

Audience attitude toward your subject How does your audience feel about your subject? This assessment is especially important if you want to try to change a belief or move the audience to action. Audience attitudes are usually expressed by opinions. One way to discover them is to poll the members of the audience, and you may want to do that when you can. If you can't poll your specific audience, you may be able to find some idea of general attitudes by accessing public opinion polls. To access links to two respected polling organizations, use your Communicate! CD-ROM to access Web Resource 12.3: Public Opinion Polls. At other times you will have to infer the dominant audience attitude from the occasion and audience demographics. For instance, if your subject is affirmative action, you can expect that an audience of black and Hispanic working-class people are likely to favor it, whereas an audience of white working-class men are likely to be against it.

Audience attitude toward you as speaker

Before you speak, will your audience recognize your subject matter expertise, or will you have to build your credibility as you are speaking? Your success in informing or persuading an audience is likely to depend on whether audience members perceive you to be a credible source of information. **Credibility** is based on whether a person seems to be knowledgeable (having the necessary information to give this speech), trustworthy (being honest, dependable, and ethical), and personable (showing enthusiasm, warmth, friendliness, and concern for members of the audience).

Figure 12.3 shows a sample checklist you can use for analyzing your audience.

credibility
based on whether a person seems to be knowledgeable, trustworthy, and personable.

Subject: _____

Data

1. The average audience member's education level is ___ high school ___ college ___ postgraduate.
2. The ages range from ___ to ___. The average age is about ___.
3. The audience is approximately ___ percent male and ___ percent female.
4. My estimate of the average socioeconomic level of the audience is ___ low ___ middle ___ high.
5. Most audience members are___ of the same occupation/major ___ different occupations/majors.
6. Most audience members are ___ the same race ___ a mixture of races.
7. Most audience members are ___ the same ethnicity ___ a mixture of ethnicities.
8. Most audience members are ___ the same religion ___ a mixture of religions.
9. Most audience members are from the same ___country ___state ___city ___ neighborhood.
10. Most audience members speak ___ the same first language ___different first languages ___English as a common language ___some other common language (list).

Predictions Based on Audience Data

1. Audience knowledge of the subject will be _____ extensive_____ moderate _____ limited, because _____.
2. Audience interest in this subject is likely to be _____ high _____ moderate _____ low, because _____.
3. Audience attitude toward my subject is likely to be _____ positive _____ neutral _____ negative, because _____.
4. My initial credibility with the audience is likely to be _____high _____ medium _____ low, because _____.

Figure 12.3
An audience analysis checklist

Action Step 1.b ▶

Analyzing Your Audience

1. Fill in the audience analysis checklist, including subject, data about your classroom audience, and predictions about their reactions to your subject.

2. Make sure you have completed the "because" part of each of the four predictions.

3. Save the results. You will use the data from this checklist throughout the preparation process.

 You can complete this activity online, print it out, and, if requested, email it to your instructor. You can also see a sample of an audience analysis prepared by a student in a similar course. Use your Communicate! CD-ROM to access Skill Learning Activity 12.2.

Understanding the Speech Setting

setting
the occasion and location for your speech.

Choosing an appropriate topic and speech goal also depends on the **setting,** the occasion and location for your speech. For speeches you will give to your class, understanding the setting is easy because the type of speech you give will be assigned to you by the professor, and your class meets regularly at the same time under the same conditions. However, when you speak to different audiences, you will need to spend time understanding the setting. Answers to the following questions about the setting will help you choose a topic and a speech goal.

1. **What are the special expectations for the speech?** Every occasion provides some special expectations. At an Episcopalian Sunday service, for example, the congregation expects the minister's sermon to have a religious theme. At a political rally we expect candidates for office to explain their positions on the issues. For classroom speeches, one of the major expectations is meeting the assignment. Whether the speech assignment is defined by purpose (to inform or to persuade), by type (expository or demonstration), or by subject (book analysis or current event), your topic should be easily adaptable to the assignment.

2. **What is the appropriate length for the speech?** The time limit for classroom speeches is usually quite short, so you will want to make sure that you are not choosing a topic that is too broad and packing too much information into your speech. "Two Major Causes of Environmental Degradation" can be presented in five minutes, but "A

History of Human Impact on the Environment" cannot. Problems with time limits are not peculiar to classroom speeches. Any speech setting includes actual or implied time limits. For example, the expected length for the sermon in a Christian Sunday service may be twenty to thirty minutes; expected length for a homily in a Roman Catholic Mass may be ten minutes.

3. **How large will the audience be?** Knowing the size of your audience will help you understand how intimate or formal your presentation will need to be. If you are anticipating a small audience (up to fifty people or so), you will be close enough to all of them to talk in a normal voice and to move about. In contrast, if your audience is larger, you may need a microphone to be heard.

4. **Where will the speech be given?** Because rooms (including classrooms) vary in size, lighting, seating arrangements, and the like, consider how the physical setup will affect the speech. In a long, narrow room, you may need to speak louder than usual to reach the back row. In a darkened room, make sure the lights are on and that the blinds or shades are open to bring in as much light as possible.

   Venues outside of school settings offer even greater variations in conditions. Ask for specific information about seating capacity, shape, number of rows, nature of lighting, existence of a speaking stage or platform, distance between speaker and first row, and so on before you speak. If possible, visit the place and see it for yourself.

A. Ramey/Stock, Boston/PictureQuest

How do the setting and the occasion dictate what a speaker will talk about at a graduation ceremony?

5. **When will the speech be given?** A speech given early in the morning requires a different approach from one given right after lunch or in the evening. If a speech is scheduled after a meal, for instance, the audience may be lethargic, mellow, or even on the verge of sleep. As a result, it helps to insert more "attention getters" (examples, illustrations, and stories) to counter potential lapses of attention.

6. **Where in the program does the speech occur?** If you are the only speaker or the featured speaker, you have an obvious advantage—you are the focal point of audience attention. In the classroom, however, and at some rallies, hearings, and other events, there are many speeches, and your place on the schedule may affect how you are received. For example, if you go first, you may need to "warm up" the listeners and be prepared to meet the distraction of a few audience members strolling in late. If you speak last, you must counter the tendency of the audience to be weary from listening to several speeches.

7. **What equipment is necessary to give the speech?** For some speeches, you may need a microphone, a chalkboard, an overhead or slide projector and screen, or a hookup for your laptop computer. In most instances, speakers have some kind of speaking stand, but it is wise not to count on it. If the person who has invited you to speak has any control over the setting, be sure to explain what you need—but always have alternative plans in case what you have asked for is unavailable. It is frustrating to plan a computer PowerPoint presentation, for example, and then discover that there's no place to plug in the computer!

Action Step 1.c ▶

Understanding the Speech Setting

1. Use the Setting Checklist in Figure 12.4 to collect information about your occasion and the location of your speech.

2. Write a short statement indicating which of these seem most important to your speech preparation? Why?

3. Save the results. You will use the data from this checklist through-out the preparation process.

 You can complete this activity online, print it out, and, if requested, email it to your instructor. You can also see a sample of a setting analysis prepared by a student in a similar course. Use your Communicate! CD-ROM to access Skill Learning Activity 12.3.

Topic: _____

1. What are the special expectations for the speech? _____
2. What is the appropriate length for the speech? _____
3. How large will the audience be? _____
4. Where will the speech be given? _____
5. When will the speech be given? _____
6. Where in the program does the speech occur? _____
7. What equipment is necessary to give the speech? _____

Which of these seem most important to your speech preparation? Why?

Figure 12.4
Setting checklist

Selecting the Topic

Armed with the information you have collected on your audience and setting, you are ready to select a topic that will be appropriate to the audience and the setting and then to develop a specific speech goal. You will want to choose a topic that takes into account the current knowledge level of your average audience member. If you're speaking to a group that is unfamiliar with your subject, then you will want to select a topic that provides basic information; if you're speaking to an expert audience, then you will choose a more advanced topic.

Action Step 1.d ⟩

Selecting a Topic

1. Review the three topics that you checked from each of the lists of topics that you brainstormed in Action Step 1.a, the audience analysis you completed in Action Step 1.b, and the setting checklist you completed in Action Step 1.c.

2. From the three categories in the brainstorming list, select the subject area that you want to use for your first speech.

3. Use your understanding of your audience and speech setting to select one of the three topics you checked that you think would be of greatest benefit to your audience.

 You can go online to print out a worksheet that will help you complete this activity. Use your Communicate! CD-ROM to access Skill Learning Activity 12.4.

Developing a Specific Speech Goal

Once you have committed yourself to your selection of a topic, continue the preparation process by developing a specific speech goal that meets audience needs. For instance, if you have selected the topic of illiteracy for your speech, you still need to determine the speech goal you want to achieve through your speech.

General and Specific Goals

general speech goal
the intent of your speech.

The **general speech goal** is the intent of your speech. Most speeches can be classified as those that intend to entertain, inform, or persuade. While most speeches include material that is entertaining, informative, and persuasive, the general goal is the overarching purpose of the presentation. Consider the following examples.

Night after night, Jay Leno's opening monologue on *The Tonight Show* is intended to entertain, even though it may include material that is perceived as informative or persuasive. If Jay Leno presented a strong argument for banning SUVs in his opening monologue, we would consider it odd and inappropriate. Likewise, when President Bush addressed Congress and the American people two days after the World Trade Center attack, his general purpose was to inform Congress and the people about what the U.S. government intended to do even though at one point he urged Americans to return to their normal lives.

There are occasions (such as after dinner speeches) when the speaker's goal is primarily to entertain. But informative and persuasive speeches are the more common kinds of presentations adults give as part of their job or community activities, so these are the focus of your study in this course. In many cases the general goal is dictated by the setting, particularly the occasion (and in this course your instructor is likely to specify it).

specific goal
a single statement of the exact response the speaker wants from the audience.

Whereas the general goal is often determined by the context in which a speech is given, the **specific goal,** or specific purpose, is a single statement of the exact response the speaker wants from the audience. For a speech on the topic "Evaluating Diamonds," you could state the specific goal as "I would like the audience to understand the four major criteria used in evaluating a diamond." For a speech on "Supporting the United Way," a specific goal might be stated, "I would like the audience to increase their annual monetary donation to the University Scholarship Fund." The first example has an informative general goal, and in the second example the goal is persuasive. In addition, the first specific goal statement would be appropriate for an audience with little knowledge of precious gemstones, whereas the second statement indicates a knowledgeable audience that is predisposed to favor the scholarship fund (the specific goal to *increase* their donations suggests that they are currently donating).

Phrasing a Specific Speech Goal

The following guidelines can help you craft a well-worded specific goal.

1. **Write a first draft of your speech goal using a complete sentence that specifies the type of response you want from the audience.** For example, suppose Julia begins her first draft on the topic of illiteracy by writing,

   I want my audience to understand illiteracy.

   Julia's draft is a complete sentence, and it specifies the response she wants from the audience: *to understand* illiteracy. As phrased, we see that she is planning to give an informative speech.

2. **Revise the infinitive (and the infinitive phrase) until it indicates the specific audience reaction desired.** If you regard your goal as providing an explanation, then your intent is primarily informative, and the infinitive that expresses your desired audience reaction should take the form "to understand," "to recognize," "to distinguish," or "to appreciate." If, however, you see the goal of your speech as changing a belief or giving a call to action, then your intent is persuasive and will be reflected by the use of such infinitives as "to believe," "to change," "to value" or "to do."

   If Julia wanted to persuade her audience, her specific goal might be worded:

   I want my audience *to believe* that illiteracy is a major problem.

3. **Make sure that the goal statement encompasses only a single idea.** Suppose Julia had written,

   I would like the audience to understand why illiteracy is a problem in the workplace and to the individual.

   This statement is not a good specific goal because it includes two distinct ideas. Either one is a worthy goal. So Julia needs to decide: (a) Does she want her audience to understand the problem of illiteracy in the workplace? If so, then the following is a better reflection of her specific goal:

   I would like the audience to understand the problems illiteracy causes in the workplace.

   Or (b) does she want her audience to understand how illiteracy affects individuals? If this is what she wants, then the following specific goal statement would be appropriate:

   I would like the audience to understand the consequences of being illiterate today in the United States.

4. **Revise your first draft until the infinitive phrase includes the complete response you want from your audience.** Julia's draft, "I want my audience to understand illiteracy," is a good start, but the infinitive phrase "to understand illiteracy" is vague. Exactly *what* about illiteracy is it that Julia wants her audience to understand?

At first she might think, "I want my audience to understand what illiteracy means." But after a few seconds of reflection she realizes that the audience is composed of college students and most already understand the definition of illiteracy. So, just defining illiteracy will not meet audience needs.

As Julia works with the wording, she amends it to read,

I would like the audience to understand three aspects of the problem of illiteracy.

This draft is an improvement in at least two ways. First, from an audience standpoint she reasons that although her audience is well aware of what illiteracy is, they are not as likely to be aware of aspects of the problem of illiteracy. So she now thinks this goal will provide more of the kind of information that her audience needs to know. Second, the goal now is expanded to focusing on "three aspects." So she has made her goal more specific.

Now the question becomes, is the phrase "understand three aspects of illiteracy" specific enough? As she thinks of her audience again, she considers how she can make the goal statement even more aligned with audience needs. As Julia thinks about it, she sees that what she really wants to communicate is how illiteracy hurts people who are trying to perform in the workplace. With this in mind, she revises the goal by writing,

I would like the audience to understand three aspects of the problem of illiteracy in the workplace.

Now she has limited the goal not only in number of aspects but also by situation. Moreover, she has a goal that she believes will be considered meaningful to her classmates. That is, she believes that this college-aged audience is likely to see the importance of a speech on this topic. In addition, she believes that she will be able to talk about the topic in ways that hold their interest and further their understanding.

Figure 12.5 gives further examples of specific goals that clearly state how each speaker wants the audience to react to a particular topic. By completing Action Step 1.e you will develop a well-written specific goal statement for your speech.

Informative Goals

I would like my audience to understand the characteristics of the five common types of coastlines.

I would like my audience to understand the three basic forms of mystery stories.

Persuasive Goals

I would like my audience to believe that drug testing by business and industry should be prohibited.

I would like my audience to join Amnesty International.

Figure 12.5
Specific speech goals

Action Step 1.e

Writing a Specific Goal

Write a specific goal for your first major speech.

Type of speech? _____

1. Write a first draft of your speech goal using a complete sentence that specifies the type of response you want from the audience.

2. Test the infinitive. Does it express the kind of speech you are assigned to present? If not, write a revised infinitive.

3. Review the stated goal. If the statement contains more than one idea, revise the sentence so that the goal contains only one idea.

4. Test the infinitive phrase. Does the infinitive phrase express precisely the specific audience reaction desired? If not, revise the infinitive phrase.

Write your final wording of the specific goal that you will use in your speech:

_____

_____

_____

 You can complete this activity online with Speech Builder Express, a speech outlining program that will help you follow the action steps in this book to develop your speech. (See the end of this chapter for instructions on how to access Speech Builder Express.) If requested, you can email this activity to your instructor. Use your Communicate! CD-ROM to access Skill Learning Activity 12.6.

What Would You Do?   A QUESTION OF ETHICS

Although Glen and Adam were taking the same speech course, they were in different sections. One evening when Adam was talking with Glen about his trouble finding a topic, Glen mentioned that he was planning to speak about Internet Web sites. Because the number of different speech goals from this topic seemed unlimited, Glen didn't see any harm in showing Adam his bibliography, so he brought it up on his computer screen.

As Adam was looking at it, Glen went down the hall to get a book he had lent to a friend earlier that morning. While Glen was away, Adam thought he would take a look at what else Glen had in the file. He was soon excited to see that Glen had a complete outline on the goal "I want the class to understand the steps in designing a home page." Figuring he could save himself some time, Adam printed the outline; he justified his action on the basis that it represented a good start that would give him ideas.

As time ran short, Adam decided just to use Glen's outline for his own speech.

Later in the week, Glen's instructor happened to be talking to Adam's instructor about speeches she had heard that week. When she mentioned that Glen had given a really interesting speech on home pages, Adam's teacher said, "That's interesting, I heard a good one just this morning. Now what did you say the goal of the speech you heard was?" When the goals turned out to be the same, Glen's instructor went back to her office to get the outline

that she would be returning the next day. As the two instructors went over the outlines, they saw that the two speeches were exactly the same. They left messages for both Adam and Glen to meet with them and the department head the next day.

1. What is the ethical issue at stake?
2. Was there anything about Glen's behavior that was unethical? Anything about Adam's?
3. What should be the penalty, if any, for Glen? For Adam?

Skill Builders   Crafting a Specific Speech Goal That Meets Audience Needs

Skill	Use	Procedure	Example
The process of identifying a speech purpose that draws on speaker's knowledge and interests and is adapted to a specific audience and setting.	To identify a speaking goal where speaker interest and expertise, audience needs and interests, and setting overlap.	1. Identify topics within subject areas in which you have interest and expertise.	Subject: Exercising Topics: Yoga, Kick Boxing, Walking, Weight Training
		2. Analyze your audience's demographic characteristics, interests, and attitudes toward your subject.	Older lower income black women with little experience in exercising. Likely to be unknowledgeable and indifferent.
		3. Understand the occasion and the location for the speech.	Women's Health Fair at local community center. About twenty women will attend.
		4. Select a topic that will meet the interests and needs of your audience and setting.	Topic: Walking (easy to do, has benefits)
		5. Write a specific speech goal that clearly states the exact response you want from your audience.	I want the audience to understand four major benefits of walking three times a week.

Summary

The first step of effective speech preparation is to determine your speech goal. You begin by selecting a subject that you know something about and are interested in, such as a job, a hobby, or a contemporary issue of concern to you. To arrive at a specific topic, brainstorm a list of related words under each subject heading. When you have brainstormed at least twenty topics, you can check the specific topics under each heading that are most meaningful to you.

The next step is to analyze the audience to decide how to shape and direct your speech. Audience analysis is the study of your audience's knowledge, interests, and attitudes. Gather specific data about your audience to determine how its members are alike and how they differ. Use this information to predict audience interest in your topic, level of understanding of your topic, and attitude toward you and your topic. Also, consider how the occasion of the speech and its physical setting will affect your overall speech plan.

Once you have a specific speech topic and have accounted for your audience and setting, you can determine your speech goal and write a thesis statement. The general goal of a speech is to entertain, to inform, or to persuade. The specific goal is a complete sentence that specifies the exact response the speaker wants from the audience. Writing a specific speech goal involves the following four-step procedure: (1) Write a first draft of your speech goal using a complete sentence. (2) Revise your first draft until it states the specific response or behavior you want from your audience. (3) Make sure the goal contains only one idea. (4) Revise the infinitive phrase until it indicates the complete audience reaction desired.

Communicate! Online

N ow that you have read Chapter 12, use your Communicate! CD-ROM for quick access to the electronic resources that accompany this text. Your CD-ROM gives you access to InfoTrac College Edition, Speech Builder Express, and the Communicate! Web site. When you get to the Communicate! home page, click on "Student Book Companion Site" in the Resource box at right to access the online study aids for this chapter, including a digital glossary, review quizzes, the chapter activities, and the chapter Web Resources.

Key Terms

At the Communicate! Web site, select the chapter resources for Chapter 12. Print a copy of the glossary for this chapter and test yourself with the electronic flash cards or complete the crossword puzzle to help you master these key terms:

subject (283) audience analysis (285) setting (290)
topic (283) audience adaptation (286) general speech goal (294)
brainstorming (284) credibility (289) specific goal (294)

Review Quiz

Test your knowledge of the concepts in this chapter by taking the online quiz at the Communicate! Web site. Select the chapter resources for Chapter 12, then click on "Review Quiz." When you have completed the quiz, submit it for scoring.

Skill Learning Activities

Complete the Observe & Analyze and Action Step activities for Chapter 12 online at the Communicate! Web site. Select the chapter resources for Chapter 12, then click on "Activities." You can submit both your Observe & Analyze and Action Step answers to your instructor.

12.1: Action Step 1.a: Brainstorming for Topics (285)
12.2: Action Step 1.b: Analyzing Your Audience (290)
12.3: Action Step 1.c: Understanding the Speech Setting (292)
12.4: Action Step 1.d: Selecting a Topic (293)
12.5: Observe & Analyze: Recognizing a Specific Goal (295)
12.6: Action Step 1.e: Writing a Specific Goal (297)

Web Resources

Access the Web Resources for this chapter online at the Communicate! Web site. Select the chapter resources for Chapter 12, then click on "Web Resources."

12.1: Brainstorming (284)
12.2: Defining Your Audience (286)
12.3: Public Opinion Polls (288)

To access Speech Builder Express, use the username and password included on your Communicate! CD-ROM. Speech Builder Express is a Web-based speech outlining tool that will help you follow the Action Steps in this book to develop your speech. In this chapter, you can use this tool to complete Action Step 1.e: Writing a Specific Goal. When you log onto Speech Builder Express, you'll be prompted to set up an account with your username and password.

THOMSON
WADSWORTH

CREATE NEW ACCOUNT
STUDENT LOGIN

SpeechBuilderExpress™

Welcome to Speech Builder Express™ your personal speech coach available 24 hours a day, 7 days a week to accompany your Wadsworth/Thomson Learning communication textbook! Speech Builder Express coaches you through every step of the speech outlining process through a series of interactive activities and with the additional support of a Tutor feature based on text content, InfoTrac College Edition, an online Dictionary and Thesaurus and video speech models. Equipped with your assigned speech type or goal, a general topic and preliminary research use this program to complete your formal speech outline. You will be able to specify your specific speech purpose, identify your organizational pattern, write your thesis statement or central idea, develop your main points and support material, write transitions and develop your speech introduction, conclusion, and bibliography. You can complete, save online, export to Microsoft® Word® or email to your professor up to 5 formal speech outlines.

@2002 Thomson Wadsworth. All rights reserved. Terms of Use. Advertise Privacy Statement

Once you've logged on and created an account, you can start on your speech outline by choosing a speech type. In this way you can create and save up to five speech outlines.

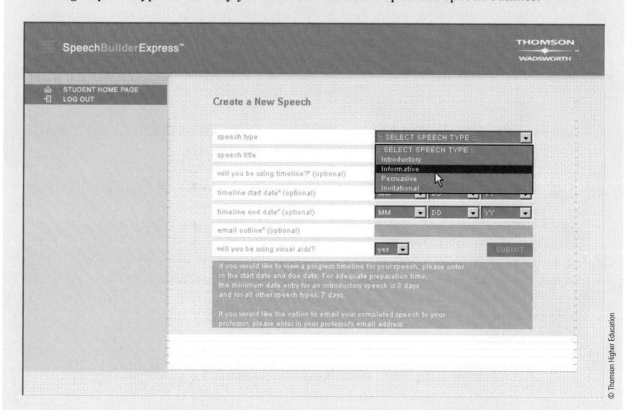

To work on your specific goal, select "Speech Goal" from the left-hand menu and follow the instructions to write and test your specific speech goal. To review information about specific goals, click on the "Tutor" button to read short reminders from this chapter.

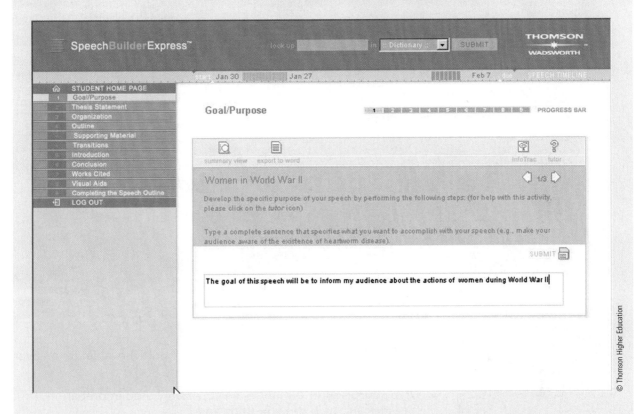

Bruce Ayers/Getty Images

13

Doing Research

eremy was concerned. He was scheduled for his first speech in a week, but he hadn't begun to find information. When he was in high school, he had written a term paper on media violence, and he was really taken with the subject. Just a couple of months ago he had read an article in a magazine at the doctor's office, but he couldn't remember the issue of the magazine the article was in. He hadn't kept a copy of his term paper, but he was still really interested in the subject. Jeremy wasn't sure exactly what to do to find the information he would need for a speech.

Jeremy's experience is not unlike that of many of us. We have strong opinions that we've formed over time as we have read and interacted with others, but we don't have the sources that support our knowledge or viewpoints at our fingertips. So when we decide to present these ideas in a public forum, we need to do some research.

In this chapter, we consider the second of the five speech plan action steps for preparing a speech: **Gather and evaluate material for use in the speech.** The information you will need must meet two criteria: it must support your specific speech goal, and it must be appropriate for the audience. To complete this step in the speech plan process, you will need to (a) locate and evaluate information sources, (b) identify and select various items of information to use in your speech, and (c) prepare to cite the information during the speech.

Locate and Evaluate Information Sources

How can you quickly find the best information related to your specific speech goal? It depends. Speakers usually start by assessing their own knowledge, experience, and personal observations. Then they move on to electronically searching for relevant books, articles, general references, and Web sites. They also look for publicly available surveys or conduct their own, and they interview knowledgeable people.

Personal Knowledge, Experience, and Observation

If you have chosen to speak on a topic you know something about, you are likely to have material that you can use as examples and personal experiences in your speech. For instance, musicians have special knowledge about music and instruments, entrepreneurs about starting up their own businesses, and marine biologists about marine reserves. So Erin, a member of the varsity volleyball team, can draw material from her own knowledge of the game and her experience in using various serving techniques for her first speech on "How to Spike a Volleyball."

For many topics, your personal knowledge from experience can be supplemented with careful observation. If, for instance, you are planning to talk about how a small claims court works or how churches help the homeless find shelter and job training, you can learn about each of these by attending small claims sessions or visiting a church's outreach center. By focusing attention on specific behaviors and taking notes of your observations, you will have a record of specifics that you can use in your speech.

Books, Articles, and General References

Most speakers use information found in books, articles, and other specialized sources. In the past speakers located books and articles by going to the library's card catalog (which listed all books) and to indexes and periodical catalogs (that listed magazines and journals). Today both books and periodicals are cataloged in **electronic databases** that can be accessed online, at the library or elsewhere, over the Internet. Electronic library systems and procedures change frequently to incorporate advances in technology, and you can avoid losing time and frustrating yourself if you ask a librarian for help. Librarians are "free" resources, experts who can demystify a knotty research problem as well as direct you to short courses and workshops designed to make your research endeavors both productive and efficient.

electronic databases *databases that can be accessed online, at the library or elsewhere, over the Internet.*

Have you ever taken a class at your library on online research? If not, consider doing so. You can save yourself lots of time and locate great sources of useful information.

Books If your topic has been around for more than six months, there are likely to be books written about it. Most libraries have their book holdings listed in an online catalog and available on site in a physical card catalog. In either form, books are cataloged by title, author, and subject. Although you may occasionally know the title or author of a book you want, more often you will be looking for books using a subject label, such as "violence in the mass media."

In addition to being able to search for author, title, and subject, most online catalogs now allow you to search by entering "key words." Even with this user-friendly system, you may find it useful to brainstorm for key words to use in the search.

For instance, Jeremy wants to find information on the subject "violence in the mass media," with a few minutes of brainstorming he could come up with several key word designations that would bring a variety of "hits"—that is, books available. Notice the differences in hits Jeremy found using each of the following key words:

media violence 95

violence in mass media 57

violence television 88

Under "violence in mass media," one book listed was *The 11 Myths of Media Violence*. Figure 13.1 shows the information about the book that was in the database. Not all of the information will be useful to you. But you certainly will want to note the *location* (many libraries have multiple branch locations and not all books are available at all locations), the *call number*

F. Pedrick/The Image Works

Author:	Potter, W. James
Title:	The 11 myths of media violence
Pub Info:	Thousand Oaks, CA: Sage Publications, c2003

Location	Call No.	Status
Langsam stacks	P96 V5 P678 2003	Available

Description:	xviii, 259p.; 24 cm
Note:	Includes bibliographical references (pp. 229–281) and Index
Subject:	Violence in Mass Media
OCLC#:	51095835
ISBN:	0761927344 (hard)
LCCN:	2002008802

Figure 13.1
Example of a library card

(which is the book's physical "address" in the library), and the *book's status* (whether it is immediately available for use or is on loan to someone else, archived, and so forth).

Another bit of useful information is found under *Note* (which tells you if the book includes bibliographical references and an index). So, in addition to providing a great deal of useful information, finding a book on your topic often leads you to additional sources. For instance, the library card for *The 11 Myths* book shows that it has twenty pages of bibliographical references, so Jeremy might find several excellent additional sources from this bibliography alone.

In addition to searching the online database for books, you can also use the call number for one book to physically locate other books on the same subject. For example, having found *The 11 Myths* book through an electronic search, when Jeremy goes to the library to retrieve it, he will find that other books on that topic have very similar call numbers (in this case P96 V5 P678 2003) and are shelved together. So he can then quickly thumb through them to check their usefulness.

periodicals
magazines and journals that appear at fixed intervals.

Articles Articles are published in **periodicals**—magazines and journals that appear at fixed intervals. The information in periodical articles is often more current than that published in books because many periodicals are published weekly, biweekly, or monthly. A periodical article is likely to be a better source if a topic is currently "in the news." Articles are also likely to be the best source of information for highly specialized topics where there may not be sufficient information for books.

Most libraries subscribe to electronic databases that index periodical articles. Check with your librarian to learn what electronic indexes your college or university subscribes to. Here are three databases that are frequently available and index many popular magazines such as *Time* and *Newsweek* as well as some of the popular academic journals such as *Communication Quarterly* and *Journal of Psychology.*

> *InfoTrac College Edition* is the electronic index that you can access from the Internet this semester if you purchased a new copy of this textbook. InfoTrac College Edition indexes articles in hundreds of popular magazines and academic journals. See the end of this chapter for instructions on how to use InfoTrac College Edition to research sources for your speech.

> *InfoTrac University Library* is an expanded version of the InfoTrac College Edition. It is available online through most college and university libraries and provides access to several hundred additional popular magazines and academic journals.

> *Periodical Abstracts,* another electronic database available online in most college and university libraries, provides access to articles in more than one thousand popular magazines and academic journals.

Offerings of these online catalogs is likely to vary from place to place, so it is wise for you to check with a librarian to see which of these and other catalogs you have access to at your university library.

When using most online indexes, you begin by entering the subject heading that you are researching. The search of an index database will result in a list of articles that are related to your subject. From these, you can then choose to read or print the individual articles or use the list of citations to locate hard copies of original articles in your library's periodical section. For instance, Rhonda has identified the drug "Ecstasy" as a topic under the heading of "designer drugs" on her brainstorming list. Rhonda's tentative speech goal is, "I want my audience to understand the dangers of the drug Ecstasy." Working from her computer at home, Rhonda opens up InfoTrac College Edition and types in "ecstasy" and finds 221 periodical references including these:

> Study: parents underestimate Ecstasy, methamphetamine risks. *Alcoholism & Drug Abuse Weekly.* June 23, 2003 v15 I24 p8(1)

> The Agony of Ecstasy: how a suburban party diversion is becoming a dangerous street drug. Benjamin Wallace-Wells. *Washington Monthly* May 2003 v35 I5 14(6)

> The Ecstasy scare: how to deal with the new threat. (Drugs). Kevin Chappell. *Ebony* Nov. 2002 v58 I1 p. 182(3)

Rhonda finds that the complete text of each of these can be printed on her own printer. At the University of Cincinnati college library Rhonda could open the extended InfoTrac University Library index or Periodical Abstracts and find article lists that include some of these same articles as well as others.

At times a search may identify articles that cannot be downloaded to your own printer. So, you will then go to your library's journal and magazine index to see whether the library has hard copies of the journal articles you want. Then you can manually access those journals.

Newspapers Newspaper articles are excellent sources of facts about and interpretations of both contemporary and historical issues. At a minimum, your library probably holds both an index of your nearest major daily newspaper and the *New York Times Index*.

Three electronic newspaper indexes that are most useful if they are available to you are (1) *National Newspaper Index*, which indexes five major newspapers: the *New York Times*, the *Wall Street Journal*, *Christian Science Monitor*, *Washington Post*, and *Los Angeles Times*; (2) *Newsbank*, which provides not only the indexes but also the text of articles from more than 450 U.S. and Canadian newspapers; and (3) InfoTrac College Edition's *National Newspaper Index*.

In addition to books and articles, a variety of general references are useful sources for some speech material. At the library, general references are shelved together in a "reference room" or on "reference shelves."

Encyclopedias An encyclopedia can be a good starting point for research. Encyclopedias give an excellent overview of many subjects, but you certainly should never limit your research to encyclopedias. General encyclopedias contain short articles about a wide variety of subjects. In addition, there are many specialized encyclopedias to choose from in areas such as art, history, religion, philosophy, and science. For instance, a college library is likely to have the *African American Encyclopedia*, *Latino Encyclopedia*, *Asian American Encyclopedia*, *Encyclopaedia Britannica*, *Encyclopedia Americana*, *World Book Encyclopedia*, *Encyclopedia of Computer Science*, *Encyclopedia of Women*, and *Encyclopedia of Women in American Politics*, as well as many more.

Many libraries have encyclopedias available online, and some encyclopedias can be accessed from the Internet. For a list of encyclopedias that are available on the Web, use your Communicate! CD-ROM to access Web Resource 13.1: Online Encyclopedias.

Statistical sources Statistical sources present numerical information on a wide variety of subjects. When you need facts about demography, continents, heads of state, weather, or similar subjects, access one of the many single-volume sources that report such data. Two of the most popular sources in this category are the *Statistical Abstract of the United States* (now available online), which provides reference material for numerical information and various aspects of American life, and the *World Almanac and Book of Facts*. You will find almanacs and other statistical resources at your library

in the reference section. For links to Web-based statistical sources, use your Communicate! CD-ROM to access Web Resource 13.2: Statistics Online.

Biographical references When you need accounts of a person's life, from thumbnail sketches to reasonably complete essays, you can turn to one of the many biographical references available. In addition to full-length books and encyclopedia entries, consult such books as *Who's Who in America* and *International Who's Who*. Your library is also likely to carry *Contemporary Black Biography*, *Dictionary of Hispanic Biography*, *Native American Women*, *Who's Who of American Women*, *Who's Who among Asian Americans*, and many more. You can also access some biographical information online. For links to popular Web-based biographical references, use your Communicate! CD-ROM to access Web Resource 13.3: Online Biographical References.

Books of quotations A good quotation can be especially provocative as well as informative, and there are times when you may want to use a quotation from a respected person. *Bartlett's Familiar Quotations* is a popular source of quotes from historical as well as contemporary figures. But there are many collections of quotations. Some you may find at your library include the *International Thesaurus of Quotations*, *Harper Book of American Quotations*, *My Soul Looks Back, 'Less I Forget: A Collection of Quotations by People of Color*, the *New Quotable Woman*, and the *Oxford Dictionary of Quotations*. For links to Web-based collections of quotations, use your Communicate! CD-ROM to access Web Resource 13.4: Quotations Online.

United States government publications Some government publications are especially useful for locating primary sources. *The Federal Register* publishes daily regulations and legal notices issued by the executive branch and all federal agencies. It is divided into sections such as rules and regulations and Sunshine Act meetings. Of special interest are announcements of hearings and investigations, committee meetings, and agency decisions and rulings. The *Monthly Catalog of United States Government Publications* covers publications of all branches of the federal government. It has semiannual and annual cumulative indexes by title, author/agency, and subject. For links to several frequently used U.S. federal government documents, use your Communicate! CD-ROM to access Web Resource 13.5: Government Publications Online. Online documents for other countries and for states and cities can be found by using a search engine.

Internet Resources

In addition to printed resources (some of which you may access online), you may find resources for your speech that are only available on the **Internet,** an international electronic collection of thousands of smaller networks. The World Wide Web (www) is one network that houses information on a broad range of topics. You can access the Internet either through your college or university library, its computer labs, or your own personal computer. Public libraries also usually provide Internet access. On the

Internet
an international electronic collection of thousands of smaller networks.

Internet you can access electronic databases, bulletin boards, scholarly and professional electronic discussion groups, as well as Web sites and Web pages that are authored by individuals and groups.

To find information on your topic, you will use a "search engine," a program that locates information that is housed on the Web. Today Google, InfoSeek, Excite, HotBox, and Alta Vista are popular search engines. You use search engines by typing in the key words for your topic. If you want to be more effective, find out which computer symbols help limit and focus your search. For example, if Jeremy is using Alta Vista and puts quotation marks around the words "media violence," he will only get hits in which these two words appear together. If he does not use quotations, he will get hits in which either word appears, which will produce lots of "hits" that aren't really relevant to his speech. Just as there are different types of print resources so too there are several types of electronic resources.

newsgroup or bulletin board
an electronic gathering place for people with similar interests.

A **newsgroup** or **bulletin board** is "an electronic gathering place for people with similar interests" (Miller, 1999, p. 187). To communicate in a newsgroup, a user posts a message (called an *article*) about some topic that is appropriate for the site. Other users read these articles and, when so disposed, respond. The result is a kind of ongoing discussion in which ten, fifty, or maybe even hundreds of users may participate. The Internet offers "more than 58,402 different sites that send and receive newsgroups" (Barnes, 2003, p. 7). Today many college classes require students to share their ideas and opinions about course-related topics in class-specific newsgroups. Bulletin boards and newsgroups maintained by scholarly organizations can be a source of new information that has yet to be published in other sources.

Hosted Web sites Most commercial and nonprofit organizations host Web sites that provide information on the organization and on issues of interest to the organization and its members. For example the Sierra Club Web site at http://sierraclub.org/ provides updates on a variety of environ-

mental issues. Hosted Web sites can be comprised of numerous Web pages and may also provide links to other related sites.

Personal Web pages Personal Web pages are created and maintained by individuals who can post any information that they choose. On the personal sites of some noted scholars, you can find links to their professional papers. On other personal sites you may find pages that support causes or points of view advocated by the site creator.

Surveys

A **survey** involves canvassing people to get information about their ideas and opinions; this information is then analyzed for trends. Survey information may be conducted in person, over the phone or Internet, or in writing. You may find surveys conducted by other people or organizations that provide information relevant to your topic; at other times you may want to conduct your own survey. If you decide to conduct your own survey, use your Communicate! CD-ROM to access Web Resource 13.6: Conducting Surveys, which will provide you with important tips for collecting good information.

survey
canvassing people to get information about their ideas and opinions and then analyzing them for trends.

Interviews

Sometimes the best source of information about your topic is an expert who you can interview. For interviews to be useful, they must be well planned so that you get the information you need. See Chapter 9 to review information about writing good questions and conducting an interview.

E. Crews/The Image Works

Interviews are a good source for personal narratives that can be used to support key ideas.

Skimming to Determine Source Value

Because you are likely to uncover far more information than you can use, you will want to skim sources to determine whether or not to read them in full. **Skimming** is a method of rapidly going through a work to determine what is covered and how. Skimming helps you decide which sources should be read in full, which should be read in part, and which should be abandoned. Minutes spent in such evaluation will save hours of reading.

skimming
a method of rapidly going through a work to determine what is covered and how.

If you are evaluating an article, spend a minute or two finding out whether it really presents information on the exact area of the topic you are exploring and whether it contains any documented statistics, examples, or quotable opinions. (We will examine the kind of information to look for in the next section.) If you are evaluating a book, read the table of contents carefully, look at the index, and skim pertinent chapters, asking the same questions as you would for a magazine article.

If you are using an electronic periodical index, you may be able to access short abstracts for each article identified by your search. Reading these abstracts can help you decide which sources you want to read in their entirety. Once you have the sources in hand, however, you still need to follow a skimming procedure.

Criteria for Judging Sources

When you rely on printed sources for the information in your speech, you can have some confidence that the information you are using is reliable if these sources are from a reputable publishing house and have been chosen by professional librarians to be part of the collection. You should be more cautious in using information that you find on the Internet. This information comes from a wide variety of sources, and no one oversees the accuracy of the information or the honesty of the people who produce it.

For instance, as the authors of *Researching Online* mention, "While the universality of the Internet can be good in that it allows previously marginalized voices to be heard, it also adds a new layer of difficulty for researchers" (Munger et al., 2000, p. 5). Why is this? Editors of academic articles and books require writers to show that the data they present meet a basic standard of reliability and relevance. The Internet lacks these gatekeepers; no one is responsible for ensuring the accuracy of Internet information. With this in mind, it's important for you to corroborate the information and authorship of material before you use it in your speech.

In evaluating any source, use these three criteria that have been suggested by a variety of research librarians.

1. **Authority.** The first test of a resource is the expertise of its author and the reputation of the publishing or sponsoring organization. A Web site that doesn't acknowledge the source for the information presented should be viewed skeptically. On the Internet, the first filter of quality is

the type of URL. Those ending in ".gov" (governmental), ".edu" (educational), and ".org" are noncommercial sites with institutional publishers. The URL ".com" indicates that the sponsor is a for-profit organization. When an author is listed, check his or her credentials through biographical references or by seeing if the author has a home page listing professional qualifications. Use the electronic periodical indexes to see whether the author has other related articles that show expertise, or check the Library of Congress to see whether the author has published books in the field.

From some sites you will find information that is anonymous or credited to someone whose background is not clear. In these cases your ability to trust the information depends on evaluating the qualifications of the sponsoring organization. If you do not know whether you can trust the sources, then do not use the information.

2. **Objectivity.** A second test of the information is how impartially it is presented. All authors have a viewpoint, but be wary of information that is overly slanted. Web documents that have been created under the sponsorship of some business, government, or public interest groups should be carefully scrutinized for obvious biases or good "public relations" fronts. For example, commercial Web sites may include corporate histories and biographical essays on founders that present the company and founders in a favorable light. So you will need other sources to give you a more accurate picture of both the company's and the founders' strengths and weaknesses. Similarly, although the Sierra Club is a well-respected environmental organization, the articles found on its Web site are unlikely to present a balanced discussion of the pros and cons of controversial environmental issues.

To evaluate the potential biases in articles and books, read the preface or identify the thesis statement. These often reveal the authors' point of view. When evaluating a Web site with which you are unfamiliar, look for the purpose of the Web site. Most home pages contain a purpose or mission statement that can help you understand why the site was created. Armed with this information you are in a better position to recognize the biases that may be contained in the information. Remember, at some level all Web pages can be seen as "infomercials," so always be concerned with who created this information and why (Kapoun, 2000).

3. **Currency.** A third test is to evaluate the currency of the information. In general, newer information is more accurate than older. When evaluating your sources, be sure to consult the latest information you can find. One of the reasons for using Web-based sources is that they can provide more up-to-date information than printed sources (Munger et al., 2000, p. 17). But just because a source is found online does not mean that the information is timely. To determine how up to date the information is, you will need to find out "when the information was placed on the Web

and how often it is revised" (Barnes, 2003, p. 82). Many authors post this information at the end of the page. If there are no dates indicated and no indications for checking the accuracy, the information should not be used.

Even some recent publications use old information. With statistics, especially, you want to know not only when the statistics were published but also when the data were collected. If, for instance, you are talking about the number of women in Congress, remember that congressional elections occur every two years. You don't want to be using data that are more than two years old, and even data from a recent publication could be wrong.

To read about additional criteria you can use to evaluate your sources, use your Communicate! CD-ROM to access Web Resource 13.7: Analyzing Information Sources.

Action Step 2.a ▶

Identify Potential Sources

The goal of this activity is to help you compile a *list* of potential sources for your speech.

1. Identify gaps in your current knowledge that you would like to fill.

2. Identify a person, an event, or a process that you could observe to broaden your personal knowledge base.

3. Brainstorm a list of key words that are related to your speech goal.

4. Working with paper or electronic versions of your library's card catalog, periodical indexes (including InfoTrac College Edition), and general references discussed in this chapter, find and list specific resources that appear to provide information for your speech.

5. Using a search engine, identify Internet sponsored and personal Web sites that may be sources of information for your speech.

6. Identify a person you could interview for additional information for this speech.

7. Skim the resources you have identified to decide which are likely to be most useful.

8. Evaluate each resource to determine how much faith you can place in the information.

You can complete this activity online, print it out, see a sample list of potential sources, and, if requested, email it to your instructor. Use your Communicate! CD-ROM to access Skill Learning Activity 13.1.

Identify and Select Relevant Information

The information that you find in your sources that you may want to use in your speech includes factual statements, expert opinions, and elaboration, including anecdotes, comparisons, and quotations.

Factual Statements

Factual statements are those that can be verified. "A recent study confirmed that preschoolers watch an average of 28 hours of television a week," "The Gateway Solo laptop comes with a CD-ROM drive," and "Johannes Gutenberg invented printing from movable type in the 1400s" are all statements of fact that can be verified. One way to verify whether the information is factual is to check it against material from another source on the same subject. Never use any information that is not carefully documented unless you have corroborating sources.

factual statements
statements that can be verified.

Examples **Examples** are specific instances that illustrate or explain a general factual statement. One or two short examples like the following are often enough to help make a generalization meaningful.

> One way a company increases its power is to buy out another company. Recently Kroger bought out Fred Meyer Inc. to make it the largest grocery firm in the country.

> Professional billiard players practice many long hours every day. Jennifer Lee practices as much as ten hours a day when she is not in a tournament.

examples
specific instances that illustrate or explain a general factual statement.

Examples are useful because they provide concrete detail that makes a general statement more meaningful to the audience.

Although most of the examples you find will be real, you may find hypothetical examples you can use. **Hypothetical examples** are those drawn from reflections about future events. They develop the idea "What if . . . ?" In the following excerpt, John A. Ahladas (1989) presents some hypothetical examples of what it will be like in the year 2039 if global warming continues:

hypothetical examples
examples drawn from reflections about future events.

> In New York, workers are building levees to hold back the rising tidal waters of the Hudson River, now lined with palm trees. In Louisiana, 100,000 acres of wetland are steadily being claimed by the sea. In Kansas, farmers learn to live with drought as a way of life and struggle to eke out an existence in the increasingly dry and dusty heartland. . . . And reports arrive from Siberia of bumper crops of corn and wheat from a longer and warmer growing season. (p. 382)

Because hypothetical examples are not themselves factual, you must be very careful to check that the facts upon which they are based are accurate.

Three principles should guide your use of examples. First, the examples should be clear and specific enough to create a clear picture for the audience. Consider the following generalization and supporting example:

Generalization: Electronics is one of the few areas in which products are significantly cheaper today than they were in the 1980s.

Supporting example: In the mid-1980s, Motorola sold cellular phones for $5,000 each; now a person can buy a Motorola cellular phone for under $90.

With this single example, the listener has a vivid picture of tremendous difference in about a twenty-year period.

Second, the examples you use should be representative. If cellular phones were the *only* electronics product for which prices were so much less over that same period, this vivid example would be misleading and unethical. Any misuse of data is unethical, especially if the user knows better.

Third, use at least one example to support every generalization.

statistics
numerical facts.

Statistics Statistics are numerical facts. Statistical statements, such as "Only five out of every ten local citizens voted in the last election" or "The cost of living rose 0.6 percent in January of 2003," enable you to pack a great deal of information into a small package. Statistics can provide impressive support for a point, but when they are poorly used in the speech, they may be boring and, in some instances, downright deceiving. Here are some guidelines for using statistics effectively.

1. **Use only statistics whose reliability you can verify.** Taking statistics from only the most reliable sources and double-checking any startling statistics with another source will guard against the use of faulty statistics.

2. **Use only recent statistics so that your audience will not be misled.** For example, if you find the statistic that only 9 of 100 members of the Senate, or 9 percent, are women (true in 1999), you would be misleading your audience if you used that statistic in a speech today. If you want to make a point about the number of women in the Senate, find the most recent statistics. Check for both the year and the range of years to which the statistics apply.

3. **Use statistics comparatively.** By themselves, statistics are hard to interpret. When we present comparative statistics, they are easier to understand. For example, in a speech on chemical waste, Donald Baeder (1980) points out that chemicals are measured in parts per billion or

How can you tell if the statistics you hear presented in a speech are reliable?

even parts per trillion. Notice how he goes on to use comparisons to put the meaning of the statistics in perspective:

One part per billion is the equivalent of one drop—one drop!—of vermouth in two 36,000 gallon tanks of gin, and that would be a very dry martini even by San Francisco standards! One part per trillion is the equivalent of one drop in two thousand tank cars. (p. 497)

4. **Do not use too many statistics.** Although statistics may be an excellent way to present a great deal of material quickly, be careful not to overuse them. A few pertinent numbers are far more effective than a battery of statistics. When you believe you must use many statistics, try preparing a visual aid, perhaps a chart, to help your audience visualize them.

Expert Opinions

Expert opinions are interpretations and judgments made by authorities in a particular subject area. "Watching 28 hours of television a week is far too much for young children," "Having a CD-ROM port on your computer is a necessity," and "The invention of printing from movable type was for all intents and purposes the start of mass communication" are all opinions based on the factual statements cited previously. Whether they are expert opinions or not depends on who made the statements.

*expert opinions
interpretations and judgments made by authorities in a particular subject area.*

How do you tell if a source is an expert? First, the expert must be a master of the specific subject. Second, experts then have engaged in long-term study of their subject. Third, an expert is recognized by other people in his or her field as being a knowledgeable and trustworthy authority. For instance, a history professor may be an expert in ancient Greek nation-states but know little about the government structure of the Aztec civilization.

When you use expert opinions in your speech, you should identify them as opinions and indicate to your audience the level of confidence that you attached to them. For instance, an informative speaker may say, "The temperatures throughout the 1990s were much higher than average. Paul Jorgenson, a space biologist, believes that these higher-than-average temperatures represent the first stages of the greenhouse effect, but the significance of these temperatures is still being debated."

Although opinions should not take the place of facts, expert opinions can help interpret and give weight to facts that you present.

Elaborations

Factual information and expert opinions can be elaborated upon through anecdotes and narratives, comparisons and contrasts, or quotable explanations and opinions.

Anecdotes and narratives Anecdotes are brief, often amusing stories; **narratives** are accounts, personal experiences, tales, or lengthier stories. Because holding audience interest is important in a speech and because audience attention is likely to be captured by a story, anecdotes and narratives

*anecdotes
brief, often amusing stories.*

*narratives
accounts, personal experiences, tales, or lengthier stories.*

are worth looking for, creating, and using. For a five-minute speech, you have little time to tell a detailed story, so one or two anecdotes or a very short narrative would be preferable.

The key to using stories is to make sure that the point of the story directly states or reinforces the point you make in your speech. In his speech John Howard (2000) made a point about failure to follow guidelines:

> The knight was returning to the castle after a long, hard day. His face was bruised and badly swollen. His armor was dented. The plume on his helmet was broken, and his steed was limping. He was a sad sight.
>
> The lord of the castle ran out and asked, "What hath befallen you, Sir Timothy?"
>
> "Oh, Sire," he said, "I have been laboring all day in your service, bloodying and pillaging your enemies to the West."
>
> "You've been doing what?" gasped the astonished nobleman. "I haven't any enemies to the West!"
>
> "Oh!" said Timothy. "Well, I think you do now."
>
> There is a moral to this little story. Enthusiasm is not enough. You need to have a sense of direction. (p. 618)

Good stories and narratives may be humorous, sentimental, suspenseful, or dramatic.

comparisons
illuminate a point by showing similarities.

Comparisons and contrasts
One of the best ways to give meaning to new ideas is through comparison and contrast. **Comparisons** illuminate a point by showing similarities. Although you can easily create comparisons using information you have found, you should still keep your eye open for creative comparisons developed by the authors of the books and articles you have found.

Comparisons may be literal or figurative. Literal comparisons show similarities of real things:

> The walk from the lighthouse back up the hill to the parking lot is equal to walking up the stairs of a 30-story building.

Figurative comparisons express one thing in terms normally denoting another:

> I always envisioned myself as a four-door sedan. I didn't know she was looking for a sports car!

Comparisons make ideas both clearer and more vivid. Notice how Stephen Joel Trachtenberg (1986), in a speech to the Newington High School Scholars' Breakfast, used a figurative comparison to demonstrate the importance of being willing to take risks even in the face of danger. Although the speech was given years ago, the point is timeless:

> The eagle flying high always risks being shot at by some hare-brained human with a rifle. But eagles and young eagles like you still prefer the view from that risky height to what is available flying with the turkeys far, far below. (p. 653)

Whereas comparisons suggest similarities, **contrasts** highlight differences. Notice how the following humorous contrast dramatizes the difference between "participation" and "commitment":

contrasts
highlight differences.

> If this morning you had bacon and eggs for breakfast, I think it illustrates the difference. The eggs represented "participation" on the part of the chicken. The bacon represented "total commitment" on the part of the pig! (Durst, 1989, pp. 309–310)

Quotations When you find an explanation, an opinion, or a brief anecdote that seems to be exactly what you are looking for, you may quote it directly in your speech. Because audiences want to listen to your ideas and arguments, they do not want to hear a string of long quotations. Nevertheless, a well-selected quotation might be perfect in one or two key places.

Quotations can both explain and vivify. Look for quotations that make a point in a particularly clear or vivid way. For example, in his speech "Enduring Values for a Secular Age," Hans Becherer (2000), Executive Officer at Deere & Company, used this Henry Ford quote to show the importance of enthusiasm to progress:

> Enthusiasm is at the heart of all progress. With it, there is accomplishment. Without it, there are only alibis. (p. 732)

Frequently, historical or literary quotations can reinforce a point vividly. Cynthia Opheim (2000), Chair of the Department of Political Science at Southwest Texas State University, in her speech "Making Democracy Work" quoted Mark Twain on the frustration of witnessing legislative decision making when she said:

> There are two things you should never watch being made: sausage and legislation. (p. 60)

Quotations may come from a book of quotations, from another article, or from an interview that you have conducted as part of the speech research process. Regardless of the source, however, when you use a direct quotation, you need to verbally acknowledge the person it came from. Using any quotation or close paraphrase without crediting its source is **plagiarism,** the unethical act of representing a published author's work as your own.

plagiarism
the unethical act of representing a published author's work as your own.

Drawing Information from Multiple Cultural Perspectives

How facts are perceived and what opinions are held often are influenced by a person's cultural background. Therefore, it is important to draw your information from culturally diverse perspectives by seeking sources that have differing cultural orientations and by interviewing experts with diverse cultural backgrounds. For example, when Carrie was preparing for her speech on proficiency testing in grade schools, she purposefully searched for articles written by noted Hispanic, Asian, and African American, as well as European American, authors. In addition, she interviewed two local school superintendents—one from an urban district and one from a suburban district. Because she consciously worked to develop diverse sources of information, Carrie felt more confident that her speech would more accurately reflect all sides of the debate on proficiency testing.

Dr. Molefi Kete Asante, an internationally renowned scholar, believes that limiting our research by only considering the viewpoints of those who are like us promotes racism that is then transmitted as we speak. The Spotlight on Scholars features his work.

Spotlight on Scholars ▸ Molefi Kete Asante

Professor of Africology, Temple University, on the Language of Prejudice and Racism ◆ ◆ ◆ ◆

Molefi Kete Asante is an activist scholar who believes it is not enough to know, one must act to humanize the world. Over his career Asante has sought not only to understand what he studied but also to use that knowledge to help people discover how to exert their power.

In 1968, at the age of 26, Asante completed his Ph.D. in Speech Communication from UCLA. As a graduate student, Asante studied language and the rhetoric of agitation, and in his dissertation, he analyzed the speeches of one of the most zealous agitators during the American Revolution, Samuel Adams. During the late 1960s, however, Asante focused his attention on another revolution occurring in the United States that he found more compelling. Demonstrating his insatiable appetite for intellectual work, at the same time that he was working on his dissertation he also wrote *The Rhetoric of Black Revolution,* published in 1969.

As a scholar grounded in communication and the rhetoric of agitation, Asante began to notice how racism and communication were intertwined. As his thinking evolved, he began to formulate the theory that racism in our culture is embedded in our language system.

According to Asante, racism stems from a thought system that values a particular race over

another. As a phenomenon of language, racism is demonstrated by what people say about others and how they justify their personal attitudes and beliefs. What Asante discovered is that our language reflects the "knowledge system" we are taught. In the United States and much of the world, this knowledge system reflected a European rather than a multicultural view of human events and achievements.

For instance, in most schools, the study of the arts or philosophy or science focuses only on the contributions made by Europeans or European Americans. As a result of the focus of these studies, we "learn" that nothing substantial or important originated from anywhere else. Thus we come to value the music, literature, rituals, and values of Europeans over those of other cultural groups. Since racism comes from valuing a particular race above another, Asante reasons, it was inevitable that mono-ethnic Eurocentric approaches to education would result in our developing racist thoughts and a racist language structure that reifies those thoughts.

To combat racism and racist language, Asante believes that we must first enlarge our knowledge base to accurately reflect the contributions that have been made by other racial and cultural groups. For example, the history that is taught needs to reflect the substantial contributions that Africa,

China, and other non-European groups have made to the development of humankind. Likewise, the literature and art that is studied needs to reflect and be drawn from a body that includes the work of various racial and ethnic groups. When people learn that all racial and cultural groups have made significant contributions to the development of humankind, they will be less prone to view themselves as superior or inferior to others.

As a contribution to providing the kinds of information that we all need to learn, in 1987 Asante wrote *Afrocentricity,* a book that seeks to discover, understand, and reclaim the contributions that many cultures, especially African cultures, have made to our common intellectual heritage. Since that time, Asante has focused his own learning and his scholarship on discovering, reclaiming, and sharing the contributions of African culture and philosophy.

Asante's influence has been widespread. He served as the first Director of Afro-American Studies at UCLA, Department Head of Speech Communication at SUNY Buffalo, and Chair of the Department of African American Studies at Temple University,

where he established the first Ph.D. program in African American Studies. He is internationally known for his work on Afrocentricity and African culture. He has published more than thirty books, edited nine others, and authored more than eighty book chapters and journal articles. In the process, he has led an intellectual revolution among scholars working in numerous disciplines. Although he is noted for his scholarship, Asante says, "Working with students is the centerpiece of what I do." He currently teaches undergraduate courses on the African American Church and 20th Century Mass Media in Black Communities and graduate courses in Ancient Egyptian Language and Culture and Egyptian Origins of Rhetoric. For a list of some of Asante's major publications, see the references listed at the end of the book.

His interest in his personal African heritage has caused him to trace his family ancestry back to Ghana. Recently, in Ghana, he was "enstooled," a ceremony that formally acknowledges a person as a member of Ghanaian royalty. At that ceremony he was given the name "Nano Okru Asante Peasah, Kyidomhene of Tafo."

Recording Information and Citing Written and Electronic Sources

As you find the facts, opinions, and elaborations that you want to use in your speech, you need to record the information accurately and keep a careful account of your sources so that they can be cited appropriately.

How should you keep track of the information you plan to use? Although it may seem easier to record all material from one source on a single sheet of paper (or to photocopy source material), sorting and arranging material is much easier when each item is recorded separately. So it is wise to record information on note cards that allow you to easily find, arrange, and rearrange each item of information as you prepare your speech.

In the note card method, each factual statement, expert opinion, or elaboration, along with the bibliographical information for its source, is recorded on a 3 × 5 inch or larger index card containing three types of information. First, each card should have a heading or key words that identify the subcategory to which the information belongs. Second, the specific fact, opinion, or elaboration statement should be recorded on the card. Any part of the information item that is quoted directly from the source should be enclosed with quotation marks. Third, the bibliographic publication data related to the source should be recorded.

The bibliographic data you will record depends on whether the source of the information item is a book, a periodical, a newspaper, an interview, or a Web site. For a book, include names of authors, title of the book, the place of publication and the publisher, the date of publication, and the page or pages from which the information is taken. For a periodical or newspaper, include the name of the author (if given), the title of the article, the name of the publication, the date, and the page number from which the information is taken. For online sources, include the URL for the Web site, the heading under which you found the information, and the date that you accessed the site. Specifics and samples for preparing source citations (including interviews) are shown in Chapter 14. Be sure to record enough source information so that you can relocate the material if you need to. Figure 13.2 provides a sample note card.

As your stack of information note cards grows, you can sort the material, placing each item under the heading to which it is related. For instance, for a speech on Ebola you might have note cards related to causes, symptoms, deadliness of, and treatments. The card in Figure 13.2 would be indexed under the heading "treatments."

The number of sources that you will need depends in part on the type of speech you are giving and your own expertise. For a narrative/personal experience, you will be the main, if not the only, source. For informative reports and persuasive speeches, however, speakers ordinarily draw from multiple sources. For a five-minute speech on Ebola in which you plan to talk about causes, symptoms, and treatments, you might have two or more note cards under each heading. Moreover, the note cards should come from at least three different sources. Avoid using only one source for your information because this often leads to plagiarism; furthermore, basing your speech on one or two sources suggests that you have not done sufficient research. Selecting and using information from several sources allows you to develop an original approach to your topic, ensures a broader research base, and makes it more likely that you will have uncovered the various opinions that are related to your topic.

Figure 13.2
A sample note card

Topic: Ebola
Heading: Treatments

In December of 2003, Army scientists reported taking a significant step in developing a possible treatment by successfully treating with an experimental drug monkeys that had been deliberately injected with Ebola.

Lawrence K. Altman and Judith Miller, "Scientists report progress in Ebola treatment," *New York Times*, Dec. 12, 2003, Section A, p. 36, col.1.

Action Step 2.b ▶

Identify, Select, and Record Relevant Information Items

The goal of this activity is to review the source material you identified in Action Step 2.a and to record specific items of information that you might wish to use in your speech.

1. Carefully read all print and electronic sources (including Web material) that you have identified and evaluated as appropriate sources for your speech. Review your notes and tapes from all interviews and observations.

2. As you read an item (fact, opinion, example, illustration, statistic, anecdote, narrative, comparison/contrast, quotation, definition, or description) that you think might be useful in your speech, record the item on a 3 X 5 note card or on the appropriate online note card form for this activity, available at the Communicate! Web site. (If you are using an article that originally appeared in a periodical but that you read online, use the periodical note card form.)

> You can complete this activity online and, if requested, email it to your instructor. You can also view a sample of three note cards prepared by another student, use online forms to prepare your own note cards, and print them out for use in preparing your speech. Use your Communicate! CD-ROM to access **Skill Learning Activity 13.2.**

Preparing to Cite Sources in the Speech

In your speeches, as in any communication in which you use ideas that are not your own, you need to acknowledge the sources of your ideas and statements. Specifically mentioning your sources not only helps the audience evaluate the content but also adds to your credibility. In addition, citing sources will give concrete evidence of the depth of your research. Failure to cite sources, especially when you are presenting information that is meant to substantiate a controversial point, is unethical.

In a written report, ideas taken from other sources are credited in footnotes; in a speech, these notations must be included in your verbal statement of the material. Although you do not want to clutter your speech with long bibliographical citations, be sure to mention the sources of your most important information. Figure 13.3 gives several examples of appropriate source citations.

"Thomas Friedman, noted international editor for the *New York Times*, stated in his book *The Lexis and the Olive Tree*..."

"In an interview with *GQ* magazine, Arnold Schwarzenegger stated..."

"According to an article about Japanese workers in last week's *Time* magazine..."

"In the latest Gallup poll cited in the February 10 issue of *Newsweek*..."

"But to get a complete picture we have to look at the statistics. According to the 2003 *Statistical Abstract*, the level of production for the European Economic Community rose from..."

"In a speech on business ethics delivered to the Public Relations Society of America last November, Preston Townly, CEO of the Conference Board, said..."

Figure 13.3
Appropriate speech source citations

Action Step 2.c ▶

Prepare to Cite Your Sources

On the back of each note card you created in Action Step 2.b, write a short phrase you can use in your speech as a verbal citation for the material on that card. This is Skill Learning Activity 13.3.

Skill Builders ▶ Gather and Evaluate Material for Your Speech

Skill	Use	Procedure	Example
The process of collecting, evaluating, and recording information items that may be appropriate for use in a speech.	To search and evaluate sources of information that may contain items related to the speech goal and to document them in a form that allows easy access to items while providing documentation for the origin of an item.	1. Locate potential sources of information including books, periodicals, reference works, Web sites, observations, and interviews.	In her research on West Nile virus, Tamika found three books, six magazine articles, one journal article, sixteen newspaper articles, several statistics from the Center for Disease Control, three Web site pages, and she interviewed a doctor who specialized in infectious disease control.

Skill	Use	Procedure	Example
		2. Scan the information to access its relevance to your speech goal.	After scanning the resources she determined that two of the books and the journal article were too technical for her specific goal.
		3. Evaluate each resource for its authority, objectivity, and currency.	Tamika eliminated five magazine articles because in the article the source of the information was not identified. She eliminated three more because they were dated. She eliminated two of the Web pages that seemed to be hysterical responses to the illness.
		4. Read all the sources and use note cards to record each item of information that might be useful in developing your speech along with the relevant bibliographic information on that source.	After reading her sources, she prepared sixteen note cards.
		5. Develop a phrase that you can use to verbally cite the source of an item in your speech.	On the back of each note card she wrote a phrase that verbally described the source of the item.

What Would You Do? A QUESTION OF ETHICS

"Dan, I was wondering whether you'd listen to the speech I'm giving in class tomorrow. It will only take about five minutes."

"Sure." [Tom and Dan found an empty classroom and Tom went through his speech.]

"What did you think?"

"Sounded pretty good to me. I could follow the speech—I knew what you wanted to do. But I was wondering about that section where you had the statistics. You didn't give any source."

"Well, the fact is I can't remember the source."

"You remember the statistics that specifically but you don't remember the source?"

"Well, I don't remember the statistics all that well, but I think I've got them about right."

"Well, you can check them, can't you?"

"Check it? Where? That would take me hours. And after all, I told you I think I have them about right."

"But, Tom, the accuracy of the statistics seems pretty important to what you said."

"Listen, trust me on this—no one is going to say anything about it. You've already said that my goal was clear, my main points were clear, and I sounded as if I know what I'm talking about. I really think that's all Goodwin is interested in."

"Well, whatever you say, Tom. I just thought I'd ask."

"No problem, thanks for listening. I thought I had it in pretty good shape, but I wanted someone to hear my last practice."

"Well, good luck!"

1. What do you think of Tom's assessment of his use of statistics that "No one is going to say anything about it"?

2. Does Tom have any further ethical obligation? If so, what is it?

Summary

Effective speaking requires high-quality information. You need to know where to look for information, what kind of information to look for, how to record it, and how to cite sources in your speeches.

To find material, begin by exploring your own knowledge, experience, and observations. Then work outward through library and electronic sources, interviewing, and surveying. Look for material in books, periodicals, newspapers, encyclopedias, statistical sources, biographical references, U. S. government publications, and the Internet. By skimming material you can quickly evaluate sources to determine whether or not to read them in full. Three criteria for evaluating sources are authority, objectivity, and currency.

When you have gathered sources, identify and select relevant information. Factual statements are presented in the form of examples and statistics. Expert opinions are interpretations of facts and judgments made by qualified authorities. Depending on your topic and speech goal, you may use facts and opinions and elaborate them with examples, anecdotes, narratives, comparisons, contrasts, and quotations.

A good method for recording material that you may want to use in your speech is to record each bit of data along with necessary bibliographical documentation on a separate note card. As your stack of information grows, sort the material under common headings. During the speech, cite the sources for the information.

Communicate! Online

N ow that you have read Chapter 13, use your Communicate! CD-ROM for quick access to the electronic resources that accompany this text. Your CD-ROM gives you access to InfoTrac College Edition, Speech Builder Express, and the Communicate! Web site. When you get to the Communicate! home page, click on "Student Book Companion Site" in the Resource box at right to access the online study aids for this chapter, including a digital glossary, review quizzes, the chapter activities, and the chapter Web Resources.

Key Terms

At the Communicate! Web site, select the chapter resources for Chapter 13. Print a copy of the glossary for this chapter and test yourself with the electronic flash cards or complete the crossword puzzle to help you master these key terms:

electronic databases (307)
periodicals (308)
Internet (311)
newsgroup or bulletin board (312)
survey (313)

skimming (314)
factual statements (317)
examples (317)
hypothetical examples (317)
statistics (318)
expert opinions (319)

anecdotes (319)
narratives (319)
comparisons (320)
contrasts (321)
plagiarism (321)

Review Quiz

Test your knowledge of the concepts in this chapter by taking the online quiz at the Communicate! Web site. Select the chapter resources for Chapter 13, then click on "Review Quiz." When you have completed the quiz, submit it for scoring.

Skill Learning Activities

Complete Action Steps 2.a and 2.b for Chapter 13 online at the Communicate! Web site. Select the chapter resources for Chapter 13, then click on "Activities." You can submit your Action Steps answers to your instructor.

13.1: Action Step 2.a: Identify Potential Sources (316)
13.2: Action Step 2.b: Identify, Select, and Record Relevant Information Items (325)
13.3: Action Step 2.c: Prepare to Cite Your Sources (326)

Web Resources

Access the Web Resources for this chapter online at the Communicate! Web site. Select the chapter resources for Chapter 13, then click on "Web Resources."

13.1: Online Encyclopedias (310)
13.2: Statistics Online (310)

The InfoTrac College Edition database contains hundreds of articles from reliable periodicals and journals. You can use this database to research sources for your speech. Use the password that accompanied a new copy of this text and your Communicate! CD-ROM to log onto InfoTrac College Edition.

Enter your speech topic into the InfoTrac College Edition keyword search box, as shown here. You can search for keywords in the title, source citation, or abstract of articles, or you can search for a keyword within the content of an article. You can also limit your search to articles published within a certain time frame, to a particular periodical, or to articles that contain certain words. When you've entered your keyword and search criteria, click on "Search."

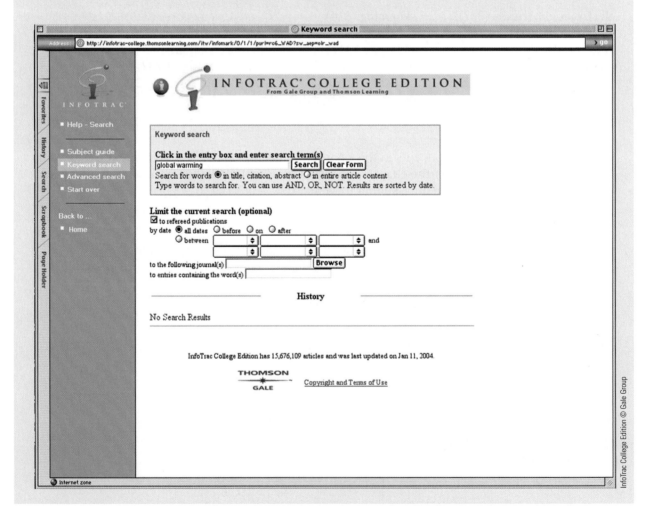

InfoTrac College Edition © Gale Group

A list of citations containing your key word search appears. Click on a link that interests you to view an article. If you want to narrow your choice of citations to work from, check the "Mark" box, then click "View Mark List" in the menu at left. A list of only the citations you selected will appear.

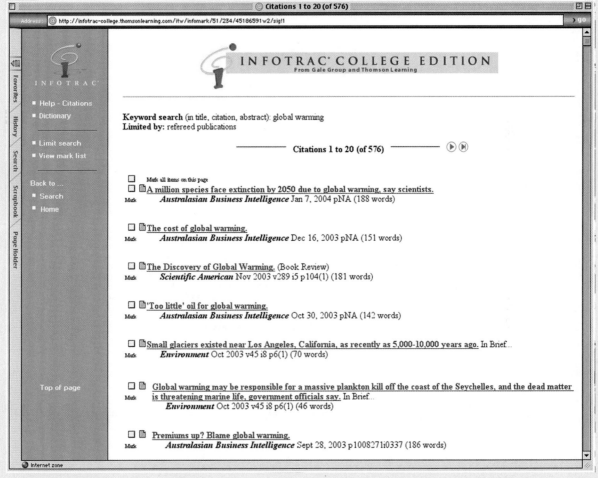

When you click to view an article, you'll see the full text of the article. The menu at the left allows you to print, email, or retrieve an Adobe Acrobat version of the article you selected. When you click on "Links," links to related articles will appear.

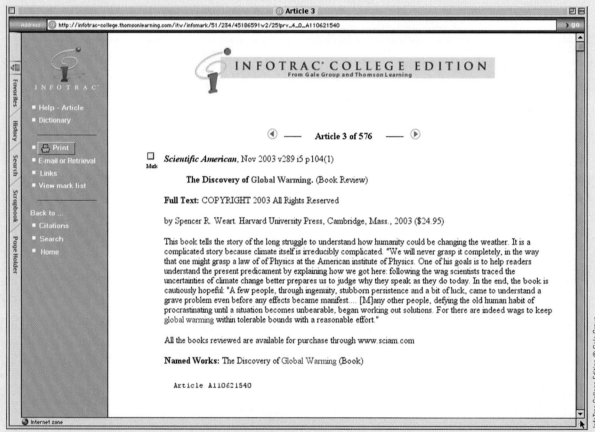

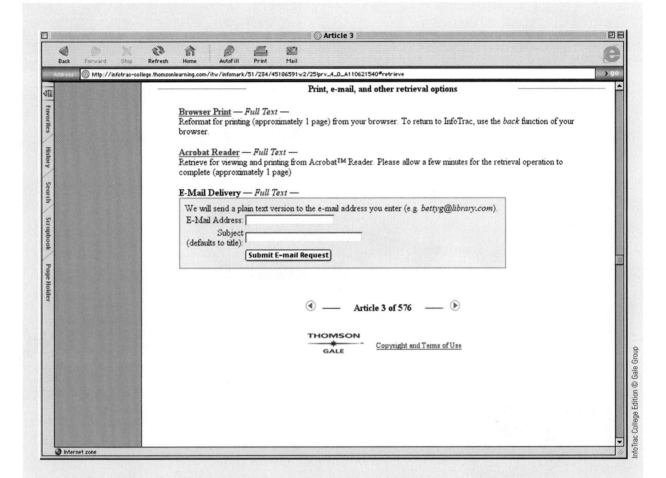

OBJECTIVES

After you have read this chapter, you should be able to answer these questions:

- How do you construct a thesis statement?
- How do you determine the main points for your speech?
- How do you determine the best order for your speech?
- What is the goal of transitions?
- What are the goals of an effective speech introduction?
- What are the most common types of speech introductions?
- What are the essentials of an effective speech conclusion?
- What are the major elements of a well-written speech outline?

14

Organizing

"Troy, that was a terrific speech. I haven't heard so many good stories in a long time."

"You're right, Brett, the stories were interesting, but I had a hard time following it."

"Well, he was talking about ways that we can help save the environment."

"Yes, but can you remember anything more than that one point about recycling."

"Let me think. Didn't he say something about fuel efficiency?"

"Yes, but can you remember what his main point was?"

"I assume he wanted us to economize—that one story he told had something to do with fuel."

"But what? I can't really recall what he was trying to get us to understand."

"Come on, you have to admit his story about the car was funny."

"Right, just about everyone laughed, but where did he go from there?"

"OK, so he didn't really give us much information, but I still enjoyed the stories."

"Let's see, what were the other key points?"

organizing
the process of selecting and arranging the main ideas and supporting material to be presented in the speech in a manner that makes it easy for the audience to understand.

speech outline
the essential features or main aspects of your speech.

roy and Brett's experience is not that unusual; even accomplished speakers sometimes give speeches that are not as clearly organized as they could be. Yet a speech that is well organized is far more likely to achieve its goal than one that is not. In this chapter, we consider the third of the five action steps: **Organize and develop speech material in a way that is best suited to your particular audience.**

Organizing is the process of selecting and arranging the main ideas and supporting material to be presented in the speech in a manner that makes it easy for the audience to understand. The quality of your organization is reflected in your **speech outline,** which includes the essential features or main aspects of your speech. Organizing involves (a) developing the body of the speech including writing a thesis statement, organizing and outlining main points, selecting and outlining supporting materials, and preparing section transitions; (b) preparing the introduction; (c) preparing the conclusion; (d) listing sources; and (e) completing the outline. The value of a speech outline is that while preparing it you consciously consider the logic of the pattern you use to organize your ideas, the material you will you use to develop your ideas, and how you will link one idea to the other. The better the outline, the better the speech is likely to be.

Developing the Body of the Speech

Because the introduction is the first part of the speech to be heard by the audience, many speakers mistakenly assume that they should begin outlining with the introduction. When you think about it, however, you will realize that it is difficult to work on an introduction before you have considered the material to be introduced. It is best to prepare the body of your speech first: Write a thesis statement, select and state the main points, and determine the best order. Once you have outlined the main points of the speech, you can select the material (examples, statistics, illustrations, quotations, and so forth) that elaborates on or supports your main points.

Writing a Thesis Statement

thesis statement
a sentence that identifies the topic of your speech and the main ideas you will present.

Having completed your research on your specific speech goal, you are ready to elaborate this goal and provide a framework for the structure of the speech. You will do this through a **thesis statement,** a sentence that identifies the topic of your speech and the main ideas you will present. Thus, the thesis statement determines the main points of a speech. For her speech goal, Erin wrote, "I want my audience to understand how to spike a volleyball effectively." Because she is a member of the women's varsity volleyball team, she already knows her subject matter well enough to write a thesis statement. Moreover, she also has talked with her coach and read some written sources on volleyball, so she feels comfortable writing the thesis statement, "The three steps for executing an effective volleyball spike are to have a good approach, a powerful swing, and a good follow-through."

Often, however, you will have collected a variety of information related to your specific speech goal. Then you have to make a decision about what main ideas will best enable you to reach your goal. Let's consider an example to illustrate how you might proceed to select the points you want to talk about now that you have found most of the information you will use in your speech.

When Emming wrote the specific goal "I would like the audience to understand the major criteria for finding a suitable credit card," he already had a few ideas about what he might focus on in the speech. But it wasn't until he completed most of his research that he really had enough information to write down seven specific ideas of what might be the key criteria for finding a suitable credit card:

interest rate
convenience
discounts
annual fee
rebates
institutional reputation
frequent flyer points

If you are able to list several potential ideas for your main points, then you can begin to evaluate them and select the ones you will use and incorporate them in your thesis statement. For instance, Emming noticed that several of his sources talked about the importance of both interest rate and annual fee. Moreover, nearly every source mentioned at least one inducement, such as rebates. Emming crossed out those criteria (topics) that did not have as much support and combined individual inducements under a single heading. At this stage, his list looked like this:

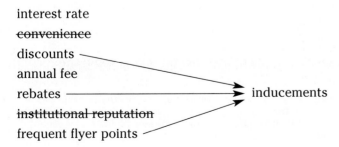

interest rate
~~convenience~~
discounts
annual fee
rebates ────────────────➤ inducements
~~institutional reputation~~
frequent flyer points

Now Emming was able to write the rough draft of his thesis statement: "Three criteria that will enable the audience to find the most suitable credit card are level of real interest rate, annual fee, and inducements." For guidance on writing analytical, expository, and persuasive thesis statements, use your Communicate! CD-ROM to access Web Resource 14.1: Writing Different Types of Thesis Statements.

Organizing and Outlining Main Points

main points
complete sentence representations of the main ideas used in your thesis statement.

Once you have determined a thesis statement, you can begin to outline the main points of your speech confidently. **Main points** are complete sentence representations of the main ideas you have used in your thesis statement. Erin identified "a good approach, a powerful swing, and a good follow-through" as the three characteristics for an effective volleyball spike, and these become her main points. Similarly, Emming determines that "interest rates, annual fee, and advertised inducements" are the three major criteria for finding a suitable credit card, and those three items become the main points in his speech.

Action Step 3.a

Writing a Thesis Statement

The goal of this activity is to develop a well-worded thesis statement for your speech.

1. Write the specific goal you developed in Chapter 12 with Speech Action Step 1.e.

2. Does this specific speech goal list a specific number of main ideas?

3. If yes, list the ideas and move to item 6.

4. If no, based on your research, identify and list the specific ideas your audience must learn about if you are to reach the specific speech goal.

5. Review this list and identify items that can be grouped together under a larger category. Then select the two to five items from your research that you believe to be the most important for this audience to understand.

6. Now write a thesis statement that identifies your topic and previews these ideas.

You can complete this activity online with Speech Builder Express, view a student sample of this activity, and, if requested, email your completed activity to your instructor. Use your Communicate! CD-ROM to access Skill Learning Activity 14.1.

Write main points as complete sentences It is important to write main points as complete sentences because only sentences can fully express the relationships associated with the key elements of the thesis statement.

Let's consider Emming's speech for which he wrote: "Three criteria you can use to find a suitable credit card are level of real interest rate, annual fee, and advertised inducements." Suppose he then wrote the first draft of his main points as follows:

I. Level of interest rate

II. Annual fee

III. Inducements

You would have some idea of what he was talking about, but you would not understand the points as criteria. To make the relationships clear, further refinement is needed. Using Roman numerals to represent main point designations, Emming might write a first draft of the main points of his speech like this:

I. Examining the interest rate is one criterion you can use to find a credit card that is suitable for where you are in life.

II. Another criterion you can use to make sure you find a credit card that is suitable for where you are in life is to examine the annual fee.

III. Finding a credit card can also depend on weighing the advertised inducements, which is the third criterion you will want to use to be sure that it is suitable for where you are in life.

Notice that we have emphasized that this is a first draft. Sometimes our first draft contains the wording we want to use. More often, however, we find that our first attempt needs revision.

Revise main points To help you improve the wording of your main points, ask yourself the following questions:

- Are main points clear?
- Are main points parallel in structure?
- Are main points meaningful?
- Are main points limited to a maximum of five?

To see how you can use these questions to refine your speech plan, let's consider Emming's main points more carefully. Emming has made a pretty good start. His three main points are complete sentences that capture the essence of the thesis statement. Now let's see how Emming might use the four questions to assure himself that he has achieved the best wording for his points.

clear

wording of main points that is likely to call up the same images in the minds of most audience members.

1. **Are the main points clear?** Main points are **clear** when their wording is likely to call up the same images in the minds of most audience members. Emming has drafted his third main point as follows:

   III. **Finding a suitable credit card can also depend on weighing the advertised inducements, which is the third criterion you will want to use to be sure that it is suitable for where you are in life.**

   As he reviews the wording of this point, he notices that it is repetitive ("suitable . . . suitable"), too general ("where you are in life"), and wordy ("which is the third criterion you will want to use to be sure that it is suitable").

   Emming could eliminate several of the problems by cutting all the words before "weighing the advertised inducements," cutting "which," and changing the rest of the sentence to "is the third criterion for finding a suitable credit card." After these changes, Emming would then have a main point written as follows:

   III. **Weighing the advertised inducements is the third criterion for finding a suitable credit card.**

parallel

wording in more than one sentence that follows the same structural pattern, often using the same introductory words.

2. **Are the main points parallel in structure?** Main points are **parallel** when their wording follows the same structural pattern, often using the same introductory words. Parallel structure helps the audience recognize main points by recalling a pattern in the wording.

   Emming notices that each of his main points begins with different wording. He now decides to begin each main point with the words "One (a second, a third) criterion for finding a suitable credit card":

   I. **One criterion for finding a suitable credit card is to examine the interest rate.**

   II. **A second criterion for finding a suitable credit card is to examine the annual fee.**

   III. **A third criterion for finding a suitable credit card is to weigh the inducements.**

   Parallelism can be achieved in many other ways. A second way is to start each sentence with an active verb. To take a different example, suppose Kenneth wants his audience to understand the steps involved in antiquing a table. He might write the following first draft of his main points:

   I. **Clean the table thoroughly.**

   II. **The base coat can be painted over the old surface.**

   III. **A stiff brush, sponge, or piece of textured material can be used to apply the antique finish.**

   IV. **Then you will want to apply two coats of shellac to harden the finish.**

After further consideration, Kenneth might revise his main points to make them parallel in structure. Note the parallel active verbs (italicized) used in his final draft:

    I. *Clean* the table thoroughly.

    II. *Paint* the base coat over the old surface.

    III. *Apply* the antique finish with a stiff brush.

    IV. *Harden* the surface with two coats of shellac.

Notice how the similarity of structure clarifies and strengthens the message. The audience can immediately identify the key steps in the process.

3. **Are the main points meaningful?** Main points are **meaningful** when they are informative. If the main points are not really meaningful, even if the audience remembers them, what is remembered may not be useful. For instance, let's go back to Emming's first main point. Suppose he had written it as follows:

    I. Thinking about the interest is one thing.

If he did word it this way, what would his audience learn from this statement? Not much. Obviously the following wording is a much better choice:

    I. One criterion for finding a suitable credit card is to examine the interest rate.

Now the audience has the opportunity to connect the idea of interest rates to a meaningful task—choosing a suitable credit card.

4. **Are main points limited to two to five in number?** As you begin to phrase prospective main points, you may find your initial list has grown to six, seven, or even ten points that seem to be main ideas. A list that long is usually a clue that some points are really subpoints or repeat other points. If you have more than five, rework your thesis statement to limit the number of main points by grouping similar points under a single heading, or determine whether some points are subpoints that can be included under main points.

Suppose you were giving a speech on shooting an effective foul shot. You might start with this list of points:

    I. Face the basket before shooting.

    II. Hold your shoulders parallel to the foul line.

    III. Spread your feet comfortably, with your knees bent.

    IV. Put your foot that is opposite to your shooting arm slightly forward.

    V. Hold the ball in your shooting hand, with your elbow bent.

    VI. Concentrate on a spot just over the rim.

meaningful
wording that is informative.

VII. Straighten your knees as you shoot the ball.

VIII. Follow through after the ball is released.

Now notice how you can make the steps even more meaningful by grouping them under three headings:

I. First, square yourself to the basket.

   A. Face the basket before shooting.

   B. Hold your shoulders parallel to the foul line.

II. Second, have proper balance.

   A. Spread your feet comfortably, with your knees bent.

   B. Put your foot that is opposite to your shooting arm slightly forward.

III. Third, deliver the ball smoothly.

   A. Hold the ball in your shooting hand, with your elbow bent.

   B. Concentrate on a spot just over the rim.

   C. Straighten your knees as you shoot the ball.

   D. Follow through after the ball is released.

Notice that this organization actually results in more items (eleven versus eight). Yet it is easier to remember two to four items under each of three subheadings than it is to remember eight separate items.

Ordering Main Points

A speech can be organized in many different ways. Your objective is to find or create the structure that will help the audience make the most sense of the material. Although speeches may follow many types of organization, three basic orders that are useful for the beginning speaker to master are topic and time for informative speeches and logical reasons for persuasive speeches.

topic order
organizing the main points of the speech by categories or divisions of a subject.

Topic order Topic order organizes the main points of the speech by categories or divisions of a subject. This is a common way of ordering main points because nearly any subject may be subdivided or categorized in many different ways. The order of the topics may go from general to specific, least important to most important, or in some other logical sequence.

In this example, the topics are presented in the order that the speaker believes is most suitable for the audience and speech goal, with the most important point at the end:

Specific Goal: I want the audience to understand three proven methods for ridding our bodies of harmful toxins.

Thesis Statement: Three proven methods for ridding our bodies of harmful toxins are reducing animal foods, hydrating, and eating natural whole foods.

Main Points:

I. One proven method for ridding our bodies of harmful toxins is reducing our intake of animal products.

II. A second proven method for ridding our bodies of harmful toxins is eating more natural whole foods.

III. A third proven method for ridding our bodies of harmful toxins is keeping well hydrated.

Emming's speech on the three criteria that will enable the audience to find the credit card that is most suitable is another example of a speech using topic order.

Time order Time order organizes main points by a chronological sequence, or by steps in a process. When you select a time order of main points, the audience understands that there is a temporal relationship among the main points. Time order is appropriate when you are explaining how to do something, how to make something, how something works, or how something happened.

Kenneth's speech on the steps in antiquing a table is an example of time order. With a time ordered speech, the order of main points is as important for audiences to remember as the content of the main points. Here is an example:

time order
organizing the main points by a chronological sequence, or by steps in a process.

Specific Goal: I want the audience to understand the four steps involved in developing a personal network.

Thesis Statement: The four steps involved in developing a personal network are to analyze your current networking potential, to position yourself in places for opportunity, to advertise yourself, and to follow up on contacts.

Main Points:

I. First, analyze your current networking potential.

II. Second, position yourself in places for opportunity.

III. Third, advertise yourself.

IV. Fourth, follow up on contacts.

Although the use of "first," "second," and so on is not a requirement when using a time order, their inclusion serves as markers that help audience members understand that the sequence is important.

Logical reasons order Logical reasons order emphasizes why the audience should believe something or behave in a particular way. Unlike the other two arrangements of main points, the logical reasons order is most appropriate for a persuasive speech.

logical reasons order
order that emphasizes why the audience should believe something or behave in a particular way.

Specific Goal: I want the audience to donate money to the United Way.

Thesis Statement: Donating to the United Way is appropriate because your one donation covers many charities, you can stipulate which specific charities you wish to support, and a high percentage of your donation goes to charities.

Main Points:

I. When you donate to the United Way, your one donation covers many charities.

II. When you donate to the United Way, you can stipulate which charities you wish to support.

III. When you donate to the United Way, you know that a high percentage of your donation goes directly to the charities.

As we mentioned earlier, these three organizational patterns are the most common ones. As you develop your public speaking skill, you may find that you will need to revise an existing pattern or create a totally different one to meet the needs of your particular subject matter or audience. In Chapter 18 we describe other organizational patterns that are commonly used in persuasive speeches.

In summary, to organize the body of your speech, (1) turn your speech goal into a thesis statement that forecasts the main points, (2) state the main points in complete sentences that are clear, parallel, meaningful, and limited to five in number, and (3) organize the main points in the pattern best

Action Step 3.b

Organizing and Outlining the Main Points of Your Speech

The goal of this activity is to help you develop your main points.

1. Write your thesis statement.

2. Underline the two to five specific ideas identified in your thesis statement that you want to communicate to your audience to achieve your goal.

3. For each underlined item, write one sentence that summarizes what you want your audience to know about that idea.

4. Review the main points as a group.

   A. Are main points clear? If not, consider why and revise.

   B. Are the main points parallel in structure? If not, consider why and revise.

   C. Are the main points meaningful? If not, consider why and revise.

5. Decide how to order these main points.

6. Write the main point statements in an order that will aid audience members in understanding your thesis and help you reach your goal.

 You can complete this activity online with Speech Builder Express, view a student sample of this activity, and, if requested, email your completed activity to your instructor. Use your Communicate! CD-ROM to access Skill Learning Activity 14.2.

suited to your material and the needs of your specific audience. To develop well-written main points for your speech, complete Action Step 3.b.

Selecting and Outlining Supporting Material

The main points provide the basic structure or skeleton of your speech. Whether your audience understands, believes, or appreciates what you have to say usually depends on how well those main points are developed using the information items you uncovered and recorded on note cards during your research. In your outline include only the basic supporting points, statements that develop your main points.

Developing supporting points Begin by considering one main point. List all the information you have found that you believe is related to that main point. Use your note cards to help you. Don't worry if ideas are out of order or don't seem to relate to each other. Your goal is to see what information you have that you can use to develop the ideas of that main point.

Organize supporting material Once you have listed the items of information related to the point, look for relationships between and among ideas. As you analyze, draw lines connecting information that fits together logically, and cross out information that seems irrelevant or doesn't really fit. You may also combine similar ideas that are stated in different words. Similar items that you have linked can often be grouped under broader headings. For example, Figure 14.1 shows Emming's list of supporting material for his first main point. It shows that Emming eliminated two items by crossing them out. It also shows how Emming linked the four statements related to specific percentages and two statements related to types of interest rate.

Peter L. Chapman Photography

Good speech development begins by selecting material from your research that supports your points. The note-card system makes it easy for you to quickly find items that may be useful.

I. One criterion for finding a suitable credit card is to examine the interest rate.

Most credit cards carry an average of 12 to 16 percent.
Some cards carry an average of as much as 18 percent.
~~Some cards offer a grace period.~~
~~Department store rates are often higher than bank rates.~~
Average rates are much higher than ordinary interest rates.
Variable rate means that the rate will change from month to month.
Fixed rate means that the rate will stay the same.
Many companies quote very low rates (4 to 6 percent) for specific periods.

Figure 14.1
Emming's supporting materials list and how he edited it

Now read this outline of Emming's first main point in which he creates two supporting points with specific information related to each. Also notice that the outline follows a consistent form: main points are designated with Roman numerals, major subpoints are designated with capital letters, and supporting points are designated with regular Arabic numbers.

I. One criterion for finding a suitable credit card is to examine the interest rate.
   A. Interest rates are the percentages that a company charges you to carry a balance on your card past the due date.
      1. Most credit cards carry an average of 14 to 16 percent, which is much higher than ordinary interest rates.
      2. Some cards carry an average of as much as 18 percent.
      3. Many companies quote very low rates (4 to 6 percent) for specific periods.
   B. Interest rates can be variable or fixed.
      1. A variable rate means that the rate will change from month to month.
      2. A fixed rate means that the rate will stay the same.

The outline includes the supporting points of a speech, but it does not include all the development. For instance, in this speech, Emming might use personal experiences, examples, illustrations, anecdotes, statistics, quotations, and other items of information he gleaned from his research. If you are giving a speech that is from four to six minutes long, you should be able to read the written outline in no more than two minutes. The other three minutes or so will be spent elaborating on the outlined information. So, although your outline will not include quotations, comparisons, sets of statistics, and so forth, you will certainly want to use these. You will add this material during your practice sessions as you work to verbally adapt your speech to your audience. The outline of the body of your speech consists only of the main points and the supporting points.

Action Step 3.c ▶

Selecting and Outlining Supporting Material

The goal of this activity is to help you develop and outline your supporting material. Complete the following steps for each of your main points.

1. List the main point.

2. Using your note cards, list the key information related to that main point that you uncovered during your research.

3. Analyze that information by crossing out information that seems less relevant or doesn't fit.

4. Look for information that seems related and can be grouped under a broader heading.

5. Try to group information until you have between two and four supporting points.

6. Write the supporting points in full sentences.

7. Repeat this process for all main points.

8. Write an outline using Roman numerals for main points, capital letters for supporting points, and Arabic numbers for material related to supporting points.

 You can complete this activity online with Speech Builder Express and, if requested, email your completed activity to your instructor. Use your Communicate! CD-ROM to access Skill Learning Activity 14.3.

Choosing developmental materials to adapt to the needs of a particular audience is discussed at length in Chapter 15. After you have developed a plan for adapting to your audience, you may revisit your outline to see if you need to incorporate other supporting material.

Planning and Outlining Section Transitions

Once you have outlined your main points and supporting material, you need to consider how you will move smoothly from one main point to another. **Transitions** are words, phrases, or sentences that show the relationship between or bridge ideas. Transitions act like tour guides, leading the audience from point to point through the speech.

Section transitions are complete sentences that show the relationship between or bridge major parts of the speech. They may summarize what has just been said or preview the next main idea. For example, suppose Kenneth has just finished the introduction of his speech on antiquing tables and is now ready to launch into his main points. Before stating his first main

transitions
words, phrases, or sentences that show the relationship between or bridge ideas.

section transitions
complete sentences that show the relationship between or bridge major parts of the speech.

Michael Newman/PhotoEdit

point he might say: "Antiquing a table is a process that has four steps. Now let's consider the first one." When his listeners hear this transition, they are signaled to be mentally prepared to listen to and remember the first main point. When he finishes his first main point, he will use another section transition to signal that he is done speaking about step one and is moving on to discuss step two: "Now that we see what is involved in cleaning the table, we can move on to the second step."

You might be thinking, "this sounds repetitive or patronizing," but section transitions are important for two reasons. First, they help the audience follow the flow of the speech. If every member of the audience were able to pay one hundred percent attention to every word, perhaps section transitions would not be needed. But as people's attention rises and falls during a speech, they often find themselves wondering where they are. Section transitions give us a mental jolt and say, "Pay attention."

Section transitions mentally prepare the audience to move to the next main idea.

Second, section transitions are important in helping us retain information. We may well remember something that was said once in a speech, but our retention is likely to increase markedly if we hear something more than once. Good transitions are important in writing, but they are even more important in speaking. If listeners get lost or think they have missed something, they cannot check back as they can with writing.

In a speech, if we forecast main points, then state each main point, and have transitions between each point, audiences are more likely to follow and to remember the organization.

On your speech outline, section transitions are written in parentheses at the junctures of the speech.

Preparing the Introduction

When the body of the speech has been developed, you can begin considering how to begin your speech. Because the introduction is critical in establishing your relationship with your audience, you will want to invest time creating two or three different introductions from which you can choose the best to use in the speech. Although your introduction may be very short, it must engage and motivate your audience to listen to all that you have to say. An introduction is generally 5 to 7 percent of the length of the entire speech, so for a five-minute speech (approximately 750 words), an introduction of 35 to 50 words is appropriate.

Action Step 3.d

Preparing Section Transitions

The goal of this exercise is to help you prepare section transitions. Section transitions appear as parenthetical statements before or after each main point. Using complete sentences:

1. Write a transition from your first main point to your second.

2. Write a transition from each of your remaining main points to the one after it.

3. Add these transitional statements to your outline.

 You can complete this activity online with Speech Builder Express, view a student sample of this activity, and, if requested, email your completed activity to your instructor. Use your Communicate! CD-ROM to access Skill Learning Activity 14.4.

Goals of the Introduction

An effective introduction meets several goals. It gets audience attention and introduces the thesis. Effective introductions also establish the speaker's credibility, set the tone for the speech, and create a bond of goodwill between the speaker and the audience.

Getting attention An audience's physical presence does not guarantee that people will actually listen to your speech. Your first goal, then, is to create an opening that will win your listeners' attention by arousing their curiosity and motivating them to continue listening. We discuss several types of attention-getting devices you can use to engage your audience later in the chapter.

Stating the thesis Early in the speech, the audience wants to know what the speech is going to be about. So it's important to share your thesis with your audience during the introduction. Because you have a well-written speech goal and a thesis statement, you have the material necessary to meet this goal. For instance, in a speech on romantic love, after you gain attention, you might draw from your thesis statement and state, "In the next five minutes, I'd like to explain to you that romantic love is comprised of three elements: passion, intimacy, and commitment." This clear statement of the thesis is appropriate unless you have some special reason for not revealing the details of the thesis, in which case you might use the specific goal: "Today, I'd like to explain the three aspects of romantic love."

Establishing your credibility   If someone hasn't formally introduced you before you speak, the audience members are going to wonder who you are and why they should pay attention to what you have to say. Although you will add to your credibility throughout the speech, your introduction should include some statement about your qualifications for speaking on this topic. For instance, after his opening sentence for his speech on romantic love, Miguel might say, "Last semester I took an interdisciplinary seminar on romantic love, and I am now doing an independent research project on commitment in relationships."

Setting a tone   The introductory remarks should reflect the emotional tone that is appropriate for the topic. A humorous opening will signal a lighthearted message; a serious opening signals a more thoughtful or somber tone appropriate for a weightier message. A speaker who starts with a rib-tickling ribald story is putting the audience in a lighthearted, devil-may-care mood. If that speaker then says, "Now let's turn to the subject of abortion (or nuclear war or drug abuse)," the audience will be confused by the preliminary introduction that signaled a far different subject.

Creating a bond of goodwill   During your first few sentences, your audience is forming an initial impression of how they feel about you as a person. If you're enthusiastic, warm, and friendly and give a sense that what you're going to talk about is in the audience's best interest, they will look forward to and be comfortable spending time listening to you.

Types of Introductions

Although some ways to introduce your speech may be inappropriate, there are also a variety of ways that will be equally effective. In fact, the ways to begin a speech are limited only by your imagination. To help you create several introductions for your speech from which you can choose one that seems appropriate, let's look at six types of introductions that can pique audience curiosity and increase audience motivation: startling statements, rhetorical questions, stories, personal references, quotations, and suspense.

Startling statement   A startling statement grabs your listeners' attention by shocking them in some way. Because of the shock of what has been said, audience members stop what they were doing or thinking and focus on the speaker. The following example illustrates the attention-getting effect of a startling statement:

> If I pointed a pistol at you, you would be justifiably scared. But at least you would know the danger to your life. Yet every day we let people fire away at us with messages that are dangerous to our pocketbooks and our minds, and we seldom say a word. I'm talking about television advertisers.
>
> Today I want to look at our choices in how we can go about letting our feelings about advertising be heard.

In just seventy-six words—about thirty seconds—this introduction grabs attention and leads into the speech.

Rhetorical question Asking a **rhetorical question**—a question seeking a mental rather than a vocal response—is another appropriate opening for a short speech. When you ask this question, audience members begin to mentally answer what you have asked and focus their attention on you and the topic. Notice how a student began her speech on counterfeiting with three short questions:

rhetorical question
a question seeking a mental rather than a vocal response.

> What would you do with this ten-dollar bill if I gave it to you? Take your friend to a movie? Treat yourself to a pizza and drinks? Well, if you did either of these things, you could get in big trouble—this bill is counterfeit!
>
> Today I want to share with you the extent of counterfeiting of American money worldwide and what our government is doing to curb it.

Again, a short opening (just seventy words—less than thirty seconds) gets attention and leads into the speech.

Story A story is an account of something that has happened. Most people enjoy a well-told story. So, if you have uncovered an interesting story in your research that is related to the goal of the speech, consider using it for your introduction.

Unfortunately, many stories are lengthy and can take more time to tell than is appropriate for the length of your speech, so only use a story if you can abbreviate it so that is just right for your speech length. Notice how the following story captures attention and leads into the topic of the speech, balancing stakeholder interests.

> A tightrope walker announced that he was going to walk across Niagara Falls. To everyone's amazement, he made it safely across, and everybody cheered. "Who believes I can ride a bicycle across?" And they all said, "Don't do it, you'll fall!" But he got on his bicycle and made it safely across. "Who believes I can push a full wheelbarrow across?" Well, by this time the crowd had seen enough to make real believers of them, and they all shouted, "We do! We do!" At that he said, "OK . . . Who wants to be the first to get in?"
>
> Well, that's how many investors feel about companies who have adopted the philosophy that balancing the interests of all stakeholders is the true route to maximum value. They go from skeptics to believers—but are very reluctant to get in that wheelbarrow.
>
> What I would like to do this afternoon is share with you Eastman's philosophy of stakeholder balance, give you some specific examples of how we're putting this philosophy into practice, and then I'll give you some results. (Deavenport, 1995, p. 49)

Personal reference Introductions that personalize the topic for audience members quickly establish how the topic is in the individual's self-interest. In addition to getting attention, a personal reference can be especially effective at engaging listeners as active participants in a speech. A personal reference opening like this one on exercise can be created for many speeches:

Say, were you panting when you got to the top of those four flights of stairs this morning? I'll bet there were a few of you who vowed you're never going to take a class on the top floor of this building again. But did you ever stop to think that maybe the problem isn't that this class is on the top floor? It just might be that you are not getting enough exercise.

Today I want to talk with you about how you can build an exercise program that will get you and keep you in shape, yet will only cost you three hours a week, and not one red cent!

Quotation A particularly vivid or thought-provoking quotation makes an excellent introduction to a speech of any length. You may need to search for appropriate quotes and use your imagination to relate the quotation to your topic. For instance, in the beginning of her introduction, notice how Suzanne Morse (2001), Director of the Pew Partnership for Civic Change, uses a quotation to get the attention of her audience:

> A few years ago one of America's foremost philosophers, Yogi Berra, remarked to his wife on a trip to the Baseball Hall of Fame in Cooperstown, New York, "We are completely lost but we are making good time." I am afraid Yogi's observation may be true for more than just his navigational skills. For Americans, our direction on the important social issues of the day finds us lost but still driving.
>
> As we think about strategies for change needed for America's third century, we must go in new directions.

As the introduction progresses, she introduces the topic of her speech, liberty versus power.

Suspense An introduction that is worded so that what is described remains uncertain or mysterious will excite the audience. When you begin your speech in a way that gets the audience to thinking, "What is she leading up to?" you have created suspense. The suspense opening is especially valuable when the topic is one that an audience does not already have an interest in hearing. Consider the attention-getting value of this introduction:

> It costs the United States more than $116 billion per year. It has cost the loss of more jobs than a recession. It accounts for nearly 100,000 deaths a year. I'm not talking about cocaine abuse—the problem is alcoholism. Today I want to show you how we can avoid this inhumane killer by abstaining from it.

Notice that by putting the problem "alcoholism" at the end, the speaker encourages the audience to try to anticipate the answer. And since the audience may well be thinking "narcotics," the revelation that the answer is alcoholism is likely to be that much more effective.

 For further discussion of these and other types of introductions, use your Communicate! CD-ROM to access Web Resource 14.2: Strategies for Introducing Speeches.

Action Step 3.e

Writing Speech Introductions

The goal of this activity is to create several introductions so you have choices for how you will begin your speech.

1. For the speech body you outlined earlier, write three different introductions for your speech chosen from these types: a startling statement, rhetorical question, story, personal reference, quotation, or suspense. Choose types that you believe would be appropriate for your speech goal and audience.

2. Of the three introductions you drafted, which do you believe is the best? Why?

3. Write that introduction in outline form.

 You can complete this activity online with Speech Builder Express, view a student sample of this activity, and, if requested, email your completed activity to your instructor. Use your Communicate! CD-ROM to access Skill Learning Activity 14.5.

Preparing the Conclusion

Shakespeare said, "All's well that ends well." A strong conclusion can heighten the impact of a good speech. A speech conclusion can have two major goals: (1) to summarize what you have said and (2) to emotionally impact the audience members so that they remember the information or consider your appeal. Like the introduction, the conclusion is a relatively small part of the speech—seldom more than 5 percent, thirty-five words or so for a 4 to 6 minute speech.

Just as with your speech introduction, you should prepare two or three conclusions and then choose the one you believe will be most effective with your audience. Four common types of conclusions are simple summaries, stories, statements of emotional impact, and appeals to action. The latter two types of conclusions are most often used in persuasive speeches.

Summary An effective speech conclusion must summarize the main points. In short speeches a summary may be the only conclusion that is necessary. Thus, a short appropriate ending for a speech on the warning signs of cancer would be, "So remember, if you experience a sudden weight loss, lack of energy, or blood in your urine or bowels, see a doctor immediately." Summaries can be used for both informative and persuasive speeches. A summary statement achieves the first goal of an effective conclusion.

When a speaker also wants to leave the audience with a vivid impression, the speaker will need to supplement the summary with one of the following concluding devices.

Story Stories or anecdotal material can reinforce the message of the speech and work just as well for the conclusion as for the introduction. Story conclusions can be used for both informative and persuasive speeches.

In his speech on corporate responsibility in the Hispanic business community, Solomon D. Trujillo (2002) ends with a story that dramatizes the importance of acting now:

> In closing, there's an old tale called "The Four Elements" from the Hispanic Southwest by my friend Rudolfo Anaya that captures my message.
>
> In the beginning, there were four elements on this earth, as well as in man. These basic elements in man and earth were Water, Fire, Wind and Honor. When the work of the creation was completed, the elements decided to separate, with each one seeking its own way. Water spoke first and said: "If you should ever need me, look for me under the earth and in the oceans." Fire then said: "If you should need me you will find me in steel and in the power of the sun." Wind whispered: "If you should need me, I will be in the heavens among the clouds." Honor, the bond of life, said: "If you lose me, don't look for me again—you will not find me."
>
> So it is for corporate responsibility. Once lost, honor cannot be replaced. It is the right thing to do . . . it is right for business . . . it is inseparable in our interdependent world. Let's act now to bring Hispanic issues to the forefront of America's agenda. (p. 406)

Emotional impact Some conclusions are designed to drive home the most important points in a way that they have an emotional impact on the audience. An emotional impact conclusion can be used in informative speeches but is likely to be used for a persuasive speech where the goal is to reinforce belief, change belief, or motivate an audience to act. Consider the way Chester Burger (2000), retired communications management consultant, ends his lengthy speech on how technology is changing the world:

> And in the earliest days of the automobile, Mercedes Benz asked its experts to analyze and forecast the future demand for cars. Their answer was, the total market for automobiles would be less than one million, because it would be impossible to find or train more than one million chauffeurs. And you'd need a chauffeur, because to drive a horseless carriage would require as much expertise and strength as driving horses.
>
> The same resistance to change, and the same narrowness of vision, is present today in most countries of the world, and in most peoples and most cultures. Never mind: fundamental changes will come, faster than we think, more profound than we can imagine, more unpredictable than were the effects of the railroad, the telephone, or electricity. In 1943, Thomas Watson, the chairman of IBM, said, "I think there is a world market for maybe five computers." Even a great visionary such as Mr. Watson couldn't foresee what would happen.

© Jeff Greenberg/PhotoEdit

When you end your speech with an emotional conclusion, you really drive your point home. Can you recall conclusions from speeches you have heard? Were they emotional?

We won't have to wait very long to see a different world. Technology is changing the world, the results showing sooner than we can conceive, pulling the whole world together, closer than Cyrus Field could ever have dreamed when the famous steamship, "Great Eastern" dropped his little copper thread underneath the North Atlantic all the way from Newfoundland to Ireland. It's a new world. (p. 712)

Appeal to action The appeal to action is a common way to end a persuasive speech. The **appeal** describes the behavior you want your listeners to follow after they have heard your arguments. Notice how Heather Ettinger (2000) concludes her speech on "Shattering the Glass Floor" with a strong appeal to action:

> We have to stop thinking someone else will change the world. We've got to get it that we're the ones.
> As you drive home tonight, remember to lift while you climb and outstretch that hand to help another woman, another girl. Let's shatter the glass floor. Let's be women donors who are leaders of fundamental change. (p. 730)

appeal
describes the behavior you want your listeners to follow after they have heard your arguments.

Listing Sources

Regardless of the type of speech or how long or how short it will be, you'll want to prepare a list of the sources you are going to use in the speech. Although you may be required to prepare this list for the course you are

Action Step 3.f

Creating Speech Conclusions

The goal of this activity is to help you create choices for how you will conclude your speech.

1. For the speech body you outlined earlier, write three different conclusions (summary, story, appeal to action, or emotional impact) that review important points you want the audience to remember and leave the audience with vivid imagery or an emotional appeal.

2. Which do you believe is the best? Why?

3. Write that conclusion in outline form.

 You can complete this activity online with Speech Builder Express, view a student sample of this activity, and, if requested, email your completed activity to your instructor. Use your Communicate! CD-ROM to access Skill Learning Activity 14.6.

taking, in real settings this list will enable you to direct audience members to the specific source of the information you have used, and it will allow you to quickly find the information at a later date. The two standard methods of organizing source lists are alphabetically by author's last name or by content category, with items listed alphabetically by author within each category. For speeches with a short list, the first method is efficient. But for long speeches with a lengthy source list, it is helpful to group sources by content categories.

There are many formal bibliographic style formats you can use in citing sources (for example, MLA, APA, Chicago, CBE), and the "correct" form differs by professional or academic discipline. Check to see if your instructor has a preference about which style you use in class.

Regardless of the particular style, however, the specific information you need to record will differ depending on whether the source is a book, a periodical, a newspaper, or an Internet source or Web site. The elements essential to all are author, title of article, title of publication, date of publication, and page numbers. Figure 14.2 gives examples of Modern Language Association (MLA) citations for the most commonly used sources. To view examples of common citations styled with the APA (American Psychological Association), *Chicago Manual of Style,* and AMA (American Medical Association) styles, use your Communicate! CD-ROM to access **Web Resource 14.3: Citation Styles.**

Book
Alley, Michael. *The Craft of Scientific Presentation: Critical Steps to Succeed and Critical Errors to Avoid.* New York: Springer-Verlag, 2003.

Edited Book
Janzen, Rod. "Five Paradigms of Ethnic Relations." *Intercultural Communication,* 10th ed. Eds. Larry Samovar and Richard Porter. Belmont, CA: Wadsworth, 2003. 36–42.

Magazine
Krauthammer, Charles. "What Makes the Bush Haters So Mad?" *Time* 22 Sept. 2003: 84.

Academic Journal
Shedletsky, Leonard J. and Joan E. Aitken. "The Paradoxes of Online Academic Work." *Communication Education* 44.2 (2001): 206–217.

Newspaper
Cohen, Richard. "Wall Street Scandal: Whatever the Market Will Bear." *The Cincinnati Enquirer* 17 Sept. 2003: C6.

Electronic Article
Friedman, Thomas L. "Connect the Dots." *New York Times.* 25 Sept. 2003. <http://www.nytimes.com/2003/09/25/opinion/25FRIED.html>.

Electronic Site
Osterweil, Neil and Michael Smith. "Does Stress Cause Breast Cancer?" *WEB M.D.Health* 24 Sept. 2003. <http://my.webmd.com/contents/article/74/89170.htm?z=3734_00000_1000_ts_01>.

Experience
Fegel's Jewelry, senior year of high school, 2003–2004.

Observation
Schoenling Brewery, April 22, 2001. Spent an hour on the floor observing the use of various machines in the total process and employees' responsibilities at each stage.

Interviews
Interview with Bruno Mueller, diamond cutter at Fegel's Jewelry, March 19, 2001.

Figure 14.2
Examples of the MLA citation form for speech sources

Action Step 3.g

Compiling a Speech Source List

The goal of this activity is to help you record the list of sources you used in the speech.

1. Review your note cards, separating those whose information you have used in your speech from those you have not.

2. List the sources whose information was used in the speech by copying the bibliographic information recorded on the note card.

3. For short lists, organize your list alphabetically by the last name of the first author. Be sure to follow the form shown in Figure 14.2. If you did not record some of the bibliographic information on your note card, you will need to revisit the library or database to find it.

 You can complete this activity online with Speech Builder Express, view a student sample of this activity, and, if requested, email your completed activity to your instructor. Use your Communicate! CD-ROM to access Skill Learning Activity 14.7.

Skill Builders

Organizing the Speech

Skill	Use	Procedure	Example
The process of determining a thesis statement, selecting the main ideas and supporting material, and developing an introduction and a conclusion.	To organize and develop material in a way that is best suited to your particular audience.	1. Write a thesis statement that identifies your main ideas.	The three aspects of romantic love are passion, intimacy, and commitment.
		2. Order, outline, and revise the main points.	I. Passion is the first aspect of romantic love to develop. II. Intimacy is the second. III. Commitment is the third.
		3. Select and outline support material for each main point.	Example for "passion": A. Passion is a compelling feeling of love. B. (Focus on function.) C. (Discuss maintenance.)
		4. Prepare section transitions.	From I to II: Although passion is essential to a relationship, passion without intimacy is just sex.
		5. Create introductions and select the best one.	What does it mean to say "I'm in love?" And how can you know whether what you are experiencing is not just a crush?
		6. Create conclusions and select the best one.	Developing romantic love involves passion, intimacy, and commitment.
		7. List sources.	Sample entry: Strenberg, Robert J. and Michael L. Barnes, eds. *The Psychology of Love*. New Haven, CT: Yale University Press, 1988.

Completing the Outline

Now that you have created all of the parts of the outline, it is time to put them together in complete outline form and edit them to make sure the outline is well organized and well worded. Use this checklist to complete the final review of the outline before you move into adaptation and rehearsal.

1. **Have I used a standard set of symbols to indicate structure?** Main points usually are indicated by Roman numerals, major subdivisions by capital letters, minor subheadings by Arabic numerals, and further subdivisions by lowercase letters.

2. **Have I written main points and major subdivisions as complete sentences?** Complete sentences help you to see (1) whether each main point actually develops your speech goal and (2) whether the wording makes your intended point. Unless the key ideas are written out in full, it will be difficult to follow the next guidelines.

3. **Do main points and major subdivisions contain a single idea?** This guideline ensures that the development of each part of the speech will be relevant to the point. Thus, rather than

    I. The park is beautiful and easy to get to.

    divide the sentence so that both parts are separate:

    I. The park is beautiful.
    II. The park is easy to get to.

    The two-point example sorts out distinct ideas so that the speaker can line up supporting material with confidence that the audience will see and understand its relationship to the main points.

4. **Does each major subdivision relate to or support its major point?** This principle is called *subordination.* Consider the following example:

    I. Proper equipment is necessary for successful play.
    A. Good gym shoes are needed for maneuverability.
    B. Padded gloves will help protect your hands.
    C. A lively ball provides sufficient bounce.
    D. And a good attitude doesn't hurt.

    This main point deals with equipment; A, B, and C (shoes, gloves, and ball) are all pieces of equipment and so are related to the main point. But D, attitude, is not a piece of equipment and it should be removed from this list.

5. **Does the outline include no more than one-third the total number of words anticipated in the speech?** An outline is only a skeleton of the speech, not a manuscript with letters and numbers. The outline

Cathy copyright 1983 Cathy Guisewite. Reprinted with permission
of Universal Press Syndicate. All rights reserved.

should be short enough to allow you to experiment with methods of development during practice periods and to adapt to audience needs during the speech itself. An easy way to judge whether your outline is about the right length is to be sure that it contains no more than one-third the number of words in the actual speech. Because approximate figures are all you need, to compute the approximate maximum words for your outline, start by assuming a speaking rate of 160 words per minute. (Last term, the speaking rate for the majority of speakers in my class was 140 to 180 words per minute.) Thus, using the average of 160 words per minute, a three- to five-minute speech would contain roughly 480 to 800 words, and the outline should be 160 to 300 words. An eight- to ten-minute speech, roughly 1,280 to 1,600 words, should have an outline of approximately 426 to 533 words.

Now that we have considered the various parts of an outline, let us put them together for a final look. The outline in Figure 14.3 illustrates the principles in practice. The commentary in the right-hand column focuses on each guideline we have considered.

Action Step 3.h

Completing the Speech Outline

Write and review a complete sentence outline of your speech, using material you've developed so far with the action steps.

You can complete this activity online with Speech Builder Express, view a student sample of this activity, and, if requested, email your completed activity to your instructor. Use your Communicate! CD-ROM to access Skill Learning Activity 14.8.

Figure 14.3
Emming's complete outline
and analysis

OUTLINE

Specific Goal: I would like the audience to understand the major criteria for finding a suitable credit card.

Introduction

I. How many of you have been hounded by credit card vendors outside the Student Union?

II. They make a credit card sound like the answer to all of your dreams, don't they?

III. Today I want to share with you three criteria you need to consider carefully before deciding on a particular credit card.

Thesis Statement: Three criteria that will enable audience members to find the credit card that is most suitable for them are level of real interest rate, annual fee, and advertised inducements.

Body

I. One criterion for finding a suitable credit card is to examine the interest rate.

   A. Interest rates are the percentages that a company charges you to carry a balance on your card past the due date.
   1. Most credit cards carry an average of 18%, which is much higher than ordinary interest rates.
   2. Some cards carry an average of as much as 21%.
   3. Many companies quote very low rates (6% to 8%) for specific periods.
   B. Interest rates can be variable or fixed.
   1. A variable rate means that the rate will change from month to month.
   2. A fixed rate means that the rate will stay the same.

(Now that we have considered rates, let's look at the next criterion.)

II. A second criterion for finding a suitable credit card is to examine the annual fee.
   A. The annual fee is the cost the company charges you for extending you credit.
   B. The charges vary widely.
   1. Some cards advertise no annual fee.
   2. Most companies charge fees that average around 25 dollars.

(After you have considered interest and fees, you can weigh the benefits that the company promises you.)

III. A third criterion for finding a suitable credit card is to weigh the inducements.
   A. Inducements are extras that you get for using a particular card.

ANALYSIS

Write your specific goal at the top of the page. Refer to the goal to test whether everything in the outline is relevant.

The heading *Introduction* sets the section apart as a separate unit. Whether or not every goal of the outline is shown in the wording of the main points, the introduction attempts to (1) get attention, (2) set a tone, (3) gain goodwill, (4) establish credibility. and (5) lead into the body.

The thesis statement states the elements that are suggested in the specific goal. In the speech, the thesis statement serves as a forecast of the main points.

The heading *Body* sets this section apart as a separate unit.
   Main point I is a complete sentence that begins a topical pattern of main points.

Two subdivisions designated by A and B indicate the equal weight of these points.

The second level subdivisions designated by 1, 2, and 3 for subpoint A and 1 and 2 for subpoint B give the necessary information for understanding the subpoints. The number of major and second level subpoints is at the discretion of the speaker.

This transition reminds listeners of the first main point and forecasts the second.

Main point II, continues the topical pattern, and is a complete, meaningful sentence paralleling the wording of main point I. Furthermore, notice that each main point considers only one major ideas.

This transition summarizes the first two criteria and forecasts the third.

Main point III continues the topical pattern and is a complete, meaningful statement paralleling the wording of main points I and II.

OUTLINE

    1. Some companies promise rebates.
    2. Some companies promise frequent flyer miles.
    3. Some companies promise discounts on "a wide variety of items."
  B. Inducements don't outweigh other criteria.

Conclusion

  I. So, getting the credit card that's right for you may be the answer to your dreams.
  II. But only if you exercise care in examining interest rates, annual fees, and inducements.

Sources

Bankrate Monitor, <http://www.Bankrate.com>
"Congratulations, Grads—You're Bankrupt: Marketing Blitz Buries Kids in Plastic Debt," *Business Week,* 21 May 2001: 48.
Lloyd, Nancy, "Charge Card Smarts," *Family Circle,* Feb. 1998: 32–33.
Orman, Suze, "Minding Your Money," *Self,* Feb. 1998: 98.
Rose, Sarah, "Prepping for College Credit," *Money,* Sep. 1998: 156–157.
Royal, Leslie E., "Smart Credit Card Use," *Black Enterprise,* Nov. 2000: 193.

ANALYSIS

Throughout the outline, notice that main points and subpoints are factual statements. The speaker adds examples, experiences, and other developmental material during practice sessions.

The heading *Conclusion* sets this section apart as a separate unit. The content of the conclusion is intended to summarize the main ideas and leave the speech on a high note.

A list of sources should always be a part of the speech outline. The sources should show where the factual material of the speech came from. The list of sources is not a total of all available sources, only those that were used directly or indirectly. Each of the sources is shown in proper form.

What Would You Do?

A QUESTION OF ETHICS

s Marna and Gloria were eating lunch together, Marna happened to ask Gloria, "How are you doing in Woodward's speech class?"

"Not bad," Gloria replied. "I'm working on this speech about product development. I think it will be really informative, but I'm having a little trouble with the opening. I just can't seem to get a good idea for getting started."

"Why not start with a story—that always worked for me in class."

"Thanks, Marna, I'll think on it."

The next day when Marna ran into Gloria again, she asked, "How's that introduction going?"

"Great. I've prepared a great story about Mary Kay—you know, the cosmetics woman? I'm going to tell about how she was terrible in school and no one thought she'd amount to anything. But she loved dabbling with cosmetics so much that she decided to start her own business—and the rest is history."

"That's a great story. I really like that part about being terrible in school. Was she really that bad?"

"I really don't know—the material I read didn't really focus on that part of her life. But I thought that angle would get people listening right away. And after all, I did it that way because you suggested starting with a story."

"Yes, but . . ."

"Listen, she did start the business. So what if the story isn't quite right? It makes the point I want to make—if people are creative and have a strong work ethic, they can make it big."

1. What are the ethical issues here?
2. Is anyone really hurt by Gloria's opening the speech with this story?
3. What are the speaker's ethical responsibilities?

Summary

A speech is organized with an introduction, a body, and a conclusion.

First, organize the body of the speech. Begin by writing a thesis statement based on the speech goal. When you have the potential main points, select the ones you will use. Main points are written as complete sentences that are specific, vivid, and written in parallel language.

A speech can be organized in many different ways depending on the type of speech and the nature of the material. Some of the most common organization patterns are time, topic, and logical reasons.

Main points are embellished with supporting material. A useful process is to begin by listing the potential material, then subordinating the material in a way that clarifies the relationship between and among subpoints and main points.

Prepare transitions to be used between points. Transitions are complete sentences that link major sections of a speech.

Second, outline the introduction to gain attention, set the tone for the speech, create goodwill, and lead into the body of the speech. Typical speech introductions include startling statements, questions, stories, personal references, quotations, or suspense.

Third, outline the conclusion. A well-designed speech conclusion ties the speech together and ends it on a high note. Typical conclusions include summaries, stories, appeals to action, and emotional impact statements.

Fourth, list the sources.

Finally, to refine the outline, use a standard set of symbols, use complete sentences for main points and major subdivisions, limit each point to a single idea, relate minor points to major points, use no more than five main points, and make sure the outline length is no more than one-third the number of words of the final speech.

Communicate! Online

Now that you have read Chapter 14, use your Communicate! CD-ROM for quick access to the electronic resources that accompany this text. Your CD-ROM gives you access to InfoTrac College Edition, Speech Builder Express, and the Communicate! Web site. When you get to the Communicate! home page, click on "Student Book Companion Site" in the Resource box at the right to access the online study aids for this chapter, including a digital glossary, review quizzes, chapter activities, and chapter Web Resources.

Key Terms

At the Communicate! Web site, select the chapter resources for Chapter 14. Print a copy of the glossary for this chapter and test yourself with the electronic flash cards or complete the crossword puzzle to help you master these key terms:

organizing (336)
speech outline (336)
thesis statement (336)
main points (338)
clear main points (340)

parallel structure of main
  points (340)
meaningful main points (341)
topic order (342)
time order (343)

logical reasons order (343)
transitions (347)
section transitions (347)
rhetorical question (351)
appeal (355)

Review Quiz

Test your knowledge of the concepts in this chapter by taking the online quiz at the Communicate! Web site. Select the chapter resources for Chapter 14, then click on "Review Quiz." When you have completed the quiz, submit it for scoring.

Skill Learning Activities

Complete the action step activities for Chapter 14 online at the Communicate! Web site. Select the chapter resources for Chapter 14, then click on "Activities." You can submit your action steps answers to your instructor.

14.1: Action Step 3.a: Writing a Thesis Statement (338)
14.2: Action Step 3.b: Organizing and Outlining the Main Points of Your Speech (344)
14.3: Action Step 3.c: Selecting and Outlining Supporting Material (347)
14.4: Action Step 3.d: Preparing Section Transitions (349)
14.5: Action Step 3.e: Writing Speech Introductions (353)
14.6: Action Step 3.f: Creating Speech Conclusions (356)
14.7: Action Step 3.g: Compiling a Speech Source List (357)
14.8: Action Step 3.h: Completing the Speech Outline (360)

Web Resources

Access the Web Resources for this chapter online at the Communicate! Web site. Select the chapter resources for Chapter 14, then click on "Web Resources."

14.1: Writing Different Types of Thesis Statements (338)
14.2: Strategies for Introducing Speeches (352)
14.3: Citation Styles (356)

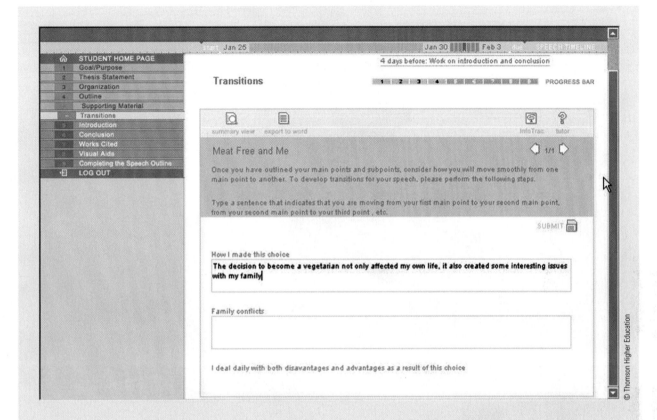

Alex Freund/Getty Images

After you have read this chapter, you should be able to answer these questions:

- What can you do to develop common ground?
- What can you do to create or build audience interest?
- What can you do to adapt to your audience's knowledge and sophistication?
- What can you do to build the audience's perception of you as a speaker?
- What can you do to reinforce or change an audience's attitude toward your topic?
- What criteria do you use to select and construct visual aids?
- What do you include in an audience adaptation strategy?

15

Adapting Verbally and Visually

Jeremy asked his friend Gloria to listen to one of his speech rehearsals. As he finished the final sentence of the speech, "So, violence does affect people in several ways—it not only desensitizes them to violence, it also contributes to making them behave more aggressively," he asked Gloria, "So, what do you think?"

"You're giving the speech to your classmates, right?"

"Yeah."

"And most of them are mass media majors, right?"

"Yeah."

"Well, you had a lot of good material, but I didn't hear anything that showed that you had members of the class in mind—you could have been giving the speech to any group of college students."

J eremy had chosen his thesis with his audience in mind, but he had forgotten something that has been recognized as long as speeches have been given: A speech is intended for a specific audience and should be developed with their needs and perspectives in mind.

audience adaptation
the active process of verbally and visually relating material directly to a specific audience.

Audience adaptation is the active process of verbally and visually relating material directly to a specific audience. You will recall that an effective speech plan is a product of five action steps. In this chapter, we consider the fourth step: **Adapt the material to your specific speech audience.** The skill of adapting involves both verbally adapting and preparing visual aids that facilitate audience understanding. These are the topics of this chapter. In Chapter 16 we describe how to incorporate the adaptations you plan as you rehearse your speech. The audience and setting analyses you completed in Action Steps 1.b and 1.c will help you as you develop your plan for adapting to the audience.

Verbally Adapting to Your Audience

You can use a variety of verbal adaptations to tailor your speech to a particular audience. In a speech verbal adaptations can help you by (1) establishing common ground, (2) building and maintaining audience interest, (3) adjusting to the audience's knowledge and sophistication, (5) building speaker credibility, (4) adapting to the audience's attitudes toward your speech goal, and (5) adjusting to audiences from different cultures and language communities.

Establishing Common Ground

Audiences have expectations that the speaker will recognize their presence by talking directly to them. Speakers meet these expectations by developing **common ground,** the perception that the speaker and the audience share the same or similar information, feelings, and experiences. Several adaptation techniques help establish common ground.

common ground
the perception that the speaker and the audience share the same or similar information, feelings, and experiences.

personal pronouns
pronouns referring directly to the one speaking, spoken to, or spoken about.

Use personal pronouns An important and easy way to let the audience know you are aware of them is to use **personal pronouns,** pronouns referring directly to the one speaking, spoken to, or spoken about. By using *you, us, we,* and *our,* you give listeners verbal signs that you are talking with them. In his speech on the effects of television violence, for example, instead of saying, "When *people* think about violence on TV, *they* often wonder how it affects viewers," Jeremy could say, "When *you* think about violence on TV, *you* may wonder how it affects viewers." The use of just these two personal pronouns in one sentence may not seem like much, but it can

Bob Daemmrich/Stock, Boston

How has the September 11th experience created common ground between the president and the people of this country?

mean the difference between audience members perceiving that this speech was prepared with them in mind or believing that it is a "canned" presentation.

Ask rhetorical questions A second method for speaking directly to the audience is to ask **rhetorical questions**—questions phrased to stimulate a mental response rather than an actual spoken response on the part of the audience. Rhetorical questions are useful in introductions, but they can also be used effectively as transitions and in other parts of the speech. For instance, to increase the audience's feelings of participation in the speech, notice how this transition phrased as a rhetorical question can draw members in:

rhetorical questions *questions phrased to stimulate a mental response rather than an actual spoken response on the part of the audience.*

> **When you watch a particularly violent TV program, have you ever asked yourself, "I wonder whether watching such violent programs has any negative effect on viewers?"**

Rhetorical questions invite mental participation, which leads audience members to become more involved in the content. To be effective, rhetorical questions must sound sincere, so it is important to practice asking them.

Share common experiences A third way of developing common ground is selecting and presenting personal experiences, examples, and illustrations that embody what you and the audience have in common. For instance, in his speech about the effects of television violence, Jeremy might say something like this:

Remember how sometimes at a key moment when you're watching a really frightening scene in a movie you may quickly shut your eyes? I remember doing that numerous times.

In this case, Jeremy calls on the audience to provide their own personal moment of fear and relates it to several he has experienced. That can be just as powerful as if he had taken the time to present the details of one particular incident.

personalize
present information it in a frame of reference that is familiar to the audience.

Personalize information A fourth way of speaking directly to the audience is to **personalize** information by presenting it in a frame of reference that is familiar to the audience. Devon, a student at the University of California, is going to give a speech on how the Japanese economy affects U.S. markets to the student chapter of the American Marketing Association. He wants to help his audience understand geographic data about Japan. He could quote these statistics from the 2001 *World Almanac*:

Japan is small and densely populated. The nation's 126 million people live in a land area of 146,000 square miles, giving them a population density of 867 persons per square mile.

Although this provides the necessary information, it is not presented in a way that acknowledges that the audience is comprised of college students in California, a large state in the United States.

Devon can easily adapt the information to the audience by putting it in terms that are familiar to them, like this:

Japan is a small, densely populated nation. Its population is 126 million— less than half that of the United States. Yet the Japanese are crowded into a land area of only 146,000 square miles—roughly the same size as California. Just think of the implications of having half the population of the United States living here in California, where 30 million now live. In fact, Japan packs 867 persons into every square mile of land, whereas in the United States we average about 74 persons per square mile. Overall, then, Japan is about 12 times as crowded as the United States.

This revision adapts the information by developing a comparison of the unknown, Japan, with the familiar, the United States and the audience's home state of California. Even though most Americans do not have the total land area of the United States on the tip of their tongue, they do know that the United States covers a great deal of territory. Likewise, a California audience would have a sense of the size of their home state compared to the rest of the nation. If Devon were speaking to an audience from another part of the country, he could adapt his comparison to a different state. This personalized information enables the audience to visualize just how small and crowded Japan is.

Adapting your information so that it speaks directly to your specific audience creating common ground takes time and thought. But well-adapted speeches never leave an audience wondering, "What does this have to do with me?" Joan Gorham, the subject of this chapter's Spotlight

Observe&Analyze

Creating Common Ground

Use your CD-ROM to access InfoTrac College Edition and search for the article "A Question of Real American Black Men," by Bailey B. Baker Jr., *Vital Speeches,* April 15, 2002. Analyze how this speaker uses personal pronouns, rhetorical questions, common experiences, and personalized information to create common ground. Write a short essay describing the conclusions of your analysis.

You can complete this activity online and, if requested, email it to your instructor. Use your Communicate! CD-ROM to access Skill Learning Activity 15.1.

on Scholars, has conducted many research projects that show the effect of adaptation, or what she calls "immediacy," on building attention and ensuring audience retention of information.

Spotlight on Scholars ▷ Joan Gorham

**Professor of Communication ◆ ◆ ◆
Studies and Associate Dean of ◆ ◆ ◆
Academic Affairs, Eberly College
of Arts and Sciences, West Virginia
University, on Immediacy**

J oan Gorham began her professional career as a high school teacher, so it is not surprising that her substantial body of research has focused on "immediacy," the use of communicative behaviors to enhance the physical and psychological closeness between teacher and student that ultimately affects student learning. Her first major work on the role of implicit communication in teaching was her dissertation at Northern Illinois University in which she contrasted how a teacher's "silent messages," those sent through nonverbal channels, affected both adult and child learners.

When Gorham accepted a position at West Virginia University, she began building on research by Jan Andersen, James McCroskey, Virginia Richmond, and others on the specific subject of immediacy. Although at that time she had not really intended to focus her lifetime research on immediacy, Gorham explained, "The research just grew out of itself. As I reported the data from one study, I found myself with many unanswered questions that motivated me to initiate new studies on different facets of the subject."

Taken together, Gorham's studies are helping teachers to understand how their communication behavior affects their relationship with their students and how it is associated significantly with student learning outcomes. Some of the early research on immediacy suggested that the learning outcome was just a perception. That is, students reported that they learned more from more immediate teachers, but these studies had not documented actual learning gains. As Gorham refined her research methods, she began to see results that supported the hypothesis that immediacy is directly correlated with learning.

Because the learning process consists of arousal, attention, and recall, Gorham believes teachers who demonstrate appropriate immediacy not only are more likely to stimulate their students to pay attention but also are more likely to increase the students' interest and motivation. As a result, students more easily understand and ultimately remember the information being presented.

From a practical sense, then, what specific behaviors must teachers use to increase their immediacy? From Gorham's studies, we learn that teachers gain immediacy in part through such nonverbal behaviors as using gestures, looking directly at students, smiling, moving around the classroom, and using variety in their vocal expressions. Moreover, Gorham's studies have shown that teachers gain immediacy through such verbal behaviors as using personal examples, relating personal experiences, using humor, using personal pronouns, addressing students by name, conversing with students outside of class, praising students' work, and soliciting students' perceptions about assignments.

Gorham's studies show that teachers can engage in behaviors that increase student motivation and ultimately student learning. Gorham has also probed the other side of the question. Are there behaviors related to immediacy that teachers exhibit that are "demotivating"—that is, behaviors that cause students to decrease attention and interest? Although students identify teacher behaviors as a factor in motivating them to do their best in college courses, Gorham found that negative teacher behaviors are perceived by students as more central to their "demotivation" than positive factors are to their motivation. Some of the most demotivating teacher behaviors noted by students are lacking a sense of humor, lacking in dynamic behavior, lacking empathy for students' perspectives, not being available for individual help, using nonimmediate nonverbal behaviors, and using too many stories or examples—engaging in overkill.

Can teachers learn to increase their immediacy and reduce nonimmediate behaviors? Gorham's research has shown that teachers can accurately monitor their own use of specific immediacy behaviors. Thus, as teachers are made aware of the critical role that immediacy plays in student motivation and learning, Gorham believes teachers can modify their own behavior and work toward incorporating the methods that lead to appropriate levels of immediacy. High-immediacy teachers are rated by students as higher in extroversion, composure, competence, and character than are low-immediacy teachers. They are rated as more similar to their students in attitude, but more expert than nonimme-

diate teachers. Students report being significantly more likely to engage in behaviors recommended by teachers who use immediacy behaviors. Thus learning the appropriate degree of immediacy between teachers and students becomes an important goal in the teaching–learning process.

In addition to her work as Associate Dean of Academic Affairs, Gorham also teaches courses in media effects, media literacy, and nonverbal and intercultural communication. In the future, Gorham plans to continue with replication and extension of her studies, but she is also interested in engaging in longitudinal studies of motivation and immediacy. For titles of several of her research publications, see the reference list at the end of this book. For more information about Gorham and her work, use your Communicate! CD-ROM to access Web Resource 15.1: Dr. Joan Gorham.

Building and Maintaining Audience Interest

Listeners' interest depends on whether they believe the information has personal impact (that it speaks to the question, "What does this have to do with me?"). Effective speakers adapt their material to build and maintain audience interest. Three adaptations that build and maintain audience interest are timeliness, proximity, and seriousness.

Timeliness   Listeners are more likely to be interested in information they perceive as **timely**—they want to know how they can use the information *now*. In a speech on "The criteria for evaluating the quality of diamonds" presented to a college audience, this introduction ties the topic to an issue that is timely for most members and will pique their interest:

> **Have you ever daydreamed about buying your mom or best girl a beautiful piece of diamond jewelry, but shied away from acting on it because you don't really know much about diamonds and didn't want to get taken? Well, today I'd like to help you out some by explaining criteria for evaluating the quality of diamonds.**

Proximity   Listeners are more likely to be interested in information that has **proximity,** a relationship to their personal space. Psychologically we pay more attention to information that affects our "territory" than to information that we perceive as remote. You have probably heard speakers say something like this: "Let me bring this closer to home by showing you . . ." Statements like this work because information becomes important to people when they perceive it as affecting "their own backyard." If, for instance,

timely
information that the audience can use now.

proximity
a relationship to the personal space of audience members.

you give a report on the difficulties the EPA is having with its environmental cleanup campaigns, you would want to focus on examples in the audience's community. If you did not find that type of information during your initial research, take time to find it. For instance, for the EPA topic, a quick visit to the EPA Web site's "Where You Live" page, or accessing your local newspaper's files, would provide information that you could use to make your speech proximal to the audience.

Seriousness Listeners are more likely to be interested in information that is **serious,** that has a physical, economic, or psychological impact on them. To build or maintain interest during a speech on toxic waste, you could show serious *physical* impact by saying "Toxic waste affects the health of all of us"; you could show serious *economic* impact by saying "Toxic waste cleanup and disposal are expensive—they raise our taxes"; or you could show serious *psychological* impact by saying "Toxic waste erodes the quality of our life and the lives of our children."

Notice how classroom attention picks up tremendously when the professor reveals that a particular piece of information is going to "be on the test." Faculty know that this potentially serious economic impact (not paying attention can cost you a lowered grade) is enough to refocus most students' interest in what they are saying.

serious
information that has a physical, economic, or psychological impact on the audience.

Adapting to the Audience's Knowledge and Sophistication

Your audience analysis should help you predict your audience's knowledge of and sophistication with your topic. You will have already selected a thesis geared to them, but individuals in the audience will vary in the knowledge and sophistication they have with a topic, so you will still want to orient them and present new information in ways that facilitate the understanding of various audience members.

Orienting listeners Because your listeners are likely to stop paying attention if they are lost at the start of your speech, a good rule of thumb is to err on the side of presenting key elementary concepts. For instance, for a speech about changes in political and economic conditions in Eastern Europe, you can be reasonably sure that everyone in your audience is aware of the breakup of the Soviet Union and Yugoslavia. However, they may not remember all of the specific countries that have been created. Before launching into your speech on current conditions, you can quickly name the countries you are going to be talking about.

A good way to present basic information without offending people by appearing to talk down to them is to acknowledge that you are reviewing information the audience remembers. By saying "As you will remember . . . ," "As we have come to find out . . . ," "As we all learned in our high school courses . . . ," your orientation will be accepted as review statements and not put-downs. For instance, for the speech on changes in political and economic conditions in Eastern Europe, you might say, "As you will recall, the former Soviet Union now consists of the following separate states." If listeners already know the information, they will see your statements as reminders. If they do not know it, they are getting the information in a way that does not call attention to their information gaps—they can act as if they do in fact remember.

The amount of orientation you give will be geared to your audience analysis. If you have chosen a thesis that is appropriate for the audience, then simple orientations should suffice to remind the audience information that they already know.

Presenting new information You will most likely be introducing your audience to new information. Use *definitions, descriptions, exemplifications,* and *comparisons* to help the audience understand and remember this new information. Audiences are comprised of individuals with different learning styles; effective speakers present information in a variety of ways to accommodate these differences. As you work on your speech, ask yourself these four questions:

1. **Have I defined all key terms carefully?** Words can have many meanings, so it is important that you define your terms. For instance, if your speech goal is, "I want my audience to understand four major problems faced by those who are functionally illiterate," early in the speech you will want to define "functionally illiterate. For example:

   By "functionally illiterate," I mean people who have trouble accomplishing transactions entailing reading and writing in which an individual wishes to engage.

2. **Have I provided vivid examples for each new concept?** Examples help audience members understand and remember abstract information. For instance, suppose that you made the statement,

   Large numbers of Americans who are functionally illiterate cannot read well enough to understand simple directions.

   You could then use the example,

   For instance, a person who is functionally illiterate might not be able to read or understand a prescription label that says "take three times a day after eating."

3. **Have I compared or contrasted new information to information my audience already understands?** You can make the unfamiliar seem

familiar with this technique. For instance, to help your audience sense what functionally illiterate people experience, you might compare their experience to ones your audience members would have surviving in a country where they weren't fluent in the language. For example:

> Many of us have taken a foreign language in school. So we figure we can visit a place where that language is spoken and "get along." Right? But when we get to that country, we often discover that even road signs are a little difficult to comprehend especially when we're under even a little pressure. For instance, while I was in Montreal last summer, I saw a sign that indicated that the women's restroom I was looking for was "à droit." At that moment, for the life of me, I couldn't remember whether "à droit" was "to the right" or "to the left," and the entry doors didn't have pictures! Just imagine what life must be like for functionally illiterate people. There are so many "simple" things where they run the risk of making a major mistake.

4. **Have I used more than one means of development for significant points I want the audience to remember?** Because your audience members learn differently, you will want to use a variety of types of development so that you increase the likelihood that each member of your audience will be able to understand and remember your point. Let's look at how we might use multiple types of development for this main point:

> Large numbers of Americans who are functionally illiterate cannot read well enough to understand simple directions.

Add one example:

> For instance, a person who is functionally illiterate might not be able to read or understand a label that says "Take three times a day after eating."

The example makes the statement more meaningful.

Now let's see how we can build that statement even further:

> A significant number of Americans are functionally illiterate. That is, large numbers of Americans—about 20 percent of the adult population, or around 35 million people—have serious difficulties with common reading tasks. They cannot read well enough to understand simple cooking instructions, directions on how to work an appliance, or rules on how to play a game. For instance, a person who is functionally illiterate might not be able to read or understand a label that says "Take three times a day after eating."

The main point statement, "A significant number of Americans are functionally illiterate," consists of eight words that are likely to be uttered in slightly less than five seconds! A listener who coughs, drops her pencil, or happens to remember an appointment she has during those five seconds will miss the entire sentence. The first expansion with an example adds twenty-five words. Now it is likely that more people will get the point. But the fully developed point contains eighty-five words and much more information. Now, even in the face of some distractions, it is likely that most listeners will have heard and registered the information and even those who knew about the problem of functional illiteracy are likely to have acquired additional information.

Building Speaker Credibility

credibility
the level of trust that an audience has in you.

If your audience has a positive attitude toward you as a speaker, then you need only try to maintain that attitude. If, however, the audience doesn't know you or for some reason has a negative impression of you, then you will want to adapt your speech so that you build your **credibility,** the level of trust that an audience has in you. There are several theories of credibility. To read an interesting article that summarizes them, use your Communicate! CD-ROM to access Web Resource 15.2: Holistic Theory of Speaker Credibility.

knowledge and expertise
your qualifications or capabilities, or what is referred to as your "track record."

Knowledge and expertise When an audience perceives you to be a knowledgeable expert, it will perceive you as credible. Their assessment of your **knowledge and expertise** includes your qualifications or capability, or what is referred to as your "track record."

The first clue an audience uses to judge your knowledge and expertise is how prepared you seem to be. Audiences have an almost instinctive sense of when a speaker is "winging it," and most audiences lose respect for a speaker who has not thought enough of them or the situation to have a well-prepared message. Therefore the first step in establishing your credibility is to prepare.

The second clue is whether you are able to demonstrate your command of the material by extemporizing high-quality examples, illustrations, and personal experiences. Recall how impressive is a professor who offers rich examples and illustrations and who is able to recall statistics without looking at notes. Compare this instructor to other faculty who seem tied to the text and notes and don't appear to know much about the subject beyond their prepared lecture. This is why it is important for you to choose a subject that you are familiar with.

A third clue is the extent to which you demonstrate your direct involvement with the topic. By demonstrating your personal involvement, your audience becomes aware of how your personal experiences have provided you with a practical understanding of the issues. For example, Brandon, who is speaking on toxic waste, will increase his credibility by sharing his personal experience of petitioning his local government for increased local environmental controls. You will be perceived to be more knowledgeable if you have real experience with your topic.

Trustworthiness The more your audience sees you as trustworthy, the more credible you will be. **Trustworthiness** refers to the extent to which the audience can believe that what you say is accurate, true, and in their best interests. To judge your trustworthiness audience members use both your character and your apparent motives for speaking.

First, listeners will make value judgments of your character based on their assessment of your moral and ethical traits. As you plan your speech, you need to ask yourself what you can do in the speech to demonstrate that you are honest, industrious, dependable, and a morally strong person. One way to demonstrate your honesty is to credit your information sources as you speak. In this way you demonstrate that you have studied the information and are not making it up. In addition, if you do a balanced job of presenting both sides of an issue instead of just the one you favor, people are likely to view you as trustworthy.

Second, listeners will consider your apparent motives. If people believe that what you are saying will benefit you but may harm them, they will be suspicious of your motives. Early in your speech, it is important to show how listeners will benefit from your speech. Then you can reemphasize your sincere interest in their well-being throughout the speech. For the speech on toxic waste, for example, Brandon could explain how a local dump site affects the community.

trustworthiness
the extent to which the audience can believe that what you say is accurate, true, and in their best interests.

Personableness A third component of credibility is **personableness,** which audiences judge based on the enthusiasm, friendliness, and warmth you project. Whether people should be or not, we are more distrustful of those we see as different. So the more your listeners see you as one of them, the more personable you will seem and the easier it will be for you to establish your trustworthiness.

Because your audience members' perceptions of this are likely to be based on their first impressions of you, how you dress, groom, and carry yourself are important. Does this mean that you should dress as your audience does? Not necessarily. Most audiences appreciate a speaker who demonstrates respect for them by careful grooming. The old compliment "He/she cleans up real good" is worth remembering. It is surprising how much appropriate dress

personableness
the enthusiasm, friendliness, and warmth you project to your audience.

Why is Rudy Guiliani considered trustworthy?

© Stone Les/CORBIS SYGMA

and good grooming will enhance the audience's perception of your personality.

In addition, audiences react favorably to a speaker who acts friendly. A smile and a pleasant tone of voice go a long way in showing warmth, which will increase your listeners' comfort with you and your ideas. We explain additional methods for demonstrating personableness (enthusiasm, eye contact, and vocal expressiveness) in Chapter 16.

Adapting to the Attitudes toward Your Speech Goal

attitude
a predisposition for or against people, places, or things, usually expressed as an opinion.

Listeners' attitudes toward your speech goal are especially important for persuasive speeches, but it can be important for informative speeches as well. An **attitude** is a predisposition for or against people, places, or things, usually expressed as an opinion.

During your audience analysis you assessed how favorably inclined your audience would be toward your topic. Suppose you determined that your listeners' attitudes toward the topic of refinishing furniture would be positive or neutral, then you will want to play up their interest. If, however, you think your listeners really view refinishing furniture as boring, then you will need to take time early in the speech to change their opinion. In Chapter 18 on persuasive speaking, we consider strategies for dealing with listeners' attitudes in depth.

Adapting to Audiences from Different Cultures and Language Communities

Western European speaking traditions inform our approach to public speaking in this book. However, public speaking is a social and cultural act so, as you would expect, public speaking traditions and perceived effectiveness varies by culture. In the United States, speakers from various subcultures draw on the traditions of their speech communities when they speak, and speakers who address audiences comprised of people from ethnic and language groups different from their own face additional challenges of adaptation. In the Diverse Voices feature, Shirley Weber explains several key features of African American speech making and how African American audiences react in public speaking settings.

DIVERSE VOICES

The Need to Be: The Socio-Cultural Significance of Black Language

by Shirley N. Weber

One of the major differences in adapting to different groups is understanding their expectations and their reactions to your words. In this excerpt, Shirley Weber describes the black perspective on the audience's role in public speaking.

To fully understand and appreciate black language and its function in the black community, it is essential to understand that while philosophies that govern the different groups in Africa vary, some general concepts are found throughout African cultures. One of the primary principles is the belief that everything has a reason for being. Nothing simply exists without purpose or consequences. This is the basis of John's explanation of the four basic elements of life, which are Muntu, mankind; Kintu, things; Hantu, place and time; and Kuntu, modality. These four elements do not exist as static objects but as forces that have consequences and influence. For instance in Hantu, the West is not merely a place defined by geographic location, but a force that influences the East, North, and South. Thus, the term "Western world" connotes a way of life that either complements or challenges other ways of life. The Western world is seen as a force and not a place. (This is applicable to the other three elements also.) Muntu, or man, is distinguished from the other three elements by his possession of Nommo, the magical power of the word. Without Nommo, nothing exists. Consequently, mankind, the possessor of Nommo, becomes the master of all things. . . .

Nommo is so powerful and respected in the black community that only those who are skillful users of the word become leaders. One of the main qualifications of leaders of black people is that they must be able to articulate the needs of the people in a most eloquent manner. And because Muntu is a force who controls Nommo, which has power and consequences, the speaker must generate and create movement and power within his listeners. One of the

ways this is done is through the use of imaginative and vivid language. Of the five canons of speech, it is said that Inventio or invention is the most utilized in black America. Molefi Asante called it the "coming to be of the novel," or the making of the new. So that while the message might be the same, the analogies, stories, images, and so forth must be fresh, new, and alive.

Because nothing exists without Nommo, it too is the force that creates a sense of community among communicators, so much so that the speaker and audience become one as senders and receivers of the message. Thus, an audience listening and responding to a message is just as important as the speaker, because without their "amens" and "right-ons" the speaker may not be successful. This interplay between speaker and listeners is called "call and response" and is a part of the African world view, which holds that all elements and forces are interrelated and indistinguishable because they work together to accomplish a common goal and to create a sense of community between the speaker and the listeners.

This difference between blacks and whites was evident, recently, in a class where I lectured on Afro-American history. During the lecture, one of my more vocal black students began to respond to the message with some encouraging remarks like "all right," "make it plain," "that all right," and "teach." She was soon joined by a few more black students who gave similar comments. I noticed that this surprised and confused some of the white students. When questioned later about this, their response was that they were not used to having more than one person talk at a time, and they really could not talk and listen at the same time. They found the comments annoying and disruptive. As the lecturer, I found the comments refreshing and inspiring. The black student who initiated the responses had no difficulty understanding what I was saying while she was reacting to it, and did not consider herself "rude."

In addition to the speaker's verbal creativity and the dynamic quality of the communication environment, black speech is very rhythmic. It flows like African languages in a consonant-vowel-consonant-vowel pattern. To achieve this rhythmic effect, some syllables are held longer and are accented stronger and differently from standard English, such as DE-troit. This rhythmic pattern is learned early by young blacks and is reinforced by the various styles it complements.

Excerpted from Shirley N. Weber, "The Need to Be: The Socio-Cultural Significance of Black Language." In Larry A. Samovar and Richard E. Porter, eds., Intercultural Communication: A Reader (7th ed., pp. 220–225). Belmont, CA: Wadsworth, 1994. Reprinted by permission of the author.

Two of the problems in adapting to different cultures and languages are speaking in a second language and a lack of a common set of experiences on which to establish common ground. Difficulty with the language includes difficulty with pronunciation, vocabulary, and idiomatic speech. Although these can make you feel self-conscious, the lack of a common set of experiences to draw from is more significant. So much of our information is gained through comparison and examples that the lack of common experiences may make drawing comparisons and using appropriate examples much more difficult.

What can you do to help yourself when you are giving a speech in a language or to a cultural group that is different? Difficulty with pronunciation might require you to speak more slowly and to articulate as clearly as possible. Also, make sure that you are comfortable with your topic. You might want to consider talking about aspects of your homeland. Because you would be providing new information, your classmates would likely look forward to hearing you speak. It would be useful for you to practice at least once with a person raised in the culture who is a native speaker of the language. Ask that person to help you by correcting any major language problems and by helping you create examples and comparisons that the audience will be able to relate to.

Most audience members understand mistakes made by people who are speaking in what is a second or even third language, and they are more forgiving of them than of mistakes made by native speakers. This will work in your favor. Also, keep in mind that the more practice you get speaking to people from this culture, the more comfortable you will become with the language and with your ability to relate to the audience members.

Action Step 4.a ▶

Adapting to Your Audience Verbally

The goal of this activity is to help you plan how you will adapt your material to the specific audience verbally.

Write your thesis statement: _____

Review the audience analysis you completed in Action Steps 1.b and 1.c. As you review your speech outline in Action Step 3.h, plan the specific tactics you will use to adapt this material to your audience by answering these questions:

1. What are the key aspects of your audience that you will need to adapt to?

2. What will you do to establish and maintain common ground?

3. What will you do to build and maintain interest?

4. What will you do to increase audience understanding and retention?

5. What will you do to build and maintain your credibility?

 Figure 15.1 presents one student's response to this activity. You can complete this activity online, view another student sample of this activity, and, if requested, email your completed activity to your instructor. Use your Communicate! CD-ROM to access Skill Learning Activity 15.2.

Roger Persson/© Thomson Higher Education

Presentation software can be used for preparing and presenting visual aids. Although visual aids are useful, verbal adaptation is vital to effective communication.

Thesis statement: Three criteria that will enable audience members to find the credit card that is most suitable for them are level of real interest rate, annual fee, and advertised inducements.

1. **What are the key aspects of your audience that you will need to adapt to?** I believe the key aspects of my audience are that there are more women than men, that they are about my same age, and that they are all college students who have somewhat similar experiences.

2. **What will you do to establish and maintain common ground?** Throughout the speech I will use personal pronouns and ask appropriate rhetorical questions. I will personalize information related to the three criteria I present.

3. **What will you do to build and maintain interest?** Audience interest is likely to be high because my classmates are at an age where credit cards are starting to become important to them. Still, there may be some who believe that because they already have a credit card they don't need to pay much attention. So I will have to present information that goes beyond what they already know. I will start with an attention-getter. Throughout the speech, I will give examples that suggest that they might have overlooked key information.

4. **What will you do to increase audience understanding and retention?** Because members of the audience are familiar with the idea of credit cards, I won't have to define them. However, most will not be familiar with how people can get caught up in credit card debt, so I will use specific examples to show what can happen if users are not careful.

5. **What will you do to build and maintain your credibility?** Because I am Asian American, I may be seen as different from the majority of the class. But I am used to associating with people of all races and ethnic backgrounds without difficulty, so I am not concerned with any problems of adapting to the class. Still, they are likely to question my expertise with the use of credit cards, so I will have to be especially careful to present information accurately and to give personal examples showing my understanding of the information.

Figure 15.1
Audience adaptation for credit card criteria speech

Adapting to Audiences Visually

visual aids
a form of speech development that enables the audience to see as well as to hear information.

As you adapt your speech to the specific needs of your audience, consider what visual material will help audience members understand and remember the material you present. **Visual aids** are a form of speech development that enables the audience to see as well as to hear information. People are likely to learn considerably more when ideas appeal to both eye and ear than when they appeal to the ear alone (Tversky, 1997, p. 258). People are likely to remember information presented with visual aids over even longer periods of time (Patterson, Danscreau, & Newbern, 1992, pp. 453–461).

Types of Visual Aids

Before you can choose what visual aids you might want to use for a specific speech, you need to learn the types of visual aids from which you can choose.

Objects Objects are three-dimensional representations of the idea that you are communicating. Objects make good visual aids (1) if they are large enough to be seen by all audience members and (2) if they are small enough to carry to the site of the speech. A volleyball or a braided rug are objects that would be appropriate in size for an audience of under fifty people. A cell phone might be OK if the goal is simply to show a phone, but it might be too small if the speaker wants to demonstrate how to key in certain specialized functions.

On occasion, *you* can be an effective visual aid object. For instance, through descriptive gestures you can show the height of tennis nets; through your posture and movement you can show the motion involved in the butterfly swimming stroke; and through your own attire you can illustrate the native dress of a different country.

Models When the exact object is too large to bring to the speech site or too small to be seen (like the cell phone), a model of the object can substitute. In a speech on the physics of bridge construction, a scale model of a suspension bridge could be an effective visual aid. Likewise, in a speech on genetic engineering, a model of the DNA double helix might help the audience to understand what happens during these microscopic procedures.

Slides and overhead transparencies get and hold attention and can be seen by the entire audience.

Still photographs If an exact reproduction of material is needed, enlarged still photographs are excellent visual aids. In a speech on "smart weapons," enlarged before and after photos of target sites would be effective in helping the audience to understand the pinpoint accuracy of these weapons.

Slides Like photographs, slides allow you to present an exact visual image to the audience. The advantage of slides over photographs is that the size of the image can be manipulated on site so that they are easy for all audience members to see. In addition, if more than one image is to be shown, slides eliminate the awkwardness associated with manually changing photographs. The remote control device allows you to

David Shopper/Stock, Boston

smoothly move from one image to the next and to talk about each image as long as you would like. One drawback to using slides, however, is that in most cases the room must be darkened for the slides to be viewed. In this situation, it is easy for the slides to become the focal point for the audience. Moreover, many novice speakers are tempted to look and talk to the slides rather than to the audience. In addition, to use slides you must bring a projector to class with you.

Film and video clips You can use short clips from films and videos to demonstrate processes or to expose audiences to important people. But because effective clips generally run one to three minutes, for most short classroom speeches they are inappropriate because they dominate the speech and speaker. In longer speeches when clips are used, speakers should make sure that the equipment is available, operative, and that they know how to run it. This means rehearsing on site with the equipment prior to giving the speech.

Simple drawings Simple drawings are easy to prepare. If you can use a compass, a straightedge, and a measure, you can draw well enough for most speech purposes. For instance, if you are making the point that water skiers must hold their arms straight, with the back straight and knees bent slightly, a stick figure (see Figure 15.2) will illustrate the point. Stick figures may not be as aesthetically pleasing as professional drawings or photographs, but to demonstrate a certain concept they can be quite effective. In fact, elaborate, detailed drawings may not be worth the time and effort, and actual photographs may be so detailed that they obscure the point you wish to make.

Once a drawing is prepared, it can be scanned and used as part of a PowerPoint presentation or as an overhead, or the drawing can be used freestanding if it is enlarged and prepared on poster board or foam core.

Maps Like drawings, maps are relatively easy to prepare. Simple maps allow you to orient audiences to landmarks (mountains, rivers, and lakes), states, cities, land routes, weather systems, and so forth. Commercial maps

Figure 15.2
Sample drawing

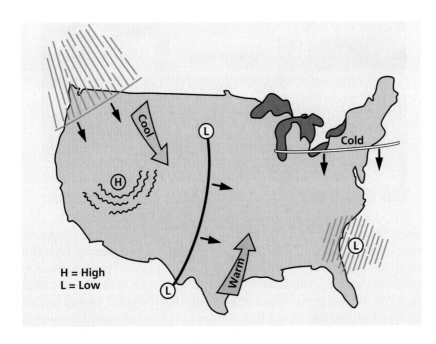

Figure 15.3
Sample map

are available that you might choose to use, but simple maps are relatively easy to prepare and can be customized so that audience members are not confused by visual information that is irrelevant to your purposes. Like drawings, maps can be used in PowerPoint presentations, as overheads, or as freestanding items. Figure 15.3 is a good example of a simple map that depicts weather systems.

Charts   A **chart** is a visual graphic representation of information that reinforces the spoken information and presents it to an audience in an easily interpreted visual format. Word charts and flow charts are two of the most common kinds of charts.

Word charts are used to preview, review, or highlight important ideas covered in a speech. In a speech on Islam, a speaker might make a word chart that lists the Five Pillars of Islam, as shown in Figure 15.4. An outline of speech main points can become a word chart.

chart
a visual graphic representation of information that reinforces the spoken information and presents it to an audience in an easily interpreted visual format.

word charts
charts used to preview, review, or highlight important ideas covered in a speech.

Five Pillars of Islam

1. Shahadah: Witness to Faith

2. Salat: Prayer

3. Sawm: Fasting

4. Zakat: Almsgiving

5. Hajj: Pilgrimage

Figure 15.4
Sample word chart

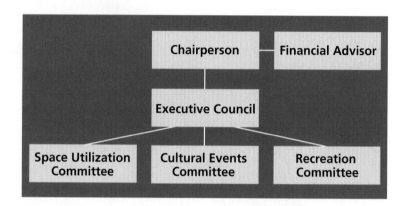

Figure 15.5
Sample organizational chart

flow charts
charts that use symbols and connecting lines to diagram the progressions through a complicated process.

Flow charts use symbols and connecting lines to diagram the progressions through a complicated process. Organizational charts, a common type of flow chart, show the flow of authority and chain of command in an organization. The chart in Figure 15.5 illustrates the organization of a student union board.

In a PowerPoint presentation you can design the chart so that each part is displayed as you talk about it. If overheads are used, multiple overheads can be "stacked" so that each overhead adds information that appears on the screen. You can also create the same effect by using a large newsprint pad with a series of charts where additional information is added on succeeding pages. Then mount the pad on an easel and, as you are talking, flip the pages to reveal more information as you discuss it.

graph
a diagram that presents numerical information.

Graphs A **graph** is a diagram that presents numerical information. Bar graphs, line graphs, and pie graphs are the most common forms of graphs.

bar graphs
diagrams that compare information with vertical or horizontal bars.

Bar graphs are diagrams that compare information with vertical or horizontal bars. These graphs can show relationships between two or more variables at the same time or at various times on one or more dimensions. For instance, in a speech highlighting the increase in exports of goods from foreign countries, Figure 15.6 shows the actual (and estimated) increases for clothing exports from China from 1998 to 2005.

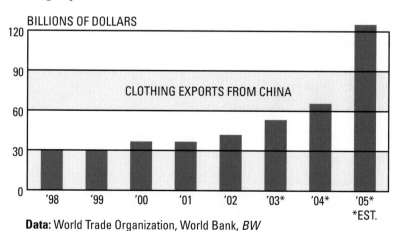

Figure 15.6
Sample bar graph

Data: World Trade Organization, World Bank, *BW*

SOURCE: *Business Week*, December 15, 2003.

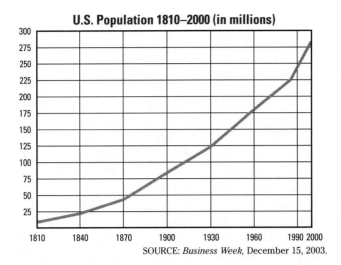

U.S. Population 1810–2000 (in millions)

SOURCE: *Business Week*, December 15, 2003.

Figure 15.7
Sample line graph

Line graphs are diagrams indicating changes in one or more variables over time. In a speech on the population of the United States, for example, the line graph in Figure 15.7 helps by showing the population increase, in millions, from 1810 to 2000.

Pie graphs are diagrams that show the relationships among parts of a single unit. In a speech on comparative family net worth, a pie graph such as the one in Figure 15.8 could be used to show the percentage of U.S. households that have achieved various levels of net worth.

Most spreadsheet computer programs allow you to easily make colorful graphs and to compare the data arrayed as a bar, line, or pie graph. This allows you to choose which display you think will be most effective for your presentation. If you prepare your graphs on the computer, you

line graphs
diagrams indicating changes in one or more variables over time.

pie graphs
diagrams that show the relationships among parts of a single unit.

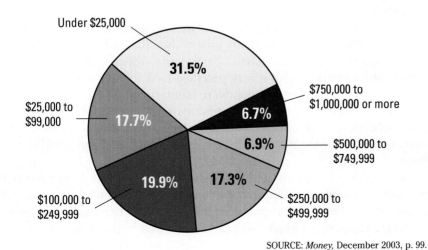

SOURCE: *Money*, December 2003, p. 99.

Figure 15.8
Sample pie graph

will be able to insert them into a PowerPoint slide or print them onto an overhead.

Methods for Displaying Visual Aids

Once you have decided on the specific visual aids for your speech, you will need to choose a method to display them. There are trade offs to be considered when choosing a method. Methods for displaying visual aids vary in the type of preparation they require, the amount of specialized training needed to use them effectively, and the professionalism they convey. Some methods, such as writing on a chalkboard, require little advance preparation. Other methods, such as computer-generated presentation aids, can require extensive preparation. Similarly, it's easy to use an object or a flipchart, but you will need training to properly set up and run a slide show or a PowerPoint presentation. Finally, the quality of your visual presentation will affect your perceived credibility. A well-run computer-generated presentation is impressive, but technical difficulties can make you look ill prepared. Hand-prepared charts and graphs that are hastily or sloppily developed mark you as an amateur, whereas professional-looking visual aids enhance your credibility. Speakers can choose from the following methods.

Computer-mediated presentation Today, in many professional settings audiences expect speakers to use computer-mediated visual aids. PowerPoint, Adobe Persuasion, and Lotus Freelance are popular presentation software. With these programs you can create your visual aids on your computer, download them to a disk or CD-ROM, and play them on a computer, a projector, or a monitor system at your speech site. Additionally, through the Internet you can find, download, and store your own "library" of images. Most presentation software allows you to insert an image from your "library" into your presentation. Using a computer scanner, you can also digitize a photograph from a book or magazine and transfer it to your computer library.

Not only can the visuals you create be displayed directly on a screen or TV monitor as a computer "slide show," but they can be used to create slides, overhead transparencies, or handouts. Visual aids developed with presentation software give a very polished look to your speech and enable you to develop complex multimedia presentations.

Today, most colleges and universities offer classes in developing and using presentation software and have dedicated classrooms or portable carts where the equipment needed to present computer-mediated visuals is housed.

Preparing visual aids with presentation software is time consuming. Smoothly presenting a computerized visual presentation takes practice. But if you start simply, over time you will become more adept at creating professional quality visuals. Well-developed and well-presented computer-mediated visual aids greatly enhance audience perceptions of speaker credibility. *Caution:* computer-mediated presentations can be addicting. Many novices overuse them, so instead of having visual *aids* (visuals that "aid" the speaker's ideas), the visuals become the show and the speaker is relegated to the role of projectionist (Humphrey, 1998, p. 470).

Overhead transparencies An easy way to display drawings, charts, and graphs is to transfer them to an acetate film and project them onto a screen via an overhead projector. With a master copy of the visual, you can make an overhead transparency using a copy machine, thermograph, color lift, or if the master is a computer document, with a computer printer. Overheads are easy and inexpensive to make, and the equipment needed to project overheads is easy to operate and likely to be available at most speech sites. Overheads work well in nearly any setting, and unlike other kinds of projections, they don't require dimming the lights in the room. Moreover, overheads can be useful for demonstrating a process because it is possible to write, trace, or draw on the transparency while you are talking. The size at which an overhead is projected can also be adjusted to the size of the room so that all audience members can see the image.

Flipcharts A **flipchart,** a large pad of paper mounted on an easel, can be an effective method for presenting visual aids. Flipcharts (and easels) are available in many sizes. For a presentation to four or five people, a small table-top version works well; for a larger audience, a larger sized pad (30" × 40") is needed.

flipchart
a large pad of paper mounted on an easel that can be an effective method for presenting visual aids.

Flipcharts are prepared before the speech using colorful markers to record the information. At times, a speaker may record some of the information before the speech begins and then add information while speaking.

When preparing flipcharts, leave several pages between each visual on the pad. If you discover a mistake or decide to revise, you can tear out that sheet without disturbing the order of the other visuals you may have prepared. After you have the visuals, tear out all but one sheet between each chart. This blank sheet serves as both a transition page and a cover sheet. Because you want your audience to focus on your words and not on visual material that is no longer being discussed, you can flip to the empty page while you are talking about material not covered by the charts. Also, the empty page between charts ensures that heavy lines or colors from the next chart will not show through.

For flipcharts to be effective, the information that is hand written or drawn, must be neat and appropriately sized. Flipchart visuals that are not neatly done detract from speaker credibility. Flipcharts can comfortably be used with smaller audiences (less than one hundred people) but are not appropriate for larger settings. It is especially important when creating flipcharts to make sure that the information is written large enough to be comfortably seen by all audience members.

Poster boards The easiest method for displaying simple drawings, charts, maps, and graphs is by preparing them on stiff cardboard or foam core. Then the visual can be placed on an easel or in a chalk tray when it is referred to during the speech. Like flipcharts, poster boards must be neat and appropriately sized. They are also limited in their use to smaller audiences.

Chalkboard Because the chalkboard is a staple in every college classroom, many novice (and ill-prepared) speakers rely on this method for displaying their visual aids. Unfortunately, the chalkboard is easy to misuse and to overuse. Moreover, chalkboards are not suitable for depicting complex material. So writing on a chalkboard is appropriate to use for very short items of information that can be written in a few seconds. Nevertheless, being able to use a chalkboard effectively should be a part of any speaker's repertoire.

Chalkboards should be written on prior to speaking or during a break in speaking. Otherwise, the visual is likely to either be illegible or partly obscured by your body as you write. Or you may end up talking to the board instead of to the audience. Should you need to draw or write on the board while you are talking, you should practice doing it. If you are right-handed, stand to the right of what you are drawing. Try to face at least part of the audience while you work. Although it may seem awkward at first, your effort will allow you to maintain contact with your audience and will allow the audience to see what you are doing while you are doing it.

"Chalk talks" are easiest to prepare, but they are the most likely to result in damage to speaker credibility. It is the rare individual who can develop well-crafted visual aids on a chalkboard. More often chalkboard visuals signal a lack of preparation.

Handouts At times it may be useful for each member of the audience to have a personal copy of the visual aid. In these situations you can prepare a handout. On the plus side, you can prepare handouts (material printed or drawn on sheets of paper) quickly, and all the people in the audience can have their own professional-quality material to refer to and take with them from the speech. On the minus side is the distraction of distributing handouts and the potential for losing audience members' attention when you want them to be looking at you. Before you decide to use handouts, carefully consider why a handout is superior to other methods. If you do decide on handouts, you may want to distribute them at the end of the speech.

Criteria for Choosing Visual Aids

Now that you understand the various types of visual aids and the methods you can use to display them, you have to decide what content needs to be depicted and the best way to do this. In this section, we focus on some of the key questions whose answers will help you decide what to present with the help of visual aids.

1. **What are the most important ideas the audience needs to understand and remember?** These ideas are ones you may want to enhance with visual aids. Visual aids are likely to be remembered, so make sure that what you present visually is what you want your audience to remember.

2. **Are there ideas that are complex or difficult to explain verbally but would be easy for members to understand visually?** The old saying "one picture is worth a thousand words" is true. At times we can help our audience by providing a visual explanation. Demonstrating the correct way to hold a golf club is much easier and clearer than simply describing the positioning of each hand and finger.

3. **How many visual aids should I consider?** Unless you are doing a slide show in which the total focus of the speech is on visual images, the number of visual aids you use should be limited. For the most part, you want the focus of the audience to be on you, the speaker. You want to use visual aids when their use will hold attention, exemplify an idea, or help the audience remember. For each of these goals, the more visual aids used, the less value they will contribute. For a five-minute speech, using three visual aids at crucial times will get attention, exemplify, and stimulate recall far better than using six or eight.

    There is another reason for keeping the visual aids to a small number. A couple of really well-crafted visual aids will maximize the power of your statements, whereas several poorly executed or poorly used visual aids may actually detract from the power of your words.

4. **How large is the audience?** The kinds of visual aids that will work for a small group of twenty or less differ from the kinds that will work for an audience of one hundred or more. For an audience of twenty or less, as in most of your classroom speeches, you can show relatively small objects and use relatively small models and everyone will be able to see. For larger audiences, you'll want projections that can be seen from 100 or 200 feet away with ease.

5. **Is necessary equipment readily available and am I adept at using it?** At times, you may be speaking in an environment that is not equipped for certain visual displays. At many colleges and universities, most rooms are equipped with only a chalkboard, an overhead projector, and electrical outlets. Anything else you want to use you will have to bring yourself or schedule through the appropriate university media office. Be prepared! In any situation in which you have scheduled equipment from an outside source, you need to prepare yourself for the possibility that the equipment may not arrive on time or may not work the way you

thought it did. Call ahead, get to your speaking location early, and have an alternative visual aid to use, just in case. For instance, if you have planned to use a computer-mediated slide presentation, you might also want to have overheads of these images.

6. **Is the time involved in making or getting the visual aid and/or equipment cost effective?** Visual aids are supplements. Their goal is to accent what you are doing verbally. If you believe that a particular visual aid will help you better achieve your goal, then the time spent is well worth it.

    You'll notice that most of the visual aids we've discussed can be obtained or prepared relatively easily. But because some procedures are "so easy," we find ourselves getting lost in making them. Visual aids definitely make a speech more interesting and engaging, but the benefit should be weighed against the cost.

In summary, use the following guidelines when choosing visual aids:

■ Take a few minutes to consider your visual aid strategy. Where would some kind of visual aid make the most sense? What kind of visual aid is most appropriate?

■ Adapt your visuals to your situation, speech topic, and audience needs.

■ Choose visuals with which you are both comfortable and competent.

■ Check out the audiovisual resources of the speaking site before you start preparing your visual aids.

■ Be discriminating in the number of visual aids you use and the key points that they support.

 For a thorough discussion of the methods and guidelines for using visual aids, use your Communicate! CD-ROM to access Web Resource 15.3: Visual Aids.

Action Step 4.b ▶

Adapting to Your Audience Visually

The goal of this activity is to help you decide what visual aids you will use in your speech.

1. Identify the key ideas in your speech for which you believe a visual presentation would increase audience interest, understanding, or retention.

2. For each idea you have identified, list the type of visual you think would be most appropriate to develop and use.

3. For each visual you have identified, decide on the method you will use to present it.

4. Write a brief paragraph describing why you chose the types and methods that you did. Be sure to consider how your choices will affect your preparation time and the audience's perception of your credibility.

 You can use your Student Workbook or Speech Builder Express to complete this activity, or you can complete it online, download a Visual Aids Planning Chart to help you organize your visual aids, view a student sample of this activity, and, if requested, email your work to your instructor. Use your Communicate! CD-ROM to access Skill Learning Activity 15.3.

Principles for Creating Effective Visual Aids

Once you have planned the visual aids you want to use, you need to create them. In this section we suggest eight principles for designing effective visual aids. Then, we look at several examples that illustrate these principles.

1. **Use a print or type size that can be seen easily by your entire audience.** If you're designing a hand-drawn poster board, check the lettering for size by moving as far away from the visual aid you've created as the farthest person in your audience will be sitting. If you can read the lettering and see the details from that distance, then both are large enough; if not, draw another sample and check it for size.

   When you project a typeface from an overhead onto a screen, the lettering on the screen will be much larger than the lettering on the overhead itself. The rule of thumb for overhead lettering is to use 36-point type for major headings, 24-point for subheadings, and 18-point for text. Figure 15.9 shows how these sizes look on paper. The 36-point type will project to about two to three inches on the screen; 24-point will project to about one to two inches; 18-point will project to one inch. Most presentation software will prompt you if you have chosen a font size that is too small.

2. **Use a typeface that is easy to read and pleasing to the eye.** Modern software packages, such as Microsoft Word, come with a variety of typeface fonts, yet only a few of them work well in projections. In general,

36 Major Headings

24 Subheads

18 Text material

Figure 15.9
Visual aid print sizes

avoid fonts that have heavy serifs or curly cues. Figure 15.10 shows a sample of four standard typefaces in regular and boldface 18-point size. Most other typefaces are designed for special situations.

Which of these typefaces seems easiest to read and most pleasing to your eye? Perhaps you'll decide that you'd like to use one typeface for the heading and another for the text. In general, you will not want to use more than two typefaces—headings in one, text in another. You want the typefaces to call attention to the material, not to themselves.

3. **Use upper- and lowercase type.** The combination of upper- and lower-case is easier to read. Some people think that printing in all capital letters

Helvetica	Selecting Typefaces **Selecting Typefaces**
Times	Selecting Typefaces **Selecting Typefaces**
Frutiger	Selecting Typefaces **Selecting Typefaces**
Palatino	Selecting Typefaces **Selecting Typefaces**

Figure 15.10
Visual aid print sizes

CARAT: THE WEIGHT OF A DIAMOND

Carat: The Weight of a Diamond

Figure 15.11
All capitals versus upper- and lowercase lettering

creates emphasis. Although that may be true in some instances, ideas printed in all capital letters are more difficult to read—even when the ideas are written in short phrases (see Figure 15.11).

4. **Limit the lines of type to less than seven.** You don't want the audience to spend a long time reading your visual aid—you want them listening to you. Limit the total number of lines to six or fewer and write points as phrases rather than as complete sentences. The visual aid is a reinforcement and summary of what you say, not the exact words you say. You don't want the audience to have to spend more than six or eight seconds "getting" your visual aid.

5. **Include only items of information that you will emphasize in your speech.** We often get ideas for visual aids from other sources, and the tendency is to include all the material that was in the original. But for speech purposes, keep the aid as simple as possible. Include only the key information, and eliminate anything that distracts or takes emphasis away from the point you want to make.

   Because the tendency to clutter is likely to present a special problem on graphs, let's consider two graphs that show college enrollment by age of students (see Figure 15.12), based on figures reported in the *Chronicle of Higher Education*. The graph on the left shows all eleven age categories mentioned; the graph on the right simplifies this information by combining age ranges with small percentages. The graph on the right is not only easier to read but also emphasizes the highest percentage classifications.

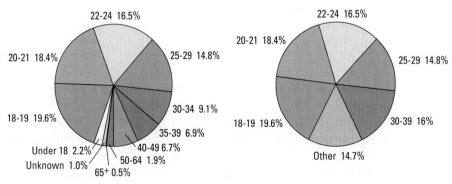

SOURCE: *Chronicle of Higher Education*, Almanac Issues, August 28, 1998, p. 18.

Figure 15.12
Comparative graphs

6. **Make sure information is laid out on the visual aid in a way that is aesthetically pleasing.** Layout involves leaving white space around the whole message, indenting subordinate ideas, and using different type sizes as well as different treatments, such as bolding and underlining.

7. **Add pictures or "clip art" where appropriate to add interest.** If you are using presentation software, consider adding pictures or clip art. Most software packages have a wide variety of clip art that you can import to your document. You can also buy relatively inexpensive software packages that contain thousands of clip art images. A relevant piece of clip art can make the image look both more professional and more dramatic. Be careful, though; clip art can be overdone. Don't let your message be overpowered by distracting pictures.

8. **Use color strategically.** Although black and white can work well for your visual aids, you should consider using color. Color can be used strategically to emphasize points. Follow these suggestions when incorporating color in your graphics:

   ■ Use color to show similarities and differences between ideas.
   ■ Use the same color background for each visual. Avoid dark backgrounds.
   ■ Use bright colors, such as red, to highlight important information.
   ■ Use black or deep blue for lettering, especially on flipcharts.
   ■ When using yellow or orange for lettering, outline the letters with a darker color so they can be seen well from a distance.
   ■ Use no more than four colors; two or three is even better.
   ■ When you want to get into more complex color usage, use a color wheel to select harmonizing colors.
   ■ Don't crowd. Let the background color separate lettering and clip art.
   ■ Always make a quick template before you prepare your visual aids. Pretend you are your audience. Sit as far away as they will be sitting, and evaluate the colors you have chosen for their readability and appeal.

   Let's see if we can put all of this advice to work. Figure 15.13 contains a lot of important information that the speaker has presented, but notice how unpleasant this is to the eye. As you can see, this visual aid ignores all the principles for effective presentation. However, with some thoughtful simplification, this speaker could produce the visual aid shown in Figure 15.14, which sharpens the focus by emphasizing the key words (reduce, reuse, recycle), highlighting the major details, and adding clip art for a professional touch.

I WANT YOU TO REMEMBER THE THREE R'S OF RECYCLING

Reduce the amount of waste people produce like overpacking or using material that won't recycle.

Reuse by relying on cloth towels rather than paper towels, earthenware dishes rather than paper or plastic plates, and glass bottles rather than aluminum cans.

Recycle by collecting recyclable products, sorting them appropriately, and getting them to the appropriate recycling agency.

Figure 15.13
A cluttered and cumbersome visual aid

Remember the three R's of recycling

Reduce waste

Reuse
    cloth towels
    dishes
    glass bottles

Recycle
    collect
    sort
    deliver

Figure 15.14
A simple but effective visual aid

Now that you have created a plan for using visual aids in your speech and understand the principles for creating high-quality visual aids, you are in a position to visually adapt your speech to your particular audience. In the next chapter we describe a process for practicing your speech. You will want to have your visual aids ready to use during your practice sessions.

What Would You Do?   A QUESTION OF ETHICS

endra, I heard you telling Jim about the speech you're giving tomorrow. You think it's a winner, huh?"

"You got that right, Omar. I'm going to have Bardston eating out of the palm of my hand."

"You sound confident."

"This time I have reason to be. See, Professor Bardston's been talking about the importance of audience adaptation. These last two weeks that's all we've heard—adaptation, adaptation."

"What does she mean?"

"Talking about something in a way that really relates to people personally."

"OK—so how are you going to do that?"

"Well, you see, I'm giving this speech on abortion. Now here's the kick. Bardston let it slip that she's a supporter of Right to Life. So what I'm

going to do is give this informative speech on the Right to Life movement. But I'm going to discuss the major beliefs of the movement in a way that'll get her to think that I'm a supporter. I'm going to mention aspects of the movement that I know she'll like."

"But I've heard you talk about how you're pro-choice."

"I am—all the way. But by keeping the information positive, she'll think I'm a supporter. It isn't as if I'm going to be telling any lies or anything."

1. In a speech, is it ethical to adapt in a way that resonates with your audience but isn't in keeping with what you really believe?

2. Could Kendra have achieved her goal using a different method? How?

Summary

Audience adaptation is the active process of verbally and visually relating material directly to a specific audience. Speakers adapt to their audiences verbally by establishing common ground using personal pronouns, rhetorical questions, common experiences, and personalized information to speak directly to audience members. They also plan how to incorporate timely, proximate, and serious material that will build and maintain audience interest. They adjust to the audience's knowledge and sophistication with their topic by orienting listeners to old material, and by clarifying new material through careful defining, vivid examples, comparisons and contrasts to familiar concepts, and multiple means for developing significant points.

They build their credibility through demonstrating expertise, trustworthiness, and personality. They understand and adapt to the audience's attitude toward their speech goal. They adjust to audiences from different cultures and language communities by drawing on common experiences and by practicing to eliminate problems stemming from vocabulary, idiomatic, or pronunciation difficulties.

Visual aids allow audiences to see as well as hear information. They are useful when they help audience members understand or remember important information and when their quality enhances speaker credibility. The most common types of visual aids are objects, models, photographs, slides, film and video clips, simple drawings, maps, charts, and graphs. Speakers can use various methods to present visual aids, including computer-mediated presentation, overhead transparencies, flipcharts, poster boards, chalkboards, and handouts. When planning the visual aids you will use with a speech, consider the time and cost of preparation, the impact on audience understanding and memory, and the effect on speaker credibility.

Design your visual aids with the following principles in mind: use printing or a type size that can be seen easily by your entire audience; use a typeface that is easy to read and pleasing to the eye; use upper- and lowercase type; limit the lines of type to six or less; include only items of information that you will emphasize in your speech; present information in short phrases rather than complete sentences; use an aesthetically pleasing layout; add clip art where appropriate; use color strategically.

Communicate! Online

Now that you have read Chapter 15, use your Communicate! CD-ROM for quick access to the electronic resources that accompany this text. Your CD-ROM gives you access to InfoTrac College Edition, Speech Builder Express, and the Communicate! Web site. When you get to the Communicate! home page, click on "Student Book Companion Site" in the Resource box at the right to access the online study aids for this chapter, including a digital glossary, review quizzes, chapter activities, and chapter Web Resources.

Key Terms

At the Communicate! Web site, select the chapter resources for Chapter 15. Print a copy of the glossary for this chapter and test yourself with the electronic flash cards or complete the crossword puzzle to help you master these key terms:

audience adaptation (368)
common ground (368)
personal pronouns (368)
rhetorical questions (369)
personalize (370)
timely (372)
proximity (372)
serious (373)

credibility (376)
knowledge and expertise (376)
trustworthiness (376)
personableness (377)
attitude (378)
visual aids (382)
chart (385)
word charts (385)

flow charts (386)
graph (386)
bar graphs (386)
line graphs (387)
pie graphs (387)
flipchart (389)

Review Quiz

Test your knowledge of the concepts in this chapter by taking the online quiz at the Communicate! Web site. Select the chapter resources for Chapter 15, then click on "Review Quiz." When you have completed the quiz, submit it for scoring.

Skill Learning Activities

Complete the Observe & Analyze and Action Step activities for Chapter 15 online at the Communicate! Web site. Select the chapter resources for Chapter 15, then click on "Activities." You can submit both your Observe & Analyze and Action Steps answers to your instructor.

15.1: Observe & Analyze: Creating Common Ground (370)
15.2: Action Step 4.a: Adapting to Your Audience Verbally (381)
15.3: Action Step 4.b: Adapting to Your Audience Visually (392)

Web Resources

Access the Web Resources for this chapter online at the Communicate! Web site. Select the chapter resources for Chapter 15, then click on "Web Resources."

15.1: Dr. Joan Gorham (372)
15.2: Holistic Theory of Speaker Credibility (376)
15.3: Visual Aids (392)

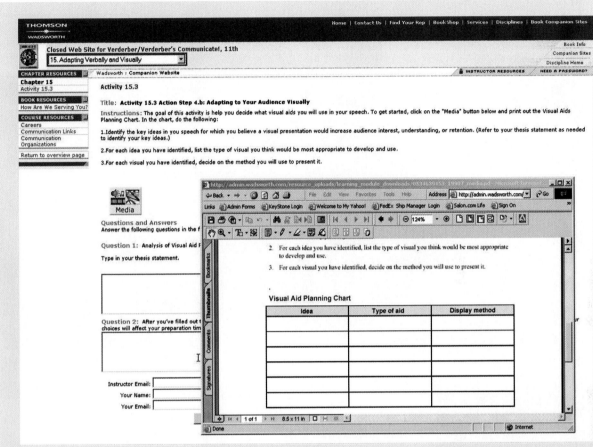

16

Practicing the Presentation of Your Speech

When Nadia finished, everyone in the audience burst into spontaneous applause and whistles.

"I don't understand it, Maurice. I thought my speech was every bit as good as Nadia's, but when I got done all I got was the ordinary polite applause that everyone gets regardless of what they've done. Of course, I'm not as pretty as Nadia."

"Come on, Sylvia get off it. Yeah, OK, she's a looker, but that's not why they gave it up for her. Your speech was OK. You had an interesting topic, lots of good information, and were well organized. But I'll tell you, girl, you didn't deliver your speech anywhere near as well as she did. She *rocked!*"

Maurice recognized what has been well-known throughout the ages: Delivery is the difference between a mediocre speech and an outstanding one. Why? Because the manner in which a speech is delivered greatly affects the audience's interest, understanding, attitudes, and memory. Although delivery cannot compensate for poorly researched, organized, or developed ideas, it can make the most of those ideas. And for those of us who are not naturally fluent or dynamic, practicing our speech will improve our delivery immensely.

In this chapter, we consider the fifth action step of an effective speech plan: **Practicing the speech.** The goal of your speech practice should be to rehearse wording of your speech ideas so that they are clear, vivid, and emphatic. In addition, as you practice, you can work on speaking in a conversational style that displays enthusiasm, spontaneity, fluency, and directness.

Speeches can be delivered by a variety of methods. If you are called on to give a very important speech that has grave consequences, you may completely script it and deliver it by reading a full manuscript, or write it out and then memorize it so that you deliver it word for word. In some settings you will be called on to share your ideas in speeches that are delivered impromptu, on the spur of the moment without any prior preparation. You are likely, however, to give most of your speeches **extemporaneously;** that is, you will have carefully prepared and practiced, but the exact wording of what you will say happens as you speak.

This chapter assumes that you will be delivering your speech extemporaneously. So we begin by describing what to practice so that the verbal presentation of your ideas is vivid and emphatic (should you deliver a speech from manuscript or memory, you will need to incorporate these ideas in your written text) and then discussing how to create a conversational quality in speaking. Next we outline several guidelines for rehearsing your speech. Then, we discuss how you can overcome nervousness about speaking. Finally, we explain criteria you can use for evaluating your speech and others you might hear and, as an example, we apply the criteria to a sample speech.

extemporaneously
speaking without having the exact wording carefully prepared and practiced.

Developing Verbal Vividness and Emphasis

Listeners cannot "reread" what you have said. To be an effective speaker, it is important to use specific, concrete, and precise words (as discussed in Chapter 3), but you will also want to work to make your wording vivid and emphatic.

Vividness

Vividness means full of life, vigorous, bright, and intense. For example, a novice baseball announcer might say, "Jackson made a great catch," but a more experienced commentator's vivid account would be, "Jackson leaped and made a spectacular one-hand catch just as he crashed into the center field wall." The words *spectacular, leaped, one-handed catch,* and *crashed* paint an intense verbal picture of the action. Vivid speech begins with vivid thought. You are much more likely to *express* yourself vividly if you can physically or psychologically *sense* the meanings you are trying to convey.

Vividness can be achieved quickly through similes and metaphors. A **simile** is a direct comparison of dissimilar things and is usually expressed with the words *like* or *as*. Clichés such as "She walks like a duck" and "She sings like a nightingale" are both similes. An elementary school teacher provided a more vivid simile when she said that being back at school after a long absence "was like trying to hold 35 corks under water at the same time" (Hensley, 1995, p. 703). This is a fresh, imaginative simile for a public school teacher's job.

A **metaphor** is a comparison that establishes a figurative identity between objects being compared. Instead of saying that one thing is like another, a metaphor says that one thing is another. Thus, problem cars are "lemons" and a team's porous infield is a "sieve." A more original metaphor in a reply to the statement that TV is just a toaster with pictures might be "This particular toaster is not just browning bread. It is cooking our country's goose" (Hundt, 1995, p. 675).

As you think about and try to develop similes and metaphors, stay away from trite clichés. Instead, develop original metaphors for your speech. Try practicing one or two different metaphors or similes when you rehearse to see which works best.

Finally, although your goal is to be vivid, make sure you use words that are understood by all your listeners. Novice speakers can mistakenly believe they will be more impressive if they use a large vocabulary, but using "big" words can be off putting to the audience and make the speaker seem pompous, affected, or stilted. When you have a choice between a common vivid word or image and one that is more obscure, choose the more common.

vividness
speech that is full of life, vigorous, bright, and intense.

simile
a direct comparison of dissimilar things usually expressed with the words like *or* as.

metaphor
a comparison that establishes a figurative identity between objects being compared.

Emphasis

Emphasis is the weight or importance given to certain words or ideas. Emphasis tells the audience what it should seriously pay attention to. Ideas are emphasized through proportion, repetition, and use of transitions.

Proportion You emphasize an idea by the amount of time you spend discussing it. Ideas to which you devote more time are perceived by listeners to be more important, whereas ideas that are quickly mentioned are

emphasis
the weight or importance given to certain words or ideas.

Observe&Analyze

Similes and Metaphors

Over the next three days, as you read books, newspapers, and magazine articles and listen to people around you talk, make notes of both the trite and original similes and metaphors you hear. Choose three that you think are particularly vivid. Write a paragraph in which you briefly describe how and why they impressed you.

 You can complete this activity online and, if requested, email it to your instructor. Use your Communicate! CD-ROM to access Skill Learning Activity 16.1.

perceived to be less important. So as you practice, monitor the amount of time you devote to each idea you discuss so that you emphasize the material that is most crucial.

Repetition Emphasizing by repeating means saying important words or ideas more than once. You can either repeat the exact words, "A ring-shaped coral island almost or completely surrounding a lagoon is called an atoll—the word is atoll," or you can restate the idea in different language, "The test will comprise about four essay questions; that is, all the questions on the test will be the kind that require you to discuss material in some detail." As you practice, try repeating or restating your main ideas or important supporting points.

Transitions Emphasizing through transitions means using words that show and emphasize idea relationships. In Chapter 14, we talked about section transitions that summarize, clarify, and forecast. Word transitions can be used to serve these additional functions:

- *To add material:* also, and, likewise, again, in addition, moreover, similarly, further
- *To add up consequences, summarize, or show results:* therefore, and so, so, finally, all in all, on the whole, in short, thus, as a result
- *To indicate changes in direction or contrasts:* but, however, on the other hand, still, although, while, no doubt
- *To indicate reasons:* because, for
- *To show causal or time relationships:* then, since, as
- *To explain, exemplify, or limit:* in other words, in fact, for example, that is to say, more specifically

Creating a Conversational Quality

conversational quality
a style of presentation that sounds like conversation to your listeners.

In your speech practice, as well as in the speech itself, the final measure of your presentation is whether the vocal and body action behaviors you use create a **conversational quality,** a style of presentation that *sounds* like conversation to your listeners. In this section we briefly discuss vocal characteristics and bodily action behaviors that need to be managed as you deliver your speech, and then we explain how these are used to create the conversational qualities of enthusiasm, spontaneity, fluency, and directness (eye contact).

Vocal Characteristics

The two vocal characteristics that must be well managed to create a conversational quality while speaking are voice and articulation.

Voice **Voice** includes pitch (highness and lowness on a scale), volume (loudness), rate (speed of speech), and quality (tone, timbre, or sound of voice). Although vocal quality is difficult to change, you will want to make sure that you use your voice effectively. Monitor yourself so that your voice is pleasant to listen to: neither too high nor too low; too loud nor too soft; too fast nor too slow.

Articulation **Articulation** is using the tongue, palate, teeth, jaw movement, and lips to shape vocalized sounds that combine to produce a word. Articulation should not be confused with **pronunciation**—the form and accent of various syllables of a word. In the word *statistics,* for instance, articulation refers to the shaping of the ten sounds (s-t-a-t-i-s-t-i-k-s); pronunciation refers to the grouping and accenting of the sounds (sta-tis´-tiks). If you are unsure of how to pronounce a word in a speech, consult a dictionary for the proper pronunciation.

Many speakers suffer from minor articulation problems such as adding a sound where none appears (ath*a*lete for athlete), leaving out a sound where one occurs (libary for library), transposing sounds (re*v*alent for rel-*e*vant), and distorting sounds (tru*f* for tru*th*). Although some people have consistent articulation problems that require speech therapy (such as substituting *th* for *s* consistently in speech), some of us have become careless in how we articulate particular sounds. Others of us come from families where we learned to misarticulate certain sounds. Each of these problems can be corrected with attentiveness.

Two of the most annoying articulation problems that audiences encounter in speakers are slurring sounds (running sounds and words together) and leaving off word endings. Spoken English always contains some running together of sounds. For instance, most people are likely to say "tha-table" for "that table." It is difficult to make two "t" sounds in a row. But if we aren't careful, we can slur sounds and drop word endings to excess, making it difficult for listeners to understand us. "Who ya gonna see?" for "Who are you going to see?" illustrates both of these errors.

To cure a mild case of "sluritis," spend ten to fifteen minutes three days a week reading passages aloud, overaccentuating each sound. Recall that we form sounds with our tongue, lips, teeth, palate, and jaw movement, so work at "chewing" your words—that is, making sure that lips, jaw, and tongue move carefully for each sound you make. As with most other problems of delivery, to improve, speakers must work conscientiously for days, weeks, or months depending on the severity of the problem.

voice
the pitch (highness and lowness on a scale), volume (loudness), rate (speed of speech), and quality (tone, timbre, or sound of voice) of speaking.

articulation
using the tongue, palate, teeth, jaw movement, and lips to shape vocalized sounds that combine to produce a word.

pronunciation
the form and accent of various syllables of a word.

"LADIES AND GENTLEMEN... IS *THAT* MY VOICE?... I NEVER HEARD IT AMPLIFIED BEFORE. IT SOUNDS SO WEIRD. HELLO. HELLO. I CAN'T BELIEVE IT'S ME. WHAT A STRANGE SENSATION. ONE, TWO, THREE... HELLO. WOW..."

accent
patterns of articulation typical of the natives of a geographical area.

Some articulation problems are the result of speech **accent**—patterns of articulation typical of the natives of a geographical area. Accents can make it difficult for audience members to understand a speaker. If you are faced with speaking to an audience unaccustomed to listening to someone with your particular accent, consider rehearsing with someone who can help you correct the most serious articulation errors related to your accent.

Bodily Action

Your facial expressions, gestures, posture, and movement affect your audience's perception of the conversational quality of your speaking.

facial expressions
eye and mouth movement.

Facial expressions Your **facial expressions,** eye and mouth movement, convey your personableness, and audiences expect them to be appropriate to what you are saying. Speaker's who do not vary their facial expressions during their speech but who wear deadpan expressions, perpetual grins, or scowls will be perceived by their audience as boring, insincere, or stern. Audiences respond positively to natural facial expressions that reflect what you are saying and how you feel about it.

gestures
movements of your hands, arms, and fingers that describe and emphasize.

Gestures Your **gestures,** movements of your hands, arms, and fingers that describe and emphasize, should flow naturally. Some of us gesture a lot in our casual conversations; others do not. If gesturing does not come easily to you, don't force yourself to gesture in a speech. Many people, however, who normally use gestures find that because they have clasped their hands behind their backs, put their hands in their pockets, or gripped the speaker's stand, they are unable to gracefully pry them free to gesture. As a result, they look stiff. To avoid this problem, when you practice and speak, leave your hands free so that they can be available to gesture as you normally do.

movement
changing the position of the body while speaking.

Movement Movement is changing the position of the body. In a speech, movement can enhance or distract from the conversational quality. Movement that accompanies a section transition or is used to emphasize an idea or calls attention to a particular aspect of a speech is effective. But

Test Your Competence ▶

Articulation Exercises

The goal of this activity is to have you practice articulating difficult word combinations. Use your Communicate! CD-ROM to access Web Resource 16.1: Articulation Exercises. There you will find a list of sentences that are difficult to articulate.

Practice saying each of these sentences until you can do so without error. Then write a short paragraph describing your experience.

 You can complete this activity online by using your Communicate! CD-ROM to access Skill Learning Activity 16.2.

unfocused movement such as bobbing and weaving, shifting from foot to foot, or pacing from one side of the room to the other distracts and can irritate the audience. As you practice your speech, try moving during transitions and to emphasize key points. Try to balance your weight on both of your feet to avoid unfocused movement.

Poise A **poised** speaker appears to be composed and in control of what he or she says and does. An audience's perception of your poise is affected by your mannerisms and your posture. A speaker who is composed avoids distracting mannerisms such as jiggling pocket change, licking lips, wringing hands, or scratching. A mannerism that is distracting detracts from the message. As you practice, be aware of any distractions you may be causing and work to eliminate them. Many of our distracting mannerisms stem from nervousness. Poised speakers control speech nervousness. Later in the chapter we present several techniques you can use to reduce your nervousness.

poised
being composed and in control of what one says and does.

Posture Your **posture** refers to the position or bearing of the body. In speeches, an upright stance and squared shoulders communicate a sense of poise to an audience. Speakers who slouch may give an unfavorable impression of themselves, including the impression of limited self-confidence and an uncaring attitude. As you practice, be aware of your posture and adjust it so that you remain upright with your weight equally distributed on both feet. To read a thought-provoking discussion of how various body motions, including posture, affect audience attention during a speech, use your Communicate! CD-ROM to access **Web Resource 16.2: Body Motions and Audience Attention.**

posture
the position or bearing of the body.

    Some of these vocal characteristics and bodily actions may be difficult for speakers with specific handicaps to achieve, but all speakers need to practice so that they are as effective at using their voice and body to create a conversational quality to their speaking as they can be. The Diverse Voices selection describes one woman's journey to build confidence and success.

DIVERSE VOICES

You're Short, Besides!

by Dr. Sucheng Chan

Although nearly everyone shows nervousness at the thought of speaking in public, some people face more difficult situations than others. In this excerpt, Dr. Chan tells us about problems that to many would seem nearly impossible to surmount. She not only overcame apparent problems but used them as motivation to succeed.

I was stricken simultaneously with pneumonia and polio at the age of four. Uncertain whether I had polio of the lungs, seven of the eight doctors who attended me—all practitioners of Western medicine—told my parents they should not feel optimistic about my survival. A Chinese fortune teller my mother consulted also gave a grim prognosis. All these pessimistic predictions notwithstanding, I hung onto life, if only by a thread. Being confined to bed was thus a mental agony as great as my physical pain. But I was determined to walk.

We left China as the Communist forces swept across the country in victory. We found an apartment in Hong Kong. After a year and a half in Hong Kong, we moved to Malaysia. The years in Malaysia were the happiest of my childhood even though I was consistently fending off children who ran after me calling, *"Baikah! Baikah!"* ("Cripple! Cripple!" in the Hokkien dialect commonly spoken in Malaysia). The taunts of children mattered little because I was a star pupil. I won one award after another for general scholarship as well as for art and public speaking. Whenever the school had important visitors, my teacher always called on me to recite in front of the class.

A significant event that marked me indelibly occurred when I was twelve. That year my school held a music recital and I was one of the students chosen to play the piano. I managed to get up the steps to the stage without any problem, but as I walked across the stage, I fell. Out of the audience, a voice said loudly and clearly, "Ayah! a *baikah* shouldn't be allowed to perform in public." I got up before anyone could get on stage to help me and, with tears streaming uncontrollably down my face, I rushed to the piano and began to play. That I managed to do so made me feel really strong. I never again feared ridicule.

Regardless of racial or cultural background, most handicapped people have to learn to find a balance between the desire to attain physical independence and the need to take care of ourselves by not overtaxing our bodies.

I've often wondered if I would have been a different person had I not been physically handicapped. I really don't know, though there is no question that being handicapped has marked me. But at the same time I usually do not *feel* handicapped—and consequently, I do not *act* handicapped. People are therefore less likely to treat me as a handicapped person. There is no doubt, however, that the lives of my parents, sister, husband, other family members, and some close friends have been affected by my physical condition. They have had to learn not to hide me away at home, not to feel embarrassed by how I look or react to people who say silly things to me, and not to resent me for the extra demands my condition makes on them. Perhaps the hardest thing for those who live with handicapped people is to know when and how to offer help.

So, has being physically handicapped been a handicap? It all depends on one's attitude. Some years ago, I told a friend that I had once said to an affirmative action compliance officer (somewhat sardonically since I do not believe in the head count approach to affirmative action) that the institution which employs me is triply lucky because it can count me as nonwhite, female, and handicapped. He responded, "Why don't you tell them to count you four times? . . . Remember, you're short, besides!"

Excerpted from Making Waves *by Asian Women United.* ©1989 *by Asian Women United. Reprinted by permission of the author.*

Enthusiasm

enthusiasm
the excitement or passion you feel about your topic.

monotone
a voice in which the pitch, volume, and rate remain constant, with no word, idea, or sentence differing significantly from any other.

Enthusiasm is the excitement or passion you feel about your topic. In casual conversation when we are excited about something, we sound and look energized. A speaker who looks and sounds enthusiastic will be listened to, and that speaker's ideas will be remembered (Williams & Ware, 1976, p. 50). We convey our enthusiasm through the vocal variety we display and by our facial expressions. When someone speaks in a **monotone,** a voice in which the pitch, volume, and rate remain constant, with no word, idea, or sentence differing significantly from any other, the speaker sounds disinterested.

When someone speaks softly or mumbles, the speaker can sound bored. If someone fidgets, or stands rigidly behind a podium, the individual appears distracted or remote. If the speaker slouches and gazes out the window, we sense the speaker's boredom.

But when you vary your tone, rate, pitch, and volume, we can hear excitement, sorrow, awe, and joy. We hear your emotions and we perceive that you are excited about what you are saying. Similarly, when you stand erect and look us in the eye, we sense that you are energized by what you are saying.

Spontaneity

Speakers who are enthusiastic and vocally expressive are also likely to present their speeches in a way that sounds spontaneous. **Spontaneity** is naturalness that seems unrehearsed and does not sound memorized. How can you carefully research, outline, develop, and practice a speech yet still sound spontaneous as you deliver it before your audience? The key is to learn the *ideas* and the *order* in which you will present them in the speech while *not* memorizing the words. Suppose someone asks you to recount the route you take on your drive to work. Because you "know" the route, you can describe it spontaneously. You develop spontaneity in your speeches by getting to know the ideas in your speech. When you are comfortable that you know them as well as you know the route you take to work, you will be able to talk about them with your audience in the same conversational tone you would use to discuss ideas with a group of friends.

spontaneity
naturalness that seems unrehearsed and does not sound memorized.

Fluency

Effective presentations are also fluent. **Fluency** is speech that flows easily without hesitation or vocal interferences such as *uh, er, well, OK, you know,* and *like* (see Chapter 4). Train yourself to hear your interferences by getting a friend to listen to practice sessions and call attention to them. As you learn to hear them, you will find that you can start to eliminate them from your speech practices and eventually from the speech itself.

fluency
speech that flows easily without hesitation or vocal interferences.

Eye Contact

Eye contact is speaking in a manner that conveys openness, truthfulness, candor, and sincerity. Norms about eye contact vary by cultural group, but in the United States directness in public speaking is conveyed through direct eye contact with audience members. This eye contact is perceived as a sign of sincerity, and speakers who fail to maintain eye contact with audiences are perceived as ill at ease and often as insincere or dishonest (Burgoon, Coker, & Coker, 1986).

In a speech effective eye contact is gazing at various groups of people in *all parts* of an audience throughout a speech. To establish effective eye contact, mentally divide your audience into small groups scattered around the

eye contact
looking at the audience in a manner that conveys openness, truthfulness, candor, and sincerity.

room. Then pick a group at random, and direct your remarks for ten to fifteen seconds to members in each group. Perhaps start with a Z pattern. Talk with the group in the back left for a few seconds, then glance at people in the far right for a few seconds, and then move to a group in the middle, a group in the front left, and then a group in the front right. Then perhaps reverse the order, starting in the back right. Eventually you will find yourself going in a random pattern in which you look at all groups over a period of a few minutes. Such a pattern ensures that you do not spend a disproportionate amount of your time talking with those in front of you or in the center of the room.

Maintaining eye contact also helps you gain insight into how the audience is understanding and reacting to what you are saying. With this feedback, you can adjust immediately to better meet your audience's needs. Listeners who are bored yawn, look out the window, slouch in their chairs, and may even sleep. If audience members are confused, they will look puzzled; if they agree with what you say or understand it, they will nod their heads. By monitoring your audience's behavior, you can adjust by becoming more animated, offering additional examples, or moving more quickly through a point. If you are well prepared, you will be better equipped to make the adjustments and adapt to the needs of your audience.

Rehearsal

rehearsing
practicing the presentation of your speech aloud.

Rehearsing is practicing the presentation of your speech aloud. In this section, we describe how to schedule your preparation and practice, how to prepare and use notes, tips for handling your visual aids, and guidelines for effective rehearsing.

What advantage is there to practicing a speech in the space in which it will be presented?

Dave Shaefer/Jeroboam

7 days (or more) before	Select topic; begin research.
6 days before	Continue research.
5 days before	Outline body of speech.
4 days before	Work on introduction and conclusion.
3 days before	Finish outline; find additional material if needed; have all visual aids completed.
2 days before	First rehearsal session.
1 day before	Second rehearsal session.
Due date	Give speech.

Figure 16.1
Timetable for preparing a classroom speech

Scheduling and Conducting Practice Sessions

Inexperienced speakers often believe they are ready to present the speech once they have finished their outline. But a speech that is not practiced is likely to be far less effective than it would have been had you given yourself sufficient practice time. In general, if you are not an experienced speaker, try to complete the outline at least two days before the speech is to be presented so that you have sufficient practice time to revise, evaluate, and mull over all aspects of the speech. Figure 16.1 provides a useful timetable for preparing a classroom speech.

Is it really necessary to practice a speech out loud? A study by Menzel and Carrell (1994) supports this notion and concludes that "the significance of rehearsing out loud probably reflects the fact that verbalization clarifies thought. As a result, oral rehearsal helps lead to success in the actual delivery of a speech" (p. 23).

Preparing Speaking Notes

Prior to your first rehearsal session, prepare a draft of your speech notes. **Speech notes** are a word or phrase outline of the speech, plus hard-to-remember information such as quotations and statistics. Appropriate notes are composed of key words or phrases that help trigger your memory. Notes will be most useful to you when they consist of the fewest words possible written in lettering large enough to be seen instantly at a distance. Many speakers condense their written preparatory outline into a brief word or phrase outline.

For a three- to five-minute speech, one or two 3 × 5 inch note cards will be sufficient for recording your notes. For a five- to ten-minute speech, two to four 3 × 5 inch note cards should be enough: one card for goal and introduction, one or two cards for the body, and one card for the conclusion. When your speech contains a particularly good quotation or a complicated set of statistics, you may want to write them in detail on separate cards. A typical set of note cards made from the body of the speech outline presented in Chapter 14 is shown in Figure 16.2.

speech notes
a word or phrase outline of the speech, plus hard-to-remember information such as quotations and statistics put onto note cards.

Introduction
How many hounded by vendors?

Three criteria: IR, Fee, Induce

Body

1st C: Examine interest rates
 IR's are % that a company charges to carry on balance
  • Average of 18%
  • As much as 21%
  • Start low 6 to 8%—but contain restrictions
 IR's variable or fixed
  • Variable—change month to month
  • Fixed stay same
 (Considered IR's: look at next criterion)

2d C: Examine annual fee
AF charges vary
 • Some, no annual
 • Most companies average around $25
  (After considered interest and fees, weigh benefits)

3d C: Weigh inducements—extras
 • Rebates
 • Freq flier miles
 • Discounts
Inducements not outweigh factors

Conclusion
So, 3 criteria IR, Ann. Fee, Inducements

Figure 16.2
Note cards for the credit criteria speech

During practice sessions, use the notes as you would in the speech. If you will use a podium, set the notes on the speaker's stand or, alternatively, hold them in one hand and refer to them only when needed. Speakers often find that the act of making a note card is so effective in helping cement ideas in the mind that during practice, or later during the speech itself, they do not need to use the notes at all.

Practice Handling Visual Aids during the Speech

Many speakers think that once they have prepared good visual aids they will have no trouble using them in the speech. However, many speeches with good visual aids have become shambles because the aids were not well handled. Here are several tips for handling your visual aids.

1. **Carefully plan when to use visual aids.** Indicate on your outline (and mark in your speaking notes) exactly when you will display the visual aid and when you will remove it. Practice introducing each visual aid, and practice different ways of displaying the visual aids until you are satisfied that everyone in the audience will be able to see them.

2. **Consider audience needs carefully.** As you practice, if you realize that a visual aid you have planned to use does not contribute substantially and directly to the audience's attention to, understanding of, or retention of information on your topic, then drop it.

3. **Display a visual aid only when talking about it.** Because visual aids will draw audience attention, practice showing them only when you are talking about them, and remove visual aids from sight when they are no longer the focus of attention.

    Often a single visual aid contains several bits of information. To keep audience attention where you want it, you can prepare the visual aid so that you only expose the portion containing the information you are currently discussing.

4. **Describe specific aspects of the visual aid while showing it.** Practice helping your audience understand the visual aid by verbally telling them what to look for, explaining the various parts, and interpreting figures, symbols, and percentages.

5. **Display visual aids so that everyone in the audience can see them.** If you hold the visual aid, practice until you can position it away from your body and point it toward the various parts of the audience. If you place your visual aid on a chalkboard or easel or mount it in some way, practice standing to one side and point with the arm nearest the visual aid. If it is necessary to roll or fold the visual aid, bring some transparent tape

© Syracuse Newspapers/The Image Works

What are the risks of using living things as visual aids?

to mount it to the chalkboard or wall so that it does not roll or wrinkle. If you are projecting your visual aid, try to practice in the space where you will give your speech so that you know how to position the equipment so that the image is the appropriate size and in focus. If you cannot practice ahead of the date, be sure to arrive early enough on the day of the presentation to practice with the equipment you will use.

6. **Talk to your audience, not to the visual aid.** You may need to look at the visual aid occasionally, but it is important to maintain eye contact with your audience as much as possible—in part so that you can gauge how they are reacting to your visual material. When speakers become too engrossed in their visual aids, looking at them instead of the audience, they tend to lose contact with the audience entirely. As you practice, resist the urge to stare at your visual aid.

7. **Avoid passing objects around the audience.** People look at, read, handle, and think about whatever they hold in their hands. While they are so occupied, they are not likely to be listening to you. So, if you must pass a visual aid among the audience members, carefully consider when and how to do this.

Guidelines for Effective Rehearsing

The goals of your rehearsals are threefold. First you practice wording your ideas so that they are vivid and emphatic. Second, you experiment with your voice and bodily action until you have developed a good conversational quality to your presentation. Finally, you practice the speech, analyzing how it went, and practicing it again until you feel confident that you can fluently present your ideas in a manner that will engage your audience.

First practice session

1. Audiotape your practice session. If you do not own a tape recorder, try to borrow one. You may also want to have a friend sit in on your practice.

2. Read through your sentence outline once or twice to refresh your memory. Then put the outline out of sight and practice the speech using note cards you have prepared.

3. Make the practice as similar to the speech situation as possible, including using the visual aids you've prepared. Stand up and face your imaginary audience. Pretend that the chairs, lamps, books, and other objects in your practice room are people.

4. Write down the time that you begin.

5. Begin speaking. Regardless of what happens, keep going until you have presented the entire speech. If you goof, make a repair as you would if you were actually delivering the speech to an audience.

6. Write down the time you finish. Compute the length of the speech for this first practice.

Analysis Listen to the tape and look at your complete outline. Did you leave out any key ideas? Did you talk too long on any one point and not long enough on another? Did you clarify each of your points? Did you try to adapt to your anticipated audience? (If you had a friend or relative listen to your practices, have him or her help with your analysis.) Were your note cards effective? Make any necessary changes before your second practice.

Second practice Repeat the six steps as outlined for the first practice. By practicing a second time right after your analysis, you are more likely to make the kind of adjustments that begin to improve the speech.

Additional rehearsals After you have completed one full rehearsal session, consisting of two practices and analysis, put the speech away until that night or the next day. Although you should rehearse the speech at least one more time, you will not benefit if you cram all the practices into one long rehearsal time. You may find that a final practice right before you go to bed will be very helpful; while you are sleeping, your subconscious will continue to work on the speech. As a result, you are likely to find significant improvement in your mastery of the speech when you practice again the next day.

How many times you practice depends on many variables, including your experience, your familiarity with the subject, and the length of your speech.

Ensuring spontaneity When practicing, try to learn the speech ideas, not memorize specific phrasings. Recall that memorizing the speech involves saying the speech the same way each time until you can give it word for word without notes. **Learning the speech** involves understanding the ideas of the speech but having the freedom to word the ideas differently during each practice.

learning the speech
understanding the ideas of the speech but having the freedom to word the ideas differently during each practice.

To illustrate the method of learning a speech, let's use a short portion of the speech outline for the credit card criteria speech as the basis for the practice. That portion of the outline reads as follows:

A. Interest rates are the percentages that a company charges you to carry a balance on your card past the due date.
   1. Most credit cards carry an average of 18%.

Now let's consider three practices that focus on this small portion of the outline.

First practice: "Interest rates are the percentages that a company charges you to carry a balance on your card past the due date. Most credit cards carry an average of 18 percent. Did you hear that? 18 percent!"

Second practice: "Interest rates are the percentages that a company charges you when you don't pay the balance in full and thus still owe the company money. Most credit cards carry an average of 18 percent—think of that, 18 percent. So, if you leave a balance every month, before you know it you're going to be paying a lot more money than you thought you would."

Third practice: "Interest rates are the percentages that a company charges you when you don't pay the balance in full—you can rack up a lot of debt by not paying on time. Most credit cards carry an average of 18 percent. Did you hear that? A whopping 18 percent at a time when you can get about any kind of a loan for less than 10 percent."

Notice that point A and subpoint 1 of the outline are in all three versions. As this illustrates, the essence of the outline will be a part of all your practices. Because you have made slight variations each time, when you finally give the speech, there will be that sense of spontaneity. In your speech, you probably will use wording that is most meaningful to you, and yet you will be assured that you are likely to get the key point across.

Action Step 5 ▶

Rehearsing Your Speech

The goal of this activity is to rehearse your speech, analyze it, and rehearse it again. One complete rehearsal includes (1) a practice, (2) an analysis, and (3) a second practice.

1. Find a place where you can be alone to practice your speech. Follow the six points of the First Practice as listed on pages 416–417.

2. Listen to the tape. Review your outline as you listen and then answer the following questions.

   Are you satisfied with how well:

   The introduction got attention and led into the speech? _____

   The main points were clearly stated? _____ And well developed? _____

   The material adapted to the audience? _____

   The section transitions were present? _____ And clear? _____

   The conclusion summarized the main points? _____ Left the speech on a high note? _____

Visual aids were used? _____

The ideas were expressed vividly? _____ And emphatically? _____

You maintained a conversational tone throughout? _____

Sounding enthusiastic? _____ Sounding spontaneous? _____

Speaking fluently? _____

List the three most important changes you will make in your next practice session.

One:

Two:

Three:

3. Go through the six steps outlined for the first practice again. Then assess: Did you achieve the goals you set for the second practice? _____

Reevaluate the speech using the checklist and continue to practice until you are satisfied with all parts of your presentation.

You can use your Student Workbook to complete this activity, or you can complete it online, print out copies of the Rehearsal Analysis Sheet, see a student sample of a practice round, and, if requested, email your work to your instructor. Use your Communicate! CD-ROM to access Skill Learning Activity 16.3.

Public Speaking Apprehension

People probably have feared speaking in public since they first began doing it. And those who teach others to speak have been concerned with helping students overcome their fears almost as long. **Public speaking apprehension,** a type of communication anxiety (or nervousness), is the level of fear a person experiences when anticipating or actually speaking to an audience. Much of what we know about fear of speaking comes from the research of James McCroskey and his colleagues. The Spotlight on Scholars feature provides a brief summary of his work.

Almost all of us have some level of public speaking apprehension, but about 15 percent of the U.S. population experiences high levels of apprehension (Richmond & McCroskey, 1995, p. 98). Today we benefit from the results of a significant amount of research on public speaking apprehension and methods for helping us overcome it.

public speaking apprehension
a type of communication anxiety (or nervousness) that reflects the level of fear a person experiences when anticipating or actually speaking to an audience.

Spotlight on Scholars

James McCroskey

Professor and Former Chair of the Department of Communication at West Virginia University, on Communication Apprehension

Jim McCroskey's academic interest had been in public speaking and debate, so it was somewhat by chance that he became involved in the study of what was to become a focus of his lifelong scholarship. One day McCroskey got a call from a therapist at the university's Psychology Center who was concerned about a student who was suicidal and kept repeating "I just can't face giving my speech." The thought that some people's fear of speaking in public was so profound that they considered suicide preferable to speaking was so compelling to McCroskey that he began an in-depth study of what he eventually called "communication apprehension."

Although a lot had been written about what was then called "stage fright," McCroskey found that there was no agreement about its causes and no way to go about measuring it. Since that time, McCroskey has made a significant contribution to our understanding of communication apprehension and ways of measuring it. When instruments for measuring a variable are developed, they must be both valid and reliable—*valid* in that the instrument must be proved to measure apprehension and not other related things, and *reliable* so that people with similar amounts of apprehension will score the same and that people who are measured more than once will receive a similar score. McCroskey and his colleagues' work culminated in what is considered the primary measure of communication apprehension, the Personal Report of Communication Apprehension (PRCA). McCroskey first published this self-report instrument in 1970. Since then, there have been several versions.

Although apprehension can be measured by observation (examining the behaviors exhibited during communication) and physiological response (outfitting people with measuring devices to record physiological information during speech), McCroskey found that the self-report instrument (having people fill out a questionnaire detailing their feelings and opinions) was the most valid and reliable. In laypersons' terms, he explains, "Many times the people we

observe may be terrified, but show no outward signs. Likewise, many times people register tremendous physiological reaction to the thought of public speaking, but when questioned, some of these people don't recognize their reactions as fear. Rather, they report excitement or other feelings that aren't at all debilitating. On the other hand, when people report, 'I'm scared stiff,' you can pretty well believe that they are."

From the research that uses the PRCA, we have learned that 15 to 20 percent of the U.S. population experiences high levels of "trait" communication apprehension. "Trait apprehension" means that some people seem to be predisposed to be apprehensive and will show high levels of nervousness in all forms of speech including public speaking, interpersonal communication, and group communication. Likewise, we have learned that nearly everyone experiences times of high "state" communication apprehension. "State apprehension" means that under some circumstances people will show high levels of nervousness in a single communication context such as public speaking.

McCroskey's research has made it possible to identify high communication apprehension students and provide appropriate intervention programs. Through these programs, people with high communication apprehension do not eliminate their fears but rather learn to reduce their tension so that they can function competently.

Later, McCroskey's interest in communication apprehension led him to related studies in talking frequency (verbal activity, talkativeness, compulsive communicators) and preference to approach or avoid communication (reticence, unwillingness to communicate, and willingness to communicate). During the last twenty years, he has validated scales for measuring both willingness to communicate and talkativeness.

What is next for McCroskey? Recently, he has begun to study genetic causes of apprehension. Although we can now identify those who suffer from communication apprehension and help them reduce their fears, there seem to be limits to how much reduction can take place for particular individuals. He believes genetic study is the wave of the future and may ultimately provide answers to dealing completely with communication apprehension.

Over the last forty years, McCroskey has published more than 175 articles, 40 books, 40 book chapters, and presented more than 250 convention papers. Currently he teaches courses in communication in instruction, organizational communication, interpersonal communication, nonverbal communication, and a graduate seminar.

As we might expect, McCroskey has received many awards for his scholarship, including the pres-tigious Robert J. Kibler Memorial Award of the National Communication Association and the Distinguished Research Award from the National Association of Teacher Educators. For a partial list of McCroskey's publications in communication apprehension, see the references at the end of this book.

McCroskey's scholarship—from identifying those with communication apprehension to finding ways to help people reduce their apprehension—has helped tremendous numbers of people become more competent communicators. For more information about McCroskey and his work, see http://www.as.wvu.edu/~jmccrosk/jcmhp.html

Symptoms and Causes

The signs of public speaking apprehension vary from individual to individual, and symptoms range from mild to debilitating. Symptoms include physical, emotional, and cognitive reactions. Physical signs may be stomach upset (or butterflies), flushed skin, sweating, shaking, light headedness, rapid or heavy heart beats, and verbal disfluencies including stuttering and vocalized pauses ("like," "you know," "ah," "um," and so forth). Emotional symptoms include feeling anxious, worried, or upset. Symptoms can also include specific negative cognitions or thought patterns. For example, a highly apprehensive person might dwell on thoughts such as "I'm going to make a fool of myself," or "I just know that I'll blow it."

The level of public speaking apprehension we feel varies over the course of speaking. Researchers have identified three phases of reaction that speakers proceed through: anticipation reaction, confrontation reaction, and adaptation reaction (Behnke & Carlile, 1971, p. 66). **Anticipation reaction** is the level of anxiety you experience prior to giving the speech, including the nervousness you feel while preparing and waiting to speak. Your **confrontation reaction** is the surge in your anxiety level that you feel as you begin your speech. This level begins to fall about a minute or so into your speech and will level off at your prespeaking level about five minutes into your presentation. Your **adaptation reaction** is the gradual decline of your anxiety level that begins about one minute into the presentation and results in your anxiety level declining to its prespeaking level in about five minutes.

The causes of public speaking apprehension are still being studied, but several sources have been suggested including the idea that speaking apprehension may have a genetic component. Two other explanations for apprehension are negative reinforcement and underdeveloped skills.

anticipation reaction
the level of anxiety you experience prior to giving the speech.

confrontation reaction
the surge in your anxiety level that you feel as you begin your speech.

adaptation reaction
the gradual decline of your anxiety level that begins about one minute into the presentation.

Negative reinforcement concerns how others have responded to your public speaking endeavors in the past. If you have experienced negative reactions, you will probably be more apprehensive about speaking in public than if you have been praised for your efforts (Motley, 1997, p. 2). But these feelings do not have to handicap future performances.

Underdeveloped skills (or skill deficit theory) was the earliest explanation for apprehension and continues to receive the attention of researchers. It suggests that many of us become apprehensive because we don't understand or do the basic tasks associated with effective speech making. Luckily, the speech plan process you have been studying is designed to give you the skills you need to be successful. In addition, you can learn to manage and reduce your apprehension.

Managing Your Apprehension

Many of us believe that we would be better off if we could be totally free from nervousness and apprehension. But based on years of study, Gerald Phillips (1977) has concluded that nervousness is not necessarily negative. He notes that "learning proceeds best when the organism is in a state of tension" (p. 37). In fact, it helps to be a little nervous to do your best: If you are lackadaisical about giving a speech, you probably will not do a good job (Motley, 1997, p. 27).

Research also has confirmed that although most students in speaking courses experience apprehension, nearly all learn to cope with the nervousness (Phillips, 1997, p. 37). So how does this apply to you?

1. **Recognize that despite your apprehension you can make it through your speech.** Very few people are so afflicted by public speaking apprehension that they are unable to function. You may not enjoy the "flutters" you experience, but you can still deliver an effective speech. In the years we've been teaching, only two students were so frightened that they were unable to give the speech. We have seen speakers forget some of what they planned to say, and some have strayed from their planned speech, but they all finished speaking. Moreover, we have had students who reported being scared stiff who actually gave excellent speeches.

2. **Realize that listeners may not perceive that you are anxious or nervous.** Some people increase their apprehension because they mistakenly think the audience will detect their fear. But the fact is that audience members are seldom aware of how nervous a person is. For instance, a classic study found that even speech instructors greatly underrate the amount of stage fright they believe a person has (Clevenger, 1959, p. 136).

3. **Understand that with careful preparation and rehearsal apprehension will decrease.** If you follow the speech plan action steps that you have

learned in this text, you will find yourself paying less attention to your apprehension as you become engrossed in the challenges of communicating with your particular audience. Moreover, by practicing for a speech, you'll reduce the anxiety you can expect to have if you are "winging it." A study by Kathleen Ellis (1995) reinforces previous research findings that students who believe they are competent speakers experience less public speaking apprehension than those who do not (p. 73).

Techniques for Reducing Apprehension

Because there are multiple causes of public speaking apprehension, several specific techniques are used to help people reduce their anxiety. Some techniques are targeted at reducing apprehension that results from worrisome thoughts and irrational beliefs. Other techniques are aimed at reducing the physical symptoms of anxiety. Yet others focus on helping people overcome the skill deficiencies that lead to stress. In this section we review three approaches to reducing public speaking apprehension that have been effective with some speakers.

1. **Visualization techniques** reduce apprehension by helping speakers develop a mental picture of themselves giving a masterful speech. Joe Ayres and Theodore S. Hopf (1990), two scholars who have conducted extensive research on visualization, have found that if people can visualize themselves going through an entire process, they will have a much better chance of succeeding when they are in the situation (p. 77).

visualization techniques
techniques to reduce apprehension by helping speakers develop a mental picture of themselves giving a masterful speech.

Bob Daemmrich/Stock, Boston

Do you use positive self-talk to pump yourself up before you have an important event? Do the same before you speak. If you believe you can, you will.

Visualization has been used as a major means of improving sports skills. Studies of the use of visualization techniques in sport have found that those who only visualized practicing improved almost as much as those who practiced (Scott, 1997, p. 99). Imagine what happens when you visualize and practice as well!

By visualizing speech making, not only do people seem to lower their general apprehension but they also report fewer negative thoughts when they actually speak (Ayres, Hopf, & Ayres, 1994, p. 256). Visualization activities are a part of effective speech preparation. For visualization tips on athletic performance that you can also apply to public speaking, read "Visualization: The Mental Road to Accomplishment," available through InfoTrac College Edition. Use your Communicate! CD-ROM to access Web Resource 16.3: Mental Road to Accomplishment.

systematic desensitization
a technique in which people first learn procedures for relaxation, and then learn to apply these to the anxiety they feel when they imagine giving a speech.

2. **Systematic desensitization** is a technique in which people first learn procedures for relaxation, and then learn to apply these to the anxiety they feel when they imagine giving a speech, so that they can remain relaxed when they actually give the speech (Richmond & McCroskey, 1995). This technique is designed to help people overcome the physical symptoms of public speaking apprehension. Since "relaxing" is easier said than done, these programs focus on teaching deep muscle relaxation procedures. The process involves consciously tensing and then relaxing muscle groups to learn to recognize the difference between the two states. Then, while in a relaxed state, you imagine yourself in successively more stressful situations—for example, researching a speech topic in the library, practicing the speech out loud to a roommate, and finally giving a speech. The ultimate goal of systematic desensitization is to have people transfer the calm feelings they attain while visualizing to the actual speaking event. Calmness on command—and it works.

public speaking skills training
systematically teaching the skills associated with the processes involved in preparing and delivering an effective public speech with the intention of improving speaking competence as a means of reducing public speaking apprehension.

3. **Public speaking skills training** is systematically teaching the skills associated with the processes involved in preparing and delivering an effective public speech with the intention of improving speaking competence as a means of reducing public speaking apprehension. Skills training is based on the assumption that some of our anxiety about speaking in public is due to our realization that we do not know how to be success-

Test Your Competence

Visualizing Your Success

Visualize your success by imagining yourself effectively delivering your speech. Complete this activity in an environment free of distractions.

To complete this activity, use your Communicate! CD-ROM to access Skill Learning Activity 16.4. Follow the directions to listen to an audiotape that will help you visualize. You can also write a short paragraph describing this experience and email it to your instructor.

ful, that we lack the knowledge and behaviors to be effective. Therefore, if we learn the processes and behaviors associated with effective speech making, then we will be less anxious about speaking in public (Kelly, Phillips, & Keaen, 1995, pp. 11–13). Research on the impact of basic courses on communication apprehension has shown that experience in a public speaking course can reduce students' communication apprehension scores.

These three techniques for reducing public speaking apprehension have all been successful at helping people reduce their anxiety. Researchers are just beginning to conduct studies to identify which techniques are most appropriate for a particular person. A study conducted by Karen Kangas Dwyer (2000) suggests that the most effective program for combating apprehension is one that uses a variety of techniques, but individualizes these so that the techniques are used in an order that corresponds to the order in which the individual experiences apprehension (p. 79). So, for example, when facing a speaking situation if your immediate reaction is to feel physical sensations (nausea, rapid heart beat, and so forth) before thinking about the event, you would benefit from learning systematic desensitization techniques before working with visualization or receiving skills training. To reduce your public speaking apprehension, you will want to use all these techniques, but use them in an order that matches the order in which you experience apprehension.

Criteria for Evaluating Speeches

In addition to learning to prepare and present speeches, you are learning to evaluate (critically analyze) the speeches you hear. Critical analysis of speeches not only provides the speaker with both an analysis of where the speech went right and where it went wrong but also gives you, the critic, insight into the methods that you want to incorporate or, perhaps, avoid in presenting your own speeches.

Although speech criticism is context specific (analyzing the effectiveness of an informative demonstration speech differs from analyzing the effectiveness of a persuasive action speech), in this section we look at criteria for evaluating public speaking in general. Classroom speeches are usually evaluated on the basis of how well the speaker has met specific criteria of effective speaking.

In Chapters 12 through 16, as you have been learning the speech plan action steps, you have also been learning the criteria by which speeches are measured. The critical assumption is that if a speech has good content, is well organized and adapted to the audience, and is delivered well, it is

Thinking Critically about Speeches

Check all items that were accomplished effectively.

Content

_____ 1. Was the goal of the speech clear?
_____ 2. Did the speaker have high-quality information?
_____ 3. Did the speaker use a variety of kinds of developmental material?
_____ 4. Were visual aids appropriate and well used?
_____ 5. Did the speaker establish common ground and adapt the content to the audience's interests, knowledge, and attitudes?

Organization

_____ 6. Did the introduction gain attention, gain goodwill for the speaker, and lead into the speech?
_____ 7. Were the main points clear, parallel, and in meaningful complete sentences?
_____ 8. Did transitions lead smoothly from one point to another?
_____ 9. Did the conclusion tie the speech together?

Presentation

_____ 10. Was the language clear?
_____ 11. Was the language vivid?
_____ 12. Was the language emphatic?
_____ 13. Did the speaker sound enthusiastic?
_____ 14. Did the speaker show sufficient vocal expressiveness?
_____ 15. Was the presentation spontaneous?
_____ 16. Was the presentation fluent?
_____ 17. Did the speaker look at the audience?
_____ 18. Were the pronunciation and articulation acceptable?
_____ 19. Did the speaker have good posture?
_____ 20. Was speaker movement appropriate?
_____ 21. Did the speaker have sufficient poise?

Based on these criteria, evaluate the speech as (check one):
_____ excellent, _____ good, _____ satisfactory, _____ fair, _____ poor.

Figure 16.3
Speech critique checklist

likely to achieve its goal. Thus, you can evaluate any speech by answering questions that relate to the basics of content, organization, and presentation. Figure 16.3 is a diagnostic speech checklist. You can use this checklist to analyze your first speech during your rehearsal period and to critique the sample student speech at the end of this chapter.

Test Your Competence

Presenting Your First Speech

1. Follow the speech plan action steps to prepare an informative or persuasive speech. The time and other parameters for this assignment will be announced by your instructor.
2. Criteria for evaluation include all the essentials of topic and purpose, content, organization, and presentation, but special emphasis will be placed on clarity of goal, clarity and appropriateness of main points, and delivery. As you practice your speech, use the diagnostic speech critique sheet as a checklist to ensure that you are meeting the basic criteria in your speech.
3. Prior to presenting your speech, prepare a complete sentence outline and a written plan for

adapting your speech to the audience. If you have used Speech Builder Express to complete the action step activities online, you will be able to print out a copy of your completed outline. Your adaptation plan should describe how you plan to verbally and visually adapt your material to the audience and should address how you will (1) indicate key aspects of the audience that you will need to adapt to, (2) establish common ground, (3) build and maintain audience inter- est, (4) adjust to the audience's knowledge and sophistication, (5) build speaker credibility, (6) adapt to audience's attitudes toward your speech goal, (7) adapt to audiences from differ- ent cultures and language communities (if rele- vant for you in this speech), and (8) use visual aids to enhance audience understanding and memory. If you completed the action step activi- ties in Chapter 15, you can use them to form the basis of your written adaptation plan.

Sample Speech: Catching, Throwing, and Cradling a Lacrosse Ball, by Anthony Masturzo*

Courtesy Anthony Masturzo

1. Review the adaptation plan and outline developed by Anthony Masturzo in preparing this speech on lacrosse.

2. Then read the transcript of Anthony's speech.

3. Use the Speech Critique Checklist from Figure 16.3 to help you evaluate this speech.

4. Use your Communicate! CD-ROM to watch a video clip of Anthony pre- senting his speech in class. Click on the "Speech Interactive" icon in the menu at the left, then click on "Speech Menu" in the menu bar at the top of the screen. Select Informative Speech: Lacrosse to watch the video (it takes a minute for the video to load).

5. Write a paragraph of feedback to Anthony describing the strengths of his presentation and what you think he might do next time to be more effective.

You can use your Communicate! CD-ROM to prepare your critique checklist and your feedback, then compare your answers to those of the authors'. To complete the checklist electronically, click on "Evaluation" in the menu bar at the top of the screen. To prepare your feedback electroni- cally, click on "Analysis" in the menu bar. To compare your answers to those provided by the authors, click the "Done" button.

You can use your Student Workbook to complete this activity, or you can complete it online, print a copy of the Speech Critique Checklist, and, if requested, email your work to your instructor. Access Skill Learning Activity 16.6.

*Delivered in speech class at the University of Cincinnati. Used with permission of Anthony Masturzo.

Adaptation Plan

1. **Key aspects of audience:** Since there are more men than women in the class and since men are usually willing to be interested in talking about and listening for information on most any sport, I think the men will receive my sport topic favorably. My true test is gaining and retaining the interest of women.

2. **Establishing and maintaining common ground:** My main way of establishing common ground will be by using personal pronouns.

3. **Building and maintaining interest:** Since interest is not automatic, I will use an actual demonstration to perk audience interest.

4. **Audience knowledge and sophistication:** Since most of the class will never have participated or have knowledge of the game, I will focus on aspects of the game that they'll be able to understand even if they don't fully know how the game is played. I believe that by repeating key points and by using visual aids to demonstrate points that students will be more likely to retain the information.

5. **Building credibility:** Early in the speech I will talk about how I have played the game extensively and have in-depth knowledge. I will also use various examples to show my competence with skills.

6. **Audience attitudes:** Since my audience has more men, they are likely to be interested in the topic. After all lacrosse is a growing sport. To adapt to the women, I will suggest that lacrosse is great exercise and can be played by women as well as men.

7. **Adapt to audiences from different cultures and language communities:** All audience members come from the same culture and language community that I do. The only thing I have to watch is not slipping into "lacrosse lingo."

8. **Use visual aids to enhance audience understanding and memory:** I will demonstrate the techniques using my lacrosse stick. I think a demonstration will be effective since the class is small and everyone can see. Demonstrating should also increase my credibility with the audience.

Speech Outline

Specific Goal: I want my audience to learn the skills necessary to play the game of lacrosse.

Introduction
I. Although the national sport of Canada is hockey, an almost equally popular sport is lacrosse.
II. Lacrosse is similar to hockey in that it has similar rules and penalties but is played on a soccer field with the same number of position players.

Thesis Statement: Three skills necessary to play the game of lacrosse are catching, throwing, and cradling the ball.

Body

I. One skill necessary to play the game of lacrosse is catching the ball.
   A. Catching the ball is accomplished with a series of steps.
      1. Your feet should be shoulder length apart.
      2. You hold the stick in a ready position.
      3. You adjust the height and length of the stick to meet the ball.
      4. Once the ball is in the crosse, you give with the ball.
   B. The common problems that hinder your effectiveness are as follows.
      1. No hand eye coordination.
      2. A tendency to swat at the ball.
      3. Improper hold on the stick.

II. The second skill necessary to play the game of lacrosse is throwing the ball.
   A. Throwing the ball is accomplished with a series of steps.
      1. Your feet should be shoulder length apart.
      2. Turn your body to give appropriate back swing.
      3. Step, twist body, release dominant arm and retrieve weak arm.
      4. Snap wrist.
      5. Follow through.
   B. The common problems that hinder your effectiveness are as follows.
      1. No follow through.
      2. Poor form.

III. The final skill necessary to play the game of lacrosse is to cradle the ball while running.
   A. Cradling the ball is accomplished with a series of steps.
      1. Hold the stick in a ready position.
      2. Twist your wrist in and out.
      3. Arm should move naturally.
   B. The common problems that hinder your effectiveness are as follows.
      1. Herky-jerky wrist and arm movement.
      2. Unbalanced stick.

Conclusion

I. The skills necessary to play the game are catching, throwing, and cradling.
II. Once you have mastered these, you can go on to strategy and shooting.

Sources

Personal Experience: 3 yr. Varsity Letterman, Walsh Jesuit Lacrosse Team.

Interview: Brian Masturzo, Defensive Captain, Walsh Jesuit Varsity Lacrosse Team.

Research: www.lacrossenetwork.com/outsidersguide/history

Speech and Analysis

Speech	Analysis
When you think of Canadian sports, what's the first thing that comes to mind? You're right, it is hockey. But did you know that one of Canada's national sports is also lacrosse?	Anthony opens with a rhetorical question to get the audience thinking with him.
Lacrosse network.Com writes, "Created by indigenous Americans, this sport was considered an excellent practice for war. The sport pitted tribe against tribe in a game where each tried to place a feather stuffed deerskin ball past a goalie." Of course nowadays, we've Americanized the sport. We no longer use a deerskin stuffed ball—we use hard rubber. The sticks are actually made of graphite and plastic—no long sticks entwined.	In this introduction he contrasts current equipment with the original. Notice that both Anthony's outline and his adaptation plan mentioned his three years as a varsity letterman in lacrosse. For some reason, perhaps nervousness, he failed to mention it in the speech itself.
What I want to show you today are the three skills that are necessary to learn the game of lacrosse.	Here Anthony uses a transition to lead into the points of the body of the speech.
The first skill that's necessary is catching the lacrosse ball. Very simple. It all starts with proper form. You want your feet about shoulder length apart, you want good positioning on the stick, two hands with the crosse facing out. As the ball comes in you need to give with the ball.	Anthony states his first main point in a clear, complete sentence. Throughout the speech, Anthony uses himself, the stick, and the ball as visual aids.
A lot of common mistakes occur with catching. The first is the absence of hand–eye coordination—if you have no coordination, this game becomes very difficult. The second is improper holding of the stick. You may have a turn, you may have too tight of a grip, and you're not ready for the ball.	Throughout the speech Anthony divides his main points into first explaining the process and then showing common mistakes.

Speech

The third problem is the tendency to swat at the ball rather than to give when you're trying to catch it.

The second skill that's necessary to learn the game of lacrosse is throwing the ball.

Once again you have the stick in a ready position. But this time since you have a ball in the net, you'll have a tendency to hold it a little farther back. Then you need to step with the opposite foot, snap your wrist and follow through. The follow-through is what is the key with throwing the lacrosse ball.

The main problem when you throw—when you first start—is you tend to stop early with no follow through. You just want to get rid of the ball. Going through the complete process improves with experience.

The final skill necessary in playing the game of lacrosse is cradling the ball.

Cradling means keeping the ball inside the stick—inside the crosse.

The game of lacrosse is played on a soccer field with the same positions as in soccer. In order to advance the ball, a lot of the times you'll need to run with the ball. Now, defenders—the opponents—are going to attempt to knock the ball loose. They do that with stick checks and with body checks.

You need to find a way to keep the ball in here no matter what occurs.

Analysis

Here Anthony needs a transition to lead into the second main point of the speech.

Again, his main point is stated clearly.

Notice that his explanations are very clear and easy to follow.

Here and throughout the speech Anthony does a good job of talking directly with the audience.

Again, he could use an internal transition.

Again, a clear statement of the main point.

Notice how he defines "cradling" to make sure that we can follow his explanation.

Comparison to soccer in this section helps us to get a better understanding of how lacrosse is played.

He continues to be very conscious of his audience. He continues to be

Speech

So, in order to keep the ball in here, you need to do what's called a cradle. Notice, what you're doing is pulling the ball across your body and back, but you're doing it as you run. Just like this.

Problems with cradling. Uh, I would say the number one problem is a herky-jerky motion where you tend to snap the ball rather than to comfortably bring it across your body.

So, to summarize, throwing the ball, catching the ball and cradling the ball are the three skills that are necessary to master in order to play the game of lacrosse. Once you've mastered these skills, you can then work on other skills such as strategy and shooting.

Analysis

careful in showing us how these skills are accomplished.

"Problems with cradling" is a heading. He needs to build this into a meaningful complete sentence.

Good closing summary.

This is a strong first speech. The structure of the speech is especially good. His use of visual aids, including himself, helps us to follow his directions very easily.

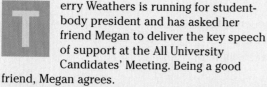

What Would You Do?   ▸ A QUESTION OF ETHICS

Terry Weathers is running for student-body president and has asked her friend Megan to deliver the key speech of support at the All University Candidates' Meeting. Being a good friend, Megan agrees.

Megan works several days developing the speech, and she believes she has prepared a really good one. The problem is that although Megan can prepare excellent speeches she suffers from stage fright. She is scared to death to give this one in front of such a large audience. So, she asks Donnell Gates, a guy in her speech class who wows audiences with his engaging manner, to deliver the speech for her at the event.

Donnell thought about her request and left the following message on her voice mail: "Listen, you know I'm not crazy about Terry, so I would never vote for her. But since I don't really care who wins this election, I'll give the speech. Hey, I just enjoy the power I have over an audience!"

1. Now that Megan knows that Donnell doesn't care for Terry, should she let him give the speech?

2. And what about Donnell? Should he give such a speech knowing that he wouldn't support Terry himself?

Summary

Although speeches may be presented impromptu, by manuscript, or by memory, the material you have been reading is designed to help you present your speeches extemporaneously—that is, carefully prepared and practiced but with the exact wording determined at the time of utterance.

The verbal components of effective presentation are clarity, vividness, and emphasis. The nonverbal elements of presentation include voice, articulation, and bodily action.

Effective speaking uses verbal and nonverbal components to achieve a conversational quality that includes vocal characteristics, bodily action, enthusiasm, spontaneity, fluency, and eye contact.

To rehearse an extemporaneous speech, complete the outline at least two days in advance. Between the time the outline has been completed and the time the speech is to be given, practice the speech several times, weighing what you did and how you did it after each practice. You may wish to use brief notes, especially for longer speeches, as long as they do not interfere with your delivery. Also make sure that you have considered means of handling visual aids.

All speakers feel nervous as they approach their first speech. Some nervousness is cognitive (in the mind) and some is behavioral (physically displayed). Rather than being an either-or matter, nervousness is a matter of degree.

Because at least some tension is constructive, our goal is not to get rid of nervousness but to learn how to cope with it. First, realize that nervousness is normal. Second, you can use several specific behaviors to help control excessive nervousness. And, if you're well prepared, you will be able to achieve a more relaxed presentation.

If nervousness is truly detrimental to your performance, see your professor outside of class and talk with him or her about what you are experiencing. Your professor should be able to offer suggestions for people you can see or programs you can attend.

Speeches are evaluated on how well they meet the guidelines for effective content, organization, language, and delivery.

Communicate! Online

Now that you have read Chapter 16, use your Communicate! CD-ROM for quick access to the electronic resources that accompany this text. Your CD-ROM gives you access to the video of Anthony's speech, InfoTrac College Edition, and the Communicate! Web site. When you get to the Communicate! home page, click on "Student Book Companion Site"

in the Resource box at the right to access the online study aids for this chapter, including a digital glossary, review quizzes, chapter activities, and chapter Web Resources.

Key Terms

At the Communicate! Web site, select the chapter resources for Chapter 16. Print a copy of the glossary for this chapter and test yourself with the electronic flash cards or complete the crossword puzzle to help you master these key terms:

extemporaneously (404)
vividness (405)
simile (405)
metaphor (405)
emphasis (405)
conversational quality (406)
voice (407)
articulation (407)
pronunciation (407)
accent (408)
facial expressions (408)
gestures (408)

movement (408)
poised (409)
posture (409)
enthusiasm (410)
monotone (410)
spontaneity (411)
fluency (411)
eye contact (411)
rehearsing (412)
speech notes (413)
learning the speech (417)

public speaking apprehension (419)
anticipation reaction (421)
confrontation reaction (421)
adaptation reaction (421)
visualization techniques (423)
systematic desensitization (424)
public speaking skills training (424)

Review Quiz

Test your knowledge of the concepts in this chapter by taking the online quiz at the Communicate! Web site. Select the chapter resources for Chapter 16, then click on "Review Quiz." When you have completed the quiz, submit it for scoring.

Skill Learning Activities

Complete the Observe & Analyze, Test Your Competence, Action Step, and Speech and Analysis activities for Chapter 16 online at the Communicate! Web site. Select the chapter resources for Chapter 16, then click on "Activities." You can submit your Observe & Analyze, Action Step, and Speech and Analysis answers to your instructor, and compare your Test Your Competence and Speech and Analysis answers to those provided by the authors.

16.1: Observe & Analyze: Similes and Metaphors (406)
16.2: Test Your Competence: Articulation Exercises (408)
16.3: Action Step 5: Rehearsing Your Speech (418)
16.4: Test Your Competence: Visualizing Your Success (424)
16.5: Observe & Analyze: Controlling Nervousness (425)
16.6: Speech and Analysis: Lacrosse, by Anthony Masturzo (427)

Web Resources

Access the Web Resources for this chapter online at the Communicate! Web site. Select the chapter resources for Chapter 16, then click on "Web Resources."

16.1: Articulation Exercises (408)
16.2: Body Motions and Audience Attention (409)
16.3: Mental Road to Accomplishment (424)

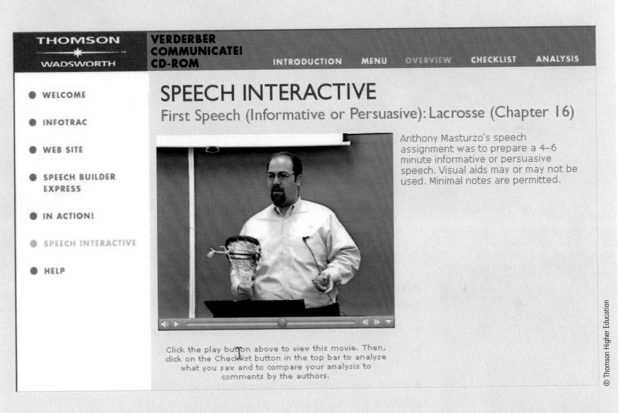

Joel Gordon

OBJECTIVES

After you have read this chapter, you should be able to answer these questions:

- What are the tests of presenting ideas creatively?
- How can you proceed to leave the impression that what you have said is new and relevant?
- What key techniques can you use to emphasize information?
- What are the major methods of informing?
- What are the key criteria for evaluating an informative speech?

Informative Speaking

For several months, a major architectural firm had been working on designs for the arts center to be built in the middle of downtown. Members of the city council and guests from various constituencies in the city, as well as a number of concerned citizens, were taking seats, as the long-anticipated presentation was about to begin. As Linda Garner, mayor and presiding officer of the city council, finished her introduction, Donald Harper, the principal architect of the project, walked to the microphone to begin his speech describing the proposed design.

his is but one of many scenarios played out every day when expert speakers present information to help others understand complex information. In the previous public speaking chapters we described the basic speech plan action steps that underlie any effective speech preparation. In this chapter, we develop the specific principles and skills that must be mastered to present an effective speech whose general goal is to inform the audience about the topic.

As an informative speaker, you have a special burden to present new information and face the challenge of holding audience interest, facilitating their understanding, and increasing the likelihood of their remembering what may be complicated information. We begin our discussion of informative speaking by introducing basic principles of informative speaking. Then we describe three different methods effective speakers use to present their ideas.

Principles of Informing

You will be a more effective informative speaker if you apply the principles of intellectual stimulation, creativity, relevance, and emphasis.

Intellectual Stimulation

Principle 1: Audiences are more likely to listen to information they perceive to be intellectually stimulating.

intellectually stimulating
information new to audience members that the audience perceives they have a deep-seated need to know.

Information will be perceived as **intellectually stimulating** when it is new to audience members and when the audience perceives a deep-seated need to know. When we say *new,* we mean that either the information is not familiar to most of the audience or that the way in which the information is developed gives audience members new insight into a familiar topic. If you choose a topic in which you already have some expertise, you may already know information that most of your audience is unacquainted with. If you suspect that this is not the case, as you research your topic, you will want to identify information that will be new to a majority of your audience. For example, the "date rape drug," rohypnol, is something that most college students may have heard of. However, it is a very important topic for students, especially women, to learn more about. Even the audience members who have heard of rohypnol may not know much about its history, or chemical properties, and the extent of the danger associated with this drug.

When you choose to talk about a topic that most of the people in your audience are familiar with, you will need to find a new angle, new application, or new perspective if you are going to "inform" them. For instance, if your topic is basketball, and your audience is a group of college students who occasionally attend games, a speech on identifying a jump shot is likely

John Elk III/Stock, Boston

Rangers, guides, and interpreters at parks and museums work to become experts so that they can tailor their presentations to the needs of specific audiences. If you were listening to this ranger, what would you want to know?

to be uninformative. But if you're a basketball fanatic and really want to talk about the sport, explaining the "pick and roll" maneuver, "matchup zone defenses," "using the press," or how the latest rule changes are likely to affect the game are likely to provide new information to the casual fan.

Presenting new information is important, but the information must also satisfy an audience's curiosity and hunger for information or insight. Part of the informative speaker's job is to satisfy that curiosity and feed that hunger. Every day we are titillated by ideas and issues that we may not fully grasp and don't have time to pursue. For instance, several years ago scientists discovered an "ice man" buried in a glacier of the southern Alps. This well-preserved body was of a man who lived between four and five thousand years ago. Newspaper headlines and TV announcers hyped the discovery. Readers and viewers were momentarily excited by the information, but few of us pursued the story beyond the headlines of the time. So, suppose you're an anthropology major with a special interest in early human forms, you could develop an informative speech on this "ice man" that would captivate your audience and satisfy a curiosity they may have been too busy to sate themselves.

Let's consider a less esoteric example. Suppose you love cars and want to give a speech on the topic of new cars. Well, most audience members are aware that SUVs have become the "hot" car to have, and some audience members may drive SUVs. So how could you identify a specific goal that would be interesting and informative on this topic? Well, it wouldn't take much research to discover several angles from which you could approach this topic. For instance, we are aware that SUVs are prone to flipping, use more gasoline, and create more damage to other vehicles in an accident.

But how are U.S. automakers and government regulators responding to these problems? How can SUVs be made less top heavy? What is being done to reduce their fuel consumption, and are there any efforts under way to make them less destructive to things that they hit? A speech updating the audience on any of these issues would likely be intellectually stimulating to the audience.

In informative speaking you have a special burden to choose specific goals that take into account what the audience is likely to already know so that you *inform* rather than *bore* them.

Creativity

Principle 2: Audiences are more likely to listen to, understand, and remember information that is presented creatively.

creativity
a person's ability to produce new or original ideas and insights.

Creativity can be defined as a person's ability to produce new or original ideas and insights. Although you may be thinking, "I'm just not a creative person," all of us can be creative in developing information in a speech. Let's consider how you can proceed that will result in creative speaking.

1. **Gather enough high-quality information to provide a broad base from which to work.** Contrary to what many of us may think, creativity is a product of perspiration not inspiration. The more deeply you have researched your topic, the more information you will have. With more information, you are in a better position to have choices of how to creatively present your ideas.

2. **Give yourself enough time for the creative process to work.** Many speakers (especially students in a speaking course) finish preparing their basic outline just in time to "go over the speech" once before they present it. Rarely do creative ideas come in the face of a time crunch. Your mind is a miraculous organ, capable of generating a myriad of creative ideas. But to work, it needs time. This is why we recommended completing your outline for a classroom speech *at least* two days before the actual presentation. During those two days, you are likely to find that after an early uninspiring practice you suddenly have two or three fresh ideas about how to approach a particular main point. While you are sleeping, your unconscious mind will continue to work on the speech. When you are walking across campus or driving to work, you'll find your thoughts drifting to your speech topic and at times you'll find yourself saying, "Yes, that's it, that'll work! Why didn't I think of that sooner?" You can increase your likelihood of creating fascinating ways to present your information by simply giving your mind the time it needs to work.

3. **Be prepared to pursue a creative idea when it comes.** When you have given yourself "time to think," have you ever noticed how ideas seem to come at odd times—while you are cleaning your room, mulching the garden, or waiting at a stoplight? Have you also noticed that if you don't immediately "capture" them, those "great" ideas are likely to slip away?

Many "creative" people carry pencil and paper with them at all times. When an idea comes up, they capture it to use later. It sounds silly, but you'll discover that you are more creative than you suspected if you will simply secure your good ideas before they fade from your memory. Not all creative ideas pan out, but most of them are at least worth exploring. If you cannot remember your creative ideas, you will never know whether they are good.

4. **Create alternative choices.** In the article "Thinking Like a Genius," available through InfoTrac College Edition, author Michael Michalko describes eight techniques that stimulate what he called "productive" not "reproductive" thought. (To read this article, access Web Resource 17.1: Thinking Like a Genius.) According to Michalko, **reproductive thought** occurs when we rely only on our past experience to guide our current action. So in working to develop an informative speech topic, a reproductive thinker would look at how the topic has been approached by others in the past and would model the speech on that tried and true pattern. By contrast a productive thinker would ask, "How many different ways can I think of to present this information?" **Productive thought** occurs when we work to think about something from a variety of perspectives. Then, with numerous ideas to choose from, the productive thinker selects the ones that are best suited to a particular audience. Michalko identifies eight specific tactics that you can use to become a productive thinker and generate many different ways for developing your ideas.

reproductive thought
relying only on our past experience to guide our current actions.

productive thought
thinking about something from a variety of perspectives.

Let's look at an example of how productive thought can lead to alternative ways of presenting information. Suppose you are planning to give a speech on climatic variation in the United States and that in your research you ran across the data shown in Figure 17.1.

City	Yearly Temperature (in degrees Fahrenheit)		Precipitation (in inches)	
	High	Low	July	Annual
Chicago	95	–21	3.7	35
Cincinnati	98	–7	3.3	39
Denver	104	–3	1.9	15
Los Angeles	104	40	trace	15
Miami	96	50	5.7	56
Minneapolis	95	–27	3.5	28
New Orleans	95	26	6.1	62
New York	98	–2	4.4	42
Phoenix	117	35	0.8	7
Portland, ME	94	–18	3.1	44
St. Louis	97	–9	3.9	37
San Francisco	94	35	trace	19
Seattle	94	23	0.9	38

Figure 17.1
Temperature and precipitation highs and lows in selected U.S. cities

Creative thought can spark several lines of development from the same information source. Study the information in Figure 17.1. What unusual or noteworthy things do you notice? First, you might notice that yearly high temperatures in U.S. cities vary less than yearly low temperatures. The yearly highs in July were about 96 degrees for Miami and 95 for Minneapolis, whereas the yearly lows were 50 degrees in Miami and –27 degrees in Minneapolis—a 77-degree difference! Most of us who don't know a lot about weather would think that high temperatures should vary nearly as much as low temperatures, and we would be curious about why this was not so.

You might also notice that it hardly ever rains on the west coast in the summer. Two of the three west coast cities listed, Los Angeles and San Francisco, show only a trace of rain in July, and a third, Seattle—a city often considered a rainy city—shows nine-tenths of an inch in July. This is almost three inches less than any eastern city and five inches less than Miami. Why is there so little rain on the west coast in July? Why is there so much more rain in the east? These are interesting ideas to pursue.

Finally, most of us think of July as a hot dry month, but these data indicate that the major cities cited in the east and in the Midwest experience more than the average one-twelfth of the annual precipitation in July. So why do we perceive July to be a dry month when it isn't? Or is it?

So, as we study the data in just this one chart, we can generate at least three different lines of development for an informative speech on climate: Why are summer highs more similar than winter lows for cities in different regions? Why do the Midwest and the East experience more summer rain than does the West? Why is July perceived to be a "dry" month when it gets more than its share of annual rainfall?

Creative thought can develop alternative ways to make the same point. Using the information from the climatic data in Figure 17.1, we can quickly create two ways to support the point "Yearly high temperatures in U.S. cities vary far less than yearly low temperatures."

A. Of the thirteen cities selected, ten (77 percent) had yearly highs between 90 and 100 degrees. Four (30 percent) had yearly lows above freezing; two (15 percent) had yearly lows between zero and 32 degrees; and seven (54 percent) had low temperatures below zero.

B. Cincinnati, Miami, Minneapolis, New York, and St. Louis—cities at different latitudes—all had yearly high temperatures of 95 to 98 degrees. In contrast, the lowest temperature for Miami was 50 degrees, and the lowest temperatures for Cincinnati, Minneapolis, New York, and St. Louis were –7, –27, –2, and –9 degrees, respectively.

5. **Force your creativity through practicing sections of the speech in different ways.** Too often, when our outline is finished, we prematurely stop thinking creatively and act as if the speech is cast in stone. Then we keep going over it the same way "to learn it." As a result, the creative process that could be helping us to improve our speech is short-circuited. As you practice, allow yourself the freedom to try new ideas.

And as you gain experience, you will begin to trust yourself to change your development while presenting the speech if a novel thought that is better than what you had planned occurs to you.

Relevance

Principle 3: Audiences are more likely to listen to and remember information they perceive as relevant.

Rather than acting like sponges that absorb every bit of information, most of us act more like filters: We listen only to information we perceive to be relevant. **Relevance** is the extent to which audience members find personal value in the information presented. Information will be seen as relevant when it relates to audience members' needs and interests.

relevance
the extent to which audience members find personal value in the information presented.

Characteristics	Dropout Rate (%)
Average Total	**4.7**
Sex	
Male	4.3
Female	5.1
Race and Hispanic Origin	
White	4.4
White non-Hispanic	3.8
Black	6.0
Asian and Pacific Islander	4.8
Hispanic (of any race)	7.1
Family Income	
Less than $20,000	9.0
$20,000–$39,000	3.8
$40,000 and over	2.3
Grade Level	
10th grade	2.7
11th grade	3.7
12th grade	8.5

SOURCE: U.S. Census Bureau, Current Population Survey, October 1999.

Figure 17.2
Annual dropout rates of U.S. high school students, 1999

vital information
information the audience perceives as a matter of life or death.

Finding **vital information**—information the audience perceives as a matter of life or death—may be the ultimate in relevance. Police cadets, for instance, will see information explaining what they should do when attacked as vital. Similarly, students may perceive information that is necessary to their passing a test as vital. When speakers show listeners that information is critical to their well-being, they have a compelling reason to listen.

Of course, information does not have to be a life or death situation to be perceived as relevant. But you will want to connect the information you are presenting to the audience's needs or interests. For example, in a speech on Japanese cultural practices, a topic that may seem distant from the audience members' needs and concerns, you can make the information relevant by reminding the audience of significant Japanese corporations that have located facilities in your community, of job opportunities with Japanese employers, or of the likelihood that they may have occasion to travel to Japan to do business. If you are speaking on funeral rituals in Tibet, you can make them more relevant by comparing them to your local funeral customs. In an informative speech, one of your responsibilities is to demonstrate how the information relates to the audience's needs and interests.

Although you will want to demonstrate the relevance of your information throughout the speech, if you are speaking on a topic whose relevance to your audience is not self-evident, it is critical that your introduction address relevance in some way. Notice how this opening for a speech on high-speed rail transportation establishes relevance:

> **Have you been stuck in a traffic jam lately? Have you started what you had hoped would be a pleasant vacation only to be trampled at the airport, or worse, to discover when you got to your destination that your luggage hadn't? We're all aware that every year our highways and our airways are getting more congested. At the same time, we are facing a rapidly decreasing supply of petroleum. Today, I'm going to tell you about one of the most practical means for solving these problems—high-speed rail transportation.**

Emphasis

Principle 4: Audiences are more likely to understand and to remember information that is emphasized.

Audiences will remember only some of the content presented in a speech; over time, the rest is likely to be forgotten. If a speech is really informative, the audience is hearing a lot of new material. So it is your responsibility to decide what you want the audience to remember and then to use various techniques to highlight that information.

Ordinarily, the highest-priority information in your speech includes the specific goal, the main points, and key facts that give meaning to the main points. So, if you were giving a speech on Roquefort cheese, you would want to make sure the audience remembered this information:

- **The goal:** to understand the three distinct elements of Roquefort cheese
- **The main points:** Roquefort cheese is trademarked, Roquefort cheese is made exclusively from ewe's milk, and Roquefort cheese is colored and flavored from molds grown only in caves located in Roquefort-sur-Soulzon.
- **Important facts:** For a salad dressing to be labeled "Roquefort," it must contain at least 15 percent legislated Roquefort. It takes 800,000 ewes to provide the milk necessary to keep Roquefort cheesemakers in business. The mold grown in caves is cultivated in bread, ground, and injected into the cheese to give the distinctive color and flavor.

Once you have decided what you want the audience to remember, there are a number of techniques that you can use to emphasize it.

1. **Use visual aids.** When we see and hear, we remember more. In an informative speech where a lot of information is presented, visual aids should be strategically chosen to reinforce the ideas you want your audience to remember. Avoid the temptation to present a graphic visual of a minor point. Your audience is likely to remember the visual and forget what you would really like them to retain.

2. **Repeat important words and ideas.** Because some audience members may be momentarily inattentive and because we remember what is repeated, one of the easiest ways to ensure that your audience remembers a piece of information is to say it more than once. You can repeat the idea word for word, "The first dimension of romantic love is passion. Passion." You can also paraphrase the idea, "The first dimension of romantic love is passion. That is, it can't really be romantic love, if there is no sexual attraction." Audiences appreciate some repetition, but like any tactic, too much repetition will bore the audience while making everything seem equally important.

3. **Use transitions to guide audience thinking.** If you are reading and you "get lost," you can go back and reread. Those listening to your speech cannot go back if they get lost. So it is especially important for you to orient your audience by verbally pointing out where you have been and where you are going. Transitions are important in all speech making, but they are crucial in informative speeches that usually have subpoints to each main point. So, in the introduction of a speech on romantic love, the speaker previews what will be covered:

   Today, I'm going to explain the three characteristics of romantic love, how the Investment Theory of Romantic Relationships explains how some people are able to keep love alive, and five "investments" you can make in your loving relationships so that they continue to thrive.

Then, as the speaker moves from the first to the second of these long main points the speaker summarizes and orients:

So there are three aspects of romantic love: passion, intimacy, and commitment. Now, let's see how people keep the love alive. The investment theory of romantic relationships suggests that . . .

And during the conclusion the speaker summarizes the main ideas:

So today you've learned that romantic love is comprised of passion, intimacy, and commitment. You've also learned that if we are satisfied with our romantic relationships we continue to be committed to them and make "investments" in them. Finally you heard about five specific investments you can make to keep the love alive. These were engaging in small talk, being supportive of your partner, openly sharing your ideas and feelings, engaging in self-development, and observing relationship rituals.

The value of using transitions to clarify the structure of an informative speech and help audience members remember the important material cannot be overstated. Think of how difficult you find it to take notes during some classes. Your instructor may understand the main points being presented and know that you should remember them, but if you have trouble taking notes, you are unlikely to recall them.

4. **Use humor to reinforce key points.** Effective speakers recognize that humor not only increases audience interest but, used strategically, can also aid memory. People remember information presented as a humorous story. For instance, in a speech on reducing stress, one of the main points the speaker wished to emphasize was "keeping things in perspective." So the speaker used this story to reinforce the point:

Keep in mind that a problem that seems enormous at the moment might turn out to be minor in a few days, so being able to put events into perspective saves a great deal of psychological wear and tear. Consider this example: a first-time visitor to the races bet two dollars on the first race on a horse that had the same name as his elementary school. The horse won and the man was ten dollars ahead. In each of the next several races, he bet on horses such as "Apple Pie," his favorite, and "Kathie's Prize," after his wife's name, and he kept winning. By the end of the sixth race he was 700 dollars ahead. He was about to go home when he noticed that in the seventh race, Seventh Veil was scheduled to race in the number seven position, and was currently going off at odds of seven to one. The man couldn't resist. So he bet his entire 700 dollars. And . . . sure enough, the horse came in seventh. When he got home his wife asked, "How did you do?" Very calmly he looked at his wife and said, "Not bad—I lost two dollars."

Now that's perspective.

5. **Create and use memory aids for your audience.** You can help your listeners retain more of your speech by using **mnemonics,** memory aids. For example, in an informative speech on evaluating diamonds, you could refer to the four criteria as weight, clarity, tint, and shape. But the audience would be more likely to remember the criteria if you referred

mnemonics
memory aids such as acronyms.

to them as the "Four Cs" and used the words "carat," "clarity," "color," and "cutting." Why? Because now you've created a memory aid—each criterion begins with the letter "C."

Acronyms can also be used as mnemonics. Acronyms can be (1) words formed from initial letters of each of the successive parts of a compound term (NATO—North Atlantic Treaty Organization, OPEC—Organization of Petroleum Exporting Countries); (2) common words made up of the first letters of objects or concepts (SMART for the five group goals: *s*pecific, *m*easurable, *a*ction-oriented, *r*easonable, and *t*ime-bound); or (3) sentences made up of words whose initial letters signal something else (Every Good Boy Does Fine for the five musical notes that set on lines in the treble clef of the scale). For example, in her speech on the healing power of listening, Carol Koehler (1998), a professor of communication and medicine, used the word *CARE* as an acronym for the skills of a therapeutic communicator: *c*oncentrate, *a*cknowledge, *r*espond, and display *e*motional control (pp. 543–544).

Memory aids work through **association,** the tendency for one thought to stimulate recall of another, similar thought. Suppose you are trying to help the audience remember the value of color in a diamond. Because blue is the most highly prized tint and yellow or brown tints lower a diamond's value, you might associate blue tint with "the blue-ribbon prize" and yellow (or brown) tint with "a lemon." The association makes it easy for the audience to remember that the best diamond gets the "blue ribbon," and the worst diamond is a "lemon."

acronyms
words formed from initial letters of each of the successive parts of a compound term, common words made up of the first letters of objects or concepts, or sentences made up of words whose initial letters signal something else.

association
the tendency for one thought to stimulate recall of another, similar thought.

© Reuters NewMedia Inc./CORBIS

How do mnemonic devices help audiences remember information?

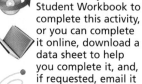

synonyms
words that have the same or nearly the same meanings.

antonyms
words that have opposite meanings.

Methods of Informing

Now that you understand the fundamental principles of informative speaking, we will describe specific methods used to inform. We can inform through definition, demonstration (or process explanation), or exposition. Each of these methods can be thought of as a type of informative speech or as an informative development skill. When you use one of these methods as the pattern for arranging your main points, it is a type of informative speech. When you use one of these methods to develop one main point and a different one to develop another main point, it can be thought of as a skill. Let's look more closely at each of these patterns.

Definition

One way to inform is through carefully defining a concept whether that concept is the topic or a key term used in the speech. For instance, the speech you read in Web Resource 17.2: Change Agents was entirely devoted to defining what "an effective change agent" is. Occasionally you may give a speech like that one whose sole purpose is to define a concept. But it is more likely that you will develop extended definitions or provide short definitions in the speeches you give.

Short definitions Short definitions clarify concepts in just a few words. Effective speakers are skillful at defining a term by using synonym and antonym, classification and differentiation, use or function, and etymological references.

1. **Synonyms and antonyms.** Using a synonym or an antonym is the quickest way to define a word, giving an approximate, if not exact, meaning in a single word or phrase. **Synonyms** are words that have the same or nearly the same meanings; **antonyms** are words that have opposite meanings. Defining by synonym is defining by association: For a word that does not bring up an immediate concrete meaning, we provide one that does. Synonyms for *prolix* include *long, wordy,* and *verbose.* Its antonyms are *short* and *concise.* Synonyms are not duplicates for the word being defined, but they do give a good idea of what the word means. Of course, the synonym or antonym must be familiar to the audience or its use defeats its purpose.

2. **Classification and differentiation.** When you define by classification, you give the boundaries of the particular idea and focus on the single feature that differentiates that idea from others that are similar. Most dictionary definitions are of the classification and differentiation variety. For instance, a dog may be defined as "a carnivorous, domesticated mammal of the family Canidae." "Carnivorous," "mammal," and "family

Canidae" limit the boundaries to dogs, jackals, foxes, and wolves. "Domesticated" differentiates dogs from the other three.

3. **Use or function.** A third short way to define is by explaining the use or function of the object or idea. Thus, when you say "A *plane* is a hand-powered tool that is used to smooth the edges of boards" or "A *scythe* is a piece of steel shaped in a half circle with a handle attached that is used to cut weeds or high grass," you are defining tools by indicating their use. Similarly, when you state "Education is the process of acquiring knowledge," you are defining how it functions.

4. **Etymology. Etymology** is the history or derivation of a particular word. Because meanings of words change over time, a description of the origin of a word may reveal very little about modern meaning. In some instances, however, the history of a word used to represent an idea adds insight that can help the audience understand the richness of the idea. For instance, in explaining why some people object to filling out a census form, a speaker might draw on the etymology of the word *censor*. A censor was originally one of two Roman magistrates appointed to take the census and, later, to supervise public morals. So even today, some people fear that the information from a census may be used to censor. *The Oxford English Dictionary* is an excellent source for discovering the etymology of words.

etymology
the history or derivation of a particular word.

5. **Making abstract ideas concrete.** Some ideas are intangible, they can't be directly seen, heard, touched, tasted, or smelled, so they can be difficult for an audience to understand unless we do something to make them **concrete,** able to be understood by the senses. Consider the concept *just*. In a speech we might begin by defining it by synonym: "You are being *just* in your dealings with another when you deal *honorably* and *fairly*." But "honorably" and "fairly" are equally abstract terms. So we add, "If Paul and Mary do the same amount of work and we reward them by giving them an equal amount of money, our dealings will be just; if, on the other hand, we give Paul more money because he's a man, our dealings will be unjust or unfair." Now we have taken the abstract concept of justice and made it concrete by giving an example that compares just to unjust behavior. For some concepts, a single example or comparison will be enough to clarify the concept, but for others several examples or comparisons may be needed.

concrete
able to be understood by the senses.

Extended definitions Sometimes understanding the definition of a concept is so important to a speech that it becomes a main point or the specific goal of the entire speech. In these cases the speaker will develop extended definitions.

An extended definition begins with a single-sentence dictionary definition or stipulated definition. For example, *Webster's Third New International Dictionary* defines *jazz* as "American music characterized by improvisation, syncopated rhythms, contrapuntal ensemble playing, and special melodic features peculiar to the individual interpretation of the player." This definition suggests four characteristics ("improvisation," "syncopation," "ensemble," and "special melodies") that could be the main points of a speech.

In a speech of definition or when using extended definition as the method for developing a main point, the key is to describe and explain the concept using examples, illustrations, comparisons, personal experiences, and observations.

Process Explanation or Demonstration

In many informative speeches a process needs to be explained or demonstrated. You may want to explain the process of how something is done, made, or works. For instance, a loan officer might explain the steps in applying for a mortgage. An engineer may describe how a turbojet works, or an author might discuss the process of writing a book. Whereas a process explanation verbally describes the steps and may use visual aids, a demonstration involves a live, hands-on visual portrayal of the process. So a **demonstration** is an explanation of a process accompanied by a physical exhibition of its steps. For example, during a popular cooking show on TV the chef demonstrates how to prepare a particular dish. A computer trainer might demonstrate how to use a new piece of software, or a golfer might demonstrate how to hold a club. Sometimes a demonstration will be a real-time hands-on enactment of each step in the process; at other times there is a partial demonstration with visual aids that depict parts of the process that are not physically enacted.

Effective process explanations or demonstrations require speakers to have carefully delineated the steps and the order in which they occur. Then speakers need to develop concrete explanations of each step.

When the process is a simple one, such as how to get more power on a forehand table tennis shot, you may want to try a **complete demonstration,** going through the complete process in front of the audience. If so, practice until you can do it smoothly and easily under the pressure of facing an actual audience. Because the actual demonstration is likely to take longer than in practice (you are likely to have to make some modifications during the speech to enable everyone in the room to see the demonstration), you may want to make sure that the final practice is somewhat shorter than the maximum time limit you will have for the speech.

For a relatively complicated process, you may want to consider the **modified demonstration,** in which you complete various stages of the demonstration at home and do only part of the actual work in front of the audience. Suppose you were going to demonstrate construction of a floral display. Actually performing the construction from scratch is too complex and time-consuming for a speech-length presentation. Instead, you could prepare a complete set of materials to begin the demonstration, a mock-up

demonstration
an explanation of a process accompanied by a physical exhibition of its steps.

complete demonstration
going through the complete process in front of the audience.

modified demonstration
various stages of the demonstration are completed at home and only part of the actual work is shown in front of the audience.

© David H. Wells/CORBIS

A carefully prepared and well-organized demonstration can help listeners retain information. At times, it could save a life.

of the basic floral triangle, and a completed floral display. During the speech, you would describe the materials needed and then begin demonstrating how to make the basic floral triangle. Rather than trying to get everything together perfectly in a few seconds, you could remove, from a bag or some concealed place, a partially completed arrangement illustrating the floral triangle. You would then use this in your demonstration, adding flowers as if you were planning to complete it. Then, from another bag, you could remove the completed arrangement to illustrate one of the effects you were discussing. Conducting a modified demonstration of this type is often easier than trying to complete an entire demonstration in a limited time.

Throughout a demonstration, speak slowly and repeat key ideas often. We learn best by doing, so if you can include audience participation, you may be even more successful. In a speech on origami, or Japanese paper folding, you could explain the principles, then pass out paper and have audience members each make a figure. Actual participation will increase interest and ensure recall. Finally, through other visual aids, you could show how these principles are used in more elaborate projects.

Although your audience may be able to visualize a process through vivid word pictures (in fact, in your impromptu explanations in ordinary conversation, it is the only way you can proceed), most effective process explanations and demonstrations use visual aids. More than with any other kind of informative speech, carefully prepared visual materials are essential to listeners' understanding in demonstration or process speeches.

Exposition

Throughout history, people have had an insatiable need to know. Unanswered questions stimulate research; research yields facts; and facts, when properly ordered and developed, yield understanding. Exposition is the method used to present information that explains complex ideas.

Although any speech of explanation is in a sense an expository speech, in this section an **expository speech** is defined as one that seeks to provide in-depth information about a complex idea gleaned through careful research. For example, "the causes and consequences of not finishing high school" "the sects of Islam," and "the origin and classifications of nursery rhymes" are all examples of topics for expository speaking.

expository speech
a speech that provides in-depth information about a complex idea gleaned through careful research.

Criteria for Evaluating Informative Speeches

In this chapter, we have been looking at the principles of informative speaking and methods for informing. Many of the general criteria for evaluating public speaking presented in Chapter 16 apply to informative speeches, but the primary criteria include specific elements that are critical to audience understanding and memory. Figure 17.3 provides a checklist for critical evaluation of an informative speech. The general criteria section highlights elements necessary for any effective speech.

Check all items that were accomplished effectively.

Primary Criteria
____ 1. Was the specific goal designed to increase audience information?
____ 2. Did the speaker show creativity in idea development?
____ 3. Was the information intellectually stimulating?
____ 4. Did the speaker show the relevance of the information?
____ 5. Did the speaker emphasize the information?
____ 6. Were the methods used to present the information appropriate for the ideas presented?

General Criteria
____ 1. Was the specific goal clear?
____ 2. Was the introduction effective?
____ 3. Were the main points clear?
____ 4. Was the conclusion effective?
____ 5. Was the language clear, vivid, and emphatic?
____ 6. Was the speech delivered enthusiastically, with vocal expressiveness, spontaneously, fluently, and with eye contact?

Evaluate the speech as (check one):
____ excellent ____ good ____ average ____ fair ____ poor

Figure 17.3
Informative speech critique checklist

Test Your Competence ▶

An Informative Speech

1. Follow the speech plan action steps to prepare an informative speech. Your instructor will announce the time limit and other parameters for this assignment.
2. Criteria for evaluation include all the general criteria of topic and purpose, content, organization, presentation, but special emphasis will be placed on how intellectually stimulating the topic is made for the audience, how creatively ideas are presented, how well the relevance of this topic for the audience is conveyed, and how clearly the important information is emphasized. Use the informative speech critique checklist in Figure 17.3 to critique yourself as you practice your speech.
3. Prior to presenting your speech, prepare a complete sentence outline and source list (bibliography) as well as a written plan for adapting your speech to the audience. If you have used Speech Builder Express to complete the action step activities online, you will be able to print out a copy of your completed outline and source list. Your adaptation plan should describe how you plan to verbally and visually adapt your material to the audience and should address how you will (1) establish common ground, (2) build and maintain audience interest, (3) adjust to the audience's knowledge and sophistication, (4) build speaker credibility, (5) adapt to audiences' attitudes toward your speech goal, (6) adapt to audiences from different cultures and language communities (if relevant for you in this speech), and (7) use visual aids to enhance audience understanding and memory.

Sample Speech: Women in World War II, by Lindsey Degenhardt*

This section presents a sample informative expository speech adaptation plan, outline, and transcript given by a student in an introductory speaking course.

1. Review the outline and adaptation plan developed by Lindsey Degenhardt in preparing her speech on women in World War II.

2. Then read the transcript of Lindsey's speech.

3. Use the informative speech critique checklist from Figure 17.3 to help you evaluate this speech.

4. Use your Communicate! CD ROM to watch a video clip of Lindsey presenting her speech in class. Click on the "Speech Interactive" icon in the menu at left, then click on "Speech Menu" in the menu bar at the top of the screen. Select "Informative Speech: Women in WWII" to watch the video (it takes a minute for the video to load).

5. Write a paragraph of feedback to Lindsey describing the strengths of her presentation and what you think she might do next time to be more effective.

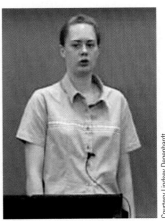
Courtesy Lindsey Degenhardt

*Delivered in speech class at the University of Cincinnati. Used with permission of Lindsey Degenhardt.

You can use your Communicate! CD-ROM to prepare your critique checklist and your feedback, then compare your answers to those of the authors'. To complete the checklist electronically, click on "Evaluation" in the menu bar at the top of the screen. To prepare your feedback electronically, click on "Analysis" in the menu bar. To compare your answers to those provided by the authors, click the "Done" button.

You can also use your Student Workbook to complete this activity, or you can complete it online, print a copy of the Informative Speech Critique Checklist, and, if requested, email your work to your instructor. Access Skill Learning Activity 17.3.

Adaptation Plan

1. **Speaking directly to members of the audience:** I will use rhetorical questions and personal pronouns to show audience I am talking to them directly.

2. **Building credibility:** I will use documented sources to show that I have good information, and I will use an example of my grandmother's experience to show that I have personal knowledge of events.

3. **Getting and maintaining interest:** Since the audience interest level will not be high, I will compare the 1940s to now and show that some of the fads now are the same as the fads then. I will try to show that although World War II happened a long time ago, the results have affected our current culture. I will also try to make my delivery enthusiastic.

4. **Facilitating understanding:** I will present the information clearly. I will use repetition and transitions to make my points clearer. I will also use examples and show visual aids.

5. **Increasing retention:** I will repeat my main points three times throughout the speech, in the introduction, in the body, and in the conclusion. I will use sectional transitions to reinforce retention of main points. I will tell stories and use visual aids to help the audience retain the information. I will also tell how the 1940s have had an impact on our culture today.

6. **Visual aids:** I will show graphs to help my audience understand.

Speech Outline

Specific Goal: I would like the audience to understand the three ways that women helped the war effort during World War II.

Introduction
    I. Do you think that World War II happened so long ago that it has no effect on us now?

II. Some of our music is based on 1940s swing, and several recent movies are based on 1940s events

III. Today I am going to share with you the roles that women played during World War II.

Thesis Statement: Three ways in which women helped the war effort during World War II were by working at home, working outside of the home, and enlisting in the military.

Body

I. One way in which women helped the war effort was by working at home.
  A. Women rationed food and supplies.
    1. They cut back on their use of sugar, canned goods, silk, and gasoline.
    2. They donated their pots and pans.
  B. Women planted "Victory Gardens."

(Now that we have seen how women helped from their homes, let's see how they helped outside of their homes.)

II. A second way in which women helped the war effort was by working outside of the home.
  A. Before the war, only 20% of women, about 13 million, worked outside the home.
  B. During the war, the number increased dramatically.
    1. By 1945, almost 19 million women were working.
    2. Women made up 40% of the workforce in aircraft assembly in 1944.

(We have now seen how women helped the war effort by getting jobs. Let me tell you the third way in which women helped.)

III. A third way in which women helped the war effort was by enlisting in the military.
  A. The Army and Navy Nurse Corps were started in the early 1900s.
    1. During World War II, 31.3% of all active nurses were women.
  B. By January 1943, all of the branches of the United States military included women.
    1. There were three positions that women could be trained in: radio operators, storekeepers, and secretaries.
    2. To be in the WAVES, women had to meet higher standards and be older than males to enlist.
    3. My grandmother was in the WAVES, the women's branch of the Navy.

Conclusion

I. Women helped at home, at work, and in the military.
II. If women had not helped in the war, there might not be so many women enrolled in college right now.

Sources

Creedy, Brooks Spive, *Women Behind the Lines.* New York: The Women's Press, 1949.

Hartmann, Susan M., *Home Front and Beyond.* Boston: Twain Publishers, 1982.

Historical Statistics of the United States Colonial Times to 1957. U.S. Bureau of the Census.

O'Neill, William L., *A Democracy at War.* New York: The Free Press, 1993.

Statistical Abstract of the United States. U. S. Census Bureau, 2000.

Stein, Conrad R., *World at the Home Front.* Chicago: Children's Press, 1986.

Weatherford, Doris, *American Women and World War II.* New York: Facts on File, 1990.

Speech and Analysis

Speech	Analysis
When someone mentions World War II, do you groan and think, "I don't want to hear about World War II, that happened such a long time ago and it doesn't have anything to do with me"?	Lindsey begins her speech with a rhetorical question.
Did you know that swing dancing and swing music similar to that played by Big Daddy Little Daddy was popular in the 1940s? Even some recent movies such as *Pearl Harbor* are based on 1940s events.	Her goal in this part of the introduction is to get the class to wondering what she is going to talk about in the speech.
Since so many more movies are portraying the roles that men played during the war, I'm going to share with you the roles women played during World War II. There are three ways in which women helped the war effort during World War II. They worked at home, worked outside of the home, and enlisted in the military.	After stating her goal, Lindsey clearly previews the three ways women helped the war effort.
The first way in which women helped the war effort was by working at home. To help the soldiers, women rationed food and supplies. They cut back on their use of sugar, canned goods, soap, and	Here Lindsey states her first main point, that women worked at home. Then she gets on to her first subpoint, that women rationed food and supplies. This subpoint needed to be stated more specifi-

Speech

gasoline. The canned goods and sugar went to feed the soldiers. The soap was used to make parachutes. And the gasoline was used to fuel tanks and airplanes. When the military had a shortage of aluminum, women donated pots and pans so that the military could make tanks, planes, and artillery.

Another way in which women helped at home was—they grew Victory Gardens. Victory Gardens are just normal vegetable gardens, um carrots, beans, cucumbers—that sort of thing.

But the reason that women planted these was they thought that if they grew their own food, they wouldn't buy so much food from the store, and the surplus could be used to feed the soldiers.

Now that we've seen how women helped from their homes, let's see how they helped outside of their homes.

A second way in which women helped the war effort was working outside of their homes. Before the war started, not very many women were employed. According to the New York Census, less than 14 million women were employed in 1940 compared to 42 million men. When women worked during this time they were usually teachers, secretaries, or librarians. But during the war a lot of men were either drafted or enlisted, so a lot of the factory jobs opened up, and no one but women were there to work. So women became crane operators, hydraulic press operators, tractor drivers, and miners.

Analysis

cally. She then supports this point with specific examples.

Now she states her second subpoint more clearly than the first: that women helped by growing Victory Gardens.

Notice how she explains how this was important to the war effort.

"Now that we've seen . . ." is a good transition to the second main point.

Here Lindsey clearly states her second main point. She develops her point by showing how women stepped in to do jobs that were held by the men who were drafted or who enlisted.

Speech

According to Conrad Stein, author of *World at the Home Front,* by 1944 40% of the workforce was made up of women and 12% in shipyards. In 1945, 19 million women worked compared to 46 million men.

So now the ratio is getting a little closer. And compare that to today when 65 million women worked in 1999 compared to 75 million men.

Now we have seen how women helped on the home front by getting jobs, let me tell you about another way women helped.

A third way that women helped the war effort was by enlisting in the military. In the early 1900s the Army/Navy Nurse Corps was started. And according to Susan Hartmann, author of *Home Front and Beyond,* during World War II, 31.3% of all active nurses were women. And Doris Weatherford, author of *American Women and World War II,* stated in her book that by January 1943 all of the branches of the United States military included women. Now not only could they be nurses, they could also be radio operators, secretaries, and storekeepers. But although women were now allowed in the military, they had to be of higher standards and also had to be older to enlist. And they couldn't actually use guns and fight in other countries.

For instance, my grandmother was in WAVES and she was positioned in Texas. But she couldn't be, even though she went to two years of college, she couldn't be a commissioned officer. She had to have a degree to be a commissioned

Analysis

In this section she documents the statistics she uses to develop her main point.

Here Lindsey creates a clear transition to her third main point.

She now clearly states her third main point.

In this section she gives examples of the kinds of roles women filled in the military to help free men to engage in the fighting.

Here Lindsey presents the ironic point that although women did the necessary work, they were prevented from becoming commissioned officers.

Speech

officer—but she was a noncommissioned officer.

On January 26, 1945, Japan surrendered. This defeat might not have been possible without the help of women at home, at work, and in the military. Not only did women have an effect on the outcome of the war, women also, the women of the '40s also had an effect on our culture today. Because if women had just gone back to their housewife positions after working in factories there might not be so many women with college degrees today.

Analysis

After a short review of the three roles women fulfilled, she concludes with a statement that shows that doing this kind of work opened many occupational possibilities for women from then on.

This is a very good expository speech. She has a good introduction that captures attention and leads into the speech; she gives three clearly stated and well-developed main points using high-quality information; and she provides a good conclusion that not only summarizes the main points but also shows the effects of their efforts on our culture today.

What Would You Do? ▶ A QUESTION OF ETHICS

 fter class, as Gina and Paul were discussing what they intended to talk about for their first speeches, Paul said, "I think I'm going to talk about the Mayan ruins."

"That sounds interesting, Paul, but I didn't know that you were a history buff."

"I'm not. But Gina, the way I see it, Professor Henderson will really be impressed with my speech because my topic will be so academic."

"That may be," Gina replied, "but didn't he stress that for the first speech we should talk about a topic that was important to us and that we knew a lot about?"

"Right," Paul said sarcastically, "he wants to hear me talk about basketball? Not on your life. Trust me on this one—when I get the good grade, you'll know what I mean."

1. Is Paul's proposed behavior unethical? Why?

2. What should Gina say to challenge Paul's last statement?

▮ Summary

Informative speeches are those in which the primary goal is to create understanding. As an informative speaker, your rhetorical challenge is to present information in a way that facilitates attending, understanding, and remembering.

To accomplish these goals, speakers must master several principles. Audiences are more likely to show interest in, understand, and remember information (1) if they perceive it to be intellectually stimulating, (2) if it is presented creatively, (3) if they perceive it to be relevant, and (4) if it is emphasized.

New information has even greater impact when it is perceived as being novel. Productive thinking stimulates creativity that enables speakers to present information in new ways. Information is perceived as relevant if it is vital or important. Information is likely to be remembered if it is repeated, if it is introduced with external transitions, if it is associated, or if it is presented humorously.

Methods of informing include defining, demonstrating or explaining, and explicating complex ideas that are based on extensive research. Defining is giving the meaning of a word or concept through classification and differentiation, synonym and antonym, use and function, or etymology. Defining can be enhanced with the use of examples and comparisons. Demonstrating or explaining a process provides step-by-step information on how something is done, made, or works. Both demonstrations and explanation of process require visual aids. Exposition is an in-depth presentation of well-researched information relating to a complex idea. Expository speeches require careful attention and creativity to ensure that the information presented is understood and remembered by the audience.

Communicate! Online

N ow that you have read Chapter 17, use your Communicate! CD-ROM for quick access to the electronic resources that accompany this text. Your CD-ROM gives you access to the video of Lindsey's speech on pages 456–459, InfoTrac College Edition, and the Communicate! Web site. When you get to the Communicate! home page, click on "Student Book Companion Site" in the Resource box at right to access the online study aids for this chapter, including a digital glossary, review quizzes, chapter activities, and chapter Web Resources.

Key Terms

At the Communicate! Web site, select the chapter resources for Chapter 17. Print a copy of the glossary for this chapter and test yourself with the electronic flash cards or complete the crossword puzzle to help you master these key terms:

intellectually stimulating (438)	mnemonics (446)	concrete (449)
creativity (440)	acronyms (447)	demonstration (450)
reproductive thought (441)	association (447)	complete demonstration (450)
productive thought (441)	synonyms (448)	modified demonstration (450)
relevance (443)	antonyms (448)	expository speech (452)
vital information (444)	etymology (449)	

Review Quiz

Test your knowledge of the concepts in this chapter by taking the online quiz at the Communicate! Web site. Select the chapter resources for Chapter 17, then click on "Review Quiz." When you have completed the quiz, submit it for scoring.

Skill Learning Activities

Complete the Observe & Analyze, Test Your Competence, and Speech and Analysis activities for Chapter 17 online at the Communicate! Web site. Select the chapter resources for Chapter 17, then click on "Activities." You can submit your Observe & Analyze and Speech and Analysis answers to your instructor, and compare your Test Your Competence and Speech and Analysis answers to those provided by the authors.

17.1: Test Your Competence: Creating Through Productive Thinking (443)
17.2: Observe & Analyze: Techniques to Emphasize Important Information (448)
17.3: Speech and Analysis: Women in World War II, by Lindsey Degenhardt (453)

Web Resources

Access the Web Resources for this chapter online at the Communicate! Web site. Select the chapter resources for Chapter 17, then click on "Web Resources."

17.1: Thinking Like a Genius (441)
17.2: Change Agents (448)

OBJECTIVES

After you have read this chapter, you should be able to answer these questions:

- What is the difference between affecting attitudes and beliefs and moving to action?
- What is the value of assessing audience attitude toward the goal?
- What are good reasons?
- What kinds of material give support to reasons?
- What are some common fallacies?
- What are typical persuasive speaking organizational patterns?
- What does a persuasive speaker do to motivate an audience?
- What are major ethical guidelines?

18

Persuasive Speaking

er audience seemed enchanted by her every word. As she finished her speech, the entire audience rose as a body and cheered. Over the din, the chair shouted, "All those in favor, say 'aye,'" and as one everyone roared "aye" as a testament to her lucid and persuasive argument. As she walked to her seat, people reached to pat her on the back, and those who could not touch her chanted her name: "Sheila . . . Sheila . . . !"

"Sheila! Wake up," Denny said as he shook her shoulder, "you're supposed to be working on your speech."

persuasive speaking
a process of influencing an audience to feel, believe, or act in accord with the position advocated by the speaker.

erhaps you've been stirred by an issue and imagined yourself giving a rousing speech that your audience cheered wildly and that moved them to act. Although it is easy to fantasize this scenario, our real-life attempts to persuade require careful planning and diligent preparation. **Persuasive speaking** is a process of influencing an audience to feel, believe, or act in accord with the position advocated by the speaker. It is perhaps the most demanding speech challenge. In this chapter we begin by explaining each of the principles of persuasive speaking and then we describe methods or organizational patterns that are commonly used in forming persuasive speeches.

Principles of Persuasive Speaking

The following principles focus on what you can do to increase the probability of being an effective persuasive speaker.

Write a Specific Goal

Principle 1: You are more likely to persuade audience members when you can articulate specifically what you want your audience to believe or do.

Your persuasive speeches are likely to be designed to establish or change beliefs or to move to action. Although a speech goal that is phrased *to establish or change a belief* may result in having listeners act upon that belief, your primary emphasis is on having them agree with you that the belief you present is reasonable. Here are some goal statements written specifically to seek audience acceptance of a belief:

> I want my audience to believe that the city should build a downtown entertainment center.

> I want my audience to believe that small schools are better for insecure students than are large schools.

> I want my audience to believe that recycling is necessary to reduce waste.

Notice that in each case you would be advocating what you want the audience to *believe*—not what audience members should *do* as a result of that belief.

Speeches designed to *move an audience to action* go beyond gaining agreement on a belief—they state exactly what you want your audience to do. Here are some goal statements that seek action.

> I want my audience to donate money to the food bank drive.

> I want the members of my audience to write to their congressional representative to support legislation in favor of gun control.

> I want my audience members to attend the school's production of *Grease*.

Audience Attitude

Principle 2: You are more likely to be able to persuade when you direct your goal and your information to the audience's attitude.

Persuasion is more likely to take place when your arguments are fitted to the initial attitude of members of your audience, so it is crucial to assess the direction and strength of audience members' attitudes before you speak. An **attitude** is "a general or enduring positive or negative feeling about some person, object, or issue" (Petty & Cacioppo, 1996, p. 7). People's attitudes are usually expressed verbally as **opinions.** Thus, saying "I think physical fitness is important" is an opinion that reflects a favorable attitude about physical fitness.

Because much of the success of a speech depends on determining how an audience is likely to react to your goal, you must find out where the audience stands. You make such judgments based on demographic information and opinion polls (see Chapter 12). The more data you have about your audience and the more experience you have in analyzing audiences, the better are your chances of judging audience attitudes accurately.

Audience attitudes (expressed by opinions) may be distributed along a continuum from highly favorable to hostile (Figure 18.1). Even though any given audience may have one or a few individuals' opinions at nearly every point along the distribution, audience opinion tends to cluster at a particular point. That cluster point represents the general audience attitude for that topic. Because it would be impossible to direct your speech to all the various shades of attitudes held by the members of your audience, you must classify audience attitude as predominantly "in favor" (already

attitude
a general or enduring positive or negative feeling about some person, object, or issue.

opinion
the verbal expression of a person's attitude.

© Thomson Higher Education

What type of audience would this be for a speaker whose goal was to convince them to abstain from premarital sex? What led you to your conclusion?

holding a particular belief), "no opinion" (uninformed, neutral, or apathetic), or "opposed" (holding an opposite point of view) so you can develop a strategy that adapts to that attitude.

Now let us consider specific strategies for adapting to audiences. Suppose your goal is written, "I want my audience to believe that they should alter their intake of saturated fats." As you will see, your assessment of audience attitude may affect how you phrase your goal and how you select your information.

In favor When your audience has a positive attitude toward your speech goal, your task is to reinforce their beliefs or motivate them to act. Because beliefs are spread along a continuum, an audience that is generally in favor of your specific goal may still need to be reminded of the reasons for holding this belief. The audience can become further committed to the belief by hearing additional or new arguments and evidence that support the belief. So, if your audience poll shows that most audience members accept the idea that lowering saturated fats reduces heart disease, then you may want to reinforce this belief by providing evidence from the most recent studies and theories. Some of your audience will be familiar with some of your arguments, but the current evidence you provide will reinforce and strengthen audience attitudes.

At times, if you believe your listeners strongly support your belief, then you may want to change your specific goal to motivating the audience to act on their belief. For instance, if members of your audience strongly support the idea that their intake of saturated fats will reduce heart disease, then you might change your specific goal to motivating them to adopt a specific diet that is low in saturated fats. When you believe your listeners are on your side, try to crystallize their attitudes, recommit them to a particular direction, or suggest a specific course of action that will serve as a rallying point. The presentation of a thoughtful and specific solution increases the likelihood of audience action.

No opinion If your audience analysis indicates that your listeners have no opinion about your specific goal, you will want to figure out whether it is because they are uninformed, neutral, or apathetic about your goal. This will enable you to choose arguments that are likely to move audiences to support your belief. If you find your audience has no opinion because it is *uninformed*, you will need to provide enough information to help your audience understand the subject before you develop persuasive appeals directed toward establishing a belief or moving your listeners to action. For

Figure 18.1
Opinion continuum

| Hostile | Opposed | Mildly opposed | Neither in favor nor opposed | Mildly in favor | In favor | Highly in favor (positive) |

Robert Brenner/PhotoEdit

Is it more challenging to try to change the attitude of a hostile audience or to persuade people who are neutral to give money to a cause?

instance, if you believe your audience is uninformed about the need to lower saturated fat intake, then early in the speech you need to define "saturated fat," talk about how cholesterol is formed, and share medical evidence about its effects on the human body. Then the audience will be equipped to listen to the arguments you make. Novice speakers sometimes spend so much time explaining the basics to an uninformed audience that they shortchange the time they can devote to developing the reasons for believing.

You may find that your audience is informed, but has no opinion because it is *neutral*. A neutral audience is able to reason objectively and accept sound reasoning. It is not prejudiced, holds no preconceived opinions, and is open minded. In this case, you will present the strongest arguments and support them with the best information you can find.

You may find that your audience members have no opinion because they are *apathetic*. An apathetic audience has no opinion because it is uninterested, unconcerned, or indifferent to your goal. To convince this audience type, you will begin by motivating them to recognize the importance or urgency of your topic. By using the adaptation technique of personalizing, members of an apathetic audience may begin to identify with your speech goal. For example, if members of your audience know what saturated fat is, know how cholesterol is formed, and even understand the medical information on negative effects, but do not seem to care, you can overcome their apathy by personalizing statistics, by choosing stories about people they can identify with, and by choosing material that is directed to your listeners' personal needs.

Opposed If you find that your listeners are opposed to your speech goal, then you need to determine whether their attitude is slightly negative or totally hostile. If you believe your listeners are *slightly opposed* to your goal, you can approach them directly with your arguments, hoping that the weight of your evidence will be sufficient to change their attitudes and swing them to your side. If your audience is slightly opposed to your goal of lowering their saturated fat intake by eliminating all fried foods, you can present good reasons and strong evidence to support the proposal.

If an audience is *mildly opposed* to your goal, you will want to present your arguments carefully so that you reduce your listeners' negative attitudes without arousing their hostility. Take care to present your arguments objectively, and make your case clearly enough that those members who are only mildly negative will consider the proposal and those who are very negative will at least understand your position.

If you believe your audience is *hostile* toward your specific speech goal, you will want to approach the topic indirectly or to consider a less ambitious goal. A complete shift in attitude or behavior as a result of one speech is probably unrealistic. Instead, you will want to present a modest proposal that seeks a slight change in attitude. With this strategy you will be able to get an audience to consider your arguments. In later speeches, you can try to move the audience further. For instance, suppose the audience is comprised of obese people who have tried diet after diet and who are "fed up" with appeals to restrict their food intake. Trying to convince them that they should eliminate all saturated fat from their diet would be a hopeless task. You might, however, convince them to avoid French fries cooked in animal fat.

Figure 18.2 summarizes the strategy choices we have reviewed for audiences with different attitudes toward your topic.

Give Good Reasons and Sound Evidence

Principle 3: You are more likely to persuade an audience when the body of your speech contains good reasons and strong evidence that support your specific speech goal.

Human beings take pride in being rational; we seldom do anything without some real or imagined grounds. Since the 1980s, persuasive speech theory has focused sharply on the cognitive activity (the way people think) that leads a person to be persuaded. Scholars believe that people form cognitive structures or "mental maps" that guide them as they understand and create meaning from their experiences (Deaux, Dane, & Wrightsman, 1993, p. 19). So, to influence audience members, effective speakers provide mental maps for the audience in the form of logical reasons.

reasons
statements that answer why you should believe or do something.

Finding reasons **Reasons** are statements that answer *why* you should believe or do something. For most persuasive speeches, you will discover many reasons that support your specific goal as you do your research. For example, for a specific goal phrased "I want the audience to believe that home ownership should be encouraged," you might uncover these six reasons:

Figure 18.2
Adapting persuasive speech strategies to audience attitudes

AUDIENCE ATTITUDES		STRATEGY CHOICES
If audience members are ...	**then they may ...**	**and you can ...**
Highly in favor	■ be ready to act	■ provide practical suggestions
		■ put emphasis on motivation rather than on information and reasoning
In favor	■ already share many of your beliefs	■ crystallize and reinforce existing beliefs and attitudes to lead them to a course of action
Mildly in favor	■ be inclined to accept your view, but with little commitment	■ strengthen positive beliefs by emphasizing supporting reasons
Neither in favor nor opposed	■ be uninformed	■ emphasize information relevant to a belief or move to action
	■ be neutral	■ emphasize reasons relevant to belief or action
	■ be apathetic	■ concentrate on motivating them to see the importance of the proposition or seriousness of the problem
Mildly opposed	■ have doubts about the wisdom of your position	■ give them reasons and evidence that will help them to consider your position
Opposed	■ have beliefs and attitudes contrary to yours	■ emphasize sound arguments
		■ concentrate on shifting beliefs rather than on moving to action
		■ be objective to avoid arousing hostility
Hostile	■ be totally unreceptive to your position	■ plant the "seeds of persuasion"
		■ try to get them to understand your position

Observe&Analyze

A Specific Goal Statement in a Persuasive Speech

The goal of this activity is to find and analyze a specific goal statement.
1. Use your Communicate! CD-ROM to access Web Resource 18.1: Maintaining the Faith and read "Terrorism and Islam: Maintaining the Faith," a speech by Mahathir Bin Mohamad, Prime Minister of Malaysia, given at the OIC Conference of Ministers of Endowments and Islamic Affairs, May 7, 2002. This speech is available through InfoTrac College Edition. Identify the specific goal statement.
2. Given the composition of the audience, what do you think their initial attitude was toward the speaker's position?
3. Write a paragraph in which you analyze this goal statement. What type of specific speech goal is this? Does this goal seem appropriate for this audience? Explain your reasoning.

You can complete this activity online and, if requested, email it to your instructor. Use your Communicate! CD-ROM to access Skill Learning Activity 18.1.

I. Home ownership builds strong communities.
II. Home ownership reduces crime.
III. Home ownership increases individual wealth.
IV. Home ownership increases individual self-esteem.
V. Home ownership improves the value of a neighborhood.
VI. Home ownership is growing in the suburbs.

Once you have a list of possible reasons, you will weigh and evaluate them in order to select the three or four that will create the best mental map for your audience. You can use the following criteria to evaluate the reasons that you uncover.

1. **Is the reason supportable?** Some reasons that sound impressive are not supported with facts. For example, the first reason, "Home ownership builds strong communities," sounds like a good one; but what facts can you find to support it directly? What is a strong community? The only evidence that you may have for reasons like this are the opinions of prominent people. If your research has revealed little systematic study to verify the claim, you will want to look for reasons with stronger support.

2. **Is the reason relevant to the position advocated in the speech goal?** Sometimes statements look like reasons, but closer inspection reveals that they are unrelated or tangential to proving the position you are advocating. For instance, "Home ownership is growing in the suburbs" may sound like a reason for encouraging home ownership, but why home ownership growth in suburbs should be a reason to support home ownership is a mystery. If a reason does not provide a direct rationale for believing or acting in accord with your position, it is not a reason for this speech.

3. **Will the reason have an impact on the intended audience?** Suppose you have a great deal of factual evidence to back up the statement "Home ownership encourages self-esteem." Even if it is a well-supported reason, it will not be convincing if the majority of the audience are bankers who find self-esteem arguments bogus. On the other hand, it might be a compelling reason to an audience that includes many people who are in the helping professions.

The Spotlight on Scholars feature discusses Richard Petty's research on attitude change and behavior.

Finding evidence to support your reasons By themselves, reasons are only unsupported statements. Some reasons are self-explanatory and occasionally have a persuasive effect without further support, but most listeners expect reasons to be backed up by facts and expert opinions before they will accept or act on them.

The strongest support for a reason is verifiable facts. Suppose you are giving a speech whose goal is to motivate audience members to donate money for Alzheimer's research. If you give the reason "Alzheimer's disease is a major killer," the follow-up statement, "According to statistics presented in an article in a recent issue of the *Journal of the American Medical Association,* Alzheimer's disease is the fourth leading cause of death for adults," is factual support.

Expert opinions are supporting statements from people who have good reputations for their knowledge on the subject. An example of expert opinion in support of the reason "Alzheimer's disease is a major killer" is the statement, "According to the Surgeon General, 'By 2050 Alzheimer's disease may afflict 14 million people a year.'"

Spotlight on Scholars ▶ Richard Petty

Professor of Psychology, the Ohio State University, on Attitude Change

As an undergraduate political science major, Richard Petty got so interested in how people change their attitudes that he chose to minor in psychology where he could not only take more courses in attitude change but also learn empirical research methods. He then decided to go on to graduate work in psychology at the Ohio State University, focusing his studies on attitude change and persuasion. Like many scholars, the subject of his doctoral dissertation—attitude change induced by persuasive communications—laid the foundation for a career of research.

When Petty began his research, the psychological scholarship of the previous forty years had been unable to demonstrate a relationship between people's attitudes and their behavior. Petty believed this was because some attitudes were consistently related to behavior but other attitudes were not. The key was to understand how attitudes were formed and which processes led to strong rather than weak attitudes. Now Petty's work is in the forefront of scholars who have demonstrated that attitude change and behavior are in fact related, but in a complex way.

During the last twenty years, Petty has published scores of research articles on his own and with colleagues on various aspects of attitude and persuasion to find out under what circumstances attitudes affect behavior. His work with various collaborators has been so successful that he has gained international acclaim. Not only have many of his works been published worldwide, but the theory of the Elaboration Likelihood Model (ELM) of persuasion that he developed in collaboration with John Cacioppo has become the most cited theoretical approach to attitude and persuasion.

In its most basic form, Petty and Cacioppo's theory says that attitude change is likely to occur from one of just two relatively distinct "routes to persuasion." The first type, the central route, occurs as a result of a person's careful and thoughtful consideration of the true merits of the information presented in support of a claim. The second type, the

peripheral route, occurs as a result of simple cues in the persuasion context (such as an attractive source) that induce change without necessitating scrutiny of the central merits of the claim. Following their initial speculation about these two routes to persuasion, Petty and Cacioppo developed, researched, and refined the theory supporting the ELM.

The ELM "is a theory about the processes responsible for attitude change and the strength of the attitudes that result from those processes." The ELM hypothesizes that what is persuasive to a person and how lasting any attitude change is likely to be are dependent on how motivated and able people are to assess the merits of a speaker, an issue, or a position. People who are highly motivated and are able to think are likely to study available information about the claim. As a result, they are more likely to arrive at a reasoned attitude that is well articulated and bolstered by information received via the central route. For people who are less motivated or able to study information related to the claim, attitude change can result from a number of less resource-demanding processes that do not require effortful evaluation of the relevant information. They are affected more by information through the peripheral route, but these attitude changes are likely to be weaker in endurance and prediction of behavior.

So what impact does Petty's research have on speakers who seek to persuade? First, speakers must recognize that attitude change is a result of a combination of choices of the means of persuasion as well as choices made by members of the audience on how deeply they wish to probe into the information. Using the ELM, speakers can better understand and predict the variables that will affect attitudes and the consequences of these attitudes. Thus sound reasons and supporting evidence adapted to audience needs should account for attitude change when listener thinking is expected to be deep. In contrast, apparent credibility and emotional images should be more likely to account for change when listener thinking is expected to be superficial. Moreover, the attitudes changed by considerable mental effort tend to be stronger than those changed by little thought.

This complexity of attitude change suggests that not only must a speaker have the necessary information to form well-constructed arguments, but the speaker must also have the artistic sense to understand important aspects of the audience (locus of belief, time constraints, interest, and so forth) and have the artistic power to, as Aristotle once said, use available means of persuasion effectively.

Where is Petty going from here? He will certainly continue working on aspects of attitude change because, as he says, "I never finish a project without discovering at least two unanswered questions arising from the research." In addition, in a series of studies with Duane Wegener, he is interested in finding out how people behave when they believe their judgments might have been inappropriate or biased.

Currently Petty teaches both graduate and undergraduate courses in attitudes and persuasion, research methods, and theories of social psychology. Petty has written scores of research articles and several books dealing with aspects of attitude, attitude change, and persuasion. For titles of several of his publications, see the references at the end of this book. For more information about Richard Petty and his work, go to http://www.psy.ohio-state.edu/petty/.

Whether the evidence you use to support your reason are facts or opinion, you will want to ask at least three questions to assure yourself that what you present is "good" evidence.

1. **What is the quality of the evidence?** This question includes assessing the sources of the evidence, the people who offered the opinions or compiled the facts as well as the reputation of the source in which they were reported. Just as some people's opinions are more reliable than others, so are some printed sources more reliable than others. If evidence comes from a person of questionable expertise or from an unreliable or biased source, seek additional verification of its accuracy from other sources, or don't use it in the speech.

2. **Is the evidence recent?** In general your audience is more likely to be persuaded when the evidence you offer represents the latest thinking and research on an issue. If you want to convince your audience that car exhaust represents the greatest threat to air quality, you are unlikely to convince them if the support you offer is based on ten-year-old data from the Environmental Protection Agency. A recent copyright date is no guarantee that information is current. Information in a book published today may be as much as five years out of date. Some magazines use old data that has been archived or is available without cost. So, as you gather support, you will want to uncover and use the most recent information you can find.

3. **Is the evidence relevant?** Don't be tempted to use an interesting "fact" that is only tangentially related to your reason. Using irrelevant information can lose the audience. Your task is to help them make the right mental map, so don't confuse them with an unnecessary detour. Make sure your evidence directly supports the reason. If it does not, leave it out of the speech.

Testing reasoning So far, we have concentrated on presenting good reasons and supporting them well. To test the validity of your reasoning more completely, however, look at the relationship between the reasons and the evidence given in support. When you do that, you can ask questions to test the logic of the reasoning.

Several kinds of reasoning links can be established between reasons and their evidence or between reasons, evidence, and the speech goal.

1. **Generalization from examples.** You are **reasoning by generalization from example** when you argue that what is true in some instances/examples (evidence) is true in all instances (conclusion). Generalization links are the basis for polls and predictions. For example, here is a statement of some factual evidence, "Tom, Jack, and Bill studied and got A's," and the conclusion based on it is "Anyone who studies will get an A." The reasoning link can be stated, "What is true in these representative instances will be true in all instances." To test this kind of argument, you should ask, "Were enough instances (examples) cited? Were the instances typical? Are negative instances accounted for? If the answer to any of these questions is "No," the reasoning is not sound.

2. **Causation.** You are **reasoning by causation** when your conclusion is presented as the effect of a single circumstance or set of circumstances. Causation links are among the most prevalent types of arguments you will discover. Here is an example: "We've had a very dry spring" (evidence); "The wheat crop will be lower than usual" (conclusion). The reasoning link can be stated, "The lack of sufficient rain causes a poor crop." To test this kind of argument, you should ask, "Are the conditions described by the data (evidence) alone important enough to bring about the particular conclusion? If we eliminate these conditions, would we eliminate the effect?" If the answer to one of these questions is "No," the reasoning is not sound. You can also ask, "Do some other conditions that accompany the ones cited in the evidence cause the effect?" If so, the reasoning is not sound.

3. **Analogy.** You are **reasoning by analogy** when your conclusion is the result of a comparison with a similar set of circumstances. Although reasoning by analogy is very popular, it is regarded as the weakest form of reasoning. The analogy link is often stated, "What is true or will work in one set of circumstances is true or will work

reasoning by generalization from example
arguing that what is true in some instances/examples (evidence) is true in all instances (conclusion).

reasoning by causation
presenting your conclusion as the effect of a single circumstance or set of circumstances.

reasoning by analogy
presenting your conclusion as the result of a comparison with a similar set of circumstances.

When the government makes manufacturers place warning labels on products, it is trying to influence consumers through reasoning by causation.

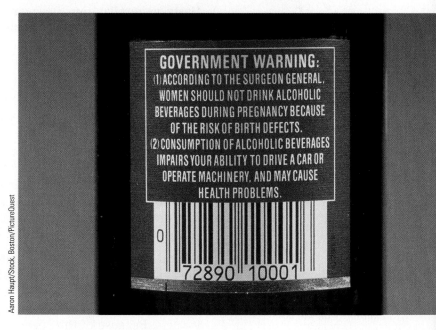

Aaron Haupt/Stock, Boston/PictureQuest

in a comparable set of circumstances." Here is an example: "Off-track betting has proved very effective in New York" (evidence); "off-track betting will prove effective in raising state revenues in Ohio" (conclusion). The reasoning link can be stated, "If something works in New York, it will work in Ohio because Ohio and New York are so similar." To test this kind of argument, you should ask, "Are the subjects really comparable? Are the subjects being compared really similar in all important ways?" If the answer to these questions is "No," the reasoning is not sound. You can also ask, "Are any of the ways that the subjects are dissimilar important to the conclusion?" If so, the reasoning is not sound.

reasoning by sign
basing your conclusion on the presence of observable data that usually or always accompany other unobserved variables.

4. **Sign.** You are **reasoning by sign** when your conclusion is based on the presence of observable data that usually or always accompany other unobserved variables. If, for example, you see longer lines at the downtown soup kitchen, the presence of that condition (longer lines) is usually or always an indicator of something else (the worsening of the recession), and we can predict the existence of this unobserved variable. Signs are often confused with causes, but signs are indications and sometimes effects, not causes. Longer lines at soup kitchens are a sign of the worsening recession. The longer lines may be an effect of a recession, but they do not cause the recession. To test this kind of argument, you should ask, "Do the data cited always or usually indicate the conclusion drawn? Are sufficient signs present?" If not, the reasoning is not sound.

Avoiding fallacies When you think you have finished constructing reasons, take a minute to make sure that you have not been guilty of any of the four common fallacies.

hasty generalization
presenting a generalization (perhaps a reason) that is either not supported with evidence or perhaps is supported with only one weak example.

1. **Hasty generalization.** Because the instances cited should represent most to all possibilities, enough must be cited to satisfy the listeners that the instances are not isolated or hand-picked. **Hasty generalization,** presenting a generalization (perhaps a reason) that is either not supported with evidence or perhaps is supported with only one weak example, is a very common fallacy of reasoning.

false cause
occurs when the alleged cause fails to be related to, or to produce, the effect.

2. **False cause. False cause** occurs when the alleged cause fails to be related to, or to produce, the effect. It is human nature to look for causes for events, but the tendency to identify and label something that happened or existed before the event or at the time of the event as the cause is often a fallacy. Think of the people who blame loss of money, sickness, and problems at work on black cats that ran in front of them or mirrors that broke or ladders they walked under. We recognize these as false cause superstitions.

appeal to authority
fallacy wherein the testimony is from a person who is not an authority on the issue.

3. **Appeal to authority.** Attempting to argue from authority can lead to the **appeal to authority** fallacy wherein the testimony is from a person who is not an authority on the issue. For instance, advertisers are well aware that the public idolizes athletes, movie stars, and television performers. Because of this, people are likely to accept the word of these

famous folks on subjects they may know little about. When a celebrity tries to get the viewer to purchase a car based on the celebrity's supposed "expert" knowledge, the argument is a fallacy.

4. **Ad hominem argument.** An **ad hominem argument** attacks the person making the argument rather than the argument itself. Literally, *ad hominem* means "to the man." For instance, if Bill Bradley, the former U.S. senator as well as former New York Knicks basketball player, presented the argument that athletics are important to the development of the total person, the reply "Great, all we need is some jock justifying his own existence" would be an example of an ad hominem argument.

Such a personal attack often is made as a smokescreen to cover a lack of good reasons and evidence. Ad hominem name-calling is used to try to encourage the audience to ignore a lack of evidence, and it is often used in political campaigns. Make no mistake, ridicule, name-calling, and other personal attacks are at times highly successful, but they are almost always fallacious.

ad hominem argument
attacks the person making the argument rather than the argument itself.

Motivation

Principle 4: You are more likely to persuade an audience when your language motivates them.

Reasoning provides a logical base for persuasion and a rationale for changing an audience's attitude: motivation brings an audience to action. **Motivation,** "forces acting on or within an organism to initiate and direct behavior" (Petri, 1996, p. 3), is often a result of incentives and emotional language.

motivation
forces acting on or within an organism to initiate and direct behavior.

Incentives An **incentive** is simply "a goal that satisfies a need" (Lefton, 2001, p. 210). Thus, if a speaker says that in addition to helping clean up the environment by collecting aluminum cans and glass and plastic bottles you can earn money by turning them in to a recycling center, you might see earning money for your efforts as an incentive to recycling.

incentive
a goal that satisfies a need.

For an incentive to have value, it must be meaningful. *Meaningfulness* involves an emotional reaction. Ordinarily, people pursue those objects, events, and experiences that are emotionally important for them. Recycling would be a meaningful goal for someone looking for ways to participate in cleaning up the environment but not for someone who does not care about the environment or about earning small amounts of money. An incentive is most powerful when it is part of a meaningful goal.

1. **Weighing incentives.** People are more likely to act when the speech goal presents incentives that outweigh costs. An incentive is "a goal objective that motivates" (Petri, 1996, p. 185). Incentives (rewards) include economic gain, good feelings, prestige, or other positive outcomes. Thus, if you can earn money by turning in cans and bottles to a recycling center, then you might see earning money as an incentive to recycle. Earning money may be a meaningful incentive for someone short of cash, but not

costs
units of expenditure such as time, energy, money, or other negative outcomes.

Observe&Analyze

Giving Good Reasons and Evidence

The goal of this activity is to analyze reasons and evidence.

1. Use your Communicate! CD-ROM to access Web Resource 18.1: Maintaining the Faith and read the speech "Terrorism and Islam: Maintaining the Faith" by Mahathir Bin Mohamad, available through InfoTrac College Edition. Identify each of the main points or reasons the speaker offers in support of his thesis.

2. Are his reasons "good"? Are they supported? Relevant? Adapted to the audience?

3. Analyze his supporting evidence. Assess the quality, currency, and relevance to his reasons.

4. Identify two kinds of reasoning links that he uses, and then test them using the appropriate questions. Are the links you tested logical? Explain.

5. Are there any fallacies that you can detect in his argument? Explain.

 You can complete this activity online and, if requested, email it to your instructor. Use your Communicate! CD-ROM to access Skill Learning Activity 18.2.

---

necessarily meaningful for someone who has money or who doesn't care about earning relatively small amounts of money.

People are more likely to be motivated by incentives (rewards) if they outweigh the costs. **Costs** are units of expenditure such as time, energy, money, or other negative outcomes.

According to Thibaut and Kelley (1986, p. 10), each of us seeks situations in which our behavior will yield us rewards in excess of the costs; or, conversely, each of us will continue our present behavior unless we are shown that either lower costs or higher rewards will come from changing a particular behavior. Consider an example. Suppose you are asking your audience to volunteer an hour a week to help adults learn to read. The time you are asking them to give is likely to be perceived as a cost rather than as an incentive; however, you may be able to describe volunteering in a way that is perceived as a reward, a meaningful incentive. That is, you may be able to get members of the audience to feel civic-minded, responsible, or helpful as a result of volunteering time for such a worthy cause. In the speech, if you can show that those rewards or incentives outweigh the cost, you can increase the likelihood of volunteering.

In your speech, then, you must achieve one of the following: (1) show that the time, energy, or money investment is small, or (2) show that the benefits in good feelings, prestige, economic gain, or other possible rewards are high.

2. **Using incentives to meet basic needs.** Many theorists who take a humanistic approach to psychology have argued that incentives are most powerful when they meet basic needs. One of the most popular needs theories is that of Abraham Maslow (1954). His theory suggests that people are more likely to act when a speaker's incentive satisfies a strong unmet need.

Maslow devised a hierarchy of needs that is particularly useful in providing a framework for needs analysis. Maslow divided basic human needs into seven categories arranged in a hierarchy that begins with the most fundamental needs. The seven categories are illustrated in Figure 18.3: physiological needs, including food, drink, and life-sustaining temperature; safety and security needs, including long-term survival and stability; belongingness and love needs, including the need to identify with friends, loved ones, and family; esteem needs, including the quest for material goods, recognition, and power or influence; cognitive needs, including the need for knowledge and understanding; aesthetic needs, including the need for order and beauty; and self-actualization needs, including the need to develop one's self to realize one's full potential. By placing these needs in a hierarchy, Maslow suggested that one set of needs must be met or satisfied before the next set of needs emerges. In theory, then, a person will not be motivated to meet an esteem need of gaining recognition until basic physiological, safety, and belongingness and love needs have been met.

What is the value of this analysis to you as a speaker? First, it suggests the kinds of needs you may want to appeal to in your speeches. Second, it

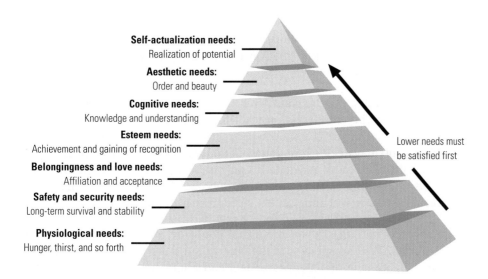

Figure 18.3
Maslow's hierarchy of needs

The pyramid, from bottom to top:

Self-actualization needs:
Realization of potential

Aesthetic needs:
Order and beauty

Cognitive needs:
Knowledge and understanding

Esteem needs:
Achievement and gaining of recognition

Belongingness and love needs:
Affiliation and acceptance

Safety and security needs:
Long-term survival and stability

Physiological needs:
Hunger, thirst, and so forth

Lower needs must
be satisfied first

enables you to understand why a line of development will work on one audience and fail with another. For instance, in difficult economic times, people are more concerned with physiological and safety needs and are less responsive to appeals to affiliation and altruism. Thus, in times of economic recession, fund-raisers for the arts experience far more resistance to giving than they do during economic upswings. Third, and perhaps most crucial, it alerts you to the need for analysis. When your proposition conflicts with a felt need, you have to be prepared with a strong alternative in the same category or in a more fundamental category. For instance, if your proposal is going to cost people money (higher taxes), you will have to show how the proposal satisfies a comparable need (perhaps by increasing their security).

Arousing emotions through language Even with good incentives directed to basic needs, to motivate an audience to act, you must appeal to their emotions. An **emotion** (anger, fear, surprise, joy) is a subjective response (feeling), usually accompanied by a physiological change, which is interpreted in a particular way by the individual and often leads to a change in behavior (Lefton, 2001, p. 223). Effective persuasive speech development entails both logical and emotional elements that act interdependently. Therefore, we need to look for good reasons and for support that will, if properly phrased, arouse these emotions.

emotion
a subjective response (feeling), usually accompanied by a physiological change, which is interpreted in a particular way by the individual and often leads to a change in behavior.

Vividly moving narratives or examples can elicit emotional responses in audience members and move them to action.

© Rudy Von Briel/PhotoEdit

As you work on your speeches, you will want to determine the emotions that you want to arouse, the kinds of information necessary to arouse those emotions, and how the information can be phrased for maximum effect. Let's consider each of these.

1. **What emotion(s) do you want your audience to experience as you make your point?** The emotions you want to arouse will differ from speech to speech. For instance, in a speech calling for more humane treatment of the elderly, you may decide that you want your listeners to feel sadness, anger, grief, caring, and perhaps, guilt. In contrast, in a speech designed to get the audience to attend your school's production of a musical, you may want your listeners to feel anticipation, excitement, or enthusiasm.

2. **What information do you have that could be used to stimulate those emotions?** For the speech on the elderly, suppose you have determined that you want your listeners to feel sad about how people in nursing homes are treated. Your information might include data from interviews with elderly individuals whose only talk of the future is the inevitability of death; accounts of social workers explaining that many elderly live totally in the past and are reluctant to talk about or even think about the future; or statistics that show few nursing homes have programs that give their clients anything to look forward to.

3. **How can you phrase your information to elicit those emotions?** How well you motivate is likely to depend on how well you phrase your information, but remember to keep ethical considerations in mind when you try to tap into powerful emotions.

   For the speech on the elderly, you might be considering an introduction like this one:

   > Currently, elderly people are alienated from society. A high percentage live in nursing homes, live on small fixed incomes, and exist out of the mainstream of society.

But with just the addition of a question and language that creates more vivid pictures, you could make this statement much more emotionally powerful:

> Currently, elderly people are alienated from the society that they worked their entire lives to support. What happens to elderly people in America? They become the forgotten segment of society. They are often relegated to "old people's homes" so that they can live out their lives and die without being "a bother" to their sons and daughters. Because they must exist on relatively small fixed incomes, they are confined to a life that for many means separation from the very society they helped to create.

You are likely to find that some of your best opportunities for using meaningful emotional appeals occur in the introduction and conclusion of your speech. Notice how emotional appeals heighten the power of the following introduction and conclusion in a student speech on euthanasia.* She began her speech as follows:

> **Let's pretend for a moment. Suppose that on the upper right-hand corner of your desk there is a button. You have the power by pushing that button to quickly and painlessly end the life of one you love: your brother or father. This loved one has terminal cancer and will be confined to a hospital for his remaining days. Would you push the button now? His condition worsens. He is in constant pain, and he is hooked up to a life-support machine. He first requests, but as the pain increases he pleads for you to help. Now would you push that button? Each day you watch him deteriorate until he reaches a point where he cannot talk, he cannot see, he cannot hear—he is only alive by that machine. Now would you push that button?**

After giving reasons for changing our laws on euthanasia, she concluded her speech as follows:

> **I ask again, how long could you take walking into that hospital room and looking at your brother or father in a coma, knowing he would rather be allowed to die a natural death than to be kept alive in such a degrading manner? I've crossed that doorstep—I've gone into that hospital room, and let me tell you, it's hell. I think it's time we reconsider our laws concerning euthanasia. Don't you?**

Regardless of your beliefs about the subject of euthanasia, you probably will have to agree that you would be inclined to experience sadness as you empathize with her feelings.

Building the Credibility of Your Arguments

Principle 5: You are more likely to persuade an audience when they view your arguments as credible.

As we have seen, maintaining credibility is important to speaker effectiveness in all types of speaking. In previous chapters, we have outlined the nature of credibility and the characteristics that you need to develop to be perceived as a credible speaker. In persuasive speaking you have a special burden to behave ethically and to present arguments that are credible. You can do this by following these four guidelines.

1. **Tell the truth.** Of all the guidelines, this may be the most important. An audience that consents to listen to you is extending you its trust and expects that you will be honest with them. Consequently, if people believe you are lying to them or if they later learn that you have lied, they will reject you and your ideas. But telling the truth means more than avoiding deliberate, outright lies. If you are not sure whether information is true, do not use it until you have verified it. Ignorance is seldom accepted as an excuse.

2. **Keep your information in perspective.** Novice speakers can become so excited about their information that they exaggerate its importance. Although a little exaggeration might be accepted as a normal product

*By permission of Betsy Burke.

Observe&Analyze

Motivating Audiences

The goal of this activity is to analyze motivational tactics.

1. Use your Communicate! CD-ROM to access Web Resource 18.1: Maintaining the Faith and read the speech "Terrorism and Islam: Maintaining the Faith" by Mahathir Bin Mohamad, available through InfoTrac College Edition. Analyze the incentives that Mahathir presents.

2. What emotions do you think he hopes to arouse? What information does he present to stimulate emotions? Does he seem to phrase the ideas in a way that elicits those emotions? Explain.

 You can complete this activity online and, if requested, email it to your instructor. Use your Communicate! CD-ROM to access Skill Learning Activity 18.3.

of human nature, when the exaggeration is perceived as distortion, most people will consider it the same as lying. For instance, suppose you discover that capital punishment has lowered the murder rates in a few states but that in many other states the statistics are inconclusive. In your speech, if you assert that statistics show that murder rates are lower in states with capital punishment, you would be distorting the evidence. Because the line between some exaggeration and gross exaggeration or distortion is often difficult to distinguish, most people see any exaggeration as unethical.

3. **Resist personal attacks against those who oppose your ideas.** There seems to be almost universal agreement that name-calling and other irrelevant personal attacks are detrimental to a speaker's trustworthiness. Responsible listeners recognize that such tactics do not contribute to the speaker's argument and represent an abuse of the privileged status the speaker enjoys.

4. **Give the source for all damning information.** Where ideas originate is often as important as the ideas themselves, especially when a statement is damning. If you are going to discuss wrongdoing by individuals or organizations or condemn an idea by relying on the words or ideas of others, provide the sources of your information and arguments. Moreover, because the mention of wrongdoing brings communication to the edge of what is legally defined as slander, speakers should be aware of the legal as well as the ethical pitfalls of making damning statements without proof.

Methods of Organizing Persuasive Arguments

Statement of logical reasons, problem solution, comparative advantages, and motivational patterns are organizational methods for persuasive speeches that are designed to be used with specific types of audiences and propositions. In the discussion that follows we will describe each method, illustrate it, explain the audience attitudes for which it is most applicable, and identify the logic underlying the organization. So that you can contrast the methods and better understand their use, we illustrate each pattern using the same proposition (specific goal) and the same (or similar) reasons.

Statement of Logical Reasons Pattern

statement of logical reasons
a straightforward organization in which you present the best-supported reasons you can find following an order of second-strongest first, strongest last, and other reason(s) in between.

The **statement of logical reasons** is a straightforward organization in which you present the best-supported reasons you can find following an order of second-strongest first, strongest last, and other reason(s) in between. It will work when your listeners have no opinion on the subject, are apathetic, or are perhaps only mildly in favor or opposed.

> **Proposition:** I want my audience to vote in favor of the school tax levy on the November ballot.

I. Income will enable the schools to restore vital programs. (second strongest)
II. Income will enable the schools to give teachers the raises they need to keep up with the cost of living.
III. The actual cost to each member of the community will be very small. (strongest)

The assumption underlying the use of the statement of logical reasons pattern is this: When good reasons and evidence are presented supporting a proposal, the proposal should be adopted.

Problem Solution Pattern

The **problem solution pattern** is a framework for clarifying the nature of the problem and for illustrating why a given proposal is the best one. The problem solution pattern is organized around three general reasons: (1) there is a problem that requires action, (2) the proposal will solve the problem, and (3) the proposal is the best solution to the problem because it will provide positive consequences. This pattern works well for a topic that is relatively unfamiliar to an audience—one in which they are unaware that a problem exists—or for an audience that has no opinion or is mildly pro or con. A problem solution organization for the school tax levy proposition might look like this:

> **Proposition:** I want my audience to vote in favor of the school tax levy on the November ballot.

I. The shortage of money is resulting in serious problems for public education. (statement of problem)
II. The proposed increase is large enough to solve those problems. (solution)
III. For now, a tax levy is the best method of solving the schools' problems. (consequences)

The assumption underlying the use of the problem solution pattern is this: When a problem is presented that is not or cannot be solved with current measures and the proposal can solve the problem practically and beneficially, then the proposal should be adopted.

problem solution pattern
a framework for clarifying the nature of the problem and for illustrating why a given proposal is the best one.

Comparative Advantages Pattern

The **comparative advantages pattern** is an organizational pattern in which a proposed change is compared to the status quo and demonstrated to be superior. Rather than presenting the proposition as a solution to a grave problem, it presents the proposition as one that ought to be adopted solely on the basis of the advantages of that proposition over what is currently being done. Although this pattern can work for any audience attitude, it works best when the audience agrees that change may be necessary. A comparative advantages approach to the school tax levy proposition would look like this:

> **Proposition:** I want my audience to vote in favor of the school tax levy on the November ballot.

comparative advantages pattern
an organizational pattern in which a proposed change is compared to the status quo and demonstrated to be superior.

I. Income from a tax levy will enable schools to raise the standards of their programs. (advantage 1)

II. Income from a tax levy will enable schools to hire better teachers. (advantage 2)

III. Income from a tax levy will enable schools to better the educational environment. (advantage 3)

The assumption underlying the use of the comparative advantages pattern is this: When reasons are presented that show a proposal is a significant improvement over what is being done, then the proposal should be adopted.

Motivational Pattern

The **motivational pattern,** articulated by Allan Monroe who was a professor of Speech at Purdue University, combines problem solving and motivation. It follows a problem solution pattern but includes required steps designed to heighten the motivational effect of the organization. Motivational patterns usually include a five-step, unified sequence that replaces the normal introduction-body-conclusion model: (1) an attention step, (2) a need step that fully explains the nature of the problem, (3) a satisfaction step that explains how the proposal solves the problem in a satisfactory manner, (4) a visualization step that provides a personal application of the proposal, and (5) an action appeal step that emphasizes the specific direction listener action should take. A motivational pattern for the school tax levy proposition would look like this:

Proposition: I want my audience to vote in favor of the school tax levy on the November ballot.

I. Comparisons of worldwide test scores in math and science have refocused our attention on education. (attention)

II. The shortage of money is resulting in cost-saving measures that compromise our ability to teach basic academic subjects well. (need, statement of problem)

III. The proposed increase is large enough to solve those problems in ways that allow for increased emphasis on academic need areas. (satisfaction, how the proposal solves the problem)

IV. Think of the contribution you will be making not only to the education of your future children but also to efforts to return our educational system to the world level it once held. (visualization of personal application)

V. Here are "Vote Yes" buttons that you can wear to show you are willing to support this much-needed tax levy. (action appeal showing specific direction)

Because motivational patterns are variations of problem solution patterns, the underlying assumption is similar: When the current means are not solving the problem, a new solution that does solve the problem should be adopted.

motivational pattern
an organization pattern that combines problem solving and motivation.

Observe&Analyze

Persuasive Organizational Methods

The goal of this activity is to analyze organizational patterns.

1. Use your Communicate! CD-ROM to access Web Resource 18.1: Maintaining the Faith and read the speech "Terrorism and Islam: Maintaining the Faith" by Mahathir Bin Mohamad, available through InfoTrac College Edition. Analyze the organizational methods Mahathir uses.

2. How well does his pattern fit the attitudes you believe his audience holds toward his position? Are there other patterns that might have served him better?

 You can complete this activity online and, if requested, email it to your instructor. Use your Communicate! CD-ROM to access Skill Learning Activity 18.4.

Criteria for Evaluating Persuasive Speeches

In this chapter, we have been looking at principles of persuasive speaking. Now let's apply those principles to evaluating and presenting a persuasive speech. Figure 18.4 outlines the criteria for evaluating a persuasive speech.

Sample Speech: Capital Punishment, by Eric Wais*

This section presents a sample speech adaptation plan, outline, and transcript given by a student in an introductory speaking course as his first major speech.

1. Review the outline and adaptation plan developed by Eric Wais in preparing his speech on Capital Punishment.

2. Then read the transcript of Eric's speech.

3. Use the persuasive speech critique checklist from Figure 18.4 to help you evaluate this speech.

4. Use your Communicate! CD-ROM to watch a video clip of Eric presenting his speech in class. Click on the "Speech Interactive" icon in the menu at

* Used with permission of Eric Wais.

Check all items that were accomplished effectively.

Primary Criteria
_____ 1. Was the specific goal designed to affect a belief or move an audience to action?
_____ 2. Did the speaker present clearly stated reasons?
_____ 3. Did the speaker use facts and expert opinions to support these reasons?
_____ 4. Was the organizational pattern appropriate for the type of goal and assumed attitude of the audience?
_____ 5. Did the speaker use emotional language to motivate the audience?
_____ 6. Was the speaker effective in establishing his or her credibility on this topic?
_____ 7. Was the speaker ethical in handling material?

General Criteria
_____ 1. Was the specific goal clear?
_____ 2. Was the introduction effective?
_____ 3. Was the organizational pattern appropriate for the intent and content of the speech?
_____ 5. Was the conclusion effective?
_____ 6. Was the language clear, vivid, emphatic, and appropriate?
_____ 7. Was the delivery convincing?

Evaluate the speech as (check one):
_____ excellent _____ good _____ average _____ fair _____ poor

Figure 18.4
Persuasive speech critique checklist

Test Your Competence ▶

A Persuasive Speech

1. Follow the speech plan action steps to prepare a persuasive speech in which you affect audience belief or move your audience to action. Your instructor will announce the time limit and other parameters for this assignment.

2. Criteria for evaluation include all the general criteria of topic and purpose, content, organization, presentation, but special emphasis will be placed on the primary persuasive criteria of how well the speech's specific goal was adapted to the audience's initial attitude toward the topic, the soundness of the reasons, the evidence cited in support of them, the use of motivational language, and the credibility of the arguments.

3. Use the persuasive speech critique checklist in Figure 18.4 to critique yourself as you practice your speech.

4. Prior to presenting your speech, prepare a complete sentence outline and source list (bibliography). If you have used Speech Builder Express to complete the action step activities online, you will be able to print out a copy of your completed outline and source list. Also prepare a written plan for adapting your speech to the audience. Your adaptation plan should address the following issues:
   a. How does your goal adapt to whether your prevailing audience attitude is in favor, no opinion, or opposed?
   b. What reasons will you use, and how will the organizational pattern you select fit your topic and audience?
   c. How will you establish your credibility with this audience?
   d. How will you motivate your audience by using incentives or by appealing to their emotions?

the left, then click on "Speech Menu" in the menu bar at the top of the screen. Select "Persuasive Speech: Capital Punishment" to watch the video (it takes a minute for the video to load).

5. Write a paragraph of feedback to Eric describing the strengths of his presentation and what you think he might do next time to be more effective.

You can use your Communicate! CD-ROM to prepare your critique checklist and your feedback, then compare your answers to those of the authors'. To complete the checklist electronically, click on "Evaluation" in the menu bar at the top of the screen. To prepare your feedback electronically, click on "Analysis" in the menu bar. To compare your answers to those provided by the authors, click the "Done" button.

You can use your Student Workbook to complete this activity, or you can complete it online, print a copy of the Persuasive Speech Critique Checklist, and, if requested, email your work to your instructor. Access Skill Learning Activity 18.5.

Adaptation Plan

1. **How your goal adapts to whether your prevailing audience attitude is in favor, no opinion, or opposed.** I believe that being college students, most of the audience will lean toward a slightly more liberal view of the topic of capital punishment. While I believe that it is the majority opinion in this country to be in favor of the death penalty, I think most

of the audience will at worst be toward the liberal end of that opinion and not be strongly opposed to my goal. But since I do expect the audience to oppose my goal, I plan on focusing on hard statistics rather than opinion. It is hard for the audience's pre-existing opinions to get in the way of accepting facts from reputable sources such as the FBI and Department of Justice.

2. **What reasons you will use, and how the organizational pattern you have selected is appropriate to your topic and audience.** Again, I chose the logical reasons pattern because I feel the best way to deal with an audience I expect to be mildly opposed to my proposition is to keep it as straightforward as possible. I chose the reasons that were least emotional and most logical so that I could back them up with as many facts and statistics as possible without losing their impact.

3. **How you will establish your credibility with this audience.** Since I have no personal credibility myself, I will have to rely on finding the most reliable and reputable sources I can. While some of my more opinionated points are supported by more partisan sources (Death Penalty Information Center, etc.), all of my hard facts come from the FBI and the Department of Justice, which are the most reliable sources of such information available and difficult to dispute.

4. **How you will motivate your audience by appealing to their emotions.** Even though I have chosen to make my speech as logical as possible, I still believe there is a strong element of emotion to the topic of capital punishment. I will try to contain all of my emotional appeals to the introduction and conclusion to avoid conflicting with the hard facts in the body of my speech. But in the introduction and conclusion I will try to appeal to the idea that capital punishment amounts to state-sanctioned murder and that any act of the state is an act of its people and, therefore, an act of the audience themselves. I think this is an element of the topic often overlooked and will therefore appeal to the audience's emotions.

Speech Outline

Specific Goal: I want to convince the audience that capital punishment is not effective.

Introduction
 I. It is natural to feel anger toward murderers and to want vengeance.
 II. But can we really justify the state-sanctioned murder that capital punishment amounts to?

Thesis Statement: Capital punishment should be abolished because it is not only used in cases of clear guilt, it does not help reduce prison overcrowding and expenses, and it does not deter violent crime.

Body

I. The death penalty is not used only in the cases of clear guilt.
   A. Large numbers of people have been released when their convictions have been overturned.
   B. Some people have been released because they did not have a fair trial.
   C. Many other people sitting on death row may be innocent.
II. The death penalty does not help reduce prison overcrowding and expenses.
   A. Since reinstatement of the death penalty in 1977, only 722 people have been executed.
   B. The cost of incarceration is much less than the cost of execution.
III. The death penalty does not deter crime.
   A. Murder rates in death penalty states are highest per capita.
      1. In 1999, murder rates per capita were 3.6 in non–death penalty states as compared to 5.5 in death penalty states. (FBI)
      2. In neighboring states, the non–death penalty neighbor always has a lower murder rate. (FBI)
   B. Death penalty may actually increase murder rates due to a brutalizing effect.
   C. That death penalty does not deter crime is believed by over 80% of criminologists.

Conclusion

I. All of these (not only used in cases of clear guilt, not reducing prison overcrowding and expenses, and not deterring crime) show that capital punishment is ineffective.
II. The real issue then is a moral one: the state is an extension of your will and power—when the state executes someone, you are responsible.
III. Webster defines murder as "the unlawful taking of a human life"—when you lawfully take a human life it is vengeance, not justice.

Sources

Akers, R. and M. Radelet, "Deterrence and the Death Penalty? The View of the Experts," 1995.

Death Penalty Information Center, http://www.fbi.gov/

FBI Uniform Crime Reports, http://www.fbi.gov/

Hoppe, Christy, "Executions cost Texas millions," *Dallas Morning Star,* March 8, 1992, p. 1A.

Isikoff, Michael and Evan Thomas, "Waiting for Justice," *Newsweek,* May 21, 2001, p. 23.

Thomson, Ernie, "Deterrence Versus Brutalization," *Homicide Studies,* May 1977.

U.S. Department of Justice, Bureau of Justice Statistics, http://www.ojp.usdoj.gov/bjs/

Speech and Analysis

Speech

I know it's natural to feel anger and to want vengeance toward people who commit murder, violent crimes and horrible atrocities that we hear about in the news: Timothy McVeigh and people like this. And they're all human emotions—we all feel them from time to time. And there's nothing wrong with that, but as a modern society can we really justify the state sanctioned murder that capital punishment amounts to?

You're going to hear three major arguments from supporters of the death penalty as to why it should exist in this country. But I'm going to try to show you today that the death penalty is not only used in cases of clear guilt, that it does not help overcrowded prisons and expenses, and it does not deter violent crime. And for these reasons it should be abolished in this country.

One thing you'll hear often is that the death penalty is only handed down in cases where we're sure of the suspect's guilt. Now I know that even being raised in a conservative family, one of the things I always had a problem with even as a child about the death penalty is what happens if they've got the wrong guy? They can't really fix that, they can't correct their mistakes and you're all probably aware that the government does not like to admit its mistakes, and it certainly doesn't like to publicize its mistakes, but does make them.

Analysis

In this introduction, Eric tries to get the audience to share common feelings.

Notice the strategy Eric uses to frame his reasons for abolishing capital punishment. First, he presents the reasons that are most widely used to justify capital punishment. Then he gives counterarguments for each of these reasons.

Eric presents the first reason that is often mentioned in support of capital punishment. Then working with his own personal experience, he begins to show that many times the death penalty is handed down in cases where the accused is not really guilty.

Speech

Since 1977 when the death penalty was reinstated by the Supreme Court, 93 people have been released, 35 since 1994 alone, all after being proven innocent of the crimes they were originally convicted of. I'll give you a couple of good examples. Donald Paradese was convicted in Idaho of murder in 1981. He was scheduled for execution three times. Each time he came within days of being killed. He was finally released this year after twenty years in prison when it was found that prosecutors and police had destroyed key evidence that had showed his innocence. And that his court appointed attorney who put on a three-hour defense in his original trial had never tried a case or had never studied criminal law before.

Some people aren't so lucky. Leo Jones was convicted of murdering a police officer in Florida, also in 1981. He was executed in 1998 by lethal injection. He was convicted only because of a confession he signed after eight hours of police interrogation by an officer who was later convicted of physically torturing suspects to coerce false confessions.

These are the people we know about. There are many other cases—and we have no idea how many other mistakes we might have made or how many people are sitting on death row right now who may be innocent of what they were accused of. But some people say that these are the rare cases. And that the death penalty serves other functions and is still viable.

One of the things they say is that our prisons are overcrowded and

Analysis

Here Eric provides statistics to show that many mistakes have been made in the past.

Then he moves to two specific examples to dramatize his argument. But to clarify his reasoning he needed to state that in one example the person was saved, but in the other the person was executed before it could be shown that he was innocent.

Notice how Eric is able to dramatize his examples enough so that we empathize with the suffering of the people involved.

Eric's statement of another reason offered by supporters of capital punishment serves as a transition to his next argument.

In this section he raises questions about the argument that because

Speech

that it costs too much to house these convicted murderers for forty or fifty years at a time. But the statement really doesn't make a whole lot of sense, especially when dealing with prisoner overcrowding.

It's so amazing when I hear that argument, and I do still hear that argument because since 1977 only 722 people have been executed in this country. Last year alone there were over a million people in our prison systems. Seven hundred and twenty-two beds over twenty-five years is not making all the difference in the world.

And that's not to mention that our prisons right now in this country as of 2000 according to the U.S. Department of Justice are only at 94% capacity. And have not been above capacity in almost a decade. And it's actually steadily going down.

The other thing you hear is that we shouldn't be expected to pay for these people who sit in prison for forty or fifty years. What you don't hear about is the price of executions themselves. The price of building the execution equipment, of maintaining the execution equipment, of manning these death houses, of actually performing executions.

According to a *Dallas Morning Star* article in 1992, in Texas, a single execution cost 2.3 million dollars. That's three times what it cost to imprison someone for forty years at a maximum security prison in a single cell. Three times what it cost to imprison someone for life in a maximum security prison just to kill them.

Analysis

of overcrowding it costs too much to house convicted murderers.

First, Eric does a good job of emphasizing the small number of those actually put to death.
    Notice how his repetition emphasizes the point he is making.

Then he quotes a Department of Justice statistic to show that jails are not overcrowded.

Here Eric moves into the second part of his argument, the costs involved.

Eric uses an example of a Texas execution to show that a single execution costs three times as much as keeping a person in jail for forty years. He then repeats the thrust of his point for emphasis. Still, his argument would be stronger if he could show that this example truly reflects the costs of executions.

Speech

Now a lot of people will say, It's not about the money—it's not about prison debts, a death penalty performs a very significant task in our society, it deters violent crime—it helps keep people from committing murders. And this sounds logical to everyone. I know it sounds logical to me. If you tell me, you do this you'll be killed, I'm certainly going to think twice about it. Unfortunately, when it comes to homicides, statistics just don't connect it up.

According to the FBI, over 75 percent of homicides in this country are aggravated. That means they're not cold, calculated, premeditated crimes. They're crimes of passion and they're crimes where people aren't thinking about the consequences of their actions. It doesn't mean they don't deserve to be punished, and be held responsible for those actions. But it means that they're really not taking into consideration, you know, I wonder if the death penalty may be applied toward my case later on in this.

In 1999, according to the FBI's crime reports in non–death penalty states in which there are twelve in this country, murders per capita were 3.6 compared to 5.5 in the rest of the 38 states that did have murderers. This has been consistent ever since the death penalty was reinstated in 1977.

Non–death penalty states have always had lower murder rates than death penalty states. There have been some studies such as one done by Dr. Ernie Thompson of the University of Arizona that have shown that there may actu-

Analysis

In this third point, Eric counters the argument that the presence of the threat of capital punishment deters crime. Notice how this final reason is the strongest and most important.

He begins with statements that seem to support the argument. Then he announces the real problem—that capital punishment is not a deterrent.

Then he shows that most capital crimes are those of passion, where the guilty aren't thinking about what they've done.

Then he goes on to compare statistics of those states with capital punishment to those states without, showing that the murder rates are actually lower in states without capital punishment!

Here Eric adds further strength to his argument by presenting a reason capital punishment may even have an opposite effect—it may make murder more likely.

Speech

ally be a brutalizing effect from capital punishment that actually increases murder rates in death penalty states. He's shown that in months after executions, murder rates in these states skyrocket. It has something to do with the state's use of violence against people which somehow is desensitizing and almost encouraging violence in its citizens. Now, according to a poll done by Homicide Studies in the *National Criminology Journal*, in 1999, over 80 percent of professional criminologists do not believe that the death penalty effectively deters violent crime. That's 80 percent of professionals who study crime and the psychology of crime, all saying that executing prisoners does not deter violent crime.

Now all of these are logical reasons why the death penalty doesn't do the job it's supposed to. It's flawed. It often is used against people whom we are not positive of their guilt, it does not help overcrowding of prisons, it does not cut down on expenses, and all signs point to the fact that it does not effectively deter violent crime.

But the real issue here is a moral one. You have to remember that when a state executes someone, it's an extension of your will and your power. And if you wouldn't be comfortable flipping a switch or pulling a trigger, or putting the noose around the neck yourself, how can you really justify having the state do it for you. Webster defines murder as the unlawful taking of a human life. The lawful taking of human life is vengeance—not justice.

Analysis

In his conclusion, Eric reviews his arguments and concludes with an emotional appeal linking capital punishment not with justice, but with vengeance.

In this speech, Eric does a very good job of presenting reasons why capital punishment should be abolished that counter opposition reasons of why it should be retained. Some excellent documentation and good use of examples.

What Would You Do?   A QUESTION OF ETHICS

lejandro had decided that for his final speech he would motivate members of the class to donate money to the Downtown Food Bank. He was excited about this topic because when he was a senior in high school he had volunteered at the Food Bank, and he had seen firsthand the face of hunger in this community.

He planned to support his speech with three reasons: (1) that an increasing number of people in the community needed food, (2) that government agencies were unable to provide sufficient help, and (3) that a high percentage of every dollar donated to the Food Bank went to buy food.

As he researched these points, however, he discovered that the number of families in need had not really risen in the past two years and that government sponsorship of the Food Bank had increased. Then, when he examined the Food Bank's financial statements, he discovered that only 68 percent of every dollar donated was actually spent on food. Faced with this evidence, he just didn't think his reasons and evidence were very strong.

Yet, because of his experience, he still thought the Food Bank was a cause that deserved financial support, so he decided to focus his entire speech on the heartwarming case of the Hernando family. Ineligible for government assistance, over the years this family of ten had managed to survive because of the aid they received from the Food Bank. Today, several of the children have graduated from college, and one is a physician working in the barrio. By telling this story of one family's struggle to survive, Alejandro thought he would be successful in persuading the class.

Would it be ethical for Alejandro to give his speech in this way? If so, why? If not, what would he need to do to make the speech ethical?

Summary

This chapter presented five principles of persuasive speaking and four organizational patterns.

The first principle is that you are more likely to persuade audience members when you can articulate specifically what you want them to believe or do.

The second principle is that you are more likely to be able to persuade when you direct your goal and your information to the audience's attitude. How you proceed will depend in whether your audience is in favor, has no opinion, or is opposed to your goal. Each position requires you to proceed somewhat differently.

The third principle is that you are more likely to persuade an audience when the body of your speech contains good reasons and strong evidence that support your specific speech goal. You evaluate reasons on the basis of whether they are supportable, relevant, and have an impact. You support your reasons with evidence that is of high quality, recent, and relevant. Then you test the reasons by looking at the reasons and the evidence given in support.

The fourth principle is that you are more likely to persuade an audience when your language motivates them. Motivation often results from strong incentives and use of emotional language.

The fifth principle is that you are more likely to persuade an audience when they view your arguments as credible; that is, you proceed by telling the truth, keeping your information in perspective, resisting the use of personal attacks, and providing sources for your arguments.

Once you have gathered the necessary information you have four methods of organizing persuasive arguments. First is a statement of logical reasons pattern in which you present the best-supported reasons you can find. The second is a problem solution pattern in which you introduce the problem, offer a proposal to solve it, and show why it is the best solution. The third is the comparative advantages pattern in which you show each of the advantages of your solution. Fourth is the motivational pattern, which extends the pattern by giving an attention step, a need step, a satisfaction step, a visualization step, and an appeal step.

Communicate! Online

Now that you have read Chapter 18, use your Communicate! CD-ROM for quick access to the electronic resources that accompany this text. Your CD-ROM gives you access to the video of Eric's speech on pages 487–491, InfoTrac College Edition, and the Communicate! Web site. When you get to the Communicate! home page, click on "Student Book Companion Site" in the Resource box at the right to access the online study aids for this chapter, including a digital glossary, review quizzes, chapter activities, and chapter Web Resources.

Key Terms

At the Communicate! Web site, select the chapter resources for Chapter 18. Print a copy of the glossary for this chapter and test yourself with the electronic flash cards or complete the crossword puzzle to help you master these key terms:

persuasive speaking (464)
attitude (465)
opinion (465)
reasons (468)
reasoning by generalization
   from example (473)
reasoning by causation (473)
reasoning by analogy (473)

reasoning by sign (474)
hasty generalization (474)
false cause (474)
appeal to authority (474)
ad hominem argument (475)
motivation (475)
incentive (475)
costs (476)

emotions (477)
statement of logical reasons
   (480)
problem solution pattern (481)
comparative advantages
   pattern (481)
motivational pattern (482)

Review Quiz

Test your knowledge of the concepts in this chapter by taking the online quiz at the Communicate! Web site. Select the chapter resources for Chapter 18, then click on "Review Quiz." When you have completed the quiz, submit it for scoring.

Skill Learning Activities

Complete the Observe & Analyze and Speech and Analysis activities for Chapter 18 online at the Communicate! Web site. Select the chapter resources for Chapter 18, then click on "Activities." You can submit your Observe & Analyze and Speech and Analysis answers to your instructor, and compare your Speech and Analysis answers to those provided by the authors.

18.1: Observe & Analyze: A Specific Goal Statement in a Persuasive Speech (469)
18.2: Observe & Analyze: Giving Good Reasons and Evidence (476)
18.3: Observe & Analyze: Motivating Audiences (479)
18.4: Observe & Analyze: Persuasive Organizational Methods (482)
18.5: Speech and Analysis: Capital Punishment, by Eric Wais (487)

Web Resources

Access the Web Resources for this chapter online at the Communicate! Web site. Select the chapter resources for Chapter 18, then click on "Web Resources."

18.1: Maintaining the Faith (479)

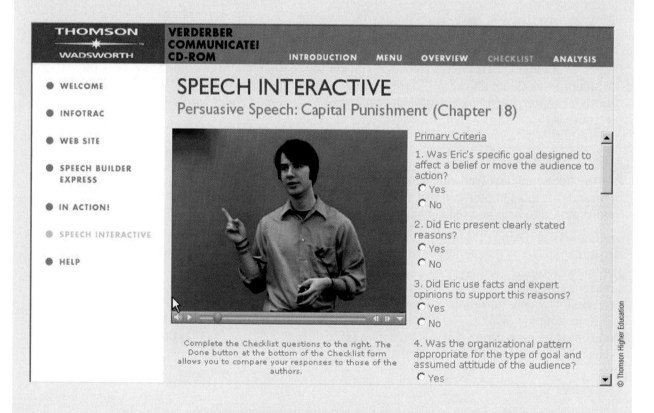

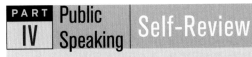

PART IV Public Speaking | Self-Review

Public Speaking Chapters 12 through 18

What kind of a public speaker are you? The following analysis looks at eleven specifics that are basic to a public speaking profile. On the line provided for each statement, indicate the response that best captures your behavior: 1, almost always; 2, often; 3, occasionally; 4, rarely; 5, never.

_____ When I am asked to speak, I am able to select a topic and determine a speech goal with confidence. (Ch. 12)

_____ When I speak, I use material from a variety of sources. (Ch. 13)

_____ In my preparation, I construct clear main points and organize them to follow some consistent pattern. (Ch. 14)

_____ In my preparation, I am careful to be sure that I have developed ideas to meet audience needs. (Ch. 15)

_____ When I speak, I sense that my audience perceives my language as clear and vivid. (Ch. 16)

_____ I look directly at members of my audience when I speak. (Ch. 16)

_____ My public speaking voice shows variation in pitch, speed, and loudness. (Ch. 16)

_____ When I speak, my bodily actions help supplement or reinforce my ideas; I feel and look involved. (Ch. 16)

_____ I have confidence in my ability to speak in public. (Ch. 16)

_____ When I give informative speeches, I am careful to use techniques designed to get audience attention, create audience understanding, and increase audience retention. (Ch. 17)

_____ When I give persuasive speeches, I am careful to use techniques designed to build my credibility, prove my reasons, and motivate my audience. (Ch. 18)

Based on your responses, select the public speaking behavior you would most like to change. Write a communication improvement plan similar to the sample in Chapter 1 (page 22). If you would like verification of your self-analysis before you write a goal statement, have a friend or a coworker complete this same analysis for you.

 You can complete this Self-Review online and, if requested, email it to your instructor. Use your Communicate! CD-ROM to access **Part IV Self-Review** at the Communicate! Web site. Select the chapter resources for Chapter 18, then click on "Part IV Self-Review."

REFERENCES

Adler, R. B. (1977). *Confidence in communication: A guide to assertive and social skills.* New York: Holt, Rinehart & Winston.

Affifi, W. A., & Guerrero, L. K. (2000). Motivations underlying topic avoidance in close relationships. In S. Petronio (Ed.), *Balancing the secrets of private disclosures* (pp. 165–180). Mahwah, NJ: Erlbaum.

Ahladas, J. (1989, April 1). Global warming. *Vital Speeches of the Day, 381–384.*

Alberti, R. E., & Emmons, M. L. (1995). *Your perfect right: A guide to assertive living* (7th ed.). San Luis Obispo, CA: Impact.

Anderson, J. (1988). Communication competency in the small group. In R. Cathcart & L. Samovar (Eds.), *Small group communication: A reader.* Dubuque, IA: Wm. Brown.

Andrews, P. H. (1992). Sex and gender differences in group communication: Impact on the facilitation process. *Small Group Research, 23,* 90.

Aries, E. (1998). Gender differences in interaction: A reexamination. In D. J. Canary & K. Dindia (Eds.), *Sex differences and similarities in communication: Critical essays and empirical investigations of sex a gender in interaction* (pp. 65–81). Mahwah, NJ: Erlbaum.

Aronson, E. (1999). *The social animal.* New York: Worth.

Asante, M. K. (2002). *American history: A journey of liberation.* Maywood, NJ: Peoples Publishing Group, Inc.

Asante, M. K. (2002). *Culture and customs of Egypt.* Westport, CN: Greenwood Press.

Asante, M. K. (2003). *Afrocentricity: The theory of social change.* Chicago: African American Images.

Asante, M. K. (2003). *Erasing racism: The survival of the American nation.* Amherst, NY: Prometheus Books.

Axtell, R. E. (1999). *Gestures: The do's and taboos of body language around the world* (Rev. ed.). New York: Wiley.

Ayres, J., & Hopf, T. S. (1990, January). The long-term effect of visualization in the classroom: A brief research report. *Communication Education, 39,* 75–78.

Ayres, J., Hopf, T. S., & Ayres, D. M. (1994, July). An examination of whether imaging ability enhances the effectiveness of an intervention designed to reduce speech anxiety. *Communication Education, 43,* 252–258.

Bach, K., & Harnish, R. M. (1979). *Linguistic communication and speech acts.* Cambridge, MA: MIT Press.

Baeder, D. L. (1980, June 1). Chemical wastes. *Vital Speeches of the Day,* 496–500.

Bales, R. F. (1971). *Personality and interpersonal behavior.* New York: Holt, Rinehart & Winston.

Balgopal, P. R., Ephross, P. H., & Vassil, T. V. (1986). Self help groups and professional helpers. *Small Group Research, 17,* 123–137.

Banks, M. A. (1997). *Web psychos, stalkers and pranksters.* Scottsdale, AZ: Coriolis Groups.

Barnes, S. B. (2003). *Computer-mediated communication: Human-to-human communication across the Internet.* Boston, MA: Allyn & Bacon.

Baron, R. A., & Bryne, D. (2000). *Social psychology* (9th ed.). Boston: Allyn & Bacon.

Becherer, H. W. (2000, September 15). Enduring values for a secular age: Faith, hope and love. *Vital Speeches of the Day,* 732–744.

Beebe, M. B., Anthony, T., Salas, E., & Driskell, J. E. (1994). Group cohesiveness and quality of decision making. *Small Group Research, 25,* 189–204.

Behnke, R. R., & Carlile, L. W. (1971). Heart rate as an index of speech anxiety. *Speech Monographs, 38,* 66.

Berger, C. R., & Brada, J. J. (1982). *Language and social knowledge: Uncertainty in interpersonal relations.* London: Arnold.

Bigelow, J. D. (1999). The Web as an organizational behavior learning medium. *Journal of Management Education, 23,* 635–650.

Bormann, E. (1990). *Small group communication: Theory and practice.* New York: Harper & Row.

Bostrom, R. (1970). Patterns of communicative interaction in small groups. *Speech Monographs, 37,* 257–263.

Brown, P., & Levinson, S. (1987). *Politeness: Some universals in language usage.* Cambridge, U.K.: Cambridge University Press.

Brownell, J. (2002). *Listening: Attitudes, principles, and skills* (2nd ed.). Boston: Allyn & Bacon.

Burger, C. (2000, September 15). Sooner than you think. *Vital Speeches of the Day,* 710–712.

Burgoon, J. K., & Bacue, A. E. (2003). Nonverbal communication skills. In J. O. Greene & B. R. Burleson (Eds.), *Handbook of communication and social interaction skills* (pp. 179–220). Mahwah, NJ: Erlbaum.

Burgoon, J. K., & Burgoon, M. (2002). Expectancy theories. In W. P Robinson & H. Giles (Eds.), *The new handbook of language and social psychology.* New York: Wiley.

Burgoon, J. K., Coker, D. A., & Coker, R. A. (1986). Communicative effects of gaze behavior: A test of two contrasting explanations. *Human Communication Research, 12,* 495–524.

Burgoon, J. K., Dunbar, N. E., & Segrin, C. (2002). Nonverbal influence. In J. P. Dillard & M. Pfau (Eds.), *The persuasion handbook: Developments in theory and practice.* Thousand Oaks, CA: Sage.

Burgoon, J. K., & Hoobler, G. D. (2002). Nonverbal signals. In M. L. Knapp & J. A. Daly (Eds.), *Handbook of interpersonal communication* (3rd ed., pp. 240–299). Thousand Oaks, CA: Sage.

Burleson, B. R. (2003). Emotional support skills. In J. O. Green & B. R. Burleson (Eds.), *Handbook of communication and social interaction skills* (pp. 551–594). Mahwah, NJ: Erlbaum.

Burleson, B. R., & Goldsmith, D. J. (1998). How the comforting process works: Alleviating emotional distress through conversationally induced reappraisals. In P. A. Andersen & L. K. Guerrero (Eds.), *Handbook of communication and emotion: Research, theory, applications, and contexts* (pp. 248–280). San Diego, CA: Academic Press.

Burleson, B. R., & MacGeorge, E. L. (2002). Supportive communication. In M. L. Knapp, J. A. Daly, & G. R. Miller (Eds.), *Handbook of interpersonal communication* (3rd ed., pp. 374–424). Thousand Oaks, CA: Sage.

Burleson, B. R., & Samter, W. (1990). Effects of cognitive complexity on the perceived importance of communication skills in friends. *Communication Research, 17,* 165–182.

Cahn, D. D. (1990). Intimates in conflict: A research review. In D. D. Cahn (Ed.), *Intimates in conflict: A communication perspective* (pp. 1–24). Hillsdale, NJ: Erlbaum.

Canary, D. J., & Hause, K. (1993). Is there any reason to research sex differences in communication? *Communication Quarterly, 41,* 129–144.

Canary, D. J., Cupach, W. R., & Messman, S. J. (1995). *Relationship conflict: Conflict in parent-child, friendship, and romantic relationships.* Thousand Oaks, CA: Sage.

Cegala, D. J., & Sillars, A. L. (1989). Further examination of nonverbal manifestations of interaction involvement. *Communication Reports, 2,* 45.

Clark, N. (1994). *Teambuilding: A practical guide for trainers.* New York: McGraw-Hill.

Clevenger, T., Jr. (1959, April). A synthesis of experimental research in stage fright. *Quarterly Journal of Speech, 45,* 134–145.

Cloven, D. H., & Roloff, M. E. (1991). Sense-making activities and interpersonal conflict: Communicative cures for the mulling blues. *Western Journal of Speech Communication, 55,* 134–158.

Cornog, M. W. (1998). *Merriam Webster's vocabulary builder.* Springfield, MA: Merriam Webster.

Criscito, P. (2000). *Résumés in cyberspace* (2nd ed.). Hauppauge, NY: Barron's Educational Series, Inc.

Crumlish, C. (1997). *The Internet for busy people* (2nd ed.). Berkeley, CA: Osborne/McGraw-Hill.

Cupach, W. R., & Canary, D. J. (1997). *Competence in interpersonal conflict.* New York: McGraw-Hill.

Dale, P. (1999). *"Did you say something, Susan?" How any woman can gain confidence with assertive communication.* Secaucus, NJ: Carol.

Darling, A. L., & Dannels, D. P. (2003, January). Practicing engineers talk about the importance of talk: A report on the role of oral communication in the workplace. *Communication Education, 52,* 1–16.

Deaux, K., Dane, F. C., & Wrightsman, L. S. (1993). *Social psychology in the '90s* (6th ed.). Pacific Grove, CA: Brooks/Cole.

Deavenport, E. W. (1995, July 15). Walking the high wire: Balancing stakeholder interests. *Vital Speeches of the Day,* 595–597.

Demo, D. H. (1987). Family relations and the self-esteem of adolescents and their parents. *Journal of Marriage and the Family, 49,* 705–715.

Dennis, A. R. (1996). Information exchange and use in small group decision making. *Small Group Research, 27,* 532–550.

Derlega, V. J., Metts, S., Petronio, S., & Margulis, S. T. (1993). *Self-disclosure.* Newbury Park, CA: Sage.

Dindia, K. (2000a). Relational maintenance. In C. Hendrick & S. S. Hendrick (Eds.), *Close relationships: A sourcebook* (pp. 287–300). Thousand Oaks, CA: Sage.

Dindia, K. (2000b). Sex differences in self-disclosure, reciprocity of self-disclosure, and self-disclosure and liking: Three meta-analyses reviewed. In S. Petronio (Ed.), *Balancing the secrets of private disclosures* (pp. 21–36). Mahwah, NJ: Erlbaum.

Dindia, K., Fitzpatrick, M. A., & Kenny, D. A. (1997). Self-disclosure in spouse and stranger interaction: A social relations analysis. *Human Communication Research, 23,* 388–412.

Dindia, K., & Timmerman, L. (2003). Accomplishing romantic relationships. In J. O. Greene & B. R. Burleson (Eds.), *Handbook of communication and social interaction* (pp. 685–722). Mahway, NJ: Erlbaum.

Duck, S. (1987). How to lose friends without influencing people. In M. E. Roloff & G. R. Miller (Eds.), *Interpersonal processes: New directions in communication research.* Beverly Hills, CA: Sage.

DuFrene, D. D., & Lehman, C. M. (2002). Persuasive appeal for clean language. *Business Communication Quarterly, 65*(March), 48–56. [Available on InfoTrac College Edition]

Durst, G. M. (1989, March 1). The manager as a developer. *Vital Speeches of the Day,* 309–314.

Dwyer, K. K. (2000, January). The multidimensional model: Teaching students to self-manage high communication apprehension buy self-selecting treatments. *Communication Education, 49,* 79.

Eggins, S., & Slade, D. (1997). *Analyzing casual conversation.* Washington, DC: Cassell.

Ekman, P., & Friesen, W. V. (1969). The repertoire of nonverbal behavior: Categories, origins, usage, and coding. *Semiotica, I,* 49–98.

Ellis, K. (1995, January). Apprehension, self-perceived competency, and teacher immediacy in the laboratory-supported public speaking course: Trends and relationships. *Communication Education, 44,* 64–78.

Encyclopedia.com. (2002). [Online]. Available: www.encyclopedia.com

Estes, W. K. (1989). Learning theory. In A. Lesgold & R. Glaser (Eds.), *Foundations for a psychology of education* (pp. 1–49). Hillsdale, NJ: Erlbaum.

Ettinger, H. R. (2000, September 15). Shattering the glass floor: Women donors as leaders of fundamental change. *Vital Speeches of the Day,* 727–730.

Evans, C., & Dion, K. (1991). Group cohesion and performance: A meta-analysis. *Small Group Research, 22,* 175–186.

Fairhurst, G. T. (2001). Dualism in leadership. In F. M. Jablin & Putnam (Eds.), *The new handbook of organizational communication* (pp. 379–439). Thousand Oaks, CA: Sage.

Fairhurst, G. T., & Sarr, R. A. (1996). *The art of framing.* San Francisco: Jossey-Bass.

Flaherty, L. M., Pearce, K. J., & Rubin, R. B. (1998). Internet and face-to-face communication: Not functional alternatives. *Communication Quarterly, 46*(Summer), 250–268.

Floyd, K., & Morman, M. T. (1998). The measurement of affectionate communication. *Communication Quarterly, 46* (Spring), 144–162.

Ford, C. E., Fox, B. A., & Thompson, S. A. (2002). Introduction. In C. E. Ford, B. A. Fox, & S. A. Thompson (Eds.), *The language of turn and sequence* (pp. 3–13). New York: Oxford University Press.

Forgas, J. P. (1991). Affect and person perception. In J. P. Forgas (Ed.), *Emotion and social judgments* (pp. 387–406). New York: Pergamon Press.

Forgas, J. P. (2000). Feelings and thinking: Summary and integration. In J. P. Forgas (Ed.), *Feeling and thinking: The role of affect in social cognition* (pp. 387–406). New York: Cambridge Press.

Freedman, J. L., Klevansky, S., & Ehrich, P. R. (1971). The effect of crowding on human task performance. *Journal of Applied Psychology, 1*(1), 7–25.

Gentry, G. (1980). Group size and attitudes towards the simulation experience. *Simulation and Games, 11,* 451–460.

Geyer, G. A. (1999, September 15). Dressing in the name of respect. *Cincinnati Enquirer,* p. A12.

Globus, S. (2002, February 28). The good and bad and the Internet: Like it or not, life is happening more and more in cyberspace. *Current Health,* 13–17.

Gmelch, S. B. (1998). *Gender on campus: Issues for college women.* New Brunswick, NJ: Rutgers University Press.

Goldberg, B. (1999). *Overcoming high-tech anxiety: Thriving in a wired world.* San Francisco, CA: Jossey-Bass.

Goleman, D. (1998). *Working with emotional intelligence.* New York: Bantam Books.

Gordon, T. (1971). *The basic modules of the instructor outline for effectiveness training courses.* Pasadena, CA: Effectiveness Training Associates.

Gorham, J., & Christophel, D. M. (1995). A test-retest analysis of student motivation, teacher immediacy, and perceived sources of motivation and demotivation in college classes. *Communication Education, 44,* 292–307.

Gorham, J., Cohen, S. H., & Morris, T. L. (1997). Fashion in the classroom II: Instructor immediacy and attire. *Communication Research Reports, 14,* 11–24.

Gorham, J., Morris, T. L., & Tracy, L. (1999). Fashion in the classroom III: Effects of instructor attire and immediacy in natural classroom interactions. *Communication Quarterly,* Summer, 281–299.

Gouran, D. S., & Hirokawa, R. Y. (1996). Functional theory and communication in decision-making groups: An expanded view. In R. Y. Hirokawa & M. S. Poole (Eds.), *Communication and group decision making* (2nd ed., pp. 55–80). Thousand Oaks, CA: Sage.

Grice, H. P. (1975). Logic and conversation. In P. Cole & J. L. Morgan (Eds.), *Syntax and semantics, volume 3, speech acts.* New York: Academic Press.

Griffiths, M. (1998). Internet addiction: Does it really exist? In J. Gackenbach (Ed.), *Psychology and the Internet: Intrapersonal, interpersonal, and transpersonal implications* (pp. 61–76). San Diego, CA: Academic Press.

Gudykunst, W. B., & Kim, Y. Y. (2003). *Communicating with strangers: An approach to intercultural communication* (4th ed.). Boston: Allyn & Bacon.

Gudykunst, W. B., & Matsumoto, Y. (1996). Cross-cultural variability of communication in personal relationships. In W. B. Gudykunst, S. Ting-Toomey, & T. Nishida (Eds.), *Communication in personal relationships across cultures* (pp. 19–56). Thousand Oaks, CA: Sage.

Guerrero, L. K., & Andersen, P. A. (2000). Cross-cultural variability of communication in personal relationships. In C. Hendrick & S. S. Hendrick (Eds.), *Close relationships: A sourcebook* (pp. 287–300). Thousand Oaks, CA: Sage.

Guidelines for meeting participants. (1998, Fall). Unpublished manuscript developed by students in BAD 305, Understanding behavior in organizations. Northern Kentucky University.

Hall, B. J. (2002). *Among cultures: The challenge of communication.* Belmont, CA: Wadsworth.

Hall, E. T. (1959). *The silent language.* Greenwich, CT: Fawcett.

Hall, E. T. (1969). *The hidden dimension.* Garden City, NY: Doubleday.

Hall, J. A. (1998). How big are nonverbal sex differences? The case of smiling and sensitivity to nonverbal cues. In D. J. Canary & K. Dindia (Eds.), *Sex differences and similarities in communication: Critical essays and empirical investigations of sex and gender in interaction* (pp. 155–178). Mahwah, NJ: Erlbaum.

Hattie, J. (1992). *Self-concept.* Hillsdale, NJ: Erlbaum.

Hawkins, K. W. (1995). Effects of gender and communication content on leadership emergence in small, task-oriented groups. *Small Group Research, 26,* 234–249.

Hayes, J. (2002). *Interpersonal skills at work* (2nd ed.). New York: Routledge.

Helgesen, S. (1990). *The female advantage: Women's ways of leadership.* New York: Doubleday.

Hensley, C. W. (1995, September 1). Speak with style and watch the impact: Make things happen. *Vital Speeches of the Day,* 703.

Hirokawa, R. Y. (1987). Why informed groups make faulty decisions. *Small Group Behavior, 18,* 3–29.

Hirokawa, R. Y. (1988). Group communication and decision-making performance: A continued test of the functional perspective. *Human Communication Research, 14,* 487–515.

Hollman, T. D. (1972). Employment interviewer's errors in processing positive and negative information. *Journal of Psychology, 56,* 130–134.

Holtgraves, T. (2002). *Language as social action: Social psychology and language use.* Mahwah, NJ: Erlbaum.

Howard, J. A. (2000, August 1). Principles in default: Rediscovered and reapplied. *Vital Speeches of the Day,* 618–619.

Humphrey, J. (1998, May 15). Executive eloquence: A seven-fold path to inspirational leadership, *Vital Speeches of the Day,* 470.

Hundt, R. E. (1995, September 1). Serving kids and the community: Do we want TV to help or hurt children? *Vital Speeches of the Day,* 675.

Jandt, F. E. (2001). *Intercultural communication: An introduction* (3rd ed.). Thousand Oaks, CA: Sage.

Janis, I. L. (1982). *Groupthink: Psychological studies of policy decisions and fiascoes.* Boston: Houghton Mifflin.

Janis, I. L. (1989). *Crucial decisions: Leadership in policy making and crisis management.* New York: Free Press.

Jensen, A. D., & Chilberg, J. C. (1991). *Small group communication: Theory and application.* Belmont, CA: Wadsworth.

Johnson, D., & Johnson, F. (2003). *Joining together: Group theory and group skills* (8th ed.). Boston: Allyn & Bacon.

Jones, M. (2002). *Social psychology of prejudice.* Upper Saddle River, NJ: Prentice-Hall.

Jurma, W. E., & Wright, B. C. (1990). Follower reactions to male and female leaders who maintain or lose reward power. *Small Group Research, 21,* 110.

Jussim, L. J., McCauley, C. R., & Lee, Y-T. (1995). Why study stereotype accuracy and inaccuracy? In Y-T Lee, L. J. Jussim, & C. R. McCauley, *Stereotype accuracy: Toward appreciating group differences* (pp. 3–28). Washington, DC: American Psychological Association.

Kaplan, R. M. (2002). How to say it in your job search: Choice words, phrases, sentences and paragraphs for résumés, cover letters and interviews. Patamus, NJ: Prentice-Hall.

Kapoun, J. (2000, January 25). *Teaching undergraduates Web evaluation: A guide for library instruction* [Online]. Available: http://www.ala.org/acrl/undwebev.htm [Accessed October 17, 2001]

Kelly, L., Phillips, G. M., & Keaen, J. A. (1995). *Teaching people to speak well: Training and remediation of communication reticence.* Cresskill, NJ: Hampton.

Kennedy C. W., & Camden, C. T. (1983). A new look at interruptions. *Western Journal of Speech Communication, 47,* 55.

Keyton, J. (1993). Group termination: Completing the study of group development. *Small Group Research, 24,* 84–100.

Knapp, M. L., & Hall, J. A. (2002). *Nonverbal communication in human interaction* (5th ed.). Belmont, CA: Wadsworth/ Thomson Learning.

Koehler, C. (1998, June 15). Mending the body by lending an ear: The healing power of listening. *Vital Speeches of the Day,* 543–544.

Kramer, J., & Kramarae, C. (1997). Gendered ethics on the Internet. In J. M. Makau & R. C. Arnett (Eds.), *Communication ethics in the age of diversity* (pp. 226–244). Chicago: University of Illinois Press.

Kunkel, A. W., & Burleson, B. R. (1999). Assessing explanations for sex differences in emotional support: A test of the different cultures and skill specialization accounts. *Human Communication Research, 25,* 307–340.

Leary, M. R. (2002). When selves collide: The nature of the self and the dynamics of interpersonal relationships. In A. Tesser, D. A. Stapel, & J. V. Wood (Eds.), *Self and motivation: Emerging psychological perspectives* (pp. 119–145). Washington, DC: American Psychological Association.

Leathers, D. (1997). *Successful nonverbal communication: Principles and applications* (3rd ed.). Boston: Allyn & Bacon.

Lefton, L. A. (2001). *Interactive psychology online.* Boston: Allyn & Bacon.

Listening Factoid. (2003). [Online]. International Listening Association. Available: http://www.listen.org/pages/factoids.html

Littlejohn, S. W. (2002). *Theories of human communication* (7th ed.). Belmont, CA: Wadsworth.

Luft, J. (1970). *Group processes: An introduction to group dynamics.* Palo Alto, CA: Mayfield.

Lulofs, R. S., & Cahn, D. D. (2000). *Conflict: From theory to action* (2nd ed.). Boston: Allyn & Bacon.

Martin, J. N., & Nakayama, T. K. (2000). *Intercultural communication in contexts* (2nd ed.). Mountain View, CA: Mayfield.

Martin, M. M., Anderson, C. M., & Horvath, C. L. (1996). Feelings about verbal aggression: Justifications for sending and hurt from receiving verbally aggressive messages. *Communication Research Reports, 13*(1), 19–26.

Maslow, A. H. (1954). *Motivation and personality.* New York: Harper & Row.

Masters, M. F., & Albright, R. R. (2002). *The complete guide to conflict resolution in the workplace.* New York: Amacom.

McCroskey, J. C., & Beatty, M. J. (1998). Communication apprehension. In J. C. McCroskey, J. A. Daley, M. M. Martin, & M. J. Beatty (Eds.), *Communication and personality: Trait perspectives* (pp. 215–232). Cresshill, NJ: Hampton Press.

McCroskey, J. C., & McCroskey, L. L. (2002). Willingness to communicate and communication apprehension in the classroom. In J. L. Chesebro & J. C. McCroskey (Eds.), *Communication for teachers.* Boston: Allyn & Bacon.

McCroskey, J. C., & Neuliep, J. W. (1997). The development in intercultural and interethnic communication apprehension scales. *Communication Research Reports, 14,* 145–157.

McCroskey, J. C., & Tenin, J. J. (1999). Goodwill: A re-examination of the construct and its measurement. *Communication Monographs, 66,* 90–103.

Menzel, K. E., & Carrell, L. J. (1994). The relationship between preparation and performance in public speaking. *Communication Education, 43,* 17–26.

Michener, H. A., & DeLamater, J. D. (1999). *Social psychology* (4th ed.). Orlando, FL: Harcourt Brace.

Miller, M. (1999). *The Lycos personal Internet guide.* Indianapolis, IN: Que Corporation.

Morse, S. (2001, January 1). The rap of change: A new generation of solutions. *Vital Speeches of the Day,* 186–189.

Motley, M. (1997). COM Therapy. In J. A. Daly, J. C. McCroskey, J. Ayres, T. Hopf, & D. M. Ayres (Eds.), *Avoiding communication: Shyness, reticence, and communication apprehension* (2nd ed., pp. 379–400). Cresskill, NJ: Hampton Press.

Mruk, C. (1999). *Self-esteem: Research, theory, and practice* (2nd ed.). New York: Springer.

Mulac, A. (1998). The gender-linked language effect: Do language differences really make a difference? In D. J. Canary & K. Dindia (Eds.), *Sex differences and similarities in communication: Critical essays and empirical investigations of sex and gender in interaction* (pp. 127–154). Mahway, NJ: Erlbaum.

Munger, D., Anderson, D., Benjamin, B., Busiel, C., & Pardes-Holt, B. (2000). *Researching online* (3rd ed.). New York: Longman.

Napier, R. W., & Gershenfeld, M. K. (1999). *Groups: Theory and experience* (6th ed.). Boston, MA: Houghton Mifflin Company.

Nieto, S. (2000). *Affirming diversity: The sociological context of multicultural education* (3rd ed.). New York: Longman.

O'Connor, J. V. (2000). FAQs #1 Cuss Control Academy [Online]. Available: http://www.cusscontrol.com/faqs.html

Ogden, C. K., & Richards, I. A. (1923). *The meaning of meaning.* London: Kegan, Paul, Trench, Trubner.

Okrent, D. (1999, May 10). Raising kids online: what can parents do? *Time,* pp. 38–43.

Omdahl, B. L. (1995). *Cognitive appraisal, emotion, and empathy.* Mahwah, NJ: Erlbaum.

Opheim, C. (2000, November 1). Making democracy work: Your responsibility to society. *Vital Speeches of the Day,* 60–61.

Patterson, B. R., Bettini, L., & Nussbaum, J. F. (1993). The meaning of friendship across the life-span: Two studies. *Communication Quarterly, 41,* 145.

Patterson, M. E., Danscreau, D. F., & Newbern, D. (1992). Effects of communication aids on cooperative teaching. *Journal of Educational Psychology, 84,* 453–461.

Pearson, J. C., West, R. L., & Turner, L. H. (1995), *Gender & communication* (3rd ed.). Dubuque, IA: Brown & Benchmark.

Petri, H. L. (1996). *Motivation: Theory, research, and applications* (4th ed.). Belmont, CA: Wadsworth.

Petty, R. E., & Cacioppo, J. (1996). *Attitudes and persuasion: Classic and contemporary approaches.* Boulder, CO: Westview.

Petty, R. E., DeSteno, D., & Rucker, D. (2001). The role of affect in persuasion and attitude change. In J. Forgas (Ed.), *Handbook of affect and social cognition* (pp. 212–233). Mahwah, NJ: Erlbaum.

Petty, R. E., Wheeler, S. C., & Bizer, G. Y. (2000). Attitude functions and persuasion: An elaboration likelihood approach to matched versus mismatched messages. In G. R. Maio & J. M. Olson (Eds.), *Why we evaluate: Functions of attitudes* (pp. 133–162). Mahwah, NJ: Erlbaum.

Phillips, G. (1977). Rhetoritherapy versus the medical model: Dealing with reticence. *Communication Education, 26,* 34–43.

Preece, J. (2000). *Online communities.* New York: Wiley.

Random House Dictionary of the English Language (2nd ed.). (1983). New York: Random House.

Rayner, S. G. (2001). Aspects of the self as learner: Perception, concept, and esteem. In R. J. Riding & S. G. Rayner (Eds.), *Self perception: International perspectives on individual differences* (Vol. 2). Westport, CN: Ablex.

Reis, H. T. (1998). Gender differences in intimacy and related behaviors: Context and process. In D. J. Canary & K. Dindia (Eds.), *Sex differences and similarities in communication: Critical essays and empirical investigations of sex and gender in interaction* (pp. 203–232). Mahwah, NJ: Erlbaum.

Renz, M. A., & Greg, J. B. (2000). *Effective small group communication in theory and practice.* Boston: Allyn & Bacon.

Richmond, V. P., & McCroskey, J. C. (1995). *Communication: Apprehension, avoidance, and effectiveness* (4th ed.). Scottsdale, AZ: Gorsuch Scarisbrick.

Richmond, V. P., & McCroskey, J. C. (2000). *Communication: Apprehension, avoidance, and effectiveness* (5th ed.). Scottsdale, AZ: Gorsuch Scarisbrick.

Rosenfeld, L. B. (2000). Overview of the ways privacy, secrecy, and disclosure are balanced in today's society. In S. Petronio (Ed.), *Balancing the secrets of private disclosures* (pp. 3–18). Mahwah, NJ: Erlbaum.

Rothwell, J. D. (1998). *In mixed company* (3rd ed.). Fort Worth, TX: Harcourt Brace.

Samovar, L. A., & Porter, R. E. (2001). *Communication between cultures* (4th ed.). Belmont, CA: Wadsworth.

Samovar, L. A., & Porter, R. E. (2003). Understanding intercultural communication: An introduction and overview. In L. A. Samovar & R. E. Porter (Eds.), *Intercultural communication: A reader* (10th ed., pp. 6–17). Belmont, CA: Wadsworth.

Sampson, E. E. (1999). *Dealing with differences: An introduction to the social psychology of prejudice.* Fort Worth, TX: Harcourt Brace.

Schimanoff, S. B. (1980). *Communication rules: Theory and research.* Beverly Hills, CA: Sage.

Schmidt, W. V., & Conaway, R. N. (1999). *Results-oriented interviewing: Principles, practices, and procedures.* Boston: Allyn & Bacon.

Scott, P. (1997, January–February). Mind of a champion. *Natural Health, 27,* 99.

Shaw, M. E. (1981). *Group dynamics: The psychology of small group behavior* (3rd ed.). New York: McGraw-Hill.

Shimanoff, M. (1992). Group interaction and communication rules. In R. Cathcart & L. Samovar (Eds.), *Small group communication: A reader.* Dubuque, IA: Wm. Brown.

Spitzberg, B. H. (2000). A model of intercultural communication competence. In L. A. Samovar & R. E. Porter (Eds.), *Intercultural communication: A reader* (9th ed., pp. 375–387). Belmont, CA: Wadsworth.

Spitzberg, B. H. (2003). Methods of interpersonal skill assessment. In J. O. Greene & B. R. Burleson (Eds.), *Handbook of communication and social interaction skills* (pp. 93–134). Mahwah, NJ: Erlbaum.

Spitzberg, B. H., & Cupach, W. R. (2002). Interpersonal skills. In M. L. Knapp & J. A. Daly (Eds.), *Handbook of interpersonal communication* (pp. 564–611). Thousand Oaks, CA: Sage.

Stewart, C. J., & Cash, W. B. (2000). *Interviewing: Principles and practices* (9th ed.). Dubuque, IA: William C. Brown.

Stewart, L. P., Cooper, P. J., Stewart, A. D., & Friedley, S. A. (1998). *Communication and gender* (3rd ed.). Boston: Allyn & Bacon.

Stiff, J. B., Dillard, J. P., Somera, L., Kim, H., & Sleight, C. (1988). Empathy, communication and prosocial behavior. *Communication Monographs, 55,* 198–213.

Sundstrom, E., DeMeuse, K. P., & Futrell, D. (1990, February). Work teams: Applications and effectiveness. *American Psychologist,* 120–133.

Tannen, D. (2003). "Put that paper down and talk to me!": Rapport-talk and report-talk. In K. M. Galvin & P. J. Cooper (Eds.), *Making connections: Readings in relational communication* (3rd ed., pp. 91–102). Los Angeles: Roxbury.

Taylor, D. A., & Altman, I. (1987). Communication in interpersonal relationships: Social penetration theory. In M. E. Roloff & G. R. Miller (Eds.), *Interpersonal processes: New directions in communication research* (pp. 257–277). Beverly Hills, CA: Sage.

Temple, L. E., & Loewen, K. R. (1993). Perceptions of power: First impressions of a woman wearing a jacket, *Perceptual and Motor Skills, 76,* 345.

Tengler, C. D., & Jablin, F. M. (1983). Effects of question type, orientation, and sequencing in the employment screening interview. *Communication Monographs. 50,* 261.

Terkel, S. N., & Duval, R. S. (Eds.). (1999). *Encyclopedia of ethics.* New York: Facts on File.

Thibaut, J. W., & Kelley, H. H. (1986). *The social psychology of groups* (reprint). New Brunswick, NJ: Transaction Books.

Trachtenberg, S. J. (1986, August 15). Five ways in which thinking is dangerous. *Vital Speeches of the Day, 653.*

Tracy, K. (2002). *Everyday talk: Building and reflecting identities.* New York: Guilford Press.

Trujillo, S. D. (2002, April 15). The Hispanic destiny: Corporate responsibility. *Vital Speeches of the Day, 406.*

Tuckman, B. W. (1965). Developmental sequence in small groups. *Psychological Bulletin, 6393,* 384–399.

Turk, D. R., & Monahan, J. L. (1999). "Here I go again": An examination of repetitive behaviors during interpersonal conflicts. *Southern Communication Journal, 64*(Spring), 232–244.

Turner, M. M., Mazur, M. A., Wendel, N., & Winslow, R. (2003). Relational ruin or social glue? The joint effect of relationship type and gossip valence on liking, trust, and expertise. *Communication Monographs, 70*(2), 129–141.

Tversky, B. (1997). Memory for pictures, maps, environments, and graphs. In D. G. Payne & F. G. Conrad (Eds.), *Intersections in basic and applied memory research* (pp. 257–277). Mahwah, NJ: Erlbaum.

Valacich, J. S., George, J. F., Nonamaker, J. F., Jr., & Vogel, D. R. (1994). Idea generation in computer based groups: A new ending to an old story. *Small Group Research, 25,* 83–104.

Vangelisti, A. L. (2002). Interpersonal processes in romantic relationship. In M. L. Knapp & J. A. Daly (Eds.), *Handbook of interpersonal communication* (3rd ed., pp. 643–679). Thousand Oaks, CA: Sage.

Waldeck, J. H., Kearney, P., & Plax, T. G. (2001). Teacher e-mail message strategies and students' willingness to communicate. *Journal of Applied Communication Research, 29,* 54–70.

Weaver, J. B., III, & Kirtley, M. B. (1995). Listening styles and empathy. *The Southern Communication Journal, 60,* 131–140.

Weiten, W. (1998). *Psychology: Themes and variations* (4th ed.). Pacific Grove, CA: Brooks/Cole.

Wheelen, S. A., & Hochberger, J. M. (1996). Validation studies of the group development questionnaire. *Small Group Research, 27*(1), 143–170.

Whetten, D. A., & Cameron, K. S. (2002). *Developing management skills* (5th ed.). Upper Saddle River, NJ: Prentice-Hall.

Widmer, W. N., & Williams, J. M. (1991). Predicting cohesion in a coacting sport. *Small Group Research, 22,* 548–570.

Williams, R. G., & Ware, J. E., Jr. (1976). Validity of student ratings of instruction under different incentive conditions: A further study of the Dr. Fox effect. *Journal of Educational Psychology, 68,* 48–56.

Winstead, B. A., Derlega, V. J., & Rose, S. (1997). *Gender and close relationships.* Thousand Oaks, CA: Sage.

Wolvin, A., & Coakley, C. G. (1996*). Listening* (5th ed.). Dubuque, IA: Brown & Benchmark.

Wood, J. T. (2003). *Gendered lives: Communication, gender, and culture* (5th ed.). Belmont, CA: Wadsworth.

Wood, J. T., & Dindia, K. (1998). What's the difference? A dialogue about differences and similarities between women and men. In D. J. Canary & K. Dindia (Eds.), *Sex differences and similarities in communication: Critical essays and empirical investigations of sex and gender in interaction* (pp. 19–40). Mahwah, NJ: Erlbaum.

Young, K. S., Wood, J. T., Phillips, G. M., & Pederson, J. D. (2000). *Group discussion: A practical guide to participation and leadership* (3rd ed.). Prospect Heights, IL: Waveland Press.

INDEX

CREDITS

Chapter 1 2: Martin Barraud/Getty Images **5:** Karen Kapoor/Getty Images **11:** Steve Dunwell/Getty Images **14:** Michael Keller/The Stock Market **18:** © George Simian/CORBIS **19:** Courtesy Brian Spitzberg **25:** © Thomson Higher Education

Chapter 2 26: Charles Gupton/Getty Images **32:** © David Young-Wolff/PhotoEdit **36:** © BSIP Agency/Index Stock Imagery/PictureQuest **40:** Bob Daemmrich/Stock, Boston **45:** CNN **49:** © Thomson Higher Education

Chapter 3 50: © David Young-Wolff/PhotoEdit/PictureQuest **57:** FRANK & ERNEST reprinted by permission of Newspaper Enterprise Association, Inc. **61:** © nonstock/untitled **63:** Shoe by Jeff MacNelly; reprinted by permission of Tribune Media Services. **66:** CNN **69:** © Thomson Higher Education

Chapter 4 70: Adam Crowley/Getty Images **72:** © 2004 by Sidney Harris **74:** © Mark L. Stephenson/CORBIS **79:** © Matthew McKee/Eye Ubiquitous/CORBIS **80:** Reprinted from Christy Haubegger, "I'm Not Fat, I'm Latina." In M. Adams, W. J. Blumenfeld, R. Castaneda, H. W. Hackman, M. L. Peters, & X. Zuniga (Eds.), *Readings for Diversity and Social Justice: An Anthology on Racism, Anti-Semitism, Sexism, Heterosexism, Ableism, and Classism* (pp. 242–243). New York: Routledge, 2000. **85:** Robert Azzi/Woodfin Camp & Associates **86:** Courtesy Judee K. Burgoon **92:** © Thomson Higher Education

Chapter 5 94: © Tom & Dee Ann McCarthy/CORBIS **100:** © Rhoda Sidney/PhotoEdit **102:** Excerpted from Dr. Gwendolyn Gong, "When Mississippi Chinese Talk." In A. Gonzalez, M. Houston, & Victoria Chen (Eds.), *Our Voices: Essays in Culture, Ethnicity, and Communication* (pp. 110–116). Los Angeles: Roxbury Publishing Company, © 1994. Reprinted by permission of the publisher. **104:** Julie Toy/Getty Images **112:** Jason Harris/© Thomson Higher Education **114:** AP/Wide World Photos **116, 117:** Jason Harris/© Thomson Higher Education **121:** © Thomson Higher Education

Chapter 6 122: Mark Richard/PhotoEdit **125:** © The New Yorker Collection 1999 from cartoonbank.com. All Rights Reserved. **131:** Dana White/PictureQuest **135:** Courtesy Brant Burleson **137:** Brian Bailey/Getty Images **139:** Michael Newman/PhotoEdit **142, 143, 144:** Jason Harris/© Thomson Higher Education **147:** © Thomson Higher Education

Chapter 7 148: Rob Nelson/PictureQuest **152:** From Nieto, Sonia, *Affirming Diversity: The Sociopolitical Context of Multicultural Education,* 3/e. Published by Allyn & Bacon, Boston, MA. Copyright © 2000 by Pearson Education. Adapted by permission of the publisher. **153:** © Jack Hollingsworth/CORBIS **156:** Jason Harris/© Thomson Higher Education 165: Bruce Ayers/Getty Images **169:** Jason Harris/© Thomson Higher Education **170, 171, 173:** © Thomson Higher Education

Chapter 8 174: Mark Scott/Getty Images **177:** © Thomson Higher Education **184:** Michael Newman/PhotoEdit **186:** Bruce Ayers/Getty Images **189:** Jason Harris/© Thomson Higher Education **193:** Courtesy Daniel J. Canary **195:** © Baby Blues Partnership. Reprinted with special Permission of King Features Syndicate. **199:** © Thomson Higher Education **200, 201:** Jason Harris/© Thomson Higher Education **203:** © Thomson Higher Education

Chapter 9 204: Jeff Cadge/Getty Images **209:** © Dana White/PhotoEdit **213:** Jason Harris/© Thomson Higher Education **220:** Michael Newman/PhotoEdit **221, 222:** Jason Harris/© Thomson Higher Education **226:** Monster.com

Chapter 10 228: Steve Smith/Getty Images **231:** DILBERT reprinted by permission of United Features Syndicate, Inc. **232:** Nita Winter Photography **245:** © Jeff Greenberg/PhotoEdit **253:** © Thomson Higher Education

Chapter 11 254: Photodisc Collection/Getty Images **258:** Nita Winter Photography **262:** © Tony Freeman/PhotoEdit **266:** Courtesy Gail T. Fairhurst **270:** © Frozen Images/The Image Works **272, 273, 279:** © Thomson Higher Education

Chapter 12 280: © Will Hart/PhotoEdit/PictureQuest **284:** © Thomson Higher Education **286:** Jeff Greenberg/PhotoEdit **291:** A. Ramey/Stock, Boston/PictureQuest **301, 302, 303:** © Thomson Higher Education

Chapter 13 304: Bruce Ayers/Getty Images **307:** F. Pedrick/The Image Works **312:** © 2004 Peter Mueller from cartoonbank.com. All Rights Reserved. **313:** E. Crews/The Image Works **318:** C. Orrico/Superstock, Inc. **322:** Courtesy Molefi Kete Asante **330, 331, 332, 333:** InfoTrac College Edition © Gale Group

Chapter 14 334, 345: © Peter L. Chapman Photography **348:** Michael Newman/PhotoEdit **355:** © Jeff Greenberg/PhotoEdit **360:** CATHY © 1983 Cathy Guisewite. Reprinted with permission of UNIVERSAL PRESS SYNDICATE. All rights reserved. **365:** © Thomson Higher Education

Chapter 15 366: Alex Freund/Getty Images **369:** Bob Daemmrich/Stock, Boston **371:** Courtesy Joan Gorham **377:** © Stone Les/CORBIS SYGMA **381:** Roger Persson/© Thomson Higher Education **383:** David Shopper/Stock, Boston **401:** © Thomson Higher Education

Chapter 16 402: Michael Newman/PhotoEdit **407:** © 2004 by Sidney Harris **410:** Excerpted from *Making Waves* by Asian Women United. © 1989 by Asian Women United. Reprinted by permission of the author. **412:** Dave Shaefer/Jeroboam **415:** © Syracuse Newspapers/The Image Works **420:** Courtesy James McCroskey **423:** Bob Daemmrich/Stock, Boston **427:** Courtesy Anthony Masturzo **435:** © Thomson Higher Education

Chapter 17 436: Joel Gordon **439:** John Elk III/Stock, Boston **447:** © Reuters NewMedia Inc./CORBIS **451:** © David H. Wells/CORBIS **453:** Used with permission of Lindsey Degenhardt **461:** © Thomson Higher Education

Chapter 18 462: © David Young-Wolff/PhotoEdit **465:** © Thomson Higher Education **467:** Robert Brenner/PhotoEdit **471:** Courtesy Richard Petty **473:** Aaron Haupt/Stock, Boston/PictureQuest **477:** © Rudi Von Briel/PhotoEdit **483:** Used with permission of Eric Wais **494:** © Thomson Higher Education